Homer 4Aeschylus Sophocles Euripides

o 7Aristotle I 8Aris... II 0Hippocrates

11Lucretius Epicte... ...urelius

Ptolemy Copernicus Kepler ...ugustine

19Dante Chaucer 20Calvin 21Machiavelli

he 24Shakespeare I 25Shakespeare II

28Francis Bacon Descartes Spinoza

32Newton Huygens 33Locke Berkeley

Montesquieu Rousseau 36Adam Smith

World

of the

0American State Papers The Federalist

Western

day 43Hegel Kierkegaard Nietzsche

en George Eliot 47Dickens 48Melville

51Tolstoy 52Dostoevsky Ibsen

es Bergson Dewey Whitehead Russell

Planck Whitehead Einstein Eddington

bzhansky Waddington 57Veblen Tawney

Strauss 59Henry James Shaw Conrad

nn Joyce 60Woolf Kafka Lawrence

Brecht Hemingway Orwell Beckett

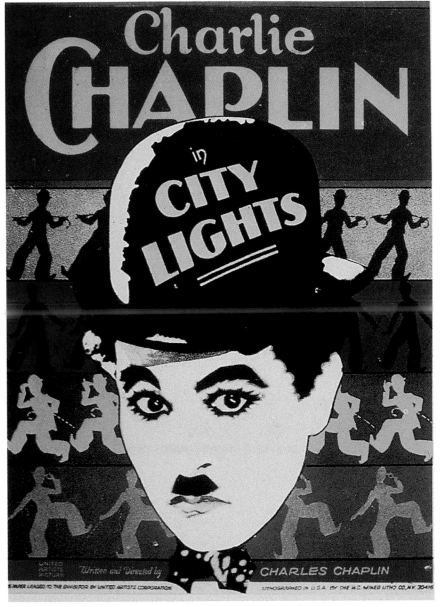

Poster for Charlie Chaplin's 1931 film City Lights.

The Great Ideas Today

1995

Encyclopædia Britannica, Inc.

Chicago · Auckland · London · Madrid · Manila · Paris · Rome · Seoul · Sydney · Tokyo · Toronto

Some of this material first appeared in *The Culture of Time and
Space* published by Harvard University Press, 1983.

Library of Congress Number: 61-65561
International Standard Book Number: 0-85229-614-2
International Standard Serial Number: 0072-7288

A NOTE ON REFERENCE STYLE

In the following pages, passages in *Great Books of the Western World* are referred to by the initials "*GBWW*," followed by a roman numeral (indicating the first edition of 1952 [I] or the second edition of 1990 [II]) with volume and page number. Thus, "*GBWW* I: 5, 100; II: 4, 112*" refers to a passage from Sophocles' *Oedipus the King,* which is on page 100 in Volume 5 of the first edition, and on page 112 in Volume 4 of the second edition. Sometimes only one reference will be given, since the contents of the first and second editions differ. Also note that passages quoted in an article may differ from the translation of that passage in either the first or second edition, since newer translations of some works are included in the second edition.

Gateway to the Great Books is referred to by the initials "*GGB*," followed by volume and page number. Thus, "*GGB* 10, 39–57" refers to pages 39 through 57 of Volume 10 of *Gateway to the Great Books,* which is James's essay, "The Will to Believe."

The Great Ideas Today is referred to by the initials "*GIT*," followed by the year and page number. Thus, "*GIT* 1968, 210" refers to page 210 of the 1968 edition of *The Great Ideas Today.*

Contents

1
2
3
4

Preface

This year's edition of *The Great Ideas Today* goes out, as have all recent ones, with brave if not foolhardy reliance on at least the remnants of a common culture in the Western world, assuming—that is, the editors assume—that we can talk about the same things with one another and be understood in the same way. Understanding is not the same as agreement, of course, which is something, more or less, being in certain instances achieved without true understanding of any kind.

The belief that understanding lies within our power as human beings is the basis on which the set of *Great Books* was created in the first place and the one that created the *Syntopicon*—the index of ideas that relies on our ability to transcend the differences of language, background, taste, and education that otherwise divide us when it comes to talk about serious matters. This notion is much in doubt at the moment; the cultural climate that prevails is inhospitable to it. However, we make the assumption that it can be done.

Why it may be difficult, and possibly doomed, is suggested by several of the articles in this year's book. For example, Alfred Corn, a fine lyric poet in his own right, asked to indicate the best such poets writing in English at the moment, reports that there *is* no English in the sense the word once conveyed, or that, if there is, it reflects national, race, and gender meanings so diverse as to make its meanings different even where its words are the same when used by poets who seem to think they can. The business of his survey of contemporary poetry is to suggest how this is so—though happily he exaggerates somewhat (or his own abilities at exposition are great)—for we can read all the poets he cites (and there are wonderful ones among them) with pleasure and comprehension.

A similar kind of doubt that we talk the same language anymore is reported by Deal Hudson in the second part of his essay on human nature, of which the first appeared last year. This year's account is of the challenges to the *idea* of human nature which lie in gender and ethnic studies, whose adherents argue that the differences they represent are so radical as to defy any argument for a single human species, at least in cultural and possibly even in biological terms. Mr. Hudson does not himself agree with these adherents, but he restates their views impartially, acknowledging the injustices, the condescension, the sheer ignorance of the cultural tradition represented by the *Great Books,* which they oppose.

Yet a more hopeful view of what might be described as an evolving culture in what, for all its angry differences is a single world, will be found in James O'Toole's essay, "Goods in Common." This addresses itself to new ways in which the human commonalty, so apparently in a process of breaking down, may be revived (if not for the first time really achieved)—the ways being indicated by the terms "efficiency" and "community" which Mr. O'Toole takes up. These are new concepts—at least relatively new—in the West but well established in the East, where they have long questioned the ideas of "liberty" and "equality" on which the West has relied for its constitutions as being too individualistic for a sustainable body politic. Perhaps all four ideas can be reconciled, as we should like, if they are good ones. Mr. O'Toole suggests how they could, and what it would mean to us if they were.

Other contributions to this volume are hopeful with respect to schisms in our thought which are of long standing, but which are seen as, at any rate, not irremediable. Thus, John Polkinghorne suggests that the breach between science and theology, evident since the seventeenth century, if not the late Middle Ages, is not beyond repair unless we take science to require a disbelief in God, which would be a quite unscientific, because quite unprovable, assumption. If such a belief is out aside, then we have the scientific universe, on the one hand, and God, who—or which—is of a different order, a different sort of eternity, if one likes. Whatever it is, it cannot be put to the test, as science puts things to the test, but must be thought of in another way—a way that does not deny science, though it may underlie it, or even transcend it. The natural order is perfectly capable of taking care of itself, without a deus ex machina. But what of what lies outside it, if anything does—and what of ourselves, who are certainly part of it, but also possibly part of something else? These are among the questions that Mr. Polkinghorne, who is a scientist as well as a theologian, invites us to consider.

To think about ourselves as eternal beings, and as biological ones, is difficult enough, but we have also as human creatures to think about ourselves in social terms. This oddly may entail a sense of the world in which we live which we would otherwise say belongs to science. Stephen Kern, writing on what he calls "The Spaces of Democracy," suggests that the sense of we have of ourselves in our age is a function of certain changes which came about at the end of the last century and the beginning of this one in our apprehension of space and time. These both underwent a profound enlargement or extension, with consequent effects upon the birth of what he calls democracy, by which he means, however, not much more than the conditions of mass existence in a technological world under almost any kind of government or state. That is far from the "democracy" that so many of the contributors to this volumes over the years have tried to distinguish—a lesser usage of the word which, however familiar it is to us, should not be confused with the greater one that Mr. O'Toole, for example, is at pains to preserve.

Our "Special Features" this year comprise still another fine examination by George Anastaplo of a culture outside the West—in this case that of sub-Saharan Africa, where the subject is made difficult, as in the case of the case of the American "Indian," by the fact that the prevailing languages are none of them literate ones, so that there is no body of written thought to consult. Perhaps we should not complain if we in the West have trouble understanding one another. What if there are no documents to understand? Yet Mr. Anastaplo, who is undiscourageable, has managed somehow to suggest the spirit of that African world, sometimes using folktales, which makes us think we know it, or at any rate are not as ignorant of it as we were before, having some means to compare it with our own.

Our other special feature is a discussion by Thomas Simpson of Charlie Chaplin, in particular *City Lights* (1925) and *Modern Times* (1936), which are among the most eloquent and moving films that Chaplin ever made. It is now hard to remember that Chaplin at the time these films were made was the most famous man in the world—at a time when a visual art could achieve such a state, as distinct from the electronic ones that now make Michael Jackson, say, as well known in Tibet as he is in Texas. The world *saw* Chaplin, and knew him as a figure of extraordinary depth and meaning, though the sense of this was mostly instinctive. What lay within that sense, and how its creation in the psyche of the world was Chaplin's achievement, is Mr. Simpson's subject, which he makes as instructive and entertaining a are the photographs that accompany it.

We have only two "Additions to the Great Books Library" this year, both of them whole books, or rather, in one case, a whole part of a book. *Part One* of *The Pilgrim's Progress* appeared last year, and in *Part Two,* the protagonist of the story is Christiana, wife of Christian who has achieved his salvation at the gates of heaven, and returns to her a dream, bidding her to collect their family and lead them to the same end. This tale is more social, less allegorical, than its predecessor, but the same energy is evident in it, and its closing pages, in which the members of the party, whom we have got to know, one by one enter the river of death so as to be born again, is a moving business—the best part of the whole work.

Of the remaining work in this section, W. E. B. Du Bois's *The Souls of Black Folk* (1903), much could and has been said. It may still be, a hundred years after it appeared, the best account of what we nowadays would call black psychology as it has developed in America—in North America, at least. It is certainly, still, a wrenching, because uncompromising, account of what it means to *be* black in a white man's world—and if we think we already know something about that, it is from later books which have built on what their authors learned first from Du Bois. Not the least of its distinctions is that it treats with extraordinary perception the songs that blacks sang during their long enslavement and the far from equal freedom they have since achieved. No reader can read these pages without being moved—well, one could say to tears, except that the pain and deprivation they set forth has a kind of transcendence beyond mere emotion, is the stuff truly of the soul and not of the whipped, starved, beaten, despised, exploited body. *The Souls of Black Folk* may be a great book in itself, so powerful is it, and yet so elusive in some respects. It is good to have it here.

Current Developments in the Arts and Sciences

1
2
3
4

Contemporary Poetry's Mother Tongues

Alfred Corn

Introduction

A decade and a half ago, when commissioned to give an overview of contemporary poetry in English for *The Great Ideas Today,* British critic John Bayley chose to discuss only three figures, Philip Larkin, Robert Lowell, and John Berryman (*GIT* 1975; 204–54). Regarded from our perspective, the choice seems strange, not only because Lowell's and Berryman's place at the center of recent poetic achievement has been seriously contested since their deaths but also because all three of Bayley's representative poets are male and Anglo-Saxon.

The figure from Lowell's generation most often discussed and praised today is Elizabeth Bishop (who died in 1979); her poetry is still an important shaping influence on many contemporary poets. Some critics have been concerned with her as a woman poet, others—following her own disavowal of any special consideration based on gender—have not. Perhaps Bishop herself would have been the most surprised by her remarkable present-day ascendancy, given how little sympathy she had for what might be called the pretentiousness of greatness. Wouldn't being "great" necessarily involve some sort of pomposity, and shouldn't poetry prefer wry spontaneity, luminous accuracy, and uninsistent mystery? Bishop's very disaffection with everything grand, romantic, or weighty matches our own end-of-century preference for modest scale, conversational tone, and the "merely human." In this connection it probably *is* appropriate to speak of women's repudiation of patriarchal attitudes and giant, universalist ambitions—to see Bishop as a woman poet, great by not being grand, with the humor and economy of, say, a Haydn instead of the metaphysical ambitions and conspicuous consumption of a Wagner.

Still, we do have evidence of authentic ambition among living poets. In fact, there are so many reckonable figures, no three of any description could adequately represent the diversity of contemporary poetry in English. Or should we say English*es,* since several variants of English are now available for literary composition?

Poets are writing in British and American English, certainly, but in Irish English, as well as East and West Indian English, Australian, and Canadian English. When Larkin noted that the title character in "Mr. Bleaney," one of his best-known poems, "kept on plugging at the four aways," most non-British readers probably scratched their heads—unless they happened to know that by "four aways" Larkin meant the four football games (or, in American speech, "soccer") played out of town (occasions for Mr. Bleaney's chronically futile betting). On the other hand, when Derek Walcott has a character say, "I taking a sea bath, I gone down the road" ("The Schooner *Flight*"), we grasp (at least, generally) what the character means; but we are also aware that Walcott is using a speech variant that falls strangely on a non-Caribbean ear. Examples from Irish, Australian, or East Indian poets could be found as well, but even without citing them, it should be clear that in any discussion of contemporary poetry on a global scale, English must be understood as spanning a wide linguistic range.

(Overleaf)
The Last
Symposium
by Arthur
Tress

Variant speech norms are only one index of diversity. Social commentators have been pointing out for some time that the world trend is not toward a unified, global civilization but instead toward ethnic particularity. Each nation—and each minority within national boundaries—seeks to affirm the value of its special identity, even at the sacrifice of easy communication with other groups. Poetry has always been a convenient index of what is going on in the minds of the population in general, so there's no surprise if it has become common to speak of "women's poetry," "African-American poetry," "gay (or lesbian) poetry," "Native-American poetry," or "Chicano poetry"—and this in the United States alone. (Or not so united; it's also routine to hear mentions of "Arizona poets," "Ohio poets," and so on down the list of all fifty states.) Boston and New York City, with a nod to San Francisco and Chicago, used to sum up the American poetry scene, but those days are now at an end. Every major American city has regularly scheduled public readings of poetry at universities and other forums, and there are small presses in every state publishing the work of new or established poets. Add to this the flourishing "poetry slam" movement, in which poets of wildly varying degrees of professionalism perform wherever and whenever bookstores or coffee houses will allow them, and you have what looks like an astonishingly diverse group of poets actively seeking an audience, even if we consider the United States alone. One practical consequence is that no single poet can command all of the audience for contemporary poetry; he or she may hope to interest more than one splinter group, but certainly not all of them.

Another circumstance worth pondering is the permanent or semipermanent presence in the United States of several internationally renowned poets from other countries. Three of these are Nobel Prize winners. Derek Walcott, born in Saint Lucia in the West Indies, spends most of the year in Boston, teaching at Boston University. Czesław Miłosz, a Lithuanian native writing in Polish, has been translated since the late seventies by American poets (themselves also distinguished) and has been published in the U.S. to great acclaim. Miłosz has lived as an American citizen in California for several decades and is one of the poets most often referred to in current journals and quarterlies. Joseph Brodsky, the third resident Nobel laureate, is also an American citizen but writes most of his poems in Russian and translates them or has them translated by other notable American poets as soon as they are written. Brodsky has lived in America nearly as long as Miłosz. The Irish poet Seamus Heaney, a Nobel finalist, should be mentioned too, since he teaches half the year at Harvard and has an enthusiastic American following. And finally, there is Thom Gunn, a highly regarded English poet who has lived in California since the 1950s; his poetry incorporates strengths from both English and American traditions. So pervasive has the influence of these nonnative artists been, it is fair to consider them "honorary American poets," regardless of their nationality or first language.

Perhaps we can compare the present situation to the pervasive "climate of opinion" that English-born poet W. H. Auden (who was a naturalized citizen) created during his three decades of residence in the United States; but otherwise it has no precedent in our literary history. Among American poets perhaps only John Ashbery has an international reputation comparable to the nonnative poets just listed, but Ashbery is not a Nobel laureate, and his importance is still contested by a high percentage of the poetry audience. Nor do there seem to be any other contemporary American poets likely to be awarded what is usually regarded as the most significant international literary honor.

There are, of course, a number of Americans who have earned high marks for their achievements even if they are not as well known abroad than the Nobel Prize recipients and candidates. Critic Harold Bloom rates James' Merrill and A. R. Ammons as high as John Ashbery, and poets Richard Wilbur, Anthony Hecht, Adrienne Rich, Mona Van Duyn, John Hollander, W. S. Merwin, Philip Levine, Richard Howard, Gwendolyn Brooks, Galway Kinnell, Mark Strand, and Amy Clampitt (who died in 1994) have strong followings as well. This is the older generation, all above age sixty, but, if we turn to those in their fifties, Charles Wright, Marilyn Hacker, Charles Simic, Robert Pinsky, Frank Bidart, Louise Glück, and Sandra MacPherson are also frequently mentioned as among our most valued poets. Rita Dove is the only poet in her forties to achieve a significant reputation, but there are enough promising talents to suggest that contemporary American poetry is thriving.

If we turn to England, the question is whether any other major poet has emerged in the aftermath of Larkin's death. Some would cite Ted Hughes, even though his reputation has been under a cloud ever since the suicide of his former wife Sylvia Plath. Even on its own terms, Hughes's poetry has not seemed to achieve as much as his talents promised when he began writing in the late 1950s. His contemporary Geoffrey Hill is for many critics, including Bloom, a much more important figure. Yet, because of the difficulties of Hill's late-modernist style and his unusual subject matter (the bare survival of religious consciousness in a secularist and brutal age), Hill has not seemed to attract many followers, and his peculiar mixture of violence, delicacy, and brooding obscurity has come to seem more like a beautiful side chapel blackened by destructive fires during the wars of religion than the great cathedral of poetry it at first promised to be. Among younger English poets, Tony Harrison, James Fenton, and Craig Raine are notable, but it is too soon to measure their achievement. One Scottish poet, Douglas Dunn, merits attention even though he has not published much in recent years. Finally, there is the Australian poet Les Murray, who has made a good start and is still in mid-career.

Thom Gunn

Because he was born in England but lives in America, Thom Gunn might be a good starting point for understanding poetry written in English today. His status as an "honorary American" is based not only on his forty-year residence in the U.S., but also on his apprenticeship with the poet and critic Yvor Winters and his close association with American contemporaries like Robert Duncan. Gunn began publishing as a Cambridge undergraduate in the 1950s

Thom Gunn

with a combative volume appropriately titled *Fighting Terms.* His poems all used the prosody of tradition with exact rhymes and clear, concise sentences that recalled late-Renaissance poets Ben Johnson and Fulke Greville—when not, however glancingly, Shakespeare. Even so, the poems felt modern, but it was a modernity based on stance and mood, not on the ephemera of contemporaneity. His philosophical assumptions were up-to-date, basically the same as those of the French existentialists of the late '40s and '50s: there is no God, and solitary, reflective consciousness is the sole arbiter of human choice. Choice for an artist ought to be carried off with "style" and, above all, with no self-pity. In this line, Stendhal and Albert Camus were important models for Gunn; he also has the impassive, Flaubertian eye, noting a wide range of human behavior down to its least detail, never shocked by anything he sees, and offering admiration only with a due sense of proportion. Abstract and timeless settings were the norm for Gunn's early poems, a lightly subversive irony setting the tone, as in these lines from "The Wind in the Street":

> The same faces, and then the same scandals
> Confront me inside the talking shop which I
> Frequent for my own good. So the assistant
> Points to the old cogwheels, the old handles
> Set in machines which to buy would be to buy
> The same faces, and then the same scandals.
>
> I climb by the same stairs to a square attic.
> And I gasp, for surely this is something new!
> So square, so simple. It is new to be so simple.
> Then I see the same sky through the skylight, static
> Cloudless, the same artificial toylike blue.
> The same stairs led to the same attic. [1]

The "talking shop" is poetry, or one version of it, which the narrator visits at first with boredom. That is momentarily dispelled by the newness of simplicity: and then the "same sky," "static/Cloudless," appears, the vast, azure realm devoid of divine sanctions. The narrator goes on to say, "What I wanted would have been what I found." He allows for the possibility that he might return some day, but "meanwhile, I'll look elsewhere."

Looking elsewhere for Gunn meant, among other things, going to the U.S. and studying with Winters—who, on the other hand, is possibly the most English-sounding poet America has ever produced. Gunn's next volume was titled *The Sense of Movement,* which seemed to confirm his close association with the poets in England (Philip Larkin, Kingsley Amis, John Wain) grouped in the '50s under the journalistic label of "The Movement." In fact, these were not close associates of Gunn's, their main resemblance nothing more than a shared preference for traditional prosody and a dislike of modernist or late-Romantic obscurity. Would the other Movement poets have chosen, as Gunn did in "On the Move," leather-jacketed motorcyclists as emblematic, exemplary figures? Probably not, and only he could have written the poem's concluding stanza:

A minute holds them, who have come to go:
The self-defined, astride the created will
They burst away; the towns they travel through
Are home for neither bird nor holiness,
For birds and saints complete their purposes.
At worst, one is in motion; and at best,
Reaching no absolute, in which to rest,
One is always nearer by not keeping still. [2]

In practical terms, the stated preference here for motion and change has meant that Gunn's poems have shown variety of form as well as content. Like other contemporaries, Gunn began experimenting with loosely metered or unmetered poetry in the '60s, and his practice since then has been to write alternately with and without meter (and rhyme) in keeping with the poem's subject. It was only natural that the social upheavals of the '60s in California—leftist politics, drugs, rock music, the expanding definition of what constituted a disenfranchised minority to include women, lesbians, and gay men—would have an impact on a temperament as open to change as Gunn's. His poems about drug experience are still probably the best in English, and his poems about same-sex relationships are also among the most perfect since the Latin poets. Sometimes both experiences combine, as in "Tom-Dobbin," a sequence with the subtitle "centaur poems."

Ruthlessly gentle, gently ruthless we move
As if through water with delaying limb.
We circle clasping round an unmarked centre
Gradually closing in, until we enter
The haze together—which is me, which him?
Selves floating in the one flesh we are of. [3]

This section of the poem is strictly metered and rhymed, as some of the others are not; the blending of two selves, of drug hallucination and reality, and of the divided centaur nature, find a counterpart in the mixed metrical form of the whole. Perhaps Gunn's dual identity as English *and* American poet is suggested as well, a "haze" of selfhood available to more than one formal and linguistic impulse.

In the '70s another aspect of Gunn's ability appeared. He began writing brief verse portraits, a range of human characters almost Chaucerian in abundance, though there is a discernible preference for marginalized identities; for example, the handsome young thief Jim in "The Idea of Trust," the heroin addict of "Faustus Triumphant," or the collector of broken dolls in "Dolly." Character portrayal was extended to the animal kingdom in "Yoko," a poem written from the point of view of a dog, and to the vegetable kingdom in "The Cherry Tree," where human sensations and feelings are attributed—with dreamlike effectiveness—to a tree as it moves through seasons and the cycle of generation.

The appearance of alternate selves in Gunn's work perhaps attests to the lessening drama of a mostly settled life, after defining choices have already been made. It is no surprise to discover as well a few quite specific poems of retrospection sparked by a sojourn in England and the set of memories stirred by the return. "The sniff of the real," he calls it in "Autobiography," detectable as well in "Hampstead: the Horse Chestnut Trees," and "Breaking Ground," an elegy for an older female relative (his grandmother?) that concludes with an outdoor pop concert in Monterey, Calif. The poet recognizes that, in some sense, the deceased person is present in the scene, that this is his true homecoming. The poem concludes with some phrases from Raleigh's "The 21th: and last booke of the Ocean to Scinthia," a paean to Elizabeth I: "Shee/is gonn, Shee is lost,/Shee is found, Shee/is ever faire." [4]

Gunn's poems in the early '80s were mostly a holding action, and it was not until the outbreak of the AIDS epidemic that he found what may turn out to be his greatest subject. His gifts for unsentimental portraiture and for metered poetry join to produce elegies with the requisite accuracy and gravity, as well as a tone that still has room for irony and the "laughter in the soul." That the dying were also gay men, most substituting a certain stoic self-reliance for the consolations of traditional religion, must have stirred Gunn's first sympathies with these doomed agonists, brothers of the "Sad Captains" of his early existential poems. The tempering action of time, though, has worked a transformation on the poet as well, so that he never seems arrogant or cold—but never sentimental, either. Consider this passage from "Lament":

And when at last the whole death was assured,
Drugs having failed, and when you had endured
Two weeks of an abominable constraint,
You faced it equably, without complaint,
Unwhimpering, but not at peace with it. [5]

The friend's physical distress, his patient, slow-burning resistance, and refusal to complain, are qualities Gunn allows himself and us to admire in these heroic couplets without falling into pathos or unearned complicity. "Lament," "The Man With Night Sweats," "Words for Some Ash," and "Sacred Heart" are probably the best poems written about the AIDS epidemic and those struck down by it. They offer only as much consolation as art can reasonably provide, but that, joined to the sense of lives lived with intensity and daring, is not a negligible achievement. Fortunately, Gunn himself does not have the disease—instead, an uncomplacent mind that refuses absolutes and accepts the provisional order of art as the only credible faith. Gunn is only sixty-five, and it is likely that his best poems are still to come.

Derek Walcott

The obstacles to poetic achievement must have seemed unusually daunting to the young Derek Walcott, born in Saint Lucia, a small island of the Lesser Antilles in the West Indies, when he began writing poems as a middle-class adolescent in the 1940s. Some of the problems facing him were inherited from history. The West Indies, wrested from the indigenous Aruacs (who gradually died out) during the colonial era and populated by European colonists and African slaves (at a later date, by imported Indian and Chinese laborers), have had for several centuries a disputed national identity, which recent independence from Europe has made only more perplexing. Should the loyalty of a contemporary resident of what Walcott refers to as "the archipelago" go to the extinct Aruacs, to European culture, to Africa?—and if the latter, to which country or tribe of Africa? Or should cues for identity and aesthetics be borrowed from the superpower to the north, especially since the African-American influence is so strong in cultural exports from the U.S.? And where do the Indian and Chinese minorities figure in the West Indian panorama? For a poet (or prose writer, like V. S. Naipaul, Walcott's younger compatriot) these questions are posed in quite specific terms: out of what cultural *mythos* shall I write, and in what kind of language?

Because of the traditional education offered to Saint Lucians, Walcott's first loyalties were to European culture and British English. Although two West Indian poets, Saint-John Perse and Aimé Césaire, were among his early models, still it must be noted that these poets wrote in standard French and achieved ready recognition outside the Caribbean as important poets. Because of the interracial marriages of both sets of grandparents, Walcott is

Derek Walcott

both African and European in origin, but Africanism came to him mostly outside the classroom in the form of African-influenced vernacular—variants of both French and English are spoken by the populace of Saint Lucia— and a few social and cultural remnants which were African in origin. "A Far Cry from Africa," a poem in Walcott's first full collection (*In a Green Night*, published in 1962), poses the dilemma of a mixed racial and cultural heritage with painful intensity:

> I who am poisoned with the blood of both,
> Where shall I turn, divided to the vein?
> I who have cursed
> The drunken officer of British rule, how choose
> Between this Africa and the English tongue I love?
> Betray them both, or give back what they give?
> How can I face such slaughter and be cool?
> How can I turn from Africa and live? [6]

The immediate occasion of the poem—slaughter of white colonials (including children) in Kenya during the struggle for national independence—leads the poet to broader considerations. He inherits the genius and violence of both races; he indicts colonial history and slavery no less than the slaughter of children; and yet he loves "the English tongue," as, indeed, the high rhetoric of the poem attests. Nevertheless, to "turn from Africa" would be a kind of suicide, an amputation of identity.

Because this dilemma can never be entirely resolved, Walcott has been given an inexhaustible subject matter, renegotiated over several decades of a writer's public and private life. Even when he is most critical of the historical injustice of Europe, whose art is implicated in its misdeeds, he never abandons European literary tradition. In an essay about the Caribbean writer, Walcott asserts that, "by openly fighting tradition we perpetuate it, that revolutionary literature is a filial impulse, and that maturity is the assimilation of the features of every ancestor." [7] Assimilation in his case meant adapting for his own purposes stylistic features of the three M's of English poetry, Christopher Marlowe, John Milton, and Andrew Marvell (whose "Bermudas" gave Walcott the title for his first book: "He hangs in shades the orange bright/Like golden lamps in a green night. . . .").

Furthermore, to help convey the Caribbean condition, three archetypal characters from Western tradition appear again and again in his poems; one from myth and two from post-Renaissance English literature. First, there is Adam of Genesis's creation narrative, who is brought to life in an idyllic setting with no previous history and assigned the task of naming all other creatures around him. Then, there is the mooncalf Caliban from Shakespeare's *The Tempest* (*GBWW* I: 27, 524–48; II: 25, 524–48), Prospero's not fully humanized (and in many ways comic) servant, who nevertheless has an original and engaging way of speaking. The Prospero-Caliban pair form a neat analogy for the British overlord and exploited African populace of the West Indies. A third archetype is Daniel Defoe's Robinson Crusoe, resembling Adam in his idyllic solitude, yet burdened with the memory of the lost culture and accompanied not by Eve but by the African whom he names Friday, an equal in the sense that both are human beings ship-wrecked far from home.

There is a conceptual overlap in all three of these characters, in fact, Walcott spells it out in an early poem titled "Crusoe's Journal," describing Defoe's novel as

> ... our first book, our profane Genesis
>   whose Adam speaks that prose
> which, blessing some sea-rock, startles itself
>   with poetry's surprise,
> in a green world, one without metaphors;
>   like Christofer he bears
> in speech mnemonic as a missionary's
>   the Word to savages,
> its shape an earthen, water-bearing vessel's
>   whose sprinkling alters us
> into good Fridays who recite His praise,
>   parroting our master's
> style and voice, we make his language ours,
>   converted cannibals
> we learn with him to eat the flesh of Christ. [8]

Crusoe saved the life of his shipwrecked companion on a Friday, hence the name conferred; but Walcott's poem activates one of the ironies only implicit in the novel. The saving Word, or Logos, of Christ (along with the hope of eternal life) is given by Crusoe to the African at the same moment that Friday is deprived of his original name and language, transforming him into a "parrot" who will henceforth also be a servant. In this servitude he is made to resemble Christ, the Suffering Servant, who became a slave even to the point of voluntary death—and on a Friday that tradition has called "Good." The final irony is that the Caliban-like cannibal is taught not to eat human flesh even as he is directed in symbolic ritual to "eat the flesh of Christ." Meanwhile, the overlord's exploitation of the bodies of slaves itself amounts to legalized cannibalism since the slaves' forced labor feeds the slaveowner.

Because of Christianity's historical complicity with slavery and oppression, it became impossible for Walcott to sustain the Methodist religion of his childhood, and yet his poetry often glows with an apocalyptic aura, much as the abandoned Protestantism of the English Romantic poets resurfaced in the form of a reverence for nature and a belief in the transcendent power of the individual soul. Walcott wrote an autobiographical long poem titled *Another Life* (1973), which is modeled on Wordsworth's *The Prelude* and, moreover, describes an experience comparable to one of Wordsworth's "spots of time," moments of solitary revelation in a natural setting. The narrator, in his fourteenth year, has walked by himself to a vantage point overlooking a valley outside the town.

> Afternoon light ripened the valley,
> rifling smoke climbed from the small labourers' houses,

and I dissolved into a trance.
I was seized by a pity more profound
than my young body could bear, I climbed
with the labouring smoke,
I drowned in labouring breakers of bright cloud,
then uncontrollably I began to weep,
inwardly, without tears, with a serene extinction
of all sense; I felt compelled to kneel,
I wept for nothing and for everything, [9]

The experience and the language recall similar moments in Wordsworth, but there is an important difference. The smoke rising like incense of religious ritual is in this case smoke from "small labourers' houses," and the passage eventually goes on to say, "something still fastens us forever to the poor." The Romantics' transcendental moments were revelations made to the solitary soul, setting it apart from other people and even from Nature herself. But Walcott's vision establishes a bond of pity and solidarity with the poor; and it *is* a visionary bond, as the word "forever" in the line just quoted suggests. Some of the passage's transcendental intentions resonate in the word "labour," variously contextualized as "labourers' houses," "labouring smoke," and "labouring breakers of bright cloud." From the houses of the poor a kind of incense arises, like the ascending vision of the poet, who is carried upward into the ethereal realm of the clouds where he is "drowned," or merged with all that is. "Labour," apart from a general reference to the working people of Saint Lucia—and of the world at large, with whose constructive activity Walcott wishes to associate his own writing—also recalls the "labour" of childbearing. Something is being brought to birth here, a vision that is like the Nativity, which of course also occurred in a humble setting. As the Saint Lucians have been the collective parents of a native identity, Walcott wishes to give birth to himself as poet, one unified with his people. It was in early adolescence that he began writing the verse that appeared in his first (self-published) chapbook of poems, some four years after the experience described here.

The recognition of solidarity's engendering power may not, of course, be mutual. Walcott has always cared about Saint Lucia's citizens, but he is sometimes troubled by a doubt that he matters to *them,* since, after all, the majority of the populace does not read poetry, its spiritual life entrusted almost entirely to the church. The theme appears in an early poem like "Crusoe's Island" and a later one titled "The Light of the World," so it is not merely a passing quibble for the poet. Without ever returning to the faith of his childhood, Walcott has from time to time used Christian symbols in his work (for example, in the late poem "Pentecost"), but it is not likely that Christian references have made his poetry more accessible to churchgoing Saint Lucians or that those references will seem fully authentic, apart from an active faith, to the largely secular audience for contemporary poetry.

Perhaps the single most effective step that Walcott has taken in order to unite himself with the underclasses of the West Indies was his work in theater, beginning in 1959, when he founded the Trinidad Theatre Workshop, serving as its director and principal playwright until 1976. He was able to develop a viable folk theater that interested both the educated and the uneducated. Inevitably, this theatrical experience (which merits a study of its own, apart from his verse writings) influenced his work as a poet, and, after all, the greatest poet in English was also a playwright.

What we see in Walcott's poems of the '60s and '70s, especially in the autobiographical *Another Life,* is an increasing concern with character and drama. Eventually native speech variants began to affect the language of the poems as well—Saint Lucia's French patois in "Sainte Lucie" and West Indian English in "The Schooner *Flight.*" The latter is a long narrative poem in the voice of a sailor named Shabine, a working-class alter ego for Walcott, as can be judged from this passage, which duplicates (in reductive terms) several biographical facts in the poet's life:

> I'm just a red nigger who love the sea,
> I had a sound colonial education,
> I have Dutch, nigger, and English in me,
> and either I'm nobody, or I'm a nation. [10]

Shabine's "sound colonial education" might explain the literary (and allusive) quality of many lines in the poem, which, among other antecedents, invoke *Piers Ploughman* and has Shabine assert, "I had no nation now but the imagination," a surprising conceptual leap for a sailor to make. Despite the gritty veracity of its details, the poem is not a piece of naturalism; instead, it is an extended self-portrait in allegorical terms. Still, Walcott's familiarity with "ordinary life" of the West Indies lends non-allegorical vividness of incident and pungency of speech to the poem, which counts as one of the most successful in his middle period.

The poet spent a year in New York City on a Rockefeller grant in the early '60s and made a number of subsequent visits to the U.S. in the years following. Beginning in the late seventies, he accepted a series of teaching posts at several American universities, including Columbia and Harvard, which led to a permanent appointment at Boston University. His 1981 volume *The Fortunate Traveller* registered the influence of the American scene and American poets, especially Lowell. Critics are made uncomfortable by sudden change, and the book had a decidedly mixed reception, yet from this distance it is clear that the book contains some of Wolcott's best work, including the title poem and "Old New England," "Piano Practice," "North and South," and "The Hotel Normandie Pool." This poem allegorizes a fellow lounger at a resort as Ovid, author of *Tristia,* which is Latin poetry's emblematic treatment of the theme of exile. Walcott's variation on the theme is no disgrace to its predecessor:

> Turn to us, Ovid. Our emerald sands
> are stained with sewage from each tin-shacked Rome;
> corruption, censorship, and arrogance
> make exile seem a happier thought than home. [11]

It was during these years that Walcott befriended Joseph Brodsky, himself an exile from the Soviet Union, and a new concern for Russian literature appeared in Walcott's writing, along with a heightened sense of the burden that Stalinist terror as well as the Holocaust has placed on all poets with serious ambitions to understand and represent the twentieth century.

Walcott's new cosmopolitanism did not please all his critics, yet it has been balanced between global range and the local, West Indian reality. For him exile has been broken by frequent returns to the Caribbean, and, when he composed a poem of epic length, its setting was once again Saint Lucia. The title *Omeros* obviously invokes the author of the *Iliad,* and several of the characters of this book-length narrative have Greek names, beginning with Helen, a beautiful black working-class wife, who is also a sort of muse figure for the poem. As local and realistic as the poem is, with its gallery of Saint Lucian types, it nevertheless makes several gestures toward wider relevance. Literary relevance is broadened through its allusions to Greek literature and political relevance through the connection established between the extinction of the Aruacs, the approximate genocide of slavery, and the destruction of Indian nations in North America.

Mass murder haunts the consciousness directing this poem, figured at the literary level in allusions to the destruction of Troy in the *Iliad* (*GBWW* I: 4, 3–178; II: 3, 1–306). The poem's narrator, close to Walcott himself, makes several cameo appearances in its pages, so that a palpable autobiographical dimension is also present in the work. Its verse form, tercets sometimes rhymed as Italian *terza rima,* recalls Dante's *Commedia* (*GBWW* I: 21; II: 19, 1–167), the first autobiographical epic; yet Walcott has rejected that term for his longest poem, remarking that epic is an idealizing genre, while his goal is to present his characters realistically, with all their faults. Doesn't the character Helen—physically beautiful, fiercely independent—have an ideal aspect, despite her infidelity to her husband Achille? Yes, but then she must also figure as the quintessence of Saint Lucia, a product of the African diaspora, anti-authoritarian, and one seamless substance with her tropical surround. Sea, sand, and palm trees join to compose a frame that in Walcott's poem stands as a rough equivalent to Beatrice's heavenly amphitheater.

Walcott is only in his sixties, and we can expect more poems from him, yet it seems clear that he has already produced a body of work that, despite its faults, qualifies him as a poet sufficiently great, even in a literary climate accustomed to repudiate greatness as a form of pretension. If it is true that the poetry audience (at least until the Nobel Prize) has acknowledged Walcott's achievement only grudgingly, his gifts and instincts have ignored the fact and gone ahead to produce a poetry wider and deeper than his era was fully prepared to receive.

Anthony Hecht

Shakespearean amplitude and a concern with history's murderous injustices might not seem a likely pairing in a contemporary poet, and yet Walcott shares them with a slightly older contemporary, Anthony Hecht, whom he otherwise resembles very little. Hecht, brought up in New York City as the elder son of an upper-middle-class Jewish family, published his first collection of poems, titled *A Summoning of Stones,* in the mid-fifties and was immediately associated with a postwar generation of young poets like Richard Wilbur, Adrienne Rich, W. S. Merwin, and James Merrill, who had followed Auden's lead by returning to the meter, rhyme, and verseforms that modernist poets had mostly abandoned three decades earlier. Traditional prosody, joined with an elevated diction and cultural allusiveness, helped these poets produce poems in an elegant, almost Augustan mode. In Hecht's case there was the difference that, hard by poems with Shakespearean diction and high formal gloss, stood poems of terror and horror, like "Christmas Is Coming," in which an unidentified narrator in an unnamed locale crawls through cold and darkness in an effort to avoid bullets of roving soldiers in the winter hills. That it should be Christmas, the season when (at least in theory) peace came into the world, is an irony essential to the poem's meaning. During Hecht's term of army service in the last year of World War II, he participated in the liberation of one of the Nazi death camps, an experience that left an indelible mark. The history of Christian intolerance to Jews, culminating in the camps, has permanently tarnished one of the central holidays in the Christian calendar for Hecht and others. Hecht returned several times to this theme in later (and more effective) poems like "Rites and Ceremonies," "The Book of Yolek," "Apprehensions," and "Persistences," with no sense that the emotion latent in the topic had been exhausted for him.

The blasted landscape of "Christmas Is Coming" also reappears in Hecht's work in other contexts as more or less an equivalent for T. S. Eliot's Waste Land or the *paese guasto* (waste country) of Canto XIV in Dante's *Inferno.* Yet it is not always an entirely terrible apparition. In a poem titled "A Hill" (from Hecht's second collection, *The Hard Hours,* published in 1967), the narrator, who may or may not be the poet, describes a stroll through an outdoor market in a Roman piazza. The carefully rendered scene is suddenly interrupted by a sort of waking dream in which actual surroundings are supplanted by a winter hill in a barren landscape. Not knowing what to make of this odd event, the narrator shrugs it off. Years later the visual picture of the hill returns to him and recalls where he first encountered it:

> I remembered that hill; it lies just to the left
> Of the road north of Poughkeepsie; and as a boy
> I stood before it for hours in wintertime. [12]

In a letter to a critic, Hecht gives his sense of the landscape's meaning:

> "In my poem I am really writing about a pronounced feeling of loneliness and abandonment in childhood, which I associate with a cold and unpeopled landscape. . . . I have always felt that desolation, that hell itself, is most powerfully expressed in an uninhabited natural landscape at its bleakest." [13]

And so the waste landscapes of this poem, of "The Short End," "The Feast of Stephen," "Auspices," and "Exile" are accounted for, at least partly. A careful reader will nevertheless recognize that the wintry hill in Hecht's early poem evidences not only an infernal aspect, but a transcendental one as well. It is a vision powerful enough to replace a superficially pretty scene drawn from actuality, and a memory resonant enough to endure through several decades, so that, despite the prevailing mood of desolation, it has a steadying effect on the writer and the reader.

Anthony Hecht

Grasping the hill's full meaning requires a reflection on the category of *negative* transcendence. The divine may be revealed to humankind either by a vision of beauty and joy like the Paradise Dante caught a glimpse of or by the terrifying voice out of the whirlwind that came to Job. For a religious philosopher like Spinoza, the very presence of inexplicable evil in the world was evidence of a Godhead that surpasses limited human understanding and expectations: God is infinite, and therefore no human boundaries—even humane ones—may be set for the divine will. Hecht has been rightly described as one of our darkest poets, but his darkness is religiously grounded, distinct from mere nihilism. The hill is a site comparable to Mount Horeb or Mount Sinai, where Moses received first his vocation, and then the Law.

Significant, too, is the fact that the hill is assigned a rather homely locality. It is not in Dante's Italy or contemporary Rome: it is just north of Poughkeepsie, New York in the United States. Although Hecht has from the first been perfectly at ease with European history and culture, his poetry is often written in an American vein as well. He grew up in New York City, and for him to be American is to be Jewish-American. The complex history and culture of European Jewry is only glancingly mentioned in Hecht's poetry, which alludes to the Old World mainly in classical or Christian terms. Meanwhile, the America Hecht is inspired by is neither Native-American culture nor New England nor Thomas Jefferson nor Ralph Waldo Emerson but instead the witty, deflationary, slangy, New York-flavored matrix that produced comics like Groucho Marx, or writers like S. J. Perelman, George S. Kaufman, and Ben Hecht, or performers like Bob Hope and Fred Astaire.

This part of Hecht's sensibility is most to the fore in his second book in poems like "The Dover Bitch," "The Man Who Married Magdalene," and "Third Avenue in Sunlight." The last poem tells the story of a fellow schoolmate of the poet's, a perennial misfit and barfly, who eventually has a breakdown during which he hallucinates an attack by Indians:

> They entered his hotel room, tomahawks
> Flashing like barracuda. He tried to pray.
> Three years of treatment. Occasionally he talks
> About how he almost didn't get away.
>
> Daily the prowling sunlight whets its knife
> Along the sidewalk, We almost never meet.
> In the Rembrandt dark he lifts his amber life.
> My bar is somewhat farther down the street. [14]

The narrator manages to keep a faintly satiric tone, despite the disturbing events recounted; and once we know that Hecht himself spent several months in a sanatorium recovering from depression after the breakup of his first marriage, the poem acquires an extra dimension of meaning.

There are a few Hecht poems in which a note of redemptive happiness is struck, in particular the radiant "Peripateia," which appeared in his third book, *Million of Strange Shadows* (1977). The poem's narrator is watching a performance of *The Tempest* when, stage play modulating into dream, the young Miranda leaves the proscenium, comes down into the audience, takes his hand, and leads him from the theater out into freedom and happiness. This fable was Hecht's way of imaging emotions attendant on his second marriage (which has lasted). The poet numbers among those on whom the world's beauty is not lost, and who sees in the birth of a son by his second marriage something compensatory in the face of suffering, madness, and death.

In some of his poems, intimations of beauty and misery actually cohabit to produce a strange, multivalent amalgam that remains a Hecht patent. For example, the title poem of *The Venetian Vespers* (1979), a long, characterized monologue in the voice of a solitary, self-belittling American who lives in Venice.

> In these late days
> I find myself frequently at the window,
> Its glass a cooling comfort to my temple.
> And I lift up mine eyes, not to the hills
> Of which there are not any, but to the clouds.
> Here is a sky determined to maintain
> The reputation of Tiepolo,
> A moving vision of a shapely mist,
> Full of the splendor of the insubstantial. [15]

A gorgeous description of sunset clouds follows, but, for all its rich diction and imagery, we are meant to regard it as useless and "insubstantial," probably because it isn't balanced by negative transcendence: no hills are present. If the speaker of the poem has led a life quite different from Hecht's, the question immediately posed is, Why did he choose to write this poem, the longest in his oeuvre? One answer might be that the Shakespearean gifts for characterization evident here are sufficient excuse for the work; it adds to our grasp of the human comedy. Another is that the character's failings represent dangerous possibilities the author has sometimes felt drawn to; the poem would amount then to a sort of exorcism, useful to the author and to others after him. For Hecht is above all a moralist, aware of the fragility of order, justice, beauty, and happiness. Human hopes of achieving them are small and always threatened by adversarial powers. And yet the effort must be made, by public servants on one hand, and by poets on the other—or at least by poets who are not themselves adversaries to justice, order, and beauty.

Adrienne Rich

Justice, order, beauty: What sounds incontrovertible becomes moot when guardians of the good do not agree on what the good is—or when their estimate changes during the course of a life and a life work. Adrienne Rich published her first book, *A Change of World,* just before completing an undergraduate degree at Radcliffe in 1951, and she, along with Hecht, was immediately ranked with the most promising of a generation noted for elegance and prosodic conservatism. Auden, who selected the book for the Yale Younger Poets series, praised the author for qualities of neatness, modesty, and respect for elders. Yet even in this book there were storm warnings, and a poem like "Aunt Jennifer's Tigers" could focus on the hidden contradictions found in needlework, a pastime always regarded as essentially feminine. "Aunt Jennifer" is a placid practitioner of it, but her subject is tigers, not flowers.

> Aunt Jennifer's fingers fluttering through her wool
> Find even the ivory needle hard to pull.
> The massive weight of Uncle's wedding band
> Sits heavily upon Aunt Jennifer's hand.
>
> When Aunt is dead, her terrified hands will lie
> Still ringed with ordeals she was mastered by.
> The tigers in the panel that she made
> Will go on prancing, proud and unafraid. [16]

The needlepoint tigers, but no other facts about Aunt Jennifer, win the poet's admiration. The early Rich tended to mock mid-century American women for the dilemma they had allowed to entrap them. In the title poem of the pivotal volume *Snapshots of a Daughter-in-Law* (1963), her trademark irony is already active in the designation of the female character described in the poem's first section, whose identity is conferred by marriage, not by any achievement of her own.

> Your mind now, mouldering like wedding-cake,
> heavy with useless experience, rich

with suspicion, rumor, fantasy,
crumbling to pieces under the knife-edge
of mere fact. In the prime of your life.

Nervy, glowering, your daughter
wipes the teaspoons, grows another way. [17]

Herself a daughter who has grown "another way," the author brings to bear a variety of reflections and citations concerning the social condition of women, very much in the light of Mary Wollstonecraft's writings and Simone de Beauvoir's pioneering study, *The Second Sex.* The poem concludes in its tenth section with something like a paean to female potential, the lines as proud and prancing as Aunt Jennifer's tigers but meant to inspire present rather than posthumous achievement—"her cargo/no promise then:/delivered/palpable/ours." [18] The poem takes its place beside Marianne Moore's "Marriage" and Bishop's "Roosters" as one of the century's most acute presentations of the obstacles women must confront in order to achieve independence.

Rich had been married for a decade when this volume appeared, managing to be wife and mother of three children while she wrote her poems. Signs of marital strain, always well worded, appeared in due course; for example, "A Marriage in the 'Sixties," written perhaps as an update of Lowell's "Man and Wife," the emblematic poem of marriage in "the tranquilized Fifties." A decade after Lowell, Rich treats the subject from the wife's point of view:

Some mote of history has flown into your eye.
Will nothing ever be the same,
even our quarrels take a different key,
our dreams exhume new metaphors?
The world breathes underneath our bed.
Don't look. We're at each other's mercy too. [19]

What frightening revelations do the poet and her husband hold at bay or sweep under the bed? The reader has to accept the disappointment as well as the relief of never being told in full and be content to watch (figuratively) the silent movie of an angry discussion. The subtitles Rich provides here are doubtless more interesting than the suppressed words themselves would have been. Still, anger and confrontation are seen as necessary phases in the process of "exhuming new metaphors," that is, writing new poems.

Rich's critique of hindering marital convention found its counterpart in the social upheavals of the '60s, the Vietnam War, and, finally, the launching of a new feminist initiative. Her next three books—*Necessities of Life* (1966), *Leaflets* (1969), and *The Will to Change* (1971)—portray their autobiographical author against the animated frieze of the counterculture, positioning herself among conflicting public and private claims, insisting on social justice, on her right to pleasure, on the importance of women's thinking and women's art. Beginning in the '60s, Rich appended the date of composition to each poem, so the sense of immediacy, of poems written

directly after political demonstra-
tions or the newest movie by Jean-
Luc Godard, is strong. As *sudden*
as this poetry is, it keeps the ironic
wit and lapidary phrasing that Rich
developed during her decade of
apprenticeship.

*Adrienne
Rich*

Possibly it was her work in the
Head Start Program at the City
University of New York, a reme-
dial education project for inner city
students, that led her to one of
her most painful insights: her poetry, written in the dialect of the
university-educated white middle
class, was not easily comprehensible to the disadvantaged groups
it was meant to assist. The 1968
"The Burning of Paper Instead of
Children" begins with an anecdote
about her young son burning a math textbook and receiving a reprimand
from a neighbor. The poem, written in five sections, begins with an im-
provisational revery about various classics in the Western tradition and an
evocation of Jeanne d'Arc at the stake; then it moves on to a fragmented
presentation of her own life and a quoted excerpt from a student paper.
Despite faulty grammar, the excerpt affectingly describes the condition of
the inner city poor; phrases drawn from it reappear with deepened cogency
in later sections of the poem. The student's halting English and the poem's
fragmented method make a strangely appropriate pair, as if faulty grammar
were a kind of art and a fragmented poetics akin to illiteracy. The last section,
which depicts the author at her typewriter, is blocked as prose:

> In America we have only the present tense. I am in danger. You are
> in danger. The burning of a book arouses no sensation in me. I know
> it hurts to burn. There are flames of napalm in Catonsville, Maryland.
> I know it hurts to burn. The typewriter is overheated, my mouth is
> burning, I cannot touch you and this is the oppressor's language. [20]

The "oppressor's language" includes not only standard English but also
the whole apparatus of literary allusion and irony that only a few readers can
follow. If encouraging the disadvantaged in their struggle for social justice is
the goal, the author is forced to realize that her poems aren't likely to do so,
even as she asserts the priority of children's lives over mere "paper."

The option of simplifying her language and form so that her poems
would have the direct appeal of placards in a political demonstration was
apparently never an option for Rich. Her next book, *Diving into the Wreck*
(1973), is among her most involuted, partly because of the use of disjunctive

fragments and partly because she seems to have attempted to write without a "censor," so that every feeling could claim its place on the page. Her husband committed suicide in 1972, a misfortune that makes her willingness to publish a poem like "The Phenomenology of Anger" even more impressive. Not too many poems (excepting dramatic literature) have included the line "I hate you," but this one does, as an element in Rich's fierce panorama of marital disaster. It is as though the author's commitment to truth and the truth of feeling had become so strong that ordinary decorum had to be dismissed, otherwise the proposed revolution in male-female relationships had no chance of succeeding. Feminism became the overriding subject of Rich's poetry because it mattered supremely to her and because she recognized that most of her audience consisted of educated middle-class women who could understand "the oppressor's language" she used. Political efforts on behalf of the underclasses and for disenfranchised nonwhites could be made outside the poetry, and references to their plight could appear in it, but they are not for the most part Rich's audience.

Although her next book was titled *The Dream of a Common Language* (1978), Rich was nevertheless aware that the dream of a common language was precisely that. The book is less complex than earlier ones, but only comparatively so. In the magisterial "Transcendental Etude" she envisions "a whole new poetry beginning here," [21] its newness posited less on its simplicity than on its status as a poetry written by women for women—and not distinct from erotic passion between them. For, at some point in her investigative experiment, Rich had discovered her own lesbian sexual orientation, and she concluded that the transfer of erotic energy would necessarily involve a shift from a male to a female muse. To sense how far she has come, all we need do is compare the poet's mocking attitudes toward the mother in "Snapshots of a Daughter-in-Law" a decade earlier, written with the intention of being overheard by male readers, to "Sibling Mysteries," a poem addressed to her sister.

> Remind me how we loved our mother's body
> our mouths drawing the first
> thin sweetness from her nipples
>
> our faces dreaming hour on hour
> in the salt smell of her lap Remind me
> how her touch melted childgrief
>
> how she floated great and tender in our dark
> or stood guard over us
> against our willing [22]

Women performing traditional roles are no longer to be ridiculed but rather understood as products of an oppressive order, with valuable qualities. The terms of evaluation chosen here may strike some readers as verging on sentimentality, but definitions of sentimentality are always culturally determined: it is not a timeless, abstract quality. (When the word "sentimental" was coined in the eighteenth century, it was used in praiseful contexts.)

Direct expression of tender feelings in these lines is perhaps part of the women's aesthetic that Rich has been searching for. In any case, the poem has renounced most of the irony and intellectual artillery of her earlier work. If writing tenderly means losing some readers, Rich is prepared to do so, on the chance that she may be making available feelings formerly dismissed as unacceptable for art. Any occasion for reexamining aesthetic strictures ought to be welcomed. Do we go to poetry mainly to sharpen the psychic (or conversational) defenses useful in daily life or to gain access to feelings we have not, for whatever reason, acknowledged?

Rich no longer wishes to attack other women, but meanwhile there is no shortage of targeted opponents, those who perpetuate—by violence or legal coercion—the patriarchal order. We trust Rich, I think, when she says she would prefer not to have to attack *anyone* if circumstances did not require it. The centerpiece of the book is an exploration of tenderness between women, the "Twenty-One Love Poems." These are from ten to sixteen lines each and recall the Elizabethan sonnet sequence, but they are more forthright about the physical details of lovemaking and end with a final separation of the lovers. If joy and triumph were the notes struck at the sequence's conclusion, it would have been more effective as an allegory for Rich's successful "will to change," but that would apparently have meant falsifying the facts of her life. The sequence first records ecstatic discovery and fulfillment, a fulfillment eventually replaced by resignation as love ends and the couple breaks apart. Possibly Rich wants to suggest that even rewarding love relationships are not women's sole chance for happiness. A purely affirmative mood is reserved for the volume's final poem, the "Transcendental Etude," which celebrates women as artists, authors of "a whole new poetry." And, once more, small-scale domestic activity and comfort are regarded with kindly respect, part of a distinctly female sensibility that the poet wishes to celebrate.

No dramatic shifts have taken place in Rich's writing since this watershed book. Instead, she has continued to explore other aspects of her central theme, focusing her inquiry on the question of her own identity—as woman and artist, certainly, but also as an American and as a person of Jewish descent (Rich's father was Jewish). In the volume *Your Native Land, Your Life* (1986), the poem, "Sources" is a quest for the origin of selfhood, a sequence in twenty-three sections, some of them written in prose. Among the most interesting are the sections addressed to her father, in which his situation as an assimilated Jew is explored. The poet is finally able to see an analogy between her oppression as a woman and the distress her father, even though male, felt as an outsider. This insight allows her in turn to confront (in writing) feelings about the suicide of her husband, who was also Jewish, a subject not taken up in her poetry before. Section XXII of the sequence, one of the prose passages, is addressed to him and concludes:

"I think you thought there was no such place for you, and perhaps there was none then, and perhaps there is none now; but we will have to make it, we who want an end to suffering, who want to change the laws of history, if we are not to *give ourselves away.*" [23]

The resolve to change the social order is paired here with a willingness to make common cause with all those whom society has harmed, men along with women, so long as ground rules of equality and cooperation apply. Extremes of rage like those in "The Phenomenology of Anger" are not recorded again, and the poet who emerges from Rich's latest books *Time's Power* (1989) and *An Atlas of the Difficult World* (1991) is one who has settled on a consistent political stance and a flexible, collage-like poetic method, resolutely critical without being violent, celebratory when the poet finds a place or person that moves her, and receptive to new insights as they appear on the horizon of consciousness.

Seamus Heaney

Is it sheer coincidence that the Irish poet Seamus Heaney is among the most tender poets writing today and that his imagination is deeply involved with female archetypes? Even those unfamiliar with Jungian psychology are aware of the primal association of Nature, Earth, and Mother. That association was intrinsic to the early Celtic religion of Ireland and has persisted in Roman Catholicism's cult of the Virgin. Though Heaney is not now a practicing Catholic, he was brought up in rural Northern Ireland, where religion goes without saying, the psychic substratum of farming communities organically bound to Earth's seasonal cycle and its counterpart in the church calendar. Traditional male archetypes center around high promontories and dry land; but Heaney has made the mud of the Irish bog his sacred precinct, a wet opening in the earth that yields "turf" (peat) for fuel and cultural artifacts from earlier epochs. In his poem, "Bogland," he says, "The bogholes might be Atlantic seepage./The wet centre is bottomless." [24]

The word "bottomless" is tinged with ambivalence, and Heaney would

*Seamus
Heaney*

have amounted to an Irish genre painter only if his adherence to Earth and the pastoral perspective had been unqualified. In fact, the early part of his career is a negotiation of the tension between his sense of poetic vocation and his loyalties to family and the farming community in County Derry in Northern Ireland where he grew up. His first book is titled *Death of a Naturalist* (1966); the "naturalist" in question is Heaney himself, who sees that he must on one level repudiate the purely natural order of Earth if he wants to evade the dissolution earthly phenomena inherit. Like the narrator of Yeats's

"Sailing to Byzantium," he must leave the country of the young, with its surplus of generative and transitory physicality, in order to attain the realm of art and permanence. This is an aesthetic or metaphysical stance, but for Heaney there was also a purely practical side to it. Choosing this writerly vocation meant not becoming a farmer like his father; and an alternative became available with Northern Ireland's 1947 Education Act, which offered scholarships to promising students from rural areas. In the early poem "Digging," Heaney describes, in terms of praise, his father's and grandfather's skill with a spade, used both for digging potatoes and cutting turf from the bogs. He admires their skill with this instrument,

> But I've no spade to follow men like them.
>
> Between my finger and my thumb
> The squat pen rests.
> I'll dig with it. [25]

At least the pen is "squat," avoiding the slender elegance of any writing that might ignore Heaney's country background—which he perceives as both an asset and a burden. If he has no spade to "follow" men like his ancestors, he even so describes, in "Follower," his childhood habit of trailing along behind his father during ploughing season, hoping one day to match parental speed and accuracy at the task.

> I was a nuisance, tripping, falling,
> Yapping always. But today
> It is my father who keeps stumbling
> Behind me, and will not go away. [26]

The last two lines present a purely figurative equivalent for the guilt of the son who goes beyond his ancestors' place in the scheme of things, but Heaney had to accept that guilt in order to become a writer.

More painful still for Heaney has been the question of his political role as part of the disenfranchised Catholic minority in Northern Ireland. During his years at the University of Belfast, Heaney joined the Gaelic Society, possibly as an assertion of his minority identity in the Protestant capital of the North. But he did not choose to become a Gaelic-language writer as other contemporaries did. Since his mother tongue is an Irish variant of English, he considers it his birthright, offering him a better chance of achievement than a language acquired by pronunciation practice and memorizing verb tenses would. He has also been willing to be influenced by English poets as well as Irish on the assumption that poetry finally belongs not to any particular nationality but instead to whoever reads it with pleasure and instruction. (A useful comparison can be made here with Derek Walcott's views concerning the English poetic tradition.)

One of the paradoxes of Heaney's early development is that he began to take himself seriously under the tutelage of a minor British poet named Philip Hobsbaum who had come to live in Belfast in 1965—a mentor who, though reasonably cosmopolitan, asserted that parochialism was "universal" because it dealt with fundamental aspects of experience available to all. Hobsbaum's view helped Heaney toward his first subject, childhood memories of County Derry. *Death of a Naturalist,* published in 1966, launched him as one among several new authors in what has turned out to be a sort of poetry renaissance in Northern Ireland. The grace period during which political questions could be assigned lower priority for poets came to an end in 1969, however, when relations between Protestants and Catholics took a violent turn. Heaney's second volume *Door into the Dark* had just appeared, and he was in Spain when news of the clash reached him. It is just possible that some of the militant minority had been stirred by a poem in the book titled "Requiem for the Croppies," a characterized monologue spoken by one of the Irish rebels of 1798 known as "croppies" because of their cropped hair. A story from that time tells how the insurgents put handfuls of barley in their pockets as convenient provisions to be eaten while on the march. Little more than cannon fodder, the defeated quickly came to their end, as Heaney's narrator recounts:

> Terraced thousands died, shaking scythes at cannon.
> The hillside blushed, soaked in our broken wave.
> They buried us without shroud or coffin
> And in August the barley grew up out of the grave. [27]

The "croppies" become then a metaphoric crop, dragon's teeth that, once sown, can produce new combatants—as late as 1969 if need be. It may, however, have been the mythic resonance of this story, rather than its political potential that most interested Heaney. For the event also recapitulates ancient fertility rituals of Northern European religion, in which devotees were slain in order to guarantee the return of vegetation in spring. The theme returns in a poem titled "The Tollund Man" in Heaney's next book *Wintering Out,* published in 1972. It describes a bog, this time one in Denmark, from which archaeologists exhumed the preserved corpse of a man sacrificed as part of a fertility ritual, long before the Christian era. After some brilliant description of the "Bridegroom to the goddess," Heaney says,

> I could risk blasphemy,
> Consecrate the cauldron bog
> Our holy ground and pray
> Him to make germinate
>
> The scattered, ambushed
> Flesh of labourers,
> Stockinged corpses
> Laid out in farmyards,
>
> Tell-tale skin and teeth
> Flecking the sleepers
> Of four young brothers, trailed
> For miles along the lines. [28]

The "sleepers" are railway ties along which partisans were dragged until dead. If Heaney is almost willing to "risk blasphemy," in speaking of them that is perhaps because Christianity also contains elements of the same archetypes in the death and resurrection of Christ, liturgically reenacted each church year during the season when foliage returns. It was no accident that the Easter Rising of 1916 (the occasion of one of Yeats's best-known poems) occurred when it did. Since Catholicism constitutes part of his minority identity, Heaney never directly repudiates it, but he prefers to locate spiritual perspectives in the older cults.

The bog and human remains taken from it reappear in several later poems collected in *North* (1975), including "Bog Queen," "The Grauballe Man," "Punishment," and "Strange Fruit," occasions for some of Heaney's most elaborate visual descriptions. It serves as one of the central metaphors of his early poetry not only because of its associations with Mother Earth and the Druid goddess but also because a place of decay and dissolution in this instance is paradoxically divine love's mansion and a site of preservation as well. In it the human bridegroom, though dead, is given a relative immortality, preserved by bog tannin for a later era to discover. Here is one resolution of the tension Heaney felt between his poetic vocation, with its promise of textual permanence, and his nostalgia for rural earth, the world of his childhood. Yeats said the poet must die a little in life in order to live a little in death, and the bog's sacrificial victims constitute an excellent metaphoric embodiment of that assertion. Beyond that, ritual sacrifice could also be linked to the new troubles in Northern Ireland (as it is again in "Punishment"); but this is a function secondary in Heaney's imagination to its larger mythic and poetic meanings. Human sympathies with those caught up directly in the struggle for autonomy led him to write poems with political content, but he was never willing to attempt a poetry of slogans, despite pressures exerted on him to produce them.

Heaney is more likely to approach all subjects in poetry as first and foremost problems in language—problems or, just as often, pleasures. Names, for instance, are likely to reveal whole histories once their etymons are looked into. The Heaney farm was called "Mossbawn," a compound of *moss,* a Scottish word, and *bawn,* English for *fortified farm.* Heaney notes that his family pronounced bawn as bann, which is Gaelic for *white.* So the centuries-old clash of ethnic identities can be exhumed from a single name, which Heaney uses as the title for one of his poems recollecting childhood. He also sees (or implies) an overlap with Anglo-Saxon *ban hus* or *bone house,* the bone-white human skeleton. In "Bone Dreams," a poem from the same volume where "Mossbawn" appeared, Heaney praises "the scop's/twang, the iron/flash of consonants/cleaving the line," reflects on his linguistic discoveries, and finally makes this exhortation:

Come back past
philology and kennings,
re-enter memory
where the bone's lair

is a love nest
in the grass. [29]

In "North," a meditation on old Norse culture, the poet is told by a Viking
longship to "Lie down/in the word-hoard," i.e., the Old English *wordhord,*
or complete treasury of the language. Heaney has obeyed the command and
made, as others have, full use of the founding language; but in his case the
activity requires "lying down," taking a horizontal position, as in sleep, lovemaking, or death. Perhaps we are meant to think of the strange multilingual
dialect Joyce, in *Finnegans Wake,* attributes to the unconscious mind during
a night's sleep. Although Heaney's poetry draws heavily on the vernacular of
County Derry, he goes beyond it to devise a tongue of his own that draws
on the blunt (or perhaps *squat*) monosyllables of Anglo-Saxon as much as
Irish English. This elemental, pastoral idiolect stands in sharp contrast to the
Latinate, abstract diction of, say, an Eliot or an Auden.

Heaney has forged what seems like the perfect linguistic embodiment of a
rural society then, but his extra achievement is to assimilate, by synesthesia,
the *sound* of words to particular landscapes as well. Consider "Anahorish," a
poem about a hill remembered from childhood:

> *Anahorish,* soft gradient
> of consonant, vowel-meadow,
>
> after-image of lamps
> swung through the yards
> on winter evenings. [30]

Or, again, "Broagh," another poem about place:

> The garden mould
> bruised easily, the shower
> gathering in your heelmark
> was the black *O*
>
> in *Broagh,*
> its low tattoo
> among the windy boortrees
> and rhubarb-blades
>
> ended almost
> suddenly, like that last
> *gh* the strangers found
> difficult to manage. [31]

The "strangers" are the British, unused to Irish sounds, and it's no coincidence that this particular name recalls the rousing Gaelic exclamation, *Erin
go bragh,* or "Ireland forever!"

In the early '70s Heaney and his wife Marie moved south to Dublin so that
they could bring up their children in an environment free of sectarian vio-

lence but probably also as a means of removing the poet from the epicenter of political upheavals that threatened his ability to write. Later in the decade, when Heaney began spending part of every year in America as a professor of poetry at Harvard, there was no doubt a further easing of the pressure placed on him to produce ad hoc position papers in verse, for which he had no gift. We do find poems with a keen political edge in *Field Work* (1979), especially "The Strand at Lough Beg," an elegy for a cousin of Heaney's killed at random by Protestants, and "Casualty," a grim but memorable depiction of meaningless sectarian slaughter and its effects on a community. Yet the centerpiece of the volume is the "Glanmore Sonnets" sequence, a celebration of the landscape around a house in County Wicklow where Heaney and his family lived for a few months. Love and war have been poetry's traditional polar extremes, so, with the diminishment of the latter theme, it is no surprise to see the subject of love assume special prominence in the sequence. Heaney's sonnets differ from their Elizabethan models in two respects: the love celebrated here is married love, and he assimilates that love to Wicklow landscapes in a meditative mode recalling the Romantic poets. Cooperating with this fusion of person and place are Celtic Earth–Mother archetypes once again; yet, in the sequence's last poem, it is mere mortals Heaney alludes to—Diarmuid and Grainne (the celebrated elopers of Irish legend) and the star-crossed lovers of *The Merchant of Venice:*

> I dreamt we slept in a moss in Donegal
> On turf banks under blankets, with our faces
> Exposed all night in a wetting drizzle,
> Pallid as the dripping sapling birches.
> Lorenzo and Jessica in a cold climate.
> Diarmuid and Grainne waiting to be found.
> Darkly asperged and censed, we were laid out
> Like breathing effigies on a raised ground. [32]

The implied connection with death here is unmistakable, but never has marriage to the archetypal goddess been portrayed as so peaceful, so moist. Keats's phrase "half in love with easeful death," comes to mind, and this death certainly seems preferable to one delivered by bullets or explosives.

Among the books published by Heaney after his association with Harvard and incorporation into the American poetry scene, *Station Island* (1984) requires special attention because of the title sequence. Station Island is an actual geographic site found in the waters of remote Lough Derg, County Donegal, and was for centuries the object of a Christian pilgrimage involving prayer, fasting, and the visitation of a series of "stations" in an itinerary called St. Patrick's Purgatory. Heaney fuses these stations with the Dantean passage up the Purgatorial mountain, envisioning it, however, as less a religious pilgrimage than a course in the poetic vocation, with scenes of instruction offered by friends and earlier Irish writers, including Joyce and Patrick Kavanagh.

One of the nonwriter characters who speaks to the poet during the stations is Colum McCartney, the cousin whose elegy Heaney had written in the

poem "The Strand at Lough Beg." This time McCartney is imagined as
speaking, his words a stinging reproach for the aestheticization of his death
in the earlier poem. Heaney makes no defensive gestures, accepting the
indictment, which, since it is composed by the author, must be connected
to guilt feelings concerning not only the elegy but also the poet's general
withdrawal from direct engagement in Northern Ireland's troubles. Other
sectarian victims appear in the poem as well to guarantee that vocational
instruction, even in this mythic setting, will not be solely aesthetic. And yet
it is Joyce's writerly directives (as Heaney imagines them) that seem most
useful to him, placed as they are in the poem's last section:

> . . . 'The English language
belongs to us. You are raking at dead fires,
>
> rehearsing the old whinges at your age.
> That subject people stuff is a cod's game,
> infantile, like this peasant's pilgrimage.
>
> You lose more of yourself than you redeem
> doing the decent thing. Keep at a tangent.
> When they make the circle wide, it's time to swim
>
> out on your own and fill the element
> with signatures on your own frequency,
> echo-soundings, searches, probes, allurements,
>
> elver-gleams in the dark of the whole sea.' [33]

During Heaney's annual teaching term at Harvard, he had deepened his
acquaintance with Lowell but seemed to have drawn more sustenance as a
poet from Bishop, who also taught there and was his friend until her death
in the late 1970s. Bishop was in her own way as "pastoral" as Heaney, the
country of the imagination located for her either in the rural Nova Scotia
of her childhood or provincial Brazil, where she lived for twenty years as
an adult. It is as though both poets, taking the measure of contemporary
poetries based on urban alienation, vaulting ambitions, or advanced literary
theory, decided to take the same backward step that Robert Frost urged and
set themselves another task—to render the daily life of characters in humble
settings, who even so embodied the interest of a rich, complex humanity.
Perhaps we see as well in Heaney's later books a move away from speech
with a strong Irish inflection to something a bit more international, a plainer
currency that is still able even so to represent County Derry.

Heaney's novelistic abilities—a flair for visual detail and for muted
drama—seem to operate only for his rural settings, but there they have a
terse, Chekhovian power in which shadow is as evocative as light. "Clearances," a sonnet sequence in *The Haw Lantern* (1987), is a portrayal of
his mother, beginning with her grandparents and moving forward through
time to the moment of her death. The seventh poem of the sequence shows
Heaney's father speaking to her shortly before she dies:

In the last minutes he said more to her
Almost than in all their life together.
'You'll be in New Row on Monday Night
And I'll come up for you and you'll be glad
When I walk in the door . . . Isn't that right?'
His head was bent down to her propped-up head.
She could not hear but we were overjoyed.
He called her good and girl. Then she was dead,
The searching for a pulsebeat was abandoned
And we all knew one thing by being there.
The space we stood around had been emptied
Into us to keep, it penetrated
Clearances that suddenly stood open.
High cries were felled and a pure change happened. [34]

The imminent departure of the remaining parent is implied in this passage, and a good many poems in Heaney's next volume of poems, *Seeing
Things* (1991), focus around his father, his father's death, and a return
to a Mossbawn no longer inhabited by the presiding figures of the poet's
childhood. The poem cited above might be a passage drawn from a novel—
up to the last four lines, in which a "metaphysics" of poetry reasserts itself.
Equally ethereal is the long sequence titled "Squarings" in the new book,
which possesses its vivid, novelistic details even while developing a helium-
light, dreamy perspective that allows past and present, memory and revery,
clarity and obscurity to associate freely in the compositional process. The
result often has a hallucinatory aura, something like medieval manuscript
illumination, as in this chiaroscuro page from childhood:

And strike this scene in gold too, in relief,
So that a greedy eye cannot exhaust it:
Stable straw, Rembrandt-gleam and burnish
Where my father bends to a tea-chest packed with salt,
The hurricane lamp held up at eye-level
In his bunched left fist, his right hand foraging

For the unbleeding, vivid-fleshed bacon,
Home-cured hocks pulled up into the light
For pondering awhile and putting back.

That night I owned the piled grain of Egypt.
I watched the sentry's torchlight on the hoard.
I stood in the door, unseen and blazed upon. [35]

Heaney evokes Rembrandt paintings both of butchers' shops with sides of
beef hung on hooks as well as Nativity scenes in numinous light. Both themes
merge here in a secular hierophany where the father's role as good provider is
epitomized in his careful tending of the cured bacon. The child spectator feels
something like religious assurance that there will always be food on the table,
that famine (an old Irish theme) will be stayed with the Biblical Egyptian
grain. The scene itself has been cured in the salt of carefully pondered poetry,

so that it provides inexhaustible sustenance for "a greedy eye." And this is the characteristic Heaney scenario, where he is not the principal actor, but rather a spectator, a beneficiary "unseen and blazed upon," who even so sees more than the principals themselves. The poet takes proper note and finds a language—his plainsong vernacular—adequate to what he sees.

1. Thom Gunn, *Collected Poems* (New York: Farrar, Straus & Giroux, 1994), p. 6.

2. Ibid., p. 40.

3. Ibid., p. 202.

4. Ibid., p. 305.

5. Ibid., p. 467.

6. Derek Walcott, *Collected Poems, 1948–84* (New York: Farrar, Straus & Giroux, 1986), p. 18.

7. Walcott, "The Muse of History," in *Is Massa Day Dead? Black Moods in the Caribbean,* ed., Orde Combs (Garden City: Anchor Books, 1974), p. 1.

8. Walcott, *CP,* pp. 92–93.

9. Ibid., pp. 184–85.

10. Ibid., p. 346.

11. Ibid., p. 442.

12. Anthony Hecht, *Collected Earlier Poems* (New York: Knopf, 1990), p. 3.

13. Quoted in J. D. McClatchy, *White Paper* (New York: Columbia University Press, 1989), p. 337–38.

14. Hecht, *CEP*, p. 4.

15. Ibid., p. 246.

16. Adrienne Rich, *Poems Selected and New, 1950-1974* (New York: Norton, 1975), p. 4.

17. Ibid., p. 47.

18. Ibid., p. 51.

19. Ibid., pp. 59–60.

20. Ibid., p. 151.

21. Rich, *The Dream of a Common Language* (New York: Norton, 1978), p. 76.

22. Ibid., p. 48.

23. Rich, *Your Native Land, Your Life* (New York: Norton, 1986), p. 25.

24. Seamus Heaney, *Selected Poems, 1966–1987,* (New York: Farrar, Straus & Giroux, 1990) p. 23.

25. Ibid., p. 4.

26. Ibid., p. 8.

27. Ibid., p. 17.

28. Ibid., pp. 39–40.

29. Ibid., p. 77.

30. Ibid., p. 29.

31. Ibid., p. 33.

32. Ibid., p. 133.

33. Ibid., p. 212.

34. Ibid., p. 252.

35. Heaney, *Seeing Things* (New York: Farrar, Straus & Giroux, 1991), p. 69.

Alfred Corn's most recent collection of poems is *Autobiographies,* which appeared in 1992. He has published five earlier volumes of poetry and a collection of literary essays entitled *The Metamorphoses of Metaphor* (1987). A teacher as well as poet and critic, he has offered classes in poetry writing at UCLA, Columbia, Yale, the City University of New York, and the University of Cincinnati.

Mr. Corn has won a number of prizes and fellowships for his work, including the Geggenheim, the NEA, *Poetry* magazine's Levinson Prize, an Award in Literature from the Academy and Institute of Arts and Letters, and one from the Academy of American Poets. His critical essays and reviews have appeared in the *The New York Times Book Review, The Washington Post Book World,* and *The New Republic.* He lives in New York City and is associated with the faculty of the Graduate Writing Division at Columbia.

The Modern Interaction of Science and Theology

John Polkinghorne

The birth pangs of modern science occurred in the late Middle Ages. By the seventeenth century science had attained maturity through the discoveries of Galileo, Kepler, and Newton. Many have suggested that Christianity was the ideological midwife of this lusty intellectual infant. [1] Because God was rational, creation would possess an intelligible regularity, but because God was free, it was necessary to inspect the world to see what form of order the divine creative will had chosen. The belief that there would be a discernible pattern of behavior in the physical world and the acknowledgment of the necessity of observation together provided the twin ingredients required to constitute the scientific enterprise. Certainly, the founding fathers of science were men to whom religion mattered, even if (like Galileo) they had trouble with the ecclesiastical authorities or (like Newton) they inclined to heterodox views.

Yet, by the end of the eighteenth century, a different spirit was abroad. The post-Newtonian generation proclaimed the triumph of mechanism. At best, the Creator was a cosmic clockmaker; at worst, he was a superfluous notion. The phenomenon of scientific atheism had begun. [2] The relation between science and religion has never been susceptible to simple characterization, [3] and in the nineteenth century there is a striking contrast between the biologists—Thomas Henry Huxley, agnostic and apostle of Darwinian evolution—and the physicists, where Faraday, Maxwell, and Lord Kelvin were all men of definite Christian conviction. Yet that century saw the widespread acceptance of an antithetical encounter between science and religion, encapsulated in the title of Andrew White's best-selling book, *A History of the Warfare of Science with Theology in Christendom.*

In the twentieth century the picture has changed again. There are significant numbers of scientists, and not just among the pious, [4] who would wish to speak of the mutual relationship in terms of friendship rather than warfare. One reason for this change lies in the death of a merely mechanical view of the world. Two advances in physics have abolished the clockwork world of the cosmic machine. The first was the discovery of quantum mechanics. [5] Some care is necessary in evaluating this development, since one of the central paradoxes of quantum theory is that, despite its great empirical success, there are still important issues of principle remaining unsettled in relation to the interpretation of the theory.

Heisenberg's uncertainty principle asserts that we cannot possess simultaneously exact knowledge of a particle's position and of its momentum. Is this to be understood as a principle of ignorance (the particle possesses a definite position and momentum but they are inaccessible to our measurement) or of indeterminacy (the unpicturable quantum world is a cloudy domain in which particles possess only potentialities, which become actual solely through the act of measurement itself)? Most physicists give the latter answer, though there is an alternative interpretation, due to David Bohm, which espouses the former point of view. [6] On the conventional understanding, the results of quantum measurements are unpredictable in detail because they are intrinsically indeterminate and radically "uncaused." Some have suggested that this rift in the web of strict causality affords the opportunity for the intervention of other kinds of agency, such as divine providence. [7] There are, however, difficulties with such a proposal. Measurements are special events, taking place only from time to time, so that agency exercised in this way would be curiously episodic. There are also problems in understanding how such microscopic events would have consequences which could be amplified to produce significant effects in the macroscopic world of everyday occurrence.

A more promising area in which to begin to look for an understanding of agency might lie in a second advance of twentieth-century physics which has also contributed to the death of mere mechanism. This is the discovery that even in classical (Newtonian) physics, there is far less predictive power than we had imagined. It turns out that the Newtonian world has in it many more clouds than clocks. That is to say, robust predictable systems, like a steadily ticking pendulum, are the exception rather than the rule. Most systems are so exquisitely sensitive to circumstances that the smallest disturbance produces uncontrollable change in their behavior, the slightest ignorance vitiates our power to predict. This first came to light in studies of models of the Earth's atmosphere and is sometimes called the butterfly effect: the weather systems are so sensitive that a butterfly stirring the air with its wings in Beijing today will have consequences for storms over North America in three or four weeks time. This astonishing discovery has been given the rather inapt name of the Theory of Chaos. [8]   The inaptness of the nomenclature arises from the fact that chaotic systems are not totally disorderly; they display in their behavior a kind of ordered-disorder as they explore, apparently randomly, a constrained set of future possibilities, called a "strange attractor."

As with quantum theory, there are unresolved questions about how to interpret this discovery. Everyone agrees that we have encountered an episte-mological barrier. Our predictive power is restricted, we can *know* less about the behavior of these systems than we had previously supposed possible.

"... the butterfly effect ... a butterfly stirring the air with its wings in Beijing today will have consequences for storms over North America in three or four weeks time."

Does this carry with it any ontological consequences? Do we need a radical revision of our basic concepts of what the physical world is actually like? It is the instinct of most scientists to feel that there should be a close connection between what we can know and what is the case. "Epistemology models Ontology" is their natural motto. This statement is an expression of the basic realist conviction which inspires the scientific endeavor: what we know (or can't know) tells us about the actual nature of the physical world. A realist belief of this kind is what motivates most physicists to opt for an interpretation of the Heisenberg uncertainty principle as involving intrinsic indeterminacy rather than mere ignorance.

It would be attractive therefore to seek to interpret chaos theory as indicating that the everyday physical world is more subtle and supple than we had previously understood. The deterministic equations of Newton would then be considered to be approximations holding in the special circumstance that parts (a pendulum bob, a single planet) can be treated as if they were isolable from their environment. In general, such isolation into bits and pieces is not possible for chaotic systems, since their exquisite sensitivity makes them vulnerable to the slightest change in their surroundings. They must be treated holistically.

Developments of metaphysical thought along these lines are necessarily speculative, but they hold out the possibility of describing a physical world in which agency could be exercised and we could recognize ourselves as being inhabitants. [9] That would be a gain for *science,* whose lifeless account has never seemed adequate to describing more than a small fraction of human experience. In such a world of open process and true becoming, it would also be coherent to consider the possibility of divine providential interaction within its flexible history. [10]

A picture is emerging which recognizes two forms of causality at work within the process of the world. One is the interchange of energy between parts, a "bottom-up" causality which science describes. But that description is not so tightly drawn as to exclude a second "top-down" causality, where the context of the whole affects the behavior of the parts. This latter form of causality is concerned with pattern rather than energy; it has been pictured as the effect of a kind of "active information." There is a glimmer of possible understanding here of how human minds may interact with the matter of human bodies. It is also a coherent possibility that this is how God interacts with creation through the continuous input of information into cosmic process, giving a hint of how science can accommodate the theological language of the Spirit "guiding" and "leading" the world. [11]

The subject of divine action is likely to be one of the most fruitful areas of interaction between science and theology in the next decade. One consequence is to emphasize the reality of time in a world of true becoming. Since God must be supposed to know everything as it is in its reality, this implies that there must be temporal knowledge within the divine mind as well as a timeless eternity. A dipolar, time/eternity, account of the divine nature has been a particular concern of process theology, which bases itself on the philosophy of Alfred North Whitehead. [12]

Much work remains to be done, but it is clear that the worldview of twentieth-century science is less rigid and more hospitable to an holistic account than was the science of previous centuries. One of the obstacles to a friendly relationship between science and theology is thereby removed. It is now necessary to turn to a more detailed description of the content of the scientific understanding of the pattern and structure of the physical world. We shall discover that many physicists find there an encouragement to look beyond their science and to acknowledge that more is going on in the universe than has met the eye of science alone. Yet in the biological community there still remains a significant degree of suspicion of religion and a continued recourse to the metaphor of warfare.

Physical scientists are very struck by the rational beauty and transparency of the physical world. "Wonder" is a word they often use to describe their reaction to the marvellous order revealed to their inquiry. Two things are particularly striking about the success of physical science. One is that mathematics is the key to discovery. Time and again it has proved to be the case that successful theories are those which can be expressed in terms of beautiful mathematical equations. The property of mathematical beauty is concerned with economy and elegance of formulation and with a "deepness" of consequence, so that apparently simple statements are found to have a profound and comprehensive fruitfulness. Mathematicians find it easy to recognize and to agree upon the presence of mathematical beauty. All the fundamental theories of physics are found to possess this characteristic. In fact, Einstein discovered general relativity (the modern theory of gravity) and P. A. M. Dirac was eventually led to the discovery of antimatter precisely through pursuing such a quest for mathematical beauty.

Yet, mathematics arises from the free exploration of the human mind. The beautiful patterns of pure mathematics are produced from human thought alone. Why is there this "unreasonable effectiveness of mathematics" (in the phrase of the Nobel prizewinning physicist Eugene Paul Wigner) which means that some of its most profound patterns are found actually to correspond to the structure of the physical world around us? There seems to be a deep-seated relationship between the reason within (the mathematical thoughts in our minds) and the reason without (the way the universe is constituted). Einstein was particularly struck by the puzzling significance of this correlation. He once said the only incomprehensible thing about the universe is that it is comprehensible. How does it come about that our minds are so perfectly attuned to the deep secrets of nature? Why is mathematics the key that turns the lock of its mysteries?

The second striking aspect of this success of physical science in understanding the world is that it seems to be of unlimited scope. We should not be surprised that our thinking is competent to cope with the world of everyday experience. We could scarcely have survived in the evolutionary struggle if that had not been the case. Yet the unreasonable effectiveness of mathematics goes far beyond anything that could be considered to have survival value. The counterintuitive quantum world is unpicturable to us, but it is not unintelligible, though its understanding requires the use of very abstract kinds of mathematics. It seems impossible to believe our ability to comprehend the behavior of subatomic entities, or to unravel the structure of cosmic curved space, has arisen simply from our ancestors having had to be able to dodge the attacks of saber-toothed tigers.

Science, of course, *assumes* the physical world will be found to be intelligible. Without this remarkable rational transparency, science would be impossible. Yet the instinct of scientists is to seek an understanding through and through and the unreasonable effectiveness of mathematics seems too remarkable a property just to treat as a brute fact about the way things are. Hence Einstein's perplexity at the universe's comprehensibility.

One could summarize this aspect of scientific experience by saying that the universe revealed to our inquiry seems shot through with signs of mind. Here the religious believer can offer an insight to answer Einstein's incomprehension. The reason within and the reason without fit together so perfectly because they have a common in the Rationality of God, whose creative will is the ground of both our physical and our mental experience. The universe is indeed shot through with signs of Mind. Science is possible because the physical world is a creation. Scientists' power to unlock its secrets is an aspect of the theological understanding that humanity is made "in the image of God" (Genesis 1: 26–27).

This discussion of the deep intelligibility of the physical world illustrates the way in which metaquestions arise from scientific experience, questions which in their nature go beyond what science itself (in its self-limited form of inquiry) can seek to explain, but which are questions that cannot be dismissed as being unworthy of further investigation. Science exploits the rational transparency of the universe, but it is not intellectually satisfying to treat that transparency as an unexplained piece of good fortune. We have seen that theology has the ability to carry the discussion further and to provide the deeper understanding which eluded science itself.

The recognition of the importance of such metaquestions and the acknowledgment that theology has something to say about their answers have given rise to a recent revival of natural theology. [13] One can define natural theology as being the attempt to learn something of God by the exercise of reason and the inspection of the world. Its two great previous periods of flowering were the late Middle Ages (Anselm, Aquinas) and the early nineteenth century (William Paley). Neither of those previous enterprises enjoyed lasting success. The logical criticisms of Hume and Kant subverted the arguments of the medievals, and Darwin destroyed Paley's version of the argument from design by showing how the evolutionary sifting of small differences through natural selection could give rise to the appearance of design without calling for the direct intervention of a Designer. After these experiences, most theologians have been wary of appeals to natural theology and the present revival is mostly taking place at the hands of the physicists. The new natural theology is also a *revised* natural theology, in two important respects.

First, it is more modest in the claims that it makes. It no longer talks about *proofs* of God, but offers intellectually satisfying theistic *insights*. Seeing the world as a creation offers an explanation of the universe's deep intelligibility, but it is not claimed that the existence of the Creator can be deduced from this consideration in a logically coercive way. We have come to recognize that grand metaphysical questions, such as the existence of God or the nonexistence of God, are not of a kind to be susceptible to such conclusive forms of discussion. We are in an area where no one, believer or unbeliever alike, has recourse to knockdown forms of argument. Instead, one must seek to build up a metaphysical picture which proves satisfying because of its simplicity and its comprehensiveness in accounting for all forms of human experience and insight. The new natural theology presents belief in God as the fulfillment of this explanatory role.

Second, the new natural theology does not point to particular occurrences in cosmic history but to the basic laws which underlie the possibility of any such occurrence. Unlike Paley, we have learned not to claim that only the direct action of a Designer could bring about the marvellous optical system of a fully-developed animal eye. How life evolved from inanimate matter, how particular structures came to be—these are scientific questions, and we have learned to expect that scientifically posable questions will receive scientifically stateable answers. To claim the contrary would be to have recourse to the discredited notion of "the God of the Gaps." Such a deity was always over the next intellectual horizon, always liable to fade away like a divine Cheshire Cat with the next advance of human knowledge. Such a conception of God was theologically unworthy. The Creator must relate to the whole of creation and not just to the scientifically murky and puzzling bits of it.

The new natural theology is not trying to be a rival to science in the latter's own domain. Rather, it is seeking to complement science, to go beyond it (metaquestions) to provide a more profound kind of understanding. It looks not to occurrences but to the given fabric of the physical universe, that which science has to assume as the given starting point for *its* explanation, but which, on investigation, does not of itself seem to be so intellectually satisfying that it can be treated as an inexplicable brute fact. We have already encountered an example of this in relation to the metaquestion of the deep mathematical intelligibility of the physical world. We must now turn to consider a second metaquestion arising from a recent insight into the amazing fruitfulness of cosmic history.

One of the reasons why cosmologists speak with considerable confidence about the early universe following the big bang is that the world was then extremely simple. It was just an almost uniform expanding ball of energy. Today, after fifteen billion years of cosmic history, the world has become richly and diversely complex, with humankind the most elaborate consequence known to us. Late twentieth-century science understands many, but not yet all, of the steps by which this amazing fruitfulness has come about. The more we understand the process, the clearer it becomes that it has depended upon a very delicate balance ("finely-tuned" one might say), built into the physical fabric of the universe. That fabric is specified by the laws of nature (e.g., the universe has a gravitational force acting within it, of a particular, inverse-square-law type) and their intrinsic strengths (e.g., specified for gravity by the magnitude of Newton's gravitational constant). It is possible for scientists to imagine what cosmic history would have been like if these specifications of physical fabric had been different. For example, one could consider a universe similar to our own except that its force of gravity was intrinsically a good deal stronger than is the case for us. Of course, things would have developed differently. Partly this would be due to the contingencies of cosmic history (we will consider that issue later) and partly it would be due to the change in physical law. Most scientists would have expected that different universe to have evolved its own kind of "people" and they would have expected the main consequence of the increased force of gravity to have been that these "people" could not grow as tall as we are. In this supposition they would have been totally mistaken. In fact, there would have been no "people" in that world at all. Such a universe would have been condemned to a boring and sterile history. Only a universe "finely-tuned" to a close similarity to ours in its given laws and circumstance would be capable of evolving the rich complexity of carbon-based life.

This very surprising insight, that a universe capable of producing *anthropoi* (beings of comparable complexity to humankind) is a very special universe indeed, is given the generic name of the Anthropic Principle. [14] Before considering what one might make of it, it is necessary to give at least some illustrative examples of the host of scientific considerations which led to its totally unanticipated conclusion.

The stars provide us with two good examples. A fruitful world requires stable long-lived stars to provide a steady source of energy over the billions of years it takes for life to evolve in a suitable planetary environment. We understand what makes a star like our Sun shine in a reliable way for up to ten billion years. It depends upon a critical balance between the effects of gravity and the effects of electromagnetic forces. If that balance were disturbed in any way (for example, by making gravity stronger) then either stars would burn up very rapidly, so that they lived for only many millions of years rather than billions of years, or they would be so faint that they could not provide adequate amounts of energy. Either consequence would be disastrous for the possibility of the development of life.

The stars have a second essential role to play. Because the very early universe is very simple, it can only produce very simple consequences. For the first three minutes of its life, the whole cosmos was hot enough to be the arena of nuclear reactions. The by-products of this hectic phase were only the two simplest chemical elements, hydrogen and helium. They do not possess a rich enough chemistry to afford the basis for life. For that, one needs heavier elements, such as carbon, with its amazing power to form the long chain molecules which are the staple of biochemistry. The only place where such elements can be made is within the nuclear furnaces of the stars.

Every atom of carbon inside our bodies was once inside a star. We are all made from the ashes of dead stars. The process of generating chemical elements in this way depends upon a very complex and delicately balanced sequence of nuclear reactions. Making carbon requires three helium nuclei to combine, and that is only possible in an appreciable quantity because of an enhancing effect of the nuclear forces (a resonance) occurring in just the right place. Some of the carbon must then go on to capture a further helium nucleus so that it turns into oxygen—but not all of it, for then one would have lost the carbon! This chain of carefully balanced consequence can only go as far as iron inside a star. To make the essential elements beyond iron (such as iodine) and to liberate into the environment the elements already made so that they become available for the evolution of planetary life, it is necessary that some stars should end their lives in the particular type of stellar explosion that we call a supernova. That process also depends upon delicate details of the nuclear forces. A universe whose nuclear forces were not finely-tuned to produce this astonishing sequence of events would be one which could not be anthropically fruitful.

One final illustration of anthropic requirements must suffice. This time it relates to the circumstance of the cosmos. Our universe is immensely big: our Sun is an ordinary star among the hundred thousand million stars of our galaxy, the Milky Way, and the Milky Way is an ordinary galaxy among the hundred thousand million galaxies of the observable universe. People have sometimes thought that such unimaginable immensity puts in question religious claims of the significance of the inhabitants of a planet which is no more than a speck of cosmic dust. Yet if the universe were not so vast, we would not be here to be daunted at the thought of it! There is a direct cosmological connection between how big a universe is and how long its history can last. It takes fifteen billion years to evolve *anthropoi,* and only a world at least as big as ours could be capable of doing it.

We live in a very special kind of universe, and we could have come to be in no other. What do we make of that? Some have said "nothing": there is only one universe and we can learn nothing from a single example. But we can *imagine* other universes, and it is precisely this exercise which has led us to the conclusion of specialness and fine-tuning. Others say merely that as we exist, it is trivial that the universe is consistent with our presence. This point of view is sometimes called the Weak Anthropic Principle. At one level, of course, it must be so, but surely it is a matter of significance, as well as surprise, that this places such very strict selective conditions on the nature of natural law. Still others have claimed that there must be a Strong Anthropic Principle at work, *requiring* the universe to produce lifelike beings. It is difficult to see what this could mean as a scientific principle (but we shall shortly reconsider it in theological terms).

The most difficult criticism to counter is one that points out that the Anthropic Principle is really the Carbon Principle. Its stringent conditions relate to the possibility of the coming-to-be of carbon-based life. Might this not be just a failure of our scientific imagination? Perhaps other kinds of universes have their own kinds of "life." Yet those who put this point are willing to draw large intellectual blank checks on unknown accounts. It seems clear that something like consciousness requires the generation of great physical complexity. The human brain, with its hundred thousand million neurons and their astonishing degree of interconnectivity, is far and away the most complicated physical system we have ever encountered in the exploration of

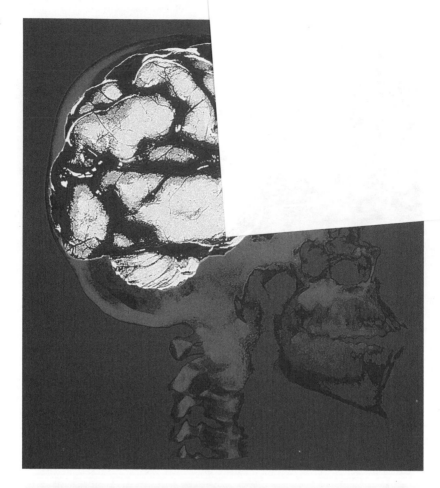

"The human brain, with its hundred thousand million neurons and their astonishing degree of interconnectivity, is far and away the most complicated physical system we have ever encountered in the exploration of our own universe."

our own universe. It would be highly surprising if there were many alternative ways of realizing such complexity.

The present author would propose the Moderate Anthropic Principle: this notes the fine-tuning necessary for a fruitful universe as being an insight of significance which calls for some sort of explanation. Theology can afford just such an explanation, for it sees the universe not as "any old world" but as a creation which has been endowed by its Creator with precisely the finely-tuned laws and circumstance that have enabled it to have so fruitful a history. This is the theological version of the Strong Anthropic Principle.

Here is a second example of the revived and revised new natural theology. It interprets the Anthropic Principle as pointing to a new version of the argument from design, relating not to occurrences of cosmic history (such as life or the human eye) but to the basic fabric of the physical world, which has been given the finely-tuned character necessary to enable the possibility of all of these or any other occurrences. Once again, there is no conflict with science—for science has to take natural laws as part of its unexplained basis—but a complementary extension and deepening of our understanding.

Hume criticized the earlier design arguments of Paley and his friends for being too anthropomorphic. They compared God's activity to human craftsmen making things. A design argument based on the anthropic fruitfulness of physical law has no human analogue and is a fitting expression of divine Creatorly activity.

The point of contact between theology and physical science to which most people seem to attach the greatest significance is the "start" of it all, the moment of the big bang itself. Yet this feeling is based on a theological mistake. The doctrine of creation in Christian theology is not concerned with temporal origin (how did it all begin?) but with ontological origin (why does it exist at all?). God is as much the Creator today as fifteen billion years ago. Consequently, although speculative notions about the very early universe are scientifically interesting, theologically they are not very significant. Stephen W. Hawking has suggested a particular way in which quantum effects might have modified gravity when the universe was less than 10^{-43} second old, with the result that, although the universe has a finite age, it does not have a datable beginning. Even if one has doubts about the detail of this proposal, the general nature of its conclusion is quite plausible. Hawking supposes this might have some relevance to theological issues, for he goes on to say, "If the universe is really completely self-contained, having no boundary or edge, it would have neither beginning nor end; it would simply be. What place then for a creator? [15]   The theist will answer "Every place—as the ordainer of that universe and as the One who holds it in being throughout its history." God is not a God of the edges alone. The Creator is not just there to light the blue touch paper of the big bang and start things off. God is concerned with creation at all times and all places.

It is certainly the case that traditional Christian belief has held the world to be of finite age and that it derived this understanding from a natural interpretation of the first two chapters of Genesis. Yet a more sophisticated theology could certainly have lived with the idea of an everlasting universe, had the steady-state theory in cosmology proved to be the case. The early Fathers of the Church knew that Genesis did not give a blow-by-blow literal account of how things came to be. Augustine recognized that the "days" must represent aeons of time and he held the view that, if the Bible and science appeared to be in conflict, this showed that one must seek another, more symbolic, interpretation of the truth of Scripture. It was only in late medieval and Reformation times that people began to adopt an ultra-literal understanding of Genesis 1 and 2. Scientific discoveries have freed us from the shackles of such a crass literalism, thereby liberating those chapters to convey afresh their primary theological message, that everything that is exists because of God's creative will alone (and God said "Let there be . . .").

Greater perplexity is occasioned for theology by science's predictions of the end of the physical universe, rather than by its account of the beginning. A cosmic struggle is going on between the expansive force of the big bang, throwing matter apart, and the attractive force of gravity, pulling matter together. They are so evenly balanced that we cannot predict which will prevail. If expansion wins, the galaxies will go on separating from each other forever. Within each galaxy, matter will condense and decay into low-grade radiation. If that is what the future holds, the universe will ultimately end in a whimper. If gravity wins, the present expansion will one day be halted and reversed. What began with the big bang will end in the fiery melting pot of the big crunch. If that is what the future holds, the universe will ultimately end in another bang. Either way, it is condemned to eventual futility. Humanity, and all forms of life, will prove to be a transient episode in its history.

These events lie tens of billions of years into the future, but they do seem to threaten the religious claim that there is a Purpose at work in cosmic history. The theist will reply that a lasting hope can rest in God alone and not in the working out of present physical process. Christianity has always placed its ultimate confidence in God's new creation (which it sees as growing from the seed of Christ's Resurrection) and not in a mere evolutionary optimism.

Between the beginning and the end lies the great sweep of cosmic history, and it is to that history the theologians must look if the claim is to be supported that God is at work as the Creator, active at all times and in all places. The most striking aspect of cosmic process revealed through scientific inquiry is that it is *evolutionary*. Here we begin to make contact with the thought of the biologists, though it is important to recognize that evolutionary insight does not refer solely to the way in which life has developed here on Earth but also to the totality of cosmic history. The universe evolved its stars and galaxies, just as the Earth evolved its biosphere.

The key feature of evolution is the interplay between chance and necessity. By "chance" is meant happenstance, the way things are, this way rather than that. It represents the contingent effect of past history, that evolution took one path and not another. Examples are the small fluctuations of matter density in the early universe ("cosmic ripples"), which were the seeds from which the galaxies grew, or the genetic mutation that brings about a novel modification of life. Chance is the engine of novelty, the way in which new possibilities arise. Yet that novelty needs also lawful "necessity" if it is to be sifted and preserved. Examples would be the force of gravity, enhancing matter fluctuations through a kind of snowballing effect, or the largely reliable transmission of genetic information from one generation to the next which gives relative stability to plant and animal species. Without necessity, all would be unfruitful chaos; without chance, all would be sterile rigidity.

Many biologists have seized upon the role of chance to claim that it subverts the religious assertion of a Purpose at work in the process of the universe. A succinct way of expressing this is to add to chance the tendentious adjective "blind." [16] It is being claimed that cosmic history is a tale told by an idiot, full of sound and fury, signifying nothing. But one does not have to read it that way. There is no unique recipe for turning physics into metaphysics. The Anglican priest and biochemist A. R. Peacocke has proposed a much more positive evaluation of the role of chance. [17] Its shuffling explorations are seen as being ways of exploring the God-given (anthropic) potentiality with which the universe has been endowed. Peacocke speaks of chance as "the search radar of God sweeping through all the possible targets of its probing." [18] Evolutionary history is then seen as a *creatio continua,* a continuous creative process. Such an idea is not foreign to the thought of the Bible found in some of the passages outside Genesis which speak of divine Creatorly activity (*e.g.,* Isaiah 45, psalm 104).

Theologically, an evolutionary universe can be understood as a creation which is allowed by its Creator to make itself. God is neither the Cosmic Tyrant, causing every event by direct fiat alone, nor the Indifferent Spectator, just watching it all happen. The God who is both loving and faithful has given to creation the twin gifts of a due regularity (necessity) and a due independence (chance). [19] Cosmic history is not the execution of an inexorable divine blueprint, but the exploration of creaturely potentiality. This insight—that creation involves God allowing the created other to be truly itself—is a very important concept in much twentieth-century theology. It affords some understanding of the problem of evil and suffering, for a world allowed to be itself and to make itself must necessarily be a world of blind alleys and ragged edges as well as fruitfulness and fulfillment. Exactly the same cellular biochemical processes which enable some cells to mutate and bring about new forms of life will also permit other cells to mutate and become cancerous. God does not bring about the act of a murder nor the incidence of a cancer, but both are allowed to be in a creation given the gift of being

Cancer cells found in the human body. "God does not bring about the act of a murder nor the incidence of a cancer, but both are allowed to be in a creation given the gift of being itself."

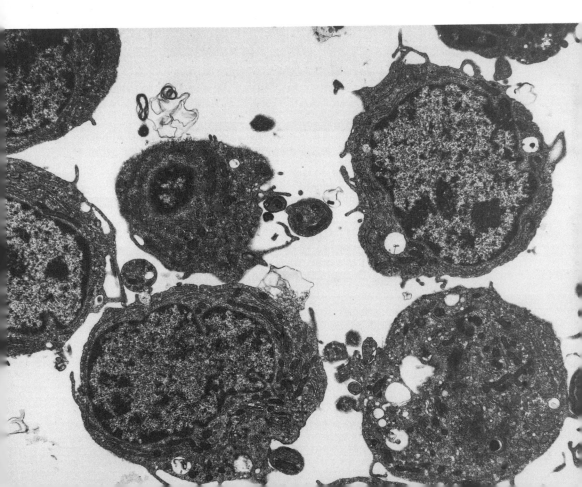

itself. The "free-will defence" in relation to moral evil must be augmented by a "free-process defence" in relation to physical evil. [20]

Fundamental to the interaction of science and theology is the question of metaphysics, that is to say, the construction of a general picture of the nature of reality which will underlie all our interpretation of experience. Scientists have often pretended not to be concerned with metaphysical questions, but in fact everyone has to have a general point of view from which to assess the world. The temptation of scientists has always been to promote the insights of their particular discipline into a rule for all. This results in various forms of reductionism; claiming that reality is "nothing but" physics, or genetics, or information processing, or whatever. [21] Here is an area in which there is certainly conflict between religion on the one hand and the claims of certain reductionist biologists or cognitive scientists on the other. If human beings are just "genetic survival machines" [22] or "computers made of meat," [23] then claims for a spiritual dimension to reality are illusory.

Those who oppose such grotesque reductionist assessments are not necessarily asserting vitalism (that an extra "ingredient" must be added to matter before it becomes living) or Cartesian dualism (that the human soul is a separable spiritual component that can exist without a body). Instead, they may well wish to accept a *constituent* reductionism (we are composed of elementary particles, like everything else), but at the same time maintain a *conceptual* antireductionism (biology and anthropology are more than complex corollaries to physics: they require their own irreducible conceptual schemes). The antireductionist's slogan is "more is different." With increasing complexity, radically new possibilities (life, consciousness) emerge as astonishing consequences of the fruitfulness of matter-in-flexible-organization. Even within physics itself one can see the emergence of radical novelty when systems become sufficiently complex. The fundamental laws of nature are reversible in character; they do not distinguish between past and future. Yet matter on the macroscopic scale exhibits a clear contrast between past and future. An irreversible direction has emerged for the "arrow of time."

The mistake of reductionism is to suppose that the whole is no more than the sum of its parts, that everything is "nothing but" the bits-and-pieces that make it up. Of course, much of value can be learned from thinking about constituents. Genetics has its valid insights into the nature of humanity without providing the total determinant of human nature. Artificial intelligence has its insights to offer, without thought being simply the computerlike execution of algorithmic procedures. [24] There is a great yawning gap, at present unbridgeable, between talk of neural networks however sophisticated, and the simplest conscious mental experience of perceiving a patch of pink. Surely if that gap is ever traversed by human understanding, it will be by the use of holistic concepts. Even physics cannot make do with a bits-and-pieces approach alone. We have already noted that chaotic systems are intrinsically unisolable in their behavior. Quantum theory provides another holistic insight through what is sometimes called the EPR phenomenon. [25] Once two quantum entities have interacted with each other, they possess a counterintuitive togetherness-in-separation (nonlocality) by which one can influence the other instantaneously, however far they have subsequently separated from each other. It seems that the universe fights back against reductionist tendencies. Even the subatomic world cannot be treated atomistically.

It is among the biologists rather than the physicists that one finds that most fervent proclamations of a mechanical reductionism. Biology has scored a stunning quantitative success by unraveling the molecular basis of genetics but in any subject, it is the mechanical aspects which are the ones first to be understood. It is much easier to figure out clocks than clouds. While the transfer of genetic information via DNA is essentially a mechanical process, that does not mean that life is no more than a reductionist interaction of individual atoms. Physics went through a similarly militant reductionist phase at the end of the eighteenth century, after its initial Newtonian triumph, when people were only too ready to proclaim that man is a machine. It has moved beyond that, as no doubt biology will in due course.

We require a balanced and ample metaphysics which can do justice to the richness and many-layered character of our experience. Science will contribute to that metaphysics, but it will not dominate it. Music is more than

"Music is more than the vibrations in the air, although that is all that science itself can tell us about it."

vibrations in the air, although that is all that science itself can tell us about it. We have access to many kinds of knowledge. Though there is certainly a cultural component in ethics, it is difficult to believe that our conviction that torturing children is wrong is simply a socially agreed convention. One of the attractions of a theistic metaphysics is that it provides an integrative basis for taking the whole gamut of experiences seriously. The rational order that science discerns is the reflection of the reason of the Creator; our experiences of beauty are a sharing in the divine joy in creation; our ethical intuitions are intimations of the perfect will of God; our religious experiences, whether mystical or numinous, are encounters with the divine presence.

So far our concern has been with the content of science and how that impinges upon the content of theology. Yet those who believe there is a clash between the two may very well locate the origin of conflict, not in content, but in style. It is not so much what scientists say, but the way that they say it. Their bright certainties threaten to put the theologians into the shade. After all, in science, questions actually get settled to universal satisfaction. At the beginning of this century there were still some physicists who did not believe in atoms. Today the question is settled for good. But in theology the debate continues, century after century, with even the basic question of the existence of God not receiving a universally affirmative answer. This contrast has led some to assert that science is the only true source of public knowledge, while religion is simply private opinion. One is fact, the other fancy. Such a judgment is mistaken on two counts, for it errs in its evaluation of both science and theology.

In neither science nor theology do we have access to facts which are of interest without their already having been interpreted. There is no clear division possible in science between experiment and theory because the detecting devices used in experiment depend upon sophisticated theory for the meaning extracted from their registrations. Moreover, all experiments are liable to be contaminated by happenings unrelated to the phenomenon under investigation, as when a cosmic ray from outside Earth triggers a reaction in a terrestrial piece of apparatus. These spurious "background" events must be eliminated if a true result is to be obtained. There is no automatic recipe for doing this; it depends upon the experimenter's judgment of what is going on, which is then evaluated using current theory. Thus the pursuit of science is not the exhibition of unchallengeable fact to be compared with the inexorable predictions of theory, but is something altogether more subtle in character, involving an interplay of fact and opinion, theory and experiment, explicit judgment and tacit skill. [26] Deep theories are not just read out of data; they involve a creative interplay between the mind of the scientist and the results that are to be interpreted.

Science never attains absolute certainty in its conclusions. It must remain open to correction. In particular, when some new regime of physical experience is opened up for exploration (higher energy reactions than have previously been observed, for example), it is often the case that surprising, and initially puzzling, new phenomena are encountered. The achievement of science is not truth but verisimilitude. A well-winnowed physical regime can be mapped in a reliable way, but when it is examined on a finer scale, a new map, with unexpected features, may well be necessary.

Thus science is a more precarious and intellectually daring enterprise than is commonly realized. This had led some philosophers of science in the twentieth century [27] to revalue its activity to the extent of seeing it as a socially constructed attempt to produce theories of empirical adequacy, not an investigation into what the physical world is actually like. The inextricable role of theory in the interpretation of experiments is held to mean that science's conclusions are just the result of an agreement (largely arrived at unconsciously) by the invisible college of scientists to see things this way.

The success of science is claimed to be a pragmatic power to get things done, using its theories as effective manners of speaking but not as realistic accounts of the way the world is.

Some philosophers and virtually all scientists reject this account. They (the present author is among them) wish to claim that science does attain a realistic account of the actual nature of the physical world, while acknowledging that account always to be partial and never total (so that verisimilitude, rather than absolute truth, is the end product) and recognizing also that there are social effects in the community of scientists, which accelerate or retard progress, without conceding that these effects ultimately determine the outcome of scientific knowledge. For the realist, the advance of science is a tightening grasp of an actual reality.

There are a number of grounds for the defense of this realist stance, which can only be sketched in this article. [28] One consideration is that it is extremely difficult to see how science could be so pragmatically successful if it did not describe some verisimilitudinous aspects of how things actually are. A second consideration arises from the experience of scientific research. It has about it the feel of discovery, not invention; the physical world frequently resists our prior expectations and is found to behave in ways which are totally surprising and unexpected. Then there is the astonishing fruitfulness of deep scientific theory. Quantum mechanics was discovered through work on atomic spectra, but it has been used to explain how stars shine and how electricity is conducted in metals.

A critical realist account of science is defensible. It shows us that the scientific method is not something unique and invulnerable, totally different from all other ways of seeking knowledge. Rather, science requires acts of judgment and of intellectual daring in supposing that things might be understood in a particular way. Scientists have to look at the world from a chosen point of view (someone said that they always wear "spectacles behind the eyes"—their image of the world is refracted by their theoretical expectations). That view must be open to correction. Yet the cumulative advance of scientific knowledge and the tightening grasp of the reality of the physical world which it has afforded encourage us to believe that this is an intellectual strategy that works. They yield, not absolute certainty, but verisimilitudinous understanding.

That is a lesson which can be transferred to other forms of rational inquiry, including theology. The latter, contrary to much popular misapprehension, is not concerned with the blind assertion of unquestionable truths. Revelation is not propositional knowledge conveyed in a mysterious and unchallengeable way; it is the record of those events and people in which the divine reality has been most perspicuously present. God is always there, but there are times and circumstance in which that divine presence is more transparently visible—just as the laws of nature are always operating, but science trades on the use of experiments, those well-contrived instances in which the effects of those laws may most clearly be discerned. Theology, like science, is concerned with the search for *motivated* belief, rather than an absolute truth.

These considerations have led many of those who have written on the interpretation of science and theology to discern a cousinly relationship between the two rational endeavors. [29]   The difference in their degrees of attainment of agreement is held to relate to the very different characters of their subject matter. Science investigates the physical universe, a world which humans transcend and which they can put to the test using science's great secret weapon of experiment. Theology, on the other hand, is concerned with God, the One who transcends us and is not to be put to the test. All forms of personal relationship—whether between human beings or between creatures and their Creator—have to be based on trust and not on testing. People can disagree in their assessment of a particular person's personality. Perhaps it is not so surprising that they can disagree also in their assessment of the nature of God.

The branches of science which exhibit the closest kinship to theology are those historical sciences, such as cosmology and evolutionary biology, which do not have direct access to experiment. There is but one cosmic history, but one biological history, to the records of which we have fragmentary access. These historical sciences seek to make sense of that partially recorded experience, not by exhibiting great predictive power, but by affording the best explanation of what appears to have been going on. The intelligibility that these sciences yield is the basis for our rational acceptance of their insights. Very much the same thing can be said for theology. It seeks the best explanation of the uniquely significant events of the life and death of Jesus Christ and their aftermath in the Resurrection and the church.

Both science and theology must speak of entities whose nature is wholly different from notions based on everyday experience and common sense (the unseen and unpicturable electron and the unseen and unpicturable God). Each, in this endeavor, must make use of exploratory models (wave and particle, Judge and Saviour) which disclose only a partial aspect of the total reality and which must sometimes be held in complementary tension with each other. Both disciplines have their own natural language: for science, it is the language of mathematics; for theology, it is the language of symbol.

Science and theology, far from being at enmity with each other, are component parts of the great human endeavor to seek a rational understanding of the nature of reality. Science can tell theology what the physical world is like in its structure and history. Theology must take account of that, for instance, in framing its doctrine of creation. The doctrine is not determined by science, but it must be consonant with science. Theology, for its part, can take the insights of science and incorporate them in a much more profound and comprehensive account. It can provide intellectually satisfying answers to those metaquestions of intelligibility and anthropic fruitfulness which arise from science but which elude the latter's self-limited power to answer. Theology can also integrate into its understanding the knowledge which we derive from aesthetics and ethics, forms of human inquiry which are deliberately bracketed out by the scientific method. As the twentieth century comes to a close, there is a widening recognition that we can rightly speak of the *friendship* of science and theology within the history of Christendom.

1. Stanley L. Jaki, *The Road of Science and the Ways to God* (Edinburgh: Scottish Academic Press, 1978); Colin A. Russell, *Cross-Currents* (Leicester: Inter-Varsity, 1984).

2. Michael J. Buckley, *At the Origins of Modern Atheism* (New Haven, Conn.: Yale University Press, 1987).

3. John Hedley Brooke, *Science and Religion* (Cambridge: Cambridge University Press, 1991).

4. *See* Paul C. W. Davies, *God and the New Physics* (London: Dent, 1983); *The Mind of God* (London: Penguin, 1992).

5. *See* e.g., John Polkinghorne, *The Quantum World* (Harlow: Longman, 1984); Alastair I. M. Rae, *Quantum Physics: Illusion or Reality?* (Cambridge: Cambridge University Press, 1986).

6. David Bohm and Basil J. Hiley, *The Undivided Universe* (London: Routledge, 1993).

7. William G. Pollard, *Transcendence and Providence* (London: Faber and Faber, 1958).

8. *See* James Gleick, *Chaos* (London: Heinemann, 1988).

9. Polkinghorne, *Reason and Reality* (London: SPCK, 1991), chap. 3.

10. Polkinghorne, *Science and Providence* (London: SPCK, 1989).

11. Arthur R. Peacocke, *Theology for a Scientific Age* (Oxford: B. Blackwell, 1990), chap. 9; Polkinghorne, notes 9 and 10; *The Faith of a Physicist* (Princeton, N.J.: Princeton University Press, 1994), chaps. 1 and 4.

12. *See* John B. Cobb, Jr., and David Ray Griffin, *Process Theology: an Introductory Exposition* (Philadelphia: Westminister Press, 1976).

13. *See* note 4 and Hugh Montefiore, *The Probability of God* (London: SCM Press, 1985); Polkinghorne, *Science and Creation* (London: SPCK, 1988), chaps. 1 and 2; *Reason,* chap. 6.

14. John D. Barrow and Frank J. Tipler, *The Anthropic Cosmological Principle* (Oxford: Oxford University Press, 1986); John Leslie, *Universes* (London: Routledge, 1989).

15. Stephen W. Hawking, *A Brief History of Time* (London: Bantam, 1988), pp. 140–41, cf. *GIT*: 1979, 33–42; 1984, 3–10; 1992, 271–304.

16. Richard Dawkins, *The Blind Watchmaker* (Harlow: Longman Scientific & Technical, 1986); Jacques Monod, *Chance and Necessity* (London: Collins, 1972).

17. Peacocke, *Creation and the World of Science* (Oxford: Oxford University Press, 1979); *God and the New Biology* (London: Dent, 1986).

18. Peacocke, *Creation,* p. 95.

19. Polkinghorne, *Creation,* chap. 4

20. Polkinghorne, *Providence,* chap. 5

21. *See* Peacocke, *New Biology,* chaps. 1 and 2.

22. Dawkins, *The Selfish Gene* (Oxford: Oxford University Press, 1976).

23. *See* Martin Lee Minsky, *The Society of Mind* (New York: Simon and Schuster, 1986).

24. *See* Roger Penrose, *The Emperor's New Mind* (Oxford: Oxford University Press, 1989), chap. 10.

25. *See* Polkinghorne, *Quantum World,* chap. 7.

26. *See* Michael Polanyi, *Personal Knowledge* (London: Routledge & Kegan Paul, 1958).

27. For a survey of the thought of many of the leading figures of twentieth-century philosophy of science, *see* W. H. Newton-Smith, *The Rationality of Science* (London: Routledge & Kegan Paul, 1981).

28. For a detailed discussion in relation to experience of elementary particle physics, *see* Polkinghorne, *Rochester Roundabout* (Harlow: Longman Scientific & Technical, 1989), chap. 21.

29. Ian G. Barbour, *Myths, Models and Paradigms* (London: SCM Press, 1974); *Religion in an Age of Science* (London: SCM Press, 1990); chaps. 2 and 3; Peacocke, *Intimations of Reality* (Notre Dame, Ind.: University of Notre Dame Press, 1986); Polkinghorne, *Reason,* chaps. 1 and 2.

John Polkinghorne received his M.A. and Ph.D. from Cambridge University. He is a Fellow of the Royal Society and has had a distinguished career as both a physicist and Anglican theologian. His academic appointments include Trinity College, the University of Edinburgh, and the University of Kent. He is a member of the Medical Ethics Committee of the British Medical Association, and is a member of the General Synod of the Church of England. Currently, Dr. Polkinghorne serves as both Canon Theologian of Liverpool Cathedral and President of Queens' College, Cambridge.

Dr. Polkinghorne has published many papers on theoretical elementary particle physics and numerous books addressing the relationship between science and theology. These include *One World* (1986), *Science and Creation* (1988), *Science and Providence* (1989), and *Quarks, Chaos and Christianity* (1994).

Reconsiderations of
Great Books and Ideas

1
2
3
4

The Spaces of Democracy

Stephen Kern

HAYE & P. D'ESPAGNAT ——— *Le Camoufleur*
Copyrigt SCHWARZ & Cⁱᵉ, 58, Rue de la Chaussée-d'Antin, PARIS

From around 1880 to the outbreak of World War I the stable and unified conception of time and space that provided the foundation for everyday life and thought began to break down. Challenges came from geometry and physics, sociology and psychology, philosophy and religion, art and literature, as well as new communication and transportation technologies such as the telephone, wireless, cinema, automobile, and airplane.

While the challengers (aside from the physicists and a few philosophers) rarely identified the thinker or philosophy against which their thought or their creative efforts were directed, the target of this new way of thinking was a simplified version of classical mechanics. That version held that time and space were *empty* or unchanging with respect to point of view or relative motion, *independent* of one another and of anything that takes place in them, *uniform* in all directions, and *universal,* that is, the same for everyone. Time and space were also thought to be *objective* dimensions of the physical world that framed the movement of matter even if no human subjects were present to observe it.

By the outbreak of World War I, the basic features of such a conception were challenged by a host of thinkers as well as artists. Time and space were not empty, but full. They were not independent of one another and were modified by relative motion and point of view as well as by what took place in them. In fact, the very notion of events occurring "in" the container of empty space was overthrown as space came to be seen as having its own positive, constitutive function. Time and space were not continuous and uniform but discontinuous and irregular. They were not homogeneous, but heterogeneous. According to sociologists, psychologists, and philosophers there were a variety of spaces and times that differed in every social system, psychological type, and human perspective.

These changes in thinking were accompanied, and in some measure influenced, by technological developments that transformed the way time and space were "lived" as well as conceived. To interpret these complementary developments, I will focus on space, which, more than time, had the more visible and public historical manifestations.

Three aspects of space underwent revolutionary change—the constituent nature of space, the form of objects in space, and the sense of distance. These changes, shaped by new communication and transportation technologies, had social and political consequences—they helped to bring about the erosion of aristocratic privilege and the rise of democracy.

(Overleaf) A page from a French war document showing an example of camouflage, which was developed by French painter Guirand de Scévola in 1914.

Political democracy refers to government by the people. Between 1880 and 1920 democracy became a reality for tens of millions of people who had never before participated in choosing their rulers. In addition to this exclusively political sense, *democratization* also refers to the erosion of the aristocracy's social, and what remained of its legal, privileges. These two phenomena have independent histories, but in this essay I am combining them under the single rubric of democratization because the essential element of a leveling of former hierarchical distinctions applies to both and because the two developments occurred throughout the Western world at around the same time and were in many ways interdependent.

This leveling of social and political hierarchy is one of a spectrum of developments in many areas of human experience beyond the social and political that can be conceived in spatial terms. My purpose is not to explain the connections between ideas about space, technological develop- ment, and political transformation (most of which I have not been able to document with evidence of direct causal influence) but to interpret the thematic or functional similarities among them as manifestations of a broad transformation of the metaphysical foundations of life and thought, one that had unmistakable political implications. Toward the end I focus on the embodiment of aristocratic Europe, Emperor Francis Joseph of Austria, whose stubborn opposition to the telephone was an unwitting but revealing recognition of the incompatibility between aristocratic social hierarchy and the democratization of communication.

The nature of space

As a young man, Albert Einstein recalled an incident from his childhood that filled him with wonder. When he was five years old his father gave him a compass. The way the needle always pointed in one direction suggested that there was "something deeply hidden" in nature that created irregularity in physical space. [1] The action of the compass suggested that space was mu- table, with orientations that varied according to its contents. The quivering needle pointed to the North Pole as well as to a revolution in physics.

New ideas from across the scholarly and artistic world indicated that space was not homogeneous, but heterogeneous. Earlier in the nineteenth century the geometricians Nikolay Lobachevsky and Bernhard Riemann developed a variety of non-Euclidean geometries, and toward the end of the century the physicists Ernst Mach and Henri Poincaré postulated a variety of different physical spaces. The biologists Élie de Cyon and Jacob von Uexküll ex- plored the space perceptions of different animals, while anthropologists such as Sir James Frazer and sociologists such as Émile Durkheim studied the spatial organizations of different cultures. The Cubist artists Pablo Picasso and Georges Braque dismantled the uniform perspectival space that had governed painting since the Renaissance and reconstructed objects as seen from several perspectives. The novelists Marcel Proust and James Joyce used multiple literary perspectives to recreate a variety of lived spaces.

The philosophers Friedrich Nietzsche and José Ortega y Gasset elaborated explicit philosophies of "perspectivism" which insisted that there are as many different spaces and truths as there are points of view. Nietzsche railed against Platonist and Christian theologians who denigrated the value of knowledge acquired through the senses. Such thinkers, he argued, "demand that we should think of an eye that is completely unthinkable, an eye turned in no particular direction." He insisted rather that there is "*only* a perspective seeing, *only* a perspective 'knowing,' . . . and the *more* eyes, different eyes, we can use to observe one thing, the more complete will be our 'concept' of this thing." [2] We must look at the world through the wrong end of the telescope as well as the right one, see things inside out and backwards, in order to achieve the highest levels of knowing.

In the twentieth century Ortega countered rationalists who insisted that there is a supreme truth that can be grasped only by factoring out the errors that arise from viewing things from subjective points of view. In 1910 he formalized his philosophy of "perspectivism" in insisting that "this supposed immutable and unique reality . . . does not exist: there are as many realities as points of view." [3] Ortega described perspectivism in terms applicable to Cubism: "The truth, the real, the universe, life . . . breaks up into innumerable facets and vertices, each of which presents a face to an individual." [4] His philosophy was based on those of Riemann, Lobachevsky, Mach, Einstein, Uexküll, Proust, and Joyce, and he shared their discomfort with conventional ideas about the sanctity of one space or a single point of view. He challenged the Western world's arrogant belief that one point of view alone was correct. Knowledge progresses and culture advances as the diversity of concrete experience is allowed to be heard.

There is a danger that such a philosophy of perspective can become a runny, undisciplined relativism, an excuse for having no point of view at all, but in this period it provided a corrective to the cultural egocentrism that had dominated Western life and thought for so long. Durkheim's theory of the social relativity of space gave value to societies outside the Western world. Ortega's philosophy of perspectivism lined up clearly on the side of pluralism and democracy against ethnocentrism and monarchy. It implied that the voices of the many, however untrained or chaotic, are a desirable check on the judgment of a single class, a single culture, or a single "expert" individual. Even Nietzsche, who had contempt for democracy and for the leveling effect of the masses, understood that the overman must achieve transcendence through a continual struggle, and hence dialogue, with them. Zarathustra repeatedly returned to the masses even though he was always misunderstood and threatened by contact with them. Even his final isolation involved loving an unnamed woman who represented his acceptance of eternal recurrence. Although these various arguments on behalf of perspectivism and the heterogeneity of space did not always address themselves explicitly to the didactic terms of social equality versus social privilege or democracy versus monarchy, they form part of a general cultural reorientation in this period that was essentially pluralistic and democratic.

Along with the *number* of spaces, another historically variable aspect of the nature of space was its *constituency*. The realization of this period was that space was not passive and empty, but active and full. This change provided the metaphysical foundation for the breakdown of aristocratic privilege, the rise of democracy, and the secularization of spiritual life. In addition to these revisions of hierarchies that had governed everyday life, a variety of other rehierarchizations took place all across the cultural spectrum as former voids, negativities, backgrounds, negative spaces, silences, empty rooms, "virgin" lands, open frontiers, profane spaces, and disenfranchised people took on more positive value. I refer to these developments collectively as democratization, by which I mean that a process that was formerly of no value (or did not count) now had a positive, constitutive function. Thus, the enfranchise-ment of people who were formerly disenfranchised becomes, in my essay, a metonym for a spectrum of "democratizing" cultural developments.

The view of space as active and full created a new conception which I refer to as "positive negative space." Art critics describe the subject of a painting (in a portrait, the figure) as *positive space,* and they describe the background (in a portrait, the space around the figure) as *negative space.* The term *positive negative space* implies that the background or surrounding space is of equal importance with the subject or figure and that that which was formerly regarded as negative now has a positive, constitutive function.

A common effect of this transvaluation was a leveling of former hierar-chical distinctions about what was primary and secondary in the space of any perceptual, artistic, social, religious, or political hierarchy. This shift can be seen as a breakdown of distinctions between the plenum of matter and the void of space in physics, between subject and background in painting, between figure and ground in perception, between the sacred and profane space of religion. The striking similarity among these changes suggests that they add up to a transformation of the metaphysical foundations of life and thought.

Physical space came to life in Einstein's field theory. In 1873 James Clerk Maxwell had hypothesized that electricity and light travel in waves through fields. These were taken to imply something tangible, and until the end of the century physicists continued to theorize about mechanical models to explain the propagation of waves through a medium of ponderable matter.* Einstein boldly abandoned that model. His special theory of 1905 removed the idea "that the electromagnetic field is to be regarded as a state of a material car-rier. The field thus becomes an irreducible element of physical description, irreducible in the same sense as the concept of matter is in the theory of Newton." In classical mechanics a particle of light moves through empty and static space. In Einstein's mechanics everything is in movement throughout the field at the same time, and space is full and dynamic and has the power of "partaking in physical events." [5] According to relativity theory, the universe is full of fields of energy in various states, and space can be thought to be as substantial as a billiard ball or as active as a bolt of lightning.

Around the turn of the century architects began to modify the way they conceived of space in relation to their constructions. Whereas formerly they tended to think of space as a negative element between the positive elements of floors, ceilings, and walls, in this period they began to consider space itself as a positive element, and they began to speak in terms of creating "spaces" and not just building "rooms." This change was facilitated by three inventions distinctive to this period—the electric light, reinforced concrete, and air-conditioning—that liberated architects from structural requirements for illumination, load-bearing, and ventilation and made it possible to sculpt

---

*For a discussion of Maxwell's *Treatise on Electricity and Magnetism,* see *GIT* 1986, 218–67.

interior space more freely. Frank Lloyd Wright exploited these inventions. He described his Larkin Soap Company building (1904) in Buffalo, N.Y., as "the original affirmative negation" in an architecture that showed "the new sense of 'the space within' as reality." [6]

Another architectural development that involved a functional use of space was the elimination of ornament, which had traditionally been added onto buildings, especially palaces, where status was visibly on display with coats of arms and other aristocratic symbols that linked the current nobility with its ancestry. Such ornamental excess and slavish historicism inspired Louis H. Sullivan to envision a "democratic architecture," as he called it, that would create new structures appropriate to the antimonarchical modern ethos. He characterized modern architecture in political terms, insisting that the "decoys of vestiture" must ultimately give way to a democratic architecture that will "pierce all feudal screens." With a vivid iconoclasm suggestive of Nietzsche, he assailed lazy historicists who consult old books for ideas and "chew this architectural cud for a stipend." In America there was a struggle between "aspirant Democracy and the inherited obsession of feudalism." Democracy would dissolve old obstructions and unite the forces of nature with the needs and values of the contemporary era. The goal of democracy

The interior of Frank Lloyd Wright's Larkin Soap Company building which was completed in 1904.

in architecture was to "liberate, broaden, intensify, and focus every human faculty." [7] Unfortunately Sullivan, himself a great creator of ornament and a sculptor of façades, did not say precisely what specific structures or styles were democratic and seemed to want ornamentation and façade eliminated altogether, which, with a functional use of space, became the new democratic spirit in architecture.

The American historian Frederick Jackson Turner argued that the empty spaces of the frontier in America had "promoted democracy." In 1903 Turner concluded: "Whenever social conditions tended to crystallize in the East, whenever capital tended to press upon labor, there was this gate of escape to the free conditions of the frontier. These lands promoted individualism, economic equality, freedom to rise, democracy." [8]

Sculpture provided the most graphic affirmation of positive negative space. Alexander Archipenko reversed the traditional notion that space was a void around the mass and maintained "that sculpture may begin where space is encircled by the material." [9] In *Woman Combing Her Hair* (1915; Perls Galleries, New York), the woman's arching arm frames the empty space that is her head. Never before in sculpture was an essential element such as a figure's head represented by completely empty space. In this work the traditional division of positive and negative space is dissolved as material, and spatial forms flow together and constitute the woman with the force of formed material.

For centuries painters had used the background to frame their subjects as a pillow frames a head. In the modern period the background took on a positive function of equal importance with the subject. The Impressionist movement took a first step in giving space its due with the painter's depictions of atmosphere. They used coastal fog, steamy summer haze, diffused forest light, and winter twilight to fuse subject and background into a single composition.

With Cubism the emergence of space as an equal constituent element is carried further. Braque and Picasso gave space the same colors, texture, and substantiality as material objects and made them interpenetrate so as to be almost indistinguishable. In an interview Braque explained that the main attraction of Cubism was "the materialization of that new space which I sensed." He discovered a "tactile space" in nature. He wanted to paint the sensation of moving around objects and give aesthetic substance to the distances between things: "This is the space that attracted me, because that was what early Cubist painting was all about—research into space." In his *Still Life with Violin and Pitcher* (1910; Kunstmuseum, Basel), the neck of the violin is fractured into sections that open into a space that is as substantial as the wood. It is impossible to distinguish clearly between subject and background as plaster, glass, wood, paper, and space are rendered in a fluid pattern of similar forms. Braque explained: "The fragmentation enabled me to establish the space and the movement within space, and I was unable to introduce the object until I had created the space." [10] The pitcher and violin are just different kinds of space, occupied by solid objects that can be simplified, geometrized, fragmented, and then reformed in space.

In 1917 the British devised a technique of painting the sides of ships with geometric patterns in contrasting colors making it difficult for submarine captains to determine a ship's size and direction of travel. John Duncan Fergusson's painting titled, "Dockyard, Portsmouth 1918," *shows evidence of Cubist style in depicting this camouflage technique that itself adapted the Cubist geometricization of forms.*

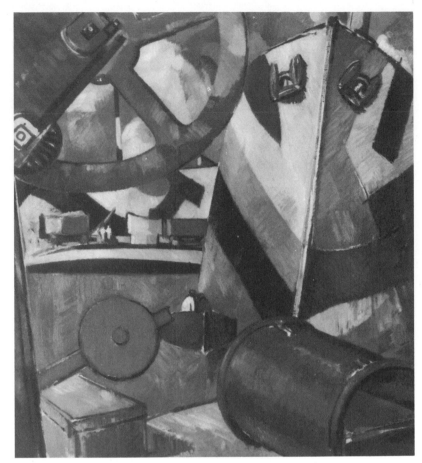

Joseph Conrad's novella *Heart of Darkness* (1899) [*GBWW* II: 59, 135–189] is about an overpowering empty space that draws the narrator, Marlow, to Africa and destroys Kurtz, the man he went to find. On his trek to the central station Marlow experiences images of dynamic negation—empty land, abandoned villages, dead carriers, and unnerving silence. He feels severed from the world he had known as he travels further into the interior. At the inner station in the heart of darkness he finds more images of negation—hungry natives, cannibals, and severed heads that were "black, dried, sunken with closed eyes." He finally locates Kurtz and discovers that negation had taken revenge within him, "because he was hollow at the core." Kurtz's final words, "The horror! The horror!" have become a cliché for nihilism in the modern world. Emptiness is the stuff of this novel, a force of darkness that rules in the wilderness and triggers the actions of men who seek to survive in it. Although it would be misleading to classify Conrad's story as democratic, it has been taken (not without dissent) as having assailed the privileges of hierarchy implicit in the nineteenth century's widespread acceptance of racism, imperialism, and Eurocentrism.

A few years after Conrad, Henry James published his story about a jungle, a journey, and the void—"The Beast in the Jungle" (1903) [*GBWW* II: 59, 1–28]. Its protagonist is John Marcher, who is convinced that a strange fate lies ahead, crouching like a beast in the jungle to leap out and slay him. He wins the affection of May Bartram, who gradually comes to understand, but does not tell him, what the beast is. When she becomes ill, he thinks that the loss he will feel over her death must be the beast, but she tells him that it has already leaped and that he failed to notice it. Her explanation is confusingly negative—"your not being aware of it is the strangeness *in* the strangeness." In the end he learns that the beast was not his love for her or his loss, but his lack of feeling for her while she was alive. He realizes further that he was "the man of his time, *the* man, to whom nothing on earth was to have happened." He had been anesthetized by the refinements of modern civilization and could not feel deeply for anyone. It was not an active spirit of negation, like Mephistopheles in Goethe's *Faust* (*GBWW* I: 47; II: 45, 1–162), but an inner emptiness, like the silence of May's grave.

In August Strindberg's *A Dream Play* (1902), there is another climactic discovery of nothing. For years an officer is obsessed with getting past a guard in order to look behind a door. "That door," he exclaims, "I can't get it out of my mind . . . What's behind it? There's got to be something behind it." When the door is finally opened, it is discovered that there is nothing behind it. The Dean of Theology interprets its significance: "Nothing. That is the key to the riddle of the world. In the beginning God created heaven and earth out of nothing." The Dean of Philosophy observes: "Out of nothing comes nothing." The Dean of Medicine makes a diagnosis as if he had just lanced a harmless boil: "Bosh! Nothing. Period." The Dean of Law suggests that the whole thing is a case of fraud. Faust had found nothing to help him affirm life from his mastery of these four fields, and Strindberg has the custodians of these fields struggle to explain away the nagging thought that the end of life is nothingness itself.

The beasts of nineteenth-century novels were generally vices, machines, institutions, or palpable forces of nature. Individuals were plagued by prostitution, alcoholism, and gambling; society was governed by railroads, factories, and coal mines; the economy was driven by materialism, capitalism, and greed. As terrifying as these things seemed, they could at least be named. The beasts of the twentieth century would be far less identifiable, existing in the mysterious realms of negativity found in the writings of Conrad, James, Strindberg, and later, Kafka. For these writers the void supplied the focus, the substance of the story. Their characters sought meaning outside themselves and found only the horror of nothingness within.

Formal as well as imaginative writers affirmed the constitutive function of perceptual space. The Gestalt psychologists Max Wertheimer, Wolfgang Köhler, and Kurt Kaffka argued that perception is an experienced whole in which the background plays an essential role in making sense out of figures in it. Considering the whole perceptual field, the smallest detail of a Gestalt may be as important as the more conspicuous figures in it, because all elements interact and give each other meaning.

Insistence on the unity of the perceptual field accorded with the radical empiricism of William James. In a discussion of the stream of consciousness from *The Principles of Psychology* (1890), he insisted on the power of negativities, as for example the silence that accompanies and outlines sound: "what we hear when the thunder crashes is not thunder pure, but thunder-breaking-upon-silence-and-contrasting-with-it." [11] The hyphens bridge the gap between words to illustrate the continuity of experience and to reverse the analytical tradition in experimental psychology. The interdependence of sound and silence is but one example of the interaction of positives and negatives in mental life. James also found constitutive negatives in his brother's novels. In a letter to his brother Henry, he wrote that the latter's style in *The American Scene* was to avoid naming something "but by dint of breathing and sighing all round and round it to arouse in the reader who may have had a similar perception already . . . the illusion of a solid object, made . . . wholly out of impalpable materials, air, and the prismatic interferences of light, ingeniously focused by mirrors upon empty space . . . Your account of America is largely one of its omissions, silences, vacancies. You work them up like solids." [12] This final characterization suggests that Henry James captured something of the American democratic spirit in giving substance to what had been an invisible background or context for noble action.

One of James's contemporary philosophers perceived the broad leveling effect in affirming the positive function of former negativities and hinted at the political significance of the "radical" in his "radical empiricism." In 1914 Horace Kallen wrote: "Pure experience has no favorites. It admits into reality . . . evil as well as good, discontinuities as well as continuities . . . [William] James . . . is the first democrat of metaphysics." James refused to detest the material world as did the idealists—nothing was more or less real or important to him than anything else. He recognized "the democratic consubstantiality of every entity in experience with every other." [13]

New constituent negativities appeared in a broad range of phenomena from physics and philosophy to sculpture and literature. Although these conceptualizations were as diverse as the many areas of life and thought from which they emerged and upon which they had influence, they shared the common feature of having resurrected the neglected "empty" spaces that formerly had had only a supporting role and brought them to the center of attention on a par with the traditional subjects. If figure and ground, bronze and empty space were equally essential to the creation of meaning, then the traditional hierarchies were open to reevaluation. The old sanctuaries of privilege and power were assailed and the value of democratization was underscored by these many affirmations of positive negative space.

Forms in space

The Victorian world was ordered in tight categories of true-false, good-bad, aristocrat-commoner, enfranchised-disenfranchised. The conviction that an inert and stable spatial order underlay experience was tersely expressed by that quintessential Victorian Samuel Smiles—"A place for everything, and everything in its place." [14] In the face of such complacency about the spatial forms of life and thought, a number of artists and intellectuals assailed the spatial integrity of numerous conventional forms. On the eve of World War I, Walter Lippmann wrote, "The sanctity of property, the patriarchal family, hereditary caste, the dogma of sin, obedience to authority—the rock of ages, in brief, has been blasted for us." [15]

The assault on the solidity of forms began at the most basic level with matter itself. In classical mechanics there was a clear distinction between the plenum of matter and the void of space. That conception was undermined by developments in electromagnetic and thermodynamic theory in the latter half of the nineteenth century. In 1896 Bergson interpreted Faraday's theory of matter as one in which the atom is a cross point for lines of energy radiating through space: "Thus each atom occupies the whole space to which gravitation extends, and all atoms are interpenetrating." He concluded that what we call an atom is "a vortex ring, ever whirling in this continuity." [16] The discovery of radioactive disintegration of matter in 1896 also eroded the stability of matter, because particles of certain elements such as radium disintegrate by throwing off energy and in time reveal a loss of mass.

Einstein's relativity theory questioned the stability of all spatially extended forms and challenged the conception of space as an inert container for the movement of stable particles of matter. In *On the Electrodynamics of Moving Bodies* (1905), he argued that when bodies are moving with respect to a stationary reference system, they change their form. A rigid body that has the form of a sphere when viewed at rest will begin to assume an ellipsoid shape when viewed in motion, and all three-dimensional objects will "shrivel up into plane figures" when their relative velocity reaches the speed of light. The general theory of relativity (1916) demolished the conventional stability of the material universe. Classical physics had taught that all bodies are elastically deformable and alter in volume with changes in temperature. But according to Einstein, every bit of matter in the universe generates a gravitational force that accelerates all material bodies in its field and modifies their apparent size.

Traditional notions of inside and outside were also changed by several new technologies from this period. Thomas Edison's discovery of the fluoroscope in 1896 made it possible to open, at least visually, the form of the body. The skin of buildings was opened up with the new supporting steel frames, walls of glass, and electric lighting which made possible new interpenetrations of indoors and outdoors. The telephone pierced the shell of privacy, as one English writer observed. While traveling in America, Arnold Bennett was overwhelmed by the ubiquity of telephones. He disliked cities "threaded under pavements and over roofs and between floors and ceilings and between walls by millions upon millions of live filaments that unite all the privacies of the organism." He also objected to European hotels in which "the dreadful curse of an active telephone" was installed in every room to invade one's privacy. [17] In 1906 a popular American writer observed how telephones and telegraphs along with rural free delivery and improved roads were mixing city and country life. The expansion of feeder railroad lines linking small towns was making it possible for workers to commute from the suburbs and thus enjoy pleasures of country living that were formerly available only to the rich.

Another new technology eroded class lines in the world of entertainment. The new cinema (first demonstrated publicly in 1896) was a uniquely democratic art form. While the theater was relatively expensive and could not reproduce itself, the cinema filled hundreds of movie houses with the same big picture for vast working class audiences. Compared to the theater, the cinema was not only far more accessible but enabled its viewers to see anywhere that a camera could be used. Metaphors reach across hierarchies and link unequals. The powerful metaphorical technology of cinema dramatized the inequalities of old hierarchies and the waste of obsolete conventions. The social and political significance of cinema was explained in an article titled "A Democratic Art," which appeared in *The Nation* in 1913. Cheap seats all at the same price, a wide range of subjects, and its appeal to "all nations, all ages, all classes, both sexes" made the cinema a truly popular art form. In New York City's early nickelodeons, which showed silent movies for a nickel, workers from all countries, even those who did not speak English, could mix with the upper classes in the dark with unprecedented proximity. The cinema makes "a direct and universal appeal to the elementary emotions" and allows everyone to be a critic as "the crowd discusses the technique of the moving-picture with as much interest as literary salons in Paris or London discuss the minutiae of the higher drama." The American director D. W. Griffith claimed that his stories and his heroes were all democratic. "Are we not making the world safe for democracy, American Democracy, through motion pictures?" he asked. In 1918 another critic speculated that cinema is "the language of democracy which reaches all strata of the population and welds them together." [18]

Class lines blurred up and down the social hierarchy. In 1912 the editor of a Parisian high society newspaper bemoaned the erosion of class lines: "Democracy, by breaking down all distinctions, has done away with the barriers which for centuries had guarded the old social hierarchy, and today our salons at their best have little individual character and at their worst are all exactly alike." [19] Snobbery was certainly not unique to this period, but its strongly defensive character was. A reactionary sociologist blamed the replacement of private cabs by streetcars for a loathsome mixing of upper and middle classes. He even faulted American cities for providing millions of free public baths. The flood of democracy ran in public water supplies, contaminating the upper classes with the detritus of the mob. If the trend continues, he warned, "the effect will be a narrowing of the esthetic space between those with position and those without." [20] A British observer saw the breakdown of classes as part of a collapse of several traditional forms. There is no longer a place for "a class with well-defined boundaries, dividing it from people of poverty on one side and people of wealth on the other." Suburbia has become a "great straggling territory" inhabited by all sorts of people. Modern restlessness has penetrated homes "like microbes through open windows," breeding chaos in the families within. [21]

Coming from an upper-middle class Jewish family and aspiring to be accepted among the high circles of the French aristocracy, Proust lived between these two classes. In *Remembrance of Things Past* (1914–27), the narrator, Marcel, aspired to be admitted to the exclusive domain of the Princess de Guermantes, but when he finally gained entry, he discovered that

> a certain complex of aristocratic prejudices, of snobbery, which in the past automatically maintained a barrier between the name of Guermantes and all that did not harmonise with it, had ceased to function. Enfeebled or broken, the springs of the machine could no longer perform their task of keeping out the crowd; a thousand alien elements made their way in and all homogeneity, all consistency of form and color was lost. [22]

Throughout this period the imagery of snobbery repeatedly involved the penetration of "pure" classes by foreign elements across formerly secure class lines.

In Austria, class boundaries at the bottom as well as on the upper levels were weakening. Carl E. Schorske has reconstructed this transformation. The multinational Habsburg Empire was being pulled apart socially along class lines as the workers, lower middle class, and peasantry began to challenge a ruling class that was itself an unsteady amalgam of a declining aristocracy and an insecure, liberal middle class that wanted to assimilate into the nobility. This structure began to come apart around the turn of the century as the ruling class lost its hold. Schorske traces this sweeping social and cultural disordering in Austrian drama, city planning, architecture, psychiatry, and art, culminating with the "explosion in the garden" of rationality with Oskar Kokoschka's tempestuous painting and Arnold Schoenberg's rejection of tonality that had served as the structural center of music since the Renaissance. [23]

The breakdown of a formal artistic distinction graphically illustrates another important assault on aristocratic privilege. That formal distinction is between subject and background, or between the positive space of the figure and the negative space around it. The Cubists wiped out that distinction. In their paintings objects do not have uninterrupted outlines, and in some places they open into the surrounding space. Parts of objects are broken off, colors bleed into neighboring objects, and translucent facets of space with multiple light sources cut shadows across bounding surfaces. Cubists removed sections of faces and reassembled what remained to create grotesque open forms in violation of natural appearance. In Picasso's *Les Demoiselles d'Avignon* (1907; Museum of Modern Art, New York), the five bodies of the prostitutes are from left to right ever less sharply contoured, as though Picasso were giving a step-by-step demonstration of how to dismantle the human form. In his *Girl with a Mandolin* (1910; Museum of Modern Art, New York), he disjointed the right elbow like a mad surgeon grafting chips of

bone onto chunks of space. Such portraits proclaimed the triumph of open forms floating in unframed space.

The Cubist assault on the closed form was one of the most graphic and significant of this period. It was more than a shift in artistic style, such as the one from Realism to Impressionism, because it involved a transformation in the very purpose of art from the interpretation of optically perceived reality to the recreation of an aesthetically conceived one. The Cubists discovered that they could deform objects and reform the artistic value of empty space in deference to artistic sensibilities alone. If those sensibilities required that an elbow open into the space around it, then they cut it open. For them, the breakdown of the closed form was a declaration of independence of art over visual appearance, one that had social and political implications if not direct causally related consequences. Their fracturing of objects and splicing them into space can be interpreted as a repudiation of the older conventions that separated subject and background, as well as those that insisted that the artist defer to the appearance of objects in reality. The cracked elbow of Picasso's mandolin player broke down the distinction between positive and negative space, proclaimed the autonomy of the artist, and put visual reality in a sling.

Cubism also had a direct impact on one manifestation of aristocratic authority in the fighting of war in 1914. The armies of the nineteenth century wore bright colors to display wealth and discipline and so to intimidate the enemy. But with the increased range and accuracy of the new breech-loading rifle and the increased firepower of machine guns, colorful uniforms were suicidal. The British switched to khaki during the Boer War, and by the outbreak of World War I the Germans wore field gray. But in 1914 the French still wore the red cap and pantaloons. After the August and September slaughters, however, the proud and aristocratic officer corps, which at first had protested against making French soldiers disappear into the background, now desperately looked for a way to make them invisible.

In September 1914 the French painter Guirand de Scévola was working as a telephone operator for an artillery unit at the Battle of the Marne.

Just after transmitting an order from telephone headquarters to his unit, it was hit by enemy fire, and he realized that it had been spotted. As he later wrote, "At this instant, vaguely at first, then ever more precisely, the idea of camouflage was born. There must be, I thought a practical way to dissimulate not only our gun but also the men who operated it . . . My first thought was to render the form and color of the material less visible." He concealed the artillery gun with a net covered with earth colors. Marshall Joffre was impressed with the idea and authorized him to create a camouflage section and to find other ways to conceal equipment and men. Soon the red cap and pantaloons were replaced by horizon blue. Scévola recalled the connection between Cubism and his discovery. "In order to totally deform objects, I employed the means Cubists used to represent them—later this permitted me . . . to hire in my [camouflage] section some painters, who, because of their very special vision, had an aptitude for denaturing any kind of form whatsoever." [24] In 1915 Picasso observed the connection between his artistic discovery and camouflage, as Gertrude Stein recalled. "I very well remember . . . being with Picasso on the Boulevard Raspail when the first camouflaged truck passed. It was at night, we had heard of camouflage but we had not yet seen it and Picasso amazed looked at it and then cried out, yes it is we who made it, that is cubism." [25] Picasso had given space the same colors, textures, and substantiality as material objects and made objects and space interpenetrate so as to be almost indistinguishable. His Cubism wiped out the hierarchical distinction between the more important subject and the less important background. This was associated with older social hierarchies, such as the one that regulated the studio of Sir Joshua Reynolds, the eighteenth-century portraitist who depicted the British upper classes. The critical part of Reynolds' portraits—the pose and the face—were executed by Sir Joshua himself, while the subjects' clothing and the background were done by an assistant. That hierarchical studio arrangement mirrored the hierarchical aristocratic world of the eighteenth century. The Cubists wiped out that hierarchy in their paintings, and thus democratized the picture surface.

(Left and above) Guirand de Scévola, an artist influenced by Cubism, created these examples of camouflage for French soldiers in 1914.

The introduction of camouflage into the military wiped out the hierarchical social implications of rank associated with differently coded uniforms, and hence had an analogous democratizing function. The abandonment of the old, brightly colored uniform, so intimately associated with aristocratic society and its emphasis on tradition and appearance, compromised the convention of deference to rank in the army and in the civilized world. Henceforth, troops and artillery guns, like pictorial objects, would be given prominence only if the situation required, not because of outmoded military traditions or artistic conventions. Cubism and camouflage leveled older hierarchies in order to rehierarchize the world in ways that suited the urgent demands of the current situation; together they implied that traditional ways are not necessarily the best ways of ordering men and guns on a battlefield or objects in pictorial space or, with some interpretive stretching, classes in a social hierarchy or voters in the electoral process.

Distance: The "annihilation" of space

New transportation and communication technologies beginning at the end of the nineteenth century had the effect, as numerous contemporary observers noted, of "annihilating" time and, especially, space. Improvements in the safety and comfort of the bicycle and reduction of its cost created a "bicycle boom" in the 1890s that enabled the masses to travel more freely. [26] An article in the *Minneapolis Tribune* in 1895 welcomed the "most democratic of all vehicles" that allowed people of all classes to amuse themselves in the same way. Another journalist was carried away with praise for the bicycle which was a "great leveller" and an instrument of social equality. [27] Stefan Zweig commented on the democratizing effect of the automobile along with other new transportation technologies: "The bicycle, the automobile, and the electric trains had shortened distances and given the world a new spaciousness . . . Whereas formerly only the privileged few had ventured abroad, now bank clerks and small tradespeople would visit France and Italy." [28] In an essay of 1898 titled *The Morality of Sport*, the French critic Paul Adam commented on the way automobiles expanded consciousness: the ease of traveling over large distances engendered an exchange of ideas, stimulated the intellect, broke up prejudices, and diminished provincialism. [29]

The telephone, invented in 1876, affected every aspect of human relationships from courting and proposing marriage to conducting diplomacy and fighting war. It expanded the range, mobility, and contact points between which messages could be sent, drawing millions of people into an instantaneous network that overcame former separations between people. By the outbreak of war in 1914 the telephone was an enormously potent technology that had the effect of democratizing the privilege of communication across vast distances—a privilege that had formerly been only for the rich and powerful. According to one report, in 1913 Germans made over 2.5 billion calls. [30] In the United States there were 10,000,000 telephones in operation by 1914. During that year it can be estimated that telephone lines were used approximately 38 billion times.

The telephone altered the quality as well as the pace and the range of human communication. In a study of city life, motion pictures, and the telephone titled *Crowds: A Moving Picture of Democracy,* Gerald Stanley Lee noted that "the telephone changes the structure of the brain. Men live in wider distances, and think in larger figures, and become eligible for nobler and wider motives." Lee welcomed all the new technology that brought crowds together, leveling former hierarchical distinctions. He viewed electricity itself as the current of the democratic ideal because "it takes all power that belongs to individual places and puts it on a wire and carries it to all places." The newly invented elevator he regarded, ironically, as a great leveler, "giving first floors to everybody and putting all men on a level at the same price." [31] Proust saw telephone conversation as an "admirable sorcery" which brings before us, "invisible but present, the person to whom we have been wishing to speak," and he imagined telephone operators to be "priestesses of the Invisible," who bring us the sound of "distance overcome." [32]

In 1901 H. G. Wells observed that "the world grows smaller and smaller, the telegraph and telephone go everywhere, wireless telegraphy opens wider

"In the United States there were 10,000,000 telephones in operation by 1914."

and wider possibilities to the imagination." Technology demolishes "obsolescent particularisms" such as class distinctions as well as national boundaries and will someday lead to the creation of a "world-state at peace with itself." [33] This latter prediction was one of Wells's most inaccurate, as the world went off to war in 1914 at unprecedentedly high speed, in part caused by the use of new transportation and communication technologies.

During the crisis in July 1914, just prior to the outbreak of war, the men in power lost their bearings in the hectic rush of telegrams, telephone conversations, memos, and press releases. Hard-boiled politicians broke down, and seasoned negotiators cracked under the pressure of tense confrontations and sleepless nights, agonizing over the probable disastrous consequences of their snap judgments and hasty actions. During the climactic period between July 23 and August 4, there were five ultimatums from various governments with ever shorter time limits, all implying or explicitly threatening war if demands were not met. In the final days, the pressing requirements of mobilization timetables, themselves dependent on railroad timetables, frayed the last shreds of patience, and European capitals responded to the rush of information as if they were so many outlets along a telephone party line, jumping at the jingle in every foreign office.

An event in the life of the Emperor Francis Joseph during the war reveals the effect of the telephone in "annihilating" the social space that had protected aristocratic privilege for so long. Up to the beginning of World War I, rule by the noble class in the Austro-Hungarian Empire was legitimized in laws that preserved royal authority and the privileges of nobility. An aristocracy of birth set itself above everyone lacking sixteen noble quarterings. Aristocrats lived secluded in hundreds of castles throughout the empire. They monopolized the higher posts in the army and diplomatic corps, controlled the conservative politics of the empire, upheld the power of the Catholic Church, and set the standard for decorum, dress, and furniture for the rest of aristocratic Europe.

That overbearing hierarchical world became the target of numerous artists and intellectuals who appreciated the revolutionary significance of the breakdown of social forms and the new sense of social proximity that were made possible by the new communications technology. Recognition of the potential threat of that technology to aristocratic society and its continued influence over the rest of society is illustrated by the Emperor's reluctance to allow any newfangled gadgetry into the royal palace. Reared under the rigid formalism of military life and the exacting requirements of one of the oldest surviving royal dynasties, convinced of his divine right to rule, hostile to incursions of popular government and the rise of democracy, isolated socially in a circle of high nobility, and contemptuous of everyone of low birth, Francis Joseph was an embodiment of the hierarchical world of the European aristocracy. In the Hofburg in Vienna, the favorite Habsburg palace for 600 years, he allowed no electric lights, and kerosene lamps provided, with gas, the only illumination. The Emperor shunned the use of typewriters and permitted no automobiles. Most revealing, was his refusal to install telephones.

The telephone, first affordable only to the rich, [34] rapidly became a democratic instrument, leveling class lines and binding nations into a single network. It created new contact points for communication across space and democratized that communication by making it unnecessary to hire a highly trained and expensive telegraph operator, thus making instantaneous communication accessible to a greater number of people. It was particularly incompatible with the aristocratic principle that certain persons have special importance by virtue of their proximity to the monarch. Telephones radically altered the experience of social distance. They broke down spatial barriers horizontally across the face of the land and vertically across social strata. They made all places equidistant from the seat of power and hence of equal value. The elaborate protocol of introductions, calling cards, invitations, and appointments was obviated by the telephone's instantaneity; and the protective function of doors, waiting rooms, servants, and armed guards was diminished by the piercing of their intrusive ring. Telephones penetrated and thus profaned all places; hence there were none in churches. The older geographical and social boundaries of the Austro-Hungarian Empire were incompatible with the new universality, irreverence, and pugnacity of the telephone. In refusing to allow telephones into the Habsburg palace, the old Emperor knew what he was about.

Technology and democracy

I have argued that affirmations of the heterogeneity of space, the breakdown of forms, and the "annihilation" of distance leveled older hierarchies, including the social hierarchy at the top of which lived a privileged aristocracy of birth. I argued further that new transportation and communication technologies made a palpable reality of these changing modes of space and contributed concretely to the intellectual, artistic, and social changes that I tagged as democratization. By way of conclusion I would like to consider whether such technologies, in particular communication technologies, are fundamentally democratic or whether their pluralizing and democratizing effect on life and thought around the turn of the century was an accidental consequence of unique historical circumstances of that period.

An easy answer would be that communication technology is value-free, that its particular use either for or against democracy is an accident of time and place. But I believe that the technology of speedy communication is not value-free, that it is inherently democratic and makes certain social hierarchies and political forms impossible, as Francis Joseph understood intuitively.

One might argue that this technology is not inherently democratic, that in the twentieth century more advanced communications technologies such as radio and television have been used to dominate or brainwash the masses and reduce democratic pluralism to undemocratic totalitarianism. The most disturbing images of such an effect are those of Hitler addressing Nazi party rallies, spitting into loudspeakers his racist and antidemocratic message. But

I would reply that although Hitler used mass communication effectively, including radio broadcasts which reached millions of listeners, that use was a corruption of electronic communication that subverted its inherently pluralistic and democratic nature. Nazis monitored and hence blocked the free use of telephones by the masses. And in their own distinctive use of telephones— not to exchange information but to give orders—they negated its purpose. Hitler did not so much use the telephone as abuse it, and that abuse on behalf of antidemocracy illustrates the inherently democratic function of the proper and free use of telephone communication.

Perhaps the most infamous image of the abuse of television communication is that of Big Brother in George Orwell's *1984,* peering out of a screen monitor into every home, spying on private life and regulating thinking in the maintenance of a totalitarian dictatorship. But again Orwell has given us an image of double corruption of a technology's communicative function. Television allows people to *see* (to gather information), not to be seen (to have information gathered about them), and the fullest exploitation of the technology involves not a single channel peering out at viewers, but a variety of channels, a democratic choice of channels—for people to discover a variety of things about the world.

Some recent developments in television technology that appear to be in the service of democracy, however, have raised doubts as to their value. Although these developments are in the service of a wider dissemination of information, they have compromised the very processes that they were designed to serve. Television news polls, television cameras in the houses of government, and television cameras in courtrooms heighten the problems created when judgments that require wisdom are submitted to the inexperienced for a determinative vote.

Television polls and the introduction of TV cameras into Congress have resulted in chronic political temperature taking and year-round campaigning instead of thoughtful statesmanship and bold leadership. Political thinking has been cramped into whatever fits the two or three-second sound bite, and so the complex thinking necessary to deal with complex problems has suffered.

Cameras in the courtroom may compromise justice in individual cases, but they educate the population about the system of law and so work to safeguard violation of basic individual liberties. It would be unfortunate if people were tried on television, not because television spreads too much information, but too little. Justice cannot be left in the hands of viewers because, among many other reasons, we cannot be as certain that they would receive as much information from television (which they could always turn off) as jurors receive in courtrooms.

Communication has an inherent function of spreading technology information faster and cheaper to more people. The world over, people have sought out such technologies in response to what I believe is a fundamental human desire to know. And since that desire takes the inquiring mind into places (and palaces) where aristocratic traditions may formerly have blocked access, that desire is inherently antiaristocratic and democratic. The

Senator Edward Kennedy testifies in the 1991 televised trial of his nephew, William Kennedy Smith. Smith, who was accused of rape, won an acquittal.

new communication technologies of the late nineteenth century assailed the palaces of privileged information and worked in the direction of democratizing life and thought. We may welcome that assault on some forms of inherited privilege. However, we must also recognize that privileged elites based on training and skill must also be given a proper forum for their creative activities, one that is protected from the tabloid newspaper approach to jurisprudence that is fueled by televising celebrity murder trials.

1. Albert Einstein, "Autobiographical Notes," in *Albert Einstein: Philosopher-Scientist,* ed. Paul Arthur Schlipp (Evanston: Library of Living Philosophers, 1949), pp. 9–11.

2. Friedrich Nietzsche, *On the Genealogy of Morals* (New York: Vintage Books, 1967), p. 119.

3. José Ortega y Gasset, "Adán en el Paraíso," in *Obras Completas de José Orlegay Gasset*(1910; rpt. Madrid: Revista de Occidente, 1946), tomo I, p. 471.

4. Gasset, "Verdad y perspectiva," in *El Espectador,* tomo I (Madrid, 1916; rpt. Madrid, 1960), p. 116.

5. Albert Einstein, *Relativity* (New York: Crown Publishers, 1961), p. 150; "The Problem of Space, Ether, and the Field in Physics," in *Ideas and Opinions* (1934; rpt. New York: Crown Publishers, 1976), p. 274.

6. Frank Lloyd Wright, "A Testament" in Edgar Kaufmann and Ben Raeburn, *Frank Lloyd Wright: Writings and Buildings* (New York: Meridian Books, 1960), p. 314.

7. Louis H. Sullivan, *Kindergarten Chats and Other Writings* (New York: Dover Publications, 1979), pp. 105, 163, 39, 73 (cf. *GIT:* 1993, 393–431).

8. Frederick Jackson Turner, "Contributions of the West to American Democracy," in *The Frontier in American History* (New York: Henry Holt and Company, 1921), p. 259.

9. Alexander Archipenko, *Archipenko: Fifty Creative Years 1908–1958* (New York: TEKHNE, 1960), pp. 51–56.

10. Dora Vallier, "Braque, la peinture et nous: Propos de l'artiste recueillis," in *Cahiers d'art,* 29 (October 1954) pp. 15–16.

11. William James, *The Letters of William James* (Boston: Boston, Little, Brown, 1926), vol. II, pp. 277–78.

12. William James, *The Principle of Psychology* (New York: Dover Publications, 1950), vol. I, p. 240.

13. Horace Meyer Kallen, *William James and Henry Bergson: A Study in Contrasting Theories of Life* (Chicago: University of Chicago Press, 1914), pp. 11, 30, 105. James organized a collection of his essays under the title "Essays in Radical Empiricism," although they were never published under that title during his life.

14. Samuel Smiles, *Thrift* (London: J. Murray, 1876), p. 70.

15. Walter Lippmann, *Drift and Mastery* (New York: M. Kennerley, 1914), p. xvii.

16. Henri Bergson, *Matter and Memory* (1896; rpt. Garden City, New York: Doubleday, 1959), pp. 192, 196–97.

17. Arnold Bennett, "Your United States," *Harper's Monthly Magazine* (July 1912), p. 191.

18. I am indebted to Lary May for these sources on the democratic meaning of cinema in *Screening Out the Past: The Birth of Mass Culture and the Motion Picture Industry* (New York: Oxford University Press, 1980); "A Democratic Art," *The Nation* (Aug. 28, 1913), p. 193; D. W. Griffith, "Radio Speech," (Griffith File, Museum of Modern Art Film Library, New York); Herbert Francis Sherwood, "Democracy and the Movies," *Bookman* (March 1918), p. 238.

19. Arthur Meyer, *Forty Years of Parisian Society* (London: E. Nash, 1912), p. 111.

20. Edward Alsworth Ross, *Changing America* (New York: The Century Co., 1912), p. 8.

21. Philip Gibbs, *The New Man* (London: Sir Issac Pitman & Sons, Ltd., 1913), pp. 44–48.

22. Marcel Proust, *The Past Recaptured* (1927; rpt. New York: Random House, 1970).

23. Carl E. Schorske, *Fin-de-siècle Vienna* (New York: Knopf, 1979), pp. 296, 285.

24. Guirand de Scévola, "Souvenirs du camouflage (1914–1918)," *La revue,* (Christmas 1950), pp. 719–20. This source and additional information is in Elizabeth Kahn Baldewicz, "Les Camoufleurs: The Mobilization of Art and the Artist in Wartime France, 1914–1918," PhD. diss., University of California, Los Angeles, 1980.

25. Gertrude Stein, *Picasso* (1938; rpt. Boston: Beacon, 1959), p. 41.

26. Gary Allan Tobin, "The Bicycle Boom of the 1890's: The Development of Private Transportation and the Birth of the Modern Tourist," *Journal of Popular Culture* (Spring 1974), pp. 838–49.

27. Articles cited by Robert A. Smith, *A Social History of the Bicycle* (New York: McGraw-Hill, 1972), p. 112.

28. Stefan Zweig, *The World of Yesterday* (Lincoln: University of Nebraska Press, 1964), pp. 193–94.

29. Paul Adam, *La morale des sports* (Paris, 1898), pp. 115–24.

30. John Brooks, *Telephone: The First Hundred Years* (New York: Harper & Row, 1975), p. 93; Friedrich Ludwig Vocke, *Die Entwickelung des Nachrichtenschnellverkehrs und das Strassenwesen* (Heidelberg, 1917), p. 92.

31. Gerald Stanley Lee, *Crowds: A Moving-Picture of Democracy* (Garden City, New York: Doubleday, 1913), pp. 4, 19, 65, 274–78.

32. Marcel Proust, *The Guermantes Way* (1920; rpt. New York: Vintage Books, 1970), pp. 93–94.

33. H. G. Wells, *Anticipations* (1901; rpt. London: Chapman & Hall, 1914), pp. 216–17, 267, and the chapter titled "The Larger Synthesis."

34. In 1896 in New York City phone service cost $20 a month, while the average income of a worker was $38.50 a month. *See* Ithiel de Sola Pool, "Retrospective Technology Assessment of the Telephone" (A Report to the National Science Foundation, 1977), vol. I, p. 252.

Stephen Kern is a Distinguished Research Professor at Northern Illinois University. Since receiving his doctorate at Columbia University in 1970, he has been teaching European intellectual history at Northern Illinois University. His approach involves adapting phenomenology to interpret historical change, specifically the shifting modes of essential elements within human experience.

In four books he has applied that method to the history of embodiment, time and space, love, and vision: *Anatomy and Destiny: A Cultural History of the Human Body* (1975); *the Culture of Time and Space: 1880–1918* (1983); *The Culture of Love: Victorians to Moderns* (1992); and *Eyes of Love: The Gaze in Anglo-French Paintings and Novels, 1840–1900* (forthcoming).

Goods in Common: Efficiency and Community

James O'Toole

I n the early 1990s, Lee Kuan Yew established his reputation as the highest-profile critic of Western values. In a series of public addresses and published articles, the former prime minister of Singapore castigated the West for its slavish devotion to civil rights, political liberty, and democracy. The Cambridge-educated Lee argued that the West's obsession with individualistic values leads to self-indulgence, disrespect for authority, slow economic growth, political disorder, and, ultimately, the disintegration of society. In his view, the crime, drugs, illegitimacy, and graffiti-covered slums found in many British and American cities are the direct result of uncompromising Anglo-American individualism. Lee thus appealed to other Third World leaders—particularly his fellow Asians—to reject the wrong turn the West had taken during the Enlightenment and, instead, to embrace the values of Confucianism, which he claimed were responsible for the exemplary economic growth of his orderly city-state.

As a passionate believer in liberty, democracy, and individual rights, I do not share his philosophy and strongly object to his strong-arm practices. Yet, all men and women are prisoners of their own cultures, and that is as true for us in the West as it is for Lee in the East. Hence, we must admit that his unpalatable protestations against the essence of Western society at least serve to remind us that we, as much as Lee, wear cultural blinders. Those in the Anglo-American tradition who wholeheartedly subscribe to the values of the Enlightenment need to be reminded that there are other values at work in the rest of the world—indeed, there are even important Western values that we have been culturally conditioned to ignore. In the pages that follow, I show that two "Asian" values advocated by Lee were, in fact, also dominant in the West for over two thousand years and are now reasserting themselves as the result of a concatenation of social, political, economic, and historical forces. We shall see that these ancient and universal values, efficiency and community, are concerned with goods that members of society share in common, as opposed to rights that each of us possesses individually.

(Overleaf)
Detail from
Pre-studies
Toward a
Synthesis: or:
The Develop-
mental
History of
a Drawing;
or: The
Capitol and
its Suburbs;
or: Rich
and Poor—
Power and
Powerlessness
by
Hans-Georg
Rauch

The legacy of the Enlightenment: Liberty *versus* equality

Significantly, "efficiency" and "community" were not included among the 102 great ideas identified by Mortimer Adler and his colleagues in the early 1950s when they created the Syntopical Index of Ideas to the *Great Books of the Western World*. (Adler "missed" these because his choice was determined by the frequency with which ideas were cited in that particular set of books). Other Westerners are blind to the importance of these two values because, for many of us, real history—history that affects us personally today—began with the Enlightenment. Since roughly the time of Hobbes, political philosophers and political economists, regardless of ideological persuasion, have been primarily concerned with securing individual rights. For example, disciples of John Locke, Immanuel Kant, and Adam Smith have focused on the individual's right to liberty. In contrast, disciples of Rousseau, Marx, and the utopian socialists (who foresaw the modern welfare state) have focused on the individual's right to equality. Because libertarians have equated the good society with a maximum amount of freedom, and egalitarians have equated social justice with equal access to the goods needed to satisfy basic human needs, politics in the West seem to have boiled down to arguments between these two ideological camps over which rights—and how much of each—individuals are entitled to claim from society.

These two camps are clearly at odds; nonetheless, they are both concerned with that same realm of individual rights. That is, while Rousseauians and Lockeans disagree over which rights individuals are entitled to, both schools of thought share a common starting point: they both believe that all individuals, by virtue of their humanity, possess natural rights. Yet, being constantly at political loggerheads causes people to all but forget this common tie that binds them. It has mattered little that a few great thinkers—most notably Thomas Jefferson—believed that liberty and equality are companionable; to libertarians and egalitarians alike, the fundamental fact of political life is that society must choose between one or the other of those irreconcilable values. In the words of the Social Darwinist William Graham Sumner:

> Let it be understood that we cannot go outside of this alternative: liberty, inequality, survival of the fittest; not-liberty, equality, survival of the unfittest. The former carries society forward and favors all its best members; the latter carries society downwards and favors all its worst members. [1]

Nearly every leading thinker in the nineteenth and early twentieth centuries held that society faces an inescapable choice between liberty and equality. Even today, the political historian Isaiah Berlin is among the majority of scholars who still argue that there is a terrible and inescapable trade-off between these two values. [2] That is, for each increment of equality gained in society there will be a subsequent loss of an increment of liberty, and vice versa. Two examples illustrate that trade-off. In the most relentlessly egalitarian modern society—Maoist China—where the ratio of the incomes of the highest paid individual to the lowest paid individual was possibly as low as 4:1, equality was achieved at the cost of a nearly total loss of liberty (the confiscation of property, censorship, banishment, and even death to dissenters); in the most libertarian of modern societies—Victorian England— liberty was achieved at the cost of enormous economic inequalities (the ratio of the incomes of the richest individual to the poorest individual was as high as 400,000:1). These two examples illustrate why liberty versus equality has been viewed as society's most painful trade-off.

Indeed, because effecting this trade-off has been the preoccupation of almost all modern politics, other values have paled in significance. Chinese Communists would murder tens of thousands in the name of equality, and Americans would proudly associate themselves with Patrick Henry's willingness to pay the ultimate price for liberty. But the Marxists rejected Confucian responsibility, while Americans would think it ridiculous to proclaim "Give me efficiency or give me death."

Both libertarians and egalitarians could afford to hear what anthropologists say, which is that liberty and equality are far from being universal or ancient values. In fact, they were meaningless words in traditional, preliterate societies. However, the concept of community is the very essence of social thought in such small-scale human groups. (*GBWW* II: 58, 1–236, 405–533) And the provision of efficiency—when understood as the orderly structuring of the community to ensure a constant and sufficient supply of food and other economic necessities—has been the major function of all human institutions since our species evolved. The same is true for what are called civilizations. In most traditional Asian cultures the concepts of liberty and equality were also nonexistent. Even today, Asian societies are driven by nothing more than the pursuit of efficiency and community which, as Lee notes, are key philosophical ideas of Confucianism.

Scholars oriented toward Western tradition concede this fact about Asian society. What they deny are the historical and continuing power of the concepts of efficiency and community in *Western* social thought, and they do not concede that these ideas are morally equivalent to liberty and equality as motivators of human behavior. It is against those arguments that I take my stand in this article. I show below that, in fact, these ideas have deep roots in the Western philosophical tradition. According to Plato, efficiency is the sine qua non of the good society, and Aristotle was a brilliant explicator of the centrality of the value of community. Moreover, these values are of practical importance today in that they constitute the core of two fast-growing ideological currents, what I here call corporatism and communitarianism. Corporatists are those who take efficiency as their highest goal—including Japanese and European business and government leaders, as well as American executives in the computer industry (and their allies in academia) who believe in a partnership between business and government and in the need for an explicit national industrial policy. Communitarians include not only humanists participating in a rising American movement known by that name but also advocates of efforts to improve the quality of work life. Most significantly, Greens and other environmentalists are, at their core, communitarians.

Singapore became the most prosperous nation in Southeast Asia while Lee Kuan Yew (right) was prime minister.

Moreover, I suggest below that these two values are related to each other—much as liberty is related to equality—as polar ends of the same dimension. Both efficiency and community are concerned with common goods and, at the extremes, political trade-offs thus are required in order to strike a balance between the two. At the extremes, efficiency and community are also incompatible with liberty and equality, almost as Lee argues. Yet, in moderation, all of these values are perfectly compatible. In fact, a basic requirement for justice in society is the simultaneous pursuit of all four values.

In sum, the standard Anglo-American two-factor model of political economy, in which liberty and equality are viewed as the central points of tension, should be rejected because it is too limited to accommodate the complexities of the modern era. In its place, I offer a model reflecting tension between four major social values; liberty, equality, community, and efficiency. This model is of particular necessity today because, since the demise of Marxist egalitarianism, the ascendent Anglo-American libertarianism has been declared "victor" of the ideological wars, and all other values but freedom are now commonly denigrated in many corners of Western society. [3]

The idea of efficiency

The concept of efficiency is, on one level, too simple to require more than a passing philosophical explanation. After all, how can a society be called good (or just) if its citizens do not have the wherewithal to meet their basic needs? But the word means more than simply the effective ordering of the institutions and activities that provide food, clothing, and shelter. Efficiency is also used by economists in several different ways to explain quite complex concepts and, more important for this discussion, it stands as shorthand for a specific political philosophy.

In the 1980s, reports emanating from the U.S.S.R. and its former Eastern European satellites indicated that it was low incomes, empty stores, and long queues for necessities which led to the fatal erosion of confidence in the communist system. If those reports were true, then the dramatic abandonment of Marxist egalitarianism was due more to a desire for a higher standard of living than to a love of liberty. After the events of the 1980s, there can be little doubt that a widespread desire for economic efficiency exists among the citizens of those nations. While that desire may not be as self-evident as the yearning for freedom or equality, there is now powerful evidence that efficiency is equated with the good society much in the way liberty and equality are traditionally valued.

Economic efficiency—when defined as increasing the wealth of a nation through the most productive application of labor and capital—is a modern notion derived from Adam Smith's pathbreaking insights into the true sources of economic growth. But the philosophical groundwork for Smith had been laid two millennia earlier in the writings of Aristotle and, more directly, Plato. While Aristotle understood such proto-Smithian concepts as markets, the division of labor, financial speculation, and economies-of-scale, it was Plato who anticipated the modern corporate state and, even, the modern business corporation. As we shall see, not only is the famous pin factory described in the opening pages of Smith's *Wealth of Nations* a Platonic organization; so is General Motors!

Plato was no friend of liberty or equality—at least, not as a modern democrat would use those terms. In *The Republic,* Plato's dramatic voice, Socrates, says of democracy that it creates a city "full of freedom and frankness— a man may say and do what he likes . . . where freedom is, the individual is clearly able to order for himself his own life as he pleases." (*GBWW* I: 7, 409; II 6, 409) While such a state sounds agreeable to the modern libertarian, to Socrates it was tantamount to anarchy. Worse, political liberty leads to political equality, a situation that is unjust because people are not, by nature, equal. "Democracy," Socrates says, "[is] full of variety and disorder, and dispens[es] a sort of equality to equals and unequals alike." (*GBWW* I: 7, 409; II: 6, 409) That might sound desirable to modern egalitarians, but Socrates found it to be the second least-acceptable form of government, only one rung above tyranny.

The Platonic ideal was the "well-ordered state," a government characterized by "the rule of the few." Importantly, this ruling elite—or oligarchy— is not composed of hereditary aristocrats who owe their positions to birth, wealth, force, or the inclination to power. No, that is the stuff of tyranny, and Plato would have none of it. Instead, the "guardians" of his ideal Republic rule by force of their rigorous "virtue." The characteristics of this leadership elite are their knowledge, wisdom, competence, talent, and ability. In short, Plato proposes a non-democratic state that is nonetheless just and legitimate because it is a meritocracy in which the leaders practice "the science of government"—which, he tells us, is "among the greatest of all sciences and most difficult to acquire." Because the mastery of this science is so rarely achieved, "any true form of government can only be supposed to be the government of one, two, or, at any rate, of a few . . . really found to possess science." (*GBWW* I: 7, 599; II: 6, 599)

Plato's elite rule not for themselves but for the good of society as a whole. Plato has Socrates say that the purpose of the Republic "is not the disproportionate happiness of any one class, but the greatest happiness of the whole." Socrates admits that many people will not like living in his Republic—nonetheless, they should appreciate that it provides what is best for the greatest number of the citizenry (in this he anticipates the nineteenth-century utilitarianism discussed below).

But to what specific end do the guardians rule the Republic? Here Plato talks about "virtue," "truth," and "order"—but he does not say what these words might mean, other than what the guardians themselves define them to mean in their selfless quest for the good society. In the realm of economy, the rulers seem to be charged with providing a high standard of living—not for themselves, but for the ruled. When Socrates posits a mere subsistence economy for the Republic, the pragmatic Glaucon counters that this would only be "providing a city of pigs." Glaucon argues that much more than bare necessities are required for

"the ordinary conveniences of life. People who are to be comfortable
are accustomed to lie on sofas, and dine off tables, and they should have
sauces and sweets in the modern style." (*GBWW* I: 7, 318; II: 6, 318)

Taking his clue from Glaucon, Socrates gets into the luxury-provisioning
business himself, describing a "state at fever heat" economically, one that
doesn't stop with necessities

"such as houses, and clothes, and shoes: the arts of the painter and the
embroiderer will have to be set in motion, and gold and ivory and all
sorts of materials must be procured." (*GBWW* I: 7, 318; II: 6, 318)

While it seems clear that Socrates is personally averse to such displays of
conspicuous consumption, others wish to make the Republic "as great and
as rich as possible." And Plato's system of guardianship is nothing if not
consistent with that end. (*GBWW* I: 7, 401–16; II: 6, 401–16)

Plato's Republic is readily recognizable as the meritocratic ideal to which
many of the world's leading religious, military, and academic institutions
aspire. Indeed, the guardians of the Republic also might be seen as analogous to the managers of modern, publicly held corporations. These men
and women hold their positions not by dint of ownership, heredity, force,
or election. Instead, in theory at least, they are a meritocratic elite who
sit atop their hierarchies thanks to their manifest virtue—their skill, talent,
intelligence, experience, and wisdom. Corporate managers should be those
most qualified to guide the organization in pursuit of the common good of
its constituencies. Moreover, like Plato's guardians, they must sacrifice their
personal self-interest in order to maximize the wealth of those they serve—
the shareholders. (John Kenneth Galbraith calls this paradoxical self-sacrifice
by professional profit maximizers "the approved contradiction.") [4]

Inherent in Plato's scheme is the notion of hierarchy. Efficiency requires
a division of labor; an orderly division requires an hierarchy based on
ability; and an hierarchical system will be, by definition, "class" stratified.
Plato was unapologetic about the antiegalitarian, antidemocratic nature of
his Republic. He agreed with Aristotle that inequality based on merit was
how things *should* be run. Moreover, Plato agreed with Aristotle that the
state takes precedence over the individual. In Aristotle's view, "the state is
by nature clearly prior to [superior to] the family and to the individual."
(*GBWW* I: 9, 446; II: 8, 446) And, from classical Athens to the present day,
all subsequent hierarchies have been justified in terms of their efficiency and
the necessity of putting the organization ahead of the individual in order to
achieve collective progress.

Corporatism: The belief that efficiency is the highest social value

Whereas the individual is the measure of liberty and equality, the focus of
efficiency is the state or organization. The most extreme expression of this

"corporatist" view was advanced by Hobbes, who argued that human beings are willing to abandon their natural liberty and equality for the security of the state. He believed that individuals form a combination (literally, a corporation) in the guise of the Leviathan which is superior to the individual—in effect, "an artificial man, though of greater stature and strength than the natural, for whose protection and defence it was intended." (*GBWW* I: 23, 47; II: 21, 47) [We recognize this today in the legal notion that a corporation is "an artificial person."]

The function of the Leviathan is to foster the safety necessary for economic progress. Despotic rule is found to be preferable to natural freedom on the grounds of efficiency. For in the state of nature,

> . . . there is no place for industry, because the fruit thereof is uncertain: and consequently no culture of the earth; no navigation; nor use of the commodities that may be imported by sea; no commodious building; no instruments of moving and removing such things as require much force; no knowledge of the face of the earth; no account of time; no arts; no letters; no society. . . . (*GBWW* I: 23, 85; II 21, 85)

While modern corporatists part company with Hobbes on the granting of total power to a Leviathan for the collective good, they accept his view that a well-ordered organization is the fount of progress, a necessity for the advance of civilization. Moreover, such organizations and societies require the rule of one, or at most a few, wise and benevolent individuals.

This view has a long philosophical lineage, even in the post-Renaissance West. After demolishing the Leviathan (in the person of Charles I), Cromwell and his supporters did not turn to democracy. Instead, they argued that there is a "natural aristocracy" of rulers, based on ownership of land. [5] A century later, Edmund Burke—no lover of tyranny—advanced the principle of "virtual representation," in which the best interests of the disfranchised working class would be represented in Parliament by their economic betters (who were, by definition, also their superiors in talent and education). One of the greatest of all liberals, J. S. Mill, so believed in the value of an intellectual aristocracy that he advocated proportional voting weighted by the amount of schooling each individual had received. (*GBWW* I: 43, 327–442; II: 40, 327–442) At about the same time, Tocqueville, too, was writing in a Platonic mode, "An aristocracy is infinitely more skillful in the science of legislation than democracy can ever be." (*GBWW* II: 44, 120) Even the American founders had oligarchic leanings. According to Madison, the U.S. Constitution aims "to obtain for rulers men who possess most wisdom to discern, and most virtue to pursue, the common good of the society." (*GBWW* I: 43, 176; II: 40, 176) Although the basis of American representative rule—an elite elected by the people—is far different from the Cromwellian elite of landed aristocrats, to critics of corporatism it amounts to the same thing: inequality. Corporatist society, in whatever form, is oligarchic. Said Marx, "Democracy is the executive committee of the ruling class."

Living in China roughly at the time of Socrates, Confucius drew many of the same conclusions as did the ancient Greeks, believing, for example, in the superiority of meritocratic oligarchy. Confucius' ideal state, as described in the *Analects,* is ruled by a meritocratic group of Mandarin "gentlemen," remarkably similar to Plato's guardians. These rulers, like their Greek counterparts, are set apart from the masses by their manifest virtue: they rule not for their own benefit, but to enrich and "bring comfort to the whole populace."

As with Hobbes, Confucius' motivation in advocating such a form of government was his fear of disorder. Indeed, throughout history and across cultures, the dominant view has been that the only realistic alternative to anarchy, on the one hand, and tyranny, on the other, is benevolent despotism. Both Socrates and Confucius are certain that they can create a system of education to ensure a benevolent ruling class—a class, not surprisingly, with traits identical to those Socrates and Confucius prided themselves on possessing! As Confucius' disciple Mencius put it, in proper Platonic terms, "If Heaven wishes peace and order for the world, who is there besides me to bring it about?" Relatively few philosophers at any time or in any culture have placed much faith in the efficacy of another possibility: democracy.

Singapore's Lee is thus both a Confucian and a Platonic ruler. Lee and Singapore have been advanced as exemplars of an alternative to Jeffersonian democracy, a view that is increasingly popular in many corporate, government, and academic circles in the West. Francis Fukuyama, author of the influential *The End of History and the Last Man,* argues that in the wake of Marxism's demise Singapore "is the one potential competitor to Western liberal democracy, and its strength and legitimacy is growing daily." [6]

One can see why. Singapore is an island populated by three million obsessively hard-working people, 78% of whom are ethnic Chinese. The nation's per capita GNP is equal to that of the United States, and it boasts the second highest standard of living in Asia, after Japan. There is no unemployment, crime, drug problem, pornography, litter, or graffiti, and there are no unwed mothers or illiterate sixteen-year-olds.

Most remarkably, Lee and his government are honest. Singapore is free of the graft and corruption commonplace throughout the developing world. Lee serves not to enrich himself but to increase the standard of living of his people. When he assumed power in 1965, Singapore was on the verge of civil war, beset by continuing racial unrest between Chinese and Malayans, and with an economy in postcolonial shambles. Lee quickly changed all that, single-handedly resolving the short-term political crisis and putting into place the necessary structure for the long-term transformation of Singapore's economy into the world-beater it has since become. Lee has been cited often as a model leader since he turned Singapore into a capitalist utopia that runs like clockwork. To many businesspeople he represents the classic corporate turn-around chief executive—the "take-charge" guy who knows what needs to be done and has the intestinal fortitude to see that his vision is carried out.

Indeed, Lee brooks little opposition to his will. Singapore's impressive efficiency comes at the price of civil liberty: the nation has no bill of rights, no dissent, no democracy. The country's Internal Security Act allows the government to lock up dissenters without trial. Even its admirable cleanliness is achieved by the draconian enforcement of laws against littering (there is a $625 penalty) and other forms of antisocial behavior (a $94 fine is imposed on those who fail to flush public toilets). The freedoms of its residents are limited in large things and small (chewing gum is banned, and there is a $312 fine for eating on the subway). Lee argues in *The Economist* that the economic efficiency of Singapore has resulted from his enlightened leadership, which has steered a course between the anarchic democracy of the West and the self-serving despotism of the Third World:

> What a country needs to develop is discipline rather than democracy . . .
> The exuberance of democracy leads to undisciplined and disorderly
> conditions which are inimical to development.

Admirers of Lee are more than willing to overlook his despotic ways. In his defense, they say, "Be realistic, the alternatives to Lee's strong leadership are either chaos or communism."

The science of economic efficiency

While rule by a meritocratic elite is an essential feature of corporatism, what also distinguishes its ideology from both libertarianism and egalitarianism is its largely economic focus. Whereas Adam Smith was of two minds about his pin factory, finding it both useful for its efficiency and immoral for the social costs it produced, true corporatists are concerned only with the efficiency side of the equation. Corporatists agree with Smith-the-economist when he writes that the goals of economic policy are, "first, to provide a plentiful revenue or subsistence for the people, or more properly to enable them to provide such a revenue or subsistence for themselves; and secondly, to supply the state or commonwealth with a revenue for the public services." Like Plato, there is a hint here of a higher good; that is, efficiency may be the means to some greater end. But that end is not made explicit, and there is a strong emphasis on the economic means. Says Smith in the next breath, the aim is "to enrich both the people and the sovereign." (*GBWW* I: 39, 182; II: 36, 204) Perhaps in church we may think about the higher implications of what we do, but in the real world of affairs, it all comes down to "cheapness and plenty"—Smith's concise statement of the intended results of efficiency.

The irony, of course, is that Smith was not a corporatist. Not only was the prime concern of Smith-the-moralist the welfare of the individual; his analytical point of departure was the entrepreneur who he saw as the basic productive unit in an economy. In contrast, not only do corporatists focus on groups (as opposed to individuals), they look upon the motivation inherent in direct ownership as being irrelevant to the question of efficiency. Publicly held corporations, combined state and private partnerships—even state ownership under certain circumstances—can be made proper vehicles for the maximization of the wealth of the nation.

While libertarians and egalitarians argue that wealth creation is a positive value in that a high standard of living is a *means* to greater liberty or equality, corporatists are incorrigibly pragmatic. Men and women of practical mind have always been drawn to the position that economic efficiency is a worthy end in itself. For example, that quintessential realist, Samuel Johnson, said to Boswell upon reading Rousseau's call for equality, "Sir, you may make the experiment. Go into the street, and give one man a lecture on morality, and another a shilling, and see which will respect you most." (*GBWW* I: 44, 125; II: 41, 125)

Such cynicism aside, it seems wrong to dismiss the pursuit of efficiency as totally lacking in moral justification. As the former leaders of communist states learned, and as the current leaders of impoverished Third World nations must be aware, the efficient production and distribution of goods is not an insignificant *moral* value. It leads to employment and, thus, to the overall well-being of a nation. (If Dr. Johnson were alive today, he might ask Boswell if he would be respected more in Ethiopia if he brought that country a General Motors plant or a democratic parliament.) Consequently, economic growth—the annual increase in gross national product—has become the major measure of success in almost all modern nations, and, for many governments, it has become the primary end they pursue.

Alexander Hamilton was the first to put economic efficiency on the national agenda in America, recognizing that there would be a loss of liberty in so doing. He believed that the threat of war "will compel nations the most attached to liberty to resort for repose and security to institutions which have a tendency to destroy their civil and political rights. To be more safe, they at length become willing to run the risk of being less free." (*GBWW* I: 43, 45; II: 40, 45) As secretary of the treasury during Washington's first administration, Hamilton sent Congress a "Report on Manufactures" in December 1791 which called upon the U.S. to abandon its agrarian bias and embrace industrialism. In order to increase national wealth, Hamilton advocated using the power of government to provide the infrastructure and other incentives needed to establish of modern textile factories in the U.S. In putting forth this "national industrial policy," Hamilton argued that America would, by means of a combined public and private partnership, free itself of economic dependence on Europe. In making his argument, Hamilton simultaneously attacked Adam Smith with his right hand—calling Smith's laissez-faire approach to business hopelessly naive in a complex world of international cartels and government-supported industry—and Jefferson with his left— arguing that the Sage of Monticello was living in the past if he thought that agriculture could ever be as productive or profitable as manufacturing. Hamilton urged America to join the industrial revolution and to follow Britain in the introduction of the cotton mill:

> In consequence of it, all the different processes for spinning cotton are
> performed by means of machines, which are put in motion by water,
> and attended chiefly by women and children; and by a smaller number
> of persons, in the whole, than are requisite in the ordinary mode of

spinning. And it is an advantage of great moment that the operations of this mill continue with convenience, during the night, as well as through the day. The prodigious effect of such a machine is easily conceived.

Hamilton contrasted the productive, urban-based textile factory with the less-efficient, rural-based agricultural system favored by Jefferson and concluded that the former offered numerous unique benefits:

> It is worthy of particular remark, that, in general, women and children
> are rendered more useful, and the latter more early useful, by manu-
> facturing establishments, than they would otherwise be. Of the number
> of persons employed in the cotton manufactories of Great Britain,
> it is computed that four-sevenths nearly, are women and children,
> of whom the greatest proportion are children, and many of them of
> a tender age. [7]

In America's chronic mythologizing about liberty, it is forgotten that Hamilton's view prevailed over the views of Smith and Jefferson. During the next two centuries, the American government intervened in the economy to give domestic industries a "level playing field" in world markets. Through such devices as tariffs, subsidies, support to colleges for industrial research and development, subsidization of railroads, and, in particular, the judicious use of tax incentives, the free-market America of myth was, in fact, a corporatist society.

Moreover, Hamilton's advocacy of the importation of "dark, satanic mills" into the United States was also successful. A kind of Faustian bargain was struck. The Industrial Revolution entailed an exchange of Jefferson's world of "virtuous, self-sufficient" farmers for the Dickensian world of grinding poverty in industrial cities (or, put positively, an exchange of what Marx had called "the idiocy of rural life" for a world of material progress). Yet, no one—not Marx, not Jefferson, not Dickens—argued in the final analysis that the bargain was a bad one. It is difficult to find a serious author who does not admit that industrialism was a necessary stage in human progress. Indeed, in *The Communist Manifesto,* Marx devotes pages to praise of the capitalists who created the world of mass manufacturing and the great increases in wealth that resulted from their efforts. In his own way, Marx was as enthusiastic as Hamilton on the subject of manufacturing efficiency.

While Marx found modern industrial practices inherently evil because they were based on the exploitation of labor, he nonetheless extolled the wealth-creating virtues of industrialism. Lenin would go much further in his enthusiasm. The Soviet leader was a great admirer of two exemplary American corporatists of his era: Henry Ford and Frederick Winslow Taylor. So taken was Lenin with the efficiency of the assembly line that he sought a Ford truck plant for the U.S.S.R., and so struck was he with the possibilities of "scientific management" that he urged Soviet factories to adopt Taylor's "time and motion" methods. In the mid-1800s—an era when almost all businesses were small, local operations—Marx had predicted the development of giant, multinational corporations. Lenin again followed Marx, outdoing his master in the application of his ideas. In fact, Lenin even surpassed Western corporatists in seeking economies-of-scale through the creation of the world's largest factories in the Soviet Union.

Efficiency in the modern era

By the early twentieth century, the value of efficiency had become dominant in the Western world, in communist and capitalist countries alike. Max Weber and other social scientists were even advocating the introduction of bureaucracy—formal, scientific hierarchy—in public and private institutions in the name of efficiency and the good society. By then, almost all economists had rejected as simplistic the Smithian philosophical approach to political economy in favor of Alfred Marshall's new "scientific" demonstration that efficiency could be defined as the point where the market "clears" (that is, the good society is achieved at the point on a graph where supply and demand curves intersect). Perhaps even more influential from a corporatist point of view was the work of the Italian Vilfredo Pareto who, early in the twentieth century, introduced the concept of mathematical "optimality." Pareto's mathematical formulas for determining the optimal allocation of resources in society, coupled with his Platonic belief in the superiority of elites, laid the basis for a modern school of corporatist economics.

Credit Marshall or Pareto; the task for economists in the first seventy years of the twentieth century became removing the "imperfections" that blocked the achievement of market clearing. Paradoxically, Smith and the libertarians had posited that such imperfections were the result of government interference in the economy, whereas corporatists were not reluctant to use government as a tool to correct market outcomes. For example, Keynes worried that untoward savings could lead to insufficient demand—to market sub-optimization, as it were. His revolutionary idea was to have government shore up demand (through borrowing and spending) in order to cover the shortfall. In effect, through correcting market inefficiencies, he sought to achieve the ideal state of "full employment." Hamiltonian to his core, Keynes gave libertarians fits.

Most singularly, the managers of Fortune 500 companies became corporatists in the post-World War II era. They took their lead from the philosophy of managerial efficiency outlined by Alfred P. Sloan in his influential book, *My Years with General Motors.* [8] Sloan uses the word efficiency (or its engineering and economic synonyms) as many as five times on a given page. Yet, nowhere in the book—not even when describing GM's pivotal role in the U.S. war effort—does he make even passing reference to liberty, equality, democracy, or any other social value. The book describes what was to become the curriculum of American business schools in the decades that followed.

While most leaders of large, publicly held American businesses may be corporatist in their thinking, their public pronouncements of that belief have been muted since the early 1980s when they came under attack from libertarians for a supposed lack of concern for "shareholder rights." Consequently, the clearest expressions of contemporary corporatism come from the academic community. In the writings of Peter Drucker, Michael Porter, Herbert Simon, Lester Thurow, Robert Reich, and, most notably, J. K. Galbraith, we find descriptions of corporatist behavior and assumptions (even if the personal views of most of these authors may not be corporatist).

In the writings of these authors it is clear that the highest corporatist values are efficiency, productivity, international competitiveness, a high standard of living, and economic growth. In order to enhance the process of wealth creation, corporatists believe in the necessity of economies of scale, particularly in industries competing in international markets. They argue that the world has become one financially and economically and that competition in some industries is as much country-versus-country as it is company-versus-company. Like Hamilton before them, they ask government to secure "a level playing field" for global competition. In particular, corporatists believe that governments must be advocates of business and should do all they can to advance the cause of domestic companies in world markets (labor unions, too, should be part of a grand national "social partnership").

Modern Asian corporatism

As Asian nations adopted Western technology and Western-style economies during the post-World War II period, they gravitated toward the corporatist pole, finding it not only compatible with Confucianism but more effective than libertarianism at stimulating investment and employment. *The Atlantic Monthly*'s James Fallows has become a forceful advocate of Confucian corporatism, which he argues is more moral and efficient than a system fueled by free-market self-interest. [9] Fallows' contribution has been to call attention to the fact that Japanese corporatism draws more heavily on the work of an obscure nineteenth-century German economist, Friedrich List, than on the writings of Adam Smith and his better-known Anglo-American disciples. List, in a manner more Asian than Anglo, advocated economic principles aimed at the welfare of the group, as opposed to the freedom of the individual. His emphasis on planning, government/industry partnership, and production and savings (as opposed to consumer-oriented consumption) struck a responsive chord in the Confucian East. Whereas Anglo-American economists argued that individuals must be completely free to choose whether to invest or to consume, List argued that nations devoted to long-term full-employment should set interest rates to encourage savings. Fallows illustrates List's corporatist philosophy with reference to Korea's successful development in the 1980s:

> The goal is to get people to save more of their paychecks, and banks to lend more money for long-term industrial expansion, than normal market forces would allow. . . . Under Anglo-American theory the country

would just let these two forces fight it out until they reached the natural equilibrium. . . . That is, in order for Korea to get enough money into the hands of its industries, it needed to bend the rules [of free-market economics]. [10]

Fallows argues that the Asian and European countries that have been most successful in achieving job creation through rapid economic growth have been those nations most willing to break the "laws" of libertarian free-market economics. Yet, he points out, Anglo-Americans "often act as if Adam Smith's theories were the only theories still in play":

Today's Americans and Britons may not like this new system, which makes their economic life more challenging and confusing than it would otherwise be. They are not obliged to try to imitate its structure, which in many ways fits the social circumstances of East Asia better than those of the modern United States or Britain. But the English-speaking world should stop ignoring the existence of this system—and stop pretending that it doesn't work. [11]

While most English-speaking economists and philosophers have ignored corporatism—or dismissed it as unworkable because it violates the laws of Adam Smith's "science"—List's system has secured a firm toehold not only in Asia but also in the European Community. Yet, this practical success of corporatism does not make it any more correct than the theoretical soundness of libertarianism validates the approach of Adam Smith. Indeed, corporatism has a tendency toward bureaucracy and, at the extreme, toward fascism. According to William Pfaff, List's philosophy spread to France after the Franco-Prussian War because it emphasized "the primacy of community over 'hedonism' and selfish individualism . . . this 'corporatism' was meant to replace 'anarchic' individualism and put limits on the greed of capitalism." Pfaff argues that these intellectual roots—most profoundly realized in Vichy France—"still feed France and Europe":

France is in many respects a corporatist society today. National social and economic policy is set in consultation with the "social partners." Much of the economy is still dominated by the state, precisely because many on both right and left see capitalism as socially irresponsible . . . Some of these forces still affect not only contemporary France but what the European Union has become. Thus Brussel's corporatism, emphasis on disinterested technocratic administration and distrust of totally uncontrolled market forces, refect these influences. [12]

A practical philosophy

When Hamilton spoke in 1791 of making young children "more early useful," he was using the language of utilitarianism which had been introduced two years earlier by the influential British philosopher and economist Jeremy Bentham. In fine Platonic fashion, utilitarians defined the good society as "the greatest good for the greatest number." J. S. Mill, who early in his career had been Bentham's prime disciple, came to worry about the justice of a system so bent on the scientific calculation of "the greatest good" that it ignored the feelings of the members of society—particularly, the feelings of those who were not part of "the greatest number." In his *Autobiography,* Mill came to conclude that no philosophy that could be used as justification for the employment of children could be considered moral—no matter how "scientifically" that justification was made.

Corporatism, whether evolved from Bentham or Pareto, has always been attractive to those, who like Sloan, have a scientific bent. One of its chief attractions is the absence of sentimentality, ideology, or superstition in its core beliefs. From the beginning, corporatists have spoken the language of *realpolitik.* During the Peloponnesian Wars, when the Melians were offered the choice between subjugation by Athens or total annihilation, the besieging Athenians sought to persuade the hopelessly outmanned Melians to be "realists"—that is, to accept the fact of life that "might makes right" and that it was better to be Athenian than dead. The Athenians reasoned that the Melians should "aim at what is feasible" as opposed to what is idealistic. (*GBWW* I: 6, 505; II: 5, 505) Two thousand years later, Machiavelli offered similar practical advice in *The Prince,* a treatise that was the first to warrant the term "political science."

Like Machiavelli, corporatists have little patience with such "unscientific" notions as natural rights, in either their strong egalitarian or weaker libertarian sense. What the corporatist belief comes down to is that there is no such thing as universal moral or philosophical "truth"; only that which can be demonstrated scientifically can be called true. For example, when corporatist executives disagree with a proposed government regulation, they do so not on ideological grounds or on the grounds of ethical justice; instead, they argue pragmatically that it does not matter what the law should is, as long as the law remains the same for all their competitors, domestic and foreign.

On this and many other points, corporatism and libertarianism sound enough alike to cause the two to be confused in the minds of many. For assistance in clarifying the differences between the two values, we may now refer to the values quadrant depicted on the accompanying page. Here we see the four primary values of political economy displayed as polar forces in constant tension with each other. On this compass card, efficiency is on a different axis than liberty and equality. Hence, while efficiency differs from liberty, it cannot logically do so in the same manner by which equality differs from liberty. Since efficiency and liberty are not in direct opposition but are, instead, adjoining values, we will find that the two overlap in certain respects. For instance, both libertarians and corporatists generally celebrate the value of economic markets.

While the two values thus overlap, they are, nonetheless, distinct. This difference may be illustrated by two examples. First, visualize the difference between the laissez-faire social, political, and economic system found in the American West during the Gold Rush, and then contrast that system to the guided capitalism found in Lee's post-World War II Singapore. Second,

The Four Poles of the Good Society

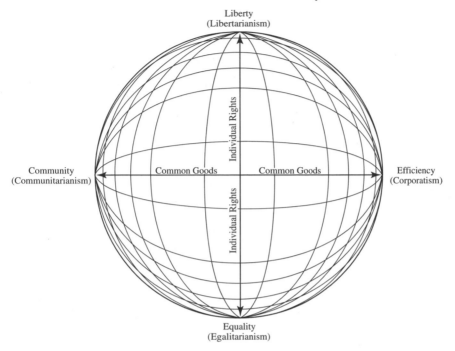

Liberty
(Libertarianism)

Individual Rights

Community   Common Goods   Common Goods   Efficiency
(Communitarianism)   (Corporatism)

Individual Rights

Equality
(Egalitarianism)

consider the well-documented differences in the pro-free-market behavior, attitudes, and political preferences of small-business owners, and the more conciliatory behavior and attitudes toward government of professional managers of Fortune 500 firms.

With these examples in mind, we see that while libertarians value the economic effects of a free market, they reserve their highest praise for systems that promote *individualism*—whether that individualism be social, political, or economic. In contrast, while corporatists also value market mechanisms, they reserve their greatest praise for systems that promote the order and efficiency of the *whole*. Where libertarians talk about entrepreneurship and individual preferences, the language of corporatism is that of planning, technology, optimization, power, and organization.

Similarly, while there is some blurring of the values of efficiency and equality, a clear distinction between the two can be drawn based on the respective definitions of the good society offered by corporatists and egalitarians. While both groups look favorably on planning and on coordination between firms, unions, and government—and both are willing, on occasion, to sacrifice the niceties of civil liberties in order to achieve what they consider higher ends—nonetheless, their goals are dissimilar. To the corporatist, the good society is a well-ordered, efficient state with an overall high standard of living, the benefits of which are distributed unequally on a meritocratic basis. In contrast, the egalitarian defines the good society as a state in which all individuals have inalienable political and economic rights, and inequalities in the enjoyment of those rights are minimized as far as reasonably possible. Thus, we should not confuse the divergent goals of corporatist Singapore with those of egalitarian Denmark.

Yet, as we now see, the distinctions between one state dedicated to efficiency and another dedicated to community are more difficult to draw. In the following discussion of communitarianism, we find that Plato was not simply a corporatist.

The idea of community

For most of this century, corporatist values have been dominant in the Western world. But, as Newton demonstrated, for every force there is an equal and countervailing reaction. Beginning in the 1960s, the "Green" reaction to corporatism has been concerned with the quality of life. Libertarians, egalitarians, and corporatists all agree that economic efficiency is necessary, either as the means to the attainment of higher ends or as an end in itself, providing citizens with a high standard of living. But in the eyes of communitarians, traditionally defined economic progress requires a pact with the devil. Hamilton's embrace of the Industrial Revolution illustrates three such Faustian exchanges. First is a trade-off of the dignity of human labor for efficiency. When Adam Smith advocated the further and continuing division and redivision of work tasks in order to improve manufacturing efficiency, he nonetheless conceded that

> . . . in the progress of the division of labor, the employment of the far
> greater part of those who live by labor . . . comes to be confined to
> a few very simple operations, frequently to one or two . . . The man
> whose whole life is spent in performing a few simple operations . . . has
> no occasion to exert his understanding or to exercise his invention . . .
> He naturally loses, therefore, the habit of such exertion, and generally
> becomes as stupid and ignorant as it is possible for a human creature to
> become. (*GBWW* I: 39, 340; II: 36, 382)

Second is a trade-off of the sense of community for efficiency. Tocqueville argued that industrialism was inevitable because, as democracy spreads, "the demand for manufactured commodities becomes more general and extensive." Yet, he warned, the very social equality which was generating increased demand for manufactured goods would be undercut by the system that provided them. Industrialization would destroy the unique American condition of rural equality by creating "an aristocracy of manufacturers." Hence, to Tocqueville, early nineteenth-century America was introducing invidious European-style social stratification in what theretofore had been a class-free society. In a factory town, he wrote, there is "no real bond" between the owner and the worker:

> These two men see each other at the factory but do not know each other
> otherwise, and though there is one point of contact, in all other respects

they stand far apart. The industrialist only asks the workman for his work, and the latter only asks him for his pay. The one contracts no obligation to protect, nor the other to defend, and they are not linked in any permanent fashion either by custom or duty. (*GBWW* II: 44, 300)

The third trade-off is that of a clean and healthy environment for efficiency. While Jefferson eventually conceded the need for manufacturing to free America from its dependence on European military powers, he nonetheless refused to accept the proposition that abandoning the high quality of rural life for the teeming, smoky, urban industrial arena was a net gain. "The mobs of great cities add just so much to the support of pure government as sores do to the strength of the human body." [13]

In the American myth, political tension is portrayed as a pitched battle between libertarians and egalitarians. In fact, it has been at least as much a battle between Hamiltonian lovers of urban-industrial efficiency and Jeffersonian lovers of rural community. In the late 1960s, economists turned their attention to measuring the consequences of pursuing both the Hamiltonian and Jeffersonian alternatives. They demonstrated that for every increment of environmental quality a society gains, a measure of efficiency is lost (as when a scrubber is placed on an industrial smokestack). The opposite is true as well—gains in efficiency from power plants endanger the quality of life of host communities. Thus, in the modern industrial state, every environmental, consumer, health, or safety regulation enforced entails a trade-off between the values of community and efficiency.

To increasing numbers of individuals in developed countries, exchanges of the quality of life to obtain a high standard of living have become morally unacceptable. In the last two dozen years, most of these dissenters have been called environmentalists. Yet, their value system—which seems so contemporary—actually is rooted deeply in the ancient humanistic, naturalistic belief that all humankind consists of a global *community*. For that reason, some of these individuals now call themselves communitarians.

Historically, Americans believed that pursuit of the end of either liberty or efficiency would lead to the good society, and that the means to those different ends was the effective application of technology. But when communitarians examine what technology has wrought, they see a degraded and abused physical and social environment. A contemporary communitarian, Neil Postman, argues that, "The uncontrolled growth of technology destroys the vital sources of our humanity. It creates a culture without a moral foundation. It undermines certain mental processes and social relations that make human life worth living." The culprit is the corporatist belief that "the primary, if not the only, goal of human labor and thought is efficiency." [14]

The second culprit is the libertarian assumption of *homo economicus*—Adam Smith's belief that the good society depends on humankind's "propensity to barter, truck and exchange one thing for another." This premise was challenged in the broadest expression of modern communitarianism, E. F. Schumacher's 1973 book, *Small is Beautiful*, subtitled, *Economics as if People Mattered*. [15] Schumacher advocated policies to conserve natural resources, end pollution, and to create opportunities for "good work" for all citizens of the globe. To this end, he called for greater social control of industry—but not necessarily state control (which he feared would lead to bureaucratization and regimentation, which are inimical to the quality of life). Schumacher's fundamental assumption was that humans are the measure of all things and, thus, traditional economic measures lead to *in*efficiency. He illustrated the difference between economic inefficiency and what he called "social inefficiency." An unregulated market creates social inefficiencies because it does not produce enough public goods, is short-term oriented, produces "externalities" such as pollution, and treats people as things (to the economist, land, labor, and capital are fungible; the environmentalist/humanist treats all three differently, because some "land" is a renewable resource, other land is nonrenewable, and humans are never to be treated as means).

Communitarian origins: The question of property

The origins of Schumacher's communitarianism can be traced to Aristotle. The Macedonian philosopher is particularly clear on questions of fundamental values, as he is on the related differences between ends and means. The end to which we should all obtain is "the good life," by which he means the use of our highest human faculties. His logic is simple: everything should aim to fulfill its highest potential. Since some animals are stronger than people, animals should do physical labor. Since only humans can reason, the proper end for humans is to use fully that capacity that distinguishes them from beasts. Therefore, "the good life" consists of intellectual and political activity—that which beasts cannot do. Since society is composed of reasoning humans, the "state exists for the sake of a good life." (*GBWW* I: 9, 477; II: 8, 477) Those who participate in the activities that constitute the good life are the citizens of the *polis*. In the *polis*, justice consists of actions for "the common advantage," that is, for the good of others; *in*justice consists of actions that despoil the sense of community, that do harm to others. "Justice, alone of the virtues, is thought to be 'another's good,' because it is related to our neighbor." (*GBWW* I: 9, 377; II: 8, 377) Here we find the germ of communitarianism, the humanistic valuing of the shared "good life."

Alas, to modern communitarians, Aristotle had a bit more to say on the subject of the collective quality of life. When discussing exactly who constituted the community—that is, who should enjoy the good life—he cautioned, "we ought not to include everybody." (*GBWW* I: 9, 530; II: 8, 530) Those "included out" (to use Samuel Goldwyn's apt if infelicitous phrase) were more numerous than those included in. Among the outs were: women, artisans, slaves, and foreigners. Thus are modern communitarians disappointed by the old master. Yet they point to him to show how the concept of community has expanded over time and how it must continue to expand further in the future. For example, Jefferson's concept was not much more inclusive than Aristotle's—he included artisans and immigrants—but it was a small step in the right direction.

Traditionally, communitarians have meant two things when they say "community": first, the Jeffersonian face-to-face community of neighbors; second, the broader world community, the "brotherhood of man." Like egalitarians, they have argued that Aristotle overstated the importance of the differences among humans, much as he understated the importance of the similarities—that is, the common humanity that unites the species. Yet, today, a strain of radical communitarianism emphasizes the differences among the world's many and diverse ethnic and racial *communities,* each with its own inviolable and unique culture. Tension between these opposing views— between those who stress the *pluribus* and those who stress the *unum* as the chief value of American society—constitutes a major controversy inside academia today. On a more violent stage, the issue currently is being played out in the ethnic conflicts of Eastern Europe.

Aristotle built his restricted notion of community from the ground up, based on his observations of nature. Like Locke and Rousseau, who would follow his lead, Aristotle believed that the family is the natural building block of a community. Families are "instinctive" to Aristotle ("like swarms of bees"), while to Rousseau they are held together by necessity. To Locke the family "draws with it mutual support and assistance, and a communion of interests, too." And in the minds of all three philosophers, the "natural" progression is family→village→state, all of which are bound together by "a communion of interests"—not only common *interests* but, perhaps, common *responsibilities* as well. In Locke's words:

> Every one, as he is bound to preserve himself, and not quit his station willfully, so, by the like reason, when his own preservation comes not in competition, ought he as much as he can to preserve the rest of mankind, and not unless it be to do justice to an offender, take away or impair the life, or what tends to be the preservation of the life, the liberty, health, limb or goods of another. (*GBWW* I: 35, 26; II: 33, 26)

Here Locke goes at least as far as Mill would five generations later in asserting the human responsibility to not harm others. In addition, there is here and in his other writings a hint of "Locke-the-communitarian." This is ironic because Locke has long been a bête noire to environmentalists for having advanced private claims to "the commons." After all, it was Locke who said, "Whatsoever, then, he removes out of the state that Nature hath provided and left it in, he hath mixed his labor with it, and joined to it something that is his own, and thereby makes it his property." But it was also Locke who said that no one could take more from nature than he could personally use, "at least where there is enough . . . left in common for others." (*GBWW* I: 35, 30; II: 33, 30)

For communitarians, the issue is to distinguish what is rightly *mine* from what is rightly *ours.* Of course, in the state of nature (which is the communitarians' particular base of reference) *everything is ours.* That is why communitarians often are accused by critics of being utopian, of irrationally longing to return to the state of nature, to the Garden of Eden, in which all was pristine and fecund. As depicted by Rousseau, this was the Golden Age in which "the produce of the earth furnished [humankind] with all he needed, and instinct told him how to use it," and where "singing and dancing, the true offspring of love and leisure, became the amusement, or rather the occupation, of men and women thus assembled together with nothing else to do." (*GBWW* I: 38, 348–51; II: 35, 348–51)

This was the age when, in Locke's phrase, "All the world was America"— undeveloped, uncivilized, unspoiled, and unpopulated. (When it came to the property rights of American Indians, Locke clearly had an attitude.) At any rate, this Eden was lost, according to Rousseau, "when property was introduced." That was "some fatal accident, which, for the public good, should never have happened." This "fatal accident" is somewhat analogous to the Biblical Fall when, along with private property, the afflictions of necessity were introduced; some people gained property, and others were forced to labor for these individuals. The consequent division of labor brought toil and drudgery (labor, after all, is Adam's curse).

The quality of life begins with good work

Labor is the curse, at least for *some* men and women, specifically, those who do not own property. Thus, the Fall—the leaving of nature—introduces a distinction between the classes that will forever divide the once-united community between those who toil and those who do not (or, in Marxist terms, between labor and capital). To non-Marxists like Locke, those who do not "labor" can still be said to "work" when they invest their capital. Aristotle revealed a related point when he made a distinction between "good work" and "bad work." Bad work is *labor,* manual work that should only be done by beasts, slaves (or women!). In contrast, good work is closer to leisure; it is mental work that can only be done by people who are free of the need to toil. Manual labor is instrumental in that it provides the extrinsic means to support the leisure for *others* to engage in dignified work, while leisure-work is an end in itself and provides intrinsic rewards to those who engage in it themselves. Marxists therefore ask for an equal distribution of property to end the manifest injustice of this two-class system.

Modern communitarians claim that it is possible to design all work in such a way that it is intrinsically rewarding for those who do it. Aristotle had the idea first, but he thought that a utopian state could only be achieved through automation. In the fourth century B.C., he raised the possibility of a future in which "the shuttle would weave and the plectrum touch the lyre without a hand to guide them," and, when that was possible, "chief workmen would not want servants, nor masters slaves." (*GBWW* I: 9, 447; II: 8, 447) Automation thus would free all men and women from the tyranny of necessity, and all could then participate in leisure-work. In this prescient passage we find the seeds of a modern paradox. Machine progress, the bane of communitarians like Schumacher and Postman, is at once the cause of the problem they identify and the solution. Indeed, modern technologists tell us that it is necessary to go through the enslaving stage of "dark satanic mills" to get to the age of the labor-saving robot. In 1930 Keynes readdressed Aristotle's question and predicted that automation would finally free all of humankind from the dictates of necessity in a mere five generations. Until then, Keynes said we would have unhappily, to continue playing by the economists' basic principle that necessity requires self-interested dog-eat-dog competition.

> For at least another hundred years we must pretend to ourselves and to every one that fair is foul and foul is fair; for foul is useful and fair is not. Avarice and usury and precaution must be our gods for a little longer still. For only they can lead us out of the tunnel of economic necessity into daylight. [16]

Keynes sounds a bit like Aristotle in his tolerance of injustice while waiting for the deus ex machina of abundance. Yet to Aristotle, Keynes's admonition might smack of moral confusion of ends and means. In Aristotle's view, some of the mental work undertaken by Keynes-the-scholar—who was a successful stock-market speculator on the side—might not have qualified as "good work." To Aristotle, wealth should not be accumulated endlessly for its own sake, but merely to provide the means to support the good life. Thus, to the extent that Keynes-the-speculator invested in order to support his research and writing, Aristotle would have approved; but had Keynes speculated in order to engage in conspicuous consumption, Aristotle would have condemned him.

Marxism contrasted with communitarianism: Standard of living *versus* quality of life

In either event, Marx would have denounced Keynes as a "parasite." Marx might have conceded that financiers like Keynes can be said to increase the overall wealth of the nation by putting their capital to productive work, but, in so doing, they degrade the unity of society. To Marx, the increase in the wealth of the few reduces the dignity of the many who are forced to labor to support them. Worse, the worker becomes a mere cog in an industrial machine that "converts the laborer into a crippled monstrosity, by forcing his detail dexterity at the expense of a world of productive capabilities and instincts." (*GBWW* I: 50, 176; II: 50, 176) Echoing Smith, Marx not only says that craftsmanship has been replaced by the dull rote of industrial work but, worse, that the worker has no leisure time for recreation. They become like an Aristotelian machine or slave—a "wage slave"—while the owner-capitalist extracts the surplus value and enjoys the leisure. Marx's description of a two-class society is remarkably like Aristotle's—except that Marx stresses the injustice inherent in the plight of the have-nots, whereas Aristotle extols the good life of the haves. While Marx would agree with Aristotle (and Keynes) on what the good life entails, it bothered him morally that the "wage slave" is denied the freedom, education, and wherewithal to be a participating member in Aristotle's *polis*—the community.

Here we must make an important distinction. Because Marxists are concerned primarily with achieving a high standard of living for all, they focus on the necessity of a just distribution of property; because communitarians are concerned primarily with achieving a high quality of life for all, they focus on the necessity of a just distribution of good work. What this difference means in practice was revealed in the late 1980s in reports from Eastern Europe. There, communist rulers believed that justice had been served fully when factories were owned collectively—even though the working conditions in those factories were Dickensian and the factories spewed tons of pollution into the environment. That is why communitarians do not believe that state ownership of the means of production, in and of itself, will address quality of life issues. And that is why for three generations communitarians have sought to improve the quality of life in workplaces regardless of who owns them. In the early part of this century, the economist Veblen called for greater attention to be paid to the common "instinct of workmanship" and for greater sensitivity to the inherent human "taste for effective work." (*GBWW* II: 57, 7) He believed that all men and women have a strong desire to find a sense of mastery, self-esteem, and competence in their individual work. This communitarian concern was pursued in earnest by a subsequent generation of workplace humanists, including Abraham Maslow and Douglas McGregor.

Contemporary workplace humanism stems from the efforts of the early nineteenth-century industrialist Robert Owen, who, in his textile factory in New Lanark, Scotland, created a modern business in which he was the first to introduce relatively short working hours, a grievance procedure, and guaranteed employment during times of economic downturn. He invented contributory health, disability, and retirement plans and provided clean, decent housing for his workers and their families. Most singularly, he took young children out of his factory and put them in a school that was the first to stress learning as a pleasurable experience. Owen is also credited with having established both the consumer and producer cooperative movements. He argued that social conditions were not determined by laws of the market, but by choices made by society. For his efforts, regarded as futile in their aim to reform capitalism, he was singled out by Marx and Engels for special scorn and condemnation in *The Communist Manifesto.*

In the final analysis, then, communitarians differ from Marxists in their humanistic (as opposed to economic) orientation. They believe in putting men and women—dignified, rational, altruistic humans—at the center of their philosophy. They believe that the peculiarly human qualities of reasoning and speech not only grant natural rights to every individual, but that they unite the entire species in a greater *commonwealth*. Mill made this communitarian point most strongly when he said that human beings differ from other animals:

> First, in being capable of sympathising, not solely with their offspring, or, like some of the more noble animals, with some superior animal who is kind to them, but with all human, and even with all sentient, beings. Secondly, in having a more developed intelligence, which gives

a wider range to the whole of their sentiments, whether self-regarding or sympathetic. By virtue of his superior intelligence, even apart from his superior range of sympathy, a human being is capable of apprehending a community of interest between himself and the human society of which he forms a part . . . (*GBWW* I: 43, 469; II: 40, 469)

Libertarianism contrasted with communitarianism: Rights *versus* responsibilities

Communitarians differ greatly from egalitarians—and from libertarians and corporatists—in their belief that humans are not only sympathetic but also capable of altruism on behalf of their fellows. For this, communitarians are said to be "idealistic" and to fail to understand that human nature is, at base, "self-interested." (Mill answered that charge in this way, "The deep-rooted selfishness which forms the general character of the existing state of society, is so deeply rooted, only because the whole course of existing institutions tends to foster it.") Libertarians, in particular, scorn communitarian willingness to sacrifice individuality to obtain the collective good. But when Mill speaks above of community, he does not mean *sameness*. Among moral philosophers, Mill was the most concerned with the repressive effects of society, "the tyranny of custom" that crushes individuality. He recognized (before Mao and Eastern European communists proved the point) that uniformity does not enhance the quality of life.

A major distinction between libertarianism and communitarianism is this: liberty has to do with independence; community with interdependence. Another way of seeing the difference is that libertarians stress individual rights, while communitarians stress common responsibilities. Mill, who had so much to say about the necessity of rights in preserving individual liberty, also saw that rampant individualism would undermine the very sense of community that separates humans from beasts. Consequently, Mill stressed the issue of balance between individual rights and community responsibilities. For instance, he believed that the right of a British subject to a trial by jury was balanced by a concomitant responsibility to serve on a jury. Mill argued that citizens have numerous responsibilities: to pay taxes, to educate their children, to serve in the army, and to provide "other joint work necessary to the interest of society." Indeed, on the communitarian issue of responsibility he went much further than any other writer (at least, further than any other communitarian who was also a libertarian!). In fact, he would have required much more of citizens than is required in America today. He argued that citizens have a duty "to perform certain acts of individual beneficence, such as saving a fellow creature's life, or interposing to protect the defenceless against ill-usage, things which whenever it is obviously a man's duty to do, he may rightfully be made responsible to society for not doing." (*GBWW* I: 43, 272; II: 40, 272)

It is on such Millian principles of responsibility that the new American communitarian movement is based. In 1991 communitarianism was formalized as a movement with the publication of "The Responsive Communitarian Platform," a Tocquevillian call for the reinvigoration of families, neighborhoods, and such secondary institutions as professional, social, religious, and ethnic-based voluntary associations. [17] Since such organizations stress responsibilities, duties, sharing, and serving others, communitarians see them as effective counterbalances to the prevailing American ethic of private self-interest. The communitarian platform also calls for rewriting divorce laws to insure child support, for making workplaces more family oriented, for national and local service for youth, and for strict limits on gun ownership. To these individuals, the essential source of community comes close to what Christians mean by charity, humanistic psychologists mean by empathy, the French revolutionaries meant by *fraternité,* and the Japanese mean by *amae.* But this was best described by Aristotle: "when men are friends they have no need of justice." (*GBWW* I: 9, 406; II: 8, 406)

Locke had similarly characterized natural society as "men living together according to reason without a common superior on earth, with authority to judge between them." (*GBWW* I: 3, 225; II: 2, 179) But, of course, humankind then altered nature and, thus, lost that common bond of fraternity. The solution was clear to Rousseau. He advocated a return to the state of nature, calling on human beings to divest themselves of the artifices of civilization, "renouncing its advances in order to renounce its vices." (*GBWW* I: 3, 226; II: 2, 180) Marx partially agreed. While he thought it impossible to go back to a lost historical era, he nonetheless felt it necessary to move through industrialism to the next, and higher, stage of civilization where humans would gain a new—and advanced—sense of community. Of course, much of what Marx had to say on this subject was as naive and impractical as Rousseau's views.

Marx was, nonetheless, the first to understand that economic progress has vast social implications. Where corporatists saw the industrial revolution as merely a shift in the mechanical modes of production, Marx called attention to such consequent changes as the destruction of entire social classes, the altering of relations among nations, and even demographic transformations. (If he failed to call attention directly to the problems of environmental degradation, he nonetheless noted the effects of factory life on the mortality and morbidity of urban workers.) In short, Rousseau, Locke, and Marx emphasized that human actions altered nature, and not necessarily for the better.

Environmentalism

All the great philosophers saw humankind as *a part* of nature—yet, somehow, *apart* from it as well by virtue of the intellectual superiority of the race. It was Darwin who placed humans squarely *in* nature—calling attention to our anatomic, physiological, and behavioral commonalities with other animals. This new perspective would lead, in subsequent generations, to a refocusing of communitarianism. For if we are a part of nature, does this not mean that we despoil ourselves when we despoil nature? Significantly, this connection was first made not by Westerners but by Asians and Native Americans.

Nearly a hundred years after Darwin, Westerners finally made the ecological connection between human behavior and the natural environment. In 1962 Rachel Carson brought the issue of environmental responsibility to light in her book *Silent Spring:*

"In 1962 Rachel Carson brought the issue of environmental responsibility to light in her book *Silent Spring.*"

> The history of life on earth has been a history of interaction between living things and their surroundings. To a large extent, the physical form and the habits of the earth's vegetation and its animal life have been molded by the environment. Considering the whole span of earthly time, the opposite effect, in which life actually modifies its surroundings, has been relatively slight. Only within the moment of time represented by the present century has one species—man—acquired significant power to alter the nature of his world. [18]

Here the two intellectual threads—humans apart from nature and humans a part of nature—combine in the notion of trusteeship, or social responsibility. Here, also, the issues of human community and community with nature are combined in the concept of the quality of life, and economic and industrial practices are shown to affect both. Here, too, we see the illogic of Aristotle's limited view of community; environmental problems know no boundaries of social class or national origin. They are problems we *all* have in common. We are united, finally, say the environmentalists, on "spaceship earth." Yet, again, we find the seeds of this "new idea" in the writings of the ancients. Building on Aristotle's continuum of family→village→state, Marcus Aurelius took the next logical step in the progression→globe. He wrote (*c.* A.D. 150):

> If our intellectual part is common, the reason also, in respect of which we are rational beings, is common: if this is so, common also is the reason which commands us what to do, and what not to do; if this is so, there is a common law also; if this is so, we are fellow-citizens; if this is so, we are members of some political community; if this is so, the world is in a manner a state. (*GBWW* I: 12, 264; II: 11, 249)

To Aristotle, the family is a "domestic community" and a state is a "political community." Both are communities in that they are composed of individuals associated for a common purpose. Logically, then, a "global community" must have a common purpose. To the environmentalist/humanist, that purpose is the protection of the biosphere, the insuring of its safety so that all who will be born in the future can lead Aristotle's good life. And since the protection of the environment requires cooperation among nations—indeed, truly *united nations*—the modern communitarian echoes Epictetus who, some fifty years before Aurelius, had written that, ". . . what else remains for men to do than what Socrates did? Never in reply to the question, to what country you belong, say that you are an Athenian or a Corinthian, but that you are a citizen of the world." (*GBWW* I: 12, 114; II: 11, 108)

Communitarians thus part company with libertarians, egalitarians, and corporatists on yet another significant issue; their philosophy does not assume the sovereignty of the nation state. Like Aristotle, communitarians start with family obligations, but they move quickly to duties owed neighbors and, most singularly, to duties owed strangers. These strangers include not only people from other communities and from other races and religions but people beyond the borders of their own nations. With considerable effort, traditional libertarianism, egalitarianism, and corporatism can be interpreted to encompass such a broad perspective, but communitarianism nonetheless is different from the other philosophies in that it is predicated on the assumption of globalism.

Perhaps the most eloquent spokesman for this, the broadest view of communitarianism, is the president of the Czech Republic, Vaclav Havel. On July 4, 1994, he received the Philadelphia Liberty Medal at Independence Hall. There, in a widely quoted address, he called for the identification of transcendent values to unite a world rent by ethnic discord and ideological diversity:

> The central political task of the final years of this century . . . is the creation of a new model of coexistence among the various cultures, peoples, races, and religious spheres within a single interconnected civilization. Many believe that this can be accomplished through technical means—the invention of new organizational, political and diplomatic instruments.
>
> Yes, it is clearly necessary to invent organizational structures appropriate to the multicultural age. But such efforts are doomed to failure if they do not grow out of something deeper, out of generally held values.
>
> In searching for the most natural source for the creation of a new world order, we usually look to an area that is the traditional foundation of modern justice and a great achievement of the modern age: to a set of values that were first declared in this building. I am referring to respect for the unique human being and his or her liberties and inalienable rights . . .

At this point in his talk, Havel took a tack that would have astounded Jefferson and other children of the Enlightenment. Havel said that the fundamental ideas of modern democracy were not enough: "We must go farther and deeper. Today, we are in a different place and facing a different situation, one to which classically modern solutions do not give a satisfactory response." He explained that the search for self-transcendence in the postmodern world requires the renewal of "lost integrity," the sense that "we are mysteriously connected to the universe, we are mirrored in it, just as the entire evolution of the universe is mirrored in us." Havel then referred to the "Gaia hypothesis," that "the dense network of mutual interactions between the organic and inorganic portions of the Earth's surface form a single system, a kind of mega-organism":

> According to the Gaia hypothesis, we are parts of a greater whole. Our destiny is not dependent merely on what we do for ourselves but also on what we do for Gaia as a whole. If we endanger her, she will dispense with us in the interests of a higher value—life itself.

In proper communitarian fashion, Havel concluded:

> Only someone who submits to the authority of the universal order and of creation, who values the right to be a part of it and a participant in it, can genuinely value himself and his neighbors and thus honor their rights as well. [19]

In light of these many differences, it might be concluded that the pursuit of community is not comparable with the pursuit of liberty, equality, and efficiency. Yet, that would be to ignore the many overlaps and complementarities between community and the three other values. For instance, communitarians line up easily with egalitarians on matters of natural rights and social equality. They line up readily with libertarians on matters of civil liberties, traditional family values, entrepreneurialism, decentralized decision-making, and voluntary associations. On many other important matters, the differences between community and the adjoining values to the north and south of it are matters more of degree than of kind. Whereas libertarians stress competition, communitarians stress

"Perhaps the most eloquent spokesman for . . . communitarianism, is the president of the Czech Republic, Vaclav Havel."

cooperation, and whereas egalitarians stress rights, communitarians stress responsibilities. These are not either/or distinctions but, more precisely, differences of emphasis that blur at the edges.

Remarkably, there is also a blurring among the desires of those who pursue efficiency and those who pursue community. Although these values are "opposed" on our compass card, there are nonetheless places where they come together (much like the relationship of liberty and equality). A close re-reading of *The Republic* illustrates the point. Our earlier corporatist interpretation of Plato's ideal state can be complemented with a communitarian interpretation which is almost as convincing. Plato's desire for efficiency and effectiveness is matched, to nearly an equal degree, by his desire for social coordination and harmony. Indeed, he attempts to bring these two poles together by defining the good society as an efficient *and* harmonious whole. While Plato is not completely successful in this attempt to fuse efficiency and community—and no Westerner has ever been successful in doing so—the reconciliation of these "opposites" is comparatively effortless in Asian cultures. In examining the rise of the successful business culture in East Asia after World War II, Tu Wei-Ming notes that the Confucian perspective incorporates a marriage of efficiency and community. [20] One might say that contemporary Japan almost does the trick—being slightly out-of-balance on the efficiency side (and failing miserably, of course, when it comes to accepting duties to those outside its borders).

In contrast, American history has been played out largely on the liberty/equality axis. The tensions between these two values have been so profound that it is often difficult for Americans to accept that our history is rather unique in this regard. Indeed, until the Enlightenment in the West—and for the rest of the world before and after that time—social, political, and economic history has been enacted mainly along the community/efficiency axis. The prime concern of all preliterate societies was to achieve sufficient social harmony to mount an effective collective front in "the battle against nature." Preliterate peoples were all members of "communities," the function of which was to provide the cohesion required for the survival of the group. The Western emphasis on the individual caused this focus to be lost, while in the process "winning the war against nature" by way of the creation of modern science and technology. In contrast, Asians gradually accepted modern science without losing as much of traditional community values as did the West.

Again, this is a matter of degree and emphasis. The tension between efficiency and community never fully disappeared in the West—witness the struggle between Hamilton and Jefferson. Nonetheless, the emphasis in the West for the past two hundred years has been on the tension between liberty and equality—with both capitalists and communists agreed on the value of efficiency. Now, with a concatenation of developments—the worldwide population explosion, periodic resource crises, the collapse of communism, to cite just three—concerns along the community/efficiency axis have surfaced with a force that is surprising to Westerners who had been preoccupied for two centuries with an entirely different agenda.

Conclusions

The preceding philosophical discussion of efficiency and community is, in the end, a practical one, especially for Britons and Americans. For we, the chief inheritors of Enlightenment values, are preoccupied with the following question; Why is it that for all our technological and economic progress, we are getting no closer to creating the good society? The answer seems clear. We shall never do so as long as we have a blinkered, limited view of what the characteristics of such a society would be. In particular, no society can be called good or just if it fails to treat all legitimate values as important. Thus, if we ignore community and efficiency, society will be no more just than if we were to overlook the values of liberty or equality.

Since liberty, equality, efficiency, and community are all "good things," a just society would tend toward creating policies that provide as much of all four values as possible. Evidence of the citizenry's near-boundless desire for all of these values is illustrated by the fact that there are few ideologues who would be satisfied with absolute equality at the cost of all other objectives, or who would want 100 percent efficiency at the expense of everything else. Most modern men and women want as much liberty, equality, efficiency, and community as they can reasonably get.

Hence, the good society aims at the creation of "moral symmetry" among these competing values. To use a phrase of George Will's, the goal is "an equilibrium based on justice." This equilibrium would be unattainable if a nation were to pursue one or the other of the various extreme courses advocated by libertarians, egalitarians, corporatists, and communitarians. For example, the adoption of laissez-faire would be anathema to those who sought greater social equality and security, protection for consumers, desired clean air and water, and wished to build the national infrastructure needed for global competitiveness. Similarly, undiluted egalitarian programs would create unacceptable consequences in the eyes of libertarians, corporatists, and communitarians (in terms of decreased incentives for performance, increased bureaucracy, and an overall decline in both the standard of living and quality of life). Extreme corporatist solutions, too, would fail to generate support at the other three "poles" because the thing many people fear more than the power of big government (or big business, or big labor) is the possibility of these three forces combining their power in unholy consort. And many communitarian policies designed to enhance the quality of life would be rejected by their opponents on the grounds that they are "elitist"—that is, serve only the interests of a minority that is wealthy enough to be unconcerned with improving its own material standard of living (or insensitive to the desires of others for material progress). Thus, policies put forward by members of each extreme ideological camp will fail because they are primarily either/or propositions that exclude, or at least subordinate, the interests of all other factions. In essence, extreme solutions are seen as unjust because they do violence to the legitimate values of the majority.

While narrowly focused ideological movements start out as essentially moral in intent, they end up being immoral in practice when imposed on those with differing views, needs, and beliefs. Isaiah Berlin writes that libertarianism and egalitarianism are noble in conception, but immoral in practice: "Both liberty and equality are among the primary goals pursued by human beings through many centuries; but total liberty for wolves is death to the lambs." [21] And total equality is poison for wolves. He concludes that democratic pluralism protects society's lambs and wolves from the tyrannical realization of either one's most noble dreams. This is far better than the totalitarian alternative, yet Berlin admits that there is nonetheless something intrinsically dissatisfying about pluralism; while giving both lambs and wolves due process, neither party will have its way. In effect, democracy will produce neither perfect liberty nor perfect equality; instead, it will provide dissatisfying amounts of both. This is "bad," of course, because both liberty and equality are "good." Berlin thus concludes that the "collisions of values" inherent in democracy are inevitable and tragic: "We are doomed to choose, and every choice may entail an irreparable loss." [22]

This tradition of "the tragic trade-off" is compelling. Indeed, it forms the basis not only for modern political philosophy, but for the discipline of economics, as well. But is such a tragic compromise absolutely necessary? In his book *Haves Without Have-Nots,* Mortimer Adler offers an answer to that question:

> When both liberty and equality are limited by the restraints of justice, they are not incompatible. The conflict is between libertarianism, which asks for unlimited liberty, and egalitarianism, which asks for complete equality and no inequality. It is never between limited liberty and equality combined with inequality. [23]

From this, we can deduce a moral or ethical standard for justice in society. Extreme policies that obviate the possibility of achieving other legitimate objectives are immoral. Thus, the pursuit of liberty is always moral, while the pursuit of radical libertarianism is immoral if that pursuit denies to others the realization of the values of equality, efficiency, and community. Adler himself suggests the following principle of justice:

> (a) No one should have more liberty than justice allows, which is to say, no more than individuals can use without injuring anyone else or the general welfare of society; and (b) No society should establish more equality than justice requires . . . all haves (that is, no have-nots, no persons *deprived* of a decent livelihood), but among the haves, some *having more* and some *having less* according to the degree to which they contribute to the economic welfare of society as a whole. [24]

What Adler is saying in philosophical terms is that liberty and equality are not ends in themselves but rather means to a higher end—the good society. Hence, when liberty and equality are mistakenly pursued as ends, they lead not to the good society but to injustice. Similarly, we could add here, a nation needs as much community and efficiency as are necessary to achieve the good society, and that means that these two goods can not be enjoyed in limitless amounts. The central political question then, is how much community or efficiency is enough?

Significantly, it was Aristotle who first asked, How much wealth does an *individual* need? His answer was, as much as one needs to live the good life. How much is that? The specifics, he tells us, will emerge from informed deliberations among the best and brightest—the most virtuous—politicians and philosophers in his oligarchic utopia. What he does not tell us is how much of any value *we need collectively* to create the good society.

The answer to that question he did not—and could not—offer because he was blind to the potential of a well-functioning democracy. It is through the never-ending process of democratic deliberations that we collectively decide the proper limits to place on the individual rights and collective goods of society. There is thus no single, eternal answer to the question. What is clear is that democracy is the only legitimate process by which to make the complex decisions entailed in determining how much the haves and have-nots need, and how much efficiency the society needs at the expense of the environment.

Of course, no democracy has realized the ideal of the good society. In practice, each decision democratically made—each law passed, and each regulation formulated—causes one value to be favored over the others but, importantly, *not the same value every time.* Consequently, the various constituencies of a democracy find themselves alternatively pleased and displeased by the policies that emanate from the system. But even when displeased, they should never grow so irrevocably disenchanted as to challenge its legitimacy. If the decision-making process is open and fair, democracy is a condition of continuing tension and periodic dissatisfaction. It is also the only condition that modern men and women accept as just.

Indeed, here is where Lee goes terribly wrong. It is not that his valuing of efficiency is objectively better or worse than a Westerner's valuing of liberty, but his benevolent despotism is, in the final analysis, unjust because it denies the legitimacy of those whose values differ from his own. Unlike the utopian ideological world of Lee—or the equally utopian worlds of ideologically extreme libertarians, egalitarians, and communitarians—there is no final "solution" to the problem of democracy, and that is why it is so dissatisfying a form of government to those who think in narrow and finite terms. Importantly, it is not a Western concept to place pluralism and respect for the values of others at the heart of the philosophical definition of justice. Lee is discovering this himself in Singapore as demands for liberty grow there among a population who have long-since satisfied their basic economic needs. In the real—and moral—world of democracy, there is no optimal mix of programs, no final resting place on the values quadrant that will produce a utopia permanently acceptable to the entire citizenry. As long as people have different values, and as long as conditions of society are susceptible to change, the realization of the good society through democracy will remain a dynamic process. The resources of a nation must be constantly managed; expanded then gathered, gathered then distributed, with each person or group sometimes gaining, sometimes losing, but always treated fairly and with respect and above all, always heard. When the process is working in this way, even those who have the least success in realizing their objectives will conclude that the system itself is just.

We can easily make the same mistake as Lee. Currently, there is danger in America and Britain where those in power feel free to ignore citizens who value efficiency and community and to dismiss as ancient history those who continue to believe in equality. In taking such a blinkered and unjust view, we run the risk of alienating significant parts of the body politic. In so doing we would cause democracy itself to be seen as illegitimate, and in that process destroy the only known vehicle for achieving the good society.

For a similar treatment of the values of liberty and equality, see my book, *The Executive Compass,* (Oxford University Press: 1993).

1. William Graham Sumner, "The Challenge of Facts," in *The Challenge of Facts and Other Essays,* ed. Albert Galloway Keller (New Haven: Yale University Press, 1914), p. 25.

2. Isaiah Berlin, *The Crooked Timber of Humanity* (London: Fontana, 1991).

3. Francis Fukuyama, *The End of History and the Last Man* (Harmondsworth: Penguin, 1992).

4. John Kenneth Galbraith, *The New Industrial State,* chap. X (Boston: Houghton Mifflin, 1985).

5. "An Agreement of the People (Debate Between Cromwellians and the Levellers)," in *Puritanism and Liberty,* ed. A. S. P. Woodhouse (London: J. M. Dent and Sons, Ltd., 1938).

6. Fukuyama citation in "Is Singapore a Model for the West?," by Jay Branegan, *Time* (Jan. 18, 1993), p. 36.

7. Alexander Hamilton, *Report of the Secretary of the Treasury of the United States, on the Subject of Manufactures,* presented to the House of Representatives, Dec. 5, 1791 (London: Printed for J. Debrett, 1793), pp. 21–23.

8. Alfred P. Sloan, *My Years With General Motors,* ed. John McDonald with Catherine Stevens (Garden City, N.Y.: Doubleday, 1963).

9. James Fallows, "How the World Works," *The Atlantic Monthly* (December 1993).

10. Ibid., p. 87.

11. Ibid.

12. William Pfaff, *The International Herald Tribune* (Oct. 19, 1994), p. 9.

13. Thomas Jefferson, Letter to Benjamin Austin, Jan. 9, 1816, in *Writings of Thomas Jefferson,* ed. H. A. Washington, Vol. VI (New York: H. W. Derby, 1861).

14. Neil Postman, *Technology: The Surrender of Culture* (New York: Knopf, 1992), pp. xiii and 51.

15. E. F. Schumacher, *Small is Beautiful: Economics as if People Mattered* (New York: Harper & Row, 1973).

16. Robert Heilbroner, *The Worldly Philosophers* (New York: Simon and Schuster, 1953).

17. Amita Etzioni, *The Spirit of Community* (New York: Crown Publishers, 1993).

18. Rachel Carson, *Silent Spring* (New York: Fawcett Crest, 1962), p. 5.

19. Adapted from an address at Independence Hall on July 4, 1994, when awarded the Philadelphia Liberty Medal. Reprinted in *International Herald Tribune* (July 11, 1994), p. 6.

20. Wei-Ming Tu, "A Confucian Perspective on the Rise of Industrial East Asia," in *The American Academy of Arts and Sciences Bulletin* (October 1988).

21. Berlin, op. cit. p. 12.

22. Ibid., p. 13.

23. Mortimer J. Adler, *Haves Without Have-Nots* (New York: Macmillan, 1991), p. 17.

24. Ibid., pp. 17–21.

James O'Toole was a member of the faculty of the Graduate School of Business at the University of Southern California for over twenty years. He has also served on the Board of Editors of the *Encyclopædia Britannica.* Currently, Mr. O'Toole is Vice President of the Aspen Institute where he heads all seminar programs, including the renowned Executive Seminar.

Mr. O'Toole is the author of twelve books and over seventy articles. His research and writings have been in the areas of business and society, corporate culture, and leadership. Among his publications, *Vanguard Management* (1985) was highly praised in the business industry. His latest book, *Leading Change,* is forthcoming.

Human Nature, Gender, and Ethnicity

(Part Two)

Deal W. Hudson

Empirical research on gender differences

The human body cannot in the long run experience itself only as the
receiver of sense stimuli; it always turns to becoming the portrayer,
the actor of itself in all the relationships it enters. Thus, its natural
drive always combines with a specific system of ideas and feelings, and
through the centuries this idealizing is like a fountain that rises and
falls. Today it is close to its deepest point. . . .

(Robert Musil, *Woman Yesterday and Tomorrow*) [1]

In Part One (*GIT* 1994, 127–67) we investigated the postmodern and feminist
critique of the classical notion of human nature. It was seen how modern
scholars are revising their account of the history of philosophy in accord
with their concerns for the bias of gender, class, and ethnicity. Some of
these revisionists are more radical than others. Some simply carry forward
the liberal concern of equality before the law while others seek to remove
the injustice they see inscribed on the very heart of Western society and
jurisprudence itself.

If there is a common denominator to these concerns, it is a critique of
human reason and rationality itself. The very notion of reasonableness as a
moral and political justification has fallen into disrepute: Reason, it is said,
is always *interested,* not in finding the truth of things but in protecting the
power and well-being of the one who reasons.

As has been said before, one does not have to look very far to see the
shadow of Nietzsche falling over these proceedings. But it is a fact worth repeating so that we may recognize the profound change occurring in the midst
of the present culture. Given the pervasive influence of the ideas described in
this report, it is clear that the present generation is disposed toward a kind of
uncritical skepticism in regard to knowing human nature and all that flows
from it. One may venture that if past generations dogmatically asserted more
than they knew, the present one asserts less. Those who may be tempted to
call this humility should consider that for human beings to deny knowledge
of the principles directing their actions entails a lack of self-knowledge. True
humility, it can be argued, is founded upon the opposite.

At the core of both multiculturalism and ethnocentrism is the basic mistrust of any universal claims about human nature and justice. Such claims
have to be understood and measured in terms of the disparate cultural
traditions producing them. Taken as a reminder that all knowledge and
values are historically conditioned, some forms of multiculturalism are fairly
traditional. But as will be seen after a brief overview of the scientific findings
regarding gender differences, the trajectory of multiculturalist thinking appears to be moving in a postmodern direction.

As Mortimer J. Adler has shown, the immaterial intellect is the decisive
mark of a human being—the distinctively human acts, such as language, are
made possible by the abstraction and use of concepts. If empirical research
were to uncover the fact that some group of people, distinguishable by gender
or race, did not possess conceptual thinking, then a difference in essence
could be posited. As will be seen, the present state of scientific research does

corroborate some of the most commonly held opinions about the differences between men and women. But, once again, these are differences of second nature; they do not indicate any difference at all in the basic potentialities of human intelligence.

The relevant issue of gender studies is the extent to which gender differences are caused by biological factors or nurtural factors. Some feminists would welcome the news that distinction in gender is entirely nurtural; others, who celebrate the feminine, would be quite comfortable finding that biological causes are determinative.

The findings do not really give comfort to one side of the feminist cause or the other. Empirical studies have addressed sexual divergence in intelligence, anatomy, perception, and social aptitude. IQ tests do not reveal any difference in basic intelligence between men and women. Testing does reveal, however, that men and women are disposed toward different kinds of intelligent acts: men tend to show higher degrees of visual-spatial intelligence, while women, at least at a young age, score higher on verbal tests. Since both skills require conceptual knowledge, a difference in first nature is not at issue, but some second nature differences may in fact be possible to specify. Some studies have shown that females are more oriented toward hearing, while men are more sensitive to the visual, but these differences are minimal and can be reduced through education.

A recent survey of the empirical research concludes that cross-cultural studies establish an "irreducible core of anatomical differences" between males and females. [2] Males everywhere are born larger, with greater muscle tissue and a larger bone structure. The difference becomes pronounced at puberty when males become stronger and faster and develop larger hearts and lungs. However, male babies are more physically vulnerable to death than females, perhaps, as it has been argued, because the male fetus evokes an antibody in the female uterus. [3]

The influence of hormones is the most common biological cause given to explain gender differences. Hormones, it appears, both sensitize the fetus and actuate behavior as we age. Because of the influence of sex hormones on behavior, men tend to be more aggressive and violent than women. As they grow older, girls will seek approval and boys will compete for success. But since most of the data have been derived from animal research, it is thought premature to come to any fixed conclusion—"The hormone system is an open system," Carol N. Jacklin says. [4] Although hormonal development does push the male child in one direction and the female in another, nurture can bring genders back toward one another. Child-rearing patterns as well as early educational practices are crucial in this regard.

The long view of this research suggests that gender differences are much less pronounced than were originally thought. Studies published by Eleanor E. Maccoby and Carol N. Jacklin in 1974 undercut much of the previous folklore about the differences between the sexes. [5] At that time it was argued that very few characteristics differed consistently on a gender basis. Maccoby revised her findings later, saying that her earlier work had been colored by the feminist thinking of the time. [6]

Her revised conclusions, however, are not dramatically different from those earlier ones. Verbal differences are less than thought, but mathematical and spatial abilities remain marked. Men are more often prone to aggressive action, but can also be more altruistic. However, when it comes to patterns of same-sex group interactions, boys act more egoistically, while girls are more facilitative. Among adults, this disposition leads men to express agreement much less frequently than women do. When the sexes interact, women are not treated with the reciprocity they receive from other women, making it easier for men to adapt to women than vice versa. As Maccoby says, this might explain why men report falling in love faster and report feeling more in love earlier than women do.

In mixed-sex groups, men do more of the initiating and interrupting than women; they speak more loudly, are less influenced by others, and oblige women to listen to them. Just as when they were children, men tend to direct the activities of any group they participate in. Women, in mixed groups, may attempt to assert themselves by exaggerated forms of female behavior such as smiling, agreeing, and signs of attentiveness. Moreover, it has been shown that patterns of social influence are strongly influenced by individual beauty, regardless of gender.

In relations between parents and children, women exercise the social habits learned as children and, thus, are more closely attuned to the needs of young children. Fathers generally become more involved after the age of two. Women also show more equanimity in the treatment of male and female children alike, whereas men differentiate by gender, especially as boys grow older and fathers become friendly rivals. As a result, some psychologists suggest that men and boys should be encouraged to nurture young children in order to dilute their aggressive disposition—as the saying goes, "you are the company you keep."

But, as Jacklin points out, using these findings to influence socialization, especially to reduce sexism, can backfire. She discusses the media coverage of studies in the early eighties showing that girls scored consistently lower than boys in math tests. The findings turned out to be exaggerated, but the media coverage only worsened the situation, since a mother's belief in the ability of her child to perform well affects the outcome more than any other factor. [7]

Some researchers have begun to explain these gender differences in terms of "gender scheme" theories, contending that before the age of three, children learn to categorize people, objects, activities, and quantities by gender. [8] Once this categorization is complete, the child begins to sort his or her experiences according to this pattern. These associations become more complex and subtle as children grow older, affecting how they speak, play, choose friends, express tastes, etc. The innovation of this theory is that children are said to develop gender categories well before the age of five or six, when they understand that sexual differentiation is permanent. It may be that the kind of binarism so much despised by feminists is a natural part of human development that each of us then learns to apply with self-conscious flexibility.

The underlying issue remains whether these and other seeming cross-cultural differences are still cultural in origin. What appears natural to male intelligence and female intelligence may, it has been suggested, in fact be a genetic disposition created by centuries of male spear-carrying and female child-rearing. [9] Inbred forms of behavior may have affected female brain lateralization in which verbal ability, belonging to the left brain, resulted in the detriment of the visual-spatial ability of the right brain.

In spite of what can be established about these differences, the similarities between the behavior of men and women far outweigh the differences. In fact, the point made earlier about the difference between a shared potential and its actualization can be applied to the scientific findings. John Nicolson, for example, says that both male and female have the "raw material" for growing breasts: "What happens is that both sexes receive sets of instructions dealing with breast development, but in only one sex are the instructions acted upon. The same applies for all the other physical characteristics which obviously distinguish men from women: genitals, shape, muscle growth, voice-box development, body hair, and so on." [10] The study of embryology reinforces this viewpoint: the basic pattern of fetal development after conception is identical for male and female until the sixth week when the sex glands, ovaries or testes, appear. The slow process of sexual differentiation occurs under the influence of the respective hormonal secretions.

What do these findings say about the sex-gender distinction assumed in most feminist theory? What can be said about the relation of biological factors in the development of values, attitudes, and behavior? Undoubtedly there are discernible global patterns in male and female development. At least some of the differences in development can be traced to causal factors that are biological, not social. Nothing about the evidence, of course, suggests a difference in first nature, which would posit that women, or men, lack conceptual reasoning altogether. The difference between spatial-mathematical and verbal reasoning is irrelevant to this issue, since both require a sophisticated use of concepts.

But what about differences in second nature? One of the traditional ways of viewing gender difference is complementarity. Just as it requires a male and a female to propagate the species, so it requires both genders to constitute a complete human community and society—male aggressiveness complements female compliance, and so forth. Seen in this way, second nature differences are not so much constructions as they are biologically ingrained dispositions that ensure a wholeness and balance in the life of the species.

Few suggestions raise feminist ire more quickly, since a complementarity that places men in the public sphere and woman in the private is contrary to their stated political purposes. It is not surprising, then, that such uses of biology, called sociobiology, have been a main target of feminist criticism. Nothing could be more counter to the political purpose of feminist theory than the notion that gender differences are ultimately determined by biological evolution.

Controversy arises when normative conclusions about social and moral practices are drawn from a universal human nature. The entire domain of morality, properly speaking, exists only because human beings are capable of voluntary action and freely pursue their happiness. And it is clear that the moral, if not the social, implications of our animal nature cannot be denied. Food, clothing, shelter, health care—all are basic needs of the human body. In one way or another, our access to them is protected by law and custom. No one argues that a person requires an ordinate, unobstructed relation to these basic goods of life. There is no difference between men and women on these grounds, but the evidence suggests that there are some intractable and cross-cultural differences at the level of social attitudes and practice.

Use of this empirical evidence depends a great deal on how much confidence one puts in technology. Feminists only have to recount the social changes encouraged by new methods of contraception to make this point. Medical technology is slowly neutralizing the determinism of a woman's biological makeup. Women can enter public life with less concern for the onslaught of maternal responsibility. They can decide where, when, and if children will be born. With the techniques of in vitro fertilization women, have less and less to fear from their "biological clock." As families become dependent on women's salaries, men have been taking on the role of nurturer to the children. Whether male biology will ever be altered enough to carry a child, to give birth, or to suckle remains to be seen. Men can become women, and vice versa, through surgery and hormone injections, but procreative functions have yet to be transplanted.

No doubt there are more than a few radical feminists who would like to see this state of affairs actually come about. The technology already exists, however, that can provide men, if they wish, the "virtual reality" of the birth experience. Is it outlandish to think that virtual reality might be the way future schools and businesses "sensitize" male students and employees to what being a woman is like? The suggestion is not as radical as might be thought. The feminist Donna Haraway is already using the fictional "cyborg"—part human, part machine—as the standard for understanding the future of gender relations: "The cyborg is our ontology; it gives us our politics." [11] Her point in insisting upon the cyborg is that the cyborg represents human existence without any reference to the natural, the whole, or the organic. Technology, therefore, can and should be placed at the service of political end, of empowerment.

Virtual reality experiences, in fact, may prove a good testing ground for determining how much the hormonally directed differences actually determine gender. How well male subjects adapt to and take pleasure in "exclusively" female experiences can provide data for scientists to study the flexibility in attitudinal dispositions. Such a study would be analogous to the way in which films are commonly sorted into women's and men's movies.

Even if we find out that gender differences, without technological intervention, are irradicable, what social implications can be drawn? Are women who chose never to become mothers denying the natural desire of their sex? Are women who become aggressive, success-driven entrepreneurs out of sync with their second natures? Have men who like to raise children become feminized, perhaps through lack of hormonal development? Is there a natural law of sorts at work in sexual difference which implies, in effect, that women and men should take care in ignoring these realities? These questions take us back into the heart of the relationship between human nature and politics, an issue to which we will return.

Ethnocentrism and multiculturalism

> In America the majority raises formidable barriers around the liberty of opinion; within these barriers, an author may write what he pleases, but woe to him if he goes beyond them. Not that he is in danger of an *auto da fé*, but he is exposed to continued obloquy and persecution.
> (Alexis de Tocqueville, *Democracy in America*) [12]

In the 1970s Sir Kenneth Clark hosted a television series entitled *Civilisation*, which became so popular that it significantly broadened the audience for public television. Looking back at that series now, from a distance of over twenty years, it is apparent that *Civilisation* could not be made today. Both its assurance in the superiority of Western culture and its indifference to gender and ethnicity would be found offensive. For example, in contrasting the outstanding aesthetic qualities of an African mask with the head of the Apollo of Belvedere, Clark comments:

> I don't think there is any doubt that the Apollo embodies a higher state of civilisation than the mask. They both represent spirits, messengers from another world—that is to say, from a world of our own imagining. To the Negro imagination it is a world of fear and darkness, ready to inflict horrible punishment for the smallest infringement of a taboo. To the Hellenistic imagination, it is a world of light and confidence, in which the gods are like ourselves, only more beautiful, and descend to earth in order to teach men reason and the laws of harmony. [13]

The value judgments that once were taken for granted now make some people cringe. The consensus among the educated on the highs and lows of civilization has been weakened. Men like Clark, or Walter Pater and Matthew Arnold before him, no longer arbitrate the standards of taste according the measure of the Italian Renaissance. Advocates of ethnicity and multiculturalism have shaken our belief in the superior "light and harmony" of Western civilization.

The present interest in ethnicity also directly challenges the long-revered ideal of America as "the melting pot." The dream of the last century was precisely that—to leave the old world behind, a world offering little hope for the future, and to start again. It is well known, for example, that Irish immigrants went to great lengths in adopting the social habits of their new country. Becoming an American outweighed any nostalgia for their Irish heritage. This desire for assimilation was celebrated for decades by filmmakers, themselves the children of immigrants, such as Frank Capra in his classic *It's a Wonderful Life*.

No doubt there are still many immigrants and their descendants who would rather be called Americans than anything else. But from the standpoint of ethnocentrism this can be seen as a perverse desire for domination, a cultural masochism that results in an individual loss of meaning. At the core of ethnocentrism is the conviction that one's pride in cultural identity is constitutive of a person's self-esteem and happiness. Thus, no one should have a particular cultural identity imposed upon them. In fact, the 1974 Ethnic Heritage Program Act guarantees the right of every citizen to choose his or her own ethnic identity.

At first glance one would think that individuals descending from multiple generations born in the United States are ethnically "American," regardless of their race. But increasing numbers are looking beyond the country of their birth for sources of identity; blacks are looking to Africa, Hispanics to South America, and, yes, the Irish to Ireland. Clubs, cultural centers, and journals, all devoted to celebrating and remembering particular cultural traditions are multiplying. In addition, ethnic groups are demanding that established cultural institutions reflect their particular origins—all schools, museums, orchestras, theaters, public art, and monuments, should be multicultural.

They maintain that a diversity of images will provide everyone, particularly children, with the opportunity for identification, the building of self-esteem, and the selection of "role models." The cry against "dead white males" is being used to criticize what is found to be far too dominant and predictable in the curriculum of Western education. In many cases, multiculturalists have joined forces with feminists in revealing the prejudices within Western culture against the inclusion of nonmale, nonwhite perspectives.

Like most reform movements, the basic insights behind this protest are not new. They began to emerge, paradoxically, at the same time that Europe began its global expansion. In the midst of the Spanish exploration of the Americas in the 1500s, there were those, such as Bishop Bartolomé de Las Casas, who objected to the treatment of the native inhabitants and questioned the motives of their fellow Europeans. And a few days before he died in 1549, Fray Domingo de Betanzos, a former chaplain to the conquistadores, repented of his belief that the Indians of the New World were "beasts." These indigenous people had been labeled "natural slaves" by the humanists of the Old World. Las Casas argued that such a label contradicts the principle that mankind is one. "Every nation, no matter how barbaric, has the right to defend itself against a more civilized one that wants to conquer it and take away its freedom." [14]

Perhaps nothing better illustrates the importance of the intellectual tradition in political progress than the way in which the justification of natural slavery was unraveled by subsequent generations reflecting on human nature and political liberty. The idea of slavery in the West has a long and complicated history. [15] But a sifting and refining of traditional ideas toward abolitionism is evident in the use Las Casas made of his own Aristotelian-Thomistic education. As it turns out, much of what is at present held dear in natural rights theory originated in the late scholasticism of sixteenth-century Spain.

Aristotle's argument for natural slavery is the standard against which this development takes place. Natural slaves are those who, being deficient in reason, are unable to either govern themselves or participate in the state. The deficiencies of Aristotle's thinking have been corrected by later writers. For example, Aquinas corroborates and reinforces much of Aristotle's position. Yet, in eliminating the condition of slavery from Eden, as a "first intention of nature" (*Summa Theologica,* Supp. Q.52.a.1), Aquinas opens the door to doubts about slavery as a corrupt social practice lacking natural justification. Aquinas shows how one idea of the natural can supplant another. In his case, the naturalness of the prelapsarian state serves as the measure of the nature of postlapsarian existence. Aquinas does not pursue this insight and finds other grounds to affirm the status quo. But his thoughts severely weaken the claims that some human beings are by nature servile and therefore unable to participate in self-governance at any level. The political history of "nature" is by no means entirely conservative; eventually the idea of human equality, unqualified by a criterion of rational agency, emerges with all of its revolutionary energy.

Another step toward equality arrives with Locke's *Two Treatises of Government* (1690). But the kind of contradictions seen in Aquinas are still apparent even at this stage of development toward abolitionism. Locke referred to slavery as "vile and miserable" (*First Treatise of Government,* Ch. 1) but assisted Lord Ashley in drafting the Fundamental Constitutions of Carolina that gave freemen "absolute power and authority over his negro slaves." [16] Locke apparently completed this task without any sign of resistence or repulsion. Locke, in fact, justified slavery as an ongoing condition of war existing outside the boundaries of the social contract (*Second Treatise of Civil Government,* Ch. 4; *GBWW* I: 35, 29–30; II: 33, 29–30).

This inconsistency might surprise those who identify Locke with human rights and individual liberty. But that is precisely the point that both feminists and ethnocentrists want to make. Ideas like "rationality" and "freedom" do not deliver what they offer at face value. The full meaning of an idea can only be grasped by observing how it is put to use *politically* in a given culture or society. To realize that ideas have a political life is to affirm that the actual import of ideas will be refracted through culture. After all, the early American society which so proudly espoused liberty also preserved the right to own chattel slaves.

It took two centuries and an American Civil War to reveal the full meaning of liberty and equality in Western political thought. Feminists consider Western philosophy and culture largely to blame for the subordination of women. Ethnocentrists and multiculturalists often dismiss Western culture for its justification of slavery. It is well known that in recent years the civil rights movement has become more ethnocentric in its thinking and more impatient with the humanism of Martin Luther King, Jr. In his famous "letter from the Birmingham jail," King derives most of his inspiration and argument against racial prejudice and injustice from the western tradition— the Bible, Socrates, Aquinas, T. S. Eliot, Reinhold Niebuhr. His immersion in Western and Christian reflection on the meaning of human life and society appears so complete, so animating to his vision, that his protest seems impossible without it. The fact that Aquinas talked about natural slaves (or that Western philosophy belongs to a culture that countenanced slavery until the nineteenth century) did not keep King from making use of Aquinas' principle that a civil law is unjust if it is not rooted in natural and eternal law (*Summa Theologica* 1–2.Q.96.a.4; *GBWW* I: 20, 233; II: 18, 233) to provide warrant for his civil disobedience.

Just as there are feminists who want to distance themselves from any part of a tradition which once espoused misogyny, there are multiculturalists who consider the Western tradition corrupted by its advocacy of slavery. Ideas, from this perspective, are not innocent of a political structure that supports patriarchy or slavery. Ideas have no meaning, no import, transcending their context. The history of great ideas from a historic viewpoint is an account of how political power structures have employed ideas as instruments of domination. Thus, claims about the common good of humanity, if deconstructed, reveal a dark underbelly of excluded classes. It is time, the multiculturalists say, for those of European descent to give up their pretensions to a "higher civilization" and to admit their own and their descendants' collaboration in barbarism.

As evident in the case of Las Casas, self-criticism has long been part of the arsenal among Western intellectuals themselves. Montaigne employs a vast classical learning in lowering the self-estimation of his learned readership several rungs toward so-called savages and animals. It would not be long before Montaigne's skepticism about the superiority of European civilization, and humanity in general, prepared the way for the Enlightenment, with its habit of "seeing one's own civilization through the eyes of others in order to attack it." [17] If another culture failed to provide a strong enough contrast, failed to underline sufficiently the evils of civilized life, one could construct a Utopia, like that of St. Thomas More, as an instrument of social criticism. And surely it is no historical accident that during this same century the Christian church would be divided in half by the protest of an Augustinian monk against the most powerful institution in Europe.

One of the hallmarks of modern European intellectual life, insofar as one is able to generalize about it, is its capacity for self-criticism and its value of tolerance. Are we aware of any other cultural traditions that so strongly endorse such postures? Could theories of ethnocentrism and multiculturalism be generated in any other known culture?

The skeptical temper of eighteenth-century humanism has remained intact, fueled by the repeated failures of its own optimism. The essays of George Steiner in *Language and Silence* ask what can be left of our confidence in European humanism after the Holocaust. This was an atrocity, he points out, committed in the heart of Europe, in a country arguably more "civilized" than any other. The ovens were designed and administered by highly educated men who read Goethe and listened to Bach in the evening after their day's work. After the Holocaust, how can the West continue to have confidence that classical education imparts moral values? [18]

In spite of this fundamental skepticism, Steiner has resisted the path taken by many contemporary intellectuals who have opted for the postmodern view that behind any claims to a hierarchy of values stands a willing oppressor. In his recent appeal to affirm a meaning transcending the relativism of cultural boundaries and interpretative standpoints, Steiner holds fast to the principles of humanism that make meaningful communication possible in the first place. "I am wagering, both in a Cartesian and a Pascalian vein, on the informing pressure of a real presence in the semantic makers. . . . " [19]

Without a language of "real presence," as Steiner puts it, the argument against cultural rights loses its ontological force and becomes pragmatic. Outrage against injustice, or atrocity at its extreme, can be met with the injunction to "mind your own business." One must question whether cooperation between nations can endure without some philosophical agreements on human nature, with only a practical consensus on a list of human rights. Such an approach to cross-cultural organization has become necessary to excise the deepening skepticism about a universal human nature which has developed since the eighteenth and nineteenth centuries. During this period nationalist movements replaced universal man with the particular man. Human nature, thus, was only credited in its specific cultural context. With the rise of nationalism, nations sought to justify their desire for self-governance by generating notions of their own differences and identity to distinguish themselves as a people [*Volk*] from others of the same nature.

The thought of Johann Gottfried von Herder (1744–1803) is the earliest explicit articulation of this position. Rejecting the notion of a common human teleology, he maintains that every individual and every nation has an original way of expressing their humanity. "Not a man, not a country, not a people, not the past of a people, not a state are like one another. Consequently, the true, the beautiful and the good in them are also not alike." [20] The normative issue from this standpoint is not whether an individual or nation can follow some measure imposed by the ideal of an abstract human nature, but whether they can be true to themselves. [21] Historians should attempt to understand other cultures from the inside, rather than unwittingly apply preconceived and foreign notions of humanity and value on their people, institutions, and artifacts.

There is no direct line of influence running between Herder and the politics of racial purity and eugenics leading to the Holocaust. But it is clear that contextualism implies a morality formulated in terms of benefit for the group declaring itself the "nation" or the "people." The nation, in this way, can justify its rejection of heteronomous interference. The happiness of man *qua* man, man as universal, can make no claim against the insular values of a particular nationality.

Given this assumption, the morally normative view of human nature is set aside. Hitler's Third Reich enacted the worst possibility inherent in Herder's distinction between universal nature and a particular *Volk*. By reducing the frame of moral vision to a particular nation, idolatry was encouraged, the exclusion of undesirables and subhumans continued, and the sources of moral self-corrective protest were shut off. But in spite of this warning, the direction of protest against the West was set.

Popular with the radicals of the late sixties, Frantz Fanon's *The Wretched of the Earth* is credited with portraying how imperialism employs deprecating images of the colonial people in order to subjugate them. The need for revolution, thus understood, becomes more than an overthrowing of sheer military and economic power; it involves eradicating alien ideals of humanity and barbarism that have been imposed by colonial powers. As Jean-Paul Sartre writes in his preface to Fanon, "There is nothing more consistent than a racist humanism, since the European has only been able to become a man through creating slaves and monsters." [22].

Sartre's attitude has become more widespread. The 500th anniversary of the "discovery" of the Americas by Christopher Columbus was celebrated in quite a different spirit from the one that animates Clark's *Civilisation.* Protests against quincentennial celebrations accused Columbus of everything from slavery to genocide, destroying the native culture, ravaging the land, introducing foreign diseases into a medically-pristine environment, and other atrocities. In marked contrast to the traditional view of Columbus, the explorer was portrayed as representative of a lethal civilization imposing itself on an exquisite, indigenous people. [23]

The character of major exhibitions in Washington, D.C., reflected the force of these protests, as did an official statement by the National Council of Churches. Berkeley, Calif., officially changed Columbus Day to "Indigenous Peoples' Day." The student senate at the University of Cincinnati voted to rid the campus of the "Columbus-myth-free Campus." Kirkpatrick Sale published his revisionist biography, *The Conquest of Paradise: Christopher Columbus and the Columbian Legacy.* Chosen as a main selection of the Book-of-the-Month Club, it called for Americans to give up their European ways and reappropriate the values of "the original Americans" or else risk the destruction of the Earth. [24] Sale repeats the feminist critique of patriarchal destructiveness, only the European rather than the male has become the aggressor.

The fact, as Robert Royal has said, that "pessimistic Americans see in Columbus an image of everything wrong with contemporary American life" [25] is symptomatic of their doubts about the Eurocentric nature of educational institutions and their new interest in multicultural curriculums. Although the desire to appreciate the value of indigenous cultures has led some researchers to either ignore or minimize practices that would be universally condemned in the West, such as the ritual sacrifice of human life, the reasons motivating the interest are compelling. Perhaps the idea of human nature, as it has been taught in the Western tradition, disposes its adherents toward the destruction of the natural world, subjection of women and minorities, and militaristic control of "barbarian" nations? Is it not possible, given the suffering inflicted in the name of Western civility, that there are other ideas of humanity as good, or in some ways better?

Edward Said shows in his *Orientalism* that the same kind of binary oppositions that have been used to subordinate women have been used to divide the world between "us" and "them," between the humane "civilized" and the so-called "barbarians," a conceptual construction of the Greeks. [26] "Orientalism" refers to the reality of life in the Near and Far East as constructed by European culture after the Enlightenment. The European version of the

Orient created built-in limitations on what could be said, thought, and written about those cultures. This dominance, Said tries to argue, is symptomatic of European and American power over the Eastern peoples—they submitted, as it were, to being Orientalized. This construct puts the Westerner in a whole series of possible relations with the Orient without ever losing him the relative upper hand. [27]

Why did the West extend its domination? It was due not to any particular European malevolence but to the fact that Europeans were studying nations that were colonies (such as India and Egypt) and this variable of imperialism could never be factored out. Said's point is that no scholar is ever free from the influence of historical circumstance, particularly his or her ethnic identity. Pure knowledge across cultures is impossible—the result will always be politicized in indirect ways. The academy, clinging to the idol of specialization, has yet to recognize the role that political imperialism has played in scholarship, whether in the interpretation of history, literature, philosophy, or science. In a later work, Said writes, "The job facing the cultural intellectual is therefore not to accept the politics of identity as given, but to show how all representations are constructed, for what purpose, by whom, and with what components." [28].

A woodcut from 1493 showing Christopher Columbus arriving at the New World. "Protests against quincentennial celebrations accused Columbus of everything from slavery to genocide, destroying the native culture, ravaging the land, introducing foreign diseases . . . and other atrocities."

The unwillingness of Western intellectuals to inspect critically the assumptions informing their research, it has been said, reveals a pretension about their place in the world. Library shelves are filled with books about the responsibility of intellectuals to society, and these books are filled with phrases such as that used by Edmund Husserl to describe his philosophers as "functionaries of humanity." Paul Feyerabend comments: "I think it shows an astounding ignorance (what does Husserl know of the 'true being of the Nuer'?), a phenomenal conceit (is there any single individual who has sufficient knowledge of all races, cultures, civilizations to be able to speak of 'the true being of humanity'?) and, of course, a sizeable contempt for anybody who lives and thinks along different lines." [29]

Feyerabend reflects the postmodern disregard for "totalizing" perspectives, for attempts at forcing together incommensurate cultural elements in metaphysical syntheses, whether Thomistic or Hegelian. Attempts at speaking for the totality of humanity amount to nothing more than speaking about oneself. Members of the academy, Feyerabend remarks, are doubly handicapped—they are not only cut off from the diversity of world cultures but also the diversity of their own popular cultures, which they often disdain.

Critical response to ethnocentrism has been gathering momentum. Much of the recent work of Charles Taylor is devoted to tracing the origins and implications of this "culture of authenticity" and its investment in the principles of difference, diversity, and multiculturalism. [30] Generally Taylor traces this change to a loss of meaning, a loss of freedom, and an eclipse of ends as reflected in individualism, social fragmentation, and instrumental reason, respectively. Value is increasingly understood entirely in terms of choice itself—there is no external or preexisting measure of worthwhile choice and action.

The problem with this situation, according to Taylor, is that defending the ideal of authenticity itself collapses horizons of significance, i.e., Steiner's real presence. "Even the sense that the significance of my life comes from its being chosen—the case where authenticity is actually grounded on self-determining freedom—depends on the understanding that *independent of my will* there is something noble, courageous, and hence significant in giving shape to my own life." [31] Even authenticity demands some sort of measure external to the self, some measure of meaning that is given.

However, Taylor describes a cultural situation where the only necessary external factor is recognition by others. This is the recognition that any self or community, its values and its artifacts, is equal in worth to any other. The denial of recognition is considered a form of oppression, a danger to self-esteem. Thus, in what seems to be a highly individualistic posture, choice is not enough to validate one's identity; recognition by other selves is required.

Although Taylor thinks there is an important claim being made about the "dialogical" character of identity, he argues that such a recognition cannot be honestly given where there is no shared view of what counts for being human. In the case of the feminist critique, for example, "if men and women are equal, it is not because they are different, but because overriding the difference are some properties, common or complementary, which are of value." [32] The source of the problem is a reductivism, the narrowing of focus to a single concern, namely, recognition. "A favorable judgment on demand is nonsense. . . . No one can really mean it as a genuine act of respect." [33] Here Taylor uncovers the legitimate complaint against "political correctness"—the insistence that everything be considered of equal worth can result in a socially enforced uniformity.

This is doubly ironic given the fact that, as Taylor points out, aesthetic creativity has become the paradigm of the moral life. Individual creativity, arising from the depths of each person's inscrutable subjectivity, not obedience to natural law or the extrinsic principles of human action, is at the core of this generation's investment in authenticity. Another critic of this rage for innovation, Thomas Fleming, comments, "There is nothing wrong with originality, but what is missing from the modern scene are all the powerful restraints, the governors that control the speed of social change, the filters of experience and tradition that sort out the practical from the merely clever." [34] The gist of this argument is that the overthrow of humanistic traditions entails the loss of our knowledge about human nature.

The wholesale rejection of any specific tradition in the name of universalism may in fact represent a temptation to become "barbarians in the strictest sense." [35] The first act of totalitarian dictators is to appropriate all the institutions in which traditional values and mores are passed on to the next generation, the family, the schools, and the church. Most westerners have little to fear from tyrants, but fail to notice the cultural homogenization occurring through the alliance of technology and the media.

The growing reliance on the electronic media can only deepen the impression that moral and political values are, at core, aesthetic matter, reducible to preferences in taste. Taylor points out that arguments about "all cultures being equal" usually begin with comparisons of cultural artifacts. If other values have become aestheticized, then genuine differences can be submerged under a thick glaze of cultural toleration: "It [cultural universalism] contradicts itself if its generosity extends to ignoring differences between universalism and exclusivity, tolerance and intolerance, itself and the barbarity; and it contradicts itself if, in order to avoid the temptations of barbarity, it concedes *to others* their right to be barbarians." [36]

As Taylor has argued, some have taken the aesthetic option and treat all differences in values and practices as matters of personal preference. Tolerance, however, does not require this kind of hazardous consistency because it is based upon the capacity of self-criticism built into the European mentality that gave it birth. Thus, being tolerant still allows a person from a certain tradition to assert its superiority in certain instances, although never finally and without some iota of doubt.

Tradition contains those thoughts about humanity and its institutions that have stood the test of time and experience. Academic theorists in the humanities have got in the habit of caring only how their theory relates to other theories, considering it progress if they correct one abstract theory by the application of another. Asking whether their theories correspond to what is "out there," in the reality under discussion, is a question rarely heard.

Having become the methodological norm, nominalism leads many in the academy to scoff at such realist assumptions. Instead, they prefer to consider their job to be the shaping of human nature and history, not merely understanding it. "Nature has become, in a way, the enemy. . . . Once human nature is rejected, it will be replaced by something designed by science." [37] Since the nature of human nature is no longer considered fixed and stable, a clear invitation has been issued to those modern theorists who feel compelled to change social structures under a banner promising a more perfect and happier world.

Fleming's argument for the stability of human nature, like that of many paleoconservatives, is taken from the historical record of attempts to ignore human nature and the lessons learned from those attempts. The obvious, and most recent, examples are this century's failed experiments in Marxism and communism. We are now witnessing the slow and painful attempt to revitalize the very institutions, such as the family and the church, whose influence these regimes did so much to destroy. (Does Fleming remember the damage done to them before by capitalism, which Marx pointed out?) The expressed intention of these ideologies, of course, is to do good, but the actual outcome "is as if a man with a sore throat were to take large doses of antibiotics only to realize that the wonder drugs had destroyed the bacteria responsible for his digestion." [38]

From this perspective, it is less important that the state supply programs to perfect society than it is for the state to avoid doing anything that will subvert the instinctual motivation human beings possess to help themselves. Once that instinct is weakened, or lost, the state is unable to do for persons what they alone can do for themselves. The historical record of the species, properly understood, reveals not only the human good, but also a hierarchy of natural social institutions, starting with the family, through which this good is effectively pursued.

Feminism, like ethnocentrism, has been accused of considering human beings in the abstract, as monadic individuals with no vital connection to families and communities. Elizabeth Fox-Genovese, herself a leading feminist, addresses the reasons behind the widening gap between those women who celebrate the deconstruction of the Western tradition and those who, considering feminism an outright rejection of everything that it means to be a woman, continue to uncritically appropriate the West's traditional roles. The unwillingness of many women to embrace feminism arises from a simultaneous unwillingness to accept its radical individualism. "Here I am arguing that individualism actually perverts the idea of socially obligated and personally responsible freedom that constitutes the only freedom worthy of the name or indeed historically possible," writes Fox-Genovese. [39]

Like Aristotle, she argues that social existence is natural, it exists prior to the rights of the individual, and that understanding this is crucial to establishing some principal of limit for the will. Even more, she thinks that this disposition to community is historically more evident in women's lives, because of their involvement in family life, than in men's. But this raises a contradiction within the feminist agenda: on the one hand, women's family experience is an antidote to the influence of individualism; on the other, the same experience is the anchor, as it were, around their necks that keeps them excluded from the seats of power.

The main tendency of feminist theory has been to assert independence from oppressive communities and to declare individual rights. Building on the insights of Jean Bethke Elshtain, Fox-Genovese urges feminism to retreat from its development along the lines proposed by individualism, which only strengthens the power of the state, and to reaffirm the necessity of reconceiving life within community, especially within the family. She does not mean this in a sentimental or reactionary way, but rather as a "new vision of legally sanctioned communities that protect rather than exploit sexual and gender symmetry and that foster internal equality." [40]

Commenting on similar divisions among black Americans, Cornel West calls Afrocentricism misguided, saying that what is needed is "a frank acknowledgment of the basic humanness and Americanness of each of us." [41] He bemoans the erosion of community, the growth of extreme individualism, and the spiral downward into a self-destructive hedonism. He calls for a renewed focus on the common good in discussions of race. A "prophetic framework" of moral qualities must infuse the public conversation with the kind of self-love and self-respect exhibited by blacks in the face of racism. [42] Like Fox-Genovese, West regards the suffering of the oppressed as a source of wisdom, one that should be expressed within the dominant culture in hopes of breaking the deadlock in discussions of injustice.

This appeal to discover the wisdom, not simply the anger, in suffering pertains to the American Founders themselves. Arthur Schlesinger makes this point when he points out that the injustices fueling multicultural protest have been just those addressed first and foremost in the West:

> There remains, however, a crucial difference between the Western tradition and the others. The crimes of the West have produced their own antidotes. They have provoked great movements to end slavery, to raise the status of women, to abolish torture, to combat racism, to defend freedom of inquiry and expression, to advance personal liberty and human rights.
>
> Whatever the particular crimes of Europe, that continent is also the source—the *unique* source—of those liberating ideas of individual liberty, political democracy, the rule of law, human rights, and cultural freedom that constitute our most precious legacy and to which most of the world today aspires. These are *European* ideas, not Asian, nor African, nor Middle Eastern ideas, except by adoption. [43]

Schlesinger laments, in particular, the tendency toward the biological determinism in the proponents of Afrocentricism. Why, he asks, did the United States struggle so painfully toward the ideal of equality only to be told by black scholars that the melanin of black skin provides that person with a unique mentality and character? [44] Ethnocentrism, in this extreme form, encourages the kind of racial logic once employed by the Ku Klux Klan, only now the natural hierarchy has been reversed.

Ironically, what begins as a protest against the political use of human nature can end up self-consciously employing the same tactics. In the case of multiculturalism, the Afrocentric version of history becomes an instrument for overthrowing traditional scholarship and, supposedly, encouraging self-esteem and identity among black children. (The parallels with the feminist treatment of intellectual history are apparent.) Schlesinger repudiates any therapeutic aim in teaching history: the "facts" of history are distorted, and children are deprived of their intellectual freedom.

Worst of all, those ideas that have historically been most effective in defeating injustice—tolerance, democracy, human rights—are stripped of their proper meaning. As Taylor illustrates, an insistence upon a proper meaning of moral terms contradicts the therapeutic mode of recognition-on-demand. Tolerance, properly understood, does not extend to the behavior of a sadist; rights are not accorded to cannibals. Democracy, in short, cannot survive without a distinction between the lawful and unlawful. The limits of the "proper" in moral discourse, of course, are set by human nature treated as an ethical norm.

Critics of feminism and ethnocentrism are defenders of human nature. Although they differ in the weight of their claims, each insists that to be human is to be rational in a political way. They issue a collective warning against the loss of confidence in a universal human nature and against any further fragmentation of our sense of common humanity. Neither the injustices done for reasons of race nor those done for reasons of gender are worth the consequences they are held to have caused.

The critics appeal to a common humanity but avoid the homogenizing tendencies of universalism; they appeal to rational standards but recognize that humans exercise their distinctive rationality in community; and they appeal to the common good but realize consensus does not await the next philosophical system.

But without a common nature, human beings cannot possess a common good, except in a conventional sense. A common good represents the goods that individuals share—it extends the significance of human nature in the political sphere. As was said in Part One, if the body and soul are a hylomorphic unity, then the rational essence of the soul infuses all human activities, including pursuit and possession of the goods of life. Lower animals who live in groups also have goods in common, but, lacking conceptual reason and freedom of will, they have no duties or obligations, no political community.

For example, when Taylor calls human existence "dialogical" he is linking politics and rationality, because to exist "through reasoning" entails the give-and-take of conversation and communication about the ends of human life and how they can be attained. To participate in the *logos,* then, is not simply to think but to converse, to communicate, which requires a city. In other words, it simply is not imaginable that an isolated individual could come close to seeking the good life without the help of others, whether one thinks of a family supplying basic needs or a tradition providing instruction in the virtues. Even the physical needs of human life are scarcely obtainable without help from others, except to maintain the barest subsistence. The necessity of a common good demonstrates that any defense of individualism based upon a state of nature in which rights are prior to society cannot be sustained.

The individual versus the community is one aspect of the basic pattern of conceptual tensions that can be discerned in the contemporary debate over human nature. The other prominent theme is the notorious conflict between nature and nurture, one which has shadowed this question since it was argued by Socrates and the Sophists. Some Aristotelians, notably Adler, think this question is answered to a large extent by simply reminding us of the difference between a potentiality and its actualization.

Other problems arise, however, when one attempts more precision in discussing the actual role that locality and particularity play in reducing the human potential to act. How can it be determined that a given culture has developed practices that are, putting it softly, undesirable or, strongly, barbarous? This is the problem of *discernment.* How can a people be called to live in accord with the dignity of their universal nature, by persons standing outside of their culture, when all anyone supposedly knows about human nature is what they have learned within a given culture?

The other question is the *developmental* question: given that some practices have been found undesirable, how is the moral and political development of a society to be encouraged? Is it possible to raise another culture's standard of living when its individuals have no lived history or consciousness of the values or habits at the core of development in more "advanced" cultures?

Aristotle himself was acutely aware of this problem. The measure of what is morally good is the morally good person, but virtue results from the nurture of a virtuous family and city (*GBWW* I: 9, 340; II: 8, 340). Since the virtues themselves are dispositions, not principles, they cannot be taught. A grown adult who is deprived of a virtuous upbringing suffers perhaps the greatest misfortune; without the moral formation that families and intimate communities provide, he or she is deprived of the foundation of a happy life.

Some cultural conservatives in this debate believe so strongly in the role of locality that they, like the contextualists, consider it to be misguided benevolence to interfere in a foreign culture in order to encourage more virtuous practices. There are times when the rhetoric of multiculturalists can sound like someone defending the agrarian South against the industrialized North in the 1870s. What both have in common is a defense of unique forms of life, undergirded by traditions of custom and language, against the hegemony of Western Enlightenment reason and its technological and economic sprawl.

Internationalism, from this perspective, exercises its power of discernment while ignoring the problem of development. For an inhumane practice to be abolished in culture, that culture's entire *ethos* has to be addressed. An honest recognition of an injustice and the process of moral rehabituation go together. The internationalist who wants to impose change weakens the already existing social and moral order by tampering with the rootedness of local traditions.

This awareness of moral development lies at the heart of skepticism about seeking human progress through world cooperation and, specifically, the enforcing of a human rights policy worldwide. But, it must be stressed, that does not necessarily count as an objection to the conception of a universal human nature. Why? Because the common nature posited by Aristotle is a nature *both* rational and political, that is, dialogical. These elements represent a permanent tension, one that combines the problems of discernment and development. Rationality grasps at the essence of things, including the knowledge of human goodness, but what we know must wait, as it were, upon what our communities are at present. Political wisdom adjusts to the tension between its vision and the conditions necessary to its embodiment.

Internationalism can rightfully exude a metaphysical and epistemological confidence—namely, that human intelligence is capable, regardless of its cultural matrix, of making sense out of human life. Human beings can transcend their circumstances and see what would be better for themselves than what is now known and practiced. The same optimism, however, does not entail a neglect of the role of locality in cultivating right desire and ordinate behavior.

Defenders of local traditions are obviously not all of the same stripe; they are not necessarily the enemies of a universal human nature. Some, like Fleming, simply warn against forgetting that a rational nature requires a tradition for its ordinate practices. Others, like the defenders of cultural rights, make more serious claims—their defense of local traditions is based upon a relativism of human ends, with an implied rejection of a common human nature.

The last underlying issue in disagreements over human nature is the question of *ends*. It is best illustrated by the difference between Aristotle and Nietzsche. The rational-political account of human nature in Aristotle is teleologically directed at a single, final end, or happiness. The aesthetic individualism of Nietzsche, in contrast, contends that individuals create their own values and reject the imposition of any extrinsic measure of goodness. The questions raised between the two accounts are as follows: Are human beings obliged to a common form of happiness prior to their free choices? Or, are they free as sovereign individuals to choose their own forms of obligation, and then, if they wish, change their minds about them and choose again?

To understand the force of these questions, notice the different conceptions of freedom that they imply. For Aristotle, freedom consists in an ordinate relation to a natural end. For Nietzsche, freedom begins with the overthrowing of heteronomous vales and natures at the birth of the childlike overman who "wills his own will." [45] Some postmodern feminists, remember, regard either use of the word "freedom" as if not laughable then politically dangerous. It suggests the kind of human ends that have consistently been used to ignore the determinism of history and to continue patterns of exclusion, criminalization, enslavement, and oppression.

At the same time, classical liberals, including the liberal feminists, take a middle ground, arguing that individualism must be curtailed by the state precisely so that individuals can pursue their chosen ends without obstacle or harm. Here the common good is conceived along the lines of noninterference, as opposed to a conception of positive acts of goodness. The problem with maintaining this conception has been the general deterioration in consensual agreement about what "pursuits of happiness" should be inhibited or allowed. In other words, the dilemma of liberalism, like that of the postmodernism, is the question of discernment, which in turn implies the question of ends.

Therefore, just as the question of ends is unavoidable in politics, as in all communal life, so the issue of human nature cannot be avoided. Our politics are established by our idea of human nature; it establishes what counts as a premise to a political conclusion. [46] Those theorists who deny a common human nature but still espouse political purposes are left in an awkward position. How can a postmodern pursue an ideal, say, of justice in society without some theoretical warrant, some explicit criterion of judgment? This inconsistency recently has lead Jacques Derrida to discuss justice as a universal goal that stands apart from postmodern and historicist assumptions. [47]

The fact that the founder of deconstruction has the courage to admit the shortcomings of his philosophical premises for political theory is encouraging. Much of what has been surveyed about recent perspectives on human nature is built upon the assumption that all human thought is determined by factors of history, race, class, and gender. This raises a problem about human freedom, specifically a person's capacity to think and to imagine outside the limitations and patterns imposed by these factors. That form of historicism implies a denial of the active subject and the autonomy of consciousness; each is merely a social construct. It assumes that human beings are in fact constituted by categories imposed on them, largely by the accidents of their birth, above all, by race, class, and gender.

It was said earlier that whether man differs in degree or in kind is still the crucial issue in human nature. The pervasive belief that humans differ only in degree from animals makes historicism possible. Animalists are materialists in the sense that all human powers, including intelligence, are subject to instinctual and deterministic forces. The knowledge of a given epoch and a given society, therefore, cannot rise above, or gain a significance beyond, the material factors determining the conditions of existence. The individual mind cannot transcend its circumstances. Without a difference in kind, attributable to an immaterial power, human intelligence will fail to think beyond the data at hand.

Since there is no transcendent viewpoint in history, historicist assumptions provide revisionist historians with the warrant to deconstruct and reconstruct history with an eye, if they wish, to promoting their ungrounded political aims. All that one can say about human nature in history is, as Michel Foucault writes, "that we are difference, that our reason is the difference of discourses, our history the difference of times, our selves the difference of masks. That difference, far from being the forgotten and recovered origin, is this dispersion that we are and make." [48]

Following Foucault, we can refer to the dispute over the ends of human nature as identity versus difference. Whereas the Aristotelian temper of mind is to find patterns of intelligibility common to all human action, it is the postmodern temper to uncover and to tease out those differences that defy traditional rationality and classification. From an Aristotelian perspective, this pursuit of difference is an exercise of intelligence against itself, against the natural grain of the intellect and the structure of its object, against that which exists. For the postmodern, this is intelligence set free from the past, not only from its imposed canons of rationality, but also from its political crimes.

Conclusion: Can *homo sapiens* survive?

> Celebrate if you will
> The triumph of your genes:
> The past is working still;
> That is all that it means.
> In every spoken word,
> Always, the past is heard.
>
> Perhaps silence is best,
> But if there must be speech,
> Then watch it closely lest
> It stretches out of reach.
> The future is too far;
> The past is all we are.
>   (C. H. Sisson, "In the Silence")[49]

Much can be said in favor of feminist and ethnocentrist scholars who are exploring the diversity of traditions indigenous to the West itself, especially those belonging to women and minorities. Could it be that female philosophers, poets, and musicians, whose output could stand alongside the established greats, await discovery? Could be it that the values used to stamp the "great" idea and "great" books are themselves unavoidably parochial?

Some will glibly respond that "quality will out" regardless of who produces it. The new scholarship promises that this will no longer have to be accepted on faith. The now notorious remark attributed to Saul Bellow, "When the Zulus produce a Tolstoy we will read him," dodges the issue of whether ingrained disregard might keep us from recognizing the existence of a great Zulu author.

Yet, also at stake is the recognized worth of the Western intellectual tradition. The danger of multiculturalism is that its adherents will sever ties with the intellectual tradition that produced their outlook. One hardly needs to point out that this cutting away from Western moorings contradicts their own principle of locality. It is no accident that the tenets of ethnocentrism and the pedagogy of multiculturalism had its origin and greatest success in Great Britain, Western Europe, and, especially, the United States. Both perspectives, in spite of their antagonism, are a product of the universalist tolerance and respect for human rights. No other rationale can be given for obliging people of disparate races and backgrounds to invest themselves in understanding each other with such particular empathy.

Perhaps for the first time, feminism and ethnocentrism make adherents of the Western tradition aware of a great irony. The same philosophical ideas of nature, rationality, and hierarchy that gave birth to Western democracy have also been employed in causes that now look grossly unjust. To measure past practices by present moral standards does limited good, but the fact that such practices persist ensures that the study of gender and ethnicity will have a long life.

What other dangers are there to avoid? The classical position that human beings possess a nature different in kind from animals, specified by a rational intellect and free will, led over a period of centuries to the recognition of their natural and unalienable rights. By overlooking the crucial difference between what belongs to human beings by their *first* nature and what belongs to them by nurture, or acculturation, we risk losing the foundation which justifies our respect for human rights in the first place. But by overlooking the role of acculturation in human development, we ignore the press in which individual and communal character receives the stamp of their *second* nature. A cultural locality may, in fact, affect the power of discernment, but it is decisive for development.

Nature is required for discernment, nurture for development. The debate over diversity has either obscured this crucial distinction by collapsing first nature into second or misunderstood it by pitting one against the other. The instability in the present American cultural climate evinces both predicaments. Protests that began long ago on behalf of the civil rights of both women and minorities were steps in political progress based upon classical, medieval, and Enlightenment ideas. Some of the radical aspects of ethnocentrism and feminism erode the affirmation of a shared human nature that grounded this political progress. As Adler writes,

> If a world cultural community is ever to come into existence, it will retain cultural pluralism of diversity with respect to all matters that are accidental in human life. . . . [But] we will have at last overcome the nurtural illusion that there is a Western mind and an Eastern mind, a European mind and an African mind, or a civilized mind and a primitive mind. There is only a human mind and it is one and the same in all human beings. [50]

Thus, for international cooperation, in any form, to be feasible, there must exist some degree of consensus about the basic ends and purposes of human life. The Universal Declaration of Human Rights testifies to a postwar agreement among developed nations which is now jeopardized by insistence on "cultural rights." The logic of such a claim contradicts the transcultural character of rights. As the political consequences of ethnocentrism are becoming apparent, the question becomes whether these trajectory of ideas can be deflected.

It is certainly a by-product of our cultural confusion that political leaders talk a great deal about "vision." Much of this rhetoric employs both the principles of feminism and ethnocentrism side-by-side with the norm of a universal human nature, with no apparent awareness of the tensions between them. Political vision, if it is to help heal this breach, must affirm both the universality of human nature and the indigenous matrix of human development. That is, politics must be idealistic about human aims and practical about their realization.

Taylor's remark about the "politics of recognition" is particularly suggestive. Yes, a part of our political nature is that recognition is integral to the mutuality that encourages political friendship. But it subverts the genuineness of all recognitions, thus all friendships, if recognition becomes obligatory, if the point of recognition becomes the elimination of self-doubt. Part of our moral practice must be the strengthening of common purposes—we are men not angels, Aristotle said. But when the good of mutuality is made to subvert the possibility of self-criticism, of intellectual discrimination beyond the *status quo,* moral criticism swallows its own tail.

Zulu children attending an open-air school in Africa. "The now notorious remark attributed to Saul Bellow, 'When the Zulus produce a Tolstoy we will read him,' dodges the issue of whether ingrained disregard might keep us from recognizing the existence of a great Zulu author."

Some critics and defenders of essentialism treat universal human nature as if persons exist ahistorically. Admittedly, there are times when universalists can seem as if they are operating in a world of abstractions. The renewal of interest in gender and ethnicity—in difference and diversity—may signal a protest against an overly formalistic attitude toward indigenous forms of life. An individual belongs to humanity, but only in an abstract sense. Humanity though real is not tangible, nor does belonging to humanity place an individual in a community with anything that concretely exists. Only families, villages, cities, and states exist, and the more localized the community, the greater will be its impact on identity and character.

These critics make another mistake in assuming it to have been held that knowledge of an essence provides an exhaustive knowledge. Recognizing

that someone is human is only the first step in knowing them individually; there is much more to know about any person than their essential nature, but it is human nature that provides the framework for discovering more. Yet, even at the level of human nature itself, once the distinctive intelligence has been specified, not all that is significant about that difference is revealed. Aristotle did not know all there was to know *about* human nature, though he knew *what* it was.

To deny the gradual historical unveiling of this significance leads us either to posit unnecessary discontinuities between our conception of the human difference and Aristotle's or to misunderstand the nature of intellectual and political progress. The abolition of slavery discredits certain aspects of Aristotle's theory. But the ideal of human equality itself was developed within the Aristotelian tradition. If Aristotle's grasp of human nature is exhaustive, there is no need for a tradition, no need to overturn his view of natural slaves and women. We can be faithful to Aristotle's basic insights without repeating his errors.

In the long view, feminism and ethnocentrism will have contributed to a further sorting out of truth from error. They will also have contributed to a deeper awareness of how ideas have consequences and will have taught an unforgettable lesson in how ideas can be the consequence of powerful interests. Some may complain that to appreciate any of these perspectives must weaken our love for Western culture. Not so. It only removes the naiveté, and, in doing so it, provides the opportunity for critical understanding of our intellectual legacy.

A new consensus, if one ever appears, will be long in coming. At present, the very suggestion of a common vision sounds oppressive to the proponents of diversity. To overcome this resistance, this fear of exclusion and subordination, universalists must reaffirm the importance of locality to the political nature of rational man. The fear of continued injustice committed under the cover of traditional rhetoric is the inner meaning of controversies over "family values" and "political correctness."

For their part, feminists and ethnocentrists must ask themselves whether or not their theories are compatible with any sound philosophical basis of governance. To continue advancing a sophisticated agnosticism concerning the common good will only lead to greater confusion and fragmentation. It is time to move beyond the project of negative critique—the challenge remains to overcome the exhausted currency of our philosophical vocabulary. If, however, these ideas can be trusted to tear down, they can also be trusted to build up.

1. Robert Musil, "Woman Yesterday and Tomorrow," in *Precision and Soul: Essays and Addresses,* trans. Burton Pike and David S. Luft (Chicago: The University of Chicago Press, 1990), p. 213.

2. Thomas Fleming, *The Politics of Human Nature* (New Brunswick, N.J.: Transaction Publishers, 1988), p. 76.

3. Carol Nagy Jacklin, "Female and Male: Issues of Gender," *American Psychologist* 44 (February 1989), p. 128.

4. Ibid., p. 130.

5. Eleanor E. Maccoby and Carol N. Jacklin, *The Psychology of Sex Differences* (Stanford: Stanford University Press, 1974).

6. Eleanor E. Maccoby, "Gender and Relationships: A Developmental Account," *American Psychologist* 45 (April 1990), pp. 513–20.

7. Jacklin, p. 127.

8. C. L. Martin, C. H. Wood, & J. K. Little, "The Development of Gender Understanding to Children's Sex-Typed Preferences and Gender Stereotypes," *Child Development* 61 (1990), pp. 1891–1904.

9. John Nicholson, *Men and Women: How Different Are They?* (New York: Oxford University Press, 1984), p. 81.

10. Ibid., p. 9.

11. Donna J. Haraway, *Simians, Cyborgs, and Women: The Reinvention of Nature* (New York: Routledge, Chapman and Hall, Inc., 1991), p. 150.

12. Alexis de Tocqueville, *Democracy in America,* Vol. 1, ed. Phillips Bradley (New York: Random House, 1990), p. 264. (*GBWW* II: 44, 132–33)

13. Kenneth Clark, *Civilisation* (New York: Harper & Row, Publishers, 1969), p. 2; for further comment, see Charles Moore, "Can K Still Stand for Civilization," *Spectator* 27 (Oct. 16, 1993), p. 8.

14. Bartolomé de Las Casas, *In Defense of the Indians,* trans. and ed. Stafford Poole (Dekalb, Ill.: Northern Illinois University Press, 1992), p. 47.

15. David Brion Davis, *The Problem of Slavery in Western Culture* (Ithaca: Cornell University Press, 1966).

16. Ibid., pp. 118–19.

17. Leszek Kolakowski, *Modernity on Endless Trial* (Chicago: The University of Chicago Press, 1990), p. 18.

18. George Steiner, *Language and Silence: Essays on Language, Literature, and the Inhuman* (New York: Atheneum, 1967); *see especially,* "To Civilize Our Gentlemen," reprinted in *The George Steiner Reader* (New York: Oxford University Press, 1984), pp. 25–36.

19. George Steiner, *Real Presences* (Chicago: The University of Chicago Press, 1989), p. 215; *see also,* pp. 165–78.

20. Quoted in Christopher J. Berry, *Human Nature* (Atlantic Highlands: Humanities Press International, Inc., 1988), p. 69.

21. Charles Taylor, *Multiculturalism and the "Politics of Recognition"* (Princeton: Princeton University Press, 1992), p. 31.

22. "Preface," to Frantz Fanon, *The Wretched of the Earth,* trans. Constance Farrington (New York: Grove, 1968; orig. French, 1961), p. 26.

23. Robert Royal, *1492 and All That: Political Manipulations of History* (Washington, D.C.: Ethics and Public Policy Center, 1992).

24. Kirkpatrick Sale, *Conquest of Paradise: Christopher Columbus and the Columbian Legacy* (New York: Alfred A. Knopf, 1990).

25. Ibid., pp. 25–6.

26. Edward W. Said, *Orientalism* (New York: Pantheon Books, 1978).

27. Ibid., p. 7.

28. Edward W. Said, *Culture and Imperialism* (New York: Alfred A. Knopf, 1993), p. 314.

29. *Farewell to Reason* (New York: Verso, 1987), p. 274.

30. Charles Taylor, *The Ethics of Authenticity* (Cambridge: Harvard University Press, 1992), p. 37. Charles Taylor, *Multiculturalism and the "Politics of Recognition"* (Princeton: Princeton University Press, 1992); for historical background, see his *Sources of the Self: The Making of Modern Identity* (Cambridge: Harvard University Press, 1989).

31. *The Ethics of Authenticity,* p. 39.

32. Ibid., p. 51.

33. *Multiculturalism and the "Politics of Recognition,"* p. 70.

34. Fleming, p. 8.

35. Kolakowski, p. 25.

36. Ibid., p. 22.

37. Fleming, p. 17.

38. Ibid., p. 16.

39. Elizabeth Fox-Genovese, *Feminism Without Illusions: A Critique of Individualism* (Chapel Hill: The University of North Carolina Press, 1991), p. 7.

40. Ibid., p. 54.

41. Cornel West, *Race Matters* (Boston: Beacon Press, 1993), p. 4.

42. Ibid., p. 29.

43. Arthur M. Schlesinger, Jr., *The Disuniting of America: Reflections on a Multicultural Society* (New York: Whittle Communications, 1991), p. 76.

44. Ibid., p. 44.

45. Friedrich Nietzsche, *Thus Spake Zarathustra,* Part I, "Of the Three Metamorphoses," trans. R. J. Hollingdale (New York: Penguin, 1961).

46. Berry, pp. 132–33.

47. Jacques Derrida, *The Other Heading,* trans. Pascale-Anne Brault and Michel B. Haas (Bloomington: Indiana University Press, 1992), pp. 70–83.

48. Michel Foucault, *The Archaeology of Knowledge,* trans. A. M. Sheridan (New York: Pantheon Books, 1972), p. 131.

49. C. H. Sisson, "In the Silence," *The New Criterion* 12 (November 1992), pp. 46–7.

50. Mortimer J. Adler, *Haves Without Have-Nots: Essays for the 21st Century on Democracy and Socialism* (New York: MacMillan, 1991) p. 242.

Deal W. Hudson is the editor of *Crisis* magazine in Washington, D.C. He is also the director of the Institutional Development for the American Academy for Liberal Education. His previous academic positions include associate professor of philosophy at Fordham University, visiting professor at New York University, and chair of the philosophy department at Mercer University.

Mr. Hudson is the author of various articles on the subjects of happiness and contemporary Thomism. He is the coeditor of *Understanding Maritain: Philosopher and Friend* (1988), and *The Future of Thomism* (1992), and is the editor of *Sigrid Undset On Saints and Sinners* (1994). He is currently editing an *Encyclopædia of Thomism,* and is writing a major work titled *Happiness and the Limits of Satisfaction.*

Special Features

1
2
3
4

An Introduction to "Ancient" African Thought

George Anastaplo

There is always something new from Africa.
—Pliny the Elder[1]

I

Two major branches of African thought have come down to us from antiquity. One stems from North Africa, principally Egypt, which had substantial contacts to the west with the Libyans, to the south with the Nubians and the Ethiopians, and to the east with the people of the Fertile Crescent in Asia Minor and, very late, with the Arabs. The other branch of African thought stems from sub-Saharan Africa, made up of hundreds of tribes or peoples, similar in their diversity to the ancient tribes of the Western hemisphere. [2] But however diverse these sub-Saharan African tribes may be, they seem (and are generally believed to be) critically different from the rest of the world which they were largely cut off from for so long. [3]

In antiquity, one "half" of Africa seems to have had little awareness of the other "half." The ancient Egyptians were part of the Mediterranean world, though deeply involved in the Nilotic world as well. The sub-Saharan Africans, although largely isolated for so long from the rest of the human race, may have a more influential worldwide presence in the coming century than the ancient Egyptians. [4] One notices in the novels of Naguib Mahfouz how little influence ancient Egypt seems to have even in the life of Egyptians in the twentieth century. [5]

We can see on display in Africa the "oldest" and the "youngest" of the races of mankind. "Human beings are widely thought to have originated in Africa." [6] It is sometimes said that the Pygmies, who roam the forests of a small part of central Africa, exhibit the earliest form of human organization. [7] In this sense the tribes of sub-Saharan Africa may show human beings in their earliest, or youngest, condition, whereas the ancient Egyptians in their later dynasties (but before the Alexandrian and Roman conquests) show what thousands of years of development, and hence aging, of a stable civil order can lead to.

My personal experiences of Africa came in the course of my service in the United States Army Air Corps at the end of the Second World War. Stationed at our air bases in Egypt and Saudi Arabia, I learned to enjoy both the Nile and the desert, as well as the sounds and smells of North Africa. My service in that part of the world included flights to Dakar (in Senegal) and to Liberia. My most vivid recollection of Liberia is when I was rebuked for paying a boy too much to climb a tree and cut a bunch of bananas. I believe I gave the boy a dime instead of a nickel. I strongly recall Dakar nights without electric lights, where I could watch people enjoying themselves around unlikely campfires on street corners. [8] My exposure to sub-Saharan Africa continues, of course, in the contacts one has in the United States with people of African descent (destined by racial prejudice to remain somewhat distinctive) who have helped convey to us some of the music, folk stories, colors, and foods of Africa.

*(Overleaf)
A young
man from
a nomadic
tribe called
Ovahimba,
plays a
simple mouth
flute. The
Ovahimba
inhabit the
Kaokoland
region in
Namibia.*

II

A special view of the Egyptian Africa of antiquity is provided by the great museums of the world—in Chicago, New York, London, Paris, Berlin, and Rome, to say nothing of what may still be seen in Egypt to this day. Ancient Egypt, which extended over some five thousand years of recorded history, [9] is distinguished by the monumental character of its structures. These structures, which are illuminated by extensive literary remains, are on a scale unmatched in the world, except perhaps for the Great Wall of China. Egyptian civilization, despite its many changes in dynasties, was remarkably stable. So extensive was the span of time evident throughout Egyptian life that the ancient Greeks could be dismissed by the Egyptians as "children." [10] Ever since decipherment of the Rosetta Stone, Egyptian history has been largely knowable by us, the moderns.

The West has long been fascinated by Egypt—and, indeed, by all of Africa, a strange place to which Westerners seem always to respond with ambivalence. Ethiopians, who represent a mixture of Egypt (including the Palestine that Egyptians long controlled) and sub-Saharan Africa, are noticed in the Greek fables of Aesop:

> A man bought an Ethiopian, thinking that his color was the result of
> the neglect of his former owner. He took him home and used all kinds
> of soap on him and tried all kinds of baths to clean him up. He couldn't
> change his color, but he made him sick with all his efforts. [11]

To this story (which can serve also as an allegory of the West's treatment of Africa in recent centuries) is added the moral, "Natures remain just as they first appear." [12] That an attempt to wash away an Ethiopian's color could be used in this way in a story attributed to Aesop (who evidently lived in the sixth century B.C.) suggests that the darker Africans were not familiar to some Greeks, although the effectiveness of the story does depend upon its audience recognizing the folly of this slave-owner's efforts.

The Egyptians, on the other hand, had long been known to the Greeks. It is likely that Herodotus, when he wrote about the Egyptians in the fifth century B.C., expressed an assessment of them already shared by other Greeks, that the Egyptians were the most religious of men. [13]

III

The great monuments of ancient Egypt, which are notable not only for their size but also for what can be called their *determination,* are devoted primarily to the care of the dead. The same can be said about many, if not most, of the literary remains of ancient Egypt. So overwhelming was the challenge of death for the Egyptians that elaborate measures were taken corpse by corpse, perhaps reinforcing thereby a radical individualism. Thus, each of the great pyramids, which could have housed the remains of all of the pharaohs, was devoted primarily to the needs of one royal corpse alone. [14]

Was death somehow to be overcome by the kind of display of energy seen in ministering to the dead? A pyramid, for example, is crystallized energy on a grand scale. Is not a preoccupation with death likely to be, in effect, a desperate effort to ensure the preservation of life? Much of what one sees and reads from ancient Egypt is dedicated to the proposition that life after death can and should continue much as it had during one's time on earth. The measures resorted to in order to preserve the corpses of the deceased testify to how vital an earthly existence is to human life, so much so that proper care of the dead permits one's spirit to come and go on earth as one wishes. (Compare the Platonic, and later the Christian, insistence upon the truly human coming into its own only when one is relieved of one's bodily attributes.) I notice in passing that an occasional ancient representation can suggest that the Egyptians were not without an openess to the erotic aspects of bodily activities and human relations, but such eroticism seems to have been consistently subordinated to their pursuit of immortality or, rather, deathlessness.

Parodies of the Egyptian approach to death may be seen in the attention lavished for decades on Lenin's corpse in the Soviet Union and in the expenditures (very much in the service of a quest for eternal youth) that are devoted in the United States to the cosmetic and celebratory aspects of the funeral industry. [15]

The dead of Egypt, it sometimes seems, do not have anything better to do than to revisit their earthly habitats. No fundamental distinction seems to be recognized between the future and the past. This can mean, in effect, that the present is both everything and nothing. This is an approach that is different both from the reincarnation expected among, say, the Hindus and some sub-Saharan Africans and from the desire for release from earthly limitations seen among, say, the Christians, the Muslims, and the seekers of Nirvana. [16]

What *is* the understanding of life, or of living, that is assumed by the Egyptians? To make as much as they do of continuing after death with everyday activity as it happens to be organized by us may be to subvert life as we can know it. Is tragedy, for example, somehow lost sight of and made virtually impossible because of the impermanence of death? [17]

On the other hand, there was among the ancient Egyptians considerable emphasis not only upon rituals and formulas but also upon the moral purity of the deceased. It was in the interest of the deceased to be able to pass muster with respect to such matters as those collected in the following recapitulation of a man's career:

> I have come from my town,
> I have descended from my nome [district],
> I have done justice for its lord,
> I have satisfied him with what he loves.
> I spoke truly, I did right,
> I spoke fairly, I repeated fairly,

I seized the right moment
So as to stand well with people.
I judged between two so as to content them,
I rescued the weak from one stronger than he
As much as was in my power.
I gave bread to the hungry, clothes to the naked,
I brought the boatless to land.
I buried him who had no son,
I made a boat for him who lacked one.
I respected my father, I pleased my mother,
I raised their children. [18]

We have no problem endorsing the merits of most, if not all, of these actions.

IV

We have noticed the recourse of the ancient Egyptians to elaborate rituals and detailed formulae, especially with a view to a proper transition of human beings to eternal life. A kind of magic seems to have been relied upon here, however reasonable and even sophisticated that people must have been with respect to such disciplines as civil engineering, mechanical and hydraulic transportation, agriculture, and masonry. Magic means, among other things, that what one knows—and hence what one says and does—can be important, even decisive, for perpetual happiness. This too reflects the role of reason in human affairs. Again and again there are prescriptions such as the following:

If this chapter be known by [the deceased] he shall come forth by day, he shall rise up to walk upon the earth among the living, and he shall never fail and come to an end, never, never, never. [19]

Another one reads:

If this composition be known [by the deceased] upon earth he shall come forth by day, and he shall have the faculty of travelling about among the living, and his name shall never perish. [20]

Still another one reads:

If this chapter be known [by the deceased] upon earth, [or if it be done] in writing upon [his] coffin, he shall come forth by day in all the forms which he is pleased [to take], and he shall enter in to [his] place and shall not be driven back. And cakes, and ale, and joints of meat upon the altar of Osiris shall be given unto him; . . . and he shall do whatsoever it pleaseth him to do, even as the company of the gods which is in the underworld, continually, and regularly, for millions of times. [21]

In these and other matters, the ancient Egyptians (like the Hindus) always "thought big," contemplating a universe with millions upon millions of years already past as well as to come. [22]

The rituals and invocations that the Egyptians relied upon were in the service of the fundamentals of their religion. These basic ideas were summed up by a Western scholar at the beginning of this century under six headings:

I. Belief in the immortality of the soul, and the recognition of relatives and friends after death.

II. Belief in the resurrection of a spiritual body, in which the soul lived after death.

III. Belief in the continued existence of the heart-soul, the ka (the double), and the shadow.

IV. Belief in the transmutation of offerings, and the efficacy of funerary sacrifices and gifts.

V. Belief in the efficacy of words of power, including names, magical and religious formulae, &c.

VI. Belief in the Judgment, the good being rewarded with everlasting life and happiness, and the wicked with annihilation. [23]

This scholar then added, "All the above appear to be indigenous [North?] African beliefs, which existed in the Predynastic Period, and are current under various forms at the present day among most of the tribes of the Sûdân who have any religious belief at all." [24]

We may well wonder what the sources were of all the information relied upon by the Egyptians. We may also wonder about the significance of the fact that such information was once known only to a relatively few in antiquity and that it has long since been either lost or abandoned. We wonder, in short, about the nature of revelation, its reception, and its staying power.

V

Critical to Egyptian thought is its understanding of the divine. A standard reference book opens its account of Egypt with these observations:

No one who strolls through the Egyptian galleries of a museum can fail to be struck by the multitude of divinities who attract attention on all sides. Colossal statues in sandstone, granite and basalt, minute statuettes in glazed composition, bronze, even in gold, portray gods and goddesses frozen in hierarchical attitudes, seated or standing. Sometimes these male or female figures have heads with human features. More often they are surmounted by the muzzle of an animal or the beak of a bird. The same divinities, receiving adoration and offerings or performing ritual gestures for the benefit of their worshipers, can be seen again on the bas-reliefs of massive sarcophagi or sculptured on funerary stelae and stone blocks stripped from temple walls. They recur on mummy cases and in the pictures which illuminate the papyri of the Book of the Dead. [25]

Further on in this account a partial list is given of the animals whose heads appear on Egyptian divinities: the bull, the cat, the cow, the crocodile, the dog-faced ape, the donkey, the falcon, the frog, the hippopotamus, the ibis, the jackal, the lion, the lioness, the ram with curved horns, the ram with wavy horns, the scarab, the scorpion, the serpent, the uraeus, the vulture, and the wolf. [26]

We are told that only the myth of Osiris, who was one of the greatest gods in the Egyptian pantheon, has been transmitted in detail to us—and this, evidently, because of the writings of Plutarch. "Plutarch, though Greek and writing of times already long past, was evidently well informed." [27] The story of Osiris' dismemberment and the subsequent reassembly of his corpse by his sorrowing mother became important in Egypt to the preservation of human corpses and to an insistence upon proper burial rites. [28]

We have noticed that knowing certain things was believed critical for the well-being of the deceased. We have also noticed that morality, or a certain kind of conduct, were considered important in the judging of the deceased. Even so, knowing things may not be the same as understanding them. The names of gods and of their parts and functions are emphasized, just as may be the proper names, not only the generic names, of, say, the various parts of the ship that is to carry the deceased to perpetual bliss. [29] But little is said in the materials we have about why these things are as they

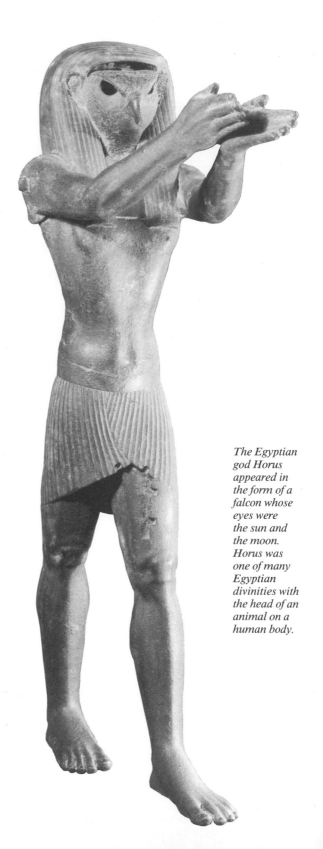

The Egyptian god Horus appeared in the form of a falcon whose eyes were the sun and the moon. Horus was one of many Egyptian divinities with the head of an animal on a human body.

Osiris was one of the greatest gods in ancient Egypt. "The story of Osiris' dismemberment and the subsequent reassembly of his corpse by his sorrowing mother became important in Egypt to the preservation of human corpses and to an insistence upon proper burial rites."

are, or even why they are named as they are. This deficiency is related to the question I have raised about the source and authority for all of this supposedly useful, indeed vital, information.

Is there in all this what we might call a parody of philosophy, or is it also a step toward philosophy, just as we see astrology as a parody of and yet a contribution to astronomy? In any effort to understand the vast Egyptian lore, especially about gods such as Osiris and about human death, one must have an awareness of what can and cannot be. [30] The same can be said about any effort to understand the stories we have from sub-Saharan Africa. It is helpful, in coming to terms with the Egyptian preoccupation with serving the dead, to recall the philosophical response exhibited by Socrates in Plato's *Apology*, where he (unconcerned about funeral rites) accepts with apparent equanimity the prospect of total annihilation of himself at death. [31] We ourselves can notice that, so far as we know, our personal nonexistence before conception was anything but distressing.

The elaborateness of both the doctrines and the rituals of the Egyptians may have eventually been self-defeating. For one thing, it must have become harder and harder to make sense of all the lore that had been accumulated in these matters—and the conditions of the country were such that there was a literate class with leisure to think about things, if so minded. [32] Furthermore, the richly-adorned corpses and tombs proved attractive to thieves, especially those criminals who could not see that any divine retribution followed from their larcenous incursions. But perhaps most important, the complexity, if not even what seems to us the inherent improbability, of their pantheon may eventually have made the Egyptians susceptible to the appeal of so single-minded, rigorous, and even pure message as that offered by Islam, a religion which (unlike Christianity) evidently has no traces of the story of the death and resurrection of a divinity such as Osiris. [33]

VI

However separated North Africa and sub-Saharan Africa were by a vast ocean-like desert, both the Nile and trans-Saharan caravans permitted some movement north and south. For example, an occasional dancing Pygmy could delight the court of a pharaoh. [34] Also, there seems always to have been some traffic in slaves and animals from south to north down the Nile. Peculiar combinations of human beings and animals could be conjured up in stories both north and south of the Sahara desert. In Egypt, we have seen, there were tales of gods with animal parts; in sub-Saharan African tales, humans and animals could also be mixed up, even sexually, without regard to species differentiations, and much could be made of animal stories.

But the differences between north and south can still be striking. There is relatively little said in the stories of the sub-Saharan Africans (whom I will now call simply Africans) about burial rites, however important the social participation in African funerals remains down to this day. [35] Also, unlike the Egyptian stories we have, the African stories are filled with resurrections of all kinds. Further distinctions from the Egyptian approach to things may be seen in the opening passage of an article, "Mythology of Black Africa":

> In Black Africa religion has nowhere reached a definitive form. Everywhere we find the worship of the forces of Nature personified—sun, moon, sky, mountains, rivers. But the undisciplined native imagination prevented the religion of Nature from expanding into poetic myths like those of India or Greece. . . .
>
> Among the Africans sorcery is very powerful. Every medical treatment has all the characteristics of exorcism, since magic remains secret while religion is open to all. Amulets and gri-gris are the usual manifestations of magic among the Africans. The object of these talismans is to protect their owner against diseases, wounds, thieves and murderers, or to increase his wealth—in brief, to procure him everything profitable.
>
> The African native thinks that the world and everything in it must be obedient to sorcerers, magicians who have the power of commanding the elements. This belief is bound up with another—the continuing existence of the soul after death. Magicians are able to call on souls to aid

their powers. The souls of the dead often transmigrate into the bodies of animals, or may even be re-incarnated in plants, when the natives think themselves bound to such by a close link of kinship. Thus the Zulus refrain from killing certain species of snakes which they think are the spirits of their relatives.

Africans attribute a spirit to every animate and inanimate object, and these spirits are the emanations of deities. Moreover, they are distinct from one another, for there are spirits of natural phenomena and spirits of the ancestors. [36]

The opinions, traits, and practices described here are drawn, for the most part, from the old stories that have come down to us. No doubt, most modern Africans have questioned, if not abandoned, many of the opinions of their ancestors about such things. It is not, however, the opinions of our contemporaries in sub-Saharan Africa or anywhere else with which we are now primarily concerned, just as it was not with the opinions of our contemporaries in Egypt. [37]

Much of the African past has long been a mystery not only to Europeans (among whom I here include Americans) but also to Africans themselves. The lack of records and of much in the way of archaeological evidence makes it difficult to piece together Africa's history. Whatever great cities, art or writing there may once have been, not many traces seem to be left with which investigators can work. In a sense for most Africans (unlike for the Egyptians) there has been heretofore neither past nor future, but only a perpetual present. [38]

Up to the twentieth century, therefore, Africa could be regarded as the Dark Continent and as a "latecomer" upon the world's stage. [39] Its problems, particularly in the raising of sufficient food for its fast-growing population, remain chronic, while famines within several countries continue to decimate the population. It is not generally recognized that the amount of arable land in regions south of the Sahara is quite small (less than ten percent). Matters are not helped by the widespread African practice of relying upon women, already burdened with household duties, for much of the agricultural work of the community. [40]

It is also hard to see Africa and Africans properly after centuries of slavery. Slavery, which seems to have been indigenous to Africa (as in other parts of the ancient world) well before the fierce depredations of the Arabs and the Europeans (and which may continue, in the hundreds of thousands, in parts of Africa today), affects how some Africans, as well as many non-Africans, regard Africans to this day. It can be hard not only to *get* past but also to *see* past such brutal subjugation and exploitation. However destructive Africans have been in wars among themselves from time to time—and they have been so—it is not likely that they have ever inflicted upon themselves the spiritual as well as the material damage that non-Africans (both Christian and Islamic) did for several centuries with their slave trade. [41] Some hope for African self-fulfillment can be gleaned, however, from the history of the successful Slavs of Eastern Europe, a people whose very name reminds everyone, including them, of their centuries of enslavement. Non-African respect can follow upon noticing what Africans (despite, if not partly because of, slavery) grasp that Westerners do not.

VII

When there is no generally authoritative text available—such as the Bible, Homer's epics, the *Gilgamesh,* the Confucian *Analects,* the *Bhagavad Gītā,* the Buddhist scriptures, or the Koran—it is difficult to determine where to begin in grasping the thought of an ancient people. [42] The principal access we have to ancient sub-Saharan thought is through the African folk stories, myths, and other tales that have been recorded, often by Europeans. These stories, collected by many outsiders for at least two centuries now, pose obvious problems with respect to the reliability of their transmission. We must do the best that we can, aware both of our shortcomings and of the weaknesses of those who collected these tales. [43] This is the approach we have to take also in our study of North American Indian thought. [44] I am somewhat reassured, in making the use I do of these very old stories for investigating ancient, *not* contemporary, African thought when I notice that these stories are repeatedly drawn upon, in a casual and relaxed fashion, in the novels and other writings of contemporary Africans, such as Chinua Achebe and Wole Soyinka. [45] This is in marked contrast to an Egyptian novelist such as Naguib Mahfouz, who barely mentions ancient Egypt in his marvelous novels of *The Cairo Trilogy*.

Chinua Achebe

One massive fact about the old African tales should be noticed: they are not, by and large, charming or attractive stories. [46] One encounters in the African tales considerable callousness, gratuitous cruelty, casual betrayal, and other severe moral limitations. To some extent these bleak responses may be traced back to prolonged adversities, especially chronic famine conditions, in much of Africa. [47]

The Western reader can find oppressive such a story as the following, which is not exceptional in the African corpus: A farmer provides refuge within his body to a snake being pursued by men. When the men leave, the snake refuses to come out of the farmer's body, finding it comfortable there. "The farmer's belly was now so puffed out that you would

have thought that he was a woman with child." The farmer enlists the help of a heron, who manages to pull the snake out of the farmer's body and to kill it. All this, with the snake's ingratitude leading to its destruction, is bad enough—but, unfortunately, the fate of the snake does not serve to make others act better toward their benefactors in turn:

> The farmer got up and said to the heron, "You have rid me of the snake, but now I want a potion to drink because he may have left some of his poison behind." "You must go and find six white fowls," said the heron, "and cook and eat them—that's the remedy." "Come to think of it," said the farmer, "you're a white fowl, so you'll do for a start."

> So saying, he seized the heron, tied it up, and carried it off home. There he hung it up in his hut while he told his wife what had happened. "I'm surprised at you," said his wife. "The bird does you a kindness, rids you of the evil in your belly, saves your life, in fact, and yet you catch it and talk of killing it." With that she released the heron and it flew away. [48]

There is something noble about this woman's response, exhibiting the important (and often dominant) role that women have in African stories, even in polygamous households. But, unfortunately for our sensibilities, this story does not end there but continues in this fashion:

> With that she released the heron and it flew away. But as it went, it gouged out one of her eyes.

I recognize that there may be something so outlandish and grotesque about such a series of betrayals that an audience could find it laughable. [49] But the teaching or moral with which this story ends is one that would apply to a significant proportion of the African stories that we have available. "When you see water flowing uphill, it means that someone is repaying a kindness." [50]

To draw such a moral is, of course, to repudiate selfishness and betrayal. But it is also to recognize, and one story after another bears this out, that one should not expect much gratitude in this world. Is not the teaching of that lesson likely to discourage kindness and self-sacrifice? The disbelief with which Westerners greet such stories is echoed in an account that reached us from Rwanda during the 1994 massacres:

> "To be in the middle of all this, to watch them turn from the most wonderful, the most smiling, the most gentle of people, to such treacherous murderers is beyond comprehension," said Dr. Per Housmann, a dentist who runs the Adventist clinic [in Kigali, Rwanda]. "It is almost as if someone flips a switch." [51]

No doubt, explanations (grounded in a long history of abuses and grievances, some of them due to colonial mismanagement) can be developed to help account for such atrocities, just as explanations can be developed to help account for what the highly cultured Germans did to millions of their victims during World War II, and what the Europeans and Americans did to millions of civilians in the bombing of cities during the same war. [52] But such explanations should not keep us from being appalled at what we witness— and from attempting to figure out what these aberrations suggest about the souls of a people.

Among the aberrations in the collections of African stories are slavery, cannibalism (with several stories even of the casual eating of mothers by their own children), and betrayals (sometimes just for the fun of it, it seems) of relatives and friends. On the other hand, an eminent Senegalese poet and statesman recorded a condemnation of white men as cannibals for what they have done to African life. [53] And Africans could describe their colonial masters as men who practiced "the art of conquering without being in the right." [54] In more ways than one, therefore, the Westerner who studies ancient African thought should be open to seeing himself better as a result of, as well as a condition for, such an inquiry. [55]

VIII

I suspect that the moral ambiguity which we find in African stories is intimately related to another peculiar feature of the old African stories: it is often difficult to figure out why things happen in the way they do. "Cause and effect" relations do not seem to be regarded the way they are in the European (or, for that matter, in the Asian and many other) stories that I happen to know. Thus one can encounter in African stories the animate instruments and the repeated spontaneous resurrections to which I have referred. This is aside from the deliberate or obvious uses in sub-Saharan Africa of magic, spirit doctors, sorcerers, and the like. [56]

This makes it difficult for us to anticipate, or to remember, what happens in many African stories. All too often they simply do not make sense to us, even though there is no indication that anything has been omitted that the audience expects. Something of this may also be seen in modern African novels, such as three by Achebe: *Things Fall Apart, The Arrow of God,* and *A Man of the People*. Here, too, it can often be said, "It is almost as if someone flips a switch"—in the sense that dramatic and largely unanticipated reversals suddenly dominate the story. [57] Things can sometimes work out well in African stories, but the European observer often does not understand why. Perhaps a benevolent but mysterious ordering of the universe is seen as occasionally at work. It may even be believed that the ultimate government of the world is well-disposed to the living things of the earth. Animism and witchcraft, for good as well as for ill, find a fertile field here. [58]

Things can be expected to work out fairly well in adverse circumstances when there are, as is sometimes assumed in African stories and is often still evident in African life, family cohesiveness, respect for elders, and what we call the work ethic. It has been pointed out that Africans have a love of justice. [59] The subordination of cause-and-effect considerations in storytelling may contribute to a kind of vitality among the Africans, a vitality reflected in the music, especially that of the drum, and in the colors and sculpture that have proved so influential in twentieth-century Western art. [60]

<h1 style="text-align:center">IX</h1>

The general order that tends to assert itself in African thought is grounded in communalism, not individualism, however self-interested the popular (somewhat Odyssean) Trickster figure may be. Such communalism can even find all forms of life to be intimately interconnected. Along with this there is in the old stories an organization of human life in fairly small communities where everyone knows everyone else who matters. [61]

One may even wonder whether the malevolent cunning and extreme selfishness in many of the old stories were a kind of reaction to, if not "compensation" for or relief from, the pervasiveness and intensity of the constraints that everyone had to live with. [62] Perhaps that intensity contributes also to the fierceness that tribal conflicts provoke. The passions and aggressiveness that are routinely suppressed among one's kin can find "legit-

Dancers from a small section of Kenya called Chuka. In all African cultures, dance, music, and song help define the role of the individual and the group within the community.

imate" expression either in stories about social relations or against outsiders who can come to be regarded as barely human. [63] In critical respects, tribalism is like individualism, but on a much larger scale: the personal and the intimate, rather than the political, color one's actions. It is no wonder, then, that a continent that is still very much dominated by tribalism as well as by a "world view" strongly influenced by beliefs in spirits and witchcraft, should generally be in chaos, politically and economically speaking. [64]

Deficiencies with respect to the political, as distinguished from the tribal, may even have contributed to the centuries-long African susceptibility to slavery at the hands of ruthless exploiters both among Africans and among outsiders. But there was also a remarkable resiliency in the African character, which permitted so many Africans to submit to and to survive (if not eventually to benefit from) North American enslavement and cruelty in a way that the perhaps more spirited (and hence less resilient) North American Indians could not. [65]

Richard Weaver has suggested that the "mind of logical simplicity," such as is promoted by modern bourgeois society, is ill-equipped to deal with those "regions where mystery and contingency are recognized," "a world of terrifying reality to which the tidy moralities" of contemporary Western life do not seem applicable. [66] He then adds:

Owambo girls shown with their fishing baskets. The people known as the Owambo, for whom the region they inhabit is named, consist of seven different tribes that populate about half of Namibia.

An anthropologist related to me that certain Negro tribes of West Africa have a symbol for the white man consisting of a figure seated on the deck of a steamer in a position of stiffest rigidity. The straight, uncompromising lines are the betrayal; the primitive artist has caught the white man's unnatural rigor, which contrasts, ominously for him, with the native's sinuous adaptation. [67]

X

What is the African grasp of that which we know as nature? This is an underlying question in our effort to understand the ancient African stories and hence African thought. The Egyptians may have blurred the distinctions between the living and the dead; the Africans may have blurred the distinctions between the human and the non-human, even between the animate and the inanimate. One form that many African stories take is that of efforts to account for what we consider natural phenomena (especially what we regard as instinctive behavior by animals) as results of "historic" events, often with acts of will (sometimes by a divinity) following upon critical events, thereby permanently establishing the characteristics of a species. [68]

The distinctions blurred here may permit, if they do not contribute to, the widespread popularity in Africa of animism and witchcraft. These can take the form among Africans in the Western hemisphere (especially when combined with Christian elements) of voodooism, the Santeira cult, and the like. [69] This is related to what I have suggested about "cause and effect"—and this, in turn, bears upon the African sense of time, which has long seemed to be markedly different (in some ways better, in some ways worse) than that in the West. This ill equips Africans for—or, should we say, this spares them from?—thoroughgoing and hence often dehumanizing industrialization. [70]

The fact that in many old African stories things somehow fit together and work out in desirable ways that we do not expect or understand may mean that the ancient African storytellers did not have the grasp of nature that we in the West do, a grasp among us that goes back in effect to philosophical and other developments in Greece and Rome (influenced thereafter by the Bible) some two thousand years ago. It may also mean, of course, that Africans grasp something about the very nature of things that we Westerners have never grasped or have had to give up in pursuit of the enlightenment and progress that we treasure. [71]

XI

The subtlety and rationality, in the Western sense, of ancient African thought are suggested by the not-infrequent recourse in African stories to well-constructed riddles of some complexity, a recourse more frequent there than in other collections of ancient stories that I have seen from other peoples.

Here is one version of the simpler riddling stories:

An old man had three children, all boys. When they had grown up to
manhood, he called them together and told them that now he was very
old and no longer able to provide, even for himself. He ordered them to
go out and bring him food and clothing.

The three brothers set out, and after a very long while they came to a
large river. As they had gone on together for such a time, they decided
that once they got across they would separate. The eldest told the
youngest to take the middle road, and the second to go to the right,
while he himself would go to the left. Then, in a year's time, they would
come back to the same spot.

So they parted, and at the end of a year, as agreed, they found their way
back to the riverside. The eldest asked the youngest what he had gotten
during his travels, and the boy replied: "I have nothing but a mirror,
but it has wonderful power. If you look into it, you can see all over the
country, no matter how far away." When asked, in turn, what he had
gotten, the second brother replied: "Only a pair of sandals that are so
full of power, that if one puts them on one can walk at once to any place
in the country in one step." Then, the eldest himself, said: "I, too, have
obtained but little, a small calabash of medicine, that is all. But let us
look into the mirror and see how father fares."

The youngest produced his mirror, and they all looked into it and saw
that their father was already dead and that even the funeral custom was
finished. Then the elder said: "Let us hasten home and see what we can
do." So the second brought out his sandals, and all three placed their
feet inside them and, immediately, they were borne to their father's
grave. Then the eldest shook the medicine out of his bag, and poured
it over the grave. At once their father arose, as if nothing had been the
matter with him. Now which of these three sons has performed the
best? [72]

Notice how the authority of, as well as a duty to, a father is taken
for granted. [73]

The African riddling story, for which there is neither an obvious nor a
"trick" solution, reflects an awareness of limitations. Considerable sophisti-
cation is exhibited. [74] What *is* obvious is that the story is so designed as to
invite and permit extended discussion among listeners. Such stories, if they
are to endure, cannot have been crafted without a reliable grasp of how things
work, if not perhaps of what makes them work as they do. [75] Audience
participation seems to be taken for granted. Perhaps that is also true for
many of the other African stories that we find puzzling or incomprehensible:
the audience may have been expected to suggest explanations and to account
otherwise for "cause and effect." Such audience participation, or rather social
involvement, might be seen in this country in the lively responses depended
upon by preachers in African-American church services. Common sense and
the general experience of the community can be brought to bear upon what
the storyteller says, thereby filling out a story in such a way as to permit the

Audience participation is common in African storytelling. "Such audience participation, or rather social involvement, might be seen in this country in the lively responses depended upon by preachers in African-American church services."

audience to consider it just as much theirs as it is the storyteller's. This can make for a richness of communal discourse that we are no longer familiar with at a time when our "entertainment" encourages us to be much more passive. It is like the difference between playing a musical recording in one's home and gathering around a piano to sing. [76]

To whom should the prize in the story of the three sons go? To the son with the mirror, to the son with the sandals, or to the son with the medicine? The answer to this question should not depend upon whether such communication, travel, or healing are now routinely possible. That is not what the story seems to be about. [77]

XII

The constancy of human nature (whether or not nature is explicitly recognized as such) may be seen in how certain stories are responded to. We can see in the African stories some that may be variations upon stories taken from the Bible. [78] Other stories are similar to, but yet sometimes quite different from, counterparts in Europe. [79]

Particularly illuminating is an African story shared with Aesop. Perhaps the two stories—one from Greece, the other from Ghana—were first put into circulation about the same time. I suspect that one of them was influenced by the other. What is more intriguing here is not which of the two might have been first, but rather what is distinctive to each version. Most intriguing of all, perhaps, is that the subtlety and humor of the episode must have appealed both to Greek and to African audiences. Here is the Greek version:

> Two friends were traveling along the same road. When a bear suddenly appeared, one of them quickly climbed a tree and hid. The other was about to be caught but fell down on the ground and played dead. When the bear put its muzzle up close and smelled all around him, he held his breath, for they say that the animal will not touch a dead body. When the bear went away, the man up in the tree asked him what the bear had said in his ear. He replied, "Not to travel in the future with friends who won't stand by you in danger." [80]

The moral associated with this Aesopian fable is, "The story shows that hardships test true friends." [81]

Now here is the African version, in which the animal is a lion:

> There were once two friends, Kwasi and Kwaku, and one day they went to the bush. They had been playing there for some time when they saw a lion coming. Straightway, Kwasi climbed the nearest tree. Kwaku tried to follow him, but he couldn't climb very well, and he had to give up. He was very frightened and called up to his friend, "Eh, Kwasi, I can't climb. What shall I do?" Kwasi said, "Ah, I don't know, you must look out for yourself."

> Now Kwaku had heard somewhere that a lion doesn't eat dead meat, so he lay down and feigned death. The lion came up to him and sniffed around for a while, and then went off. Kwasi came down from the tree and said to Kwaku, "Oh, Kwaku, I thought you were dead. What was the lion saying to you just now?"

> Kwaku told Kwasi, "Well, Kwasi, he said a lot of things to me, but the most important one was that I should choose my friends better. So when we leave here, you and I will part company for good." [82]

A few differences are worth noticing, however briefly. The African story is almost twice the length of the Greek one. [83] The personal touch is provided in the African story by naming the two friends. The African version has the desperate companion ask his friend for help, only to be explicitly rebuffed. Similarly, when the survivor of the lion's attentions reports in the African version on what the lion had said, he makes explicit what he intends to do with the lion's advice.

Is explicitness, or a kind of expansiveness, more likely in African than in Greek stories? Is there in this a kind of realism, or less reliance here upon the imagination of the audience? Or does it reflect primarily the difference between an oral and a written presentation?

I suspect that Aesop's Greek audience did not believe that the bear said anything to the "corpse," but merely nosed around it—and that the speech given to the bear is entirely the man's. What, on the other hand, would an African audience have been inclined to believe—and why? [84]

I believe that the differences between these two accounts are worth exploring. Perhaps one can begin with speculations about why the Aesop story has the two friends travelling together while the African story has them playing in the nearby bush. [85]

XIII

A few more points about the African stories that I have discussed in this essay can usefully be noticed before we conclude. Erotic relations are far less important in these African stories than they would be in stories among us today in the West. A village mentality is evident in these stories, as may be seen also in much of the life today in even the larger African (as also in the larger Greek) cities. One can easily lose sight of the "national" interest in such circumstances; it may not even be given lip-service (as may be seen in Achebe's *A Man of the People*). We are surprised to learn, in Achebe's *Things Fall Apart,* that one of the great battles (if not wars) in his hero's youth had seen only a dozen men killed. [86]

Our inquiry on this occasion obliges us to wonder, what is the truly human life? What does "Africa" contribute to the "mix" that the human race, which was once divided up more distinctly than it is now, seems to be developing worldwide? In a sense, much of what distinguishes the United States from Europe can be attributed to the contributions that Africa has made to this country, far more than it seems to have made to Europe. [87] Is the special vitality and resiliency, as well as the unpredictability, of American life in part due to the African elements among us?

All this bears upon the worldwide political and social developments to be expected in the twenty-first century. A commentary both upon traditional African thought and upon the special influence of the United States in the modern world may be found in W. E. B. Du Bois's 1897 declaration:

We are Americans, not only by birth and by citizenship, but by our political ideals, our language, our religion. Farther than that, our Americanism does not go. At that point, we are Negroes, *members of a vast historic race that from the very dawn of creation has slept,* but half awakening in the dark forests of its African fatherland. We are the first fruits of this new nation, the harbinger of that black to-morrow which is yet destined to soften the whiteness of the Teutonic to-day. We are that people whose subtle sense of song has given American fairy tales its only touch of pathos and humor amid its mad money-getting plutocracy. As such, it is our duty to conserve our physical powers, our intellectual endowments, our spiritual ideals; as a race we must strive by race organization, by race solidarity, by race unity in the realization of that broader humanity which freely recognizes differences in men, but sternly deprecates inequality in their opportunities of development. [88]

Particularly significant here, in considering how African thought is to be assessed, is Du Bois's insistence that the African-American, as "the harbinger of [a] black to-morrow," was in the vanguard of the African people of the world. This suggests that the West, or at least the United States, has provided Africans something that they, insofar as they are a distinct race, must have if they are to come to terms with the modern world. In 1903 Du Bois argued, "[T]here are to-day no truer exponents of the pure human spirit of the Declaration of Independence than the American Negroes . . ." He also said on that occasion, "[W]e black men seem the sole oasis of simple faith and reverence in a dusty desert of dollars and smartness." [89]

But one caution is in order for Africans assessing what they might usefully, and safely, take from the West. It would be a mistake for Africans to do what all too many Americans (including, of course, African-Americans) tend to do: that is, it is a mistake to make far more of *action* than of *understanding*, a tendency which does not appreciate sufficiently what the discovery of *nature* in the West suggests about the best possible life for human beings.

Even so, it is humane (as well as in our interest as a people dedicated to the pursuit of happiness)—it is humane and just to respect Colin Turnbull's loving description of the life of the Pygmies, perhaps the most "ancient" and hence the "youngest" of the peoples of Africa:

Pygmy women and children groom each other in Zaire. ". . . the Pygmies, perhaps the most 'ancient' and hence the 'youngest' of the peoples of Africa . . ."

The Pygmies were more than curiosities to be filmed, and their music was more than a quaint sound to be put on records. They were a people who had found in the forest something that made their life more than just worth living, something that made it, with all its hardships and problems and tragedies, a wonderful thing of joy and happiness and free of care. [90]

This is a people which can treasure that great song of praise, a song which Socrates would have found intriguing, "If Darkness *is*, Darkness is Good." [91]

1. Pliny the Elder, *Natural History*, VIII, 77 (an ancient Greek proverb). *See,* on race, law, and civilization, George Anastaplo, *Human Being and Citizen: Essays on Virtue, Freedom, and the Common Good* (Chicago: Swallow Press, 1975), pp. 175–99. *See also,* note 46 below.

2. *See* Anastaplo, "An Introduction to North American Indian Thought" (*GIT* 1993, 253–86). *See also,* notes 46 and 47 below.

3. Similarly, the many Christian sects (and the Jews as well) probably appeared alike in critical respects to various Asian observers first exposed to the West. Similarly, also, the Unionists and Confederates who fought each other so desperately in North America between 1861 and 1865 could appear to the rest of the world as very much alike.

4. In a sense, the sub-Saharan Africans, like the Jews and the Greeks, may have found their highest modern development in their *diaspora* rather than in their homeland.

5. *See,* e.g., Naguib Mahfouz, *The Cairo Trilogy* (New York: Doubleday, 1990–92), vol. III (*Sugar Street*), pp. 43–44.

6. "Africa," *Encyclopædia Britannica*, 15th edition, (1993 printing), vol. 1, p. 132.

7. *See,* e.g., Colin M. Turnbull, *The Forest People: A Study of the Pygmies of the Congo* (Anchor Books; Doubleday & Company, 1962), pp. 4–6. *See also,* note 62 below.

8. *See,* on my impressions of Cairo, Anastaplo, "An Introduction to Islamic Thought: The Koran" (*GIT* 1989, 278, nn. 90, 91, 93).

9. *See,* "Africa," *EB,* vol. 1, p. 133. *See also,* Edward Gibbon, *The Decline and Fall of the Roman Empire* (New York: Modern Library, n.d.), III, 179–80 (chap. 51). (*GBWW* I: 41, 253–88; II: 38, 253–88).

10. *See* Plato, *Timaeus* 22B. (*GBWW* I: 7, 444; II: 6, 444).

11. *Aesop Without Morals,* Lloyd W. Daly, trans. (New York: Thomas Yoseloff, 1961), pp. 219–20.

12. Ibid., p. 301. This is No. 11 in the Bude edition of Aesop. It does not appear to be in the Penguin edition.

13. See *Larousse Encyclopedia of Mythology* (London: Paul Hamlyn, 1959), p. 47. Still, Plutarch suggested, "the element of health [was, among the Egyptians,] no less important than that of piety." *Isis and Osiris* 383B (in *Plutarch's Moralia,* vol. V, trans. Frank Cole Babbitt [Cambridge: Loeb Classical Library; Harvard University Press, 1936]).

14. Ancient Egypt is referred to by a Mahfouz character, upon visiting the Great Pyramids, as "a nation whose most notable manifestations are tombs and corpses!" Mahfouz, *The Cairo Trilogy,* vol. II (*Palace of Desire*), p. 178. *See also,* note 33 below.

15. *See,* on the inept efforts made to preserve in perpetuity the body of Mao Tse-Tung, Zhisui Li, *The Private Life of Chairman Mao* (New York: Random House, 1994), pp. 16–25, 629–30. *See also* note 35 below. *See,* on Egyptian eroticism, Lise Manniche, *Sexual Life in Ancient Egypt* (London: KPI Ltd., 1987).

16. *See,* on the Hindus, Anastaplo, "An Introduction to Hindu Thought: The *Bhagavad Gītā*" (GIT 1985, 258–85). *See,* on the Muslims, note 8 above. *See,* on Nirvana,

Anastaplo, "An Introduction to Buddhist Thought" (*GIT* 1992, 218–47). *See,* on the African blending of the spiritual and the physical, note 42 below.

17. Christianity, for this reason, may also make tragedy impossible. Whether, however the common man was as much influenced in North Africa by the dominant ancient Egyptian priestly doctrines as he later was in Europe by the dominant Christian church doctrines is uncertain. Consider also this New Kingdom love poetry:

> If I stare hard enough at the gate
> My darling will come to me.
> Eyes on the road, ears straining,
> I wait for him who avoids me,
> Because loving him is all I can do.
> My heart won't shut up about him.
> It sends me a fleet-footed messenger
> That goes about everywhere, telling me:
> "He deceives you," and more,
> "He has found another woman
> Who dazzles his eyes."
> Why do you torture me with leaving?"

Elizabeth J. Sherman, "Delving into the mysteries of women's lives in old Egypt," *Washington Times,* Oct. 10, 1993, p. B7 (citing Papyrus Harris 500). (This author, who has a doctorate in Egyptology, dismisses Martin Bernal's *Black Athena* (1987) as "bloated and garbled" and Erich von Däniken's *Chariot of the Gods?* (1970) as "laughable." *Ibid. See also,* Jonathan Rauch, "Academic Left vs. Science," *Wall Street Journal,* April 19, 1994, p. A16. *See,* as well, note 37 below.

18. *Ancient Egyptian Literature,* Miriam Lichtheim, ed. (Berkeley: University of California Press, 1973), vol. I, p. 17. *See also, The Book of the Dead,* E. A. Wallis Budge, ed. (New York: Arkana [Penguin Group], 1989), pp. 26, 360f, 366f.

19. *The Book of the Dead,* p. 155. A dim reflection of Egyptian formulae and rituals may be seen in the Masonic rites drawn upon in Mozart's *The Magic Flute* (1791). *See* note 27 below.

20. *The Book of the Dead,* p. 236.

21. Ibid., p. 243. *See also,* ibid., pp. 233, 269, 273, 284, 302, 306, 417.

22. *See,* e.g., ibid., p. 14.

23. Ibid., p. ccxi.

24. Ibid., p. ccxi.

25. *Larousse Encyclopedia of Mythology,* p. 9.

26. Ibid., p. 48. The uraeus was a representation of the sacred asp on the headdress of ancient Egyptian rulers. It served as a symbol of sovereignty. Consider the response to all this by Plutarch, who was somewhat of a Platonist:

> But the great majority of the Egyptians, in doing service to the animals themselves and in treating them as gods, have not only filled their sacred offices with ridicule and derision, but this is the least of the evils connected with their silly practices.

Isis and Osiris 379E. *See also,* note 27 below. *See,* on "doing service to the animals" in sub-Saharan Africa, John S. Mbiti, *African Religions and Philosophy* (Garden City, New York: Anchor Books; Doubleday & Co., 1970), p. 62f. *See also,* note 42 below.

27. *Larousse Encyclopedia of Mythology,* p. 9. See *Isis and Osiris,* in Plutarch's *Moralia,* vol. V, pp. 1–191. The cult of Isis and Osiris is important both for Masonic rituals and in Mozart's *The Magic Flute. See* note 19 above.

28. The possible influences here upon later Christian imagery are obvious. The Israelites evidently recalled many Egyptian beliefs and practices that they wanted to have nothing to do with once they were liberated. One consequence to this day seems to be the Jewish practice of immediate burial without treatment of the corpse. *See* note 33 below.

29. Consider, also, the distinctions made in Homer's *Iliad* between the names used by human beings and those used by the gods for the same persons and things.

30. *See,* e.g., Hellmut Fritzsche, "Of Things That Are Not," in John A. Murley, Robert L. Stone, and William T. Braithwaite, eds., *Law and Philosophy* (Athens, Ohio: Ohio University Press, 1992), vol. I, pp. 3–18.

31. *See* Plato, *Apology* 40A sq. (*GBWW* I: 7, 211; II: 6, 211).

32. Consider, for example, Socrates' lack of concern about what should be done with his corpse. *See* Plato, *Phaedo* (*GBWW* I: 7, 220–51; II: 6, 220–51). Compare the concern about such matters exhibited in Sophocles' *Antigone* (*GBWW* I: 5, 131–42; II: 4, 159–74). *See,* on the Socratic response to Antigone's (as well as to the Egyptian?) approach to these matters, Anastaplo, "On Trial: Explorations," *Loyola University of Chicago Law Journal,* vol. 22, p. 1054, n. 348 (1991). *See also,* ibid., pp. 846–54. *See,* as well, note 26 above.

33. *See* notes 16 and 28, above. *See also,* G. W. F. Hegel, *The History of Philosophy* (New York: Dover Publications 1956), pp. 217–18. *See,* as well, note 13 above and note 46 below.

34. See *Ancient Egyptian Literature,* vol. I, pp. 26–27, 48. *See also,* Turnbull, *The Forest People,* pp. 4–6. The story of *Homo sapiens,* we are told,

> appears to begin 1.8 million years ago, in the region of Africa south of the Sahara that is said to be the cradle of humanity, judging from the wealth of ancestral bones that have been found there. It was there that a species of early human [*Homo erectus*] lived a simple foraging existence, although its way of life was no doubt considerably more sophisticated than that of any ape-like animal which had lived before.

Clive Gamble, "March of the Timewalkers," *The Independent on Sunday,* April 10, 1994. p. 66.

35. *See,* on African funerals, Mbiti, *African Religions and Philosophy,* p. 195f. Much more effort had to be made among the Africans in their sub-Saharan climate, than among the Egyptians in their climate, to preserve things, including corpses and art. (In addition, the Egyptians had much more stone to work with.) Conditions in sub-Saharan Africa led to constant improvisation by the Africans, especially as both rapid decay and a steady growth of vegetation confronted them in their more fertile areas.

36. *Larousse Encyclopedia of Mythology,* p. 480. *See also,* notes 42 and 58 below.

37. Far more is said by me in this article about sub-Saharan thought than about the much better known Egyptian thought. One opinion of a few of our contemporaries in this country is that the Egyptians are substantially Negroid in origins. Another such opinion is that these Egyptians are primarily responsible for the flowering of Greek civilization. *See,* e.g., Lerone Bennett, Jr., *Before the Mayflower: A History of Black America* (New York: Penguin Books, 1993), pp. 3–9. These are opinions for which there has yet to be developed sufficient evidence to persuade many scholars. *See,* e.g., note 17 above. More persuasive among scholars today is the argument that Joseph Conrad's influential *Heart of Darkness* is a distorted account of the life of the natives on that other great African river, the Congo. *See,* e.g., Chinua Achebe, *Hopes and Impediments* (New York: Doubleday, 1989), pp. 1–20.

38. *See,* on Edwin Muir's "The Animals," Anastaplo, *The Artist as Thinker: From Shakespeare to Joyce* (Athens, Ohio: Ohio University Press, 1983), pp. 257–63. Consider, also, the discovery of the *Gilgamesh* epic which unearthed a remarkable but long-forgotten way of life. *See* Anastaplo, "An Introduction to Mesopotamian Thought: The *Gilgamesh* Epic" (*GIT* 1986, 288–313). Compare Robert Farris Thompson, *Flash of the Spirit: African and Afro-American Art and Philosophy* (New York: Vintage Books, 1984), pp. xiv, xv, 3, 13, 227, 298 n. 1. The accomplishments of Yoruban letters, city-building, and art are summed up thus:

> Like ancient Greece, Yorubaland consisted of self-sufficient city-states characterized by artistic and poetic richness. The Yoruba themselves cherish the creators of their aesthetic world, as one of their hunters' ballads states: "not the

brave alone, they also praise those who know how to shape images in wood or compose a song."

Ibid., p. 5. *See also,* notes 50 and 91.

39. *See,* e.g., Herbert J. Storing, ed., *What Country Have I? Political Writings of Black Americans* (New York: St. Martin's Press, 1970) pp. 16, 19, 23 (Augustus Washington), 32–33, 38–40 (Frederick Douglass). Compare Josiah C. Nott, *Two Lectures on the Natural History of the Caucasian and Negro Races* (1844), in Drew Giplin Faust, ed., *The Ideology of Slavery: Proslavery Thought in the Antebellum South, 1830–1860* (Baton Rouge: Louisiana State University Press, 1981), p. 235. *See,* on nature, note 71 below. *See also,* note 1 above and notes 53, 65, and 89 below.

40. Molara Ogundipe-Leslie, a Nigerian writer, replied, upon being asked whether the African woman writer was different from her counterparts elsewhere:

> I don't know if the African woman writer is different from woman writers in other parts of the world. I can only hazard some guesses . . . Because of the definitely patriarchal arrangements of the society, publicly and privately, most women bear a double workload, if not a triple one. Hence they have even less time and leisure than their western counterparts to think or write.

Adeola James, ed., *In Their Own Voices: African Women Writers Talk* (London: James Currey, 1990), p. 67. Virginia Woolf has also developed this theme in *A Room of One's Own* (1929). Compare note 61 below.

41. *See,* on how slavery can be taken for granted in African stories, Kathleen Arnott, ed., *African Myths and Legends* (Oxford: Oxford University Press, 1989), pp. 144, 179, 184. *See also,* Howard W. French, "On Slavery, Africans Say the Guilt is Theirs, Too," *New York Times,* Dec. 27, 1994, p. A5. *See,* as well, Vincent Harding, *There Is a River: The Black Struggle for Freedom in America* (New York: Harcourt Brace Jovanovich, 1981), pp. 6–7; note 71 below.

42. *See,* on the Bible, Anastaplo, "On Trial," pp. 821f, 854f, 882f, 900f. *See,* on Homer, Anastaplo, *The Artist as Thinker,* p. 492. *See,* on the Confucian *Analects,* Anastaplo, "An Introduction to Confucian Thought" (*GIT* 1984, 125–70). *See,* on the *Bhagavad Gītā,* on the Koran, note 8 above, and on Buddhism, note 16 above. *See also,* note 46 below. It has been noticed, "Africans are notoriously religious, and each people has its own religious system with a set of beliefs and practices. . . . We speak of African traditional religions in the plural because there are about one thousand African peoples (tribes), and each has its own religious system." Mbiti, *African Religions and Philosophy,* p. 1. *See* note 26 above and note 58 below.

43. *See* "Africa," *EB,* vol. 1, p. 133.

44. *See* note 2 above and notes 46 and 47 below.

45. "Ngugi [wa Thiong'o] has argued that a study of the Oral Tradition would be 'important' not only in rehabilitating our minds, but also in helping African writers to innovate and break away from the European mainstream." Steven R. Carter, "Decolonization and Detective Fiction," in Eugene Schleh, ed., *Mysteries of Africa* (Bowling Green, Ohio: Bowling Green State University Popular Press, 1991), p. 87. Ngugi has questioned whether African experience can be honestly and fully portrayed in a European language or art form. *See* ibid., p. 74. *See,* on an advocacy of *négritude* as resistance to that European assimilationism which suppresses African culture, R. N. Egudu, *Modern African Poetry and the African Predicament* (London: Macmillan, 1978), pp. 30–32.

46. *See,* for exceptions, some of the stories in Arnott, ed., *African Myths and Legends,* e.g., pp. 32–34, 53–55. (But, it should be noticed, the stories in this collection have been "retold" by the editor.) This is quite different from the typical Western reader's impression of, say, many of the North American Indian stories (collected, as the African stories probably have been, mainly by missionaries and anthropologists). It is only prudent to record the following caution here:

> Preliterate societies have their own kinds of wisdom, no doubt, and primitive Papuans probably have a better grasp of their myths than most educated Amer-

icans have of their own literature. But without years of study we can't begin to understand a culture very different from our own. The fair thing, therefore, is to make allowance for what we outsiders cannot hope to fathom in another society and grant that, as members of the same species, primitive men are as mysterious or as monstrous as any other branch of humankind.

Saul Bellow, "Papuans and Zulus," *New York Times,* March 10, 1994, p. A12.

It is also prudent to notice the observations, a half-century ago, by an eminent anthropologist who intended "to correct the erroneous impression, still widely current, that native African folk-literature is mainly animal tales and to bring home the fact that it is possibly the most sophisticated and realistic of all aboriginal literature." Paul Radin, ed., *African Folktales* (New York: Schocken Books, 1983), p. vii. Professor Radin noticed the cynicism in some of these folktales, even as he insisted that "African realism is not always nor generally accompanied by cynicism." (Ibid., p. 5) "Yet, in the main," he added, "little romanticism is found in African myths and definitely no sentimentality. It is emphatically not a literature in which wish-fulfillment plays a great role, not one where one can assume that the hero will triumph at the end or that wrongs will always be righted. How are we to explain this?" (Ibid., p. 5) The Radin explanation includes these observations (ibid., pp. 8–9):

It goes without saying that the conflict and disorganization engendered in people by a forced acculturation extending over so many centuries would leave a permanent residue in their oral literature. Folktales which were predominantly wish-fulfillment fantasies . . . were pushed into the background. Human heroes with plots taken from purely human situations forged to the front. In the latter, with uncompromising realism, man was pitted against man, as is inevitably the case when individuals are living in an economically and politically disturbed and insecure world.

Assuredly we have the right to infer that it is largely because these people are living in an insecure and semi-chaotic world, with its loss of values and its consequent inward demoralization, that cruelty and wanton murder loom so large in many of their tales. So it does among the Eskimo, where the environment is so persistently inimical, and so it did in the Russia of the nineteenth century.

See, on the differences as well as the similarity between "the Jewish and Negro question," Anastaplo, "On Trial," p. 1058, n. 398. *See,* on the Hobbesian man evident in "an economically and politically disturbed and insecure world," Laurence Berns, "Thomas Hobbes," in Leo Strauss and Joseph Cropsey, eds., *History of Political Philosophy* (Chicago: Rand McNally, 1963), p. 354.

47. The only things comparable in the North American Indian stories are the scalping parties that young men might go on and the fiendish delight taken in the torture of prisoners before execution. But these atrocities do not dominate the Indian stories we happen to have, even though there is the reference in the Declaration of Independence to "the merciless Indian Savages." *See,* on famines being regarded as routine in Africa, Arnott, ed., *African Myths and Legends,* pp. 82, 83, 108, 124. *See,* for the foiling of the bad, ibid., pp. 15, 24, 31, 186f. *See,* for gratuitous cruelty, ibid., pp. 77, 93, 104. *See,* for the unexplained kindness of a witch, ibid., p. 148.

48. Roger D. Abrahams, ed., *African Folktales* (New York: Pantheon Books, 1983), p. 145.

49. Penina Muhando, a Tanzanian playwright has this to say about African audiences that she has observed:

There is definitely an African aesthetic, which has been down-played because of our colonial history. There are certain elements of the African traditional performance which can best be understood and enjoyed by an African audience. . . . There is still much more to be done with the African tradition. To give this simple example, I have noticed the way the African audience laughs, even when the play is tragic. The point is, that Africans are not callous people, it doesn't mean they enjoy seeing people murdered, *it means they have a different perception.* Maybe they are laughing at the perfection of the acting, seeing that the actor has managed to imitate the action so well. I don't know, but these are things to be researched.

James, ed., *In Their Own Voices,* p. 88 (emphasis added). *See,* for comparable betrayals, Aristophanes' *Birds.*

50. *See* Abrahams, ed., *African Folktales,* p. 145. Consider the comment we sometimes hear, "No good deed goes unpunished." Compare Arnott, ed., *African Myths and Legends,* p. 94f. But *see* note 46, above, ibid., pp. 29–30, 135–39, 150–52. Compare, also, the magnanimity exhibited by African warriors at the end of the 1963 movie, *Zulu. See* "The Zulu Warrior: Then and Now," *Wall Street Journal,* May 12, 1994, p. A15. Compare, as well, Thompson, *Flash of the Spirit,* p. 13:

> Generosity, the highest form of morality in Yoruba traditional terms, is suggested yet another way: by the symbolized offering of something by a person to a higher force through the act of kneeling.

See, for a more comprehensive account of Yoruban thought, ibid., pp. 5–6. *See also* note 38 above and notes 85 and 91 below.

51. William E. Schmidt, "Refugee Missionaries from Rwanda Speak of Their Terror, Grief and Guilt," *New York Times,* April 12, 1994, p. A6.

52. *See,* on the German atrocities, Anastaplo, "On Trial," 977–94. *See,* on the bombing of cities, Anastaplo, "On Freedom: Explorations," *Oklahoma City University Law Review,* vol. 17, pp. 645–66 (1992).

53. Leopold Sedar Senghor, *Prose and Poetry* (London: Oxford University Press, 1965), p. 29:

> "White men are cannibals," an old sage from my own country told me a few years ago. "They have no respect for life." It is this process of devouring which they call "humanizing nature" or more exactly "domesticating nature." "But," went on the old sage, who had seen and heard much and reflected deeply, "what they don't take into account, these whites, is that life cannot be domesticated, nor especially can God who is the source of all life, in whom all life shares." And finally: "It is life which makes human, not death. I am afraid it may all turn out very badly. The whites by their madness will in the end bring down trouble upon us."

See, on African eroticism, sensuality, and musical sense, ibid., pp. 30–32. "George Hardy wrote: 'The most civilized African, even in a dinner jacket, still quivers at the sound of a drum.' He was right." Ibid., p. 31. *See also,* note 89 below. Compare note 39 above.

54. Achebe, *Hopes and Impediments,* p. 52.

55. *See,* on the moral conditions for a sound understanding of human conduct, Anastaplo, *The Artist as Thinker,* pp. 1–14. *See,* on helpfulness that does *not* depend upon a sound understanding, Arnott, ed., *African Myths and Legends,* pp. 114, 121f. *See also,* Senghor, *Prose and Poetry,* p. 82: "Under the forms of the Lion, the Elephant, the Hyena, the Crocodile, the Hare and the Old Women, we read plainly with our ears of our social structures and our passions, the good as well as the bad." *See,* as well, ibid., p. 85.

56. The ancient Egyptian stories now available to us do not show everyday life confronting such events, however fanciful their pantheon may be.

57. *See,* on art and probability, Aristotle, *Poetics,* chap. 9. (*GBWW* I: 9, 686; II: 8, 686).

58. *See,* on animism, *Encyclopedia of Religion* (New York: Macmillan Company, 1987), vol. 1, p. 296; *Poems of Black Africa,* Wole Soyinka, ed. (New York: Hill and Wang, 1975), pp. 37f, 59f; Senghor, *Prose and Poetry,* pp. 29–30, 32, 34–35; Mbiti, *African Religions and Philosophy,* pp. 9–18, 97–118, note 36 above. *See,* on the spirit world of the ancestors in Africa, "Interview of Thomas Adeoye Lambo," *Omni,* Feb.

1992, p. 71. "In Africa, the gods are still alive." Ibid., p. 103. *See also,* Achebe, *Things Fall Apart* (London: Heineman, 1986), p. 114; note 78 below. *See,* on the curious but perhaps not irrational mixing of modern technology and traditional beliefs about spirits, the following account from Ethiopia:

> The Emperor [Haile Selassie] had lent [Lord Mountbatten's party] his personal Cadillac and motor-cycle escort, a signal honour but somewhat inconvenient, since every road they travelled was strewn with the bodies of peasants seeking to present petitions to what they imagined must be their imperial master. "Another charming habit of Ethiopians who believe themselves to be pursued by evil spirits is to dash across the road in front of the car, timing matters in such a way that they will just not be run over, while the evil spirit is of course cut off by the car."

Philip Ziegler, *Mountbatten: The Official Biography* (London: Collins, 1985), p. 511. But putting modern technology to good use, including against evil spirits, does not mean that the principles (or the ideas about nature) implicit in the modern science upon which modern technology is based are either understood or accepted. *See* note 42 above.

59. A fourteenth-century Muslim visitor to Mali reported, "The Negroes possess some admirable qualities. They are seldom unjust, and have a greater abhorrence of injustice than any other people." *See* Kevin Shillington, *History of Africa* (New York: St. Martin's Press, 1989), p. 99. *See also,* Lloyd A. Fallers, *Law without Precedent: Legal Ideas in Action in the Courts of Colonial Busoga* (Chicago: University of Chicago Press, 1969); Mbiti, *African Religions and Philosophy,* p. 266f.

60. *See* William Rubin, ed., *"Primitivism" in the 20th Century: Affinity of the Tribal and the Modern* (New York: Museum of Modern Art, 1984), e.g., vol. I, p. 125f.

61. *See* "Africa," *EB,* vol. I, p. 133. It is, we are told, an African adage. "It takes a village to raise a child." *See,* e.g., Barbara Ehrenreich, "The Bright Side of Overpopulation," *Time,* Sept. 26, 1994, p. 86. When the African community is properly constituted, we are also told, the place of woman is preeminent. *See* Senghor, *Prose and Poetry,* pp. 44–45. Compare Mwana Kupona, who lived during the first half of the nineteenth century. She sums up her advice to her daughter on how to minister to her husband with this assurance:

> Be gay with him that he be amused. Do not oppose his authority. If he brings you ill God will defend you.

Anthology of Swahili Poetry, Ali A. Jahadhmy, ed. (London: Heineman, 1977), p. 33. *See,* on nature-based standards and the practice of female circumcision (which does seem to be common in "matriarchate" Africa), Larry Arnhart, "Feminism, Primatology, and Ethical Naturalism," *Politics and the Life Sciences,* August 1992, pp. 164–66, 177–78. *See also,* Mbiti, *African Religions and Philosophy,* pp. 165–71. *See,* as well, note 40 above and note 71 below. *See* on polygamy in Africa, ibid., p. 186f. Consider, also, ibid., p. 3.

62. Those constraints are graphically described in Colin Turnbull's remarkable account of life among the Pygmies of Central Africa. *See* note 7 above. *See also,* note 49 above and the text at notes 90 and 91 below.

63. Consider how the victims of Hitler and Stalin "had" to be spoken of by their oppressors. *See,* e.g., Anastaplo, "On Trial," p. 1089, n. 720. *See also,* note 39 above.

64. *See,* on Africa today, "Darkest Africa: Bits of it are degenerating into chaos," *The Economist,* Feb. 13, 1993, p. 17; Thomas W. Hazlett, "The Forgotten Continent," *Wall Street Journal,* Mar. 17, 1993, p. A12; Bill Keller, "Blind Eye: Africa Allows Its Tragedies To Take Their Own Course," *New York Times,* Aug. 7, 1994, sec. 4, p. 1; William Pfaff, "The Europeans should go back to Africa," *Chicago Tribune,* Aug. 14, 1994, sec. 4, p. 3; Liz Sly, "Africa: The Dream Erodes," *Chicago Tribune,* July 9, 1995, sec. 1, p. 1.

65. *See* Frederick Douglass, "The Destiny of Colored Americans," in Storing, *What Country Have I?,* p. 39. Apologists for African slavery also explained in this way why the Indians could not be enslaved:

> The Indian is by nature a savage, and a beast of the forest like the Buffalo—can exist in no other state, and is exterminated by the approach of civilization. You cannot make a slave of him like a Negro, his spirit is broken and he dies like a wild animal in a cage.

Nott, *Two Lectures,* p. 235. *See* note 39 above. Consider, as well, Harding, *This Is a River,* p. 7.

66. Richard M. Weaver, *Ideas Have Consequences* (Chicago: University of Chicago Press, 1948), p. 107. *See also,* note 42 above.

67. Ibid., pp. 107–08.

68. *See,* e.g., *Poems of Black Africa,* pp. 57–58 (a sequence of creations). This sort of thing may also be seen among other places, in North American Indian stories. *See also,* note 26 above.

69. *See,* on the shaping of species, Arnott, ed., *African Myths and Legends,* pp. 21, 32–34, 39, 53–55, 63, 104, 132, 134, 150f. *See,* on witchcraft in sub-Saharan Africa, ibid., pp. 93, 142f, 280; Mbiti, *African Religions and Philosophy,* p. 153f. *See,* on the terrors addressed by the European witch trials, Anastaplo, "Church and State: Explorations," *Loyola University of Chicago Law Journal,* vol. 19, pp. 65–86 (1987). Consider, on the terror of the dark among adults reported from still another part of the world, Paul Gauguin, *Noa Noa: The Tahitian Journal* (New York: Dover Publications, 1985), pp. 33–34. *See also,* note 78 below. Compare note 91 below.

70. *See,* on Adam Smith's approach to these matters, Anastaplo, *The Constitutionalist: Notes on the First Amendment* (Dallas: Southern Methodist University Press, 1971), p. 690, n. 42.

71. *See,* on nature as a guide to right living, Anastaplo, "Natural Law or Natural Right?", *Loyola of New Orleans Law Review,* vol. 38, p. 915 (1993). *See also,* notes 41 and 61 above.

72. Abrahams, ed., *African Folktales,* pp. 114–15.

73. *See also,* ibid., pp. 125, 131, 134; note 77 below. *See,* as well, ibid., the epigraph for the Abrahams volume.

74. Consider the title story in Frank R. Stockton, *The Lady, or the Tiger? and Other Stories* (New York: Charles Scribner's Sons, 1884). *See also,* Arnott, ed., *African Myths and Legends,* pp. 40–42.

75. Consider, on the use of "second sight" in a Greek village, Anastaplo, *The American Moralist: On Law, Ethics and Government* (Athens, Ohio: Ohio University Press, 1992) p. 388. *See* note 78 below.

76. *See,* on Willa Muir and the old games and songs of Scottish school children, Anastaplo, *The Constitutionalist,* p. 556, n. 136.

77. The story, or problem, might have to be changed if the powers inherent in one or more of the sons' possessions should become routine in their operations. We notice that it is taken for granted in this story that such powers are occasionally available to human beings, although nothing is said explicitly about how the powers happened to be allocated among the three sons. We should also notice that it is the eldest son who seems to direct the action throughout, once their father has spoken.

78. Or, some might say, these are stories that provide the basis for Biblical stories. *See,* for variations on the story of Joseph and his brothers, Arnott, ed., *African Myths and Legends,* pp. 160f, 195f, 200f. *See,* on the influence of Christianity upon Yoruban art and vice versa, Thompson, *Flash of the Spirit, passim. See* on Christianity and Islam in Africa, Mbiti, *African Religions and Philosophy,* p. 299f; note 42 above. *See also,* Larry Rohter, "In a Harsh Land, Faith at Christmas," *New York Times,* Dec. 25, 1994, sec. 4, pp. 1–10. *See,* as well notes 58, 69, and 75 above.

79. *See,* e.g., Jack Berry, ed., *West African Folktales* (Evanston: Northwestern University Press, 1991), pp. 146–47 (on the most efficient sequence of ferrying vulnerable things across a river). *See,* for a happy variation of the Oedipus story, Arnott, ed., *African Myths and Legends,* p. 167f.

80. *Aesop Without Morals,* p. 120.

81. Ibid., p. 274.

82. Berry, ed. *West African Folktales,* p. 144.

83. The typical Aesop fable is far shorter than the typical African story in the collections cited in this article.

84. *See,* on a lion's leaving corpses alone, William Shakespeare, *As You Like It,* IV, iii, 115. (*GBWW* I: 26, 620; II: 24, 620)

85. For Aesop's Greeks, it seems, such encounters with wild animals were not part of everyday life at home. Do the African names used here mean anything? It should also be observed that gratitude for favors received is not uncommon in the Aesop fables. *See,* e.g., *Aesop Without Morals,* pp. 156, 209. Compare note 48 above.

86. *See* Achebe, *Things Fall Apart,* p. 141.

87. *See* note 65 above. One great European exception, however, is Alexander Pushkin, the national poet of Russia. The contributions of the Jews in the United States are also special, partly because of the status first recognized for them here. *See,* for George Washington's 1790 letter to the Hebrew Congregation in Newport, Rhode Island, Anastaplo, *The Amendments to the Constitution,* p. 407, n. 69.

88. W. E. B. Du Bois, *Writings* (New York: The Library of America, 1986), p. 822 (emphasis added).

89. Ibid., p. 370. *See also,* note 61 (end), above. *See,* on certain dubious legacies from Africa (including a tradition with an occasional human sacrifice), ibid., p. 499. *See also,* "Interview of Thomas Adeoye Lambo," *Omni,* February 1992, p. 96:

> There's no doubt human sacrifice was practiced as recently as ten years ago. Certain tribes in remote parts may still practice it. Practitioners [of human sacrifice] claim that the oracle or some other voice tells them the blood of a human must be sacrificed, otherwise the community will be wiped out by famine or another malevolent force. Men also kill to enhance their sense of maleness and potency.

See, as well, Mbiti, *African Religions and Philosophy,* p. 79. "The Africans are usually dismissed [by Western mystery writers who set their stories in Colonial Africa] as inefficient, slow, superstitious, witchcraft ridden, having so sense of time, *or just having different thought processes.*" Schleh, "Colonial Mysteries," *Mysteries of Africa,* p. 6 (emphasis added). *See,* on the African sense of time, Mbiti, *African Religions and Philosophy,* pp. 6, 19–36. The "thought processes" distinction may be at the heart of the matter, with the Africans open to a way of life which the West simply cannot appreciate. *See* Senghor, *Prose and Poetry,* pp. 33–34. *See also,* notes 49 and 53 above.

90. Turnbull, *The Forest People,* p. 17.

91. Ibid., p. 292. Consider, also, these lines from Alexander Pope's *Essay on Man* (I, 293):

> And spite of Pride, in the erring Reason's spite,
> One thing is clear, *Whatever is, is right.*

This sentiment was anticipated by Democritus' observation, "what is is right." Diogenes Laertius, *Democritus,* IX, 45. *See,* on the relation between goodness and beauty, Arnott, ed., *African Myths and Legends,* p. 92. The best among the Egyptians, the Greeks, and the Africans would have endorsed these lines from a Yoruban poem:

> A man may be very, very handsome
> Handsome as a fish within the water
> But if he has no character
> He is no more than a wooden doll.

Thompson, *Flash of the Spirit,* p. 11. Compare note 69 above. *See* note 46 above.

George Anastaplo is a professor of law at Loyola University of Chicago, lecturer in the liberal arts at the University of Chicago, and professor *emeritus* of political science and of philosophy at Rosary College. Widely known as an author and lecturer on law and public morality, especially in constitutional matters, he has also written a series of articles for *The Great Ideas Today* on non-Western cultures and religions.

Among his books are *The Constitutionalist: Notes on the First Amendment* (1971); *The Artist as Thinker: From Shakespere to Joyce* (1983); and *The American Moralist: Essays on Law, Ethics, and Government* (1992). His latest book, *The Amendments to the Constitution* (1995), includes a commentary on the Emancipation Proclamation and a defense of affirmative-action programs.

The Voice of Silence: Charlie Chaplin

Thomas K. Simpson

Introduction: Eisenstein's question

ergei Eisenstein, who had come to know Charlie Chaplin pretty well and had observed his working methods acutely, asked the right question: "With what eyes does Charlie Chaplin look on life?" [1] Eisenstein understood full well the depths his question was probing. For Chaplin sees through the eyes of the pantomime figure he has created, the unforgettable Tramp with the baggy pants; the proper jacket and bowler hat, each threadbare and a little too small; the downtrodden boots, very much too big; and the jaunty walking-stick, the staff of a comic office. Every inch, every gesture of that figure tells us something—yet as mime, he offers never a word of explanation. The task is absolutely ours, to divine his meanings or to share his insights. It is as if between the mime and the viewer there lay a secret agreement: no words will pass, yet the mime will depend utterly on the viewer to interpret his meaning and thereby to give him life. Charlie can conjure from us endless mirth, ungovernable laughter, but he is always also strangely sad; when we laugh, we laugh with him, not at him—and perhaps, finally, at ourselves. Thus Eisenstein's question comes back to haunt us: Charlie sees only what we ourselves are able to see through his eyes. The following remarks were made specifically with respect to *Modern Times,* but they speak to something more generally true of the meaning hidden within Chaplin's wordless art:

> The film as a whole means no more than Charlie Chaplin means. Nobody has ever been able to say what that is, but . . . it is something quite timeless and priceless, and more human than the best of alien words lugged in for definition. [2]

In this essay, we will look at the last two great films in which the Tramp makes his appearance, *City Lights* and *Modern Times.* [3] They are in a sense the last stand of Chaplin's art of pantomime, for the new technology of recorded sound was already sweeping the industry at the time Chaplin made the first of these films. As the issue took shape for Chaplin, it became not a question of *sound* per se, but of *words:* Chaplin in the end resolved to embrace sound but to use it in his own ways and to his own ends. It became Chaplin's triumph that in neither of these two films does a human voice speak in dialogue. It is true that in *Modern Times* machines do speak, and in the final few minutes before the Tramp walks off the screen for the last time at the close of the film, we do at last hear the mime give voice—but he mocks the new fad for dialogue to the end: the sounds he utters are not words, or are words of no recognizable language. Charlie's sounds, stripped of dialogue, become themselves a new dimension of the art of pantomime, part of the tapestry of which it falls to us to read the meaning.

In these two films, then, Chaplin presses the art of pantomime to an ultimate achievement—and in systematically forbidding us access to the easy recourse of spoken dialogue, he in a sense focuses attention all the more acutely on the questionable role of the word and on the possibility of sharing thought in an intensity of silence. Not being handed thoughts in the small

(Overleaf) "The Tramp's final, unforgettable image . . ." *seen at the conclusion of* City Lights.

change of spoken dialogue, we must spring to life, to construct these secret, silent thoughts as we go along. The pace of Chaplin's comedy is always such that we have no time to formulate wordy phrases with which thought might rest. Deeper and deeper he carries us with him into his wordless complexities. As we go mirthfully on, and the patterns become more complicated, we see more and more fully: we learn to see with Chaplin's eyes.

It will be a leading thread through this essay that, in Chaplin's hands, *comedy is a mode of thought,* and that in these two films we follow a single course of thought leading through *City Lights* to a conclusion in *Modern Times.* This wordless thought seems somehow related to that thinking which Aristotle says we have in common through our nature as human, preceding that other thought which occurs in words, which are merely conventional and tend to divide rather than unite us. Chaplin, as we shall see, was highly sensitive to the universality of his wordless art, and he was very conscious of the fact that his audience was not confined to any one nation or culture, but consisted of the people of the world. [4] Like Aristophanes, Chaplin was well aware of the political dimension of comedy, so that the trajectory of this silent thought leads him to address a world community—to address his audiences in their humanity, and to invite them to transcend the limitations and divisions of their conventional systems and existing polities.

> The silent picture . . . is a universal means of expression. Talking
> pictures necessarily have a limited field, they are held down to the
> particular tongue of particular races. . . . It is axiomatic that true drama
> must be universal in its appeal—the word elemental might be better—
> and I believe the medium of presentation should also be a universal
> rather than a restricted one. [5]

Such revolutionary implications of his art of comic pantomime ultimately drew the attention of the authorities and led Chaplin to the unwelcome distinction of reviving within our own democracy the classic stigma of political exile, and for his views he was formally deported from the United States. [6] Although the authorities may not have taken notice until Chaplin had set aside the mask of the mime and uttered words in syllables they could understand, I think we will find that the revolutionary implications which ultimately alarmed them were already fully present in these two films. We will, then, be looking at these films not only from the point of view of silent thought, but also as instances of a political dialectic of special efficacy. As a first response to Eisenstein, we may explore the possibility that Charlie sees deeply into our humanity, looking ahead to a world community, better than the one we know today.

City Lights
The Civic Sculpture

We turn to the first of the two films, *City Lights.* During the opening credits, the title of the film is spelled out in theater lights over an image of the teeming life of the City by night, to the accompaniment of a Gershwin-like clarinet glissando and a jazzy blare of trumpets. Already, the self-referential logical twister of "City Lights" spelled out in city lights is teasing us with the puzzle of the relation of word, image, and thought. If we look sharply at the background of that scene, to the end of that noisy street, we can make out a contrastingly silent group of statuary which we shall refer to as the Civic Sculpture. It is to be the scene of our first encounter with pantomime.

In the opening scene of the film, the location is the same, but bland morning daylight has replaced the fascination of the night, while the lively crowd has frozen into a dutiful civic audience—what was the spirit of Broadway has now become that of a civic forum. We have jumped back from the timeless credits to a specific moment when the Civic Sculpture was new, on the point of being unveiled. Stentorian trumpets announce the Mayor, who begins to speak from a platform erected for the event. He himself caricatures every corpulent civic orator at work at his trade, while his voice, filtered through a kazoo, tellingly catches the spirit of his words. Behind him a great tent veils the sculpture; beside him on the platform sits a woman burdened with a large bunch of flowers, evidently the Donor. His announcement is divulged in a caption: "To the people of this city we dedicate this monument, 'Peace and Prosperity.' " He turns grandly to the Donor, and she in turn, to the sound of a much higher-pitched kazoo, wishes the occasion well. A type of boy scout in a sailor suit brings the Donor her end of a very long ribbon leading to the top of the tent. She pulls it; nothing happens. She pulls it again, very firmly, and it falls off. We wait a long, awkward second, until some device unconnected to the ribbon—managed evidently by the god of comedy— mysteriously removes the tent skyward.

The sculpture of Peace and Prosperity consists of three figures: a central woman (whom I think we may identify as "Prosperity") seated above the others on a throne; a young gentleman lounging to her left (as he holds a nasty-looking dagger at an angle aloft, pointed fairly directly at her midriff, I take him to be the languid defender of "Peace"); and a standing figure facing us directly and to the right of Prosperity (his right hand is raised, palm toward us in a Stop! position, while his left hand, below his waist, has its palm cupped in a horizontal position which appears to be inviting a contribution. I take him to be, as perhaps a second supporter of Peace, the figure of "Law"). To the dismay of the assembled City, the Tramp is discovered resting comfortably in the lap of Prosperity.

(Opposite) Charlie Chaplin as "... the unforgettable Tramp with the baggy pants; the proper jacket and bowler hat, each threadbare and a little too small ..."

We have evidently awakened him; unaware of the presence of the observing City, he goes through a recognizably human series of morning motions— elevating one leg for a comfortable scratch, then a scratch of his head, another good leg-scratch, and only then a gradually dawning awareness that he is not alone. An urgent stretto in the sound track reflects the mood of the City, outraged at this desecration of its civic pride; the magic of Chaplin's pantomime, which often lets us see sounds we might otherwise hear, now shows us the citizenry crying out with a single voice of anger. The Tramp slowly acknowledges the presence of the City, to whom in a genteel gesture he tips his hat—as he does indeed to the stone figures as well—and then inquiringly wonders if the citizentry wish him to get down? Noting from their unanimous shouts of complaint that they perhaps do, he undertakes a descent. We see what is coming, as he does not, for in backing down from the lap of luxury he is inexorably presenting his undefended posterior to the upraised dagger of the lounging figure. Our expectations are enormously gratified when the inevitable occurs, and the Tramp finds himself impaled on the Sword of Peace. He is now helplessly tilted forward: he slips, suspended and grappling to recover a foothold.

Our attention has been called to a military gentleman at the front of the despairing crowd: he is commanding descent, though he, like everyone else, seems helpless to act. In the middle of his extremely vigorous gestures, he is suddenly rendered immobile: we hear the National Anthem struck up. The Tramp, good citizen, holds hat over chest and likewise stands to attention, though angularly impaled as he is by Peace, he can hardly be expected to preserve a respectful posture. He sprawls uncontrollably, innocently desecrating the sacred phrases. Only after the anthem has ended is he able to find a way to disengage himself, and in an effort to improve the situation he finds himself seated flatly on the face of Peace. He asks the City if this will be better and, assured that it is not, makes his way to new efforts involving the figure of Law.

Let us pause at this point to consider what we are learning about Chaplin's art of comedy. This is, quite literally, an instance of what is termed "montage," the conveyance of thought and feeling through juxtaposition of images—here, the image of the Tramp mounted on the images of the sculpture and juxtaposed to the images of the citizenry. Between these initially unrelated images, relations of likeness or contrast do exist, spurring and supporting thought; in the broadest sense, montage is the filmmaker's version of the poetic domain of metaphor. Since in filming the camera does not follow an uninterrupted, continuous flow of events but looks first at one object, then at another, the filmmaker must place these in their succession before the viewer in some way which makes sense, and montage becomes a device most natural to the cinema. In this case, we have met powerful visual suggestions of the relation between the spontaneous humanity of the Tramp, and the unfeeling rigidity of the City and its institutions.

Eisenstein, in his own filming as well as in his theories of film, recognized the special power of montage, and articulated a further distinction. Montage which makes only a static, intellectual statement remains merely *formal,* but montage may also move thought and feeling forward through the juxtaposition of elements in dialectical relation: this he calls *dynamic montage.* The dialectical relation is one in which one element is in some way the negation of the other, so that the two cannot simply rest together—Eisenstein says they "collide"—and out of that unrest a new, third thought is born, distinct from either of the two, but born of them and in some sense bearing them forward through transcendence.

> The foundation for this [dialectical] philosophy is a *dynamic* concept of things: Being—as a constant evolution from the interaction of two contradictory opposites. Synthesis—arising from the opposition between thesis and antithesis.
>
> A dynamic comprehension of things is also basic to the same degree, for a correct understanding of art and all art-forms. In the realm of art this dialectic principle of dynamics is embodied in CONFLICT as the fundamental principle for the existence of every art-work and every art-form.
>
> ... montage is an idea which arises from the collision of independent shots—shots even opposite to one another: the "dramatic" principle. [7]

Eisenstein quite appropriately founds his cinematic theory in the dialectical theories of Lenin and Hegel. Chaplin certainly did not learn his montage from Eisenstein, but he was fascinated by its application, for example, in Eisenstein's *Potemkin.* [8]

We have seen the Tramp's very human waking-up gestures juxtaposed to the rigidity and lifeless conformity of the stony sculpted figures. The gentility of the Tramp's manners has been set against the violent shouts and commanding gestures of officialdom. But these are not merely statements of a formal contrast: they are in every case instances of dynamic montage, montage, we might say, with strong directionality. For we as audience are caught up in a laughing alliance with the human, in what we feel from the beginning to be a universal struggle against the unseeing figures of civic rigidity. That first revelation of the Tramp ensconced, uninvited, in the lap of luxury is enough to win our good will for his cause—we laugh not *at* the Tramp, but *with* him. Such dynamic montage, then, moves us from passage to passage with strong feeling for the outcome. Each anticipated doom is a foreboding for us—not that we do not wish him stuck, for we delight in that outcome—but we delight only because we have already seen his power. We wish him well, and anticipate a new triumph. The Tramp is in command; he is the center of attraction, on a stage before the assembled City. The authorities may rant, but they are powerless against him. And his very incapacity while impaled on the civic sword becomes a comic weapon against their anthem: try as he may, he is powerless to honor this sacred symbol of the City.

Let us give a name to this inversion of powerlessness into power: *comic innocence. Each case of comic innocence invites translation into its opposite.* Literally, the Tramp cannot honor the anthem, but this innocence becomes the power to make the reversed statement with impunity. He is asserting the covert but real proposition that the "sacred" character of a national anthem—it is *our* national anthem, and we really do hear it played—is but one aspect of the lifeless apparatus of unseeing civic structures. The point is emphasized by our visual impression as the anthem renders the populace rigid. And this, in truth, is one of Chaplin's deeply held beliefs; he cared for the universality of his art, and the worldwide membership of the audience for his films, too much to give credence to claims of national divisions. His words, spoken on one occasion shortly after *City Lights* was released, were unequivocal: "Patriotism is the greatest insanity the world has ever suffered"— a bold statement to make, by many not easily understood or forgiven. [9] Yet made in this comic innocence, and at a level of thought which underlies those words which divide, all the audience can laughingly see the point. This wordless, preverbal comic thinking by way of montage is a real dialectic which escapes the defenses, we might say, of packaged convictions. It is a comic license to think thoughts we normally forbid ourselves, to see points we normally could never entertain.

A scene from The Odessa Steps, a segment of Sergei Eisenstein's Battleship Potemkin (1925). "Chaplin certainly did not learn his montage from Eisenstein, but he was fascinated by its application . . ."

We might look at the situation which Chaplin has already produced, in this way. The assemblage gathered in the forum in a demonstration of civic conformity—to celebrate those blind civic figures which deny the very goals they assert, of "peace" and "prosperity"—is the same body which, in the theater, becomes the audience of *City Lights*. Masses of people all over the world collected in theaters and took delight in these very scenes. For the most part, these people were conformists in the civic forum, by no means revolutionaries—yet in the theater, before two minutes of *City Lights* have passed, Chaplin has made revolutionaries of them all. Not that on leaving the theater they will take any part in a revolutionary act or statement, but they will have had the experience of looking at themselves from the other side of this dialectical divide, and they must be better human beings for having had that experience. Chaplin's theater, then, is liberating: it lets us see ourselves in a new perspective, and think new and larger thoughts.

It is tempting to imagine that caught up in laughter, and being thus "helpless" in Chaplin's hands, we are passive, and not actively thinking at all. The opposite seems to me true, and in that correction lies all the difference between minor comedy conceived as "entertainment," and Chaplin's work, which as it deepens in *City Lights* and *Modern Times* actively invokes all the human resources we in the audience can muster. It is as if we were endowed with unaccustomed powers of mental activity by the wake-up call of Chaplin's comedy. His fast-paced sequences keep us on our mental toes at every moment—not *following* passively, but actively *anticipating*. We are constantly being given clues, hints, and montage problems demanding solution, and all in a realm of feeling—empathy and foreboding, dismay and hope—on which the best of true thought is always nourished. Rudolph Arnheim puts this in terms of Max Wertheimer's Gestalt theory of problem solving, in which the "Aha!" of discovery becomes cue for our laughter, perhaps that "sudden glory" of which Hobbes speaks. [10] Chaplin himself speaks of the conception of his scenes as problem solving:

> Sometimes a story would present a problem and I would have difficulty in solving it. At this juncture I would lay off work and try to think . . . struggling with the problem. . . . Sometimes the solution came at the end of the day when I was in a state of despair, having thought of everything and discarded it; then the solution would suddenly reveal itself, as if a layer of dust had been swept off a marble floor—there it was, the beautiful mosaic I had been looking for. [11]

In all modesty we can say that here, as in the case of any of our great authors, our work as readers must be, as nearly as we can make it, commensurate with that of the mind which first conceived the work. And as in the case of a poem or a symphony, our efforts come to most active focus not when we are in critical retreat, but at the moment of fullest commitment to the work itself. We must acknowledge that a moment of wholehearted laughter, not necessarily unmixed with tears, may be a point of most intense intellectual insight. Fortunately, we have Plato to join Chaplin, as teacher in these matters! [12] Through the universality of pantomime, Chaplin renews our membership in the human race. We deride our own daily lifelessness when we join with the Tramp in his genteel mockery of our sacred cows.

However, he is not always altogether genteel! There is the "vulgar Chaplin," even a bawdy, Aristophanic reading of the sequence we have just described, and in the next, one which constitutes open insult to the City as a whole. Charlie stands with his nose to the Stop! hand of the Law in such a way that it is impossible to ignore the gesture. The Tramp is now unmistakably "thumbing his nose" at the entire *civitas*. He pushes the license of his comic innocence a trifle far, for he extends his leg behind him and holds his hat in front, forming the nose-thumbing image into a kind of figurehead for the ship of state, inviting the admiration of his captive audience. In all of this, we may note, not a smile is cracked, not a flicker of support is to be seen anywhere in the sea of faces. The abyss between the two manifestations of the human assemblage is total: in their civic mode, they are as unyielding as their sculpted images, while in the theater as audience, they are enveloped in peals of laughter at the Tramp's gestures and at themselves. Such are the reaches of dynamic montage.

The Newsboys' street corner

The opening confrontation of the Tramp with the assembled City has been at arm's length: we are left anticipating what may transpire when the two meet more directly. We find out immediately, for we next see the Tramp on the street corner, confronted by two of the unfeeling City's most daunting agents, two Newsboys. They attack maliciously, taunting him with that classic weapon of callous youth, the peashooter. Their sly glee in their accomplishment has no component of sympathy: Chaplin gives us at the outset this exemplar of the dark pole of laughter, laughter *at* its object. However ridiculous we find the Tramp, our response is founded in sympathy, in recognition of our common humanity. The Newsboys sense no community with this beggar, an object for them of ridicule and contempt. This brief vignette takes a measure we will need later, on the yardstick of laughter, of the abyss between the Tramp and his City. It measures as well the strength of his own pride, out of which he is able to defy them on their own ground. We will meet the Newsboys on their fated corner again at the end of the film, when their terrible laughter will cut more deeply.

On the same corner, the Tramp assumes a new role, and we take a new measure of his resources. He turns from the Newsboys to emerge as art connoisseur, for in a store window before him are two objects-d'art, one small and ambiguous, the other large, a bold nude female figure. As connoisseur, the Tramp evidences strong interest in the ambiguous object, but as human, he gives furtive appreciative glances toward the nude. We have no doubt which principle is holding his attention as he steps back elegantly for perspective, then forward for the more exacting examination. He is the perfect aristocrat of the gallery, but also we know, the very human admirer of the female figure. As he performs this ritual gallery-dance, an operation of destiny is occurring behind his back; there is a sidewalk elevator at work. Each time he steps back, it rises to the level of the pavement; each time he steps forward, it sinks, leaving a deadly gap in the pavement. Three times the dance is performed—enough to assure us of the immediate presence of the god of comedy. For we do not fear: this is the very life-assuring divine guarantee which makes it possible to laugh rather than to tremble in every comic theater, which wraps us in a cloak of confidence that in the end, all will be well.

Of course, it will not all be simple. The god adjusts the timing so that on the last retreat, the elevator begins its descent while the Tramp is still within its domain. Startled, he scrambles off as *terra firma* begins to subside, and turns to see a small workman coming up with it as it ascends. Recovering his presence, he rises to full height—not very great in the Tramp's case—and lectures the offender, indicating the near presence of a policeman who might easily be summoned. As the god raises the elevator yet further, it appears that the small Workman is in fact larger than he had appeared, and as the

Albert Einstein and his wife, Else, arrive with Charlie Chaplin at the premiere of City Lights *(1931) in Los Angeles.*

Workman finally emerges to his full and very daunting height, the Tramp's pretensions diminish in precisely inverse proportion, so that in the end he slips away as inoffensively as possible.

We might take this elegant episode as an exercise in a kind of comic algebra, in which a play of substitutions and transformations generates ever-changing symbolic forms (a sidewalk becomes an elevator, scale change converts a lecture to a hasty retreat). At each stage, a balance is being drawn, which is some new iteration of the comic equation; here with the window in front and the god's elevator behind, we have an interesting play of simultaneous equations. It seems that Chaplin himself once generated a rather cryptic account of this process, while trapped in an elevator in Paris, in which D = the derby, M = the mustache, and so on. He concludes that "$a + b = 80$," though he has neglected to mention what a and b might represent! [13] For our purposes, the suggestion is enough. Some delicate interchange and balancing is going on in all of Chaplin's compositions, whether on a small scale or large, and the solution of the comic equation probably tickles our intellects as much as it does our ribs.

In this case, the solution tells us that comic assurance exacts its price. The Tramp has been saved, but he has also been warned: his human foibles are under surveillance—in this case, Dionysus of the Elevator stood unnoticed just behind the back of the truant connoisseur. He is saved as human: he must not aspire to be more. Little latitude, it seems, is allowed for hybris. In that sense, the Newsboys and the God of the Elevator are allied in a single montage-statement, bounding the universe of possibility for the Tramp within the City—at least, so far as it will be perceived in *City Lights.*

The encounter: Reflections on pantomime

We are introduced to a flower girl, seated on a low wall in the City; only gradually do we come to realize that she is blind. By the time this brief scene has run its course, we will have seen the Tramp fall in love—and embark on a doom-laden commitment which will challenge his resources throughout the remainder of the drama. The beginning is with a fade-in to a glowing, screen-filling bunch of flowers; our eyes dwell on them for a few seconds, before we see, equally briefly, a close-up of the girl, a pensive, beautiful young woman. Each of these images stands alone; there is no caption, and no visual connection is made—the girl is as yet placed in no spatial context. This is, we might say, stark, formal montage. If that were the whole story, we might be left simply wondering—a question posed, with no hint for the mind to work on. But this is never Chaplin's way. In fact, we are given a strong clue, for the sound track has embarked on the first phrases of "La Violetera"— the "Flower Girl" (the first words of which are "Won't you buy my pretty flowers?"). Another clue suggests itself—if we were thinking in terms of the charade, of which Chaplin was excessively fond, the two images have spelled the answer: "flower" "girl." [14]

The timing here, always on the order of seconds, is deliberately kept too rapid for reflection—Chaplin keeps our minds turning fast. We see the girl seated on the wall, and the relation of the two initial images is resolved. By her side sits a small change-box which is the grim catalyst of the first two images. Chaplin could have shown us this third image directly, but we see immediately why he did not. Our minds were set questioning by the first juxtaposed images and we were left to seek their relation. In our minds we were running ahead of the camera generating the third image. In a simple way, we might say this is catching the very "birth of logos," the birth of an idea—the motion of mind, reaching forward to grasp a thought. But there is no pausing in this development in montage for formulation in words—there is no time to say to ourselves, "She is selling flowers." We are still taking in that connection as the camera moves back to show us a larger context—we are at a street corner of the City, full of the activity of busy traffic: the City is added to our montage.

A limousine—we shall see in time that it is a fate-laden vehicle—rounds the corner and stops at the curb at a little distance from the Flower Girl. Other similar vehicles follow and are stopped behind and beyond it. There is a flow of pedestrian traffic as well—three well-dressed, busy people round the corner. She offers a flower, but they hardly deign to notice, and pass on without slowing. In one shot of a few seconds, montage has begun to take on more complex significance, as we sense that it echoes that of the Civic Sculpture, the unseeing City set against the human appeal.

Now is the moment for the Tramp to walk into the scene which fate has been devising for him. We see him crossing the street, caught in the crunch we have already noticed developing. In front of him he spies a motorcycle policeman; behind him, the way is blocked. On the instant, the Tramp—always the image of resourcefulness and ingenuity—solves his problem by opening the back door of a limousine, passing through it, and emerging on the sidewalk. It is in fact that very limousine we saw pulled up in front of the Flower Girl's position. As he leaves the car, he gives the polished, solid door a brisk slam, indulging for that moment in the assumption of an owner's confident grace, and pleasing aristocratic flair. He walks off toward the corner—but then, turns back slightly. We see that he has heard the Girl offering him a flower.

Both we and the Tramp have been presented with a puzzle: why should the Flower Girl offer to sell a flower to one who is so obviously a mere Tramp? While we are still chuckling at the Tramp's elegant solution of the traffic and policeman problem, we are already addressing a new, more difficult conundrum, wondering what can now be going on? We see in pantomime that the Tramp has the same problem we do. For a moment, he is pantomiming our own thought process. The entire scene, which has required so many labored words to describe, has consumed thus far only twenty seconds—exactly long enough for the playing of the first bars of "La Violetera," the first section of which comes to a close precisely as the Tramp turns, and stands in arrested motion, his cane poised in mid-swing. A succession of vehicles rounds the corner and a flow of unnoticing pedestrians—indispensable montage for Chaplin—continues behind the Tramp's back, while he stands fast in an angular indeterminacy.

What thoughts do we read now, in the succession of gestures and expressions of the Tramp? Words are of little help in catching this next flow of reactions, imaged in a fast series of very brief shots, waves and eddies on the surface of the mind's waters, timed to the bars of the second section of the song. Do not mistake: we are not "watching" the Tramp thinking; by way of our sharp watching and his skilled pantomime, we are thinking him thinking. [15]

The camera dwells for two seconds on the Girl, as she carefully reiterates her invitation to him. We watch her speak the phrases, holding up the flower to match that word. New waves of expression now pass over his face, one after the other, in a very few seconds of close-up. First, his highly arched brows and very blank face suggest the absurdity of her request, leaning a little toward her as if he couldn't have heard quite rightly, then backing away, and closing his eyes in a message of rejection. His brow furrows in criticism of her forward behavior, his mouth tightens in something like a critical smirk, his eyes close again, as if rejecting any thought of involvement in the situation. As he turns toward her again, with a negating shake of the head, the camera turns back to her. She again appeals to him—inviting, smiling, as though politely asking his kindness, asking him not to reject her without more consideration.

The next cycle of his expressions is quite different. He must grant that this invitation is insistently directed to him. He turns directly to the camera—that is, to us—as if joining in asking, "What can be made of this?" He is clearly yielding to the situation as he turns back to her. He prepares in his most elegant manner to adopt as nearly as possible the character she is requiring of him. He straightens his tie, pulls down his coat, and in his most polished manner approaches her and leans forward to examine the flower—this last sequence in three seconds of pantomime!

We should note the montage inherent in the Tramp's very character and his dress. He incorporates both the outcast and the aristocrat in a tense, ill-fitting comic alliance. He is now permitting himself to act the role of the gentleman—fate, addressing his interest in being what the City absolutely judges he is not, has prepared a subtle trap from which he may never emerge. She offers him a choice of flowers, one in each hand. He most elegantly points to the one of his choice. When she rather stupidly as it seems offers him, again, the choice of the other, he reiterates his first choice by gently grasping that hand, reprimanding her primly for her lack of attention. He turns from her for a moment, and as he then turns back, the flower is accidentally knocked from her hand to the ground. He elegantly stoops and picks it up, but she, on her knees, continues to feel for it. At this point, if not perhaps long before, we perceive that she is blind—as the Tramp, however, has not. When she asks (in a caption) "Did you pick it up, Sir?" he is annoyed by her continuing inattention, shows her the flower which is now in his hand, and only then recognizes that she does not see. He places it directly before her eyes—his suspicion is confirmed. His feelings—a moment before so lofty, as if he had indeed been lured by these circumstances into forgetting, in a flicker of hybris, his status as a tramp—now soften utterly. In the kindest way, with

The Tramp accepts a flower from the blind Flower Girl (Virginia Cherrill).

dawning love, he guides her to her seat on the wall—and he pays her, for the flower, what is evidently his only coin.

He is the Mime; we have been reading his mind, catching the turns of his feelings. But the Tramp has had his own reading of appearances to do: the Flower Girl has innocently *pantomimed* for him her blindness. We read in Chaplin's pantomime the transformation which comes over the Tramp as he successfully reads the pantomime of the Girl's blindness. We study pantomime; but he, and we, have far more complex reading yet to do. Long before—in terms of the rapid ticking of Chaplin's film-clock—we met the overarching problem (which indeed we have had no time to articulate to ourselves) of why the Flower Girl should offer her wares to a tramp. We have seen the Tramp himself wrestle with the question. Now, though there is still no time for words, we need to sense the conclusion—blind, she has not seen the symptoms which would tell her she was dealing with a tramp. And we must recognize that by rising to mime the part of the gentleman—all too well—the Tramp has sealed that illusion. Yet there is more to come.

The fate-laden limousine is still parked at the curb. At this moment, the owner comes around the corner, enters, and is driven off. A more intricate work of fate is now pantomimed—for us, and for the Tramp. As the door closes, she turns in its direction, and says (in a caption), "Wait for your change, Sir!" The Tramp turns to it as well, and as the shot closes, both are watching the limousine depart. We know, and we know the Tramp knows, that the gentleman whose part he has been destined to play has just left the scene. The second slam of the car door reminds us of the first. There is just time, perhaps, as this shot closes and we reflect with the Tramp, to assemble our pantomimed syllogism: when the Tramp first emerged from the limousine and the girl heard the first closing of the aristocratic door, she took him for that gentleman. Her invitations, her appeals were not for the Tramp, but specifically for the mythic proprietor of the limousine, who at this moment and for the rest of the film remains fixed in her mind. And we should note, that of these most important fate-ridden sounds, the two closings of fate's door, we heard—and needed to hear—neither one! Pantomime alone has spoken far louder than any recorded sound. Perhaps this silence of the closing door speaks most directly to a quality of Chaplin's art which is in fact present throughout this scene, and which he regarded as of its essence: a special, curiously life-giving rigor of *restraint.* [16]

"La Violetera" has played the entire time, but for telling silences at moments of awareness and decision, at which the mind itself paused. We begin to realize that, from this point on, for the Flower Girl the mythic gentleman who did not wait for his change is everything, and the Tramp must never exist. The point is sharpened for the Tramp by a short postscript. Deeply in love, but realizing he must remain undetected, he silently sits at the end of her wall, leaning against a water fountain. To his concern, she approaches the fountain to change the water in her pot. Then beautifully unseeing, she tosses the potful of rinse water directly in his face. Once again, he is reduced to slinking away, dampened and chastened by his attendant god.

Conclusion of City Lights: *Fate springs the trap*

We are seeing, I suspect, how deeply that which would be "plot" in classic drama is here rooted in montage. [17] It is so as well with the film's subplot, which we cannot enter into here. The Tramp rescues an inebriated millionaire from suicide by drowning, and is rewarded by the man's inordinate friendship. This friendship, however, operates only by night; when sober, the Millionaire disdainfully disowns his erstwhile friend. In the course of the cycle, however, the Tramp is able to extract enough benefits to maintain the impression on the part of the Girl that he is indeed her gentleman. We necessarily omit here any discussion of a cornucopia of comedy which unfolds in the course of this film, in order to trace the unfolding to its conclusion of the line of thought we have watched Fate set under way.

There has been a long interval during which the Millionaire has gone to Europe. During that time, the Tramp has striven valiantly, but with little success, to gather money—and he has learned of a new urgency, for the Flower Girl and the grandmother with whom she lives are facing immediate eviction unless rent money can be found, while the Tramp has read of an operation which might give the Flower Girl the gift of sight.

The Millionaire returns from Europe, and as an evening theater performance is letting out, he appears in the crowd, inebriated, recognizes his passing friend, and embraces the Tramp with unbounded warmth and joy. The Tramp is carried off once again to the Millionaire's home, but this time Fate has an intricate preparation awaiting him. He is generously given the thousand dollars needed for the operation, but burglars are stalking the room, and at a critical moment, they strike the Millionaire unconscious and abscond with the money remaining in his wallet. Following a breathtaking comic sequence, the Tramp is accused by the butler, never his friend, of having stolen the money which was in fact a gift to him. Only the testimony of the Millionaire, now rousing from unconsciousness, can save the Tramp— and the crucial thousand dollars.

The awakening Millionaire now holds his head in both hands—we sense that a fated transformation is under way. He stares blankly at the Tramp. "Who is this man?" he asks—and we know that doom has struck. [18] This time the situation is very serious—the dollars have become *theft* rather than *gift,* albeit the Tramp's own in truth, and the only hope for the Girl's eyesight. Accepting the role of thief which Fate has assigned him, he manages to make off with the money, and deliver it to the Girl.

As he arrives to deliver this prize, he must be transformed once more into her gentleman, giving to her with every assurance of ease and generosity the gift he has now so precariously stolen from a deceitful world. He is dissembling; she is wrapped in illusion— yet as in that first scene at the wall, something more than the world's tokens of money and pantomimed style is exchanged. As she takes the bills, he wraps her hand around the gift, and holds that hand in both of his. She bows forward, and kisses his hand. He is startled, moved—and restores one last bill, which he had cravenly withheld for himself. Strangely, touch has become the truest pantomime, tainted perhaps with none of the illusion to which sight is subject. It will be the key to everything in the final scene (*GBWW* I: 8, 654–55; II: 7, 654–55).

She asks his assurance that he will return, and he answers with a "Yes" that means "No." We know that he cannot return, not because of the prison sentence which awaits him, but because he has now given her sight—by which, if she does see him, it will not be as the gentleman to whom she addresses her question, but as the Tramp.

He is indeed arrested, and though he enters the prison with a jaunty kick of the heels, he emerges some nine months later broken in spirit. His clothes are in a state of tatters, and—sure sign that he is no longer in power—he has lost his stick. He moves, not with the flair of the Tramp, but in a slinking, beaten mode. He returns to the Flower Girl's corner, but finds it empty. We hear the first strains of "La Violetera," playing darkly.

By contrast, the lilting second strain of the song accompanies our view of the Flower Girl, delivered now to the world of sight. We find her in her own

"The Tramp rescues an inebriated millionaire *(Harry C. Myers)* from suicide by drowning, and is rewarded by the man's inordinate friendship."

shop, attractively dressed, arranging flowers which she is now able to see. We may be rethinking a complex of thoughts we had entertained before, when, on recognizing her blindness, we must have realized as well that the beauty of that opening, glowing image of her flowers would have been invisible to her blindness. This thought is inverting again, as we learn to mistrust sight: she may have seen them better then than now. Did Chaplin plant that first image to pose this question?

She now knows success in the City's terms, and the City has fully captured her as its own. Fate reminds us of its imminent presence, as it knits this scene to the first encounter—a limousine pulls up before the shop, and we see her look up significantly as a handsome, elegantly attired young gentleman firmly slams the car door behind him. He comes into the shop and orders flowers, leaving his card. The Flower Girl looks intently at him; he is the image of her mythic gentleman.

The Tramp now appears outside the shop window—it is the very corner of the Newsboys. They spot him, and as before, attack mercilessly with the peashooter; he is hurt, reproachful—and this time, without resource. In the harshest of arrangements, this bitter drama is being played in front of the Flower Girl, who is seated, with her assistant beside her, arranging flowers in the shop window. The street corner has become theater; the Tramp is playing the victim in a comedy which for the Newsboys is a mocking, caustic satire. One of the boys notices a bit of white cloth hanging from the Tramp's rear pocket. As he frames his attack, the shop assistant is sweeping scraps of flowers out of the door and across the pavement. The Tramp notices a single cast-out blossom and awkwardly stoops to pick it up. The Newsboy attacks, pulling at the scrap of cloth. The Tramp is drawn backwards, one foot on the pavement, one in the gutter. He runs savagely after the boys, past the shop window. We see that the Flower Girl has been watching. Awful to acknowledge, she is joining in laughter which is something very close to the Newsboys' mocking delight. The Tramp, summoning some element of his former pride, neatly folds a bit of cloth left to him from the skirmish, lightly wipes his nose with it, and inserts it elegantly as a handkerchief in his top coat pocket. The Flower Girl watches with increasing fascination, pointing out to her assistant his ridiculous behavior. The Tramp is unaware of her presence.

Turning to the window for the first time, he now notices her, and for an instant a smile of simple, unrestrained happiness appears. Astonished, she remarks to her assistant laughingly, "I seem to have made a conquest." She sees that he is holding his one poor flower, losing the last of its petals, and, through the window, offers him a fresh one. We realize that we are seeing the opening of their relationship, the first invitation, reenacted. We have returned to the plaintive opening strains of "La Violetera," which accompanied them then. He demurs, and as in that first scene, she reiterates her invitation. As in the first instance—but now, for inverted reasons—he hesitates. She adds the offer of a coin—that dark omen of the first scene, the very theme of "La Violetera," and indeed, we know that money has been the grim catalyst of the entire film. She is, in the symmetries of this entrancing hall of mirrors, giving back the coin he first gave to her. As she moves to the door to bestow

After his release from prison, the Tramp is once again attacked by the Newsboys.

these on him—perhaps no more than a whim of kindness toward a curiously appealing tramp, mirror of his first condescending kindness to the Flower Girl—he hastens to leave, and is hurrying past the door as she emerges. He stops, she places the flower in his hand, and then he lets her hands fold his over the coin.

It is that touch, the least of signals, which instantly reverses the world she has lived in, longed for, through the entire course of their relation. Her two hands fold over his one, as his two had folded over hers when he gave her the gift of sight. Her hand now moves up his coat, questioning, up to the lapel to which she first attached her flower. The expressions which pass over her face speak of recognition, wonder, and dismay. She puts a hand to the side of her head—suggesting the transformation underway within. We see pain and disillusionment, surely; but she holds his enfolded hand to her breast, and if touch means what we suspect now that it does, there is in that gesture an affirmation of a constant devotion which has been present beneath all other appearances since their first encounter. It is the mystery of the mime—something that lies beneath, not only the words which mime rejects, but those appearances which are the stock-in-trade of the mime's own art. Something is real here. Their symmetric acts of touch are its symbol: first his as donor, enfolding her receiving hand; now hers, enfolding his.

The Tramp's final, unforgettable image takes us back to our opening question. For in his face are comprehended all the questions, all the hopes and fears, and any possibility of an answer, which Fate has packaged in this complex mosaic. He holds his flower by his lips; a smile envelops his mouth; and his eyes speak of fear, of despair, but if possible, at the same time, of joy and hope. Chaplin is preparing a molecule of thought and feeling which may be a finer vessel for the active intellect than a volume of philosophy. The Flower

Girl is searching the Tramp's expression, and he is as anxiously searching hers, on which his fate depends. We read them both, but in doing that, we must supply any hope, any devotion from our own resources. And so indeed we read ourselves. Chaplin has given us everything he can, to work with.

We must bring our discussion of *City Lights* to a close. It would be good to be able to report Eisenstein's own answer to our opening question, but this proves difficult as his essay, significantly entitled "Charlie the Kid," is long and tortured. He evidently cares very much for Chaplin and his art, but it is not a happy observation when he concludes:

> The ability to *see as a child*—is inimitably, irrepeatably inherent in Chaplin personally. Only Chaplin sees this way. [19]

Chaplin himself became concerned that his works, even *City Lights,* did not come to grips with reality. [20] If Chaplin himself sees through the Tramp's eyes, that thrust to go beyond the mythic limitation of *City Lights* may lie in the depths of the final smile, in the power of hope which glows through the "ice" which Walter Kerr perceives as sealing it. It projects us forward to *Modern Times,* and although Eisenstein does not see Chaplin becoming "Charlie the Grown-Up" until Charlie finds full voice in *The Great Dictator,* I think we may see *Modern Times* as in fact the drama in which the Tramp will gain self-consciousness, and with it, full maturity.

Modern Times
Man and machine: The factory sequence

The opening montage, accompanying the titles, sets the themes of *Modern Times* vividly, and in fact carries us through to the very threshold of the initial action. Time begins running as soon as the projector does: we see the face of a clock, the time is one minute and a half before the hour of six in the morning. This allows just time for the credits to run before the whistle blows at the Electro Steel Corporation, and the same montage clock times us as we go. We see a mass of workers pouring toward the factory, matched by a flock of sheep rushing—we can only suppose, "to the slaughter." At the center of the flock there is one black sheep: so we know that the Tramp will be among the workers. We watch them with unbroken pace flow toward the factory, down technologically sterile hallways, then branch to their workstations—and at one instant the credits are over, the whistle has blown, the clock has reached the hour, and work begins—the day and the themes of the film have been launched together. Time itself has been pantomimed, together with the time-driven life, the work process, the new technology, the herding of the human spirit—and the one black sheep!

Now the sound track—loud with a stretto, metric pace until this point—falls silent; we are in the office of the President of Electro Steel, caricature of the capitalist as if straight from the pages of Marx. With apparently no contribution to make toward production beyond speeding it up, he is passing his time with a jigsaw puzzle and a comic book, pausing only to accept the pill brought in by his primly attired Secretary. He turns to a control panel on his desk to activate a sparking high-tension coil, whose zaps mysteriously produce an image on a very large screen by means of which he evidently surveys his factory. He barks an order to an Operator, who sees the Presidential image on a receiving screen. He is specifying a speed for an assembly line, the very section on which we next find the Tramp at work. The Tramp—now denoted in the titles as a Worker, and attired in overalls—wields a pair of wrenches, with which he tightens corresponding pairs of nuts as they pass on an assembly line. Other workers down the line perform further operations on the nuts, such as hitting them with hammers. The pace, though it will accelerate throughout the day, is already hectic.

But Charlie is no ordinary worker: not for nothing did we see him prefigured as the black sheep in the flock! In him there lurks an irrepressible spirit, which will burst forth before we are through as the spirit of Pan. We need therefore to give some thought initially to the nature of this god who lurks in the modest person of the Tramp-in-overalls.

I want to suggest this initial insight: Pan is god of those natural forces which are normally contained in well-ordered human lives. [21] He is himself first a goat, and only ambiguously human—he keeps his goat ears, his goat legs, and his goatish ways, which seem to include a disposition which is both clever and disruptive. As a god, in a metaphor which seems to belong to his very concept, he is master not of agriculture, but of herds. His name means first of all "grazier" and only comes by insightful philological slippage to be taken to be PAN, or "everything." He can be devilish. The metaphor I alluded to is this: when he comes down from his dwelling place on the mountain tops, he injects confusion and madness into human affairs, making groups of men run mad as he would make herds of cattle stampede. In its human manifestation, this disruption spreads as "panic" fear. Without having any idea to what extent Chaplin had interested himself in the detailed mythology of Pan, I would suggest that there are ways in which the concept of Pan fits the structure of *Modern Times* remarkably well—and we will see Charlie emerge quite explicitly as Pan before we leave Electro Steel.

From the beginning, Charlie's style as Worker betrays goatlike agility and goatish ways. Before there is any hint of the transformation which is about to take place, in which the tramp-worker will turn into the very god, we see in his style some hints that the god dwells within him. He is, as it seems inevitably, disruptive of the regimen of the assembly line; in ways which are at first small, but with cascading consequences, he manages to throw the process off its pace, and finally, to bring the line to a halt. He needs to scratch his arm, he is troubled with a buzzing fly which seems to find its way exclusively to him. But he is also curiously devilish in his relations with fellow workers, transferring to others retributions which in justice they do not deserve. He is quite capable of administering to a coworker a quick kick, or playing a sly trick.

We detect Pan at work again in a sequence which begins with the mechanical announcement, "Relief Man passing!" For Charlie, this is an opportunity to have a cigarette and shake off the trammels of the assembly line. The Relief Man takes Charlie's place at the wrenches, and Charlie uses the men's room as a haven of peace, rather than for its intended purpose. Seated on the edge of a washbasin, he is drawing on his cigarette with intense satisfaction, when a screen appears from which the image of the President barks the order to "Quit stalling and get back to work!" Charlie obliges, but we perceive that he has yielded nothing—for when he returns to his position, he stands apart from the line, letting the Relief Man go right on doing his work, while Charlie fastidiously manicures his nails. When the Relief Man tentatively turns to complain at this injustice, thereby dropping his pace for a moment, Charlie is so ungracious as to indicate loftily that his Relief is letting his work slip, and gives one more elegant stroke to his fingernail before resuming his position. This, I suggest, is the very deviltry of Pan. We are watching a being who is sensitive to human factors the world is accustomed to ignore or suppress, and who is ready to needle his fellows for their unbecoming conformity. He is unjust to them, indeed, and altogether inconsiderate—yet in another scale of justice, one in which Pan does his weighing, they get what is coming to them. For they have lent themselves to a system which is an affront to nature—in particular, to that human nature which leads one to scratch, to rub the eyes, or to take offense at a buzzing fly.

The entire system constitutes one enormous affront to Pan. The factory is the image of the "modern"—*i.e.,* it images our film's title—a smooth-running, slick temple of power rather than the dirty steam-and-belt plant of an earlier era. It is very much in the image of those temples of power, the great hydroelectric plants of the film's era. Electricity is very much Pan's territory—for Pan can command lightning and thunder when the time is right. The quiet hum of the Electro Steel factory is the very image of Pan's energy controlled and tightly restrained under severe discipline. Such electrical sounds figure largely here—on the one hand, suppressed and inhibited while things are in good control, but ready to snap, snarl, and blast if the constraints are relaxed. We realize that the human qualities which troubled Charlie's performance on the line are of the very same sort—spontaneous energies, under tight control. The human beings are suppressed in the factory as Pan's powers are suppressed behind the switchboards: the men take this without complaint, while the President and the Secretary dress like components of the factory itself.

In Charlie's case, however, suppression is impossible—as he turns from the line, his arms uncontrollably repeat their motion, twisting imaginary wrenches. As we watch its effects, this nervous twitch beginning in his arms takes on a life of its own. When Charlie attempts to deliver a fellow worker's lunch, we see the consequences as he flings a plate of soup about. Chastened by the reprimand he then receives, Charlie determines to conquer this troublesome twitch by locking his arms very tightly. But the twitch will not be quieted; confined in one part of his body, it can be seen to work its way progressively downward, and we watch in fascination as it exits through his foot, in a frisky kick worthy of a dexterous goat. This brief pantomime makes an important statement: Pan will escape all bonds!

The Feeding Machine: The confinement of Pan

At the lunch hour, we are introduced to the Feeding Machine, an invention for feeding workers on the assembly line with minimal subtraction from productivity. We meet it first in the President's office, where a blare of trumpets announces its arrival. It is rolled in, accompanied by its inventor and two assistants, one of whom, especially significant to Chaplin, we may call "the Technician." The machine is to be presented by a recorded voice, which identifies itself as "your Mechanical Salesman." From that moment we realize that the presentation itself will be Chaplin's cutting parody of the new technology of recorded sound, the particular form in which "modern times" have brought anguish to his own doorstep as a filmmaker and artist. The machine has the effrontery to begin in an intimate style with the words, "Good morning, my friends. . .," while as it proceeds its human entourage is reduced to a puppetlike pantomime of the details as the Salesman describes them.

It had become Chaplin's absolute insistence that in any relationship between sound and the film actor, the actor must remain primary, as the true arena of the art, while the sound should derive from and follow upon the action. [22] What is to be avoided is precisely what Chaplin sees happening around him—in a craze for "talkies" and the musical extravaganza, sound and technical effects have seized the center of attention, and the actors' roles have become derivative. The Mechanical Salesman parodies precisely this inverted relation. The Inventor himself comes directly from the early Keystone days, heavily made-up and gesturing elaborately, ominously suggesting a latter-day Frankenstein who has, as we very well see, yielded his soul to his own mechanical product. The first days of film pantomime seem to have come back to mock this era of the art's agony, in which pantomime is everywhere ignominiously enslaved to the machine—everywhere, that is, but in this film in which Chaplin is co-opting the new technology, and yielding not an inch of his own artistry to these "modern times!"

The Feeding Machine is, we might say, twice-designed: once by our Frankenstein as a sacrifice on the altar of increase, but more interestingly, as a set for Chaplin's parody. We shall see how ingeniously it serves Chaplin's ends, even as it traduces those of its inventor. The rhetoric with which the Mechanical Salesman praises its features is an unparalleled spoof of both the unctuous voice of the radio announcer and the mind and message of the new technology.

This engineer's line of thought—Chaplin's version of what came to be characterized as an era, still with us, of "better things for better living"—envisions the elimination of any demand for activity on the part of the human being. These are the very times in which the automotive industry was undertaking to define the direction of "progress," and Chaplin has caught each syllable of that rhetoric to the life: a corn-feeding lathe is to shift the gears of its "synchro-mesh transmission" at "the touch of the tongue," while an automatic soup-cooler is to eliminate any unnecessary expenditure of one's energy by obviating the need for breathing upon the soup. We note that the Salesman has been allowed to give us a rather long speech—while there is to be strictly no human dialogue in this film, Chaplin grants room enough for the machines to bark their orders or praise their own virtues. This machine closes its siren song of honeyed words with the ironic and, as it proves, fate-laden remark: "Actions speak louder than words." Precisely so, as Chaplin, the pantomimist, maintains!

With its credentials thus presented at the Presidential level, the Feeding Machine proceeds to the factory floor, where it arrives at lunchtime, accompanied now by an enlarged entourage of executives, to the sound of another trumpet fanfare. Together with its imperial train, it passes in review down the assembly line, searching out that human victim on whom the technology will descend. Fate has Charlie in its sights. The President points him out with Napoleonic authority, and Charlie—protectively holding to his breast what appears to be a half-eaten crust of bread from his lunch box—in vain attempts to avert this mission. Again, however, the Presidential gesture singles him out, and he is shortly in the hands of the Inventor, who with professional assurance binds him to his place in the machine. As its function is described to him, Charlie greets each increment of the program with the subtleties of human distrust and a prescience of disaster.

As Inventor and Technician take their places, and the Feeding Machine makes its initial moves, a supreme Chaplin comic "mosaic" of counterpoised and interactive motions and sounds begins to unfold. It is at first insidiously funny, yet as it develops, without altogether shedding the aura of the comic, it becomes at the same time increasingly threatening. Ultimately, it will work its way toward sheer terror, and confront reality undefended.

Visually, we may distinguish four elements: Charlie himself; the Machine in which he is strapped and which though introduced as benefactor, clearly and inexorably reveals itself as antagonist; the Inventor; and the Technician. The roles of these latter two turn out to be significantly different. The Feeding Machine itself has several distinct components, each with a personality and a voice. There is first the table on which the components are mounted, a rotating stage quite possibly mimicking those of the new cinema extravaganzas. To it are attached four serving functions: the Soup Bowl, the Pusher Plate, the Corn Lathe, and the Dessert Dish. Finally, approaching from the side on a program of its own, there is the Mouth Wiper, representing the kind of consideration on the part of the engineering mind which is meant to assure ease and elegance to the human condition. It will have a singularly malicious effect as the dance proceeds.

We see now how far Chaplin, having made a certain tentative peace on his own terms with the new technology of film sound, even as he mocks it grants it a creatively conceived, major role: he is greatly enlarging the scope of pantomime itself. Each mechanical *persona* in this drama is assigned its distinctive voice. That which belongs to the Machine as a whole is played by the orchestra, a tightly metric phrase in the strings consisting of four short notes on a single tone, each ornamented from above with a slight grace note. The effect is of a walking motion, as of an insect. As the repeated phrase rises and falls over rather large, meaningless intervals of pitch, the suggestion might be that of a cockroach walking up and down the wall of a washbasin. One notices not only its normally steady beat, but those awful moments in which it pauses in silence. Let us call this signature of the Feeding Machine as a whole, the "crawley" theme.

Other sounds, not instrumental yet integral to Chaplin's music, are mechanical voices of the elements of the Machine: a gentle rumbling sound as the Table rotates, and a slight scraping of the elevating mechanisms for the Soup Bowl, the Pusher Plate, and the Dessert Dish. We catch only a slight liquid sound for the Soup, but a very distinct, and increasingly ominous, sound of metal sliding over ceramic as the Pusher advances across its plate. The Corn Lathe has a visible electric motor, whose sound, rising in pitch in expression of increasing speed, is viscerally recognizable as the voice of the classic dentist's drill. The Lathe has also a tiny instrumental voice, a kind of sostenuto phrase in the clarinets which becomes an obbligato to the crawley ground. One of the least voices becomes one of the most insidious: it is a restrained tick, tick, tick . . ., accompanying each swing of the menacing Mouth Wiper.

Beyond this chorus of individual voices, there are certain background sounds of actual events—rare occasions in which the microphone seems to have been left open. A sort of background humming seems to belong to this category; but the very presence of these few instances serves to remind us how seldom throughout the film Chaplin allows such intrusions of reality to interfere with his symphony. The voices Chaplin admits to his sound track are all there for purposes: they are elements of a new acoustical pantomime which in Chaplin's hands joins as full partner with the visual.

Like a piece in a chess game, each of the Feeding Machine's components has its own defining motion. The Soup Bowl rises to mouth height, and tips delicately forward so as to allow the soup to flow into the waiting orifice; when its work is done, it retreats, and settles itself on the Table with a clunk verifying its mechanical seating. The Pusher Plate similarly rises and subsides, but it is equipped with a pusher arm which slides solid food items into the waiting mouth; it repeats this linear cycle deliberately several times during each presentation of the plate. The Corn Lathe has not only its spinning motion, but a distracting linear traverse along the lathe bed. And finally, the Wiper has a double motion, first swinging into place from the side, where it lurks out of the field of vision, then passing the arc of its absorber over the mouth; the combined motion is disturbingly serpentine. All of these motions are choreographed in sequence, the Mouth Wiper following each component function with its unctuous attentions. We might suppose that the result, in its perfect operation, would be a ballet of smooth if extravagant perfection; but Chaplin's composition has a totally different effect. His ironic composition of mechanical voices and motions is permeated from the outset with a sense of insidious purpose and incipient doom. Here is no mechanical idyll, but a masterpiece of comic, dynamic montage.

Weighed against this edifice of sound and motion—that is, weighed against this metaphor for the age of electricity and the programmed device, our "modern times"—is Charlie. Charlie has, as we have seen, been penned in the Feeding Machine; thinking of Pan, we can hardly avoid seeing him as a spirited beast unadvisedly penned into a cage—so the doomed Pentheus bound Bacchus in Euripides' drama. (*GBWW* I: 5, 342; II: 4, 475) In the precarious balance of the action which is to unfold, we have on the one hand the machine with all its motions, purposes, and voices, and on the other, Charlie pinned in the Machine, immobilized from the neck down, and *voiceless*. Thus is the spirit of man matched against the Machine, with all advantage given to the Machine. All that remains to Charlie—that is, to Chaplin—is that one master art of pantomime.

There will be a third, complicating factor not included in the account we have given thus far. This is the voice of Pan, for Pan will not endure this horrid confinement, or these insulting ministrations, quietly. As Pentheus discovered, Pan will break out.

The Feeding Machine goes through its orderly, Apollonian ballet just once; the Inventor has no sooner congratulated himself on its success than the voice of Pan is first heard. What does Pan sound like? At Electro Steel, he speaks with a sharp, snapping sound; that of a chthonic short-circuit. For the Inventor has attempted in the Machine what Electro Steel has done with an entire factory, and the modern world with computerized ordering and the fast-food chain. He has confined human spontaneity to programmed channels, and Pan's energy revolts by jumping these tracks, with a spark and a snap. As the Corn Lathe is performing its revolutions, we hear two such nasty snaps overlaid upon the crawley melody, and we soon hear more as the corn begins to accelerate in its spinning. We cut to see the Inventor on the floor with his mechanism, sparks flying; there is a consultation with the Technician, advice is given, but the corn speeds and speeds, the voice of the motor rising to a shrill whine. Charlie is under open attack; kernels of corn are flying, and human endurance is being tested. The Technician arrives at the Machine, gets it stopped, relieves Charlie of the Corn Lathe—but then advises a new start. There is a sudden and violent attack, the shrill whine, and uninterrupted snapping. It stops. It starts. It stops and starts again, and now, accelerates uncontrollably; the shrill whine becoming a whooping cry— the perfect cry of Pan! The snapping has become a merciless percussion. At last it is stopped, but in the meantime we have seen the human spirit beaten with a pounding which sorely presses the limits of comedy. Yet we will see worse before the Feeding Machine is abandoned.

In all this, we have not attempted to describe the part played by Charlie. My notes say that he is alarmed, interested, concerned, defensive, anxious, intrigued, astonished, surprised, affronted, annoyed, angry, frustrated, hurting, outraged, furious. . . . A thousand adjectives could be corralled to match the waves of human reaction which pass over his face. The blandishments of the Mouth Wiper, which arrives insidiously exactly when least wanted or expected, most test his human spirit. He turns his head one way, the other, advances, tilts back, tilts down, retreats—the motions of that head can no more be captured here in prose than the expressions of the face can be recited. It is not a task for words. There is an epic in Charlie's silent communications—the epic of man's relation to the machine in our modern times. In the end, the Mouth Wiper is beating upon him, mercilessly. [23] As we finally see him slump from the Feeding Machine, his face registers horror and full terror. This is pure pain, no remnant of comedy—adumbrations of Hiroshima and Nagasaki.

One factor in this montage has yet to be mentioned—one most frightening of all, I suspect, for Chaplin. That is the role of the Technician. We see him standing at Charlie's side, intent on the diagnosis of the problems of the machine, and absolutely oblivious to the human drama which it entails. He is thoroughly rational, a cool head with sound advice to give the wretched Inventor crazed among his sparking connections. This Technician would be good at giving countdowns for—significantly enough—Apollo missions. Chaplin articulates this very simply, when he translates his pantomimed thought into words at the close of *The Great Dictator:*

We think too much, and feel too little. More than machinery, we need humanity. [24]

In a strange, premonitory way, the Technician is the central, most torment-ing image in this immensely dynamic montage. We know him all too well.

The dance of Pan

If Pan, so confined in the machines and disciplines of Electro Steel, has decided at last to break out on a grand scale, it seems that Charlie has been chosen by the god to assume his person on the factory floor. For with an afternoon speed-up of the assembly line to the barked Presidential command "Give 'er the limit!", Charlie, back on the line with his pair of wrenches, loses his wits altogether and in pursuit of his task throws himself prone on the belt whence; indifferent to his fate, he is conveyed into the very maw of the machine. Like an initiate, he is now wholly committed to the mysteries.

We next see him miraculously rise intact out of those depths and elevated into another world, the inner sanctum of the machine. This is indeed a magic machine—as we are never given any idea of what it might manufacture, it seems perfectly conceivable that it manufactures nothing at all. The insistent music of the assembly line, frenetically metrical, has yielded abruptly to an easy music-box waltz which speaks of some other, happier world. At the peak of Charlie's ascension, the machine rests long enough for Charlie, sprawled on an enormous gear, to give two nuts a ritual tightening. A mechanic then sets the magic in reverse, and we see Charlie delivered again to the assembly line from which he began his journey—but now, he is transformed. He has become the very god, Pan himself. What we have seen is a modern, comic version of ancient rites of passage, and what we are about to witness is the Dance of Pan, spirit freed from all bondage and in total mastery of the human domain.

Charlie performs a few introductory dance steps, to graceful musical phrases which rise to successive peaks; at each peak he uses his weapon, the pair of wrenches, to tweak a nose—first that of his neighbor on the assembly line, then on the next phrase, the nose of the Foreman arrived to restore order. Pan postures and pirouettes; then notices the Secretary who is passing again. He becomes altogether the goat, and with a countenance openly inviting participation in some unspeakable orgy, he advances as she retreats in what is fast becoming indeed, panic fear. Turned animal, he is crouching as he moves, and the dance—still performed to sweeping rhythms—becomes a chase. The object of what was once a twitch but has now become something close to a lust, is again the assembly line of buttons which trim the back of her prim dress. She runs in terror before him, leading him out of the factory onto a street which looks suddenly old-fashioned after the decor within the temple of power; and there, providentially, a fire hydrant offers an array of nuts even more tempting than her buttons. His pursuit is deflected, and she escapes as he wields his wrenches in a pattern of attacks on the new object of his attentions.

When we leave Electro Steel and find ourselves on a common sidewalk, it would be easy to conclude that Chaplin here has lost track of his theme—he has dropped us back into the streets of *City Lights,* and we seem no longer in touch with the times. If so, the fault worsens, for we hear an old-fashioned vamp as the Matron straight out of a Keystone Cop sequence comes toward us along the sidewalk; a naïve close-up calls our attention to her bosom, adorned with two strategically placed buttons. This is a set-up in the oldest of the silent film traditions; Charlie notices her, a little after we do, and confronts the Matron at very close quarters. She stops, turns, and begins to run, with Pan in full chase after her. Around the corner, she finds the cop who has been there since 1914; he is alerted, and begins a reverse chase, with Pan in full retreat. Pan hops around the corner back into the factory—stops on second thought to punch his time-clock, though he tosses away the ticket—and slides straight into the arms of the Operator, who takes firm hold of him. Pan, for the moment, has been captured.

We are already beginning to learn a good deal about Pan. If indeed Pan is that human spirit so tightly suppressed in the Apollonian world, it will be important to find out just what he is like. What we have seen is not necessarily comforting. He is a delightful dancer, but it may be troubling that there is certainly the mark of the animal about his style. We might rather he had not attacked not only the Foreman, but even that fellow worker who had tried to rescue him, with the painful wrench. And in his goatlike way, he is an open threat to women.

It has always been Chaplin's comic suggestion that we, beneath our good manners, share a great deal with nature as a whole, and that we are far from immune from animal impulses. (We have only to recall the connoisseur at the store window in *City Lights,* who unsuccessfully dissembled a prurient interest in the large nude figure—immediately preceding, we remind ourselves, the true delicacy of feeling in the encounter with the Flower Girl.) If in fantasy the faculty of Apollonian judgment were removed, Chaplin is suggesting we might all give chase. The reason that it is a chase, and does not give rise to a glorious *pas de deux,* is that the Secretary is bound as tightly to her role as the assembly-line drones are to theirs. And there, I suspect, lies the clue to Pan's unkind treatment of his fellow workers. It is not as *human,* but as minions of the system who have lent their humanity to the machine, that he attacks them. He will create havoc wherever the spirit is being confined; in a sense, he attacks his assembly-line neighbor much as the Pan of the Feeding Machine attacked him, in driving his attendant machine berserk.

It is only for a moment that Pan remains in the custody of the Operator; for when the clanging bell demands the Operator's attention he turns to his levers and lets loose Pan's arm. And with this begins a new, more lyric sequence. Pan is now playing; like a child in a room of toys, he mimics the Operator's purposeful moves with pulls and twists of levers and wheels governed only by impulse of the moment. The Operator is the technician of Electro Steel, the engineer who obeys orders with cold rationality and sublime indifference to the human realm, and now Pan is invading his ordered realm. Pan proves far more prolific in the generation of disorder, than the Operator does in bringing it under control. In this playful attack on the sanctum of Apollo, Pan delightedly poses in fetching attitudes and gestures—it is all a wildly rhythmic dance in the mode of the most complete comic innocence. Pan pays no attention whatever to the consequences of his interventions— though soon behind him we see his lightnings and hear thunderbolts emerging in blasts from the dynamos down the hall. For whom is he posing? It does not seem to matter that there is no one there to give him approbation: he is as innocent of any audience as he is of any consequence. This is the character of his dancing madness—to be wrapped in himself, to dance and to pose with no thought of consequence. It is as well, for throughout the entire Dance of Pan, not one of the minions of that "modern" world cracks the least smile, or shows the least sign of anything but pain, fear, annoyance, or disgust. He

Charlie is transformed and becomes caught up in ". . . the Dance of Pan, spirit freed from all bondage and in total mastery of the human domain."

is indeed the child, wrapped in an imagined part, with no thought of anyone but himself to watch.

Chaos is spreading in the factory. Upstairs, the great screen refuses to bring up a picture, while the President himself madly twists his dials in a vain effort to regain control. Abandoning his wrenches, Pan helps himself to the Operator's own icon, a great oil can, which he turns to his own purposes by promptly squirting the Operator in the face. With this new weapon begins a new phase of Pan's attack on good order. Our scene shifts from Pan at the Controls to Pan as Master of the Assembly Line. He returns to his old station, where he now confronts his fellow workers. He dances down the line squirting them one by one with his new weapon. Pan, the herdsman of the mountains, came in the old legend to spread havoc in men's herds—and just so our Pan is ingenious in turning the assembly line into pandemonium. He gains control of the master lever—he can turn off the line, but if they approach him with an eye to capture, he has only to turn it back on again and back they jump like automated ratchets to perform their frantic chores.

All this is unfolding so rapidly that in the theater it dazzles the eyes, ears, and minds of an enthralled audience. From the assembly line, Pan now scales the heights—presumably, those mountain crags from which he came. He reaches a balcony, and from there, leaps to the hook of a great overhead crane. He swings like the god he is above the heads of the outraged world below. On the factory floor appears the President himself, and for him, Pan descends. Napoleonic as ever, the President commands Pan to stand precisely before him—and Pan, complying, gives the President that one great squirt which, we might say, decisively speaks truth to power.

Standing with the President at the descent of Pan is the Policeman, forgotten in the interval, who now takes command in carrying Pan bodily out of the building. The wail of the siren of an arriving ambulance has already been heard, and as Pan with his escorts leaves the building, the ambulance swings up. The door opens, the attendant emerges and receives a deserved but unexpected squirt in the eye. When the Policeman at this point presumes to disarm Pan of his oil can, he becomes witness to Pan's infinite resourcefulness—for from his pocket, Pan neatly produces another, very small but nonetheless effective, as the Policeman quickly discovers. With this final victory behind him, Pan elegantly hands his oil can to a fellow workman who as it happens has been holding the door for him. The door closes on Pan's chariot, which with a great wail of its siren accompanied by trumpets and cymbals, drives off in absolute, comic triumph.

We have seen that Pan taunts his fellows, attacks them, disrupts their work and tweaks their noses with his wrench, squirts them with his oil can. As I have suggested, it is those workers as minions of the machine, not as persons, that he is attacking. Let us try once again to solve the comic equation, now in this new form. Pan is confined everywhere, in the geometrical discipline of the machinery's gears and belts, under the slick floorboards and behind the metered control panels of the factory. But above all, Pan is confined within each one of us, and those workers whom he attacks with oil can and wrench are themselves temples of Pan—they just do not know themselves. They can make nothing of Pan as they see him dance before their eyes. These are the "masses"—they are the sheep of the opening montage, the herds which Pan ambivalently both manages and disrupts. They are the "masses" Eisenstein had told Chaplin would if educated be "like rich new soil." [25] But they are also the masses who attend Chaplin's comedies: that is, the workers who are minions in the factory are also—in the theater, not in the factory—the real audience to the Dance of Pan. In the factory, they are Apollo's servants, and can make nothing of Pan; but in the theater, Pan has them in his power, and they are so carried away by the dance that they take no offense at injury by oil can or wrench. "If educated . . ." If "education" means being led from one place into a new and better one, is that not just what Chaplin, by the operation of the comic equation, is accomplishing? The workers triumph here, not by being led in revolt or strike out of the factory, but by being lifted out to become audience to themselves in film. We have seen how Chaplin's Pan—ever the mime—dances alone. Members of the audience, if the theater in some way reflects the society Chaplin is suggesting, are, and are not, individuals. We laugh together, yet each laughs alone. Each is absolute Pan, yet we form an audience and laugh our best in company.

We noted earlier that outside the factory, we seemed to drop into a long past—into footage as if spliced in from the Keystone era. Chaplin, I suspect, is reaching here, not only for the strength which still can be found in those old laughs, but for the continuity of the long trajectory of his art over the years. The Tramp of *City Lights* could flirt with a world of timeless myth to which he remained bound. Now a new Tramp confronts a fiercer society he cannot flirt with. Modern times have taught him to discover something in himself he had not known. At last he can glory and delight, he can be himself in the frank spontaneity of Pan unleashed. Chaplin is teaching us the first principle of dialectics: the old Tramp is at the same time both *left behind* and *present in* the new era. Hegel has terms for this which may be useful: the old Tramp has both been *canceled,* and uplifted or *transcended.* [26] He is still present, but he is not the same. And we his audience, still supplying for the mime the thoughts which give him this life, know ourselves in the spontaneity of freedom in the same new way. We follow the Tramp in this trajectory from the dependency of *City Lights* to the new autonomy of *Modern Times.*

The red flag: The Tramp as leader of the revolution

We were left with Pan triumphant, having led a very successful though absolutely individual revolution against the bonds which repress the human spirit. We must wonder whether he will remain alone in this revolution, and indeed, that question forms the subject of the next sequence—one which though it runs for only some eighty seconds, stands out as one of the finest, as well as one of the most controversial, Chaplin ever composed. It is a simple incident, an excellent "gag," yet it hides within it an intricate line of thought about the role of the Tramp in the world.

The action is quickly described. Released from the institution in which his mind has been cured, he emerges to our delight and astonishment as once

"... the Tramp takes a bold stance in the middle of the street and generously waves his red flag, attempting to get the driver's attention."

again, to all appearances the Tramp of *City Lights*. He is admonished to "take it easy," a caption immediately greeted with a dense montage of city traffic and noises, significantly including the siren already familiar to us, and set at such angles as to be as visually disturbing as possible. This is a mere editorial however, for the Tramp wanders quietly down the sidewalk; the first factory he passes has a "closed" sign on its door. He stumbles slightly at that point, looks back for a moment—and at that point what we may think of as his anthem begins. The action begins just then, and "Hallelujah, I'm a Bum!" plays in various versions from that moment to the close of the episode. Throughout, the action is conceived and timed to the bars of the song; for all its narrative character, it must be thought of as a dance, more exactingly choreographed than Pan's own dance at the factory. As a choreographed vehicle of unfolding comic thought, it will repay close attention on our part.

As he approaches the corner, and exactly as a very quiet rendition of the first section of his anthem comes to a close, a lumber truck comes around the corner, its long load marked by a warning flag. We do not need color to read the flag as red. We now watch the flag in close-up as it teeters a little on the end of a board; we know that it will fall—we cannot yet know what the significance of that fall will be. The second section of the anthem is taking stronger form, and we hear destiny (is it Pan again?) arriving in the marching beat of trap drums. Exactly as two of the four phrases of the second section end, the flag falls—it is one of the dancers (as was the lumber truck) in Chaplin's choreography. The Tramp, good citizen, picks it up, and—looking only toward the departing truck—attempts to call the driver's attention to the problem.

The Tramp steps off the sidewalk, past an open grating in the street too ominous to escape our notice, though he does not see it. Exactly as we return to the first section of the anthem, the Tramp takes a bold stance in the middle of the street and generously waves his red flag, attempting to get the driver's attention. Just at the end of the first phrase of this now confident rendition of the anthem, a demonstrating crowd makes its appearance around the corner, behind the Tramp; and as that phrase ends, at the midpoint of the stanza, the Tramp begins to walk toward the truck. The entire demonstration, at first a rag-tag group, has fallen in directly behind him. Their signs, equally in Spanish and English, read "Liberty," "Libertad," "Liberty or Death!," "Unite," "Unidad!" This is California during a spirited, populist campaign of Upton Sinclair's in which Chaplin was involved during the making of *Modern Times*—must it not be a sample of that doomed effort, up against forces, as Chaplin was witnessing, too powerful and too ruthless to resist? [27] The crowd, inspirited, is striding along in step with the music only we are hearing, and with the Tramp. The Tramp is waving the flag grandly, and all are following in the train of his red flag of revolution. He happens to be totally unaware of their presence.

Exactly as the anthem is about to come to rest on its triumphant final note, the music stops abruptly, and a look of sudden concern comes over the Tramp's face. Trumpets blare as the crowd, exhibiting alarm, comes to a stop as well. We detect the arrival of the police only by way of the alarm on all the faces, and the motions of falling back. Only as the crowd is attempting to retreat do we see, riding in from behind us and hence looming largest and suddenly in the frame, two mounted policemen. The crowd falls off to both sides of the street, leaving an open space in the center, in which the Tramp finds himself. Great, awful percussive sounds in the orchestra replace phrases of the anthem as the police push back the crowd. The Tramp is alone in his no-man's land, striving awkwardly to find cover, but there is none. We note that he is still holding the flag prominently, with none of the sense we now have of its significance in this context. For a moment, we lose track of the Tramp, as the police clear the street.

To an announcement of "Hallelujah!" in the trumpets, in the now emptied street we see the Tramp's head emerge from the manhole, flag still held aloft. The police see him, too, and grip the emerging Tramp—who tries in vain to disappear back into the depths—firmly by both shoulders. The final rendition of "Hallelujah!" begins in an ominously deep version in the trombones, as the reluctant Tramp is brought to his feet. A phrase from the police siren is interpolated in the anthem, accompanied by the caption, "So, you're the leader!"—and to the final bars of the anthem, played proudly, full orchestra with full siren obbligato, the Tramp is loaded into the patrol wagon, and driven off in even grander style than Pan in the ambulance. I cannot make out the gestures of the crowd toward him as he—alone of them all—is driven off, but I am not sure they are friendly. There is good reason why they might not be—for their signs had no direct note of communism in them: only he introduced what may have been the fatal red flag. He baited the bull of the police, *they* did not draw the full political conclusion of their outcry for "Liberty!" Might not the cossacks have let the ineffectual demonstration pass by, if it had not raised the banner of revolution? It would be hard to ignore here the significance of Chaplin's enthusiastic viewings of *Potemkin,* for there the red flag (actually painted red on the film in one version), raised high, is the symbol around which the triumphant final scene turns.

Is Chaplin saying that the Tramp is, or is not, the true leader of the Revolution? Many wise readers of the film say that this proves most certainly that the Tramp is only accidentally political, so that the sequence by extension is Chaplin's disclaimer of any responsibility for political readings of his films. This passage translates to film his assertion that he is "not a politician"— and appears neatly to respond to ascriptions of "guilt by association" in the matter of communist convictions.

We remember the principle, however, often so inescapable in other passages we have looked at, that such comic innocence has another side to it; that in innocence the Tramp can say things which are quite translatable as positive propositions. The Tramp's accidental mockery of the national anthem at the outset of *City Lights* is a nice case in point, for overt mockery of the national anthem is not taken seriously. A fool's statements "like a wild goose fly, untamed of any man" and are read as positive assertions only by those who choose to assume the responsibility the fool disclaims. We know that a positive assertion by Chaplin regarding patriotism as insanity was given to the press not long after this film was released.

I suggest that here, the principle of comic innocence gives us the right answer to the question of his intent: Chaplin is asserting both that he leads the revolution, and that he does so indirectly, and not directly. [28] Here, the Tramp—who may yet be pure Pan—becomes the real leader, taking the demonstration further to the political left than it had announced itself to go. [29] The masses then will see Pan's dance—they will see the role of the capitalist President, the attack of the Feeding Machine and the indifference of the Technician—which indeed may take their thinking further to the left than they would have expected it to go. And not, we must always add, as worded propositions, but as a trajectory of insights which avoid the taboos of the forbidden words. The conclusions draw themselves as penetrating insights which are prior to words. We are in the midst here of the intellectual play of montage. We watch here veritable montage at work: the Tramp is "mounted" before the demonstration, and, with our sense of the significance of comic innocence and the placement of the audience in the film, I think the montage-conclusions may be inescapable. To argue that he is "only accidentally" in front of the demonstration will entail arguing that he is "only accidentally" sleeping in the lap of the civic prosperity or thumbing his nose at officialdom—to take *montage* to be *accident.* A principal discovery here has been that comic montage is not accident, but the visual, and now auditory as well, vehicle of intuitive dialectical logic.

Two encounters: The Flower Girl and the Gamin

The Tramp of *Modern Times* has come a long way from the Tramp of *City Lights,* though we can see that beneath the surface one character has followed a logical trajectory from the first film to the second. The Tramp of *City Lights,* though he lived in implicit dialectical relation to the City, nonetheless saw it in mythical terms, as timeless; now the Worker, emerged again as comic leader of the revolution, has advanced to a position of open revolt. That factory-city has entered history, these "times" are new, the Feeding Machine had no counterpart in the old City, and the fact that it broke through the fabric of comedy and could not in the end be sustained as funny speaks of a new sense of reality. Chaplin as filmmaker has committed his art in a new way: *Modern Times* enters history with an intent to influence its course. The fact that Electro Steel is a factory in metaphor only does not exempt it from a place in history: Chaplin, in agreement with Aristotle, came to see poetry as the truest medium of history. [30]

Chaplin bore the problem of finding a companion for the Tramp; the Flower Girl represented one attempt, but she remained sealed within her myth; now in *Modern Times* the Tramp meets a companion of a new kind. She is, "A child of the waterfront," the *Gamin.* [31] The advance from the first film to the second can be traced in the difference of these two women. Kerr is nearly right in his reading of the final scene of *City Lights:*

. . . .The end is isolation, face to face, smiling through ice.
City Lights is an utterly stable film about total instability. Its pieces

come together in perfect harmony, shutting its people out. Without the least loss of laughter, Chaplin has remade the world in his own despairing, but unyielding, image. [32]

He misses only the sense that the montage of *City Lights* is *dynamic,* the contradiction between the Tramp and the mythic City is dialectical, and hence inherently moves beyond itself. That City may indeed be timeless, but the Tramp's relation to it is not. The human spirit which springs from him will not rest; it lies hidden in the depths of that "smile seen through ice," and carries him forward though he must leave the Flower Girl behind. And the Cry of Pan receives an answer, in the person of the Gamin.

Where we first saw the Flower Girl seated in passive hope, we meet the Gamin in the mid-course of an act of daring piracy, knife in her teeth, legs spread, commandeering bananas from a vessel and boldly flinging them to children of the waterfront. Here she is playing what is conventionally a man's part—and easily outrunning and outmaneuvering the boatman who pursues her. [33] In the shack which is her family's wretched home on the waterfront, she provides this food to her delighted little sisters, and most significantly, to her unemployed father, whose failing spirits it falls to her to sustain. He admonishes her gently for stealing the food, yet we see that there is no other in the house. She clearly has no concern whatever for the rules of a society which deprives herself and her family of food. Soon after this first scene, we meet her again in what may be the starkest encounter in any Chaplin film with reality as hard as steel. We actually see her father, somewhere in the midst of a large group of demonstrating unemployed workers, shot dead by the police—who can no longer be mistaken for the comic caricatures of the Keystone era. We see her hold him in her arms, demanding a justice which is nowhere to be found. Instead, she and her sisters are taken into custody by juvenile officers—but when a moment of opportunity appears, she successfully bolts for freedom. The Flower Girl was wedded to the timeless City and its myth; the Gamin is a fugitive from justice, defying the factory-city of modern times and its laws.

It is striking that Chaplin points to the contrast of

The Gamin (Paulette Goddard) with the bananas she has stolen to feed her family. ". . . the Gamin is a fugitive from justice, defying the factory-city of modern times and its laws."

these two companions by formally paralleling the Tramp's encounters with them; out of the formal similarity, the differences become manifest. It is as if *Modern Times* had become a retake of *City Lights* at an altogether higher level of the Tramp's consciousness: the rigid Civic Sculpture has become the factory made of motion; the Tramp's long, cautious feigning has become open revolt.

We recall that in *City Lights* the Tramp, passing on the sidewalk, received an utterly unaccountable invitation from the Girl to buy a flower. We learned that he has been called only by virtue of a misunderstanding—so that from the beginning, his relation to the Girl was based on a pretense— initially inadvertent, but ratified by his acceptance of the invitation. Though this initial invitation was in truth so incomprehensible that he could give only a querulous, delaying response, it was followed by a reiteration, more urgent and enticing. We watched his miming in detail of the waves passing through his psyche, as he turned from rejection to acceptance, and moved in her direction.

Substantively, the encounter of the Tramp of *Modern Times* with the Gamin is indeed of a totally different sort. She is carrying a loaf of bread which, in her hunger, she has stolen. But again, from the outset there is a crucial misunderstanding. The Tramp's purpose at that moment, as we in the audience well know, is to find his way back to the security of jail; in a jail cell, we have seen him enjoying ease and blessed release from the trials of a world outside in the midst of the Depression. The Tramp is trying to contrive arrest as something rather to be sought than avoided, but the Gamin cannot know that. She is accused of her theft, and having thus fallen in her flight, is about to be arrested by an arriving policeman. The Tramp, grasping the situation, deftly takes the loaf from the hands of the Gamin. We see him, as does the wide-eyed, uncomprehending girl, with the utmost show of gallantry proffer the loaf to the policeman, saying of the theft, "No, she didn't—I did!" She appears dumbfounded: she cannot comprehend the existence of such gallantry, yet no other explanation seems possible. Thus, the Tramp flies under false colors from the outset of *each* encounter—the Flower Girl cannot but believe him to be a gentleman; the Gamin cannot but believe him to be the picture of gallantry.

As the Tramp ought to have bought his flower and left, so here the two ways should part: the Tramp, now in the custody of his policeman, should go peacefully to jail, and the Gamin should be free to make good her escape. But Fate has an agent on each scene: before the Flower Girl's stand, the gentleman-owner returns to open and close his door again, winding a skein from which the Tramp cannot escape. And still in the block with the Gamin is a meddling woman, a pure ethicist, who was her initial accuser; she now insists "It was the girl, not the man!" As a consequence, the Gamin is apprehended a second time, and the Tramp loses the police custody he had sought. The Tramp having succeeded, by another, delightfully comic device, in achieving re-arrest, Fate joins them together again in a police patrol-wagon. Again the Tramp welcomes her with gallantry, offering her his seat among the other felons, with a tip of the hat and the warmest of smiles. He asks, "Remember me . . . ?" and she hesitantly acknowledges him; but despair seizes her, and she makes a desperate thrust for the back door of the van and freedom. The Tramp follows her, and in the end the Tramp, the Gamin, and a policeman end up unconscious together on the pavement. The Tramp rouses first to a sitting position, and after retrieving his hat and stick, lifts the girl, massaging her face to awaken her. Borrowing the policeman's own stick, he neatly corrects the policeman's effort to rouse as well—and then, pointing dramatically in the direction of a far street corner, urges the girl to seize this opportunity to escape. We see her depart, running fast and lightly, flying barefoot over a curb and around the corner. She has made good her freedom, and the Tramp is now in a position to continue his trip to jail; fixedly, however, he watches her leave.

Astonishingly, she reappears almost immediately at the same corner, beckoning to him to follow. Like the Flower Girl, she is acting under a complete misunderstanding—she can only believe that he wishes his freedom as she does hers, and she knows him only for his gallantry. The Tramp greets this first invitation almost precisely as he did the first invitation of the Flower Girl: he stands as if transfixed, silently asking "Me?" Exactly as had the Flower Girl, the Gamin gives him a second invitation, beckoning twice, smiling and silently saying "Come on!" And very much as he had in *City Lights,* the Tramp yields, passing through a deep crisis of decision—now, as then, he turns directly to the camera, directing his question to us, with narrowed eyes and a devilish, mincing smile which seems to say, "This is very tempting; would it be so very wrong?" A second rousing of the policeman forces the decision; the Tramp turns rapidly and decisively, and rushes toward the girl at a run which is no slower for all its awkwardness, stumblingly leaping over the curb she had cleared with her gazelle stride. We see them walking together in a shared freedom, and a companionship the Tramp had never in any film before been offered, and accepted. If "a friend is another self," it may be that only through this match with one who is at last his equal in spirit, can the Tramp be fully endowed with a "self."

The Tramp infinitely adored the Flower Girl, but he has met his companion in life in the Gamin. He invited her to life when they were traveling together in the police van; she seemed too despondent then to respond, but she did look up. His expression had conveyed good cheer, life, and hope. Her expressions now are almost designedly parallel to those of his. And we realize that she shares this most characteristic hallmark of the Tramp, with a brightness of countenance to enjoin others to life and hope. We know his invitation to her has worked, for she gives back to him the same invitation he had given to her, the same expression. He had had no thought of inviting her to join him, only to invite her to pursue her own freedom. But the very prospect he had thrown out to her, having done its work, comes back now, returned to him as an invitation to do the same.

They find themselves sitting on a curbstone, as it seems anomalously, in a bourgeois neighborhood; they are getting acquainted, falling in love. Before their amused eyes, a little caricature-drama of the bourgeois home unfolds— a husband eagerly setting out to work, his wife happily skipping back to her tasks with the housework. The man is going off to join the flock of sheep we observed in the opening montage; she is going back to a home in which her work will be, on its own scale, the image of his. To match this, Charlie conjures for the Gamin a delightful comic vision of the home they might have, and as he elaborates this dream of bourgeois bliss, we see that its little house is, on a tiny scale, the very image of the factory. At the kitchen door, a cow arrives on Charlie's summons as if on an assembly line, delivers its milk directly to a waiting jar, and then, at his signal moves on. Presumably there is an endless belt of cows available to meet his further needs, a suburban Feeding Machine. In the course of the film the Gamin contrives for them just such a little bourgeois haven in a collapsing waterfront hut, and they explore the bourgeois heaven of commodities—complete with her parody of the "fashion" segment of a newsreel straight out of the talkies—as he takes over as night watchman at a department store. In all this bracketing of human life as consumption, we see that on the personal scale the bourgeois dream is the precise counterpart of Electro Steel. Could Chaplin have suspected how totally this demon would have swallowed our society by the end of the century?

His dream of a life of peace in the jail cell had been a denial of life itself; it was an escape from that negation of the human he had met in the world of factories—but as such, it was not an affirmation, only (in Hegel's terms) a "negation of the negation." [34] She offers back to him now a true image of life, in transcendence of that negation through action and freedom. The Gamin thus personifies a new spirit of freedom, the way out of that tragic stasis in which his devotion to the Flower Girl had held him locked.

The final scene: The Tramp finds a voice

Charlie began with a job on the assembly line, one which drove him out, into the new world of the Gamin. They have gone together into the industrial era, as Charlie initially had tried to do on his own, and that new joint venture became their bourgeois home, and a new, heroic effort on Charlie's part to find work which he could do. Fate has assured that that fails, too, and now on emergence from yet another incarceration, Charlie finds that his Gamin has taken another of her distinctive initiatives. She greets him (as she once greeted her father) with good things she has garnered by her own strategies from the world: in her way, in the world of the street corner, she has found jobs—one for her, and one as well for him. We have already seen a vignette of hers: we see her first, dancing in the street to the music of a calliope. The owner of an adjacent nightclub has his eyes on her. In a montage, we see her again, dancing her same dance but this time attired as a performer, in the bright light of the city by night. The job for him will be in the same club, but while hers seems to have taken us back to the world of *City Lights,* his is laden with a terrible token of *Modern Times:* for he is not only to be a waiter, but he must sing.

In this backhanded way, Fate has brought the new era to bear on the Tramp at the most personal and decisive level. For this is the issue with which history has chosen to arrive at Charlie's door: the new technology

"... Charlie conjures for the Gamin a delightful comic vision of the home they might have, and as he elaborates this dream of bourgeois bliss, we see that its little house is, on a tiny scale, the very image of the factory."

of the electrically recorded voice—that voice which praised the Feeding Machine, the voice which barked the speed-up orders from the President's office, now demands that the Tramp deliver up his silence. The dual nature of this new job has time's arrow in it. As waiter, he will be his old self—and indeed we will see, as if drawn from film history's own scrapbook, a virtuoso performance by the Tramp.

The distinctions here are tricky: the Tramp will fail as waiter, but by the same token triumph as *comic* waiter. The distinction is Marx's: between one's true *work,* which is spontaneous activity, and a *job,* which is work for someone else, for the sake of pay. Work in the bourgeois world which Charlie and the Gamin are here making a final effort to enter, is understood in terms of the *job.* Insofar as the Tramp's work as a waiter is a *job,* the work is alien and he is a failure; but insofar as the same work becomes a fountain of *spontaneous activity,* it is a brilliant success—and earns the delight of even the jaded nightclub customers who thought they liked only singing waiters. In the second aspect of his job, he is constrained by the jaded demand for "singing waiters" (read: talking pictures). But even there, his spontaneity will break through to make something very special of it.

Many critics say that the best of *Modern Times* is the opening factory sequence, and that the film from that point draws on old material and runs downhill. [35] How far they may be from grasping the wonders of this film I think we have seen, but about this scene they would be right in saying that it reworks old material. It is the mime's last performance, ever. After that comic masterpiece, his "failure" as a waiter, his boss—it is one of Chaplin's repertory company's venerable heroes, Henry Bergman, the failed clown of *The Circus* and one of Chaplin's longest and closest friends—says only, "I hope you can sing!" and he turns to the rehearsal of "his song." For the rehearsal, the Gamin (who has been significantly absent during his entire sequence as waiter) is now at his side—seated in fact on a table, just a little above him; as his guide to the future, she is helping him get the words right. Each attempt fails: he cannot "remember" the words. Custodian of the text, she is positioned as his guide into modern times and the future. Since he, absolute mime, cannot live with the word, she is his Hermes, leading to a future which is his death.

Only a few minutes more of Charlie the Tramp in fact remain. His act is about to go on; he cannot get the words into his head. She has a bright idea— to write them on his cuff. The test is a complete success: it seems he does utter the words, but this is only the rehearsal, the sound track declines to pick them up, and we do not hear them. Now his vamp begins, he stride-glides onto the floor, and swinging about—flings off the crucial cuff. He stretches the vamp as far as it can go, looking everywhere for the cuff he cannot want to find. In panic he looks to his mentor. Already several times she has invited, urged him to a future. Now she pantomimes from the dressing room door: "Just sing—anything!" and he understands. He does his song, in itself a fooling entertainment piece out of the London music halls, in words which are not words—we hear wonderful pantomimes of words, suggesting every language, belonging to none. They mean, but they derive their meanings from the pantomime which they accompany. What greater final triumph of the art of pantomime over the art of dialogue, than to pantomime dialogue itself? The performance is a success both with us and with the filmed audience, the denizens of the new world who demanded his voice. Charlie has his job and he and the Gamin lock in a warm embrace of joy. She is on next. He hangs up his hat and stick as she goes out, radiantly, to dance.

We, however, are not allowed to indulge for more than a moment in this illusion of bourgeois success which they now share. For we have already glimpsed the next turn in the labyrinth of their destiny: the signing of an arrest warrant for the Gamin, "escaped from juvenile officers." The officers are waiting as she appears on the floor, and grasp her from behind, drawing her back into the dressing room. The Owner remonstrates, but is still weighing the claims of the law judiciously when the Gamin makes her move. For the fourth time in the film, she makes a break for freedom (first from these same

The Gamin helps Charlie the Tramp rehearse for his singing waiter performance. ". . . she is positioned as his guide into modern times and the future."

officers, then out of the patrol wagon, yet again, at Charlie's urging, from the pavement following the accident). This time she is immediately captured, but now the Tramp, divested of hat and stick and emerged for this moment simply as a man, wrestles his way between her and her captors, releases her and powerfully pushes the two brutes to the door. She instantly rushes into an inner dressing room and he as instantly follows her. He holds the door against the two solely by leaning against it: again he is exhibiting sheer force against force, unaided by any comic device. Wonderfully, he gestures with his head to her to recover his hat and stick from a hook on which he has hung them (she brings her hat as well) and as the officers burst in, Charlie and the Gamin burst out. Now after all in what is a final comic triumph— once again, invested with his art—he spreads the café chairs in the officers' path as he and the Gamin make a successful escape, leaving the pursuers to struggle in vain through the wreckage he has strewn.

How can we draw the balance sheet of this transaction? He has been meeting the "times" throughout the film; each occasion has enforced the split between its demands and the human spirit. Without the Gamin, he might have retired from the combat, and history would have left the silent Tramp behind. But in the person of the Gamin, the future has found its way to the very doorstep of the mime. Not in the form of the factory or even the streets, but in the innocuous, old-fashioned form of a little music hall act in which nothing is demanded of this masterful mime—but that he sing! And he does it—yet in his own way, which is to capture words for his own art. And the mediator of this agreement is the Gamin, who led him relentlessly into this bind, and out of it. Only through her good offices—he could not, would not have done it alone—the Tramp has made his peace with history, has passed through the doorway from the timeless world of *City Lights* to the birth of history in *Modern Times*. The price is only that in the passage, he render here his last, marvelous performance.

Conclusion: The road

Their escape made good, we find the Gamin and the Tramp seated on the side of the road. Their first such tête-à-tête was on the bourgeois curbstone, in a mode of newfound abandon together. Now they are on an open road, outside of town, and the caption and the light both tell us, "Dawn." Charlie is nursing a tired foot, exhibiting prominently the great shoe which, with the hat and stick, has been for so long the symbol of his art; he is musing. The Gamin is wrapping her few things a little tighter, staring forward—and suddenly doubles in despair. A caption speaks for her: "What's the use of trying?" Charlie, suddenly noticing, turns toward her, beautifully loving, and leans to embrace her. He lectures her just a little, pantomimes hope and especially, strength. We watch the pirate spirit flow back. The two rise to address the road. Charlie is wearing his derby, swinging his stick. They hold hands, and set out straight down the middle of the vacant road. We have a good look at their faces: she is looking resolute, strong.

Evidently that is not quite right. Charlie stops them, turns to her, and with his finger paints a smile on his face. She responds like a child, smiling his smile. Now they can return to the road, not just resolute, but laughing. For that first passage, they were coming toward us, backlit by the dawn sun; we needed to see their faces. Now we don't, we know the smile is there—and Chaplin wants us to see them off; we will watch them from behind, departing. But now especially, he wants the image backlit; we are to see them as dark figures, silhouetted against the light. They must, then, be walking into the light. But the light is the sun! This can only be accomplished by turning the world around, which is what he does. They were walking west, now they must walk east, and so it is we watch them getting smaller, two figures silhouetted jet black against the low, brilliant sun—walking firmly hand-in-hand *into the dawn,* which means of course, walking into the future. Charlie is jaunty, and to say "Good-bye," he flips his stick to his shoulder. The film whites out in that dawn light, and if I am not mistaken, one can make out on that full-white screen an afterimage of the two irrepressible figures.

And that is the end of Charlie the Tramp, born something more than two decades earlier. We must conclude by asking, "What is that road?" or perhaps, in terms closer to those of Eisenstein's question, "What has Charlie *come to see?*" The road is surely that *trajectory* of which we have been speaking; it leads now as always from a past into a future, the point of their juncture being always the present era seen historically in the guise of "modern *times.*" When in *The Circus,* the wagons left in another dawn scene, Charlie was by his own wisdom left behind to watch them go. [36] Now the road has become a vector, pointed by the directed energy of the human spirit we have seen gloriously released in the persons of Charlie as Pan and the Gamin as Pirate, and followed over their course through this film. They have left the modern times, with its mechanical metric of motion and life and its universal Feeding Machine, firmly behind them. But they are not just leaving one era, they are headed for another, which will give scope to the human spirit with which they move off as we watch. It was that very trajectory which brought us from *City Lights* to *Modern Times*—it was already implicit in the

". . . and so it is we watch them getting smaller, two figures silhouetted jet black against the low, brilliant sun . . . walking into the future."

montage which placed the Tramp in the lap of the Civic Sculpture. Chaplin will follow it from film to film in the future—each a step on the way to something which he in some way knows must be expressed. And by all the principles which have emerged in our successive efforts to solve the comic equation, it is not the Tramp and the Gamin, but we ourselves who are committed to that road.

To attempt an answer, then, to our opening question with respect to the close of *Modern Times,* should we not say that the Tramp, with the Gamin who is now essential companion to him, has come to see *ahead,* to perceive purpose in the world, and a future? [37] He may see that the spirit which lies deeper than the world of words and conventions is too splendid to accept their confinement, that there is work yet for some equivalent of his old art of pantomime. He seems to see that to be "outcast" as Tramp is not to be left out, or to be locked as in *City Lights* in timeless stasis, but to be granted a privileged position of comic power to change our minds and hearts. He might see a better future for the world, a community with the universality of his world audience, in which the human spirit can find a home, as in his theater, for mirth, love, and spontaneity. He sees he has a role in taking us there. And that is what he and the Gamin are looking at, blinded a little no doubt by the light of that wondrous, low morning sun!

Eisenstein concludes, of Chaplin in the maturity of his art:

> And thereby Chaplin stands equally and firmly in the ranks of
> the greatest masters of the age-long struggle of Satire with Darkness,
> alongside Aristophanes of Athens . . . And even, maybe, in front of the
> others. . . . [38]

Although Eisenstein believes Chaplin reached that point only one step further down the road, with *The Great Dictator,* I think we may see our two films, in which that trajectory is so singularly defined, as the finest expression of Chaplin's insight into life. And for readers of the great authors of our tradition, Eisenstein's judgment must raise the question whether Chaplin at this remove of time ought not now to be granted the recognition he deserves.

1. Sergei Eisenstein, "Charlie the Kid," in *Film Essays and a Lecture,* ed. Leyda, Jay (New York: Praeger Publishers, 1970), p. 110. On Eisenstein and Chaplin, *see* Ivor Montagu, *With Eisenstein in Hollywood* (Berlin: Seven-Seas Publishers, 1967).

2. Mark Van Doren, *The Private Reader* (New York: Henry Holt & Co., 1942), p. 316.

3. *City Lights* premiered Jan. 30, 1931; production had begun Dec. 31, 1927. *Modern Times* premiered Feb. 5, 1936; production had begun in September 1933. It is often remarked that each of these films was a very long time in production. *See* the "Filmography" in David Robinson, *Chaplin: His Life and Art* (New York: McGraw Hill, 1985), in general an excellent source of information on Chaplin. Both films are currently available on videocassette: *City Lights* (Beverly Hills, Calif: Fox Video, 1992/ 1931), 87 min.; *Modern Times* (New York: Key Video, 1989/1931), 87 min. A useful reference album on the Chaplin films in general is Gerald D. McDonald, et al., *The Films of Charlie Chaplin* (New York: Bonanza Books, 1965).

4. United States box office admissions were a minority of the total: a typical

breakdown is reported to have been 35% from the United States, 65% from the rest of the world. Chaplin was deeply impressed by his reception abroad, first on a tour of England and the continent in 1921, and again on an extended period abroad in 1930, between the premiere of *City Lights* and the beginning of work on *Modern Times*— i.e., during the gestation period of the latter. He wrote accounts of both of these experiences. *See* Robinson, op. cit., for more information and a Chaplin "Chronology." To much of the world he was affectionately known as "Charlot."

5. Chaplin, "A Rejection of the Talkies" (1931), reprinted in Donald W. McCaffrey, *Focus on Chaplin* (Englewood Cliffs, N.J.: Prentice-Hall, Inc., 1971), p. 63. This is a most interesting collection of essays on Chaplin's work including some by Chaplin himself.

6. Chaplin sailed for England in 1952 with the intention of returning to the United States. Only two days after sailing did he learn by radio that the Attorney General had rescinded his reentry permit, and that the Immigration and Naturalization Service had been ordered to hold him for hearings if he ever attempted to reenter the United States. Robinson, op. cit., p. 572. For many years he had been hounded and persecuted by agencies of the government, principally J. Edgar Hoover and the FBI, for his nonconformist political views, surely one of the darkest of the many shadows on our national conscience. Chaplin made no secret of his early and consistent support for the purposes of the Russian revolution. He said he "learned his socialism" early from Upton Sinclair; he met Max Eastman, whom some of us met in the previous issue of *GIT* (cf. *GIT* 1994, 347–81) as the literate translator of Trotsky's *The History of the Russian Revolution,* at a radical rally in Los Angeles; to attend, it had been necessary to confront a battalion of forty policemen. Eastman remained a close friend for many years. On Chaplin's political interests and activity, *see* Charles J. Maland, *Chaplin and American Culture* (Princeton: Princeton University Press, 1989), pass.; on their friendship, *see* Max Eastman, "Charlie Chaplin: Memories and Reflections" in *Great Companions* (New York: Farrar, Straus and Cudahy, 1959), pp. 206 ff., and in general, Charles Chaplin, *My Autobiography* (New York: Simon and Schuster, 1964).

7. Eisenstein, *Film Form* (New York: Harcourt Brace, 1949), pp. 45–46, 49.

8. Chaplin made striking use of montage in *The Kid* (1921), where, for example, he juxtaposed an image of Christ carrying the cross with images of the child's mother. Eisenstein's *The Battleship Potemkin,* a paradigm of Russian montage, had been only recently released when Douglas Fairbanks and Mary Pickford saw it, with great enthusiasm, in Moscow in 1926. Chaplin saw it for the first time soon afterward, and again shortly before Eisenstein's arrival in Hollywood in 1930, while *City Lights* was still in production.

9. Remark in a press interview during his period abroad in 1931; quoted in Maland, op. cit., p. 128.

10. Rudolf Arnheim, *Film as Art* (Berkeley: University of California Press, 1966), pp. 149–50. Arnheim analyzes a "gag" from *Easy Street* in terms of a Gestalt "restructuring." He refers to Max Wertheimer, *Productive Thinking* (Chicago: University of Chicago Press, 1982). Hobbes, *Leviathan* (*GBWW* I: 23, 63; II: 21, 63).

11. Maland, op. cit., pp. 187–88.

12. No finer example of montage could be found than the startling appearance of the figure of Alcibiades, evidently bearing in his person the spirit of Dionysus, at the *Symposium.* The dialogue becomes truly serious with his comic arrival. He describes Socrates as a figure who, like Chaplin, bears montage in his person, comic on the outside, divine on the inside. The dialogue closes with agreement on the essential unity of tragedy, comedy, and philosophy—close to the intent of the present essay. (*GBWW* I:7, 169–73; II: 6, 169–73)

13. Robert Payne, *The Great God Pan: A Biography of the Tramp* (New York: Hermitage House, 1952), p. 205.

14. Max Eastman describes elaborate productions of charades, speech making, and drama games in which he and Chaplin became involved: op. cit., pp. 216 ff.

15. Robinson describes the gala opening night of *City Lights,* "the greatest Hollywood had ever seen"; with enormous crowds lining the streets. The Einsteins, who had been friends of Chaplin's for some years, attended with him. On the party's entrance with great difficulty into the theater, the house rose—in honor of Einstein! (Robinson,

op. cit., p. 414). Chaplin takes time in the *Autobiography* to describe Mrs. Einstein's account to him of the birth process of relativity; the terms are much like those Chaplin used of his own search for the "mosaic." (*Autobiography*, pp. 320–23).

16. Eastman describes this as the theme of their first meeting, at the political rally described earlier (*see* note 6 above). Chaplin had sought him out in the wings after his speech.

> "You have what I consider the essence of all art," he said, "even of mine, if I may call myself an artist—restraint." "Well—did you see all those policemen?" I said. (op. cit., p. 210)

Interestingly, Eisenstein refers to the same characteristic of Chaplin's work, *Film Sense* (New York: Harcourt, Brace, 1947), p. 23.

17. The debated role of "plot" in *City Lights* is well reviewed in Gerard Molyneaux, *Charlie Chaplin's "City Lights": Its Production and Dialectical Structure* (New York: Garland Publishing, 1983), pp. 140 ff. Molyneaux's study is a great help in the study of many aspects of this film. With respect to plot, at one extreme Payne claims rather absurdly:

> *City Lights* begins with an advantage lacking in all his other longer films, there is no narration, and almost no story. It is made up of odds and ends intricately woven together. (Payne, op. cit., pp. 222–23)

18. cf. Matthew 26:72. "I do not know the man."

19. Eisenstein, *Film Essay*, p. 125.

20. Maland, op. cit., pp. 133 ff, points out that serious reviewers in the Depression period were expressing impatience with the mythic aspect of *City Lights* and notes that Chaplin expresses agreement with one of them:

> . . . I was depressed by the remark of a young critic who said that *City Lights* was very good, but that it verged on the sentimental, and that in my future films I should try to approximate realism. I myself agreeing with him. (*Autobiography*, pp. 382–83)

21. Payne, op. cit., paints a picture of Pan in relation to *Modern Times*, to which I am indebted.

22. Chaplin writes:

> " . . . pantomime . . . serves to effect the gradual transformation from farce to pathos or from comedy to tragedy much more smoothly and with less effort than speech can ever do . . . the sudden arrival of dialogue in motion pictures is causing many of our actors to forget the elementals of the art of acting. . . ."("A Rejection of the Talkies," sup., p. 64

and,

> "Dialogue, to my way of thinking, always slows action, because action must wait upon words." (Robinson, op. cit., p. 465)

Eisenstein and other Soviet filmmakers had issued a statement already in 1928 rejecting mere "talking films" and urging that *nonsynchronized sound* be treated as "a new montage element," as Chaplin does in our two films. (*Film Form*, pp. 257 ff.)

23. One can almost feel such physical pain in his outcry against the new film technology: "They're trying to force me to speak, but I will not! I will not! . . ." Payne, op. cit., p. 225.

24. The speech, which Chaplin repeated on other occasions, is included in the *Autobiography*, pp. 399 ff.

25. *Autobiography*, p. 323.

26. Terms and translations vary, but here is Hegel:

> Thus the imperfect, as involving its opposite, is a contradiction . . . which is continually annulled and solved, [transcended] . . . the inherent impulse in the

life of the soul, to break through the rind of . . . that which is alien to it, and to attain to the light of consciousness, i.e., to itself. [*Philosophy of History* (*GBWW* I: 46, 179; II: 43, 164)]

27. Sinclair, though well known as an avowed Socialist, had gained the Democratic nomination for governor of California and mounted an enthusiastic populist campaign. Chaplin defied the film industry in supporting Sinclair; he is reported to have taken time from the production of *Modern Times* to address a rally. Sinclair envisioned a state-run film industry, with Charlie Chaplin in charge of production. *See,* for example, Mitchell, Greg, "How Hollywood Fixed an Election," *American Film,* November 1988, pp. 26 ff., and Maland, op. cit., pp. 135–36.

28. Chaplin had early asserted: "Any perfectly free and profound intelligence would be Bolshevik today. . . ." (Eastman, op. cit., p. 214). He once had occasion to explain revolution to Winston Churchill:

Gandhis or Lenins do not start revolutions. They are forced up by the masses and usually voice the want of the people . . .I believe we should go with evolution to avoid revolution, and there's every evidence that the world needs a drastic change. (Maland, op. cit., p. 130)

A comic statement is not as such merely a joke: "Comedy is the most serious study in the world." Chaplin, "The Development of the Comic Story and the Tramp Character," in *Focus on Chaplin,* p. 45.

29. It is a pertinent thought that the demonstration lacked clear leadership before it encountered the Tramp; only he carried the revolutionary flag and endowed it with spirit and a forward look. Without his role, the police might not have attacked.

30. Chaplin says of Eisenstein's *Ivan the Terrible:*

He dealt with history poetically—an excellent way of dealing with it. When I realize how distorted even recent events have become, history as such only arouses my skepticism—whereas a poetic interpretation achieves a general effect of the period. After all, there are more valid facts and details in works of art than there are in history books. (*Autobiography,* p. 323)

cf. Aristotle, *Poetics* (*GBWW* I: 9, 686; II: 8, 686).

31. In good grammar, she should be the *gamine,* but I follow the film's titles here; *gamin* may in some way be appropriate. The Gamin was portrayed by Paulett Goddard, who married Chaplin in 1936.

32. Walter Kerr, *The Silent Clowns* (New York: Alfred A. Knopf, 1975), p. 352.

33. Molyneaux points out that the Gamin's "pirate" performance, as well as Pan's swinging performance on the crane, are spoofs of Chaplin's very close friend, Douglas Fairbanks.

34. Hegel could be speaking of Charlie relaxing in the comfort of this prison cell, in retreat from the world and at the same time from his own freedom:

What spirit really strives for is the realization of its ideal being; but in doing so, it hides that goal from its own vision, and is proud and well satisfied in this alienation from it. op. cit., *GBWW* I: 46, 178; II: 43, 163.

35. Thus Payne wonders why *Modern Times* "contains so much of the best and so much of the worst of Chaplin." After the factory scenes he sees the rest as "gradual decline." op. cit., p. 239.

36. *The Circus,* which premiered in early 1928, immediately preceded *City Lights.*

37. The speech referred to in an earlier note (note 24), given by the barber who is impersonating the dictator at the close of *The Great Dictator,* puts into words the vision I am suggesting here. (*Autobiography,* pp. 399 ff.)

38. Eisenstein, *Film Essays,* p. 138.

Thomas K. Simpson has written numerous articles for *The Great Ideas Today*. Until 1990, he was a tutor at St. John's College in Santa Fe, New Mexico, and Annapolis, Maryland. His education was at the Virginia Polytechnic Institute, St. John's College, Wesleyan University, and Johns Hopkins University.

During the past year, Mr. Simpson has been engaged in a project with the NEH and the Association of Science-Technology Centers, leading *Great Books* seminars with science museum personnel, as well as seminars on the exhibits themselves. These seminars are held at regional centers located in Boston, Massachusetts, St. Paul, Minnesota, and San Francisco, California. Mr. Simpson is also the inventor of a system that makes possible the visualization of objects in four-dimensional space.

1
2
3
4 Additions to the
Great Books Library

The Pilgrim's Progress

John Bunyan

Illustrations by Bascove

The Pilgrim's Progress from
This World to That Which Is to Come
The Second Part

*

Delivered Under the Similitude of a
Dream Wherein Is Set Forth the
Manner of the Setting Out of
Christian's Wife and Children,
Their Dangerous Journey, and
Safe Arrival at the Desired Country

*

by John Bunyan

"I have used similitudes." Hosea 12:10

The Author's Way of Sending Forth
His Second Part of The Pilgrim

Go, now, my little book, to every place
Where my first pilgrim has but shown his face.
Call at their door. If any say, "Who's there?"
Then answer thou, "Christiana is here."
If they bid thee come in then enter thou
With all thy boys. And then, as thou knowest how,
Tell who they are, also from whence they came.
Perhaps they'll know them, by their looks or name.
But if they should not, ask them yet again
If formerly they did not entertain
One Christian, a pilgrim; if they say
They did and was delighted in his way,
Then let them know that those related were
Unto him, yea, his wife and children are.
   Tell them that they have left their house and home,
Are turned pilgrims, seek a world to come;
That they have met with hardships in the way;
That they do meet with troubles night and day;
That they have trod on serpents, fought with devils,
Have also overcome a many evils.
Yea, tell them also of the rest, who have,
Of love to pilgrimage, been stout and brave
Defenders of that way, and how they still
Refuse this world to do their Father's will.
   Go, tell them also of those dainty things
That pilgrimage unto the pilgrim brings.
Let them acquainted be, too, how they are
Beloved of their King under his care,
What goodly mansions for them he provides.
Though they meet with rough winds and swelling tides,
How brave a calm they will enjoy at last
Who to their Lord and by his ways hold fast.
   Perhaps with heart and hand they will embrace
Thee, as they did my firstling, and will grace
Thee and thy fellows with such cheer and fair
As show will, they of pilgrims lovers are.

1 Object
   But how if they will not believe of me
That I am truly thine, 'cause some there be
That counterfeit the pilgrim and his name,
Seek by disguise to seem the very same;
And by that means have wrought themselves into
The hands and houses of I know not who.

Answer
'Tis true, some have, of late, to counterfeit
My pilgrim, to their own my title set;
Yea, others, half my name and title too
Have stitched to their book, to make them do.

But yet they by their features do declare
Themselves not mine to be, whose ere they are.
    If such thou meetst with, then thine only way
Before them all is to say out thy say
In thine own native language, which no man
Now useth, nor with ease dissemble can.
    If, after all, they still of you shall doubt,
Thinking that you like gypsies go about
In naughty-wise, the country to defile,
Or that you seek good people to beguile
With things unwarrantable, send for me
And I will testify you pilgrims be.
Yea, I will testify that only you
My pilgrims are; and that alone will do.

2 Object

    But yet, perhaps I may inquire for him
Of those that wish him damned life and limb.
What shall I do when I, at such a door,
For pilgrims ask, and they shall rage the more?

Answer

Fright not thyself, my book, for such bugbears
Are nothing else but ground for groundless fears.
My pilgrim's book has travelled sea and land,
Yet could I never come to understand
That it was slighted or turned out-of-door
By any kingdom, were they rich or poor.
    In France and Flanders, where men kill each other,
My pilgrim is esteemed a friend, a brother.
    In Holland, too, 'tis said, as I am told,
My pilgrim is with some worth more than gold.
    Highlanders and wild Irish can agree
My pilgrim should familiar with them be.
    'Tis in New England, under such advance,
Receives there so much loving countenance,
As to be trimmed, new clothed and decked with gems,
That it might show its features and its limbs
Yet more. So comely doth my pilgrim walk
That of him thousands daily sing and talk.
    If you draw nearer home, it will appear
My pilgrim knows no ground of shame or fear;
City and country will him entertain,
With welcome, pilgrim. Yea, they can't refrain
From smiling if my pilgrim be but by
Or shows his head in any company.
    Brave gallants do my pilgrim hug and love,
Esteem it much, yea, value it above
Things of a greater bulk, yea, with delight,
Say my lark's leg is better than a kite.
    Young ladies, and young gentlewomen, too,
Do no small kindness to my pilgrim show.
Their cabinets, their bosoms, and their hearts

My pilgrim has, 'cause he to them imparts
His pretty riddles in such wholesome strains
As yields them profit double to their pains
Of reading. Yea, I think I may be bold
To say some prize him far above their gold.

   The very children that do walk the street,
If they do but my holy pilgrim meet,
Salute him will, will wish him well and say
He is the only stripling* of the day.

   They that have never seen him yet admire
What they have heard of him, and much desire
To have his company and hear him tell
Those pilgrim stories which he knows so well.

   Yea, some who did not love him at the first,
But called him fool and noddy, say they must,
Now they have seen and heard him, him commend;
And to those whom they love they do him send.

   Wherefore, my second part, thou needst not be
Afraid to show thy head. None can hurt thee
That wish but well to him that went before,
'Cause thou comest after with a second store
Of things as good, as rich, as profitable,
For young, for old, for staggering and for stable.

3 Object
But some there be that say he laughs too loud;
And some do say his head is in a cloud.
Some say his words and stories are so dark
They know not how, by them, to find his mark.

Answer
   One may (I think) say both his laughs and cries
May well be guessed at by his watery eyes.
Some things are of that nature as to make
One's fancy chuckle while his heart doth ache;
When Jacob saw his Rachel with the sheep,
He did at the same time both kiss and weep.

   Whereas some say a cloud is in his head,
That doth but show how wisdom's covered
With its own mantles. And to stir the mind
To a search after what it fain would find,
Things that seem to be hid in words obscure
Do but the godly mind the more allure
To study what those sayings should contain
That speak to us in such a cloudy strain.

   I also know a dark similitude
Will on the fancy more itself intrude,
And will stick faster in the heart and head,
Than things from similies not borrowed.

   Wherefore, my book, let no discouragement

*Young boy.

Hinder thy travels. Behold, thou art sent
To friends not foes, to friends that will give place
To thee, thy pilgrims and thy words embrace.

    Besides, what my first pilgrim left concealed,
Thou, my brave second pilgrim, hast revealed;
What Christian left locked up and went his way,
Sweet Christiana opens with her key.

4 Object
But some love not the method of your first;
Romance they count it, thrown away as dust.
If I should meet with such, what should I say?
Must I slight them as they slight me, or nay?

Answer
My Christiana, if with such thou meet,
By all means, in all loving-wise, them greet;
Render them not reviling for revile.
But if they frown, I prithee on them smile.
Perhaps 'tis nature, or some ill report,
Has made them thus despise or thus retort.

    Some love no cheese, some love no fish, and some
Love not their friends, nor their own house or home;
Some start at pig, slight chicken, love not fowl
More than they love a cuckoo or an owl.
Leave such, my Christiana, to their choice,
And seek those who to find thee will rejoice;
By no means strive, but in all humblewise,
Present thee to them in thy pilgrim's guise.

    Go then, my little book, and show to all
That entertain and bid thee welcome shall,
What thou shalt keep close, shut up from the rest,
And wish what thou shalt show them may be blest
To them for good, may make them choose to be
Pilgrims better by far than thee or me.

    Go then, I say, tell all men who thou art,
Say, I am Christiana, and my part
Is now, with my four sons, to tell you what
It is for men to take a pilgrim's lot.

    Go also tell them who and what they be
That now do go on pilgrimage with thee.
Say, here's my neighbour Mercy; she is one
That has long-time with me a pilgrim gone.
Come see her in her virgin face, and learn
'Twixt idle ones and pilgrims to discern.
Yea, let young damsels learn of her to prize
The world which is to come, in any wise;
When little tripping maidens follow God,
And leave old doting sinners to his rod,
'Tis like those days wherein the young ones cried
Hosanna to whom old ones did deride.

    Next tell them of old Honest, who you found
With his white hairs treading the pilgrim's ground.

Yea, tell them how plain-hearted this man was,
How after his good Lord he bare his cross;
Perhaps with some gray head this may prevail
With Christ to fall in love, and sin bewail.
Tell them also how Master Fearing went
On pilgrimage, and how the time he spent
In solitariness with fears and cries,
And how, at last, he won the joyful prize.
He was a good man though much down in spirit;
He is a good man and doth life inherit.

Tell them of Master Feeble-mind also,
Who, not before, but still behind would go;
Show them also how he had like been slain,
And how one Great-heart did his life regain.
This man was true of heart, though weak in grace;
One might true godliness read in his face.

Then tell them of Master Ready-to-halt,
A man with crutches, but much without fault.
Tell them how Master Feeble-mind and he
Did love and in opinions much agree.
And let all know, though weakness was their chance,
Yet sometimes one could sing, the other dance.

Forget not Master Valiant-for-the-truth,
That man of courage, though a very youth.
Tell everyone his spirit was so stout
No man could ever make him face about,
And how Great-heart and he could not forbear
But put down Doubting Castle, slay Despair.
Overlook not Master Despondency
Nor Much-afraid, his daughter, though they lie
Under such mantles as may make them look
(With some) as if their God had them forsook.
They softly went, but sure, and, at the end,
Found that the Lord of pilgrims was their friend.
When thou hast told the world of all these things,
Then turn about, my book, and touch these strings
Which, if but touched will such music make,
They'll make a cripple dance, a giant quake.
Those riddles that lie couched within thy breast
Freely propound, expound; and for the rest
Of thy mysterious lines, let them remain
For those whose nimble fancies shall them gain.

Now may this little book a blessing be
To those that love this little book and me,
And may its buyer have no cause to say
His money is but lost or thrown away.
Yea, may this second pilgrim yield that fruit,
As may with each good pilgrim's fancy suit;
And may it persuade some that go astray
To turn their foot and heart to the right way.

Is the hearty prayer of the author,
John Bunyan

The Pilgrim's Progress:
In the Similitude of a Dream
The Second Part

Courteous companions, some time since, to tell you my dream that I had of Christian, the pilgrim, and of his dangerous journey toward the Celestial Country, was pleasant to me and profitable to you. I told you then also what I saw concerning his wife and children, and how unwilling they were to go with him on pilgrimage; insomuch that he was forced to go on his progress without them, for he durst not run the danger of that destruction which he feared would come by staying with them in the City of Destruction. Wherefore, as I then showed you, he left them and departed.

Now it hath so happened, through the multiplicity of business, that I have been much hindered and kept back from my wonted travels into those parts whence he went, and so could not till now obtain an opportunity to make further inquiry after whom he left behind, that I might give you an account of them. But having had some concerns that way of late, I went down again thitherward. Now, having taken up my lodgings in a wood about a mile off the place, as I slept I dreamed again.

And as I was in my dream, behold, an aged gentleman came by where I lay; and because he was to go some part of the way that I was travelling, methought I got up and went with him. So as we walked, and as travellers usually do, it was as if we fell into discourse. And our talk happened to be about Christian and his travels. For thus I began with the old man:

"Sir," said I, "what town is that there below that lieth on the left hand of our way?"

Then said Mr. Sagacity, for that was his name, "It is the City of Destruction, a populous place, but possessed with a very ill-conditioned* and idle sort of people."

"I thought that was that city," quoth I. "I went once myself through that town, and therefore know that this report you give of it is true."

SAGACITY. "Too true. I wish I could speak truth in speaking better of them that dwell therein."

"Well, sir," quoth I, "then I perceive you to be a well-meaning man, and so one that takes pleasure to hear and tell of that which is good. Pray, did you never hear what happened to a man sometime ago in this town, whose name was Christian, that went on pilgrimage up towards the higher regions?"

SAGACITY. "Hear of him! Ay, and I also heard of the molestations, troubles, wars, captivities, cries, groans, frights and fears that he met with and had in his journey. Besides, I must tell you, all our country rings of him. There are few houses that have heard of him and his doings, but have sought after and got the records of his pilgrimage. Yea, I think I may say that his hazardous journey has got a many well-wishers to his ways. For though when he was here, he was fool in every man's mouth, yet now he is gone, he is

---

*People of bad qualities.

highly commended of all. For 'tis said he lives bravely where he is. Yea, many of them that are resolved never to run his hazards, yet have their mouths water at his gains."

"They may," quoth I, "well think, if they think anything that is true, that he liveth well, where he is. For he now lives at and in the Fountain of Life, and has what he has without labour and sorrow, for there is no grief mixed therewith."

SAGACITY. "Talk! The people talk strangely about him. Some say that he now walks in white, [Revelation 3:4] that he has a chain of gold about his neck, that he has a crown of gold, beset with pearls, upon his head. Others say that the Shining Ones, that sometimes showed themselves to him in his journey, are become his companions, and that he is as familiar with them in the place where he is as here one neighbour is with another. Besides, 'tis confidently affirmed concerning him that the King of the place where he is has bestowed upon him already a very rich and pleasant dwelling at court; and that he every day eateth and drinketh, and walketh and talketh with him, and receiveth of the smiles and favours of him that is judge of all there. Moreover, it is expected of some that his Prince, the Lord of that country, will shortly come into these parts, and will know the reason, if they can give any, why his neighbours set so little by him and had him so much in derision when they perceived that he would be a pilgrim. For they say that now he is so in the affections of his Prince, and that his sovereign is so much concerned with the indignities that was cast upon Christian when he became a pilgrim, that he will look upon all as if done unto himself; and no marvel, for 'twas for the love that he had to his Prince that he ventured as he did."

"I dare say," quoth I, "I am glad on't. I am glad for the poor man's sake, for now that he has rest from his labour, [Revelation 14:13] and for that he now reapeth the benefit of his tears with joy, and for that he is got beyond the gunshot of his enemies and is out of the reach of them that hate him. I also am glad for that a rumour of these things is noised abroad in this country. Who can tell but that it may work some good effect on some that are left behind? But, pray, air, while it is fresh in my mind, do you hear anything of his wife and children? Poor hearts, I wonder in my mind what they do."

SAGACITY. "Who? Christiana and her sons? They are like to do as well as did Christian himself; for though they all played the fool at the first, and would by no means be persuaded by either the tears or entreaties of Christian, yet second thoughts have wrought wonderfully with them. So they have packed up and are also gone after him."

"Better and better," quoth I. "But, what! wife and children and all?"

SAGACITY. " 'Tis true, I can give you an account of the matter, for I was upon the spot at the instant and was thoroughly acquainted with the whole affair."

"Then," said I, "a man, it seems, may report it for a truth?"

SAGACITY. "You need not fear to affirm it. I mean that they are all gone on pilgrimage, both the good woman and her four boys. And being we are, as I perceive, going some considerable way together, I will give you an account of the whole of the matter.

"This Christiana (for that was her name from the day that she with her children betook themselves to a pilgrim's life), after her husband was gone over the river, and she could hear of him no more, her thoughts began to work in her mind. First, for that she had lost her husband, and for that the loving bond of that relation was utterly broken betwixt them. For you know," said he to me, "nature can do no less but entertain the living with many a heavy cogitation in the remembrance of the loss of loving relations. This therefore of her husband did cost her many a tear. But this was not all, for Christiana did also begin to consider with herself, whether her unbecoming behaviour towards her husband was not one cause that she saw him no more, and that in such sort he was taken away from her. And upon this, came into her mind by swarms all her unkind, unnatural, and ungodly carriages* to her dear friend, which also clogged her conscience and did load her with guilt. She was, moreover, much broken with recalling to remembrance the restless groans, brinish tears, and self-bemoanings of her husband, and how she did harden her heart against all his entreaties, and loving persuasions (of her and her sons) to go with him. Yea, there was not anything that Christian either said to her or did before her, all the while that his burden did hang on his back, but it returned upon her like a flash of lightning and rent the caul of her heart in sunder; specially that bitter outcry of his, 'What shall I do to be saved?' did ring in her ears most dolefully.

"Then said she to her children, 'Sons, we are all undone. I have sinned away your father, and he is gone. He would have had us with him, but I would not go myself. I also have hindered you of life.' With that, the boys fell all into tears and cried out to go after their father. 'Oh,' said Christiana, 'that it had been but our lot to go with him, then had it fared well with us beyond that 'tis like to do now. For though I formerly foolishly imagined, concerning the troubles of your father, that they proceeded of a foolish fancy that he had, or for that he was overrun with melancholy humours; yet now 'twill not out of my mind but that they sprang from another cause, to wit, for that the light of light was given him, by, the help of which, as I perceive, he has escaped the snares of death.' Then they all wept again, and cried out, 'Oh, woe worth the day.'

"The next night Christiana had a dream, and behold, she saw as if a broad parchment was opened before her, in which were recorded the sum of her ways, and the times, as she thought, looked very black upon her. Then she cried out aloud in her sleep, 'Lord have mercy upon me, a sinner,' and the little children heard her.

"After this she thought she saw two very ill-favoured† ones standing by her bedside, and saying, 'What shall we do with this woman? For she cries out for mercy waking and sleeping. If she be suffered to go on as she begins, we shall lose her as we have lost her husband. Wherefore we must, by one way

*Conduct.
†Ugly.

or other, seek to take her off from the thoughts of what shall be hereafter; else all the world cannot help it but she will become a pilgrim.'

"Now she awoke in a great sweat; also a trembling was upon her, but after a while she fell to sleeping again. And then she thought she saw Christian, her husband, in a place of bliss among many immortals, with an harp in his hand, standing and playing upon it before one that sat on a throne with a rainbow about his head. She saw also as if he bowed his head with his face to the paved work that was under the Prince's feet, saying, 'I heartily thank my Lord and King for bringing of me into this place.' Then shouted a company of them that stood round about and harped with their harps; [Revelation 14:2] but no man living could tell what they said but Christian and his companions.

"Next morning when she was up, had prayed to God and talked with her children awhile, one knocked hard at the door, to whom she spake out saying, 'If thou comest in God's name, come in.' So he said 'Amen,' and opened the door, and saluted her with 'Peace be to this house.' The which when he had done, he said, 'Christiana, knowest thou wherefore I am come?' Then she blushed and trembled; also her heart began to wax warm with desires to know whence he came and what was his errand to her. So he said unto her, 'My name is Secret; I dwell with those that are high. It is talked of where I dwell as if thou hadst a desire to go thither. Also there is a report that thou art aware of the evil thou hast formerly done to thy husband in hardening of thy heart against his way and in keeping of these thy babes in their ignorance. Christiana, the merciful one has sent me to tell thee that he is a God ready to forgive, and that he taketh delight to multiply pardon to offences. He also would have thee know that he inviteth thee to come into his presence, to his table, and that he will feed thee with the fat of his house and with the heritage of Jacob, thy father.

" 'There is Christian, thy husband that was, with legions more his companions, ever beholding that face that doth minister life to beholders. And they will all be glad when they shall hear the sound of thy feet step over thy Father's threshold.'

"Christiana at this was greatly abashed in herself and bowing her head to the ground. This visitor proceeded and said, 'Christiana, here is also a letter for thee which I have brought from thy husband's King.' So she took it and opened it, but it smelt after the manner of the best perfume; also it was written in letters of gold. The contents of the letter was, 'that the King would have her do as did Christian, her husband; for that was the way to come to his city, and to dwell in his presence with joy forever.' At this, the good woman was quite overcome; so she cried out to her visitor, 'Sir, will you carry me and my children with you that we also may go and worship this King?'

"Then said the visitor, 'Christiana, the bitter is before the sweet. Thou must through troubles, as did he that went before thee enter this Celestial City. Wherefore I advise thee to do as did Christian, thy husband. Go to the wicket-gate yonder, over the plain, for that stands in the head of the way up which thou must go, and I wish thee all good speed. Also I advise that thou put this letter in thy bosom, that thou read therein to thyself and to thy children until you have got it by root-of-heart. For it is one of the songs that thou must sing while thou are in this house of thy pilgrimage. [Psalms 119:54] Also this thou must deliver in at the further gate.' "

Now I saw in my dream that this old gentleman, as he told me this story, did himself seem to be greatly affected therewith. He moreover proceeded and said, "So Christiana called her sons together and began thus to address herself unto them, 'My sons, I have, as you may perceive, been of late under much exercise in my soul about the death of your father; not for that I doubt at all of his happiness, for I am satisfied now that he is well. I have also been much affected with the thoughts of mine own state and yours, which I verily believe is by nature miserable. My carriages also to your father in his distress is a great load to my conscience. For I hardened both mine own heart and yours against him and refused to go with him on pilgrimage.

" 'The thoughts of these things would now kill me outright, but that for a dream which I had last night, and but that for the encouragement that this stranger has given me this morning. Come, my children, let us pack up and be gone to the gate that leads to the Celestial Country, that we may see your father and be with him and his companions in peace according to the laws of that land.'

"Then did her children burst out into tears for joy that the heart of their mother was so inclined. So their visitor bid them farewell, and they began to prepare to set out for their journey.

"But while they were thus about to be gone, two of the women that were Christiana's neighbours came up to her house and knocked at her door. To whom she said as before, 'If you come in God's name, come in.' At this, the women were stunned, for this kind of language they used not to hear, or to perceive to drop from the lips of Christiana. Yet they came in. But, behold, they found the good woman a-preparing to be gone from her house.

"So they began and said, 'Neighbour, pray, what is your meaning by this?'

"Christiana answered and said to the eldest of them, whose name was Mrs. Timorous, 'I am preparing for a journey.' (This Timorous was daughter to him that met Christian upon the hill Difficulty; and would a had him gone back for fear of the lions.)

TIMOROUS. 'For what journey, I pray you?'

CHRISTIANA. 'Even to go after my good husband,' and with that she fell aweeping.

TIMOROUS. 'I hope not so, good neighbour. Pray, for your poor children's sake, do not so unwomanly cast away yourself.'

CHRISTIANA. 'Nay, my children shall go with me; not one of them is willing to stay behind.'

TIMOROUS. 'I wonder in my very heart, what, or who, has brought you into this mind.'

CHRISTIANA. 'Oh, neighbour, knew you but as much as I do, I doubt not but that you would go with me.'

TIMOROUS. 'Prithee, what new knowledge hast thou got that so worketh off thy mind from thy friends and that tempteth thee to go nobody knows where?"

CHRISTIANA. "Then Christiana replied, 'I have been sorely afflicted since my husband's departure from me, but specially since he went over the river. But that which troubleth me most is my churlish carriages to him when he was under his distress. Besides, I am now as he was then; nothing will serve me but going on pilgrimage. I was a-dreamed last night that I saw him. O, that my soul was with him! He dwelleth in the presence of the King of the country; he sits and eats with him at his table; he is become a companion of immortals, and has a house now given him to dwell in, to which, the best palaces on earth, if compared, seems to me to be but as a dunghill. The Prince of the place has also sent for me with promise of entertainment if I shall come to him; his messenger was here even now and has brought me a letter which invites me to come.' And with that she plucked out her letter and read it and said to them, 'What now will you say to this?'

TIMOROUS. 'Oh, the madness that has possessed thee and thy husband, to run yourselves upon such difficulties! You have heard, I am sure, what your husband did meet with, even in a manner at the first step that he took on his way as our neighbour Obstinate yet can testify; for he went along with him, yea, and Pliable too, until they, like wise men, were afraid to go any further. We also heard over and above, how he met the lions, Apollyon, the Shadow of Death, and many other things. Nor is the danger he met with at Vanity Fair to be forgotten by thee. For if he, though a man, was so hard put to it, what canst thou, being but a poor woman, do? Consider also that these four sweet babes are thy children, thy flesh and thy bones. Wherefore, though thou shouldest be so rash as to cast away thyself, yet for the sake of the fruit of thy body, keep thou at home.'

"But Christiana said unto her, 'Tempt me not, my neighbour. I have now a price put into mine hand to get gain, and I should be a fool of the greatest size if I should have no heart to strike in with the opportunity. And for that you tell me of all these troubles that I am like to meet with in the way, they are so far off from being to me a discouragement that they show I am in the right. The bitter must come before the sweet, and that also will make the sweet the sweeter. Wherefore, since you came not to my house in God's name, as I said, I pray you to be gone and not to disquiet me further.'

"Then Timorous all to reviled her, and said to her fellow, 'Come neighbour Mercy, let's leave her in her own hands, since she scorns our counsel and company.' But Mercy was at a stand and could not so readily comply with her neighbour, and that for a twofold reason. First, her bowels* yearned over Christiana. So she said within herself, 'If my neighbour will needs be gone, I will go a little way with her and help her.' Secondly, her bowels yearned over her own soul, for what Christiana had said had taken some hold upon her mind. Wherefore she said within herself again, 'I will yet have more talk with this Christiana, and if I find truth and life in what she shall say, myself with my heart shall also go with her.' Wherefore Mercy began thus to reply to her neighbour Timorous.

---

*Considered as the source of emotions such as pity, feeling, and compassion.

MERCY. 'Neighbour, I did indeed come with you to see Christiana this morning, and since she is, as you see, a-taking of her last farewell of her country, I think to walk, this sunshine morning, a little way with her to help her on the way.' But she told her not of her second reason, but kept that to herself.

TIMOROUS. 'Well, I see you have a mind to go a-fooling too; but take heed in time, and be wise. While we are out of danger we are out; but when we are in, we are in.' So Mrs. Timorous returned to her house, and Christiana betook herself to her journey. But when Timorous was got home to her house, she sends for some of her neighbours, to wit, Mrs. Bat's-eyes, Mrs. Inconsiderate, Mrs. Light-mind, and Mrs. Know-nothing. So when they were come to her house, she falls to telling of the story of Christiana and of her intended journey. And thus she began her tale,

TIMOROUS. 'Neighbours, having had little to do this morning, I went to give Christiana a visit, and when I came at the door I knocked, as you know 'tis our custom. And she answered, "If you come in God's name, come in." So in I went, thinking all was well. But when I came in, I found her preparing herself to depart the town, she and also her children. So I asked her what was her meaning by that. And she told me, in short, that she was now of a mind to go on pilgrimage as did her husband. She told me also of a dream that she had, and how the King of the country where her husband was had sent her an inviting letter to come thither.'

"Then said Mrs. Know-nothing, 'And what, Do you think she will go?'

TIMOROUS. 'Ay, go she will, whatever come on't. And methinks I know it by this: for that which was my great argument to persuade her to stay at home (to wit, the troubles she was like to meet with in the way), is one great argument with her to put her forward on her journey. For she told me in so many words, "The bitter goes before the sweet. Yea, and for as much as it so doth, it makes the sweet the sweeter." '

MRS. BAT'S-EYES. 'Oh, this blind and foolish woman,' said she. 'Will she not take warning by her husband's afflictions? For my part, I say if he was here again he would rest him content in a whole skin and never run so many hazards for nothing.'

"Mrs. Inconsiderate also replied, saying, 'Away with such fantastical fools from the town; a good riddance, for my part, I say of her. Should she stay where she dwells and retain this her mind, who could live quietly by her? For she will either be dumpish* or unneighbourly, or talk of such matters as no wise body can abide. Wherefore, for my part, I shall never be sorry for her departure. Let her go, and let better come in her room. 'Twas never a good world since these whimsical fools dwelt in it.'

"Then Mrs. Light-mind added as followeth. 'Come put this kind of talk away. I was yesterday as Madam Wanton's, where we were as merry as the maids. For who do you think should be there but I, and Mrs. Love-the-flesh, and three or four more, with Mr. Lechery, Mrs. Filth, and some others. So

*Downcast.

there we had music, and dancing, and what else was meet* to fill up the pleasure. And I dare say my lady herself is an admirably well-bred gentlewoman, and Mr. Lechery is as pretty a fellow.'

"By this time Christiana was got on her way, and Mercy went along with her. So as they went, her children being there also, Christiana began to discourse. 'And Mercy,' said Christiana, 'I take this as an unexpected favour that thou shouldest set foot out-of-doors with me to accompany me a little in my way.'

MERCY. Then said young Mercy (for she was but young), 'If I thought it would be to purpose to go with you, I would never go near the town any more.'

CHRISTIANA. 'Well, Mercy,' said Christiana, 'cast in thy lot with me. I well know what will be the end of our pilgrimage. My husband is where he would not but be for all the gold in the Spanish mines. Nor shalt thou be rejected, though thou goest but upon my invitation. The King, who hath sent for me and my children, is one that delighteth in Mercy. Besides, if thou wilt, I will hire thee, and thou shalt go along with me as my servant. Yet we will have all things in common betwixt thee and me; only go along with me.'

MERCY. 'But how shall I be ascertained that I also shall be entertained?† Had I but this hope from one that can tell, I would make no stick‡ at all, but would go, being helped by him that can help, though the way was never so tedious.'

CHRISTIANA. 'Well, loving Mercy, I will tell thee what thou shalt do. Go with me to the wicket-gate, and there I will further inquire for thee, and if there thou shalt not meet with encouragement, I will be content that thou shalt return to thy place. I also will pay thee for thy kindness which thou showest to me and my children in thy accompanying of us in our way as thou doest.'

MERCY. 'Then will I go thither and will take what shall follow, and the Lord grant that my lot may there fall even as the King of heaven shall have his heart upon me.'

"Christiana then was glad at her heart, not only that she had a companion, but also for that she had prevailed with this poor maid to fall in love with her own salvation. So they went on together, and Mercy began to weep. Then said Christiana, 'Wherefore weepeth my sister so?'

MERCY. 'Alas,' said she, 'who can but lament that shall but rightly consider what a state and condition my poor relations are in that yet remain in our sinful town? And that which makes my grief the more heavy is because they have no instructor, nor any to tell them what is to come.'

CHRISTIANA. 'Bowels becometh pilgrims. And thou dost for thy friends as my good Christian did for me when he left me. He mourned for that I would not heed nor regard him, but his Lord and ours did gather up his tears and

---

*Appropriate.
†Accepted.
‡Would not hamper.

put them into his bottle. [Psalms 56:8] And now both I and thou, and these
my sweet babes, are reaping the fruit and benefit of them. I hope, Mercy,
these tears of thine will not be lost, for the truth hath said 'That they that sow
in tears shall reap in joy, in singing. And he that goeth forth and weepeth,
hearing precious seed, shall doubtless come again with rejoicing, bringing his
sheaves with him.' [Psalms 126:5-6]

Then said Mercy,

> Let the most blessed by my guide,
> If't be his blessed will;
> Unto his gate, into his fold,
> Up to his holy hill.
>
> And let him never suffer me
> To swerve or turn aside
> From his free grace, and holy ways,
> What ere shall me betide.
>
> And let him gather them of mine,
> That I have left behind;
> Lord, make them pray they may be thine,
> With all their heart and mind.

Now my old friend proceeded and said, "But when Christiana came up
to the Slough of Despond, she began to be at a stand. 'For,' said she, 'this
is the place in which my dear husband had like to a been smothered with
mud.' She perceived also that, notwithstanding the command of the King to
make this place for pilgrims good, yet it was rather worse than formerly." So
I asked if that was true. "Yes," said the old gentleman, "too true. For that
many there be that pretend to be the King's labourers, and that say they are
for mending the King's highway, that bring dirt and dung instead of stones,
and so mar instead of mending. Here Christiana therefore, with her boys, did
make a stand. But said Mercy, 'Come, let us venture; only let us be wary.'
Then they looked well to the steps and made a shift to get staggeringly over.
Yet Christiana had like to a been in, and that not once nor twice. Now they
had no sooner got over, but they thought they heard words that said unto
them, 'Blessed is she that believeth, for there shall be a performance of the
things that have been told her from the Lord.' [Luke 1:45]

"Then they went on again, and said Mercy to Christiana, 'Had I as good
ground to hope for a loving reception at the wicket-gate as you, I think no
Slough of Despond would discourage me.'

" 'Well,' said the other, 'you know your sore, and I know mine; and, good
friend, we shall all have enough evil before we come at our journey's end.

" 'For can it be imagined that the people that design to attain such excellent glories as we do, and that are so envied that happiness as we are, but that
we shall meet with what fears and scares, with what troubles and afflictions
they can possibly assault us with, that hate us?' "

And now Mr. Sagacity left me to dream out my dream by myself. Wherefore methought I saw Christiana and Mercy, and the boys, go all of them up to the gate. To which, when they were come, they betook themselves to a short debate about how they must manage their calling at the gate and what should be said to him that did open to them. So it was concluded, since Christiana was the eldest, that she should knock for entrance, and that she should speak to him that did open, for the rest. So Christiana began to knock, and, as her poor husband did, she knocked and knocked again. But instead of any that answered, they all thought that they heard as if a dog came barking upon them, a dog, and a great one too; and this made the women and children afraid. Nor durst they for a while dare to knock any more, for fear the mastiff should fly upon them. Now, therefore, they were greatly tumbled up and down in their minds and knew not what to do. Knock they durst not, for fear of the dog; go back they durst not, for fear that the keeper of that gate should espy them as they so went, and should be offended with them. At last they thought of knocking again, and knocked more vehemently than they did at the first. Then said the keeper of the gate, "Who is there?" So the dog left off to bark, and he opened unto them.

Then Christiana made low obeisance and said, "Let not our Lord be offended with his handmaidens for that we have knocked at his princely gate." Then said the keeper, "Whence come ye, and what is that you would have?"

Christiana answered, "We are come from whence Christian did come and upon the same errand as he, to wit, to be, if it shall please you, graciously admitted by this gate into the way that leads to the Celestial City. And I answer, my Lord, in the next place, that I am Christiana, once the wife of Christian, that now is gotten above."

With that the keeper of the gate did marvel, saying, "What, is she become now a pilgrim, that but awhile ago abhorred that life?" Then she bowed her head and said, "Yes, and so are these my sweet babes also."

Then he took her by the hand and led her in, and said also, "Suffer the little children to come unto me," [Mark 10:14] and with that he shut up the gate. This done, he called to a trumpeter that was above, over the gate, to entertain Christiana with shouting and sound of trumpet for joy. So he obeyed and sounded and filled the air with his melodious notes.

Now, all this while, poor Mercy did stand without, trembling and crying for fear that she was rejected. But when Christiana had gotten admittance for herself and her boys, then she began to make intercession for Mercy.

CHRISTIANA. And she said, "My Lord, I have a companion of mine that stands yet without, that is come hither upon the same account as myself, one that is much dejected in her mind, for that she comes, as she thinks, without sending for, whereas I was sent to by my husband's King to come."

Now Mercy began to be very impatient, for each minute was as long to her as an hour; wherefore she prevented Christiana from a fuller interceding for her by knocking at the gate herself. And she knocked then so loud that she made Christiana to start. Then said the keeper of the gate, "Who is there?" And said Christiana, "It is my friend."

So he opened the gate and looked out, but Mercy was fallen down without in a swoon, for she fainted and was afraid that no gate should be opened to her.

Then he took her by the hand and said, "Damsel, I bid thee arise."

"O, sir," said she, "I am faint. There is scarce life left in me." But he answered, "That one once said, 'When my soul fainted within me I remembered the Lord, and my prayer came in unto thee, into thy Holy Temple.' [Jonah 2:7] Fear not, but stand upon thy feet and tell me wherefore thou are come."

MERCY. "I am come for that unto which I was never invited as my friend Christiana was. Hers was from the King and mine was but from her. Wherefore I fear I presume."

"Did she desire thee to come with her to this place?"

MERCY. "Yes, and as my Lord sees, I am come. And if there is any grace and forgiveness of sins to spare, I beseech that I, thy poor handmaid, may be partaker thereof."

Then he took her again by the hand and led her gently in and said, "I pray for all them that believe on me, by what means soever they come unto me." Then said he to those that stood by, "Fetch something, and give it Mercy to smell on, thereby to stay her fainting." So they fetched her a bundle of myrrh, [Song of Solomon 1:13] and awhile after she was revived.

And now was Christiana, and her boys, and Mercy received of the Lord at the head of the way and spoke kindly unto by him.

Then said they yet further unto him, "We are sorry for our sins, and beg of our Lord his pardon and further information what we must do."

"I grant pardon," said he, "by word, and deed; by word in the promise of forgiveness; by deed in the way I obtained it. Take the first from my lips with a kiss, and the other as it shall be revealed."

Now I saw in my dream that he spake many good words unto them whereby they were greatly gladdened. He also had them up to the top of the gate and showed them by what deed they were saved, and told them withal that that sight they would have again as they went along in the way, to their comfort.

So he left them awhile in a summer-parlour below, where they entered into talk by themselves. And thus Christiana began, "O Lord! How glad am I that we are got in hither!"

MERCY. "So you well may. But I, of all, have cause to leap for joy."

CHRISTIANA. "I thought, one time, as I stood at the gate (because I had knocked and none did answer), that all our labour had been lost, specially when that ugly cur made such a heavy barking against us."

MERCY. "But my worst fears was after I saw that you was taken into his favour and that I was left behind. Now, thought I, 'tis fulfilled which is written, 'Two women shall be grinding together; the one shall be taken, and the other left.' [Matthew 24:41] I had much ado to forbear crying out, 'Undone, undone.'"

"And afraid I was to knock any more; but when I looked up to what was written over the gate, I took courage. I also thought that I must either knock again or die. So I knocked; but I cannot tell how, for my spirit now struggled betwixt life and death."

CHRISTIANA. "Can you not tell how you knocked? I am sure your knocks were so earnest that the very sound of them made me start. I thought I never heard such knocking in all my life. I thought you would a come in by violent hand or a took the kingdom by storm."

MERCY. "Alas, to be in my case. Who that so was could but a done so? You saw that the door was shut upon me and that there was a most cruel dog thereabout. Who, I say, that was so faint-hearted as I, that would not a knocked with all their might? But, pray, what said my Lord to my rudeness? Was he not angry with me?"

CHRISTIANA. "When he heard your lumbering noise, he gave a wonderful innocent smile. I believe what you did pleased him well enough, for he showed no sign to the contrary. But I marvel in my heart why he keeps such a dog. Had I known that afore, I fear I should not have had heart enough to a ventured myself in this manner. But now we are in, we are in, and I am glad with all my heart."

MERCY. "I will ask, if you please, next time he comes down, why he keeps such a filthy cur in his yard. I hope he will not take it amiss."

"Ay, do," said the children, "and persuade him to hang him, for we are afraid that he will bite us when we go hence."

So at last he came down to them again, and Mercy fell to the ground on her face before him and worshipped and said, "Let my Lord accept of the sacrifice of praise which I now offer unto him, with the calves of my lips."

So he said to her, "Peace be to thee, stand up."

But she continued upon her face and said, "Righteous art thou, O Lord, when I plead with thee. Yet let me talk with thee of thy judgements. Wherefore dost thou keep so cruel a dog in thy yard, at the sight of which such women and children as we are ready to fly from thy gate for fear?" [Jeremiah 12:1–2]

He answered and said, "That dog has another owner. He also is kept close in another man's ground; only my pilgrims hear his barking. He belongs to the castle which you see there at a distance but can come up to the walls of this place. He has frighted many an honest pilgrim, from worse to better, by the great voice of his roaring. Indeed, he that owneth him doth not keep him of any good will to me or mine, but with intent to keep the pilgrims from coming to me, and that they may be afraid to knock at this gate for entrance. Sometimes also he has broken out and has worried some that I love; but I take all at present patiently. I also give my pilgrims timely help, so they are not delivered up to his power to do to them what his doggish nature would prompt him to. But what! my purchased one, I trow, hadst thou known never so much beforehand, thou wouldst not a been afraid of a dog.

"The beggars that go from door to door will, rather than they will lose a supposed alms, run the hazard of the bawling, barking, and biting, too, of a dog. And shall a dog, a dog in another man's yard, a dog whose barking I turn to the profit of pilgrims, keep any from coming to me? I deliver them from the lions, their darling from the power of the dog." [Psalms 22:20–21]

MERCY. Then said Mercy, "I confess my ignorance; I spake what I understood not; I acknowledge that thou doest all things well."

CHRISTIANA. Then Christiana began to talk of their journey and to inquire after the way. So he fed them, and washed their feet, and set them in the way of his steps, according as he had dealt with her husband before.

So I saw in my dream that they walked on in their way and had the weather very comfortable to them.

Then Christiana began to sing saying,

> Blessed be the day that I began
> A pilgrim for to be;
> And blessed also be that man
> That thereto moved me.

> 'Tis true, 'twas long ere I began
> To seek to live forever:
> But now I run fast as I can;
> 'Tis better late than never.

> Our tears to joy, our fears to faith,
> Are turned, as we see,
> Thus our beginning, as one saith,
> Shows what our end will be.

Now there was, on the other side of the wall that fenced in the way up which Christiana and her companions was to go, a garden; and that garden belonged to him whose was that barking dog of whom mention was made before. And some of the fruit-trees that grew in that garden shot their branches over the wall, and being mellow, they that found them did gather them up and oft eat of them to their hurt. So Christiana's boys, as boys are apt to do, being pleased with the trees, and with the fruit that did hang thereon, did plash* them and began to eat. Their mother did also chide them for so doing, but still the boys went on.

"Well," said she, "my sons, you transgress, for that fruit is none of ours." But she did not know that they did belong to the enemy. I'll warrant you if she had, she would a been ready to die for fear. But that passed, and they went on their way. Now by that they were gone about two bows-shot from the place that let them into the way, they espied two very ill-favoured ones coming down apace to meet them. With that, Christiana, and Mercy, her friend, covered themselves with their veils and so kept on their journey. The children also went on before, so at last they met together. Then they that came down to meet them came just up to the women, as if they would

*Bend.

embrace them; but Christiana said, "Stand back, or go peaceably by as you should." Yet these two, as men that are deaf, regarded not Christiana's words, but began to lay hands upon them. At that, Christiana, waxing very wroth, spurned at them with her feet. Mercy also, as well as she could, did what she could to shift them. Christiana again said to them, "Stand back and be gone, for we have no money to lose, being pilgrims, as ye see, and such too as live upon the charity of our friends."

ILL-FAVOURED. Then said one of the two of the men, "We make no assault upon you for money, but are come out to tell you that if you will but grant one small request which we shall ask, we will make women of you forever."

CHRISTIANA. Now Christiana, imagining what they should mean, made answer again, "We will neither hear nor regard nor yield to what you shall ask. We are in haste, cannot stay. Our business is a business of life and death." So again she and her companions made a fresh essay to go past them. But they letted them in their way.

ILL-FAVOURED. And they said, "We intend no hurt to your lives. 'Tis another thing we would have."

CHRISTIANA. "Ay," quoth Christiana, "you would have us body and soul, for I know 'tis for that you are come. But we will die rather upon the spot than suffer ourselves to be brought into such snares as shall hazard our well-being hereafter." And with that they both shrieked out and cried, "Murder, murder," and so put themselves under those laws that are provided for the protection of women. But the men still made their approach upon them, with design to prevail against them. They therefore cried out again.

Now they being, as I said, not far from the gate in at which they came, their voice was heard from where they was thither. Wherefore, some of the house came out and, knowing that it was Christiana's tongue, they made haste to her relief. But by that they was got within sight of them, the women was in a very great scuffle; the children also stood crying by. Then did he that came in for their relief call out to the ruffians saying, "What is that thing that you do? Would you make my Lord's people to transgress?" He also attempted to take them, but they did make their escape over the wall into the garden of the man to whom the great dog belonged; so the dog became their protector. This Reliever then came up to the women and asked them how they did. So they answered, "We thank thy Prince, pretty well, only we have been somewhat affrighted. We thank thee also for that thou camest in to our help, for otherwise we had been overcome."

RELIEVER. So after a few more words, this Reliever said as followeth, "I marvelled much when you was entertained at the gate above, being ye knew that ye were but weak women, that you petitioned not the lord there for a conductor. Then might you have avoided these troubles and dangers, for he would have granted you one."

CHRISTIANA. "Alas," said Christiana, "we were so taken with our present blessing that dangers to come were forgotten by us. Besides, who could have thought that so near the King's palace there should have lurked such naughty ones. Indeed, it had been well for us had we asked our Lord for one;

but, since our Lord knew 'twould be for our profit, I wonder he sent not one along with us."

RELIEVER. "It is not always necessary to grant things not asked for, lest by so doing they become of little esteem; but when the want of a thing is felt, it then comes under, in the eyes of him that feels it, that estimate that properly is its due, and so consequently will be thereafter used. Had my Lord granted you a conductor, you would not neither so have bewailed that oversight of yours in not asking for one as now you have occasion to do. So all things work for good and tend to make you more wary."

CHRISTIANA. "Shall we go back again to my Lord, and confess our folly and ask one?"

RELIEVER. "Your confession of your folly I will present him with; to go back again, you need not. For in all places where you shall come, you will find no want at all; for, in every of my Lord's lodgings which he has prepared for the reception of his pilgrims, there is sufficient to furnish them against all attempts whatsoever. But, as I said, he will be inquired of by them to do it for them, and 'tis a poor thing that is not worth asking for." [Ezekiel 36:37] When he had thus said, he went back to his place, and the pilgrims went on their way.

MERCY. Then said Mercy, "What a sudden blank is here? I made account we had now been past all danger and that we should never see sorrow more."

CHRISTIANA. "Thy innocency, my sister," said Christiana to Mercy, "may excuse thee much. But as for me, my fault is so much the greater, for that I saw this danger before I came out of the doors and yet did not provide for it where provision might a been had. I am therefore much to be blamed."

MERCY. Then said Mercy, "How knew you this before you came from home? Pray, open to me this riddle."

CHRISTIANA. "Why, I will tell you. Before I set foot out-of-doors, one night, as I lay in my bed, I had a dream about this. For methought I saw two men, as like these as ever the world they could look, stand at my beds-feet, plotting how they might prevent my salvation. I will tell you their very words. They said ('twas when I was in my troubles), 'What shall we do with this woman, for she cries out waking and sleeping for forgiveness? If she be suffered to go on as she begins, we shall lose her as we have lost her husband.' This you know might a made me take heed and have provided when provision might a been had."

MERCY. "Well," said Mercy, "as by this neglect we have an occasion ministered unto us to behold our own imperfections. So our Lord has taken occasion thereby, to make manifest the riches of his grace. For he, as we see, has followed us with unasked kindness and has delivered us from their hands that were stronger than we, of his mere good pleasure."

Thus now when they had talked away a little more time, they drew nigh to an house which stood in the way, which house was built for the relief of pilgrims as you will find more fully related in the first part of these records of the Pilgrim's Progress. So they drew on towards the house (the house of the Interpreter), and when they came to the door, they heard a great talk in the house. They then gave ear and heard, as they thought, Christiana mentioned by name. For you must know that there went along, even before her, a talk of her and her children's going on pilgrimage. And this thing was the more pleasing to them because they had heard that she was Christian's wife, that woman who was sometime ago so unwilling to hear of going on pilgrimage. Thus, therefore, they stood still and heard the good people within commending her who they little thought stood at the door. At last, Christiana knocked as she had done at the gate before. Now when she had knocked, there came to the door a young damsel and opened the door and looked, and behold, two women was there.

DAMSEL. Then said the Damsel to them, "With whom would you speak in this place?"

CHRISTIANA. Christiana answered, "We understand that this is a privileged place for those that are become pilgrims, and we now at this door are such. Wherefore we pray that we may be partakers of that for which we at this time are come; for the day, as thou seest, is very far spent, and we are loath tonight to go any further."

DAMSEL. "Pray, what may I call your name, that I may tell it to my lord within?"

CHRISTIANA. "My name is Christiana. I was the wife of that pilgrim that some years ago did travel this way, and these be his four children. This maiden also is my companion and is going on pilgrimage, too."

INNOCENT. Then ran Innocent in (for that was her name) and said to those within, "Can you think who is at the door? There is Christiana and her children and her companion, all waiting for entertainment here." Then they leaped for joy and went and told their master. So he came to the door, and, looking upon her, he said, "Art thou that Christiana, whom Christian, the good man, left behind him when he betook himself to a pilgrim's life?"

CHRISTIANA. "I am that woman that was so hard-hearted as to slight my husband's troubles, and that left him to go on in his journey alone, and these are his four children. But now I also am come, for I am convinced that no way is right but this."

INTERPRETER. "Then is fulfilled that which also is written of the man that said to his son, 'Go work today in my vineyard.' And he said to his father, 'I will not,' but afterwards repented and went." [Matthew 21:28–29]

CHRISTIANA. Then said Christiana, "Sobeit, Amen. God make it a true saying upon me, and grant that I may be found, at the last, of him in peace, without spot and blameless."

INTERPRETER. "But why standest thou thus at the door? Come in, thou daughter of Abraham; we was talking of thee but now. For tidings have come to us before how thou art become a pilgrim. Come, children, come in; come, maiden, come in." So he had them all into the house.

So when they were within, they were bidden sit down and rest them; the which when they had done, those that attended upon the pilgrims in the house came into the room to see them. And one smiled, and another smiled, and they all smiled for joy that Christiana was become a pilgrim. They also looked upon the boys; they stroked them over the faces with the hand in token of their kind reception of them. They also carried it lovingly to Mercy, and bid them all welcome into their master's house.

After a while, because supper was not ready, the Interpreter took them into his significant rooms and showed them what Christian, Christiana's husband, had seen sometime before. Here, therefore, they saw the man in the cage, the man and his dream, the man that cut his way through his enemies, and the picture of the biggest of them all, together with the rest of those things that were then so profitable to Christian.

This done, and after these things had been somewhat digested by Christiana and her company, the Interpreter takes them apart again and has them first into a room, where was a man that could look no way but downwards, with a muck-rake in his hand. There stood also one, over his head, with a celestial crown in his hand, and proffered to give him that crown for his muck-rake; but the man did neither look up nor regard, but raked to himself the straws, the small sticks, and dust of the floor.

Then said Christiana, "I persuade myself that I know somewhat the meaning of this. For this is a figure of a man of this world, is it not, good sir?"

INTERPRETER. "Thou hast said the right," said he, "and his muck-rake doth show his carnal mind. And, whereas thou seest him rather give heed to rake up straws, and sticks, and the dust of the floor, than to what he says that calls to him from above with the celestial crown in his hand, it is to show that heaven is but as a fable to some, and that things here are counted the only things substantial. Now, whereas it was also showed thee that the man could look no way but downwards, it is to let thee know that earthly things, when they are with power upon men's minds, quite carry their hearts away from God."

CHRISTIANA. Then said Christiana, "O! deliver me from this muck-rake!"

INTERPRETER. "That prayer," said the Interpreter, "has lain by till 'tis almost rusty. 'Give me not riches,' is scarce the prayer of one of ten thousand; straws, and sticks, and dust, with most, are the great things now looked after."

With that Mercy and Christiana wept and said, "It is, alas, too true."

When the Interpreter had showed them this, he has them into the very best room in the house (a very brave room it was), so he bid them look round about and see if they could find anything profitable there. Then they looked round and round, for there was nothing there to be seen but a very great spider on the wall, and that they overlooked.

MERCY. Then said Mercy, "Sir, I see nothing." But Christiana held her peace.

INTERPRETER. "But," said the Interpreter, "look again." She therefore looked again and said, "Here is not anything but an ugly spider who hangs by her hands upon the wall. Then said he, "Is there but one spider in all this spacious room?" Then the water stood in Christiana's eyes, for she was a woman quick of apprehension; and she said, "Yes, Lord, there is more than one. Yea, and spiders whose venom is far more destructive than that which is in her." The Interpreter then looked pleasantly upon her and said, "Thou hast said the truth." This made Mercy blush and the boys to cover their faces, for they all began now to understand the riddle.

Then said the Interpreter again, "The spider taketh hold with her hands, as you see, and is in king's palaces. [Proverbs 30:28] And wherefore is this recorded, but to show you that how full of the venom of sin soever you be, yet you may by the hand of faith lay hold of and dwell in the best room that belongs to the King's house above?"

CHRISTIANA. "I thought," said Christiana, "of something of this, but I could not imagine it all. I thought that we were like spiders and that we looked like ugly creatures in what fine room soever we were, but that by this spider, this venomous and ill-favoured creature, we were to learn how to act faith, that came not into my mind. And yet she has taken hold with her hands, as I see, and dwells in the best room in the house. God has made nothing in vain."

Then they seemed all to be glad, but the water stood in their eyes; yet they looked one upon another and also bowed before the Interpreter.

He had them then into another room, where was a hen and chickens, and bid them observe awhile. So one of the chickens went to the trough to drink, and every time she drank she lift up her head and her eyes towards heaven. "See," said he, "what this little chick doth, and learn of her to acknowledge whence your mercies come by receiving them with looking up. Yet again," said he, "observe and look." So they gave heed and perceived that the hen did walk in a fourfold method towards her chickens. 1. She had a common call, and that she hath all day long. 2. She had a special call, and that she had but sometimes. 3. She had a brooding note. And 4. She had an outcry.

"Now," said he, "compare this hen to your King and these chickens to his obedient ones. For answerable to her, himself has his methods which he walketh in towards his people. By his common call, he gives nothing; by his special call, he always has something to give; he has also a brooding voice, for them that are under his wing. And he has an outcry, to give the alarm when he seeth the enemy come. I chose, my darlings, to lead you into the room where such things are because you are women and they are easy for you."

CHRISTIANA. "And, sir," said Christiana, "pray, let us see some more." So he had them into the slaughter-house, where was a butcher a-killing of a sheep. And, behold, the sheep was quiet and took her death patiently. Then said the Interpreter, "You must learn of this sheep to suffer, and to put up wrongs without murmurings and complaints. Behold how quietly she takes her death, and without objecting she suffereth her skin to be pulled over her ears. Your King doth call you his sheep."

After this, he led them into his garden, where was great variety of flowers. And he said, "Do you see all these?" So Christiana said, "Yes." Then said he again, "Behold, the flowers are diverse in stature, in quality, and colour, and smell, and virtue, and some are better than some; also, where the gardener has set them, there they stand and quarrel not one with another."

Again he had them into his field which he had sowed with wheat and corn. But, when they beheld, the tops of all was cut off; only the straw remained. He said again, "This ground was dunged, and plowed, and sowed. But what shall we do with the crop?" Then said Christiana, "Burn some and make muck of the rest." Then said the Interpreter again, "Fruit you see is that thing you look for, and for want of that you condemn it to the fire and to be trodden under foot of men. Beware that in this you condemn not yourselves."

Then, as they were coming in from abroad, they espied a little robin with a great spider in his mouth. So the Interpreter said, "Look here." So they looked, and Mercy wondered. But Christiana said, "What a disparagement is it to such a little pretty bird as the robin redbreast is, he being also a bird above many that loveth to maintain a kind of sociableness with man. I had thought they had lived upon crumbs of bread or upon other such harmless matter. I like him worse than I did."

The Interpreter then replied, "This robin is an emblem very apt to set forth some professors by; for to sight they are as this robin, pretty of note, colour and carriages. They seem also to have a very great love for professors that are sincere, and above all other to desire to sociate with and to be in their company, as if they could live upon the good man's crumbs. They pretend also that therefore it is that they frequent the house of the godly and the appointments of the Lord; but when they are by themselves, as the robin, they can catch and gobble up spiders, they can change their diet, drink iniquity, and swallow down sin like water."

So when they were come again into the house, because supper as yet was not ready, Christiana again desired that the Interpreter would either show or tell of some other things that are profitable.

Then the Interpreter began and said, "The fatter the sow is, the more she desires the mire; the fatter the ox is, the more gamesomely he goes to the slaughter; and the more healthy the lusty man is, the more prone he is unto evil.

"There is a desire in women to go neat and fine, and it is a comely thing to be adorned with that that in God's sight is of great price.

" 'Tis easier watching a night or two, than to sit up a whole year together. So 'tis easier for one to begin to profess well, than to hold out as he should to the end.

"Every shipmaster, when in a storm, will willingly cast that overboard that is of the smallest value in the vessel; but who will throw the best out first? None but he that feareth not God.

"One leak will sink a ship, and one sin will destroy a sinner.

"He that forgets his friend is ungrateful unto him; but he that forgets his Saviour is unmerciful to himself.

"He that lives in sin and looks for happiness hereafter is like him that soweth cockle* and thinks to fill his barn with wheat or barley.

"If a man would live well, let him fetch his last day to him, and make it always his company-keeper.

*A weed.

"Whispering and change of thoughts proves that sin is in the world.

"If the world which God sets light by is counted a thing of that worth with men, what is heaven which God commendeth?

"If the life that is attended with so many troubles is so loath to be let go by us, what is the life above?

"Everybody will cry up the goodness of men; but who is there that is, as he should, affected with the goodness of God?

"We seldom sit down to meat, but we eat and leave. So there is in Jesus Christ more merit and righteousness than the whole world has need of."

When the Interpreter had done, he takes them out into his garden again and had them to a tree whose inside was all rotten and gone, and yet it grew and had leaves. Then said Mercy, "What means this?" "This tree," said he, "whose outside is fair and whose inside is rotten, is it to which many may be compared that are in the garden of God, who with their mouths speak high in behalf of God, but indeed will do nothing for him, whose leaves are fair, but their heart good for nothing but to be tinder for the Devil's tinder-box."

Now supper was ready, the table spread, and all things set on the board; so they sat down and did eat when one had given thanks. And the Interpreter did usually entertain those that lodged with him with music at meals, so the minstrels played. There was also one that did sing, and a very fine voice he had.

His song was this,

> The Lord is only my support,
> And he that doth me feed;
> How can I then want anything
> Whereof I stand in need?

When the song and music was ended, the Interpreter asked Christiana what it was that at first did move her to betake herself to a pilgrim's life?

Christiana answered, "First, the loss of my husband came into mind, at which I was heartily grieved, but all that was but natural affection. Then, after that, came the troubles and pilgrimage of my husband into my mind, and also how like a churl I had carried it to him as to that. So guilt took hold of my mind and would have drawn me into the pond but that opportunely I had a dream of the well-being of my husband, and a letter sent me by the King of that country where my husband dwells, to come to him. The dream and the letter together so wrought upon my mind that they forced me to this way."

INTERPRETER. "But met you with no opposition afore you set out-of-doors?"

CHRISTIANA. "Yes, a neighbour of mine, one Mrs. Timorous. (She was a kin to him that would have persuaded my husband to go back for fear of the lions.) She all-to-befooled me for, as she called it, my intended desperate adventure; she also urged what she could, to dishearten me to it, the hardships and troubles that my husband met with in the way; but all this I got over pretty well. But a dream that I had, of two ill-looked ones that I thought did plot how to make me miscarry in my journey, that hath troubled me much. Yea, it still runs in my mind and makes me afraid of everyone that I meet, lest they should meet me to do me a mischief and to turn me out of the way. Yea, I may tell my Lord, though I would not have everybody know it, that between this and the gate by which we got into the way, we were both so sorely assaulted that we were made to cry out murder, and the two that made this assault upon us were like the two that I saw in my dream."

Then said the Interpreter, "Thy beginning is good; thy latter end shall greatly increase." So he addressed himself to Mercy and said unto her, "And what moved thee to come hither, sweetheart?"

MERCY. Then Mercy blushed and trembled and for a while continued silent.

INTERPRETER. Then said he, "Be not afraid; only believe, and speak thy mind."

MERCY. So she began and said, "Truly, sir, my want of experience is that that makes me covet to be in silence, and that also that fills me with fears of coming short at last. I cannot tell of visions and dreams as my friend Christiana can; nor know I what it is to mourn for my refusing of the counsel of those that were good relations."

INTERPRETER. "What was it then, dear heart, that hath prevailed with thee to do as thou hast done?"

MERCY. "Why, when our friend here was packing up to be gone from our town, I and another went accidentally to see her. So we knocked at the door and went in. When we were within, and seeing what she was doing, we asked what was her meaning. She said she was sent for to go to her husband, and then she up and told us how she had seen him in a dream, dwelling in a curious place among immortals wearing a crown, playing upon a harp, eating and drinking at his Prince's table, and singing praises to him for bringing him thither, etc. Now methought while she was telling these things unto us, my heart burned within me. And I said in my heart, 'If this be true, I will leave my father and my mother, and the land of my nativity, and will, if I may, go along with Christiana.'

"So I asked her further of the truth of these things and if she would let me go with her, for I saw now that there was no dwelling, but with the danger of ruin, any longer in our town. But yet I came away with a heavy heart, not for that I was unwilling to come away, but for that so many of my relations were left behind. And I am come with all the desire of my heart and will go, if I may, with Christiana unto her husband and his King."

INTERPRETER. "Thy setting out is good, for thou hast given credit to the truth. Thou art a Ruth, who did for the love that she bore to Naomi, and to the Lord her God, leave father and mother, and the land of her nativity to come out and go with a people that she knew not heretofore.

'The Lord recompense thy work, and a full reward be given thee of the Lord God of Israel, under whose wings thou art come to trust.' " [Ruth 2:11–12]

Now supper was ended, and preparations was made for bed; the women were laid singly alone and the boys by themselves. Now when Mercy was in bed, she could not sleep for joy, for that now her doubts of missing at last were removed further from her than ever they were before. So she lay blessing and praising God who had had such favour for her.

In the morning they arose with the sun and prepared themselves for their departure. But the Interpreter would have them tarry awhile, "For," said he, "you must orderly go from hence." Then said he to the damsel that at first opened unto them, "Take them and have them into the garden, to the bath, and there wash them and make them clean from the soil which they have gathered by travelling. Then Innocent, the damsel, took them and had them into the garden and brought them to the bath, so she told them that there they must wash and be clean, for so her master would have the women to do that called at his house as they were going on pilgrimage. They then went in and washed, yea, they and the boys and all, and they came out of that bath not only sweet and clean, but also much enlivened and strengthened in their joints. So when they came in they looked fairer a deal than when they went out to the washing.

When they were returned out of the garden from the bath, the Interpreter took them and looked upon them and said unto them, "Fair as the moon." [Song of Solomon 6:10] Then he called for the seal wherewith they used to be sealed that were washed in his bath. So the seal was brought, and he set his mark upon them that they might be known in the places whither they were yet to go. Now the seal was the contents and sum of the Passover which the children of Israel did eat when they came out from the Land of Egypt, and the mark was set between their eyes. This seal greatly added to their beauty, for it was an ornament to their faces. It also added to their gravity and made their countenances more like them of angels.

Then said the Interpreter again to the damsel that waited upon these women, "Go into the vestry and fetch out garments for these people." So she went and fetched out white raiment and laid it down before him; so he commanded them to put it on. It was fine linen, white and clean. [Revelation 19:4,18] When the women were thus adorned they seemed to be a terror one to the other for that they could not see that glory each one on herself which they could see in each other. Now, therefore, they began to esteem each other better than themselves. For "You are fairer than I am," said one, and, "You are more comely than I am," said another. The children also stood amazed to see into what fashion they were brought.

The Interpreter then called for a manservant of his, one Great-heart, and bid him take sword, and helmet and shield, and, "Take these, my daughters," said he, "and conduct them to the house called Beautiful, at which place they will rest next." So he took his weapons and went before them, and the

Interpreter said, "Godspeed." Those also that belonged to the family sent them away with many a good wish. So they went on their way and sung,

> This place has been our second stage;
> Here we have heard and seen
> Those good things that, from age to age,
> To others hid have been.

> The dung-hill raker, spider, hen,
> The chicken, too, to me
> Hath taught a lesson; let me then
> Conformed to it be.

> The butcher, garden and the field,
> The robin and his bait,
> Also the rotten tree doth yield
> Me argument of weight;

> To move me for to watch and pray,
> To strive to be sincere,
> To take my cross up day by day,
> And serve the Lord with fear.

Now I saw in my dream that they went on, and Great-heart went before them; so they went and came to the place where Christian's burthen fell off his back and tumbled into a sepulchre. Here then they made a pause, and here also they blessed God. Now said Christiana, "It comes to my mind what was said to us at the gate, to wit, that we should have pardon, by word and deed; by word, that is, by the promise; by deed, to wit, in the way it was obtained. What the promise is of that I know something. But what is it to have pardon by deed, or in the way that it was obtained, Mr. Great-heart, I suppose you know; wherefore, if you please, let us hear you discourse thereof."

GREAT-HEART. "Pardon by the deed done is pardon obtained by some one for another that hath need thereof; not by the person pardoned, but in the way, saith another, in which I have obtained it. So then to speak to the question more large, the pardon that you and Mercy and these boys have attained was obtained by another, to wit, by him that let you in at the gate; and he hath obtained it in this double way. He has performed righteousness to cover you and spilt blood to wash you in."

CHRISTIANA. "But if he parts with his righteousness to us, what will he have for himself?"

GREAT-HEART. "He has more righteousness than you have need of or than he needeth himself."

CHRISTIANA. "Pray, make that appear."

GREAT-HEART. "With all my heart, but first I must premise that he of whom we are now about to speak is one that has not his fellow. He has two natures in one person, plain to be distinguished, impossible to be divided.

Unto each of these natures a righteousness belongeth, and each righteousness is essential to that nature. So that one may as easily cause the nature to be extinct as to separate its justice or righteousness from it. Of these righteousnesses, therefore, we are not made partakers so as that they, or any of them, should be put upon us that we might be made just and live thereby. Besides these, there is a righteousness which this person has, as these two natures are joined in one. And this is not the righteousness of the Godhead, as distinguished from the manhood, nor the righteousness of the manhood, as distinguished from the Godhead; but a righteousness which standeth in the union of both natures, and may properly be called the righteousness that is essential to his being prepared of God to the capacity of the mediatory office which he was to be intrusted with. If he parts with his first righteousness, he parts with his Godhead; if he parts with his second righteousness, he parts with the purity of his manhood; if he parts with his third, he parts with that perfection that capacitates him to the office of meditation. He has, therefore, another righteousness which standeth in performance, or obedience to a revealed will, and that is it that he puts upon sinners, and that by which their sins are covered. Wherefore he saith, 'As by one man's disobedience many were made sinners, so by the obedience of one shall many be made righteous.' " [Romans 5:19]

CHRISTIANA. "But are the other righteousnesses of no use to us?"

GREAT-HEART. "Yes, for though they are essential to his natures and office, and so cannot be communicated unto another, yet it is by virtue of them that the righteousness that justifies is for that purpose efficacious. The righteousness of his Godhead gives virtue to his obedience; the righteousness of his manhood giveth capability to his obedience to justify; and the righteousness that standeth in the union of these two natures to his office giveth authority to that righteousness to do the work for which it is ordained.

"So then, here is a righteousness that Christ, as God, has no need of, for he is God without it. Here is a righteousness that Christ, as man, has no need of to make him so, for he is perfect man without it. Again, here is a righteousness that Christ as God-man has no need of, for he is perfectly so without it. Here then is a righteousness that Christ, as God, as man, as God-man has no need of with reference to himself, and, therefore, he can spare it, a justifying righteousness, that he for himself wanteth not, and therefore he giveth it away. Hence 'tis called the 'gift of righteousness.' [Romans 5:17] This righteousness, since Christ Jesus the Lord has made himself under the law, must be given away. For the law doth not only bind him that is under it to do justly, but to use charity. Wherefore he must, he ought by the law, if he hath two coats, to give one to him that has none. Now our Lord hath indeed two coats, one for himself and one to spare. Wherefore he freely bestows one upon those that have none. And thus, Christiana, and Mercy, and the rest of you that are here, doth your pardon come by deed, or by the work of another man. Your Lord Christ is he that has worked and given away what he wrought for to the next poor beggar he meets.

"But again, in order to pardon by deed, there must something be paid to

God as a price, as well as something prepared to cover us withal. Sin has delivered us up to the just curse of a righteous law. Now from this curse we must be justified by way of redemption, a price being paid for the harms we have done, and this is by the blood of your Lord, who came and stood in your place and stead, and died your death for your transgressions. Thus has he ransomed you from your transgressions by blood and covered your polluted and deformed souls with righteousness. For the sake of which God passeth by you and will not hurt you when he comes to judge the world."

CHRISTIANA. "This is brave. Now I see that there was something to be learnt by our being pardoned by word and deed. Good Mercy, let us labour to keep this in mind, and my children, do you remember it also. But, sir, was not this it that made my good Christian's burden fall from off his shoulder and that made him give three leaps for joy?"

GREAT-HEART. "Yes, 'twas the belief of this that cut those strings that could not be cut by other means, and 'twas to give him a proof of the virtue of this that he was suffered to carry his burden to the cross."

CHRISTIANA. "I thought so, for though my heart was lightful and joyous before, yet it is ten times more lightsome and joyous now. And I am persuaded by what I have felt, though I have felt but little as yet, that if the most burdened man in the world was here and did see and believe, as I now do, 'twould make his heart the more merry and blithe."

GREAT-HEART. "There is not only comfort and the ease of a burden brought to us by the sight and consideration of these, but an endeared affection begot in us by it. For who can, if he doth but once think that pardon comes not only by promise but thus, but be affected with the way and means of his redemption, and so with the man that hath wrought it for him?"

CHRISTIANA. "True, methinks it makes my heart bleed to think that he should bleed for me. Oh, thou loving one! Oh, thou blessed one! Thou deservest to have me, thou hast bought me; thou deservest to have me all, thou has paid for me ten thousand times more than I am worth. No marvel that this made the water stand in my husband's eyes, and that it made him trudge so nimbly on. I am persuaded he wished me with him; but vile wretch that I was, I let him come all alone. O, Mercy, that thy father and mother were here, yea, and Mrs. Timorous also. Nay, I wish now with all my heart, that here was Madam Wanton, too. Surely, surely, their hearts would be affected, nor could the fear of the one, nor the powerful lusts of the other, prevail with them to go home again and to refuse to become good pilgrims."

GREAT-HEART. "You speak now in the warmth of your affections. Will it, think you, be always thus with you? Besides, this is not communicated to everyone, nor to everyone that did see your Jesus bleed. There was that stood by, and that saw the blood run from his heart to the ground, and yet was so far off this that, instead of lamenting, they laughed at him, and instead of becoming his disciples, did harden their hearts against him. So that all that you have, my daughters, you have by a peculiar impression made by a divine contemplating upon what I have spoken to you. Remember that 'twas told you that the hen, by her common call, gives no meat to her chickens. This you have, therefore, by a special grace."

Now I saw still in my dream that they went on until they were come to the place that Simple, and Sloth and Presumption lay and slept in when Christian went by on pilgrimage. And behold, they were hanged up in irons a little way off on the other side.

MERCY. Then said Mercy to him that was their guide and conductor, "What are those three men, and for what are they hanged here?"

GREAT-HEART. "These three men were men of very bad qualities. They had no mind to be pilgrims themselves, and whosoever they could they hindered. They were for sloth and folly themselves, and whoever they could persuade with they made so too, and withal taught them to presume that they should do well at last. They were asleep when Christian went by, and now you go by they are hanged."

> Behold how the slothful are a sign
> Hung up, 'cause holy ways they did decline.
> See here to how the child doth play the man,
> And weak grow strong, when Great-heart leads the van.

MERCY. "But could they persuade any to be of their opinion?"

GREAT-HEART. "Yes, they turned several out of the way. There was Slow-pace that they persuaded to do as they. They also prevailed with one Short-wind, with one No-heart, with one Linger-after-lust, and with one Sleepy-head, and with a young woman, her name was Dull, to turn out of the way and become as they. Besides, they brought up an ill report of your Lord, persuading others that he was a taskmaster. They also brought up an evil report of the good land, saying 'twas not half so good as some pretend it was. They also began to villify his servants and to count the very best of them meddlesome, troublesome busy-bodies. Further, they would call the bread of God, husks, the comforts of his children, fancies, the travel and labour of pilgrims, things to no purpose."

CHRISTIANA. "Nay," said Christiana, 'if they were such, they shall never be bewailed by me; they have but what they deserve, and I think it is well that they hang so near the highway that others may see and take warning. But had it not been well if their crimes had been engraven in some plate of iron or brass and left here, even where they did their mischiefs, for a caution to other bad men?"

GREAT-HEART. "So it is, as you well may perceive if you will go a little to the wall."

MERCY. "No, no, let them hang and their names rot, and their crimes live forever against them. I think it a high favour that they were hanged afore we came hither; who knows else what they might a done to such poor women as we are?" Then she turned it into a song, saying,

> Now then, you three, hang there and be a sign
> To all that shall against the truth combine.
> And let him that comes after fear this end,

If unto pilgrims he is not a friend.
And thou, my soul; of all such men beware,
That unto holiness opposers are.

Thus they went on till they came at the foot of the Hill Difficulty where
again their good friend, Mr. Great-heart, took an occasion to tell them of
what happened there when Christian himself went by; so he had them first to
the spring. "Lo," saith he, "this is the spring that Christian drank of before
he went up this hill, and then 'twas clear and good; but now 'tis dirty with
the feet of some that are not desirous that pilgrims here should quench their
thirst." Thereat Mercy said, "And why so envious, trow?*" But said their
guide, "It will do if taken up and put into a vessel that is sweet and good; for
then the dirt will sink to the bottom and the water come out by itself more
clear." Thus, therefore, Christiana and her companions were compelled to
do. They took it up and put it into an earthen pot and so let it stand till the
dirt was gone to the bottom, and then they drank thereof.

Next he showed them the two by-ways that were at the foot of the hill
where Formality and Hypocrisy lost themselves. "And," said he, "these
are dangerous paths. Two were cast away when Christian came by. And
although, as you see, these ways are since stopped up with chains, posts and
a ditch, yet there are that will choose to adventure here, rather than take the
pains to go up this hill."

CHRISTIANA. " 'The way of transgressors is hard.' [Proverbs 13:15] 'Tis a
wonder that they can get into those ways without danger of breaking their
necks."

GREAT-HEART. "They will venture, yea, if at any time any of the King's
servants doth happen to see them and doth call unto them and tell them
that they are in the wrong ways and do bid them beware the danger. Then
they will railingly return them answer and say, 'As for the Word that thou
hast spoken unto us in the name of the King, we will not hearken unto
thee; but we will certainly do whatsoever thing goeth out of our own mouths,
etc.' [Jeremiah 44:16–17] Nay, if you look a little farther you shall see
that these ways are made cautionary enough, not only by these posts and
ditch and chain, but also by being hedged up. Yet they will choose to go
there."

CHRISTIANA. "They are idle, they love not to take pains; uphill-way is
unpleasant to them. So it is fulfilled unto them as it is written. 'The way of
the slothful man is a hedge of thorns.' [Proverbs 15:19] Yea, they will rather
choose to walk upon a snare than to go up this hill and the rest of this
way to the city."

Then they set forward and began to go up the hill, and up the hill they
went; but before they got to the top, Christiana began to pant and said, "I
dare say this is a breathing hill, no marvel if they that love their ease more

*Phrase meaning "faith."

than their souls choose to themselves a smoother way." Then said Mercy, "I must sit down." Also the least of the children began to cry. "Come, come," said Great-heart, "sit not down here, for a little above is the Prince's arbour." Then took he the little boy by the hand, and led him up thereto.

When they were come to the arbour they were very willing to sit down, for they were all in a pelting heat. Then said Mercy, "How sweet is rest to them that labour! And how good is the Prince of pilgrims, to provide such resting places for them! Of this arbour I have heard much, but I never saw it before. But here let us beware of sleeping, for, as I have heard, for that it cost poor Christian dear."

Then said Mr. Great-heart to the little ones, "Come, my pretty boys, how do you do? What think you now of going on pilgrimage?" "Sir," said the least,* "I was almost beat out of heart, but I thank you for lending me a hand at my need. And I remember now what my mother has told me, namely, that the way to heaven is as up a ladder, and the way to hell is as down a hill. But I had rather go up the ladder to life, than down the hill to death."

Then said Mercy, "But the proverb is 'To go down the hill is easy,' " but James said (for that was his name), "The day is coming when, in my opinion, going down hill will be the hardest of all." " 'Tis a good boy," said his master, "thou hast given her a right answer." Then Mercy smiled, but the little boy did blush.

CHRISTIANA. "Come," said Christiana, "will you eat a bit, a little to sweeten your mouths, while you sit here to rest your legs? For I have here a piece of pomegranate which Mr. Interpreter put in my hand just when I came out of his doors; he gave me also a piece of an honeycomb and a little bottle of spirits." "I thought he gave you something," said Mercy, "because he called you a to-side." "Yes, so he did," said the other. "But, Mercy, it shall still be as I said it should when at first we came from home. Thou shalt be a sharer in all the good that I have because thou so willingly didst become my companion." Then she gave to them, and they did eat, both Mercy and the boys. And said Christiana to Mr. Great-heart, "Sir, will you do as we?" But he answered, "You are going on pilgrimage, and presently I shall return. Much good may what you have do to you. At home I eat the same every day." Now when they had eaten and drank, and chatted a little longer, their guide said to them, "The day wears away; if you think good, let us prepare to be going." So they got up to go, and the little boys went before, but Christiana forgot to take her bottle of spirits with her. So she sent her little boy back to fetch it. Then said Mercy, "I think this is a losing place. Here Christian lost his roll, and here Christiana left her bottle behind her. Sir, what is the cause of this?" So their guide made answer and said, "The cause is sleep, or forgetfulness. Some sleep when they should keep awake; and some forget when they should remember. And this is the very cause why, often at the resting places, some pilgrims in some things come off losers. Pilgrims should watch and remember what they have already received under their greatest

---

*The youngest.

enjoyments. But for want of doing so, ofttimes their rejoicing ends in tears and their sunshine in a cloud. Witness the story of Christian at this place."

When they were come to the place where Mistrust and Timorous met Christian to persuade him to go back for fear of the lions, they perceived as it were a stage, and before it, towards the road, a broad plate with a copy of verses written thereon, and underneath, the reason of the raising up of that stage in that place rendered. The verses were these,

> Let him that sees this stage take heed
> Unto his heart and tongue;
> Lest if he do not, here he speed,
> As some have long agone.

The words underneath the verses were, "This stage was built to punish such upon who, through timorousness or mistrust, shall be afraid to go further on pilgrimage. Also on this stage, both Mistrust and Timorous were burned through the tongue with an hot iron for endeavouring to hinder Christian in his journey."

Then said Mercy, "This is much like to the saying of the beloved, 'What shall be given unto thee? Or what shall be done unto thee, thou false tongue? Sharp arrows of the mighty, with coals of juniper.' " [Psalms 120:3–4]

So they went on till they came within sight of the lions. Now Mr. Great-heart was a strong man, so he was not afraid of a lion. But yet, when they were come up to the place where the lions were, the boys that went before were now glad to cringe behind, for they were afraid of the lions; so they stepped back and went behind. At this their guide smiled and said, "How now, my boys, do you love to go before when no danger doth approach and love to come behind so soon as the lions appear?"

Now as they went up, Mr. Great-heart drew his sword with intent to make a way for the pilgrims in spite of the lions. Then there appeared one that, it seems, had taken upon him to back the lions. And he said to the pilgrims' guide, "What is the cause of your coming hither?" Now the name of that man was Grim or Bloody-man because of his slaying of pilgrims, and he was of the race of the giants.

GREAT-HEART. Then said the pilgrims' guide, "These women and children are going on pilgrimage, and this is the way they must go, and go it they shall in spite of thee and the lions."

GRIM. "This is not their way, neither shall they go therein. I am come forth to withstand them, and to that end will back the lions."

Now to say truth, by reason of the fierceness of the lions and of the grim carriage of him that did back them, this way had of late lain much unoccupied and was almost all grown over with grass.

CHRISTIANA. Then said Christiana, "Though the highways have been unoccupied heretofore, and though the travellers have been made in time past to walk through by-paths, it must not be so now I am risen, now I am risen a mother in Israel."

GRIM. Then he swore by the lions but it should; and therefore bid them turn aside, for they should not have passage there.

GREAT-HEART. But their guide made first his approach unto Grim, and laid so heavily at him with his sword that he forced him to a retreat.

GRIM. Then said he (that attempted to back the lions), "Will you slay me upon mine own ground?"

GREAT-HEART. " 'Tis the King's highway that we are in, and in this way it is that thou hast placed thy lions. But these women and these children, though weak, shall hold on their way in spite of thy lions." And with that he gave him again a downright blow and brought him upon his knees. With this blow he also broke his helmet, and with the next he cut off his arm. Then did the giant roar so hideously that his voice frighted the women, and yet they were glad to see him lie sprawling upon the ground. Now the lions were chained, and so of themselves could do nothing. Wherefore, when old Grim that intended to back them was dead, Mr. Great-heart said to the pilgrims, "Come now and follow me, and no hurt shall happen to you from the lions." They therefore went on. But the women trembled as they passed by them; the boys also looked as if they would die. But they all got by without further hurt.

Now then they were within sight of the Porter's lodge, and they soon came up unto it; but they made the more haste after this to go thither because 'tis dangerous travelling there in the night. So when they were come to the gate the guide knocked, and the Porter cried, "Who is there?" But as soon as the guide had said, "It is I," he knew his voice and came down. (For the guide had oft before that came thither as a conductor of pilgrims.) When he was come down he opened the gate, and seeing the guide standing just before it (for he saw not the women, for they were behind), he said unto him, "How now, Mr. Great-heart, what is your business here so late tonight?" "I have brought," said he, "some pilgrims hither, where by my Lord's commandment they must lodge. I had been here some time ago had I not been opposed by the giant that did use to back the lions. But I, after a long and tedious combat with him, have cut him off and have brought the pilgrims hither in safety."

PORTER. "Will you not go in, and stay till morning?"

GREAT-HEART. "No, I will return to my Lord tonight."

CHRISTIANA. "Oh, sir, I know not how to be willing you should leave us in our pilgrimage. You have been so faithful and so loving to us, you have fought so stoutly for us, you have been so hearty in counselling of us, that I shall never forget your favour towards us."

MERCY. Then said Mercy, "O, that we might have thy company to our journey's end! How can such poor women as we hold out in a way so full of troubles as this way is without a friend and defender?"

JAMES. Then said James, the youngest of the boys, "Pray, sir, be persuaded to go with us and help us because we are so weak and the way so dangerous as it is."

GREAT-HEART. "I am at my Lord's commandment. If he shall allot me to be your guide quite through, I will willingly wait upon you. But here you failed at first; for when he bid me come thus far with you, then you should have begged me of him to have gone quite through with you, and he would have granted your request. However, at present I must withdraw; and so good Christiana, Mercy, and my brave children, adieu."

Then the Porter, Mr. Watchful, asked Christiana of her country, and of her kindred, and she said, "I came from the City of Destruction. I am a widow woman, and my husband is dead; his name was Christian, the pilgrim." "How," said the Porter, "was he your husband?" "Yes," said she, "and these are his children, and this (pointing to Mercy) is one of my townswomen." Then the Porter rang his bell, as at such times he is wont, and there came to the door one of the damsels, whose name was Humble-mind. And to her the Porter said, "Go tell it within that Christiana, the wife of Christian, and her children, are come hither on pilgrimage." She went in, therefore, and told it. But oh, what a noise for gladness was there within when the damsel did but drop that word out of her mouth!

So they came with haste to the Porter, for Christiana stood still at the door. Then some of the most grave said unto her, "Come in, Christiana; come in, thou wife of that good man, come in, thou blessed woman, come in with all that are with thee." So she went in, and they followed her that were her children and her companions. Now when they were gone in, they were had into a very large room where they were bidden to sit down. So they sat down, and the chief of the house was called to see and welcome the guests. Then they came in and, understanding who they were, did salute each one with a kiss and said, "Welcome ye vessels of the grace of God; welcome to us, your friends."

Now because it was somewhat late, and because the pilgrims were weary with their journey and also made faint with the sight of the fight and of the terrible lions, therefore, they desired as soon as might be to prepare to go to rest. "Nay," said those of the family, "refresh yourselves first with a morsel of meat." For they had prepared for them a lamb with the accustomed sauce belonging thereto. For the Porter had heard before of their coming and had told it to them within. So when they had supped and ended their prayer with a psalm, they desired they might go to rest. "But let us," said Christiana, "if we may be so bold as to choose, be in that chamber that was my husband's when he was here." So they had them up thither and they lay all in a room. When they were at rest, Christiana and Mercy entered into discourse about things that were convenient.

CHRISTIANA. "Little did I think once that when my husband went on pilgrimage I should ever a followed."

MERCY. "And you as little thought of lying in his bed and in his chamber to rest as you do now."

CHRISTIANA. "And much less did I ever think of seeing his face with comfort, and of worshipping the Lord the King with him, and yet now I believe I shall."

MERCY. "Hark, don't you hear a noise?"

CHRISTIANA. "Yes, 'tis as I believe a noise of music, for joy that we are here."

MERCY. "Wonderful! Music in the house, music in the heart, and music also in heaven, for joy that we are here."

Thus they talked awhile and then betook themselves to sleep. So in the morning, when they were awake, Christiana said to Mercy.

CHRISTIANA. "What was the matter that you did laugh in your sleep tonight? I suppose you was in a dream?"

MERCY. "So I was, and a sweet dream it was; but are you sure I laughed?"

CHRISTIANA. "Yes, you laughed heartily. But, prithee, Mercy, tell me thy dream?"

MERCY. "I was a-dreamed that I sat all alone in a solitary place and was bemoaning of the hardness of my heart. Now I had not sat there long, but methought many were gathered about me to see me and to hear what it was that I said. So they hearkened, and I went on bemoaning the hardness of my heart. At this, some of them laughed at me, some called me fool, and some began to thrust me about. With that, methought I looked up and saw one coming with wings towards me. So he came directly to me, and said, 'Mercy, what aileth thee!' Now when he had heard me make my complaint he said, 'Peace be to thee.' He also wiped mine eyes with his handkerchief and clad me in silver and gold; he put a chain about my neck, and earrings in mine ears, and a beautiful crown upon my head. [Ezekiel 16:11–13] Then he took me by my hand and said, 'Mercy, come after me.' So he went up and I followed, till we came at a golden gate. Then he knocked, and when they within had opened, the man went in and I followed him up to a throne upon which one sat, and he said to me, 'Welcome, daughter.' The place looked bright and twinkling like the stars, or rather like the sun, and I thought that I saw your husband there, so I awoke from my dream. But did I laugh?"

CHRISTIANA. "Laugh, ay, and well you might to see yourself so well. For you must give me leave to tell you that I believe it was a good dream, and that as you have begun to find the first part true, so you shall find the second at last. God speaks once, yea twice, yet man perceiveth it not. In a dream, in a vision of the night, when deep sleep falleth upon men, in slumbering upon the bed. [Job 33:14–15] We need not, when abed, lie awake to talk with God; he can visit us while we sleep and cause us then to hear his voice. Our heart of times wakes when we sleep, and God can speak to that, either by words, by proverbs, by signs and similitudes, as well as if one was awake."

MERCY. "Well, I am glad of my dream, for I hope ere long to see it fulfilled to the making of me laugh again."

CHRISTIANA. "I think it is now time to rise and to know what we must do."

MERCY. "Pray, if they invite us to stay awhile, let us willingly accept of the proffer. I am the willinger to stay awhile here to grow better acquainted with these maids. Methinks Prudence, Piety and Charity have very comely and sober countenances."

CHRISTIANA. "We shall see what they will do." So when they were up and ready, they came down. And they asked one another of their rest and if it was comfortable, or not.

MERCY. "Very good," said Mercy. "It was one of the best night's lodging that ever I had in my life."

Then said Prudence and Piety, "If you will be persuaded to stay here awhile you shall have what the house will afford."

CHARITY. "Ay, and that with a very good will," said Charity. So they consented and stayed there about a month or above and became very profitable one to another. And because Prudence would see how Christiana had brought up her children, she asked leave of her to catechise them; so she gave her free consent. Then she began at the youngest, whose name was James.

PRUDENCE. And she said, "Come, James, canst thou tell who made thee?"

JAMES. "God the Father, God the Son, and God the Holy Ghost."

PRUDENCE. "Good boy. And canst thou tell who saves thee?"

JAMES. "God the Father, God the Son, and God the Holy Ghost."

PRUDENCE. "Good boy still. But how doth God the Father save thee?"

JAMES. "By his grace."

PRUDENCE. "How doth God the Son save thee?"

JAMES. "By his righteousness, death, and blood, and life."

PRUDENCE. "And how doth God the Holy Ghost save thee?"

JAMES. "By his illumination, by his renovation, and by his preservation."

Then said Prudence to Christiana, "You are to be commended for thus bringing up your children. I suppose I need not ask the rest these questions since the youngest of them can answer them so well. I will therefore now apply myself to the youngest next."

PRUDENCE. Then she said, "Come, Joseph (for his name was Joseph), will you let me catechise you?"

JOSEPH. "With all my heart."

PRUDENCE. "What is man?"

JOSEPH. "A reasonable creature, so made by God, as my brother said."

PRUDENCE. "What is supposed by this word, 'saved'?"

JOSEPH. "That man by sin has brought himself into a state of captivity and misery."

PRUDENCE. "What is supposed by his being saved by the Trinity?"

JOSEPH. "That sin is so great and mighty a tyrant that none can pull us out of its clutches but God, and that God is so good and loving to man as to pull him indeed out of this miserable state."

PRUDENCE. "What is God's design in saving of poor men?"

JOSEPH. "The glorifying of his name, of his grace and justice, etc. And the everlasting happiness of his creature."

PRUDENCE. "Who are they that must be saved?"

JOSEPH. "Those that accept of his salvation."

PRUDENCE. "Good boy, Joseph, thy mother has taught thee well, and thou hast hearkened to what she has said unto thee."

Then said Prudence to Samuel, who was the eldest but one.

PRUDENCE. "Come, Samuel, are you willing that I should catechise you also?"

SAMUEL. "Yes, forsooth, if you please."

PRUDENCE. "What is heaven?"

SAMUEL. "A place, and state most blessed because God dwelleth there."

PRUDENCE. "What is hell?"

SAMUEL. "A place and state most woeful because it is the dwelling place of sin, the Devil, and death."

PRUDENCE. "Why wouldest thou go to heaven?"

SAMUEL. "That I may see God and serve him without weariness; that I may see Christ and love him everlastingly; that I may have that fullness of the Holy Spirit in me that I can by no means here enjoy."

PRUDENCE. "A very good boy also, and one that has learned well."

Then she addressed herself to the eldest, whose name was Matthew, and she said to him, "Come, Matthew, shall I also catechise you?"

MATTHEW. "With a very good will."

PRUDENCE. "I ask then, if there was ever anything that had a being, antecedent to or before God?"

MATTHEW. "No, for God is eternal, nor is there anything excepting himself that had a being until the beginning of the first day. For in six days the Lord made heaven and earth, the sea, and all that in them is." [Exodus 20:11]

PRUDENCE. "What do you think of the Bible?"

MATTHEW. "It is the holy Word of God."

PRUDENCE. "Is there nothing written therein but what you understand?"

MATTHEW. "Yes, a great deal."

PRUDENCE. "What do you do when you meet with such places therein that you do not understand?"

MATTHEW. "I think God is wiser than I. I pray also that he will please to let me know all therein that he knows will be for my good."

PRUDENCE. "How believe you as touching the resurrection of the dead?"

MATTHEW. "I believe they shall rise the same that was buried, the same in nature, though not in corruption. And I believe this upon a double account. First, because God has promised it; secondly, because he is able to perform it."

Then said Prudence to the boys, "You must still hearken to your mother, for she can learn you more. You must also diligently give ear to what good talk you shall hear from others, for for your sakes do they speak good things. Observe also, and that with carefulness, what the heavens and the earth do teach you; but especially be much in the meditation of that book that was the cause of your father's becoming a pilgrim. I for my part, my children, will teach you what I can while you are here, and shall be glad if you will ask me questions that tend to godly edifying."

Now by that these pilgrims had been at this place a week, Mercy had a visitor that pretended some good will unto her, and his name was Mr. Brisk, a man of some breeding, and that pretended to religion, but a man that stuck very close to the world. So he came once or twice or more to Mercy and offered love unto her. Now Mercy was of a fair countenance and therefore the more alluring.

Her mind also was to be always busying of herself in doing, for when she had nothing to do for herself, she would be making of hose and garments for others, and would bestow them upon them that had need. And Mr. Brisk, not knowing where or how she disposed of what she made, seemed to be greatly taken, for that he found her never idle. "I will warrant her a good housewife," quoth he to himself.

Mercy then revealed the business to the maidens that were of the house and inquired of them concerning him, for they did know him better than she. So they told her that he was a very busy young man, and one that pretended to religion, but was, as they feared, a stranger to the power of that which was good.

"Nay then," said Mercy, "I will look no more on him, for I purpose never to have a clog to my soul."

Prudence then replied that there needed no great matter of discouragement to be given to him; her continuing so as she had began to do for the poor would quickly cool his courage.

So the next time he comes he finds her at her old work, a-making of things for the poor. Then said he, "What, always at it?" "Yes," said she, "either for myself, or for others." "And what canst thee earn a day?" quoth he. "I do these things," said she, "that I may be rich in good works, laying up in store a good foundation against the time to come, that I may lay hold on eternal life." [I Timothy 18:19] "Why, prithee, what dost thou with them?" said he. "Clothe the naked," said she. With that his countenance fell. So he forbore to come at her again. And when he was asked the reason why he said that Mercy was a pretty lass but troubled with ill conditions.*

When he had left her, Prudence said, "Did I not tell thee that Mr. Brisk would soon forsake thee? Yea, he will raise up an ill report of thee. For notwithstanding his pretense to religion and his seeming love to Mercy, yet Mercy and he are of tempers so different that I believe they will never come together."

MERCY. "I might a had husbands afore now, though I spake not of it to any; but they were such as did not like my conditions though never did any of them find fault with my person. So they and I could not agree."

PRUDENCE. "Mercy in our days is little set by any further than as to its name; the practice, which is set forth by thy conditions, there are but few that can abide."

MERCY. "Well," said Mercy, "if nobody will have me I will die a maid or my conditions shall be to me as a husband. For I cannot change my nature, and to have one that lies cross to me in this, that I purpose never to admit of as long as I live. I had a sister named Bountiful that was married to one of these churls. But he and she could never agree but because my sister was resolved to do as she had began, that is, to show kindness to the poor. Therefore her husband first cried her down at the cross,† and then turned her out of his doors."

---

*Character.
†Bountiful's husband condemned her at a cross erected in a public place.

PRUDENCE. "And yet he was a professor,* I warrant you?"

MERCY. "Yes, such a one as he was, and of such as he the world is now full; but I am for none of them all."

Now Matthew, the eldest son of Christiana, fell sick. And his sickness was sore upon him, for he was much pained in his bowels; so that he was with it, at times, pulled as 'twere both ends together. There dwelt also not far from thence one Mr. Skill, an ancient and well-approved physician. So Christiana desired it, and they sent for him, and he came. When he was entered the room and had a little observed the boy, he concluded that he was sick of the gripes.† Then he said to his mother, "What diet has Matthew of late fed upon?" "Diet," said Christiana, "nothing but that which is wholesome." The physician answered, "This boy has been tampering with something which lies in his maw undigested and that will not away without means. And I tell you he must be purged or else he will die."

SAMUEL. Then said Samuel, "Mother, Mother, what was that which my brother did gather up and eat so soon as we were come from the gate that is, at the head of this way? You know that there was an orchard on the left hand, on the other side of the wall, and some of the trees hung over the wall, and my brother did plash and did eat."

CHRISTIANA. "True, my child," said Christiana, "he did take thereof and did eat, naughty boy as he was. I did chide him, and yet he would eat thereof."

SKILL. "I knew he had eaten something that was not wholesome food. And that food, to wit, that fruit is even the most hurtful of all. It is the fruit of Beelzebub's orchard. I do marvel that none did warn you of it; many have died thereof."

CHRISTIANA. Then Christiana began to cry, and she said, "O, naughty boy, and O, careless mother! What shall I do for my son?"

SKILL. "Come, do not be too much dejected. The boy may do well again, but he must purge and vomit."

CHRISTIANA. "Pray, sir, try the utmost of your skill with him whatever it costs."

SKILL. "Nay, I hope I shall be reasonable." So he made him a purge, but it was too weak. 'Twas said it was made of the blood of a goat, the ashes of an heifer, and with some of the juice of hyssop, etc. When Mr. Skill had seen that that purge was too weak he made him one to the purpose. 'Twas made *ex carne et sanguine Christi.*‡ (You know physicians give strange medicines to their patients.) And it was made up into pills with a promise or two and a proportionable quantity of salt. Now he was to take them three at a time, fasting, in half a quarter of a pint of the tears of repentance. When this potion was prepared and brought to the boy, he was loath to take it, though torn with the gripes as if he should be pulled in pieces. "Come, come," said the physician, "you must take it." "It goes against my stomach," said the boy.

*A professing Christian.
†Pinpricks of conscience.
‡Of the flesh and blood of Christ.

"I must have you take it," said his mother. "I shall vomit it up again," said the boy. "Pray, sir," said Christiana to Mr. Skill, "how does it taste?" "It has no ill taste," said the doctor, and with that she touched one of the pills with the tip of her tongue. "Oh, Matthew," said she, "this potion is sweeter than honey. If thou lovest thy mother, if thou lovest thy brothers, if thou lovest Mercy, if thou lovest thy life, take it." So with much ado, after a short prayer for the blessing of God upon it, he took it; and it wrought kindly with him. It caused him to purge, it caused him to sleep and rest quietly, it put him into a fine heat and breathing sweat, and did quite rid him of his gripes.

So in little time he got up, and walked about with a staff, and would go from room to room and talk with Prudence, Piety, and Charity of his distemper and how he was healed.

So when the boy was healed Christiana asked Mr. Skill saying, "Sir, what will content you for your pains and care to and of my child?" And he said, "You must pay the master of the College of Physicians according to rules made in that case and provided."

CHRISTIANA. "But, sir," said she, "what is this pill good for else?"

SKILL. "It is an universal pill. 'Tis good against all the diseases that pilgrims are incident to; and when it is well prepared it will keep good, time out of mind."

CHRISTIANA. "Pray, sir, make me up twelve boxes of them. For if I can get these, I will never take other physic."

SKILL. "These pills are good to prevent diseases, as well as to cure when one is sick. Yea, I dare say it and stand to it, that if a man will but use this physic as he should, it will make him live forever. But, good Christiana, thou must give these pills no other way but as I have prescribed; for if you do, they will do no good." So he gave unto Christiana physic for herself and her boys, and for Mercy, and bid Matthew take heed how he eat any more green plums, and kissed them and went his way.

It was told you before that Prudence bid the boys that, if at any time they would, they should ask her some questions that might be profitable, and she would say something to them.

MATTHEW. Then Matthew, who had been sick, asked her why, for the most part, physic should be bitter to our palates.

PRUDENCE. "To show how unwelcome the Word of God and the effects thereof are to a carnal heart."

MATTHEW. "Why does physic, if it does good, purge and cause that we vomit?"

PRUDENCE. "To show that the Word, when it works effectually, cleanseth the heart and mind. For look what the one doth to the body, the other doth to the soul."

MATTHEW. "What should we learn by seeing the flame of our fire go upwards, and by seeing the beams and sweet influences of the sun strike downwards?"

PRUDENCE. "By the going up of the fire, we are taught to ascend to heaven by fervent and hot desires. And by the sun his sending his heat, beams, and sweet influences downwards, we are taught that the Saviour of the world, though high, reaches down with his grace and love to us below."

MATTHEW. "Where have the clouds their water?"

PRUDENCE. "Out of the sea."

MATTHEW. "What may we learn from that?"

PRUDENCE. "That ministers should fetch their doctrine from God."

MATTHEW. "Why do they empty themselves upon the earth?"

PRUDENCE. "To show that ministers should give out what they know of God to the world."

MATTHEW. "Why is the rainbow caused by the sun?"

PRUDENCE. "To show that the covenant of God's grace is confirmed to us in Christ."

MATTHEW. "Why do the springs come from the sea to us through the earth?"

PRUDENCE. "To show that the grace of God comes to us through the body of Christ."

MATTHEW. "Why do some of the springs rise out of the tops of high hills?"

PRUDENCE. "To show that the spirit of grace shall spring up in some that are great and mighty, as well as in many that are poor and low."

MATTHEW. "Why doth the fire fasten upon the candlewick?"

PRUDENCE. "To show that unless grace doth kindle upon the heart there will be no true light of life in us."

MATTHEW. "Why is the wick and tallow and all spent to maintain the light of the candle?"

PRUDENCE. "To show that body and soul and all should be at the service of, and spend themselves to maintain in good condition, that grace of God that is in us."

MATTHEW. "Why doth the pelican pierce her own breast with her bill?"

PRUDENCE. "To nourish her young ones with her blood, and thereby to show that Christ the blessed so loveth his young, his people, as to save them from death by his blood."

MATTHEW. "What may one learn by hearing the cock to crow?"

PRUDENCE. "Learn to remember Peter's sin and Peter's repentance. The cock's crowing shows also that day is coming on. Let then the crowing of the cock put thee in mind of that last and terrible day of judgement."

Now about this time their month was out, wherefore they signified to those of the house that 'twas convenient for them to up and be going. Then said Joseph to his mother, "It is convenient that you forget not to send to the house of Mr. Interpreter to pray him to grant that Mr. Great-heart should be sent unto us that he may be our conductor the rest of our way." "Good boy," said she, "I had almost forgot." So she drew up a petition and prayed Mr. Watchful, the Porter, to send it by some fit man to her good friend Mr. Interpreter, who, when it was come and he had seen the contents of the petition, said to the messenger, "Go tell them that I will send him."

When the family where Christiana was saw that they had a purpose to go forward, they called the whole house together to give thanks to their King for sending of them such profitable guests as these. Which done, they said to

Christiana, "And shall we not show thee something, according as our custom is to do to pilgrims, on which thou mayest meditate when thou art upon the way?" So they took Christiana, her children, and Mercy into the closet and showed them one of the apples that Eve did eat of, and that she also did give to her husband, and that for the eating of which they both were turned out of Paradise, and asked her what she thought that was. Then Christiana said, " 'Tis food, or poison, I know not which." So they opened the matter to her, and she held up her hands and wondered.

Then they had her to a place and showed her Jacob's ladder. Now at that time there were some angels ascending upon it. So Christiana looked and looked to see the Angels go up, and so did the rest of the company. Then they were going into another place to show them something else; but James said to his mother, "Pray bid them stay here a little longer, for this is a curious sight." So they turned again and stood feeding their eyes with this so pleasant a prospect. After this, they had them into a place where did hang up a golden anchor; so they bid Christiana take it down. "For," said they, "you shall have it with you. For 'tis of absolute necessity that you should that you may lay hold of that within the veil and stand steadfast in case you should meet with turbulent weather." So they were glad thereof. Then they took them and had them to the mount upon which Abraham, our father, had offered up Isaac, his son, and showed them the altar, the wood, the fire, and the knife, for they remained to be seen to this very day. When they had seen it, they held up their hands and blessed themselves and said, "Oh, what a man, for love to his Master and for denial to himself, was Abraham!" After they had showed them all these things, Prudence took them into the dining-room, where stood a pair of excellent virginals; so she played upon them and turned what she had showed them into this excellent song saying:

Eve's apple we have showed you,
Of that be you aware;
You have seen Jacob's ladder, too,
Upon which angels are.

An anchor you received have,
But let not these suffice,
Until with Abr'm you have gave
Your best a sacrifice.

Now about this time one knocked at the door, so the Porter opened. And behold, Mr. Great-heart was there. But when he was come in, what joy was there? For it came now fresh again into their minds how, but a while ago, he had slain old Grim Bloodyman, the giant, and had delivered them from the lions.

Then said Mr. Great-heart to Christiana, and to Mercy, "My Lord has sent each of you a bottle of wine and also some parched corn, together with a couple of pomegranates. He has also sent the boys some figs and raisins to refresh you in your way."

Then they addressed themselves to their journey, and Prudence and Piety went along with them. When they came at the gate Christiana asked the Porter if any of late went by. He said, "No, only one some time since who also told me that of late there had been a great robbery committed on the King's highway, as you go. But," he saith, "the thieves are taken and will shortly be tried for their lives." Then Christiana and Mercy was afraid. But Matthew said, "Mother, fear nothing as long as Mr. Great-heart is to go with us and to be our conductor."

Then said Christiana to the Porter, "Sir, I am much obliged to you for all the kindnesses that you have showed me since I came hither, and also for that you have been so loving and kind to my children. I know not how to gratify your kindness, wherefore, pray, as a token of my respects to you, accept of this small mite." So she put a gold angel in his hand, and he made her a low obeisance and said, "Let thy garments be always white, and let thy head want no ointment. Let Mercy live and not die, and let not her works be few." And to the boys he said, "Do you fly youthful lusts, and follow after godliness with them that are grave and wise, so shall you put gladness into your mother's heart and obtain praise of all that are sober minded." So they thanked the Porter and departed.

Now I saw in my dream that they went forward until they were come to the brow of the hill, where Piety, bethinking herself, cried out, "Alas! I have forgot what I intended to bestow upon Christiana and her companions. I will go back and fetch it." So she ran and fetched it. While she was gone, Christiana thought she heard in a grove a little way off, on the right hand, a most curious melodious note, with words much like these,

> Through all my life thy favour is
> So frankly showed to me,
> That in thy house forevermore
> My dwelling place shall be.

And listening still she thought she heard another answer it, saying,

> For why? the Lord our God is good,
> His Mercy is forever sure.
> His truth at all times firmly stood,
> And shall from age to age endure.

So Christiana asked Prudence what 'twas that made those curious notes. "They are," said she, "our country birds. They sing these notes but seldom, except it be at the Spring, when the flowers appear and the sun shines warm. And then you may hear them all day long. I often," said she, "go out to hear them; we also ofttimes keep them tame in our house. They are very fine company for us when we are melancholy; also they make the woods, and groves, and solitary places, places desirous to be in."

By this time Piety was come again; so she said to Christiana, "Look here,

I have brought thee a scheme* of all those things that thou hast seen at our house, upon which thou mayest look when thou findest thyself forgetful, and call those things again to remembrance for thy edification and comfort."

Now they began to go down the hill into the Valley of Humiliation. It was a steep hill, and the way was slippery; but they were very careful, so they got down pretty well. When they were down in the valley, Piety said to Christiana, "This is the place where Christian, your husband, met with the foul fiend Apollyon and where they had that dreadful fight that they had. I know you cannot but have heard thereof. But be of good courage; as long as you have here Mr. Great-heart to be your guide and conductor, we hope you will fare the better." So when these two had committed the pilgrims unto the conduct of their guide he went forward, and they went after.

GREAT-HEART. Then said Mr. Great-heart, "We need not be so afraid of this valley; for here is nothing to hurt us unless we procure it to ourselves. 'Tis true, Christian did here meet with Apollyon, with whom he also had a sore combat; but that fray was the fruit of those slips that he got in his going down the hill. For they that get slips there must look for combats here. And hence it is that this valley has got so hard a name. For the common people when they hear that some frightful thing has befallen such an one in such a place are of an opinion that that place is haunted with some foul fiend or evil spirit when, alas, it is for the fruit of their doing that such things do befall them there.

"This Valley of Humiliation is of itself as fruitful a place as any the crow flies over; and I am persuaded, if we could hit upon it, we might find somewhere hereabout something that might give us an account why Christian was so hardly beset in this place."

Then James said to his mother, "Lo, yonder stands a pillar, and it looks as if something was written thereon. Let us go and see what it is." So they went and found there written, "Let Christian's slips before he came hither, and the battles that he met with in this place, be a warning to those that come after."

"Lo," said their guide, "did not I tell you that there was something hereabout that would give intimation of the reason why Christian was so hard beset in this place?" Then turning himself to Christiana, he said, "No disparagement to Christian more than to many others whose hap and lot his was. For 'tis easier going up than down this hill, and that can be said but of few hills in all these parts of the world. But we will leave the good man; he is at rest; he also had a brave victory over his enemy. Let him grant that dwelleth above that we fare no worse when we come to be tried than he.

"But we will come again to this Valley of Humiliation. It is the best and most fruitful piece of ground in all those parts. It is fat ground and, as you see, consisteth much in meadows. And if a man was to come here in the summertime, as we do now, if he knew not anything before thereof, and if he also delighted himself in the sight of his eyes, he might see that that would be delightful to him. Behold, how green this valley is, also how

*Summary.

beautified with lilies. I have also known many labouring men that have got good estates in this Valley of Humiliation. (For God resisteth the proud, but gives more, more grace to the humble.) [James 4:6] For indeed, it is a very fruitful soil and doth bring forth by handfuls. Some also have wished that the next way to their Father's house were here, that they might be troubled no more with either hills or mountains to go over; but the way is the way, and there's an end."

Now as they were going along and talking, they espied a boy feeding his father's sheep. The boy was in very mean clothes, but of a very fresh and well-favoured countenance, and as he sat by himself he sung. "Hark," said Mr. Great-heart, "to what the shepherd's boy saith." So they hearkened, and he said,

> He that is down needs fear no fall;
> He that is low, no pride;
> He that is humble, ever shall
> Have God to be his guide.
>
> I am content with what I have,
> Little be it, or much;
> And, Lord, contentment still I crave,
> Because thou savest such.
>
> Fullness to such a burden is
> That go on pilgrimage;
> Here little, and hereafter bliss,
> Is best from age to age.

Then said their guide, "Do you hear him? I will dare to say that this boy lives a merrier life and wears more of that herb called heartsease in his bosom than he that is clad in silk and velvet. But we will proceed in our discourse.

"In this valley our Lord formerly had his country-house; He loved much to be here. He loved also to walk these meadows, for he found the air was pleasant. Besides, here a man shall be free from the noise and from the hurryings of this life. All states are full of noise and confusion; only the Valley of Humiliation is that empty and solitary place. Here a man shall not be so let and hindered in his contemplation as in other places he is apt to be. This is a valley that nobody walks in but those that love a pilgrim's life. And though Christian had the hard hap to meet here with Apollyon and to enter with him a brisk encounter, yet I must tell you that in former times men have met with angels here, have found pearls here, and have in this place found the words of life.

"Did I say our Lord had here in former days his country-house and that he loved here to walk? I will add, in this place, and to the people that live and trace* these grounds, he has left a yearly revenue to be faithfully paid them

*Travel though.

at certain seasons for their maintenance by the way and for their further encouragement to go on in their pilgrimage."

SAMUEL. Now, as they went on, Samuel said to Mr. Great-heart, "Sir, I perceive that in this valley my father and Apollyon had their battle; but whereabout was the fight, for I perceive this valley is large?"

GREAT-HEART. "Your father had that battle with Apollyon at a place yonder before us, in a narrow passage just beyond Forgetful Green. And indeed that place is the most dangerous place in all these parts. For if at any time the pilgrims meet with any brunt, it is when they forget what favours they have received and how unworthy they are of them. This was the place also where others have been hard put to it. But more of the place when we are come to it; for I persuade myself that to this day there remains either some sign of the battle or some monument to testify that such a battle there was fought."

MERCY. Then said Mercy, "I think I am as well in this valley as I have been anywhere else in all our journey. The place, methinks, suits with my spirit. I love to be in such places where there is no rattling with coaches nor rumbling with wheels. Methinks here one may without much molestation be thinking what he is, whence he came, what he has done, and to what the King has called him. Here one may think, and break at heart, and melt in one's spirit, until one's eyes become like the fish pools of Heshbon. [Song of Solomon 7:4] They that go rightly through this Valley of Baca make it a well, the rain that God sends down from heaven upon them that are here also filleth the pools. This valley is that from whence also the King will give to his their vineyards, and they that go through it shall sing (as Christian did, for all he met with Apollyon).

GREAT-HEART. " 'Tis true," said their guide, "I have gone through this valley many a time and never was better than when here.

"I have also been a conduct to several pilgrims and they have confessed the same. 'To this man will I look,' saith the King, 'even to him that is poor and of a contrite spirit, and that trembles at my word.' " [Isaiah 66:2]

Now they were come to the place where the aforementioned battle was fought. Then said the guide to Christiana, her children, and Mercy, "This is the place. On this ground Christian stood, and up there came Apollyon against him. And look, did not I tell you, here is some of your husband's blood upon these stones to this day. Behold, also, how here and there are yet to be seen upon the place some of the shivers of Apollyon's broken darts. See also how they did beat the ground with their feet as they fought to make good their places against each other, how also with their by-blows they did split the very stones in pieces. Verily, Christian did here play the man, and showed himself as stout, as could, had he been here, even Hercules himself. When Apollyon was beat, he made his retreat to the next valley, that is called the Valley of the Shadow of Death, unto which we shall come anon.

"Lo, yonder also stands a monument, on which is engraven this battle and Christian's victory, to his fame throughout all ages." So because it stood just on the wayside before them, they stepped to it and read the writing, which word for word was this:

Hard by here was a battle fought,
Most strange, and yet most true;
Christian and Apollyon sought
Each other to subdue.

The man so bravely played the man,
He made the fiend to fly;
Of which a monument I stand,
The same to testify.

When they had passed by this place, they came upon the borders of the Shadow of Death, and this valley was longer than the other, a place also most strangely haunted with evil things, as many are able to testify. But these women and children went the better through it because they had daylight, and because Mr. Great-heart was their conductor.

When they were entered upon this valley, they thought that they heard a groaning as of dead men, a very great groaning. They thought also they did hear words of lamentation spoken, as of some in extreme torment. These things made the boys to quake; the women also looked pale and wan. But their guide bid them be of good comfort.

So they went on a little further, and they thought that they felt the ground begin to shake under them as if some hollow place was there. They heard also kind of a hissing as of serpents, but nothing as yet appeared. Then said the boys, "Are we not yet at the end of this doleful place?" But the guide also bid them be of good courage and look well to their feet, "Lest haply," said he, "you be taken in some snare."

Now James began to be sick, but I think the cause thereof was fear; so his mother gave him some of that glass of spirits that she had given her at the Interpreter's house, and three of these pills that Mr. Skill had prepared, and the boy began to revive. Thus they went on till they came to about the middle of the valley, and then Christiana said, "Methinks I see something yonder upon the road before us, a thing of a shape such as I have not seen." Then said Joseph, "Mother, what is it?" "An ugly thing, child, an ugly thing," said she. "But, Mother, what is it like?" said he. " 'Tis like I cannot tell what," said she. And now it was but a little way off. Then said she, "It is nigh."

"Well, well," said Mr. Great-heart, "let them that are most afraid keep close to me." So the fiend came on and the conductor met it; but when it was just come to him, it vanished to all their sights. Then remembered they what had been said sometime ago, "Resist the devil, and he will fly from you."

They went therefore on as being a little refreshed. But they had not gone far before Mercy, looking behind her, saw, as she thought, something most like a lion, and it came a great padding pace after. And it had a hollow voice of roaring, and at every roar that it gave it made all the valley echo and their hearts to ache, save the heart of him that was their guide. So it came up. And Mr. Great-heart went behind, and put the pilgrims all before him. The lion also came on apace, and Mr. Great-heart addressed himself to give him battle. But when he saw that it was determined that resistance should be made, he also drew back and came no further.

Then they went on again, and their conductor did go before them till they came at a place where was cast up a pit the whole breadth of the way; and before they could be prepared to go over that a great mist and a darkness fell upon them, so that they could not see. Then said the pilgrims, "Alas, now what shall we do?" But their guide made answer, "Fear not. Stand still and see what an end will he put to this also." So they stayed there because their path was marred. They then also thought that they did hear more apparently the noise and rushing of the enemies; the fire also and the smoke of the pit was much easier to be discerned. Then said Christiana to Mercy, "Now I see what my poor husband went through. I have heard much of this place, but I never was here afore now. Poor man, he went here all alone in the night; he had night almost quite through the way; also these fiends were busy about him as if they would have torn him in pieces. Many have spoke of it, but none can tell what the Valley of the Shadow of Death should mean until they come in it themselves. 'The heart knows its own bitterness, and a stranger intermeddleth not with its joy.' [Proverbs 14:10] To be here is a fearful thing."

GREAT-HEART. "This is like doing business in great waters, or like going down into the deep. This is like being in the heart of the sea and like going down to the bottoms of the mountains. Now it seems as if the earth with its bars were about us forever. But let them that walk in darkness and have no light, trust in the name of the Lord, and stay upon their God. [Isaiah 50:10] For my part, as I have told you already, I have gone often through this valley, and have been much harder put to it than now I am, and yet you see I am alive. I would not boast for that I am not mine own saviour. But I trust we shall have a good deliverance. Come let us pray for light to him that can lighten our darkness, and that can rebuke, not only these, but all the Satans in hell."

So they cried and prayed, and God sent light and deliverance; for there was now no let in their way, no not there, where, but now, they were stopped with a pit.

Yet they were not got through the valley. So they went on still, and, behold, great stinks and loathsome smells, to the great annoyance of them. Then said Mercy to Christiana, "There is not such pleasant being here as at the gate, or at the Interpreter's, or at the house where we lay last."

"O, but," said one of the boys, "it is not so bad to go through here as it is to abide here always. And, for ought I know, one reason why we must go this way to the house prepared for us is that our home might be made the sweeter to us."

"Well said, Samuel," quoth the guide, "thou hast now spoke like a man." "Why, if ever I get out here again," said the boy, "I think I shall prize light and good way better than ever I did in all my life." Then said the guide, "We shall be out by and by."

So on they went, and Joseph said, "Cannot we see to the end of this valley as yet?" Then said the guide, "Look to your feet, for you shall presently be among the snares." So they looked to their feet and went on; but they were troubled much with the snares. Now when they were come among the snares, they espied a man cast into the ditch on the left hand with his flesh all rent and torn. Then said the guide, "That is one Heedless that was a-going this way; he has lain there a great while. There was one Takeheed with him when he was taken and slain, but he escaped their hands. You cannot imagine how many are killed hereabout, and yet men are so foolishly venturous as to set out lightly on pilgrimage, and to come without a guide. Poor Christian, it was a wonder that he here escaped, but he was beloved of his God; also he had a good heart of his own, or else he could never a done it." Now they drew towards the end of the way, and just there, where Christian had seen the cave when he went by, out thence came forth Maul, a giant. This Maul did use to spoil young pilgrims with sophistry, and he called Great-heart by his name and said unto him, "How many times have you been forbidden to do these things?" Then said Mr. Great-heart, "What things?" "What things?" quoth the giant, "You know what things. But I will put an end to your trade." "But, pray," said Mr. Great-heart, "before we fall to it, let us understand wherefore we must fight." (Now the women and children stood trembling and knew not what to do.) Quoth the giant, "You rob the country, and rob it with the worst of thefts." "These are but generals," said Mr. Great-heart. "Come to particulars, man."

Then said the giant, "Thou practises the craft of a kidnapper. Thou gatherest up women and children and carriest them into a strange country, to the weakening of my master's kingdom." But now Great-heart replied, "I am a servant of the God of heaven; my business is to persuade sinners to repentance. I am commanded to do my endeavour to turn men, women and children, from darkness to light, and from the power of Satan to God; and if this be indeed the ground of thy quarrel, let us fall to it as soon as thou wilt."

Then the giant came up, and Mr. Great-heart went to meet him; and as he went, he drew his sword, but the giant had a club. So without more ado they fell to it. And at the first blow the giant stroke Mr. Great-heart down upon one of his knees. With that, the women and children cried out. So Mr. Great-heart, recovering himself, laid about him in full lusty manner and gave the giant a wound in his arm. Thus he fought for the space of an hour to that height of heat that the breath came out of the giant's nostrils as the heat doth out of a boiling cauldron.

Then they sat down to rest them. But Mr. Great-heart betook him to prayer; also the women and children did nothing but sigh and cry all the time that the battle did last.

When they had rested them and taken breath, they both fell to it again, and Mr. Great-heart with a full blow fetched the giant down to the ground. "Nay, hold, and let me recover," quoth he. So Mr. Great-heart fairly let him get up. So to it they went again, and the giant missed but little of all-to-breaking Mr. Great-heart's skull with his club.

Mr. Great-heart, seeing that, runs to him in the full heat of his spirit and pierceth him under the fifth rib. With that, the giant began to faint and could hold up his club no longer. Then Mr. Great-heart seconded his blow

and smote the head of the giant from his shoulders. Then the women and children rejoiced, and Mr. Great-heart also praised God for the deliverance he had wrought.

When this was done, they amongst them erected a pillar and fastened the giant's head thereon, and wrote underneath in letters that passengers might read,

He that did wear this head was one
That pilgrims did misuse;
He stopped their way, he spared none,
But did them all abuse.

Until that I, Great-heart, arose,
The pilgrim's guide to be;
Until that I did him oppose,
That was their enemy.

Now I saw that they went to the ascent that was a little way off cast up to be a prospect for pilgrims. (That was the place from whence Christian had the first sight of Faithful, his brother.) Wherefore here they sat down and rested; they also here did eat and drink, and make merry, for that they had gotten deliverance from this so dangerous an enemy. As they sat thus and did eat, Christiana asked the guide if he had caught no hurt in the battle. Then said Mr. Great-heart, "No, save a little on my flesh. Yet that also shall be so far from being to my determent that it is at present a proof of my love to my Master and you, and shall be a means by grace to increase my reward at last."

"But was you not afraid, good sir, when you see him come with his club?"

"It is my duty," said he, "to distrust mine own ability, that I may have reliance on him that is stronger than all." "But what did you think when he fetched you down to the ground at the first blow?" "Why I thought," quoth he, "that so my Master himself was served, and yet he it was that conquered at the last."

MATTHEW. "When you all have thought what you please I think God has been wonderful good unto us, both in bringing us out of this valley and in delivering us out of the hand of this enemy. For my part, I see no reason why we should distrust our God any more, since he has now, and in such a place as this, given us such testimony of his love as this."

Then they got up and went forward. Now a little before them stood an oak, and under it, when they came to it, they found and old pilgrim fast asleep; they knew that he was a pilgrim by his clothes, and his staff, and his girdle.

So the guide, Mr. Great-heart, awaked him, and the old gentleman, as he lift up his eyes, cried out, "What's the matter? Who are you, and what is your business here?"

GREAT-HEART. "Come, man, be not so hot. Here is none but friends." Yet the old man gets up and stands upon his guard and will know of them what they were. Then said the guide, "My name is Great-heart. I am the guide of these pilgrims which are going to the Celestial Country."

HONEST. Then said Mr. Honest, "I cry you mercy. I feared that you had been of the company of those that some time ago did rob Little-faith of his money; but now I look better about me, I perceive you are honester people."

GREAT-HEART. "Why, what would or could you a done to a helped yourself, if we indeed had been of that company?"

HONEST. "Done! Why I would a fought as long as breath had been in me. And had I so done, I am sure you could never have given me the worst on't, for a Christian can never be overcome unless he shall yield of himself."

GREAT-HEART. "Well said, Father Honest," quoth the guide, "for by this I know that thou art a cock of the right kind, for thou hast said the truth."

HONEST. "And by this also I know that thou knowest what true pilgrimage is, for all others do think that we are the soonest overcome of any."

GREAT-HEART. "Well, now we are so happily met, pray, let me crave your name and the name of the place you came from?"

HONEST. "My name I cannot, but I came from the Town of Stupidity; it lieth about four degrees beyond the City of Destruction."

GREAT-HEART. "Oh, are you that countryman then? I deem I have half a guess of you; your name is old Honesty, is it not?" So the old gentleman blushed and said, "Not honesty in the abstract, but Honest is my name, and I wish that my nature shall agree to what I am called."

HONEST. "But sir," said the old gentleman, "how could you guess that I am such a man, since I came from such a place?"

GREAT-HEART. "I had heard of you before, by my master, for he knows all things that are done on the earth. but I have often wondered that any should come from your place; for your town is worse than is the City of Destruction itself."

HONEST. "Yes, we lie more off from the sun, and so are more cold and senseless. But was a man in a mountain of ice, yet if the sun of righteousness will arise upon him, his frozen heart shall feel a thaw; and thus it hath been with me."

GREAT-HEART. "I believe it, Father Honest, I believe it; for I know the thing is true."

Then the old gentleman saluted all the pilgrims with a holy kiss of charity and asked them of their names and how they had fared since they set out on their pilgrimage.

CHRISTIANA. Then said Christiana, "My name I suppose you have heard of; good Christian was my husband, and these four were his children." But can you think how the old gentleman was taken when she told him who she was. He skipped, he smiled and blessed them with a thousand good wishes, saying,

HONEST. "I have heard much of your husband and of his travels and wars which he underwent in his days. Be it spoken to your comfort, the name of your husband rings all over these parts of the world. His faith, his courage, his enduring, and his sincerity under all has made his name famous." Then he turned him to the boys and asked them of their names, which they told him. And then said he unto them, "Matthew, be thou like Matthew the publican, not in vice, but virtue. Samuel," said he, "be thou like Samuel, the prophet, a man of faith and prayer. Joseph," said he, "be thou like Joseph in Potiphar's house, chaste and one that flies from temptation. And, James, be thou like James, the just, and like James, the brother of our Lord."

Then they told him of Mercy and how she had left her town and her kindred to come along with Christiana and with her sons. At that, the old honest man said, "Mercy is thy name? By mercy shalt thou be sustained and carried through all those difficulties that shall assault thee in thy way, till thou come thither where thou shalt look the Fountain of Mercy in the face with comfort."

All this while the guide, Mr. Great-heart, was very much pleased and smiled upon his companion.

Now as they walked along together the guide asked the old gentleman if he did not know one Mr. Fearing that came on pilgrimage out of his parts.

HONEST. "Yes, very well," said he. "He was a man that had the root of the matter in him, but he was one of the most troublesome pilgrims that ever I met with in all my days."

GREAT-HEART. "I perceive you knew him, for you have given a very right character of him."

HONEST. "Knew him! I was a great companion of his; I was with him most an end. When he first began to think of what would come upon us hereafter, I was with him."

GREAT-HEART. "I was his guide from my master's house to the gates of the Celestial City."

HONEST. "Then you knew him to be a troublesome one?"

GREAT-HEART. "I did so. But I could very well bear it, for men of my calling are oftentimes intrusted with the conduct of such as he was."

HONEST. "Well then, pray, let us hear a little of him and how he managed himself under your conduct."

GREAT-HEART. "Why, he was always afraid that he should come short of whither he had a desire to go. Everything frightened him that he heard anybody speak of that had the least appearance of opposition in it. I heard that he lay roaring at the Slough of Despond for above a month together, nor durst he, for all he saw several go over before him, venture, though they, many of them, offered to lend him their hand. He would not go back again neither. The Celestial City, he said, he should die if he came not to it, and yet was dejected at every difficulty, and stumbled at every straw that anybody cast in his way. Well, after he had lain at the Slough of Despond a great while, as I have told you, one sunshine morning, I do not know how, he ventured and so got over. But when he was over he would scarce believe it. He had, I think, a Slough of Despond in his mind, a slough that he carried everywhere with him, or else he cold never have been as he was. So he came up to the gate, you know what I mean, that stands at the head of this way, and there also he stood a good while before he would adventure to knock. When the gate was opened, he would give back and give place to others and say that he was not worthy. For, for all he gat before some to the gate, yet many of them went in before him. There the poor man would stand shaking and shrinking; I dare say it would have pitied one's heart to have seen him. Nor would he go back again. At last, he took the hammer that hanged on the gate in his hand and gave a small rap or two. Then one opened to him, but he shrunk back as before. He that opened stepped out after him and said, 'Thou trembling one, what wantest thou?' With that, he fell to the ground. He that spoke to him wondered to see him so faint. So he said to him, 'Peace be to thee, up, for I have set open the door to thee. Come in, for thou art blest.' With that he gat up and went in trembling, and when he was in he was ashamed to show his face. Well, after he had been entertained there awhile, as you know how the manner is, he was bid go on his way and also told the way he should take. So he came till he came to our house. But, as he behaved himself at the gate, so he did at my master the Interpreter's door. He lay thereabout in the cold a good while before he would adventure to call. Yet he would not go back. And the nights were long and cold then. Nay, he had a note of necessity in his bosom to my master to receive him and grant him the comfort of his house, and also to allow him a stout and valiant conduct because he was himself so chicken-hearted a man. And yet for all that he was afraid to call at the door. So he lay up and down thereabout, till, poor man, he was almost starved. Yes, so great was his dejection, that though he saw several others for knocking got in, yet he was afraid to venture. At last, I think I looked out of the window, and perceiving a man to be up and down about the door, I went out to him and asked what he was. But, poor man, the water stood in his eyes; so I perceived what he wanted. I went therefore in and told it in the house, and we showed the thing to our Lord. So he sent me out again to entreat him to come in, but I dare say I had hard work to do it. At last he came in, and I will say that for my Lord, he carried it wonderful lovingly to him. There were but a few good bits at the table, but some of it was laid upon his trencher. Then he presented the note, and my Lord looked thereon and said, 'His desire should be granted.' So when he had been there a good while he seemed to get some heart and to be a little more comfortable. For my master, you must know, is one of very tender bowels, especially to them that are afraid; wherefore he carried it so towards him as might tend most to his encouragement. Well, when he had had a sight of the things of the place and was ready to take his journey to go to the city, my Lord, as he did to Christian before, gave him a bottle of spirits and some comfortable things to eat. Thus we set forward, and I went before him; but the man was but of few words, only he would sigh aloud.

"When we were come to where the three fellows were hanged he said that he doubted that that would be his end also. Only he seemed glad when he saw the cross and the sepulchre. There, I confess, he desired to stay a little to look, and he seemed for awhile after to be a little cheery. When we came at the Hill Difficulty he made no stick at that, nor did he much fear the lions. For you must know that his trouble was not about such things as those; his fear was about his acceptance at last.

"I got him in at the House Beautiful, I think, before he was willing. Also, when he was in I brought him acquainted with the damsels that were of the place, but he was ashamed to make himself much for company. He desired much to be alone, yet he always loved good talk and often would get behind the screen to hear it. He also loved much to see ancient things and to be pondering them in his mind. He told me afterwards that he loved to be in those two houses from which he came last, to wit, at the gate, and that of the Interpreter's, but that he durst not be so bold to ask.

"When we went also from the House Beautiful, down the hill into the Valley of Humiliation, he went down as well as ever I saw man in my life, for he cared not how mean he was so he might be happy at last. Yea, I think there was a kind of a sympathy betwixt that valley and him, for I never saw him better in all his pilgrimage than when he was in that valley.

"Here he would lie down, embrace the ground, and kiss the very flowers that grew in this valley. He would now be up every morning by break of day, tracing and walking to and fro in this valley.

"But when he was come to the entrance of the Valley of the Shadow of Death I thought I should have lost my man, not for that he had any inclination to go back, that he always abhorred, but he was ready to die for fear. 'O, the hobgoblins will have me, the hobgoblins will have me,' cried he, and I could not beat him out on't. He made such a noise and such an outcry here that, had they but heard him 'twas enough to encourage them to come and fall upon us.

"But this I took very great notice of, that this valley was as quiet while he went through it as ever I knew it before or since. I suppose those enemies here had now a special check from our Lord and a command not to meddle until Mr. Fearing was passed over it.

"I would be too tedious to tell you of all. We will therefore only mention a passage or two more. When he was come at Vanity Fair I thought he would have fought with all the men in the fair. I feared there we should both have been knocked o'the head, so hot was he against their fooleries; upon the Enchanted Ground he also was very wakeful. But when he was come at the river where was no bridge, there again he was in a heavy case. Now, now, he said, he should be drowned forever, and so never see that face with comfort that he had come so many miles to behold.

"And here also I took notice of what was very remarkable; the water of that river was lower at this time than ever I saw it in all my life. So he went over at last, not much above wet-shod. When he was going up to the gate Mr. Great-heart began to take his leave of him and to wish him a good reception above, so he said, 'I shall, I shall.' Then parted we asunder, and I saw him no more."

HONEST. "Then it seems he was well at last."

GREAT-HEART. "Yes, yes, I never had doubt about him. He was a man of a choice spirit; only he was always kept very low, and that made his life so burthensome to himself and so troublesome to others. he was, above many, tender of sin; he was so afraid of doing injuries to others that he often would deny himself of that which was lawful because he would not offend."

HONEST. "But what should be the reason that such a good man should be all his days so much in the dark?"

GREAT-HEART. "There are two sorts of reasons for it. One is, the wise God will have it so; some must pipe, and some must weep. Now Mr. Fearing was one that played upon this bass. He and his fellows sound the sackbut, whose notes are more doleful than the notes of other music are. Though indeed some say, the bass is the ground of music. And, for my part, I care not at all for that profession* that begins not in heaviness of mind. The first string that the musician usually touches is the bass when he intends to put all in tune. God also plays upon this string first when he sets the soul in tune for himself. Only here was the imperfection of Mr. Fearing; he could play upon no other music but this till towards his latter end.

"I make bold to talk thus metaphorically for the ripening of the wits of young readers, and because in the Book of the Revelations, the saved are compared to a company of musicians that play upon their trumpets and harps and sing their songs before the throne."

HONEST. "He was a very zealous man, as one may see by what relation you have given of him. Difficulties, lions, or Vanity Fair, he feared not at all. 'Twas only sin, death and hell that was to him a terror because he had some doubts about his interest in that Celestial Country."

GREAT-HEART. "You say right. Those were the things that were his troublers; and they, as you have well observed, arose from the weakness of his mind thereabout, not from weakness of spirit as to the practical part of a pilgrim's life. I dare believe that, as the proverb is, he could have bit a firebrand had it stood in his way, but the things with which he was oppressed no man ever yet could shake off with ease."

CHRISTIANA. Then said Christiana, "This relation of Mr. Fearing has done me good. I thought nobody had been like me. But I see there was some semblance 'twixt this good man and I; only we differed in two things. His troubles were so great they broke out, but mine I kept within. His also lay so hard upon him they made him that he could not knock at the houses provided for entertainment. But my trouble was always such as made me knock the louder."

MERCY. "If I might also speak my heart I must say that something of him has also dwelt in me. For I have ever been more afraid of the lake and the loss of a place in Paradise than I have been of the loss of other things. 'Oh,' thought I, 'may I have the happiness to have a habitation there, 'tis enough, though I part with all the world to win it.' "

MATTHEW. Then said Matthew, "Fear was one thing that made me think that I was far from having that within me that accompanies salvation. But if it was so with such a good man as he, why may it not also go well with me?"

JAMES. "No fears, no grace," said James. "Though there is not always grace where there is the fear of hell, yet to be sure there is no grace where there is no fear of God."

GREAT-HEART. "Well said, James, thou hast hit the mark, for the fear of God is the beginning of wisdom. And, to be sure, they that want the beginning have neither middle nor end. But we will here conclude our discourse of Mr. Fearing, after we have sent after him this farewell."

---

*Declaration of belief.

Well, Master Fearing, thou didst fear
Thy God, and wast afraid
Of doing anything, while here,
That would have thee betrayed.
And didst thou fear the lake and pit?
Would others did so too!
For, as for them that want thy wit,
They do themselves undo.

Now I saw that they still went on in their talk. For after Mr. Great-heart had made an end with Mr. Fearing, Mr. Honest began to tell them of another, but his name was Mr. Selfwill. "He pretended himself to be a pilgrim," said Mr. Honest. "But I persuade myself he never came in at the gate that stands at the head of the way."

GREAT-HEART. "Had you ever any talk with him about it?"

HONEST. "Yes, more than once or twice, but he would always be like himself, self-willed. He neither cared for man, nor argument, nor yet example. What his mind prompted him to, that he would do, and nothing else could he be got to."

GREAT-HEART. "Pray, what principles did he hold, for I suppose you can tell?"

HONEST. "He held that a man might follow the vices as well as the virtues of the pilgrims, and that if he did both he should be certainly saved."

GREAT-HEART. "How! If he had said, 'Tis possible for the best to be guilty of the vices as well as to partake of the virtues of pilgrims,' he could not much a been blamed. For indeed, we are exempted from no vice absolutely, but on condition that we watch and strive; but this I perceive is not the thing. But if I understand you right, your meaning is that he was of that opinion that it was allowable so to be."

HONEST. "Ay, ay, so I mean, and so he believed and practised."

GREAT-HEART. "But what ground had he for his so saying?"

HONEST. "Why, he said he had the scripture for his warrant."

GREAT-HEART. "Prithee, Mr. Honest, present us with a few particulars."

HONEST. "So I will. He said to have to do with other men's wives had been practised by David, God's beloved, and therefore he could do it. He said to have more women than one was a thing that Solomon practised, and therefore he could do it. He said that Sarah and the godly midwives of Egypt lied and so did saved Rahab, and therefore he could do it. He said that the disciples went at the bidding of their Master and took away the owner's ass, and therefore, he could do so too. He said that Jacob got the inheritance of his father in a way of guile and dissimulation, and therefore he could do so too."

GREAT-HEART. "High* base, indeed. You are sure he was of this opinion?"

*Very.

HONEST. "I have heard him plead for it, bring scripture for it, bring argument for it, etc."

GREAT-HEART. "An opinion that is not fit to be, with any allowance, in the world."

HONEST. "You must understand me rightly. He did not say that any man might do this, but that those that had the virtues of those that did such things might also do the same."

GREAT-HEART. "But what more false than such a conclusion? For this is as much as to say that because good men heretofore have sinned of infirmity, therefore he had allowance to do it of a presumptuous mind. Or if because a child, by the blast of the wind, or for that it stumbled at a stone, fell down and so defiled itself in mire, therefore he might willfully lie down and wallow like a boar therein. Who could a thought that anyone could so far a been blinded by the power of lust? But what is written must be true. They stumble at the Word, being disobedient, whereunto also they were appointed." [I Peter 2:8]

"His supposing that such may have the godly man's virtues, who addict themselves to their vices, is also a delusion as strong as the other. 'Tis just as if the dog should say, 'I have, or may have, the qualities of the child because I lick up its stinking excrements.' To eat up the sin of God's people is no sign of one that is possessed with their virtues.

Nor can I believe that one that is of this opinion can at present have faith or love in him. But I know you have made strong objections against him; prithee, what can he say for himself?"

HONEST. "Why, he says, 'To do this by way of opinion seems abundance more honest than to do it and yet hold contrary to it in opinion.' "

GREAT-HEART. "A very wicked answer. For though to let loose the bridle to lusts, while our opinions are against such things, is bad; yet to sin, and plead a toleration so to do, is worse. The one stumbles beholders accidentally, the other pleads them into the snare."

HONEST. "There are many of this man's mind that have not this man's mouth, and that makes going on pilgrimage of so little esteem as it is."

GREAT-HEART. "You have said the truth, and it is to be lamented. But he that feareth the King of Paradise shall come out of them all."

CHRISTIANA. "There are strange opinions in the world. I know one that said 'twas time enough to repent when they came to die."

GREAT-HEART. "Such are not over-wise. That man would a been loath, might he have had a week to run twenty mile in for his life, to have deferred that journey to the last hour of that week."

HONEST. "You say right, and yet the generality of them that count themselves pilgrims do indeed do thus. I am, as you see, an old man, and have been a traveller in this road many a day. And I have taken notice of many things.

"I have seen some that have set out as if they would drive all the world afore them, who yet have, in few days, died as they in the wilderness and so never gat sight of the promised land.

"I have seen some that have promised nothing at first, setting out to be pilgrims, and that one would a thought could not have lived a day, that have yet proved very good pilgrims.

"I have seen some that have run hastily forward that again have, after a little time, run just as fast back again.

"I have seen some who have spoke very well of a pilgrim's life at first that, after a while, have spoken as much against it.

"I have heard some, when they first set out for Paradise, say positively, 'There is such a place,' who when they have been almost there have come back again and said there is none.

"I have heard some vaunt what they would do in case they should be opposed that have even at a false alarm fled faith, the pilgrim's way, and all."

Now as they were thus in their way there came one running to meet them and said, "Gentlemen, and you of the weaker sort, if you love life, shift for yourselves, for the robbers are before you."

GREAT-HEART. Then said Mr. Great-heart, "They be the three that set upon Little-faith heretofore. Well," said he, "we are ready for them. So they went on their way. Now they looked at every turning when they should a met with the villains. But whether they heard of Mr. Great-heart or whether they had some other game, they came not up to the pilgrims.

CHRISTIANA. Christiana then wished for an inn for herself and her children because they were weary. Then said Mr. Honest, "There is one a little before us where a very honourable disciple, one Gaius, dwells." So they all concluded to turn in thither, and the rather because the old gentleman gave him so good a report. So when they came to the door they went in, not knocking, for folks use not to knock at the door of an inn. Then they called for the master of the house, and he came to them. So they asked if they might lie there that night.

GAIUS. "Yes, gentlemen, if you be true men, for my house is for none but pilgrims." Then was Christiana, Mercy, and the boys the more glad for that the innkeeper was a lover of pilgrims. So they called for rooms. And he showed them one for Christiana, and her children, and Mercy, and another for Mr. Great-heart and the old gentlemen.

GREATH-HEART. Then said Mr. Great-heart, "Good Gaius, what hast thou for supper? For these pilgrims have come far today and are weary."

GAIUS. "It is late," said Gaius. "So we cannot conveniently go out to seek food; but such as we have you shall be welcome to, if that will content."

GREATH-HEART. "We will be content with what thou hast in the house; for as much as I have proved thee, thou art never destitute of that which is convenient."

Then he went down and spoke to the cook, whose name was Taste-that-which-is-good, to get ready supper for so many pilgrims. This done, he comes up again saying, "Come, my good friends, you are welcome to me, and I am glad that I have an house to entertain you. And while supper is making ready, if you please, let us entertain one another with some good discourse." So they all said, "Content."

GAIUS. Then said Gaius, "Whose wife is the aged matron? And whose daughter is this young damsel?"

GREAT-HEART. "The woman is the wife of one Christian, a pilgrim of former times, and these are his four children. The maid is one of her acquaintance, one that she hath persuaded to come with her on pilgrimage. The boys take all after their father and covet to tread in his steps. Yea, if they do but see any place where the old pilgrim hath lain, or any print of his foot, it ministereth joy to their hearts, and they covet to lie or tread in the same."

GAIUS. Then said Gaius, "Is this Christian's wife, and are these Christian's children? I knew your husband's father, yea, also, his father's father. Many have been good of this stock; their ancestors dwelt first at Antioch. Christian's progenitors (I suppose you have heard your husband talk of them) were very worthy men. They have, above any that I know, showed themselves men of great virtue and courage for the Lord of the pilgrims, his ways, and them that loved him. I have heard of many of your husband's relations that have stood all trials for the sake of the truth. Stephen, that was one of the first of the family from whence your husband sprang, was knocked o'the head with stones. James, another of this generation, was slain with the edge of the sword, to say nothing of Paul and Peter, men anciently of the family from whence your husband came. There was Ignatius, who was cast to the lions; Romanus, whose flesh was cut by pieces from his bones; and Polycarp, that played the man in the fire. There was he that was hanged up in a basket in the sun for the wasps to eat; and he who they put into a sack and cast him into the sea to be drowned. 'Twould be impossible, utterly, to count up all of that family that have suffered injuries and death for the love of a pilgrim's life. Nor can I but be glad to see that thy husband has left behind him four such boys as these. I hope they will bear up their father's name, and tread in their father's steps, and come to their father's end."

GREAT-HEART. "Indeed, sir, they are likely lads. They seem to choose heartily their father's ways."

GAIUS. "That is it that I said; wherefore Christian's family is like still to spread aboard upon the face of the ground, and yet to be numerous upon the face of the earth. Wherefore let Christiana look out some damsels for her sons, to whom they may be betrothed, etc., that the name of their father, and the house of his progenitors may never be forgotten in the world."

HONEST. " 'Tis pity this family should fall and be extinct."

GAIUS. "Fall it cannot, but be diminished it may. But let Christiana take my advice, and that's the way to uphold it."

"And Christiana," said this innkeeper, "I am glad to see thee and thy friend, Mercy, together here, a lovely couple. And may I advise, take Mercy into a nearer relation to thee. If she will, let her be given to Matthew, thy eldest son. 'Tis the way to preserve you a posterity in the earth." So this match was concluded, and in process of time they were married. But more of that hereafter.

Gaius also proceeded and said, "I will now speak on the behalf of women, to take away their reproach. For as death and the curse came into the world by a woman, so also did life and health. God sent forth his Son, made of a woman. [Galatians 4:4] Yea, to show how much those that came after did abhor the act of their mother, this sex, in the Old Testament, coveted children, if happily this or that woman might be the mother of the Saviour of the world. I will say again that, when the Saviour was come, women rejoiced in him before either man or angel. I read not that ever any man did give unto Christ so much as one groat, but the women followed him and ministered to him of their substance. 'Twas a woman that washed his feet with tears, and a woman that anointed his body to the burial. They were women that wept when he was going to the cross, and women that followed him from the cross, and that sat by his sepulchre when he was buried. They were women that was first with him at his resurrection morn, and women that brought tidings first to his disciples that he was risen from the dead. Women therefore are highly favoured and show by these things that they are sharers with us in the grace of life."

Now the cook sent up to signify that supper was almost ready and sent one to lay the cloth, the trenchers, and to set the salt and bread in order.

Then said Matthew, "The sight of this cloth and of this forerunner of the supper begetteth in me a greater appetite to my food than I had before."

GAIUS. "So let all ministering doctrines to thee in this life beget in thee a greater desire to sit at the supper of the great King in his kingdom. For all preaching, books, and ordinances here, are but as the laying of the trenchers, and as setting of salt upon the board when compared with the feast that our Lord will make for us when we come to his house."

So supper came up, and first a heave-shoulder and a wave-breast* was set on the table before them to show that they must begin their meal with prayer and praise to God. The heave-shoulder David lifted his heart up to God with, and with the wave-breast, where his heart lay, with that he used to lean upon his harp when he played. These two dishes were very fresh and good, and they all eat heartily-well thereof.

The next they brought up was a bottle of wine, red as blood. So Gaius said to them, "Drink freely. This is the juice of the true vine that makes glad the heart of God and man." So they drank and were merry.

The next was a dish of milk well crumbed. But Gaius said, "Let the boys have that, that they may grow thereby."

Then they brought up in course a dish of butter and honey. Then said Gaius, "Eat freely of this, for this is good to cheer up and strengthen your judgements and understandings. This was our Lord's dish when he was a child; butter and honey shall he eat, that he may know to refuse the evil, and choose the good." [Isaiah 7:15]

Then they brought them up a dish of apples, and they were very good tasted fruit. Then said Matthew, "May we eat apples, since they were such, by, and with which the serpent beguiled our first mother?"

Then said Gaius,

Apples were they with which we were beguiled;
Yet sin, not apples, hath our souls defiled.

*Sacrifice offerings.

Apples forbid, if eat, corrupt the blood;
To eat such, when commanded, does us good.
Drink of his flagons then, thou Church, his dove,
And eat his apples, who art sick of love. [Song of Solomon 2:5]

Then said Matthew, "I made the scruple because I, awhile since, was sick with eating of fruit."

GAIUS. "Forbidden fruit will make you sick, but not what our Lord has tolerated."

While they were thus talking, they were presented with another dish, and 'twas a dish of nuts. Then said some at the table, "Nuts spoil tender teeth, especially the teeth of children." Which when Gaius heard, he said,

Hard texts are nuts, (I will not call them cheaters),
Whose shells do keep their kernels from the eaters.
Ope then the shells, and you shall have the meat;
They here are brought for you to crack and eat.

Then were they very merry and sat at the table a long time, talking of many things. Then said the old gentleman, "My good landlord, while we are cracking you nuts, if you please, do you open this riddle,

A man there was, though some did count him mad,
The more he cast away, the more he had."

Then they all gave good heed, wondering what good Gaius would say. So he sat still awhile, and then thus replied,

He that bestows his goods upon the poor,
Shall have as much again, and ten times more.

Then said Joseph, "I dare say, sir, I did not think you could a found it out."

"Oh," said Gaius, "I have been trained up in this way a great while. Nothing teaches like experience. I have learned of my Lord to be kind, and have found by experience that I have gained thereby. There is that scattereth, yet increaseth; and there is that withholdeth more than is meet, but it tendeth to poverty. [Proverbs 11:24] There is that maketh himself rich, yet hath nothing; there is that maketh himself poor, yet hath great riches." [Proverbs 13:7]

Then Samuel whispered to Christiana, his mother, and said, "Mother, this is a very good man's house. Let us stay here a good while, and let my brother, Matthew, be married here to Mercy, before we go any further."

The which Gaius the host overhearing said, "With a very good will, my child."

So they stayed there more than a month, and Mercy was given to Matthew to wife.

While they stayed here Mercy, as her custom was, would be making coats and garments to give to the poor, by which she brought up a very good report upon the pilgrims.

But to return again to our story. After supper, the lads desired a bed for that they were weary with travelling. Then Gaius called to show them their chamber, but said Mercy, "I will have them to bed." So she had them to bed, and they slept well, but the rest sat up all night. For Gaius and they were such suitable company that they could not tell how to part. Then after much talk of their Lord, themselves, and their journey, old Mr. Honest, he that put forth the riddle to Gaius, began to nod. Then said Great-heart, "What, sir, you begin to be drowsy. Come rub up; now here's a riddle for you." Then said Mr. Honest, "Let's hear it."

Then said Mr. Great-heart,

He that will kill must first be overcome;
Who live abroad would, first must die at home.

"Huh," said Mr. Honest, "it is a hard one, hard to expound and harder to practise. But, come, landlord," said he, "I will, if you please, leave my part to you. Do you expound it, and I will hear what you say."

"No," said Gaius, " 'twas put to you, and 'tis expected that you should answer it."

Then said the old gentleman,

He first by grace must conquered be,
That sin would mortify;
And who, that lives, would convince me,
Unto himself must die.

"It is right," said Gaius. "Good doctrine and experience teaches this. For first, until grace displays itself and overcomes the soul with its glory, it is altogether without heart to oppose sin. Besides, if sin is Satan's cords, by which the soul lies bound, how should it make resistance before it is loosed from the infirmity?

"Secondly, nor will any that knows either reason or grace believe that such a man can be a living monument of grace that is a slave to his own corruptions.

"And now it comes in my mind, I will tell you a story worth the hearing. There were two men that went on pilgrimage, the one began when he was young, the other when he was old. The young man had strong corruptions to grapple with, the old man's were decayed with the decays of nature. The young man trod his steps as even as did the old one, and was every way as light as he. Who now, or which of them, had their graces shining clearest since both seemed to be alike?"

HONEST. "The young man's doubtless. For that which heads it against the greatest opposition gives best demonstration that it is strongest, specially when it also holdeth pace with that that meets not with half so much, as to be sure old age does not.

"Besides, I have observed that old men have blessed themselves with this mistake, namely, taking the decays of nature for a gracious conquest over corruptions, and so have been apt to beguile themselves. Indeed old men that are gracious are best able to give advice to them that are young because they have seen most of the emptiness of things. But yet, for an old and a young to set out both together, the young one has the advantage of the fairest discovery of a work of grace within him though the old man's corruptions are naturally the weakest."

Thus they sat talking till break of day. Now when the family was up, Christiana bid her son James that he should read a chapter. So he read the 53rd of Isaiah. When he had done, Mr. Honest asked why it was said that the Saviour is said to come out of a dry ground, and also that he had no form nor comeliness in him?

GREAT-HEART. Then said Mr. Great-heart, "To the first I answer, because the church of the Jews, of which Christ came, had then lost almost all the sap and spirit of religion. To the second I say, the words are spoken in the person of the unbelievers, who because they want that eye that can see into our Prince's heart, therefore they judge of him by the meanness of his outside.

"Just like those that know not that precious stones are covered over with a homely crust, who, when they have found one, because they know not what they have found, cast it again away as men do a common stone."

"Well," said Gaius, "Now you are here, and since, as I know, Mr. Great-heart is good at his weapons, if you please, after we have refreshed ourselves, we will walk into the fields to see if we can do any good. About a mile from hence there is one Slaygood, a giant, that doth much annoy the King's highway in these parts. And I know whereabout his haunt is; he is master of a number of thieves. 'Twould be well if we could clear these parts of him."

So they consented and went, Mr. Great-heart with his sword, helmet and shield, and the rest with spears and staves.

When they came to the place where he was, they found him with one Feeble-mind in his hands, whom his servants had brought unto him, having taken him in the way. Now the giant was rifling of him with a purpose, after that, to pick his bones. For he was of the nature of flesh-eaters.

Well, so soon as he saw Mr. Great-heart, and his friends at the mouth of his cave with their weapons, he demanded what they wanted.

GREAT-HEART. "We want thee. For we are come to revenge the quarrel of the many that thou hast slain of the pilgrims when thou hast dragged them out of the King's highway. Wherefore come out of thy cave." So he armed himself and came out. And to a battle they went, and fought for above an hour, and then stood still to take wind.

SLAYGOOD. Then said the giant, "Why are you here on my ground?"

GREAT-HEART. "To revenge the blood of pilgrims, as I also told thee before." So they went to it again, and the giant made Mr. Great-heart give back. But he came up again, and, in the greatness of his mind, he let fly with such stoutness at the giant's head and sides that he made him let his weapon fall out of his hand. So he smote him, and slew him, and cut off his head, and brought it away to the inn. He also took Feeble-mind, the pilgrim, and brought him with him to his lodgings. When they were come home they showed his head to the family and then set it up, as they had done others before, for a terror to those that should attempt to do as he hereafter.

Then they asked Mr. Feeble-mind how he fell into his hands.

FEEBLE-MIND. Then said the poor man, "I am a sickly man, as you see, and because death did usually once a day knock at my door, I thought I should never be well at home. So I betook myself to a pilgrim's life, and have travelled hither from the Town of Uncertain where I and my father were born. I am a man of no strength at all of body, nor yet of mind, but would, if I could, though I can but crawl, spend my life in the pilgrim's way. When I came at the gate that is at the head of the way, the lord of that place did entertain me freely. Neither objected he against my weakly looks, nor against my feeble mind, but gave me such things that were necessary for my journey and bid me hope to the end. When I came to the house of the Interpreter I received much kindness there, and because the Hill Difficulty was judged too hard for me I was carried up that by one of his servants. Indeed, I have found much relief from pilgrims though none was willing to go so softly as I am forced to do. Yet still as they came on, they bid me be of good cheer and said that it was the will of their Lord that comfort should be given to the feeble-minded, and so went on their own pace. When I was come up to Assault Lane, then this giant met with me and bid me prepare for an encounter, but, alas, feeble one that I was, I had more need of a cordial. So he came up and took me. I conceited* he should not kill me. Also when he had got me into his den, since I went not with him willingly, I believed I should come out alive again. For I have heard that not any pilgrim that is taken captive by violent hands, if he keeps heart-whole towards his Master, is by the laws of Providence to die by the hand of the enemy. Robbed, I looked to be, and robbed to be sure I am, but I am, as you see, escaped with life, for the which I thank my King as author and you as the means. Other brunts I also look for, but this I have resolved on, to wit, to run when I can, to go when I cannot run, and to creep when I cannot go. As to the main, I thank him that loves me, I am fixed. My way is before me; my mind is beyond the river that has no bridge though I am, as you see, but of a feeble mind."

HONEST. Then said old Mr. Honest, "Have not you, some time ago, been acquainted with one Mr. Fearing, a pilgrim?"

FEEBLE-MIND. "Acquainted with him, yes. He came from the town of Stupidity, which lieth four degrees to the northward of the City of Destruction

---

*Believed.

and as many off of where I was born. Yet we were well acquainted, for indeed he was mine uncle, my father's brother. He and I have been much of a temper. He was a little shorter than I, but yet we were much of a complexion."

HONEST. "I perceive you knew him, and I am apt to believe also that you were related one to another, for you have his whitely look, a cast like his with your eye, and your speech is much alike."

FEEBLE-MIND. "Most have said so that have known us both, and besides, what I have read in him I have for the most part found in myself."

GAIUS. "Come, sir," said good Gaius, "be of good cheer, you are welcome to me and to my house. And what thou hast a mind to, call for freely, and what thou wouldst have my servants do for thee, they will do it with a ready mind."

FEEBLE-MIND. Then said Mr. Feeble-mind, "This is unexpected favour, and as the sun shining out of a very dark cloud. Did giant Slaygood intend me this favour when he stopped me and resolved to let me go no further? Did he intend that after he had rifled my pockets I should go to Gaius, mine host? Yet so it is."

Now, just as Mr. Feeble-mind and Gaius was thus in talk, there comes one running and called at the door and told that about a mile and an half off, there was one Mr. Notright, a pilgrim, struck dead upon the place where he was with a thunder bolt.

FEEBLE-MIND. "Alas," said Mr. Feeble-mind, "is he slain? He overtook me some days before I came so far as hither and would be my company-keeper. He also was with me when Slaygood the giant took me, but he was nimble of his heels and escaped. But, it seems, he escaped to die, and I was took to live."

> What one would think doth seek to slay outright,
> Ofttimes delivers from the saddest plight.
> That very Providence, whose face is death,
> Doth ofttimes to the lowly life bequeath.
> I taken was, he did escape and flee;
> Hands crossed gives death to him and life to me.

Now about this time Matthew and Mercy was married. Also Gaius gave his daughter, Phoebe, to James, Matthew's brother, to wife; after which time, they yet stayed above ten days at Gaius' house, spending their time, and the seasons, like as pilgrims use to do.

When they were to depart Gaius made them a feast, and they did eat and drink and were merry. Now the hour was come that they must be gone, wherefore Mr. Great-heart called for a reckoning. But Gaius told him that at his house it was not the custom for pilgrims to pay for their entertainment. He boarded them by the year but looked for his pay from the good Samaritan, who had promised him at his return, whatsoever charge he was at with them, faithfully to repay him. Then said Mr. Great-heart to him,

GREAT-HEART. "Beloved, thou dost faithfully whatsoever thou dost to the brethren, and to strangers, which have borne witness of thy charity before the church, whom if thou (yet) bring forward on their journey after a godly sort, thou shalt do well." [3 John 5:6]

Then Gaius took his leave of them all, and of his children, and particularly of Mr. Feeble-mind. He also gave him something to drink by the way.

Now Mr. Feeble-mind, when they were going out of the door, made as if he intended to linger. The which, when Mr. Great-heart espied, he said, "Come, Mr. Feeble-mind, pray, do you go along with us. I will be your conductor, and you shall fare as the rest."

FEEBLE-MIND. "Alas, I want a suitable companion. You are all lusty and strong, but I, as you see, am weak. I choose, therefore, rather to come behind, lest, by reason of my many infirmities, I should be both a burthen to myself and to you. I am, as I said, a man of a weak and feeble mind, and shall be offended and made weak at that which others can bear. I shall like no laughing, I shall like no gay attire, I shall like no unprofitable questions. Nay, I am so weak a man as to be offended with that which others have a liberty to do. I do not yet know all the truth; I am a very ignorant Christian man. Sometimes, if I hear some rejoice in the Lord it troubles me because I cannot do so too. It is with me as it is a weak man among the strong, or as with a sick man among the healthy, or as a lamp despised. (He that is ready to slip with his feet is as a lamp despised in the thought of him that is at ease.) [Job 12:5] So that I know not what to do."

GREAT-HEART. "But, brother," said Mr. Great-heart, "I have it in commission to comfort the feeble-minded and to support the weak. You must needs go along with us. We will wait for you, we will lend you our help, we will deny ourselves of some things, both opinionative and practical, for your sake. We will not enter into doubtful disputations before you. We will be made all things to you rather than you shall be left behind."

Now all this while they were at Gaius' door. And behold, as they were thus in the heat of their discourse, Mr. Ready-to-halt came by with his crutches* in his hand, and he also was going on pilgrimage.

FEEBLE-MIND. Then said Mr. Feeble-mind to him, "Man, how camest thou hither? I was but just now complaining that I had not a suitable companion, but thou art according to my wish. Welcome, welcome, good Mr. Ready-to-halt, I hope thee and I may be some help."

READY-TO-HALT. "I shall be glad of thy company," said the other. "And, good Mr. Feeble-mind, rather than we will part, since we are thus happily met, I will lend thee one of my crutches."

FEEBLE-MIND. "Nay," said he, "though I thank thee for thy good will, I am not inclined to halt before I am lame. Howbeit, I think when occasion is it may help me against a dog."

READY-TO-HALT. "If either myself or my crutches can do thee a pleasure we are both at thy command, good Mr. Feeble-mind."

Thus, therefore, they went on. Mr. Great-heart and Mr. Honest went before, Christiana and her children went next, and Mr. Feeble-mind and

---

*Halt: lame.

Mr. Ready-to-halt came behind with his crutches. Then said Mr. Honest,

HONEST. "Pray, sir, now we are upon the road, tell us some profitable things of some that have gone on pilgrimage before us."

GREAT-HEART. "With a good will. I suppose you have heard how Christian, of old, did meet with Apollyon in the Valley of Humiliation, and also what hard work he had to go through the Valley of the Shadow of Death. Also I think you cannot but have heard how Faithful was put to it with Madam Wanton, with Adam the First, with one Discontent, and Shame, four as deceitful villains as a man can meet with upon the road."

HONEST. "Yes, I have heard of all this. But indeed, good Faithful was hardest put to it with Shame; he was an unwearied one."

GREAT-HEART. "Ay, for as the pilgrim well said, he of all men had the wrong name."

HONEST. "But, pray, sir, where was it that Christian and Faithful met Talkative? That same was also a notable one."

GREAT-HEART. "He was a confident fool, yet many follow his ways."

HONEST. "He had like to a beguiled Faithful?"

GREAT-HEART. "Ay, but Christian put him into a way quickly to find him out." Thus they went on till thy came at the place where Evangelist met with Christian and Faithful and prophesied to them of what should befall them at Vanity Fair.

GREAT-HEART. Then said their guide, "Hereabout did Christian and Faithful meet with Evangelist, who prophesied to them what troubles they should meet with at Vanity Fair."

HONEST. "Say you so! I dare say it was a hard chapter that then he did read unto them."

GREAT-HEART. " 'Twas so, but he gave them encouragement withal. But what do we talk of them? They were a couple of lion-like men; they had set their faces like flint. Don't you remember how undaunted they were when they stood before the judge?"

HONEST. "Well, Faithful, bravely suffered!"

GREAT-HEART. "So he did, and as brave things came on't. For Hopeful and some others, as the story relates it, were converted by his death."

HONEST. "Well, but, pray, go on, for you are well acquainted with things."

GREAT-HEART. "Above all that Christian met with after he had passed through Vanity Fair, one By-ends was the arch one."

HONEST. "By-ends, what was he?"

GREAT-HEART. "A very arch fellow, a downright hypocrite. One that would be religious which way ever the world went, but so cunning that he would be sure neither to lose nor suffer for it.

"He had his mode of religion for every fresh occasion, and his wife was as good at it as he. He would turn and change from opinion to opinion; yea, and plead for so doing too. But so far as I could learn, he came to an ill end with his by-ends, nor did I ever hear that any of his children were ever of any esteem with any that truly feared God."

Now by this time they were come within sight of the town of Vanity, where Vanity Fair is kept. So when they saw that they were so near the town, they consulted with one another how they should pass through the town, and some said one thing and some another. At last Mr. Great-heart said, "I have, as you may understand, often been a conductor of pilgrims through this town. Now I am acquainted with one Mr. Mnason, a Cyprusian by nation, an old disciple, at whose house we may lodge. If you think good," said he, "we will turn in there."

"Content," said old Honest; "Content," said Christiana, "Content," said Mr. Feeble-mind, and so they said all. Now you must think it was eventide by that they got to the outside of the town, but Mr. Great-heart knew the way to the old man's house. So thither they came. And he called at the door, and the old man within knew his tongue so soon as ever he heard it. So he opened, and they all came in. Then said Mnason, their host, "How far have ye come today?" So they said, "From the house of Gaius, our friend." "I promise you," said he, "you have gone a good stitch. You may well be a-weary, sit down." So they sat down.

GREAT-HEART. Then said their guide, "Come, what cheer, sirs, I dare say you are welcome to my friend."

MNASON. "I also," said Mr. Mnason, "do bid you welcome. And whatever you want, do but say, and we will do what we can to get it for you."

HONEST. "Our great want, a while since, was harbour and good company, and now I hope we have both."

MNASON. "For harbour, you see what it is, but for good company, that will appear in the trial."

GREAT-HEART. "Well," said Mr. Great-heart, "will you have the pilgrims up into their lodging?"

MNASON. "I will," said Mr. Mnason. So he had them to their respective places, and also showed them a very fair dining-room where they might be and sup together until time was come to go to rest.

Now when they were set in their places, and were a little cheery after their journey, Mr. Honest asked his landlord if there were any store of good people in the town.

MNASON. "We have a few, for indeed they are but a few when compared with them on the other side."

HONEST. "But how shall we do to see some of them? For the sight of good men to them that are going on pilgrimage is like to the appearing of the moon and the stars to them that are sailing upon the seas."

MNASON. Then Mr. Mnason stamped with his foot, and his daughter, Grace, came up. So he said unto her, "Grace, go you, tell my friends, Mr. Contrite, Mr. Holy-man, Mr. Love-saint, Mr. Dare-not-lie, and Mr. Penitent that I have a friend or two at my house that have a mind this evening to see them."

So Grace went to call them, and they came. And after salutation made, they sat down together at the table.

Then said Mr. Mnason, their landlord, "My neighbours, I have, as you see, a company of strangers come to my house; they are pilgrims. They come from afar and are going to Mount Zion. But who," quoth he, "do you think this is?" pointing with his finger to Christiana. "It is Christiana, the wife of Christian, that famous pilgrim, who with Faithful, his brother, were so shamefully handled in our town." At that they stood amazed saying, "We little thought to see Christiana, when Grace came to call us, wherefore this is a very comfortable surprise." Then they asked her of her welfare and if these young men were her husband's sons. And, when she had told them they were, they said, "The King whom you love and serve make you as your Father and bring you where he is in peace."

HONEST. Then Mr. Honest (when they were all sat down) asked Mr. Contrite and the rest in what posture their town was at present?

CONTRITE. "You may be sure we are full of hurry in fair time. 'Tis hard keeping our hearts and spirits in any good order when we are in a cumbered condition. He that lives in such a place as this is, and that has to do with such as we have, has need of an item to caution him to take heed every moment of the day."

HONEST. "But how are your neighbours for quietness?"

CONTRITE. "They are much more moderate now than formerly. You know how Christian and Faithful were used at our town; but of late, I say, they have been far more moderate. I think the blood of Faithful lieth with load upon them till now; for since they burned him, they have been ashamed to burn any more. In those days, we were afraid to walk the streets, but now we can show our heads. Then the name of a professor was odious; now, specially in some parts of our town (for you know our town is large), religion is counted honourable."

Then said Mr. Contrite to them, "Pray, how fareth it with you in your pilgrimage? How stands the country affected towards you?"

HONEST. "It happens to us as it happeneth to wayfaring men. Sometimes our way is clean, sometimes foul; sometimes uphill, sometimes downhill. We are seldom at a certainty. The wind is not always on our backs, nor is everyone a friend that we meet with in the way. We have met with some notable rubs already, and what are yet behind we know not. But for the most part we find it true that has been talked of of old, a good man must suffer trouble."

CONTRITE. "You talk of rubs; what rubs have you met withal?"

HONEST. "Nay, ask Mr. Great-heart, our guide, for he can give the best account of that."

GREAT-HEART. "We have been beset three or four times already. First, Christiana and her children were beset with two ruffians that they feared would a took away their lives. We were beset with giant Bloody-man, giant Maul, and giant Slaygood. Indeed, we did rather beset the last than were beset of him. And thus it was. After we had been some time at the house of Gaius, mine host, and of the whole church, we were minded upon a time to take our weapons with us, and go see if we could light upon any of those that were enemies to pilgrims (for we heard that there was a notable one thereabouts). Now Gaius knew his haunt better than I because he dwelt thereabout, so we looked and looked till, at last, we discerned the mouth of his cave. Then we were glad and plucked up our spirits. So we approached up to his den, and, lo, when we came there, he had dragged by mere force into his net this poor man, Mr. Feeble-mind, and was about to bring him to his end. But when he saw us, supposing, as we thought, he had had another prey, he left the poor man in his hole and came out. So we fell to it full sore, and he lustily laid about him. But, in conclusion, he was brought down to the ground, and his head cut off and set up by the wayside for a terror to such as should after practice such ungodliness. That I tell you the truth, here is the man himself to affirm it, who was as a lamb taken out of the mouth of the lion."

FEEBLE-MIND. Then said Mr. Feeble-mind, "I found this true to my cost and comfort; to my cost when he threatened to pick my bones every moment, and to my comfort when I saw Mr. Great-heart and his friends with their weapons approach so near for my deliverance."

HOLY-MAN. Then said Mr. Holy-man, "There are two things that they have need to be possessed with that go on pilgrimage, courage and an unspotted life. If they have not courage they can never hold on their way. And if their lives be loose they will make the very name of a pilgrim stink."

LOVE-SAINT. Then said Mr. Love-saint, "I hope this caution is not needful amongst you. But truly there are many that go upon the road that rather declare themselves strangers to pilgrimage than strangers and pilgrims in the earth."

DARE-NOT-LIE. Then said Mr. Dare-not-lie, " 'Tis true. They neither have the pilgrim's weed nor the pilgrim's courage. They go not uprightly, but all awry with their feet; one shoe goes inward, another outward, and their hose out behind; there a rag, and there a rent, to the disparagement of their Lord."

PENITENT. "These things," said Mr. Penitent, "they ought to be troubled for, nor are the pilgrims like to have that grace put upon them and their pilgrim's progress, as they desire, until the way is cleared of such spots and blemishes."

Thus they sat talking and spending the time until supper was set upon the table, unto which they went and refreshed their weary bodies, so they went to rest. Now they stayed in this fair a great while, at the house of this Mr. Mnason, who, in process of time, gave his daughter, Grace, unto Samuel, Christiana's son, to wife, and his daughter, Martha, to Joseph.

The time, as I said, that they lay here was long (for it was not now as in former times). Wherefore the pilgrims grew acquainted with many of the good people of the town and did them what service they could. Mercy, as she was wont, laboured much for the poor, wherefore their bellies and backs blessed her, and she was there an ornament to her profession. And to say the truth for Grace, Phoebe, and Martha, they were all of a very good nature and did much good in their place. They were also all of them very fruitful, so that Christian's name, as was said before, was like to live in the world.

While they lay here, there came a monster out of the woods and slew many of the people of the town. It would also carry away their children and teach them to suck its whelps. Now no man in the town durst so much as face this monster, but all men fled when they heard of the noise of his coming.

The monster was like unto no one beast upon the earth. Its body was like a dragon, and it had seven heads and ten horns. It made great havoc of children, and yet it was governed by a woman. This monster propounded conditions to men; and such men as loved their lives more than their souls accepted of those conditions; so they came under.

Now this Mr. Great-heart, together with these that came to visit the pilgrims at Mr. Mnason's house, entered into a covenant to go and engage this beast if perhaps they might deliver the people of this town from the paws and mouths of this so devouring a serpent.

Then did Mr. Great-heart, Mr. Contrite, Mr. Holy-man, Mr. Dare-not-lie, and Mr. Penitent, with their weapons, go forth to meet him. Now the monster at first was very rampant and looked upon these enemies with great disdain, but they so belaboured him, being sturdy men at arms, that they made him make a retreat. So they came home to Mr. Mnason's house again.

The monster, you must know, had his certain seasons to come out in and to make his attempts upon the children of the people of the town. Also these seasons did these valiant worthies watch him in and did still continually assault him, in so much, that in process of time, he became not only wounded, but lame. Also he has not made that havoc of the townsmen's children as formerly he has done. And it is verily believed by some that this beast will die of his wounds.

This, therefore, made Mr. Great-heart and his fellows of great fame in this town, so that many of the people that wanted their taste of things yet had a reverend esteem and respect for them. Upon this account, therefore, it was that these pilgrims got not much hurt here. True, there were some of the baser sort that could see no more than a mole, nor understand more than a beast. These had no reverence for these men, nor took they notice of their valour or adventures.

Well, the time drew on that the pilgrims must go on their way; wherefore they prepared for their journey. They sent for their friends; they conferred with them; they had some time set apart therein to commit each other to the protection of their Prince. There were again that brought them of such things as they had that were fit for the weak, and the strong, for the women, and the men; and so laded them with such things as was necessary.

Then they set forwards on their way. And their friends accompanying them so far as was convenient, they again committed each other to the protection of their King and parted.

They therefore that were of the pilgrims' company went on, and Mr. Great-heart went before them. Now the women and children being weakly, they were forced to go as they could bear; by this means Mr. Ready-to-halt and Mr. Feeble-mind had more to sympathize with their condition.

When they were gone from the townsmen, and when their friends had bid them farewell, they quickly came to the place where Faithful was put to death. There therefore they made a stand and thanked him that had enabled him to bear his cross so well, and the rather because they now found that they had a benefit by such a manly suffering as his was.

They went on therefore after this a good way further, talking of Christian and Faithful and how Hopeful joined himself to Christian after that Faithful was dead.

Now they were come up with the Hill Lucre, where the silver mine was which took Demas off from his pilgrimage, and into which, as some think, By-ends fell and perished; wherefore they considered that. But when they were come to the old monument that stood over against the Hill Lucre, to wit, to the pillar of salt that stood also within view of Sodom, and its stinking lake, they marvelled, as did Christian before, that men of that knowledge and ripeness of wit, as they were, should be so blinded as to turn aside here. Only they considered again that nature is not affected with the harms that others have met with, specially if that thing upon which they look has an attracting virtue upon the foolish eye.

I saw now that they went on till they came at the river that was on this side of the Delectable Mountains, to the river where the fine trees grow on both sides, and whose leaves, if taken inwardly, are good against surfeits, where the meadows are green all the year long, and where they might lie down safely.

By this riverside in the meadow there were cotes and folds for sheep, an house built for the nourishing and bringing up of those lambs, the babes of those women that go on pilgrimage. Also there was here one that was intrusted with them, who could have compassion, and that could gather these lambs with his arm and carry them in his bosom, and that could gently lead those that were with young. Now to the care of this man Christiana admonished her four daughters to commit their little ones, that by these waters they might be housed, harboured, succoured and nourished, and that none of them might be lacking in time to come. "This man, if any of them go astray or be lost, he will bring them again; he will also bind up that which was broken and will strengthen them that are sick. Here they will never want meat, and drink, and clothing. Here they will be kept from thieves and robbers, for this man will die before one of those committed to his trust shall be lost. Besides, here they shall be sure to have good nurture and admonition and shall be taught to walk in right paths, and that you know is a favour of no small account. Also here, as you see, are delicate waters, pleasant meadows, dainty flowers, variety of trees, and such as bear wholesome fruit, fruit, not like that that Matthew ate of, that fell over the wall out of Beelzebub's garden, but fruit that procureth health where there is none, and that continueth and increaseth it where it is."

So they were content to commit their little ones to him. And that which was also an encouragement to them so to do was for that all this was to be at the charge of the King, and so was an hospital to young children and orphans.

Now they went on. And when they were come to By-path Meadow, to the stile over which Christian went with his fellow, Hopeful, when they were taken by giant Despair and put into Doubting Castle, they sat down and consulted what was best to be done, to wit; now they were so strong, and had got such a man as Mr. Great-heart for their conductor, whether they had not best to make an attempt upon the giant, demolish his castle, and, if there were any pilgrims in it, to set them at liberty before they went any further. So one said one thing, and another said the contrary. One questioned if it was lawful to go upon unconsecrated ground; another said they might, provided their end was good. But Mr. Great-heart said, "Though that assertion offered last cannot be universally true, yet I have a commandment to resist sin, to overcome evil, to fight the good fight of faith. [I Timothy 6:12] And I pray, with whom should I fight this good fight if not with giant Despair? I will therefore attempt the taking away of his life and the demolishing of Doubting Castle." Then said he, "Who will go with me?" Then said old Honest, "I will." "And so will we too," said Christian's four sons, Matthew, Samuel, James, and Joseph, for they were young men and strong.

So they left the women in the road, and with them Mr. Feeble-mind, and Mr. Ready-to-halt, with his crutches, to be their guard until they came back. For in that place, though Giant Despair dwelt so near, they keeping in the road, a little child might lead them.

So Mr. Great-heart, old Honest, and the four young men, went to go up to Doubting Castle to look for Giant Despair. When they came at the castle-gate, they knocked for entrance with an unusual noise. At that, the old giant comes to the gate, and Diffidence, his wife, follows. Then said he, "Who, and what is he that is so hardy as after this manner to molest the Giant Despair?" Mr. Great-heart replied, "It is I, Great-heart, one of the King of the Celestial Country's conductors of pilgrims to their place. And I demand of thee that thou open thy gates for my entrance. Prepare thyself also to fight, for I am come to take away thy head and to demolish Doubting Castle."

Now Giant Despair, because he was a giant, thought no man could overcome him. And again, thought he, "Since heretofore I have made a conquest of angels, shall Great-heart make me afraid?" So he harnessed himself and went out. He had a cap of steel upon his head, a breastplate of fire girded to him, and he came out in iron shoes, with a great club in his hand. Then these six men made up to him and beset him behind and before. Also when Diffidence, the giantess, came up to help him, old Mr. Honest cut her down at one blow. Then they fought for their lives. And Giant Despair was brought down to the ground but was very loath to die. He struggled hard, and had, as they say, as many lives as a cat. But Great-heart was his death, for he left him not till he had severed his head from his shoulders.

Then they fell to demolishing Doubting Castle, and that, you know, might with ease be done since Giant Despair was dead. They were seven days in destroying of that, and in it of pilgrims they found one Mr. Despondency, almost starved to death, and one Much-afraid, his daughter. These two they saved alive. But it would a made you a wondered to have seen the dead bodies that lay here and there in the castle-yard, and how full of dead men's bones the dungeon was.

When Mr. Great-heart and his companions had performed this exploit, they took Mr. Despondency and his daughter, Much-afraid, into their protection, for they were honest people though they were prisoners, in Doubting Castle, to that tyrant, Giant Despair. They, therefore, I say, took with them the head of the giant (for his body they had buried under a heap of stones), and down to the road and to their companions they came and showed them what they had done. Now when Feeble-mind and Ready-to-halt saw that it was the head of Giant Despair, indeed, they were very jocund and merry. Now Christiana, if need was, could play upon the viol, and her daughter,

Mercy, upon the lute. So, since they were so merry disposed, she played them a lesson, and Ready-to-halt would dance. So he took Despondency's daughter, named Much-afraid, by the hand, and to dancing they went in the road. True, he could not dance without one crutch in his hand, but, I promise you, he footed it well; also the girl was to be commended, for she answered the music handsomely.

As for Mr. Despondency, the music was not much to him; he was for feeding rather than dancing, for that he was almost starved. So Christiana gave him some of her bottle of spirits for present relief and then prepared him something to eat. And in little time the old gentleman came to himself and began to be finely revived.

Now I saw in my dream, when all these things were finished Mr. Great-heart took the head of Giant Despair and set it upon a pole by the highway-side, right over against the pillar that Christian erected for a caution to pilgrims that came after to take heed of entering into his grounds.

> Though Doubting Castle be demolished
> And the Giant Despair has lost his head,
> Sin can rebuild the Castle, make it remain,
> And make Despair the Giant live again.

Then he writ under it upon a marble stone these verses following,

> This is the head of him, whose name only
> In former times did pilgrims terrify.
> His castle's down; and Diffidence, his wife,
> Brave Master Great-heart has bereft of life.
> Despondency, his daughter, Much-afraid,
> Great-heart for them also the man has played;
> Who hereof doubts, if he'll but cast his eye
> Up hither, may his scruples satisfy:
> This head also, when doubting cripples dance,
> Doth show from fears they have deliverance.

When these men had thus bravely showed themselves against Doubting Castle and had slain Giant Despair, they went forward and went on till they came to the Delectable Mountains, where Christian and Hopeful refreshed themselves with the varieties of the place. They also acquainted themselves with the shepherds there, who welcomed them, as they had done Christian before, unto the Delectable Mountains.

Now the shepherds seeing so great a train follow Mr. Great-heart (for with him they were well acquainted), they said unto him, "Good sir, you have got a goodly company here. Pray, where did you find all these?"

Then Mr. Great-heart replied,

> First here's Christiana and her train,
> Her sons, and her sons' wives, who like the wain,

Keep by the Pole, and do by compass steer,
From sin to grace, else they had not been here;
Next here's old Honest come on pilgrimage,
Ready-to-halt, too, who, I dare engage
True-hearted is, and so is Feeble-mind,
Who willing was not to be left behind;
Despondency, good man, is coming after,
And so also is Much-afraid, his daughter.
May we have entertainment here, or must
We further go? Let's know whereon to trust.

Then said the shepherds, "This is a comfortable company. You are welcome to us, for we have for the feeble as for the strong. Our Prince has an eye to what is done to the least of these; therefore infirmity must not be a block to our entertainment." So they had them to the palace door and then said unto them, "Come in, Mr. Feeble-mind; come in, Mr. Ready-to-halt; come in, Mr. Despondency, and Mrs. Much-afraid, his daughter. These, Mr. Great-heart," said the shepherds to the guide, "we call in by name, for that they are most subject to draw back. But as for you and the rest that are strong, we leave you to your wonted liberty." Then said Mr. Great-heart, "This day I see that grace doth shine in your faces, and that you are my Lord's shepherds indeed; for that you have not pushed these diseased neither with side nor shoulder, but have rather strewed their way into the palace with flowers, as you should."

So the feeble and weak went in, and Mr. Great-heart and the rest did follow. When they were also set down the shepherds said to those of the weakest sort, "What is it that you would have? For," said they, "all things must be managed here to the supporting of the weak as well as to the warning of the unruly."

So they made them a feast of things easy of digestion and that were pleasant to the palate and nourishing; the which when they had received, they went to their rest, each one respectively unto his proper place. When morning was come, because the mountains were high and the day clear, and because it was the custom of the shepherds to show to their pilgrims, before their departure, some rarities, therefore, after they were ready and had refreshed themselves, the shepherds took them out into the fields and showed them first what they had showed to Christian before.

Then they had them to some new places. The first was to Mount Marvel, where they looked and, behold, a man, at a distance, that tumbled the hills about with words. Then they asked the shepherds what that should mean. So they told him, that that man was the son of one Great-grace, of whom you read in the first part of the Records of the Pilgrim's Progress. And he is set there to teach pilgrims how to believe down, or to tumble out of their ways, what difficulties they shall meet with, by faith. Then said Mr. Great-heart, "I know him; he is a man above many."

Then they had them to another place called Mount Innocent. And there they saw a man clothed all in white and two men, Prejudice and Ill-will, continually casting dirt upon him. Now behold the dirt, whatsoever they cast at him, would in little time fall off again, and his garment would look as clear as if no dirt had been cast thereat.

Then said the pilgrims, "What means this?" The shepherds answered, "This man is named Godly-man, and this garment is to show the innocency of his life. Now those that throw dirt at him are such as hate his well-doing; but, as you see, the dirt will not stick upon his clothes. So it shall be with him that liveth truly innocently in the world. Whoever they be that would make such men dirty, they labour all in vain; for God, by that a little time is spent, will cause that their innocence shall break forth as the light and their righteousness as the noonday."

Then they took them, and had them to Mount Charity, where they showed them a man that had a bundle of cloth lying before him, out of which he cut coats and garments for the poor that stood about him, yet his bundle or roll of cloth was never the less.

Then said they, "What should this be?" "This is," said the shepherds, "to show you that he that has a heart to give of his labour to the poor shall never want wherewithal; he that watereth shall be watered himself. And the cake that the widow gave to the prophet did not cause that she had ever the less in her barrel."

They had them also to a place where they saw one Fool and one Want-wit washing of an Ethiopian with intention to make him white, but the more they washed him, the blacker he was. They then asked the shepherds what that should mean. So they told them saying, "Thus shall it be with the vile person. All means used to get such an one a good name shall, in conclusion, tend but to make him more abominable. Thus it was with the Pharisees, and so shall it be with all hypocrites."

Then said Mercy, the wife of Matthew, to Christiana, her mother, "Mother, I would, if it might be, see the hole in the hill, or that, commonly called, the By-way to hell." So her mother brake her mind to the shepherds. Then they went to the door, it was in the side of an hill, and they opened it and bid Mercy hearken awhile. So she hearkened and heard one saying, "Cursed be my Father for holding of my feet back from the way of peace and life." And another said, "O, that I had been torn in pieces before I had, to save my life, lost my soul." And another said, "If I were to live again, how would I deny myself rather than come to this place." Then there was as if the very earth had groaned and quaked under the feet of this young woman for fear. So she looked white and came trembling away saying, "Blessed be he and she that is delivered from this place."

Now when the shepherds had showed them all these things, then they had them back to the palace and entertained them with what the house would afford, but Mercy, being a young and breeding woman, longed for something which she saw there but was ashamed to ask. Her mother-in-law then asked her what she ailed, for she looked as one not well. Then said Mercy, "There is a looking-glass hangs up in the dining-room, off of which I cannot take my mind. If therefore I have it not, I think I shall miscarry." Then said her mother, "I will mention thy wants to the shepherds, and they will not deny it thee." "But," she said, "I am ashamed that these men should know that I longed." "Nay, my daughter," said she, "it is no shame, but a virtue, to long for such a thing as that." So Mercy said, "Then, Mother, if you please, ask the shepherds if they are willing to sell it."

Now the glass was one of a thousand. It would present a man one way with his own feature exactly, and turn it but another way, and it would show one the very face and similitude of the Prince of pilgrims himself. Yea, I have talked with them that can tell, and they have said that they have seen the very crown of thorns upon his head by looking in that glass; they have therein also seen the holes in his hands, in his feet, and his side. Yea, such an excellency is there in that glass that it will show him to one where they have a mind to see him, whether living or dead, whether in earth or heaven, whether in a state of humiliation or in his exaltation, whether coming to suffer or coming to reign.

Christiana therefore went to the shepherds apart (now the names of the shepherds are Knowledge, Experience, Watchful, and Sincere) and said unto them, "There is one of my daughters, a breeding woman, that I think doth long for something that she hath seen in this house. And she thinks she shall miscarry if she should by you be denied."

EXPERIENCE. "Call her, call her. She shall assuredly have what we can help her to." So they called her and said to her, "Mercy, what is that thing thou wouldst have?" Then she blushed and said, "The great glass that hangs up in the dining-room." So Sincere ran and fetched it, and with a joyful consent it was given her. Then she bowed her head and gave thanks and said, "By this I know that I have obtained favour in your eyes."

They also gave to the other young women such things as they desired and to their husbands great commendations for that they joined with Mr. Great-heart to the slaying of Giant Despair and the demolishing of Doubting Castle.

About Christiana's neck the shepherds put a bracelet, and so they did about the necks of her four daughters; also they put earrings in their ears and jewels on their foreheads.

When they were minded to go hence, they let them go in peace but gave not to them those certain cautions which before was given to Christian and his companion. The reason was for that these had Great-heart to be their guide, who was one that was well acquainted with things, and so could give them their cautions more seasonably, to wit, even then when the danger was nigh the approaching.

What cautions Christian and his companions had received of the shepherds they had also lost by that the time was come that they had need to put them in practice. Wherefore here was the advantage that this company had over the other.

From hence they went on singing, and they said,

Behold, how fitly are the stages set
For their relief that pilgrims are become!

And how they us receive without one let
That makes the other life our mark and home.

What novelties they have to us they give,
That we, though pilgrims, joyful lives may live;
They do upon us, too, such things bestow,
That show we pilgrims are, where'er we go.

When they were gone from the shepherds they quickly came to the place where Christian met with one Turnaway, that dwelt in the town of Apostasy. Wherefore of him Mr. Great-heart, their guide, did now put them in mind, saying, "This is the place where Christian met with one Turnaway, who carried with him the character of his rebellion at his back. And this I have to say concerning this man: he would hearken to no counsel, but once a-falling, persuasion could not stop him. When he came to the place where the cross and the sepulchre was, he did meet with one that did bid him look there, but he gnashed with his teeth and stamped, and said he was resolved to go back to his own town. Before he came to the gate he met with Evangelist, who offered to lay hands on him to turn him into the way again. But this Turnaway resisted him, and having done much despite unto him, he got away over the wall and so escaped his hand."

Then they went on, and just at the place where Little-faith formerly was robbed, there stood a man with his sword drawn and his face all bloody. Then said Mr. Great-heart, "What art thou?" The man made answer saying, "I am one whose name is Valiant-for-truth. I am a pilgrim and am going to the Celestial City. Now as I was in my way, there was three men did beset me and propounded unto me these three things: 1. Whether I would become one of them. 2. Or go back from whence I came. 3. Or die upon the place. To the first I answered I had been a true man a long season, and, therefore, it could not be expected that I now should cast in my lot with thieves. Then they demanded what I would say to the second. So I told them that the place from whence I came, had I not found incommodity there, I had not forsaken it at all; but finding it altogether unsuitable to me, and very unprofitable for me, I forsook it for this way. Then they asked me what I said to the third. And I told them my life cost more dear far than that I should lightly give it away. Besides, you have nothing to do thus to put things to my choice; wherefore at your peril be it if you meddle. Then these three, to wit, Wild-head, Inconsiderate, and Pragmatic,* drew upon me, and I also drew upon them.

"So we fell to it, one against three, for the space of above three hours. They have left upon me, as you see, some of the marks of their valour, and have also carried away with them some of mine. They are but just now gone. I suppose they might, as the saying is, hear your horse dash, and so they betook them to flight."

*Prying, snooping.

GREAT-HEART. "But here was great odds, three against one."

VALIANT. " 'Tis true, but little and more are nothing to him that has the truth on his side. 'Though an host should encamp against me,' said one, 'my heart shall not fear. Though war should rise against me, in this will I be confident, etc.' [Psalms 27:3] Besides," said he, "I have read in some records that one man has fought an army. And how many did Sampson slay with the jaw-bone of an ass?"

GREAT-HEART. Then said the guide, "Why did you not cry out, that some might a came in for your succour?"

VALIANT. "So I did, to my King, who I knew could hear and afford invisible help, and that was sufficient for me."

GREAT-HEART. Then said Great-heart to Mr. Valiant-for-truth, "Thou has worthily behaved thyself. Let me see thy sword." So he showed it him.

When he had taken it in his hand and looked thereon awhile, he said, "Ha! It is a right Jerusalem blade."

VALIANT. "It is so. Let a man have one of these blades, with a hand to wield it and skill to use it, and he may venture upon an angel with it. He need not fear its holding if he can but tell how to lay on. Its edges will never blunt; it will cut flesh, and bones, and soul, and spirit, and all."

GREAT-HEART. "But you fought a great while; I wonder you was not weary."

VALIANT. "I fought till my sword did cleave to my hand. And when they were joined together as if a sword grew out of my arm, and when the blood run through my fingers, then I fought with most courage."

GREAT-HEART. "Thou hast done well; thou hast resisted unto blood, striving against sin. Thou shalt abide by us, come in and go out with us, for we are thy companions."

Then they took him and washed his wounds and gave him of what they had to refresh him, and so they went on together. Now as they went on, because Mr. Great-heart was delighted in him (for he loved one greatly that he found to be a man of his hands), and because there was with his company them that was feeble and weak, therefore he questioned with him about many things, as first, "What countryman he was?"

VALIANT. "I am of Dark-land, for there I was born, and there my father and mother are still."

GREAT-HEART. "Dark-land," said the guide. "Doth not that lie upon the same coast with the City of Destruction?"

VALIANT. "Yes, it doth. Now that which caused me to come on pilgrimage was this: we had one Mr. Tell-true came into our parts, and he told it about what Christian had done that went from the City of Destruction, namely, how he had forsaken his wife and children and had betaken himself to a pilgrim's life. It was also confidently reported how he had killed a serpent that did come out to resist him in his journey, and how he got through to whither he intended. It was also told what welcome he had at all his Lord's lodgings, especially when he came to the gates of the Celestial City. 'For there,' said the man, 'he was received, with sound of trumpet, by a company of Shining Ones.' He told it also how all the bells in the city did ring for joy at his reception, and what golden garments he was clothed with, with many other things that now I shall forbear to relate. In a word, that man so told the story of Christian and his travels that my heart fell into a burning haste to be gone after him, nor could father or mother stay me. So I got from them and am come thus far on my way."

GREAT-HEART. "You came in at the gate, did you not?"

VALIANT. "Yes, yes. For the same man also told us that all would be nothing if we did not begin to enter this way at the gate."

GREAT-HEART. "Look you," said the guide to Christiana, "the pilgrimage of your husband, and what he has gotten thereby, is spread abroad far and near."

VALIANT. "Why, is this Christian's wife?"

GREAT-HEART. "Yes, that it is, and these are also her four sons."

VALIANT. "What, and going on pilgrimage too?"

GREAT-HEART. "Yes, verily, they are following after."

VALIANT. "It glads me at the heart! Good man, how joyful will he be when he shall see them that would not go with him yet to enter after him in at the gates into the city."

GREAT-HEART. "Without doubt it will be a comfort to him. For next to the joy of seeing himself there, it will be a joy to meet there his wife and his children."

VALIANT. "But now you are upon that, pray, let me see your opinion about it. Some make a question whether we shall know one another when we are there."

GREAT-HEART. "Do they think they shall know themselves then? Or that they shall rejoice to see themselves in that bliss? And if they think they shall know and do these, why not know others and rejoice in their welfare also?

"Again, since relations are our second self though that state will be dissolved there, yet why may it not be rationally concluded that we shall be more glad to see them there than to see they are wanting?"

VALIANT. "Well, I perceive whereabout you are as to this. Have you any more things to ask me about my beginning to come on pilgrimage?"

GREAT-HEART. "Yes, was your father and mother willing that you should become a pilgrim?"

VALIANT. "Oh, no. They used all means imaginable to persuade me to stay at home."

GREAT-HEART. "Why, what could they say against it?"

VALIANT. "They said it was an idle life, and if I myself were not inclined to sloth and laziness I would never countenance a pilgrim's condition."

GREAT-HEART. "And what did they say else?"

VALIANT. "Why, they told me that it was a dangerous way. 'Yea, the most dangerous way in the world,' said they, 'is that which the pilgrims go.' "

GREAT-HEART. "Did they show wherein this way is so dangerous?"

VALIANT. "Yes, and that in many particulars."

GREAT-HEART. "Name some of them."

VALIANT. "They told me of the Slough of Despond where Christian was well nigh smothered. They told me that there were archers standing ready in Beelzebub's Castle to shoot them that should knock at the wicket-gate for entrance. They told me also of the wood and dark mountains, of the Hill Difficulty, of the lions, and also of the three giants, Bloody-man, Maul, and Slaygood. They said, moreover, that there was a foul fiend haunted the Valley of Humiliation, and that Christian was, by him, almost bereft of life. 'Besides,' said they, 'you must go over the Valley of the Shadow of Death, where the hobgoblins are, where the light is darkness, where the way is full of snares, pits, traps and gins.' They told me also of Giant Despair, of Doubting Castle, and of the ruins that the pilgrims met with there. Further, they said, I must go over the Enchanted Ground, which was dangerous, and that after all this I should find a river, over which I should find no bridge, and that that river did lie betwixt me and the Celestial Country."

GREAT-HEART. "And was this all?"

VALIANT. "No, they also told me that this way was full of deceivers and of persons that laid await there to turn good men out of the path."

GREAT-HEART. "But how did they make that out?"

VALIANT. "They told me that Mr. Worldly Wiseman did there lie in wait to deceive. They also said that there was Formality and Hypocrisy continually on the road. They said also that By-ends, Talkative, or Demas, would go near to gather me up; that the Flatterer would catch me in his net; or that with greenheaded Ignorance I would presume to go on to the gate, from whence he always was sent back to the hole that was in the side of the hill, and made to go the by-way to hell."

GREAT-HEART. "I promise you this was enough to discourage. But did they make an end here?"

VALIANT. "No, stay. They told me also of many that had tried that way of old, and that had gone a great way therein, to see if they could find something of the glory there that so many had so much talked of from time to time; and how they came back again and befooled themselves for setting a foot out-of-doors in that path to the satisfaction of all the country. And they named several that did so, as Obstinate and Pliable, Mistrust and Timorous, Turnaway and old Atheist, with several more, who, they said, had, some of them, gone far to see if they could find. But not one of them found so much advantage by going, as amounted to the weight of a feather."

GREAT-HEART. "Said they anything more to discourage you?"

VALIANT. "Yes, they told me of one Mr. Fearing, who was a pilgrim, and how he found this way so solitary that he never had comfortable hour therein; also that Mr. Despondency had like to been starved therein. Yea, and also, which I had almost forgot, that Christian himself, about whom there has been such a noise after all his ventures for a celestial crown, was certainly drowned in the black river, and never went foot further, however it was smothered up."

GREAT-HEART. "And did none of these things discourage you?"

VALIANT. "No, they seemed but as so many nothings to me."

GREAT-HEART. "How came that about?"

VALIANT. "Why, I still believed what Mr. Tell-true had said, and that carried me beyond them all."

GREAT-HEART. "Then this was your victory, even your faith?"

VALIANT. "It was so. I believed and therefore came out, got into the way, fought all that set themselves against me, and by believing am come to this place."

Who would true valour see, .
Let him come hither;
One here will constant be,
Come wind, come weather.
There's no discouragement
Shall make him once relent
His first avowed intent
To be a pilgrim.

Who so beset him round
With dismal stories,
Do but themselves confound—
His strength the more is;
No lion can him fright,
He'll with a giant fight;
But he will have a right
To be a pilgrim.

Hobgoblin nor foul fiend
Can daunt his spirit;
He knows he at the end
Shall life inherit.
Then fancies fly away,
He'll fear not what men say;
He'll labour night and day
To be a pilgrim.

By this time, they were got to the Enchanted Ground, where the air naturally tended to make one drowsy. And that place was all grown over with briers and thorns, excepting here and there, where was an enchanted arbour, upon which, if a man sits, or in which if a man sleeps, 'tis a question, say some, whether ever they shall rise or wake again in this world. Over this forest therefore they went, both one with another. And Mr. Great-heart went before, for that he was the guide; and Mr. Valiant-for-truth, he came behind, being there a guard, for fear lest peradventure some fiend, or dragon, or giant, or thief, should fall upon their rear, and so do mischief. They went on here, each man with his sword drawn in his hand; for they knew it was a dangerous place. Also they cheered up one another as well as they could. Feeble-mind, Mr. Great-heart commanded, should come up after him, and Mr. Despondency was under the eye of Mr. Valiant.

Now they had not gone far, but a great mist and a darkness fell upon them all; so that they could scarce, for a great while, see the one the other. Wherefore they were forced, for some time, to feel for one another by words, for they walked not by sight.

But anyone must think that here was but sorry going for the best of them all, but how much worse for the women and children, who both of feet and heart were but tender. Yet so it was, that through the encouraging words of he that led in the front, and of him that brought them up behind, they made a pretty good shift to wag along.

The way also was here very wearisome, through dirt and slabbiness.* Nor was there on all this ground so much as one inn or victualling-house therein to refresh the feebler sort. Here, therefore, was grunting, and puffing, and sighing. While one tumbleth over a bush, another sticks fast in the dirt, and the children, some of them lost their shoes in the mire. While one cries out, "I am down," and another, "Ho, where are you?" and a third, "The bushes have got such fast hold on me, I think I cannot get away from them."

Then they came at an arbour, warm, and promising much refreshing to the pilgrims; for it was finely wrought above head, beautified with greens, furnished with benches and settles. It also had in it a soft couch whereon the weary might lean. This, you must think, all things considered, was tempting, for the pilgrims already began to be foiled with the badness of the way; but there was not one of them that made so much as a motion to stop there. Yea, for ought I could perceive, they continually gave so good heed to the advice of their guide, and he did so faithfully tell them of dangers, and of the nature of dangers when they were at them, that usually when they were nearest to them they did most pluck up their spirits and hearten one another to deny the flesh. This arbour was called the Slothful's Friend, on purpose to allure, if it might be, some of the pilgrims there to take up their rest when weary.

I saw then in my dream that they went on in this their solitary ground till they came to a place at which a man is apt to lose his way. Now, though when it was light their guide could well enough tell how to miss those ways that led wrong, yet in the dark he was put to a stand. But he had in his pocket a map of all ways leading to or from the Celestial City. Wherefore he struck a light (for he never goes also without his tinder-box), and takes a view of his book or map, which bids him be careful in that place to turn to the right-hand way. And had he not here been careful to look in his map, they had all, in probability, been smothered in the mud; for just a little before them, and that at the end of the cleanest way, too, was a pit, none knows how deep, full of nothing but mud, there made on purpose to destroy the pilgrims in.

Then thought I with myself, "Who that goeth on pilgrimage, but would have one of these maps about him, that he may look, when he is at a stand, which is the way he must take?"

They went on then in this Enchanted Ground till they came to where was another arbour, and it was built by the highway side. And in that arbour there lay two men, whose names were Heedless and Too-bold. These two went thus far on pilgrimage, but, here being wearied with their journey, they sat down to rest themselves, and so fell fast asleep. When the pilgrims saw them they stood still and shook their heads, for they knew that the sleepers

*Mud.

were in a pitiful case. Then they consulted what to do, whether to go on and leave them in their sleep, or to step to them and try to awake them. So they concluded to go to them and wake them, that is, if they could; but with this caution, namely, to take heed that themselves did not sit down nor embrace the offered benefit of that arbour.

So they went in and spake to the men, and called each by his name (for the guide, it seems, did know them), but there was no voice nor answer. Then the guide did shake them and do what he could to disturb them. Then said one of them, "I will pay you when I take my money," at which the guide shook his head. "I will fight so long as I can hold my sword in my hand," said the other. At that, one of the children laughed.

Then said Christiana, "What is the meaning of this?" The guide said, "They talk in their sleep. If you strike them, beat them, or whatever else you do to them, they will answer you after this fashion. Or as one of them said in old time, when the waves of the sea did beat upon him and he slept as one upon the mast of a ship, 'When I awake I will seek it again.' You know, when men talk in their sleeps they say anything; but their words are not governed either by faith or reason. There is an incoherency in their words now, as there was before, betwixt their going on pilgrimage and sitting down here. This then is the mischief on't, when heedless ones go on pilgrimage 'tis twenty to one but they are served thus. For this Enchanted Ground is one of the last refuges that the enemy to pilgrims has; wherefore it is, as you see, placed almost at the end of the way, and so it standeth against us with the more advantage. 'For when,' thinks the enemy, 'will these fools be so desirous to sit down, as when they are weary; and when so like to be weary, as when almost at their journey's end?' Therefore it is, I say, that the Enchanted Ground is placed so nigh to the Land Beulah and so near the end of their race. Wherefore let pilgrims look to themselves, lest it happen to them as it has done to these that, as you see, are fallen asleep, and none can wake them."

Then the pilgrims desired with trembling to go forward; only they prayed their guide to strike a light, that they might go the rest of their way by the help of the light of a lantern. So he struck a light, and they went by the help of that through the rest of this way though the darkness was very great.

But the children began to be sorely weary, and they cried out unto him that loveth pilgrims to make their way more comfortable. So by that they had gone a little further, a wind arose that drove away the fog, so the air became more clear.

Yet they were not off (by much) of the Enchanted Ground. Only now they could see one another better, and the way wherein they should walk.

Now when they were almost at the end of this ground, they perceived that a little before them was a solemn noise, as of one that was much concerned. So they went on and looked before them, and, behold, they saw, as they thought, a man upon his knees, with hands and eyes lift up, and speaking, as they thought, earnestly to one that was above. They drew nigh, but could not tell what he said; so they went softly till he had done. When he had done, he got up and began to run towards the Celestial City. Then Mr. Great-heart called after him saying, "So, ho, friend, let us have your company, if you go, as I suppose you do, to the Celestial City." So the man stopped, and they came up to him. But as soon as Mr. Honest saw him he said, "I know this man." Then said Mr. Valiant-for-truth, "Prithee, who is it?" " 'Tis one," said he, "that comes from whereabout I dwelt. His name is Stand-fast; he is certainly a right good pilgrim."

So they came up one to another, and presently Stand-fast said to old Honest, "Ho, Father Honest, are you there?" "Ay," said he, "that I am, as sure as you are there." "Right glad am I," said Mr. Stand-fast, "that I have found you on this road." "And as glad am I," said the other, "that I espied you upon your knees." Then Mr. Stand-fast blushed and said, "But, why, did you see me?" "Yes, that I did," quoth the other, "and with my heart was glad at the sight." "Why, what did you think?" said Stand-fast. "Think," said old Honest, "what should I think? I thought we had an honest man upon the road, and therefore should have his company by and by." "If you thought not amiss, how happy am I. But if I be not as I should, I alone must bear it." "That is true," said the other, "but your fear doth further confirm me that things are right betwixt the Prince of pilgrims and your soul. For he saith, 'Blessed is the man that feareth always.' "

VALIANT. "Well, but, brother, I pray thee tell us what was it that was the cause of thy being upon thy knees even now? Was it for that some special mercy laid obligations upon thee, or how?"

STAND-FAST. "Why we are, as you see, upon the Enchanted Ground, and as I was coming along I was musing with myself of what a dangerous road the road in this place was, and how many that had come even thus far on pilgrimage had here been stopped and been destroyed. I thought also of the manner of the death with which this place destroyeth men. Those that die here die of no violent distemper; the death which such die is not grievous to them. For he that goeth away in a sleep begins that journey with desire and pleasure. Yea, such acquiesce in the will of that disease."

HONEST. Then Mr. Honest, interrupting of him, said, "Did you see the two men asleep in the arbour?"

STAND-FAST. "Ay, ay, I saw Heedless and Too-bold there. And for ought I know, there they will lie till they rot. But let me go on in my tale. As I was thus musing, as I said, there was one in very pleasant attire, but old, that presented herself unto me and offered me three things, to wit, her body, her purse, and her bed. Now the truth is, I was both a-weary and sleepy. I am also as poor as a howlet,* and that, perhaps, the witch knew. Well, I repulsed her once and twice, but she put by my repulses and smiled. Then I began to be angry, but she mattered that nothing at all. Then she made offers again and said if I would be ruled by her, she would make me great and happy. 'For,' said she, 'I am the mistress of the world, and men are made happy by me.' Then I asked her name, and she told me it was Madam Bubble. This set me further from her; but she still followed me with enticements. Then I betook me, as you see, to my knees, and with hands lift up, and cries, I prayed to

*Owlet.

him that had said he would help. So, just as you came up, the gentlewoman went her way. Then I continued to give thanks for this my great deliverance; for I verily believe she intended no good, but rather sought to make stop of me in my journey."

HONEST. "Without doubt her designs were bad. But, stay, now you talk of her, methinks I either have seen her or have read some story of her."

STAND-FAST. "Perhaps you have done both."

HONEST. "Madam Bubble! Is she not a tall comely dame, something of a swarthy complexion?"

STAND-FAST. "Right, you hit it; she is just such an one."

HONEST. "Doth she not speak very smoothly and give you a smile at the end of a sentence?"

STAND-FAST. "You fall right upon it again, for these are her very actions."

HONEST. "Doth she not wear a great purse by her side, and is not her hand often in it fingering her money as if that was her heart's delight?"

STAND-FAST. " 'Tis just so. Had she stood by all this while, you could not more amply set her forth before me, nor have better described her features."

HONEST. "Then he that drew her picture was a good limner, and he that wrote of her said true."

GREAT-HEART. "This woman is a witch, and it is by virtue of her sorceries that this ground is enchanted. Whoever doth lay their head down in her lap had as good lay it down upon that block over which the ax doth hang; and whoever lay their eyes upon her beauty are counted the enemies of God. This is she that maintaineth in their splendour all those that are the enemies of pilgrims. Yea, this is she that has bought off many a man from a pilgrim's life. She is a great gossiper; she is always, both she and her daughters, at one pilgrim's heels or other, now commending, and then preferring, the excellencies of this life. She is a bold and impudent slut; she will talk with any man. She always laugheth poor pilgrims to scorn, but highly commends the rich. If there be one cunning to get money in a place, she will speak well of him from house to house. She loveth banqueting and feasting mainly well; she is always at one full table or another. She has given it out in some places that she is a goddess, and therefore some do worship her. She has her times and open places of feasting, and she will say and avow it that none can show a food comparable to hers. She promiseth to dwell with children's children, if they will but love and make much of her. She will cast out of her purse gold like dust, in some places and to some persons. She loves to be sought after, spoken well of, and to lie in the bosoms of men. She is never weary of commending of her commodities, and she loves them most that think best of her. She will promise to some crowns and kingdoms if they will but take her advice, yet many has she brought to the halter,* and ten thousand times more to hell."

STAND-FAST. "O," said Stand-fast, "what a mercy is it that I did resist her! For whither might she a drawn me?"

*A noose.

GREAT-HEART. "Whither! Nay, none but God knows whither. But in general, to be sure, she would a drawn thee into many foolish and hurtful lusts, which drown men in destruction and perdition. [I Timothy 6:9]

" 'Twas she that set Absalom against his father and Jeroboam against his master. 'Twas she that persuaded Judas to sell his Lord and that prevailed with Demas to forsake the godly pilgrim's life. None can tell of the mischief that she doth. She makes variance betwixt rulers and subjects, betwixt parents and children, 'twixt neighbour and neighbour, 'twixt a man and his wife, 'twixt a man and himself, 'twixt the flesh and the heart.

"Wherefore, good Master Stand-fast, be as your name is, and when you have done all, stand."

At this discourse there was among the pilgrims a mixture of joy and trembling, but at length they broke out and sang,

What danger is the pilgrim in,
How many are his foes!
How many ways there are to sin
No living mortal knows.

Some of the ditch shy are, yet can
Lie tumbling in the mire;
Some, though they shun the frying-pan,
Do leap into the fire.

After this, I beheld until they were come into the Land of Beulah, where the sun shineth night and day. Here, because they were weary, they betook themselves awhile to rest. And because this country was common for pilgrims, and because the orchards and vineyards that were here belonged to the King of the Celestial Country, therefore they were licensed to make bold with any of his things.

But a little while soon refreshed them here, for the bells did so ring, and the trumpets continually sound so melodiously, that they could not sleep, and yet they received as much refreshing as if they had slept their sleep never so soundly. Here also all the noise of them that walked the streets was, "More pilgrims are come to town." And another would answer saying, "And so many went over the water and were let in at the golden gates today." They would cry again, "There is now a legion of Shining Ones just come to town, by which we know that there are more pilgrims upon the road; for here they come to wait for them and to comfort them after all their sorrow." Then the pilgrims got up and walked to and fro. But how were their ears now filled with heavenly noises and their eyes delighted with celestial visions? In this land they heard nothing, saw nothing, felt nothing, smelt nothing, tasted nothing that was offensive to their stomach or mind. Only when they tasted of the water of the river over which they were to go, they thought that tasted a little bitterish to the palate, but it proved sweeter when 'twas down.

In this place, there was a record kept of the names of them that had been pilgrims of old, and a history of all the famous acts that they had done. It was here also much discoursed how the river to some had had its flowings, and what ebbings it has had while others have gone over. It has been in a manner dry for some, while it has overflowed its banks for others.

In this place, the children of the town would go into the King's gardens and gather nosegays for the pilgrims and bring them to them with much affection. Here also grew camphire, with spikenard, and saffron, calamus, and cinnamon, with all its trees of frankincense, myrrh, and aloes, with all chief spices. [Song of Solomon 4:13–14] With these the pilgrims' chambers were perfumed while they stayed here; and with these were their bodies anointed to prepare them to go over the river when the time appointed was come.

Now while they lay here and waited for the good hour, there was a noise in the town that there was a post* come from the Celestial City with matter of great importance to one Christiana, the wife of Christian, the pilgrim. So inquiry was made for her, and the house was found out where she was; so the post presented her with a letter the contents whereof was, "Hail, good woman, I bring thee tidings that the Master calleth for thee and expecteth that thou shouldest stand in his presence, in clothes of immortality, within this ten days."

When he had read this letter to her, he gave her therewith a sure token that he was a true messenger and was come to bid her make haste to be gone. The token was an arrow with a point sharpened with love, let easily into her heart, which by degrees wrought so effectually with her that at the time appointed she must be gone.

When Christiana saw that her time was come, and that she was the first of this company that was to go over, she called for Mr. Great-heart, her guide, and told him how matters were. So he told her he was heartily glad of the news and could a been glad had the post came for him. Then she bid that he should give advice how all things should be prepared for her journey.

So he told her saying, "Thus and thus it must be, and we that survive will accompany you to the river-side."

Then she called for her children and gave them her blessing, and told them that she yet read with comfort the mark that was set in their foreheads, and was glad to see them with her there, and that they kept their garments so white. Lastly, she bequeathed to the poor that little she had, and commanded her sons and her daughters to be ready against the messenger should come for them.

When she had spoken these words to her guide and to her children, she called for Mr. Valiant-for-truth and said unto him, "Sir, you have in all places showed yourself true-hearted; be faithful unto death and my King will give you a crown of life. I would also entreat you to have an eye to my children, and if at any time you see them faint, speak comfortably to them. For my daughters, my sons' wives, they have been faithful, and a fulfilling of the promise upon them will be their end." But she gave Mr. Stand-fast a ring.

*Messenger.

Then she called for old Mr. Honest and said of him, "Behold, an Israelite indeed, in whom is no guile." Then said he, "I wish you a fair day when you set out for Mount Zion, and shall be glad to see that you go over the river dry-shod." But she answered, "Come wet, come dry, I long to be gone. For however the weather is in my journey, I shall have time enough when I come there to sit down and rest me, and dry me."

Then came in that good man, Mr. Ready-to-halt, to see her. So she said to him, "Thy travel hither has been with difficulty, but that will make thy rest the sweeter. But watch and be ready, for at an hour when you think not the messenger may come."

After him came in Mr. Despondency, and his daughter, Much-afraid, to whom she said, "You ought, with thankfulness forever, to remember your deliverance from the hands of Giant Despair, and out of Doubting Castle. The effect of that mercy is that you are brought with safety hither. Be ye watchful, and cast away fear. Be sober, and hope to the end."

Then she said to Mr. Feeble-mind, "Thou was delivered from the mouth of Giant Slaygood that thou mightest live in the light of the living forever and see thy King with comfort. Only I advise thee to repent thee of thy aptness to fear and doubt of his goodness before he sends for thee lest thou shouldest, when he comes, be forced to stand before him for that fault with blushing."

Now the day drew on that Christiana must be gone. So the road was full of people to see her take her journey. But, behold, all the banks beyond the river were full of horses and chariots which were come down from above to accompany her to the city gate. So she came forth and entered the river with a beckon of farewell to those that followed her to the river-side. The last word she was heard to say here was, "I come, Lord, to be with thee and bless thee."

So her children and friends returned to their place for that those that waited for Christiana had carried her out of their sight. So she went and called, and entered in at the gate with all the ceremonies of joy that her husband, Christian, had done before her.

At her departure her children wept, but Mr. Great-heart and Mr. Valiant played upon the well-tuned cymbal and harp, for joy. So all departed to their respective places.

In the process of time there came a post to the town again, and his business was with Mr. Ready-to-halt. So he inquired him out and said to him, "I am come to thee in the name of him whom thou hast loved and followed though upon crutches. And my message is to tell thee that he expects thee at his table to sup with him in his kingdom the next day after Easter, wherefore prepare thyself for this journey."

Then he also gave him a token that he was a true messenger saying, "I have broken thy golden bowl and loosed thy silver cord."

After this, Mr. Ready-to-halt called for his fellow pilgrims and told them saying, "I am sent for, and God shall surely visit you also." So he desired Mr. Valiant to make his will. And because he had nothing to bequeath to them that should survive him but his crutches and his good wishes, therefore thus

he said, "These crutches I bequeath to my son that shall tread in my steps, with an hundred warm wishes that he may prove better than I have done."

Then he thanked Mr. Great-heart for his conduct and kindness and so addressed himself to his journey. When he came at the brink of the river he said, "Now I shall have no more need of these crutches since yonder are chariots and horses for me to ride on." The last words he was heard to say was, "Welcome, life." So he went his way.

After this, Mr. Feeble-mind had tidings brought him that the post sounded his horn at his chamber-door. Then he came in and told him saying, "I am come to tell thee that the Master has need of thee, and that in very little time thou must behold his face in brightness. And take this as a token of the truth of my message, 'Those that look out at the windows shall be darkened.' "

Then Mr. Feeble-mind called for his friends and told them what errand had been brought unto him, and what token he had received of the truth of the message. Then he said, "Since I have nothing to bequeath to any, to what purpose should I make a will? As for my feeble mind, that I will leave behind me, for that I shall have no need of that in the place whither I go, nor is it worth bestowing upon the poorest pilgrim. Wherefore, when I am gone, I desire that you, Mr. Valiant, would bury it in a dunghill." This done, and the day being come in which he was to depart, he entered the river as the rest. His last words were, "Hold out, faith and patience." So he went over to the other side.

When days had many of them passed away Mr. Despondency was sent for. For a post was come, and brought this message to him, "Trembling man, these are to summon thee to be ready with thy King, by the next Lord's day, to shout for joy for thy deliverance from all thy doubtings."

And said the messenger, "That my message is true take this for a proof." So he gave him, "The grasshopper to be a burthen unto him." Now Mr. Despondency's daughter, whose name was Much-afraid, said, when she heard what was done, that she would go with her father. Then Mr. Despondency said to his friends, "Myself and my daughter, you know what we have been and how troublesomely we have behaved ourselves in every company. My will and my daughter's is that our desponds and slavish fears be by no man ever received, from the day of our departure, forever; for I know that after my death they will offer themselves to others. For, to be plain with you, they are ghosts, the which we entertained when we first began to be pilgrims and could never shake them off after. And they will walk about and seek entertainment of the pilgrims, but for our sakes shut ye the doors upon them."

When the time was come for them to depart they went to the brink of the river. The last words of Mr. Despondency were, "Farewell, night; welcome, day." His daughter went through the river singing, but none would understand what she said.

Then it came to pass, a while after, that there was a post in the town that inquired for Mr. Honest. So he came to the house where he was and delivered to his hand these lines, "Thou art commanded to be ready against this day seven-night, to present thyself before thy Lord, at His Father's house. And for a token that my message is true, 'All thy daughters of music shall be brought low.' " Then Mr. Honest called for his friends and said unto them, "I die but shall make no will. As for my honesty, it shall go with me; let him that comes after be told of this." When the day that he was to be gone was come, he addressed himself to go over the river. Now the river at that time overflowed the banks in some places. But Mr. Honest in his lifetime had spoken to one Good-conscience to meet him there, the which he also did, and lent him his hand, and so helped him over. The last words of Mr. Honest were, "Grace reigns." So he left the world.

After this it was noised abroad that Mr. Valiant-for-truth was taken with a summons by the same post as the other, and had this for a token that the summons was true, "That his pitcher was broken at the fountain." When he understood it, he called for his friends and told them of it. Then said he, "I am going to my Father's, and though with great difficulty I am got hither, yet now I do not repent me of all the trouble I have been at to arrive where I am. My sword I give to him that shall succeed me in my pilgrimage, and my courage and skill to him that can get it. My marks and scars I carry with me to be a witness for me that I have fought his battles who now will be my rewarder." When the day that he must go hence was come, many accompanied him to the river-side, into which, as he went, he said, "Death, where is thy sting?" And as he went down deeper he said, "Grave, where is thy victory?" [I Corinthians 15:55] So he passed over, and the trumpets sounded for him on the other side.

Then there came forth a summons for Mr. Stand-fast (this Mr. Stand-fast was he that the rest of the pilgrims found upon his knees in the Enchanted Ground), for the post brought it him open in his hands. The contents whereof were that he must prepare for a change of life, for his Master was not willing that he should be so far from him any longer. At this, Mr. Stand-fast was put into a muse. "Nay," said the messenger, "you need not doubt of the truth of my message. For here is a token of the truth thereof. 'Thy wheel is broken at the cistern.' " Then he called to him Mr. Great-heart, who was their guide, and said unto him, "Sir, although it was not my hap to be much in your good company in the days of my pilgrimage, yet since the time I knew you, you have been profitable to me. When I came from home, I left behind me a wife and five small children. Let me entreat you, at your return (for I know that you will go and return to your master's house, in hopes that you may yet be a conductor to more of the holy pilgrims), that you send to my family and let them be acquainted with all that hath, and shall happen, unto me. Tell them, moreover, of my happy arrival to this place, and of the present late blessed condition that I am in. Tell them also of Christian, and of Christiana, his wife, and how she and her children came after her husband. Tell them also of what a happy end she made and whither she is gone. I have little or nothing to send to my family, except it be prayers and tears for them; of which it will suffice, if thou acquaint them, if peradventure they may prevail." When Mr. Stand-fast had thus set things in order, and the time being come for him to hast him away, he also went down to the river. Now there was a great calm at that time in the river; wherefore Mr. Stand-fast, when he was about half-way in, he stood awhile and talked to his companions that had waited upon him thither. And he said,

"This river has been a terror to many; yea, the thoughts of it also have often frighted me. But now, methinks, I stand easy. My foot is fixed upon that upon which the feet of the priests that bare the ark of the covenant stood while Israel went over this Jordan. The waters indeed are to the palate bitter and to the stomach cold. Yet the thoughts of what I am going to, and of the conduct that waits for me on the other side, doth lie as a glowing coal at my heart.

"I see myself now at the end of my journey; my toilsome days are ended. I am going now to see that head that was crowned with thorns and that face that was spit upon for me.

"I have formerly lived by hearsay and faith, but now I go where I shall live by sight and shall be with him in whose company I delight myself.

"I have loved to hear my Lord spoken of, and wherever I have seen the print of his shoe in the earth, there I have coveted to set my foot too.

"His name has been to me as a civet-box, yea, sweeter than all perfumes. His voice to me has been most sweet, and his countenance I have more desired than they that have most desired the light of the sun. His Word I did use to gather for my food and for antidotes against my faintings. He has held me, and I have kept me from mine iniquities. Yea, my steps hath he strengthened in his way."

Now while he was thus in discourse his countenance changed, his strong men bowed under him, and after he had said, "Take me, for I come unto thee," he ceased to be seen of them.

But glorious it was to see how the open region was filled with horses and chariots, with trumpeters and pipers, with singers and players on stringed instruments, to welcome the pilgrims as they went up and followed one another in at the beautiful gate of the city.

As for Christian's children, the four boys that Christiana brought with her, with their wives and children, I did not stay where I was till they were gone over. Also since I came away I heard one say that they were yet alive, and so would be for the increase of the Church in that place where they were for a time.

Shall it be my lot to go that way again, I may give those that desire it an account of what I here am silent about; meantime I bid my reader adieu.

Editor's Notes

The *Second Part* of *The Pilgrim's Progress,* of which the first appeared in last year's issue of *The Great Ideas Today,* was published in 1684, six years after the original work, when Bunyan was 56. Unlike its predecessor, which was written while he languished in prison for holding nonconformist religious services in defiance of laws instituted with the Restoration of the monarchy in 1660, the sequel was the work of a busy minister of a puritan church at Bedford, England, where Bunyan lived. He was also now famous as the author of the *First Part,* and had published other works as well. These depicted puritan life as it developed after the age of supression was over, when the members of the sect gradually established themselves as members of the middle class, and in one case took up again, by way of further allegory, the drama, as for Bunyan it always was, of the conversion of the individual soul, hindered partly by its own weakness, and partly by religious persecution.

In the *Second Part,* as the reader has seen, Christian tells how his wife, Christiana, and her children followed the way to salvation after him. It does not contain the same adventures, or at least not all of them—Bunyan was too good a writer to simply repeat himself—and lacks, as sequels tend always to lack, the special intensity of the *First Part.* On the other hand, it gives perhaps a better picture of the social life of the times and is something more of a novel, as distinct from a charged allegory, than the *First Part* had been. Bunyan was no less serious this time, but having established his vision, as it were, he could afford to give more to realism, the better perhaps to show the ordinary person, as distinct from the deeply devout (or perhaps deeply troubled), the way to salvation.

The *Second Part* does include, at its ending, what is generally acknowledged to be the most moving passage in the entire work. One by one, with exaltation, Christiana, her children, and the whole party accompanying them accept the summons to submit to the river of Death, from which, after they have disappeared, they are taken up by the heavenly host on the opposite bank (though the narrator says at the end that he has heard that at least Christiana and her extended family are still alive, that only the allegorical figures in the party have perished—something Bunyan might have found awkward at his own breakfast table to deny and notwithstanding that the whole thing is represented, as the *First Part* had been, in terms of a dream). Among those called is Mr. Valiant-for-truth, who willingly answers, saying "I am going to my Father's." We are told that "when the day that he must go hence was come, many accompanied him to the river-side, into which, as he went, he said, 'Death, where is thy sting?' And as he went down deeper he said, 'Grave, where is thy victory?' So he passed over, and the trumpets sounded for him ont he other side." To which Bunyan adds that "glorious it was to see how the open region was filled with horses and chariots, with trumpeters and pipers, with singers and players on stringed instruments, to welcome the pilgrims as they went up and followed one another in at the beautiful gate of the city."

We note in this—and surely it is relevant to Bunyan's reputation among ten generations of readers that we can do so—a warmth of human feeling which is not extinguished by the allegorical nature of the work. If that seems inconsistent with our notion of Puritan character, perhaps it is our notion of Puritan character which needs revising—a notion of it, in other words, as something cold and repressive. *The Pilgrim's Progress,* whatever one makes of its religious purpose, is not cold or repressive at all, but a passionate and sympathetic work, and "one would know confidently" of Bunyan himself from reading it, as F. R. Leavis has said, "that he was a tender husband and father, a steadfast friend, and a man, authoritative in his human insight and his integrity, whom a close neighborhood of the devout would naturally choose for their pastor—as the Bedford 'people of God' chose Bunyan in 1672, the year of his release from jail."

Nowhere is this more evident than in the book's evocation of everyday life—something wholly absent from Dante's *Divine Comedy,* for example. "This is especially so in *Part Two,*" Leavis adds. "The theme is pilgrimage, but the distinctive note is that of a family party, and the rendering yields abundant matter that might have been invoked in illustration by the historian John Richard Green for the enforcement of his once well-known contention: the home, as we think of it now, was the creation of the puritan." It is a paradox that *The Pilgrim's Progress,* full as it is of the spectre of damnation and the pitiless notion of the Elect, is a homely story, but so it seemed to Bunyan's public. So in some fashion it can still appear, long after that public has grown secular in its preoccupations, and has lost the passion that drove Bunyan to write.

The Souls of Black Folk

W. E. B. Du Bois

The Forethought

Herein lie buried many things which if read with patience may show the strange meaning of being black here at the dawning of the Twentieth Century. This meaning is not without interest to you, Gentle Reader; for the problem of the Twentieth Century is the problem of the color line. I pray you, then, receive my little book in all charity, studying my words with me, forgiving mistake and foible for sake of the faith and passion that is in me, and seeking the grain of truth hidden there.

I have sought here to sketch, in vague, uncertain outline, the spiritual world in which ten thousand thousand Americans live and strive. First, in two chapters I have tried to show what Emancipation meant to them, and what was its aftermath. In a third chapter I have pointed out the slow rise of personal leadership, and criticized candidly the leader who bears the chief burden of his race to-day. Then, in two other chapters I have sketched in swift outline the two worlds within and without the Veil, and thus have come to the central problem of training men for life. Venturing now into deeper detail, I have in two chapters studied the struggles of the massed millions of the black peasantry, and in another have sought to make clear the present relations of the sons of master and man. Leaving, then, the white world, I have stepped within the Veil, raising it that you may view faintly its deeper recesses,—the meaning of its religion, the passion of its human sorrow, and the struggle of its greater souls. All this I have ended with a tale twice told but seldom written, and a chapter of song.

Some of these thoughts of mine have seen the light before in other guise. For kindly consenting to their republication here, in altered and extended form, I must thank the publishers of the *Atlantic Monthly, The World's Work,* the *Dial, The New World,* and the *Annals of the American Academy of Political and Social Science.* Before each chapter, as now printed, stands a bar of the Sorrow Songs,—some echo of haunting melody from the only American music which welled up from black souls in the dark past. And, finally, need I add that I who speak here am bone of the bone and flesh of the flesh of them that live within the Veil?

W. E. B. Du B.

Atlanta, Ga., Feb. 1, 1903.

I
Of Our Spiritual Strivings

(Overleaf)
A group of former slaves assemble along a canal bank in Richmond, Virginia.

O water, voice of my heart, crying in the sand,
  All night long crying with a mournful cry,
As I lie and listen, and cannot understand
    The voice of my heart in my side or the voice of the sea,
  O water, crying for rest, is it I, is it I?
    All night long the water is crying to me.

Unresting water, there shall never be rest
  Till the last moon droop and the last tide fail,
And the fire of the end begin to burn in the west;
    And the heart shall be weary and wonder and cry like the sea,
  All life long crying without avail,
    As the water all night long is crying to me.

Arthur Symons. (1865–1945)

Between me and the other world there is ever an unasked question: unasked by some through feelings of delicacy; by others through the difficulty of rightly framing it. All, nevertheless, flutter round it. They approach me in a half-hesitant sort of way, eye me curiously or compassionately, and then, instead of saying directly, How does it feel to be a problem? they say, I know an excellent colored man in my town; or, I fought at Mechanicsville; or, Do not these Southern outrages make your blood boil? At these I smile, or am interested, or reduce the boiling to a simmer, as the occasion may require. To the real question, How does it feel to be a problem? I answer seldom a word.

And yet, being a problem is a strange experience,—peculiar even for one who has never been anything else, save perhaps in babyhood and in Europe. It is in the early days of rollicking boyhood that the revelation first bursts upon one, all in a day, as it were. I remember well when the shadow swept across me. I was a little thing, away up in the hills of New England, where the dark Housatonic winds between Hoosac and Taghkanic to the sea. In a wee wooden schoolhouse, something put it into the boys' and girls' heads to buy gorgeous visiting-cards—ten cents a package—and exchange. The exchange was merry, till one girl, a tall newcomer, refused my card,—refused it peremptorily, with a glance. Then it dawned upon me with a certain suddenness that I was different from the others; or like, mayhap, in heart and life and longing, but shut out from their world by a vast veil. I had thereafter no desire to tear down that veil, to creep through; I held all beyond it in common contempt, and lived above it in a region of blue sky and great wandering shadows. That sky was bluest when I could beat my mates at examination-time, or beat them at a foot-race, or even beat their stringy heads. Alas, with the years all this fine contempt began to fade; for the words I longed for, and all their dazzling opportunities, were theirs, not mine. But they should not keep these prizes, I said; some, all, I would wrest from them. Just how I would do it I could never decide: by reading law, by healing the sick, by telling the wonderful tales that swam in my head,—some way. With other black boys the strife was not so fiercely sunny: their youth shrunk into tasteless sycophancy, or into silent hatred of the pale world about them and mocking distrust of everything white; or wasted itself in a bitter cry, Why did God make me an outcast and a stranger in mine own house? The shades of the prison-house closed round about us all: walls strait and stubborn to the whitest, but relentlessly narrow, tall, and unscalable to sons of night who must plod darkly on in resignation, or beat unavailing palms against the stone, or steadily, half hopelessly, watch the streak of blue above.

After the Egyptian and Indian, the Greek and Roman, the Teuton and Mongolian, the Negro is a sort of seventh son, born with a veil, and gifted with second-sight in this American world,—a world which yields him no true self-consciousness, but only lets him see himself through the revelation of the other world. It is a peculiar sensation, this double-consciousness, this sense of always looking at one's self through the eyes of others, of measuring one's soul by the tape of a world that looks on in amused contempt and pity. One ever feels his twoness,—an American, a Negro; two souls, two thoughts, two

Children pose for a classroom portrait in 1902.

unreconciled strivings; two warring ideals in one dark body, whose dogged strength alone keeps it from being torn asunder.

The history of the American Negro is the history of this strife,—this longing to attain self-conscious manhood, to merge his double self into a better and truer self. In this merging he wishes neither of the older selves to be lost. He would not Africanize America, for America has too much to teach the world and Africa. He would not bleach his Negro soul in a flood of white Americanism, for he knows that Negro blood has a message for the world.

He simply wishes to make it possible for a man to be both a Negro and an American, without being cursed and spit upon by his fellows, without having the doors of Opportunity closed roughly in his face.

This, then, is the end of his striving: to be a co-worker in the kingdom of culture, to escape both death and isolation, to husband and use his best powers and his latent genius. These powers of body and mind have in the past been strangely wasted, dispersed, or forgotten. The shadow of a mighty Negro past flits through the tale of Ethiopia the Shadowy and of Egypt the Sphinx. Through history, the powers of single black men flash here and there like falling stars, and die sometimes before the world has rightly gauged their brightness. Here in America, in the few days since Emancipation, the black man's turning hither and thither in hesitant and doubtful striving has often made his very strength to lose effectiveness, to seem like absence of power, like weakness. And yet it is not weakness,—it is the contradiction of double aims. The double-aimed struggle of the black artisan—on the one hand to escape white contempt for a nation of mere hewers of wood and drawers of water, and on the other hand to plough and nail and dig for a poverty-stricken horde—could only result in making him a poor craftsman, for he had but half a heart in either cause. By the poverty and ignorance of his people, the Negro minister or doctor was tempted toward quackery and demagogy; and by the criticism of the other world, toward ideals that made him ashamed of his lowly tasks. The would-be black *savant* was confronted by the paradox that the knowledge his people needed was a twice-told tale to his white neighbors, while the knowledge which would teach the white world was Greek to his own flesh and blood. The innate love of harmony and beauty that set the ruder souls of his people a-dancing and a-singing raised but confusion and doubt in the soul of the black artist; for the beauty revealed to him was the soul-beauty of a race which his larger audience despised, and he could not articulate the message of another people. This waste of double aims, this seeking to satisfy two unreconciled ideals, has wrought sad havoc with the courage and faith and deeds of ten thousand thousand people,—has sent them often wooing false gods and invoking false means of salvation, and at times has even seemed about to make them ashamed of themselves.

Away back in the days of bondage they thought to see in one divine event the end of all doubt and disappointment; few men ever worshipped Freedom with half such unquestioning faith as did the American Negro for two centuries. To him, so far as he thought and dreamed, slavery was indeed the sum of all villainies, the cause of all sorrow, the root of all prejudice; Emancipation was the key to a promised land of sweeter beauty than ever stretched before the eyes of wearied Israelites. In song and exhortation swelled one refrain—Liberty; in his tears and curses the God he implored had Freedom in his right hand. At last it came,—suddenly, fearfully, like a dream. With one wild carnival of blood and passion came the message in his own plaintive cadences:—

"Shout, O children!
Shout, you're free!
For God has bought your liberty!"

Years have passed away since then,—ten, twenty, forty; forty years of national life, forty years of renewal and development, and yet the swarthy spectre sits in its accustomed seat at the Nation's feast. In vain do we cry to this our vastest social problem:—

"Take any shape but that, and my firm nerves
Shall never tremble!"

The Nation has not yet found peace from its sins; the freedman has not yet found in freedom his promised land. Whatever of good may have come in these years of change, the shadow of a deep disappointment rests upon the Negro people,—a disappointment all the more bitter because the unattained ideal was unbounded save by the simple ignorance of a lowly people.

The first decade was merely a prolongation of the vain search for freedom, the boon that seemed ever barely to elude their grasp,—like a tantalizing will-o'-the-wisp, maddening and misleading the headless host. The holocaust of war, the terrors of the Ku-Klux Klan, the lies of carpet-baggers, the disorganization of industry, and the contradictory advice of friends and foes, left the bewildered serf with no new watchword beyond the old cry for freedom. As the time flew, however, he began to grasp a new idea. The ideal of liberty demanded for its attainment powerful means, and these the Fifteenth Amendment gave him. The ballot, which before he had looked upon as a visible sign of freedom, he now regarded as the chief means of gaining and perfecting the liberty with which war had partially endowed him. And why not? Had not votes made war and emancipated millions? Had not votes enfranchised the freedmen? Was anything impossible to a power that had done all this? A million black men started with renewed zeal to vote themselves into the kingdom. So the decade flew away, the revolution of 1876 came, and left the half-free serf weary, wondering, but still inspired. Slowly but steadily, in the following years, a new vision began gradually to replace the dream of political power,—a powerful movement, the rise of another ideal to guide the unguided, another pillar of fire by night after a clouded day. It was the ideal of "book-learning"; the curiosity, born of compulsory ignorance, to know and test the power of the cabalistic letters of the white man, the longing to know. Here at last seemed to have been discovered the mountain path to Canaan; longer than the highway of Emancipation and law, steep and rugged, but straight, leading to heights high enough to overlook life.

Up the new path the advance guard toiled, slowly, heavily, doggedly; only those who have watched and guided the faltering feet, the misty minds, the dull understandings, of the dark pupils of these schools know how faithfully, how piteously, this people strove to learn. It was weary work. The cold statistician wrote down the inches of progress here and there, noted also where here and there a foot had slipped or some one had fallen. To the tired climbers, the horizon was ever dark, the mists were often cold, the Canaan was always dim and far away. If, however, the vistas disclosed as yet no goal, no resting-place, little but flattery and criticism, the journey at least gave leisure for reflection and self-examination; it changed the child of

Emancipation to the youth with dawning self-consciousness, self-realization, self-respect. In those sombre forests of his striving his own soul rose before him, and he saw himself,—darkly as through a veil; and yet he saw in himself some faint revelation of his power, of his mission. He began to have a dim feeling that, to attain his place in the world, he must be himself, and not another. For the first time he sought to analyze the burden he bore upon his back, that dead-weight of social degradation partially masked behind a half-named Negro problem. He felt his poverty; without a cent, without a home, without land, tools, or savings, he had entered into competition with rich, landed, skilled neighbors. To be a poor man is hard, but to be a poor race in a land of dollars is the very bottom of hardships. He felt the weight of his ignorance,—not simply of letters, but of life, of business, of the humanities; the accumulated sloth and shirking and awkwardness of decades and centuries shackled his hands and feet. Nor was his burden all poverty and ignorance. The red stain of bastardy, which two centuries of systematic legal defilement of Negro women had stamped upon his race, meant not only the loss of ancient African chastity, but also the hereditary weight of a mass of corruption from white adulterers, threatening almost the obliteration of the Negro home.

A people thus handicapped ought not to be asked to race with the world, but rather allowed to give all its time and thought to its own social problems. But alas! while sociologists gleefully count his bastards and his prostitutes, the very soul of the toiling, sweating black man is darkened by the shadow of a vast despair. Men call the shadow prejudice, and learnedly explain it as the natural defence of culture against barbarism, learning against ignorance, purity against crime, the "higher" against the "lower" races. To which the Negro cries Amen! and swears that to so much of this strange prejudice as is founded on just homage to civilization, culture, righteousness, and progress, he humble bows and meekly does obeisance. But before that nameless prejudice that leaps beyond all this he stands helpless, dismayed, and well-nigh speechless; before that personal disrespect and mockery, the ridicule and systematic humiliation, the distortion of fact and wanton license of fancy, the cynical ignoring of the better and the boisterous welcoming of the worse, the all-pervading desire to inculcate disdain for everything black, from Toussaint to the devil,—before this there rises a sickening despair that would disarm and discourage any nation save that black host to whom "discouragement" is an unwritten word.

But the facing of so vast a prejudice could not but bring the inevitable self-questioning, self-disparagement, and lowering of ideals which ever accompany repression and breed in an atmosphere of contempt and hate. Whisperings and portents came borne upon the four winds: Lo! we are diseased and dying, cried the dark hosts; we cannot write, our voting is vain; what need of education, since we must always cook and serve? And the Nation echoed and enforced this self-criticism, saying: Be content to be servants, and nothing more; what need of higher culture for half-men? Away with the black man's ballot, by force or fraud,—and behold the suicide of a race! Nevertheless, out of the evil came something of good,—the more

careful adjustment of education to real life, the clearer perception of the Negroes' social responsibilities, and the sobering realization of the meaning of
progress.

So dawned the time of *Sturm und Drang:* storm and stress to-day rocks
our little boat on the mad waters of the world-sea; there is within and without
the sound of conflict, the burning of body and rending of soul; inspiration
strives with doubt, and faith with vain questionings. The bright ideals of
the past,—physical freedom, political power, the training of brains and the
training of hands,—all these in turn have waxed and waned, until even the
last grows dim and overcast. Are they all wrong,—all false? No, not that,
but each alone was over-simple and incomplete,—the dreams of a credulous
race-childhood, or the fond imaginings of the other world which does not
know and does not want to know our power. To be really true, all these ideals
must be melted and welded into one. The training of the schools we need to-
day more than ever,—the training of deft hands, quick eyes and ears, and
above all the broader, deeper, higher culture of gifted minds and pure hearts.
The power of the ballot we need in sheer self-defence,—else what shall save
us from a second slavery? Freedom, too, the long-sought, we still seek,—
the freedom of life and limb, the freedom to work and think, the freedom
to love and aspire. Work, culture, liberty,—all these we need, not singly but
together, not successively but together, each growing and aiding each, and
all striving toward that vaster ideal that swims before the Negro people, the
ideal of human brotherhood, gained through the unifying ideal of Race; the
ideal of fostering and developing the traits and talents of the Negro, not in
opposition to or contempt for other races, but rather in large conformity
to the greater ideals of the American Republic, in order that some day on
American soil two world-races may give each to each those characteristics
both so sadly lack. We the darker ones come even now not altogether empty-
handed; there are to-day no truer exponents of the pure human spirit of
the Declaration of Independence than the American Negroes; there is no
true American music but the wild sweet melodies of the Negro slave; the
American fairy tales and folklore are Indian and African; and, all in all, we
black men seem the sole oasis of simple faith and reverence in a dusty desert
of dollars and smartness. Will America be poorer if she replace her brutal
dyspeptic blundering with light-hearted but determined Negro humility? or
her coarse and cruel wit with loving jovial good-humor? or her vulgar music
with the soul of the Sorrow Songs?

Merely a concrete test of the underlying principles of the great republic
is the Negro Problem, and the spiritual striving of the freedmen's sons is
the travail of souls whose burden is almost beyond the measure of their
strength, but who bear it in the name of an historic race, in the name
of this the land of their fathers' fathers, and in the name of human
opportunity.

And now what I have briefly sketched in large outline let me on coming
pages tell again in many ways, with loving emphasis and deeper detail, that
men may listen to the striving in the souls of black folk.

II
Of the Dawn of Freedom

Careless seems the great Avenger;
    History's lessons but record
One death-grapple in the darkness
    'Twixt old systems and the Word;
Truth forever on the scaffold,
    Wrong forever on the throne;
Yet that scaffold sways the future,
    And behind the dim unknown
Standeth God within the shadow
    Keeping watch above His own.
              James Russell Lowell. (1819–91)

The problem of the twentieth century is the problem of the color-line,—the relation of the darker to the lighter races of men in Asia and Africa, in America and the islands of the sea. It was a phase of this problem that caused the Civil War; and however much they who marched South and North in 1861 may have fixed on the technical points of union and local autonomy as a shibboleth, all nevertheless knew, as we know, that the question of Negro slavery was the real cause of the conflict. Curious it was, too, how this deeper question ever forced itself to the surface despite effort and disclaimer. No sooner had Northern armies touched Southern soil than this old question, newly guised, sprang from the earth,—What shall be done with Negroes? Peremptory military commands this way and that, could not answer the query; the Emancipation Proclamation seemed but to broaden and intensify the difficulties; and the War Amendments made the Negro problems of to-day.

It is the aim of this essay to study the period of history from 1861 to 1872 so far as it relates to the American Negro. In effect, this tale of the dawn of Freedom is an account of that government of men called the Freedmen's Bureau,—one of the most singular and interesting of the attempts made by a great nation to grapple with vast problems of race and social condition.

The war has naught to do with slaves, cried Congress, the President, and the Nation; and yet no sooner had the armies, East and West, penetrated Virginia and Tennessee than fugitive slaves appeared within their lines. They came at night, when the flickering camp-fires shone like vast unsteady stars along the black horizon: old men and thin, with gray and tufted hair;

women with frightened eyes, dragging whimpering hungry children; men and girls, stalwart and gaunt,—a horde of starving vagabonds, homeless, helpless, and pitiable, in their dark distress. Two methods of treating these newcomers seemed equally logical to opposite sorts of minds. Ben Butler*, in Virginia, quickly declared slave property contraband of war, and put the fugitives to work; while Fremont†, in Missouri, declared the slaves free under martial law. Butler's action was approved, but Fremont's was hastily countermanded, and his successor, Halleck, saw things differently. "Hereafter," he commanded, "no slaves should be allowed to come into your lines at all; if any come without your knowledge, when owners call for them deliver them." Such a policy was difficult to enforce; some of the black refugees declared themselves freemen, others showed that their masters had deserted them, and still others were captured with forts and plantations. Evidently, too, slaves were a source of strength to the Confederacy, and were being used as laborers and producers. "They constitute a military resource," wrote Secretary Cameron‡, late in 1861; "and being such, that they should not be turned over to the enemy is too plain to discuss." So gradually the tone of the army chiefs changed; Congress forbade the rendition of fugitives, and Butler's "contrabands" were welcomed as military laborers. This complicated rather than solved the problem, for now the scattering fugitives became a steady stream, which flowed faster as the armies marched.

Then the long-headed man with care-chiselled face who sat in the White House saw the inevitable, and emancipated the slaves of rebels on New Year's, 1863. A month later Congress called earnestly for the Negro soldiers whom the act of July, 1862, had half grudgingly allowed to enlist. Thus the barriers were levelled and the deed was done. The stream of fugitives swelled to a flood, and anxious army officers kept inquiring: "What must be done with slaves, arriving almost daily? Are we to find food and shelter for women and children?"

It was a Pierce∮ of Boston who pointed out the way, and thus became in a sense the founder of the Freedmen's Bureau. He was a firm friend of Secretary Chase; and when, in 1861, the care of slaves and abandoned lands devolved upon the Treasury officials, Pierce was specially detailed from the ranks to study the conditions. First, he cared for the refugees at Fortress Monroe; and then, after Sherman had captured Hilton Head, Pierce was sent there to found his Port Royal experiment of making free workingmen out of slaves. Before his experiment was barely started, however, the problem of the fugitives had assumed such proportions that it was taken from the hands of the over-burdened Treasury Department and given to the army officials. Already centres of massed freedmen were forming at Fortress Monroe, Washington, New Orleans, Vicksburg and Corinth, Columbus, Ky.,

---

*1818–93; politician, Army officer; championed blacks civil rights.
†John Charles Fremont 1813–90; politician and Army officer.
‡Simon Cameron (1799–1889); U.S. Secretary of War during the Civil War.
∮Edward Hillie Pierce (1829–97) lawyer and biographer.

and Cairo, Ill., as well as at Port Royal. Army chaplains found here new and fruitful fields; "superintendents of contrabands" multiplied, and some attempt at systematic work was made by enlisting the able-bodied men and giving work to the others.

Then came the Freedmen's Aid societies, born of the touching appeals from Pierce and from these other centres of distress. There was the American Missionary Association, sprung from the *Amistad,* and now full-grown for work; the various church organizations, the National Freedmen's Relief Association, the American Freedmen's Union, the Western Freedmen's Aid Commission,—in all fifty or more active organizations, which sent clothes, money, school-books, and teachers southward. All they did was needed, for the destitution of the freedmen was often reported as "too appalling for belief," and the situation was daily growing worse rather than better.

And daily, too, it seemed more plain that this was no ordinary matter of temporary relief, but a national crisis; for here loomed a labor problem of vast dimensions. Masses of Negroes stood idle, or, if they worked spasmodically, were never sure of pay; and if perchance they received pay, squandered the new thing thoughtlessly. In these and other ways were camp-life and the new liberty demoralizing the freedmen. The broader economic organization thus clearly demanded sprang up here and there as accident and local conditions determined. Here it was that Pierce's Port Royal plan of leased plantations and guided workmen pointed out the rough way. In Washington the military governor, at the urgent appeal of the superintendent, opened confiscated estates to the cultivation of the fugitives, and there in the shadow of the dome gathered black farm villages. General Dix gave over estates to the freedmen of Fortress Monroe, and so on, South and West. The government and benevolent societies furnished the means of cultivation, and the Negro turned again slowly to work. The systems of control, thus started, rapidly grew, here and there, into strange little governments, like that of General Banks in Louisiana, with its ninety thousand black subjects, its fifty thousand guided laborers, and its annual budget of one hundred thousand dollars and more. It made out four thousand pay-rolls a year, registered all freedmen, inquired into grievances and redressed them, laid and collected taxes, and established a system of public schools. So, too, Colonel Eaton, the superintendent of Tennessee and Arkansas, ruled over one hundred thousand freedmen, leased and cultivated seven thousand acres of cotton land, and fed ten thousand paupers a year. In South Carolina was General Saxton, with his deep interest in black folk. He succeeded Pierce and the Treasury officials, and sold forfeited estates, leased abandoned plantations, encouraged schools, and received from Sherman, after that terribly picturesque march to the sea, thousands of the wretched camp followers.

Three characteristic things one might have seen in Sherman's raid through Georgia, which threw the new situation in shadowy relief: the Conqueror, the Conquered, and the Negro. Some see all significance in the grim front of the destroyer, and some in the bitter sufferers of the Lost Cause. But to me neither soldier nor fugitive speaks with so deep a meaning as that dark human cloud that clung like remorse on the rear of those swift columns, swelling at times to half their size, almost engulfing and choking them. In vain were they ordered back, in vain were bridges hewn from beneath their feet; on they trudged and writhed and surged, until they rolled into Savannah, a starved and naked horde of tens of thousands. There too came the characteristic military remedy: "The islands from Charleston south, the abandoned rice-fields along the rivers for thirty miles back from the sea, and the country bordering the St. John's River, Florida, are reserved and set apart for the settlement of Negroes now made free by act of war." So read the celebrated "Field-order Number Fifteen."

All these experiments, orders, and systems were bound to attract and perplex the government and the nation. Directly after the Emancipation Proclamation, Representative Eliot had introduced a bill creating a Bureau of Emancipation; but it was never reported. The following June a committee of inquiry, appointed by the Secretary of War, reported in favor of a tempo-rary bureau for the "improvement, protection, and employment of refugee freedmen," on much the same lines as were afterwards followed. Petitions came in to President Lincoln from distinguished citizens and organizations, strongly urging a comprehensive and unified plan of dealing with the freed-men, under a bureau which should be "charged with the study of plans and execution of measures for easily guiding, and in every way judiciously and humanely aiding, the passage of our emancipated and yet to be emancipated blacks from the old condition of forced labor to their new state of vol-untary industry."

Some half-hearted steps were taken to accomplish this, in part, by putting the whole matter again in charge of the special Treasury agents. Laws of 1863 and 1864 directed them to take charge of and lease abandoned lands for periods not exceeding twelve months, and to "provide in such leases, or otherwise, for the employment and general welfare" of the freedmen. Most of the army officers greeted this as a welcome relief from perplexing "Negro affairs," and Secretary Fessenden, July 29, 1864, issued an excellent system of regulations, which were afterward closely followed by General Howard. Under Treasury agents, large quantities of land were leased in the Mississippi Valley, and many Negroes were employed; but in August, 1864, the new regulations were suspended for reasons of "public policy," and the army was again in control.

Meanwhile Congress had turned its attention to the subject; and in March the House passed a bill by a majority of two establishing a Bureau for Freedmen in the War Department. Charles Sumner*, who had charge of the bill in the Senate, argued that freedmen and abandoned lands ought to be under the same department, and reported a substitute for the House bill attaching the Bureau to the Treasury Department. This bill passed, but too late for action by the House. The debates wandered over the whole policy of the administration and the general question of slavery, without touching very closely the specific merits of the measure in hand. Then the national election

*1811–74; abolitionist statesman.

took place; and the administration, with a vote of renewed confidence from the country, addressed itself to the matter more seriously. A conference between the two branches of Congress agreed upon a carefully drawn measure which contained the chief provisions of Sumner's bill, but made the proposed organization a department independent of both the War and the Treasury officials. The bill was conservative, giving the new department "general superintendence of all freedmen." Its purpose was to "establish regulations" for them, protect them, lease them lands, adjust their wages, and appear in civil and military courts as their "next friend." There were many limitations attached to the powers thus granted, and the organization was made permanent. Nevertheless, the Senate defeated the bill, and a new conference committee was appointed. This committee reported a new bill, February 28, which was whirled through just as the session closed, and became the act of 1865 establishing in the War Department a "Bureau of Refugees, Freedmen, and Abandoned Lands."

This last compromise was a hasty bit of legislation, vague and uncertain in outline. A Bureau was created, "to continue during the present War of

An office of the Freedmen's Bureau in Memphis, Tennessee. The Freedmen's Bureau, which existed from 1865–72, was created by Congress to provide aide to newly freed black Americans.

Rebellion, and for one year thereafter," to which was given "the supervision and management of all abandoned lands and the control of "all subjects relating to refugees and freedmen," under "such rules and regulations as may be presented by the head of the Bureau and approved by the President." A Commissioner, appointed by the President and Senate, was to control the Bureau, with an office force not exceeding ten clerks. The President might also appoint assistant commissioners in the seceded States, and to all these offices military officials might be detailed at regular pay. The Secretary of

War could issue rations, clothing, and fuel to the destitute, and all abandoned property was placed in the hands of the Bureau for eventual lease and sale to ex-slaves in forty-acre parcels.

Thus did the United States government definitely assume charge of the emancipated Negro as the ward of the nation. It was a tremendous undertaking. Here at a stroke of the pen was erected a government of millions of men,—and not ordinary men either, but black men emasculated by a peculiarly complete system of slavery, centuries old; and now, suddenly, violently, they come into a new birthright, at a time of war and passion, in the midst of the stricken and embittered population of their former masters. Any man might well have hesitated to assume charge of such a work, with vast responsibilities, indefinite powers, and limited resources. Probably no one but a soldier would have answered such a call promptly; and, indeed, no one but a soldier could be called, for Congress had appropriated no money for salaries and expenses.

Less than a month after the weary Emancipator passed to his rest, his successor assigned Major-Gen. Oliver O. Howard to duty as Commissioner of the new Bureau. He was a Maine man, then only thirty-five years of age. He had marched with Sherman to the sea, had fought well at Gettysburg, and but the year before had been assigned to the command of the Department of Tennessee. An honest man, with too much faith in human nature, little aptitude for business and intricate detail, he had had large opportunity of becoming acquainted at first hand with much of the work before him. And of that work it has been truly said that "no approximately correct history of civilization can ever be written which does not throw out in bold relief, as one of the great landmarks of political and social progress, the organization and administration of the Freedmen's Bureau."

On May 12, 1865, Howard was appointed; and he assumed the duties of his office promptly on the 15th, and began examining the field of work. A curious mess he looked upon: little despotisms, communistic experiments, slavery, peonage, business speculations, organized charity, unorganized almsgiving,—all reeling on under the guise of helping the freedmen, and all enshrined in the smoke and blood of the war and the cursing and silence of angry men. On May 19 the new government—for a government it really was—issued its constitution; commissioners were to be appointed in each of the seceded states, who were to take charge of "all subjects relating to refugees and freedmen," and all relief and rations were to be given by their consent alone. The Bureau invited continued cooperation with benevolent societies, and declared: "It will be the object of all commissioners to introduce practicable systems of compensated labor," and to establish schools. Forthwith nine assistant commissioners were appointed. They were to hasten to their fields of work; seek gradually to close relief establishments, and make the destitute self-supporting; act as courts of law where there were no courts, or where Negroes were not recognized in them as free; establish the institution of marriage among ex-slaves, and keep records; see that freedmen were free to choose their employers, and help in making fair contracts for them; and finally, the circular said: "Simple good faith, for which we hope on all hands for those concerned in the passing away of slavery, will especially relieve the assistant commissioners in the discharge of their duties toward the freedmen, as well as promote the general welfare."

No sooner was the work thus started, and the general system and local organization in some measure begun, than two grave difficulties appeared which changed largely the theory and outcome of Bureau work. First, there were the abandoned lands of the South. It had long been the more or less definitely expressed theory of the North that all the chief problems of Emancipation might be settled by establishing the slaves on the forfeited lands of their masters,—a sort of poetic justice, said some. But this poetry done into solemn prose meant either wholesale confiscation of private property in the South, or vast appropriations. Now Congress had not appropriated a cent, and no sooner did the proclamations of general amnesty appear than the eight hundred thousand acres of abandoned lands in the hands of the Freedmen's Bureau melted quickly away. The second difficulty lay in perfecting the local organization of the Bureau throughout the wide field of work. Making a new machine and sending out officials of duly ascertained fitness for a great work of social reform is no child's task; but this task was even harder, for a new central organization had to be fitted on a heterogeneous and confused but already existing system of relief and control of ex-slaves; and the agents available for this work must be sought for in an army still busy with war operations,—men in the very nature of the case ill fitted for delicate social work,—or among the questionable camp followers of an invading host. Thus, after a year's work, vigorously as it was pushed, the problem looked even more difficult to grasp and solve than at the beginning. Nevertheless, three things that year's work did, well worth the doing: it relieved a vast amount of physical suffering; it transported seven thousand fugitives from congested centres back to the farm; and, best of all, it inaugurated the crusade of the New England schoolma'am.

The annals of this Ninth Crusade are yet to be written,—the tale of a mission that seemed to our age far more quixotic than the quest of St. Louis seemed to his. Behind the mists of ruin and rapine waved the calico dresses of women who dared, and after the hoarse mouthings of the field guns rang the rhythm of the alphabet. Rich and poor they were, serious and curious. Bereaved now of a father, now of a brother, now of more than these, they came seeking a life work in planting New England schoolhouses among the white and black of the South. They did their work well. In that first year they taught one hundred thousand souls, and more.

Evidently, Congress must soon legislate again on the hastily organized Bureau, which had so quickly grown into wide significance and vast possibilities. An institution such as that was well-nigh as difficult to end as to begin. Early in 1866 Congress took up the matter, when Senator Trumbull*, of Illinois, introduced a bill to extend the Bureau and enlarge its powers. This measure received, at the hands of Congress, far more thorough discussion

*Lyman Trumbull (1813–96); wrote text of 13th Amendment abolishing slavery.

and attention than its predecessor. The war cloud had thinned enough to allow a clearer conception of the work of Emancipation. The champions of the bill argued that the strengthening of the Freedmen's Bureau was still a military necessity; that it was needed for the proper carrying out of the Thirteenth Amendment, and was a work of sheer justice to the ex-slave, at a trifling cost to the government. The opponents of the measure declared that the war was over, and the necessity for war measures past; that the Bureau, by reason of its extraordinary powers, was clearly unconstitutional in time of peace, and was destined to irritate the South and pauperize the freedmen, at a final cost of possibly hundreds of millions. These two arguments were unanswered, and indeed unanswerable: the one that the extraordinary powers of the Bureau threatened the civil rights of all citizens; and the other that the government must have power to do what manifestly must be done, and that present abandonment of the freedmen meant their practical reenslavement. The bill which finally passed enlarged and made permanent the Freedmen's Bureau. It was promptly vetoed by President Johnson as "unconstitutional," "unnecessary," and "extrajudicial," and failed of passage over the veto. Meantime, however, the breach between Congress and the President began to broaden, and a modified form of the lost bill was finally passed over the President's second veto, July 16.

The act of 1866 gave the Freedmen's Bureau its final form,—the form by which it will be known to posterity and judged of men. It extended the existence of the Bureau to July, 1868; it authorized additional assistant commissioners, the retention of army officers mustered out of regular service, the sale of certain forfeited lands to freedmen on nominal terms, the sale of Confederate public property for Negro schools, and a wider field of judicial interpretation and cognizance. The government of the unreconstructed South was thus put very largely in the hands of the Freedmen's Bureau, especially as in many cases the departmental military commander was now made also assistant commissioner. It was thus that the Freedmen's Bureau became a full-fledged government of men. It made laws, executed them and interpreted them; it laid and collected taxes, defined and punished crime, maintained and used military force, and dictated such measures as it thought necessary and proper for the accomplishment of its varied ends. Naturally, all these powers were not exercised continuously nor to their fullest extent; and yet, as General Howard has said, "scarcely any subject that has to be legislated upon in civil society failed, at one time or another, to demand the action of this singular Bureau."

To understand and criticise intelligently so vast a work, one must not forget an instant the drift of things in the later sixties. Lee had surrendered, Lincoln was dead, and Johnson and Congress were at loggerheads; the Thirteenth Amendment was adopted, the Fourteenth pending, and the Fifteenth declared in force in 1870. Guerrilla raiding, the ever-present flickering after-flame of war, was spending its forces against the Negroes, and all the Southern land was awakening as from some wild dream to poverty and social revolution. In a time of perfect calm, amid willing neighbors and streaming wealth, the social uplifting of four million slaves to an assured and self-sustaining place in the body politic and economic would have been a herculean task; but when to the inherent difficulties of so delicate and nice a social operation were added the spite and hate of conflict, the hell of war; when suspicion and cruelty were rife, and gaunt Hunger wept beside Bereavement,—in such a case, the work of any instrument of social regeneration was in large part foredoomed to failure. The very name of the Bureau stood for a thing in the South which for two centuries and better men had refused even to argue,—that life amid free Negroes was simply unthinkable, the maddest of experiments.

The agents that the Bureau could command varied all the way from unselfish philanthropists to narrow-minded busybodies and thieves; and even though it be true that the average was far better than the worst, it was the occasional fly that helped spoil the ointment.

Then amid all crouched the freed slave, bewildered between friend and foe. He had emerged from slavery,—not the worst slavery in the world, not a slavery that made all life unbearable, rather a slavery that had here and there something of kindliness, fidelity, and happiness,—but withal slavery, which, so far as human aspiration and desert were concerned, classed the black man and the ox together. And the Negro knew full well that, whatever their deeper convictions may have been, Southern men had fought with desperate energy to perpetuate this slavery under which the black masses, with half-articulate thought, had writhed and shivered. They welcomed freedom with a cry. They shrank from the master who still strove for their chains; they fled to the friends that had freed them, even though those friends stood ready to use them as a club for driving the recalcitrant South back into loyalty. So the cleft between the white and black South grew. Idle to say it never should have been; it was as inevitable as its results were pitiable. Curiously incongruous elements were left arrayed against each other,—the North, the government, the carpet-bagger, and the slave, here; and there, all the South that was white, whether gentleman or vagabond, honest man or rascal, lawless murderer or martyr to duty.

Thus it is doubly difficult to write of this period calmly, so intense was the feeling, so mighty the human passions that swayed and blinded men. Amid it all, two figures ever stand to typify that day to coming ages,—the one, a gray-haired gentleman, whose fathers had quit themselves like men, whose sons lay in nameless graves; who bowed to the evil of slavery because its abolition threatened untold ill to all; who stood at last, in the evening of life, a blighted, ruined form, with hate in his eyes;—and the other, a form hovering dark and motherlike, her awful face black with the mists of centuries, had aforetime quailed at that white master's command, had bent in love over the cradles of his sons and daughters, and closed in death the sunken eyes of his wife,— aye, too, at his behest had laid herself low to his lust, and borne a tawny man-child to the world, only to see her dark boy's limbs scattered to the winds by midnight marauders riding after "damned Niggers." These were the saddest sights of that woeful day; and no man clasped the hands of these two passing figures of the present-past; but, hating, they went to their long home, and, hating, their children's children live today.

Here, then, was the field of work for the Freedmen's Bureau; and since, with some hesitation, it was continued by the act of 1868 until 1869, let us look upon four years of its work as a whole. There were, in 1868, nine hundred Bureau officials scattered from Washington to Texas, ruling, directly and indirectly, many millions of men. The deeds of these rulers fall mainly under seven heads: the relief of physical suffering, the overseeing of the beginnings of free labor, the buying and selling of land, the establishment of schools, the paying of bounties, the administration of justice, and the financiering of all these activities.

Up to June, 1869, over half a million patients had been treated by Bureau physicians and surgeons, and sixty hospitals and asylums had been in operation. In fifty months twenty-one million free rations were distributed at a cost of over four million dollars. Next came the difficult question of labor. First, thirty thousand black men were transported from the refuges and relief stations back to the farms, back to the critical trial of a new way of working. Plain instructions went out from Washington: the laborers must be free to choose their employers, no fixed rate of wages was prescribed, and there was to be no peonage or forced labor. So far, so good; but where local agents differed *toto cælo* in capacity and character, where the *personnel* was continually changing, the outcome was necessarily varied. The largest element of success lay in the fact that the majority of the freedmen were willing, even eager, to work. So labor contracts were written,—fifty thousand in a single State,—laborers advised, wages guaranteed, and employers supplied. In truth, the organization became a vast labor bureau,—not perfect, indeed, notably defective here and there, but on the whole successful beyond the dreams of thoughtful men. The two great obstacles which confronted the officials were the tyrant and the idler,—the slaveholder who was determined to perpetuate slavery under another name; and the freedman who regarded freedom as perpetual rest,—the Devil and the Deep Sea.

In the work of establishing the Negroes as peasant proprietors, the Bureau was from the first handicapped and at last absolutely checked. Something was done, and larger things were planned; abandoned lands were leased so long as they remained in the hands of the Bureau, and a total revenue of nearly half a million dollars derived from black tenants. Some other lands to which the nation had gained title were sold on easy terms, and public lands were opened for settlement to the very few freedmen who had tools and capital. But the vision of "forty acres and a mule"—the righteous and reasonable ambition to become a landholder, which the nation had all but categorically promised the freedmen—was destined in most cases to bitter disappointment. And those men of marvellous hindsight who are today seeking to preach the Negro back to the present peonage of the soil know well, or ought to know, that the opportunity of binding the Negro peasant willingly to the soil was lost on that day when the Commissioner of the Freedmen's Bureau had to go to South Carolina and tell the weeping freedmen, after their years of toil, that their land was not theirs, that there was a mistake—somewhere. If by 1874 the Georgia Negro alone owned three hundred and fifty thousand acres of land, it was by grace of his thrift rather than by bounty of the government.

The greatest success of the Freedmen's Bureau lay in the planting of the free school among Negroes, and the idea of free elementary education among all classes in the South. It not only called the school-mistresses through the benevolent agencies and built them schoolhouses, but it helped discover and support such apostles of human culture as Edmund Ware*, Samuel Armstrong†, and Erastus Cravath‡. The opposition to Negro education in the South was at first bitter, and showed itself in ashes, insult, and blood; for the South believed an educated Negro to be a dangerous Negro. And the South was not wholly wrong; for education among all kinds of men always has had, and always will have, an element of danger and revolution, of dissatisfaction and discontent. Nevertheless, men strive to know. Perhaps some inkling of this paradox, even in the unquiet days of the Bureau, helped the bayonets allay an opposition to human training which still to-day lies smouldering in the South, but not flaming. Fisk, Atlanta, Howard, and Hampton were founded in these days, and six million dollars were expended for educational work, seven hundred and fifty thousand dollars of which the freedmen themselves gave of their poverty.

Such contributions, together with the buying of land and various other enterprises, showed that the ex-slave was handling some free capital already. The chief initial source of this was labor in the army, and his pay and bounty as a soldier. Payments to Negro soldiers were at first complicated by the ignorance of the recipients, and the fact that the quotas of colored regiments from Northern States were largely filled by recruits from the South, unknown to their fellow soldiers. Consequently, payments were accompanied by such frauds that Congress, by joint resolution in 1867, put the whole matter in the hands of the Freedmen's Bureau. In two years six million dollars was thus distributed to five thousand claimants, and in the end the sum exceeded eight million dollars. Even in this system fraud was frequent; but still the work put needed capital in the hands of practical paupers, and some, at least, was well spent.

The most perplexing and least successful part of the Bureau's work lay in the exercise of its judicial functions. The regular Bureau court consisted of one representative of the employer, one of the Negro, and one of the Bureau. If the Bureau could have maintained a perfectly judicial attitude, this arrangement would have been ideal, and must in time have gained confidence; but the nature of its other activities and the character of its *personnel* prejudiced the Bureau in favor of the black litigants, and led without doubt to much injustice and annoyance. On the other hand, to leave the Negro in the hands of Southern courts was impossible. In a distracted land where slavery had hardly fallen, to keep the strong from wanton abuse of the weak, and the weak from gloating insolently over the half-shorn strength of the strong, was a thankless, hopeless task. The former masters of the land were peremp-

*(1837–85); abolitionist and educator.
†(1839–93) Union military commander of black troops.
‡(1833–1900); abolitionist and clergyman.

torily ordered about, seized, and imprisoned, and punished over and again, with scant courtesy from army officers. The former slaves were intimidated, beaten, raped, and butchered by angry and revengeful men. Bureau courts tended to become centres simply for punishing whites, while the regular civil courts tended to become solely institutions for perpetuating the slavery of blacks. Almost every law and method ingenuity could devise was employed by the legislatures to reduce the Negroes to serfdom,—to make them the slaves of the State, if not of individual owners; while the Bureau officials too often were found striving to put the "bottom rail on top," and gave the freedmen a power and independence which they could not yet use. It is all well enough for us of another generation to wax wise with advice to those who bore the burden in the heat of the day. It is full easy now to see that the man who lost home, fortune, and family at a stroke, and saw his land ruled by "mules and niggers," was really benefited by the passing of slavery. It is not difficult now to say to the young freedman, cheated and cuffed about who has seen his father's head beaten to a jelly and his own mother namelessly assaulted, that the meek shall inherit the earth. Above all, nothing is more convenient than to heap on the Freedmen's Bureau all the evils of that evil day, and damn it utterly for every mistake and blunder that was made.

All this is easy, but it is neither sensible nor just. Someone had blundered, but that was long before Oliver Howard was born; there was criminal aggression and heedless neglect, but without some system of control there would have been far more than there was. Had that control been from within, the Negro would have been re-enslaved, to all intents and purposes. Coming as the control did from without, perfect men and methods would have bettered all things; and even with imperfect agents and questionable methods, the work accomplished was not undeserving of commendation.

Such was the dawn of Freedom; such was the work of the Freedmen's Bureau, which, summed up in brief, may be epitomized thus: for some fifteen million dollars, beside the sums spent before 1865, and the dole of benevolent societies, this Bureau set going a system of free labor, established a beginning of peasant proprietorship, secured the recognition of black freedmen before courts of law, and founded the free common school in the South. On the other hand, it failed to begin the establishment of good-will between ex-masters and freedmen, to guard its work wholly from paternalistic methods which discouraged self-reliance, and to carry out to any considerable extent its implied promises to furnish the freedmen with land. Its successes were the result of hard work, supplemented by the aid of philanthropists and the eager striving of black men. Its failures were the result of bad local agents, the inherent difficulties of the work, and national neglect.

Such an institution, from its wide powers, great responsibilities, large control of moneys, and generally conspicuous position, was naturally open to repeated and bitter attack. It sustained a searching Congressional investigation at the instance of Fernando Wood in 1870. Its archives and few remaining functions were with blunt discourtesy transferred from Howard's control, in his absence, to the supervision of Secretary of War Belknap in 1872, on the Secretary's recommendation. Finally, in consequence of grave intimations of wrong-doing made by the Secretary and his subordinates, General Howard was court-martialed in 1874. In both of these trials the Commissioner of the Freedmen's Bureau was officially exonerated from any wilful misdoing, and his work commended. Nevertheless, many unpleasant things were brought to light,—the methods of transacting the business of the Bureau were faulty; several cases of defalcation were proved, and other frauds strongly suspected; there were some business transactions which savored of dangerous speculation, if not dishonesty; and around it all lay the smirch of the Freedmen's Bank.

Morally and practically, the Freedmen's Bank was part of the Freedmen's Bureau, although it had no legal connection with it. With the prestige of the government back of it, and a directing board of unusual respectability and national reputation, this banking institution had made a remarkable start in the development of that thrift among black folk which slavery had kept them from knowing. Then in one sad day came the crash,—all the hard-earned dollars of the freedmen disappeared; but that was the least of the loss,—all the faith in saving went too, and much of the faith in men; and that was a loss that a Nation which to-day sneers at Negro shiftlessness has never yet made good. Not even ten additional years of slavery could have done so much to throttle the thrift of the freedmen as the mismanagement and bankruptcy of the series of savings banks chartered by the Nation for their especial aid. Where all the blame should rest, it is hard to say; whether the Bureau and the Bank died chiefly by reason of the blows of its selfish friends or the dark machinations of its foes, perhaps even time will never reveal, for here lies unwritten history.

Of the foes without the Bureau, the bitterest were those who attacked not so much its conduct or policy under the law as the necessity for any such institution at all. Such attacks came primarily from the Border States and the South; and they were summed up by Senator Davis, of Kentucky, when he moved to entitle the act of 1866 a bill "to promote strife and conflict between the white and black races . . . by a grant of unconstitutional power." The argument gathered tremendous strength South and North; but its very strength was its weakness. For, argued the plain common-sense of the nation, if it is unconstitutional, unpractical, and futile for the nation to stand guardian over its helpless wards, then there is left but one alternative,—to make those wards their own guardians by arming them with the ballot. Moreover, the path of the practical politician pointed the same way; for, argued this opportunist, if we cannot peacefully reconstruct the South with white votes, we certainly can with black votes. So justice and force joined hands.

The alternative thus offered the nation was not between full and restricted Negro suffrage; else every sensible man, black and white, would easily have chosen the latter. It was rather a choice between suffrage and slavery, after endless blood and gold had flowed to sweep human bondage away. Not a single Southern legislature stood ready to admit a Negro, under any conditions, to the polls; not a single Southern legislature believed free Negro labor was possible without a system of restrictions that took all its freedom away; there was scarcely a white man in the South who did not honestly regard Emancipation as a crime, and its practical nullification as a duty. In such a situation, the granting of the ballot to the black man was a necessity, the very least a guilty nation could grant a wronged race, and the only method of compelling the South to accept the results of the war. Thus Negro suffrage ended a civil war by beginning a race feud. And some felt gratitude toward the race thus sacrificed in its swaddling clothes on the altar of national integrity; and some felt and feel only indifference and contempt.

Had political exigencies been less pressing, the opposition to government guardianship of Negroes less bitter, and the attachment to the slave system less strong, the social seer can well imagine a far better policy,—a permanent Freedmen's Bureau, with a national system of Negro schools; a carefully supervised employment and labor office; a system of impartial protection before the regular courts; and such institutions for social betterment as savings-banks, land and building associations, and social settlements. All this vast expenditure of money and brains might have formed a great school of prospective citizenship, and solved in a way we have not yet solved the most perplexing and persistent of the Negro problems.

That such an institution was unthinkable in 1870 was due in part to certain acts of the Freedmen's Bureau itself. It came to regard its work as merely temporary, and Negro suffrage as a final answer to all present perplexities. The political ambition of many of its agents and *protégés* led it far afield into questionable activities, until the South, nursing its own deep prejudices, came easily to ignore all the good deeds of the Bureau and hate its very name with perfect hatred. So the Freedmen's Bureau died, and its child was the Fifteenth Amendment.

The passing of a great human institution before its work is done, like the untimely passing of a single soul, but leaves a legacy of striving for other men. The legacy of the Freedmen's Bureau is the heavy heritage of this generation. To-day, when new and vaster problems are destined to strain every fibre of the national mind and soul, would it not be well to count this legacy honestly and carefully? For this much all men know: despite compromise, war, and struggle, the Negro is not free. In the backwoods of the Gulf States, for miles and miles, he may not leave the plantation of his birth; in well-nigh the whole rural South the black farmers are peons, bound by law and custom to an economic slavery, from which the only escape is death or the penitentiary. In the most cultured sections and cities of the South the Negroes are a segregated servile caste, with restricted rights and privileges. Before the courts, both in law and custom, they stand on a different and peculiar basis. Taxation without representation is the rule of their political life. And the result of all this is, and in nature must have been, lawlessness and crime. That is the large legacy of the Freedmen's Bureau, the work it did not do because it could not.

I have seen a land right merry with the sun, where children sing, and rolling hills lie like passioned women wanton with harvest. And there in the King's Highways sat and sits a figure veiled and bowed, by which the traveller's footsteps hasten as they go. On the tainted air broods fear. Three centuries' thought has been the raising and unveiling of that bowed human heart, and now behold a century new for the duty and the deed. The problem of the Twentieth Century is the problem of the color-line.

III
Of Mr. Booker T. Washington and Others

From birth till death enslaved; in word, in deed, unmanned!
. . . .

Hereditary bondsmen! Know ye not
Who would be free themselves must strike the blow?
                          Byron. (1778–1824) from *Childe Harold's Pilgrimage*

Easily the most striking thing in the history of the American Negro since 1876 is the ascendancy of Mr. Booker T. Washington. It began at the time when war memories and ideals were rapidly passing; a day of astonishing commercial development was dawning; a sense of doubt and hesitation overtook the freedmen's sons,—then it was that his leading began. Mr. Washington came, with a simple definite programme, at the psychological moment when the nation was a little ashamed of having bestowed so much sentiment on Negroes, and was concentrating its energies on Dollars. His programme of industrial education, conciliation of the South, and submission and silence as to civil and political rights, was not wholly original; the Free Negroes from 1830 up to war-time had striven to build industrial schools, and the American Missionary Association had from the first taught various trades; and Price and others had sought a way of honorable alliance with the best of the Southerners. But Mr. Washington first indissolubly linked these things; he put enthusiasm, unlimited energy, and perfect faith into his programme, and changed it from a by-path into a veritable Way of Life. And the tale of the methods by which he did this is a fascinating study of human life.

It startled the nation to hear a Negro advocating such a programme after many decades of bitter complaint; it startled and won the applause of the South, it interested and won the admiration of the North; and after a confused murmur of protest, it silenced if it did not convert the Negroes themselves.

To gain the sympathy and cooperation of the various elements comprising the white South was Mr. Washington's first task; and this, at the time

Tuskegee was founded, seemed, for a black man, well-nigh impossible. And yet ten years later it was done in the word spoken at Atlanta: "In all things purely social we can be as separate as the five fingers, and yet one as the hand in all things essential to mutual progress." This "Atlanta Compromise" is by all odds the most notable thing in Mr. Washington's career. The South interpreted it in different ways: the radicals received it as a complete surrender of the demand for civil and political equality; the conservatives, as a generously conceived working basis for mutual understanding. So both approved it, and to-day its author is certainly the most distinguished Southerner since Jefferson Davis, and the one with the largest personal following.

Next to this achievement comes Mr. Washington's work in gaining place and consideration in the North. Others less shrewd and tactful had formerly essayed to sit on these two stools and had fallen between them; but as Mr. Washington knew the heart of the South from birth and training, so by singular insight he intuitively grasped the spirit of the age which was dominating the North. And so thoroughly did he learn the speech and thought of triumphant commercialism, and the ideals of material prosperity, that the picture of a lone black boy poring over a French grammar amid the weeds and dirt of a neglected home soon seemed to him the acme of absurdities. One wonders what Socrates and St. Francis of Assisi would say to this.

And yet this very singleness of vision and thorough oneness with his age is a mark of the successful man. It is as though Nature must needs make men narrow in order to give them force. So Mr. Washington's cult has gained unquestioning followers, his work has wonderfully prospered, his friends are legion, and his enemies are confounded. To-day he stands as the one recognized spokesman of his ten million fellows, and one of the most notable figures in a nation of seventy millions. One hesitates, therefore, to criticise a life which, beginning with so little, has done so much. And yet the time is come when one may speak in all sincerity and utter courtesy of the mistakes and shortcomings of Mr. Washington's career, as well as of his triumphs, without being thought captious or envious, and without forgetting that it is easier to do ill than well in the world.

The criticism that has hitherto met Mr. Washington has not always been of this broad character. In the South especially has he had to walk warily to avoid the harshest judgments,—and naturally so, for he is dealing with the one subject of deepest sensitiveness to that section. Twice—once when at the Chicago celebration of the Spanish-American War he alluded to the color-prejudice that is "eating away the vitals of the South," and once when he dined with President Roosevelt—has the resulting Southern criticism been violent enough to threaten seriously his popularity. In the North the feeling has several times forced itself into words, that Mr. Washington's counsels of submission overlooked certain elements of true manhood, and that his educational programme was unnecessarily narrow. Usually, however, such criticism has not found open expression, although, too, the spiritual sons of the Abolitionists have not been prepared to acknowledge that the schools founded before Tuskegee, by men of broad ideals and self-sacrificing spirit, were wholly failures or worthy of ridicule. While, then, criticism has not failed to follow Mr. Washington, yet the prevailing public opinion of the land has been but too willing to deliver the solution of a wearisome problem into his hands, and say, "If that is all you and your race ask, take it."

Among his own people, however, Mr. Washington has encountered the strongest and most lasting opposition, amounting at times to bitterness, and even today continuing strong and insistent even though largely silenced in outward expression by the public opinion of the nation. Some of this opposition is, of course, mere envy; the disappointment of displaced demagogues and the spite of narrow minds. But aside from this, there is among educated and thoughtful colored men in all parts of the land a feeling of deep regret, sorrow, and apprehension at the wide currency and ascendancy which some of Mr. Washington's theories have gained. These same men admire his sincerity of purpose, and are willing to forgive much to honest endeavor which is doing something worth the doing. They cooperate with Mr. Washington as far as they conscientiously can; and, indeed, it is no ordinary tribute to this man's tact and power that, steering as he must between so many diverse interests and opinions, he so largely retains the respect of all.

But the hushing of the criticism of honest opponents is a dangerous thing. It leads some of the best of the critics to unfortunate silence and paralysis of effort, and others to burst into speech so passionately and intemperately as to lose listeners. Honest and earnest criticism from those whose interests are most nearly touched,—criticism of writers by readers, of government by those governed, of leaders by those led,—this is the soul of democracy and the safeguard of modern society. If the best of the American Negroes receive by outer pressure a leader whom they had not recognized before, manifestly there is here a certain palpable gain. Yet there is also irreparable loss,—a loss of that peculiarly valuable education which a group receives when by search and criticism it finds and commissions its own leaders. The way in which this is done is at once the most elementary and the nicest problem of social growth. History is but the record of such group-leadership; and yet how infinitely changeful is its type and character! And of all types and kinds, what can be more instructive than the leadership of a group within a group?—that curious double movement where real progress may be negative and actual advance be relative retrogression. All this is the social student's inspiration and despair.

Now in the past the American Negro has had instructive experience in the choosing of group leaders, founding thus a peculiar dynasty which in the light of present conditions is worth while studying. When sticks and stones and beasts form the sole environment of a people, their attitude is largely one of determined opposition to and conquest of natural forces. But when to earth and brute is added an environment of men and ideas, then the attitude of the imprisoned group may take three main forms,—a feeling of revolt and revenge; an attempt to adjust all thought and action to the will of the greater group; or, finally, a determined effort at self-realization and self-development despite environing opinion. The influence of all of these attitudes at various times can be traced in the history of the American Negro, and in the evolution of his successive leaders.

Before 1750, while the fire of African freedom still burned in the veins of the slaves, there was in all leadership or attempted leadership but the one motive of revolt and revenge,—typified in the terrible Maroons, the Danish blacks, and Cato of Stono, and veiling all the Americas in fear of insurrection. The liberalizing tendencies of the latter half of the eighteenth century brought, along with kindlier relations between black and white, thoughts of ultimate adjustment and assimilation. Such aspiration was especially voiced in the earnest songs of Phyllis, in the martyrdom of Attucks, the fighting of Salem and Poor, the intellectual accomplishments of Banneker and Derham, and the political demands of the Cuffes.

Stern financial and social stress after the war cooled much of the previous humanitarian ardor. The disappointment and impatience of the Negroes at the persistence of slavery and serfdom voiced itself in two movements. The slaves in the South, aroused undoubtedly by vague rumors of the Haytian revolt, made three fierce attempts at insurrection,—in 1800 under Gabriel in Virginia, in 1822 under Vesey in Carolina, and in 1831 again in Virginia under the terrible Nat Turner. In the Free States, on the other hand, a new and curious attempt at self-development was made. In Philadelphia and New York color-prescription led to a withdrawal of Negro communicants from white churches and the formation of a peculiar socio-religious institution among the Negroes known as the African Church,—an organization still living and controlling in its various branches over a million of men.

Walker's wild appeal against the trend of the times showed how the

Booker T. Washington (1856–1915) speaks to a group in Louisiana during his last tour of the South in 1915.

world was changing after the coming of the cotton-gin. By 1830 slavery seemed hopelessly fastened on the South, and the slaves thoroughly cowed into submission. The free Negroes of the North, inspired by the mulatto immigrants from the West Indies, began to change the basis of their demands; they recognized the slavery of slaves, but insisted that they themselves were freemen, and sought assimilation and amalgamation with the nation on the same terms with other men. Thus, Forten and Purvis of Philadelphia, Shad of Wilmington, Du Bois of New Haven, Barbadoes of Boston, and others, strove singly and together as men, they said, not as slaves; as "people of color," not as "Negroes." The trend of the times, however, refused them recognition save in individual and exceptional cases, considered them as one with all the despised blacks, and they soon found themselves striving to keep even the rights they formerly had of voting and working and moving as freemen. Schemes of migration and colonization arose among them; but these they refused to entertain, and they eventually turned to the Abolition movement as a final refuge.

Here, led by Remond, Nell, Wells-Brown, and Douglass, a new period of self-assertion and self-development dawned. To be sure, ultimate freedom and assimilation was the ideal before the leaders, but the assertion of the manhood rights of the Negro by himself was the main reliance, and John Brown's raid was the extreme of its logic. After the war and emancipation, the great form of Frederick Douglass, the greatest of American Negro leaders, still led the host. Self-assertion, especially in political lines, was the main programme, and behind Douglass came Elliot, Bruce, and Langston, and the Reconstruction politicians, and, less conspicuous but of greater social significance, Alexander Crummell and Bishop Daniel Payne*.

Then came the Revolution of 1876, the suppression of the Negro votes, the changing and shifting of ideals, and the seeking of new lights in the great night. Douglass, in his old age, still bravely stood for the ideals of his early manhood,—ultimate assimilation *through* self-assertion, and on no other terms. For a time Price arose as a new leader, destined, it seemed, not to give up, but to re-state the old ideals in a form less repugnant to the white South. But he passed away in his prime. Then came the new leader. Nearly all the former ones had become leaders by the silent suffrage of their fellows, had sought to lead their own people alone, and were usually, save Douglass, little known outside their race. But Booker T. Washington arose as essentially the leader not of one race but of two,—a compromiser between the South, the North, and the Negro. Naturally the Negroes resented, at first bitterly, signs of compromise which surrendered their civil and political rights, even though this was to be exchanged for larger chances of economic development. The rich and dominating North, however, was not only weary of the race problem, but was investing largely in Southern enterprises, and welcomed any method of peaceful cooperation. Thus, by national opinion,

---

*Figures mentioned in this paragraph were abolitionists of special importance.

the Negroes began to recognize Mr. Washington's leadership; and the voice of criticism was hushed.

Mr. Washington represents in Negro thought the old attitude of adjustment and submission; but adjustment at such a peculiar time as to make his programme unique. This is an age of unusual economic development, and Mr. Washington's programme naturally takes an economic cast, becoming a gospel of Work and Money to such an extent as apparently almost completely to overshadow the higher aims of life. Moreover, this is an age when the more advanced races are coming in closer contact with the less developed races, and the race-feeling is therefore intensified; and Mr. Washington's programme practically accepts the alleged inferiority of the Negro races. Again, in our own land, the reaction from the sentiment of war time has given impetus to race-prejudice against Negroes, and Mr. Washington withdraws many of the high demands of Negroes as men and American citizens. In other periods of intensified prejudice all the Negro's tendency to self-assertion has been called forth; at this period a policy of submission is advocated. In the history of nearly all other races and peoples the doctrine preached at such crises has been that manly self-respect is worth more than lands and houses, and that a people who voluntarily surrender such respect, or cease striving for it, are not worth civilizing.

In answer to this, it has been claimed that the Negro can survive only through submission. Mr. Washington distinctly asks that black people give up, at least for the present, three things,—

First, political power,

Second, insistence on civil rights,

Third, higher education of Negro youth,—

and concentrate all their energies on industrial education, and accumulation of wealth, and the conciliation of the South. This policy has been courageously and insistently advocated for over fifteen years, and has been triumphant for perhaps ten years. As a result of this tender of the palm-branch, what has been the return? In these years there have occurred:

1. The disfranchisement of the Negro.

2. The legal creation of a distinct status of civil inferiority for the Negro.

3. The steady withdrawal of aid from institutions for the higher training of the Negro.

These movements are not, to be sure, direct results of Mr. Washington's teachings; but his propaganda has, without a shadow of doubt, helped their speedier accomplishment. The question then comes: Is it possible, and probable, that nine millions of men can make effective progress in economic lines if they are deprived of political rights, made a servile caste, and allowed only the most meagre chance for developing their exceptional men? If history and reason give any distinct answer to these questions, it is an emphatic *No*. And Mr. Washington thus faces the triple paradox of his career:

1. He is striving nobly to make Negro artisans business men and property-owners; but it is utterly impossible, under modern competitive methods, for

workingmen and property-owners to defend their rights and exist without the right of suffrage.

2. He insists on thrift and self-respect, but at the same time counsels a silent submission to civic inferiority such as is bound to sap the manhood of any race in the long run.

3. He advocates common-school and industrial training, and depreciates institutions of higher learning; but neither the Negro common-schools, nor Tuskegee itself, could remain open a day were it not for teachers trained in Negro colleges, or trained by their graduates.

This triple paradox in Mr. Washington's position is the object of criticism by two classes of colored Americans. One class is spiritually descended from Toussaint the Savior, through Gabriel, Vesey, and Turner, and they represent the attitude of revolt and revenge; they hate the white South blindly and distrust the white race generally, and so far as they agree on definite action, think that the Negro's only hope lies in emigration beyond the borders of the United States. And yet, by the irony of fate, nothing has more effectually made this programme seem hopeless than the recent course of the United States toward weaker and darker peoples in the West Indies, Hawaii, and the Philippines,—for where in the world may we go and be safe from lying and brute force?

The other class of Negroes who cannot agree with Mr. Washington has hitherto said little aloud. They deprecate the sight of scattered counsels, of internal disagreement; and especially they dislike making their just criticism of a useful and earnest man an excuse for a general discharge of venom from small-minded opponents. Nevertheless, the questions involved are so fundamental and serious that it is difficult to see how men like the Grimkes, Kelly Miller, J. W. E. Bowen, and other representatives of this group, can much longer be silent. Such men feel in conscience bound to ask of this nation three things:

1. The right to vote.
2. Civic equality.
3. The education of youth according to ability.

They acknowledge Mr. Washington's invaluable service in counselling patience and courtesy in such demands; they do not ask that ignorant black men vote when ignorant whites are debarred, or that any reasonable restrictions in the suffrage should not be applied; they know that the low social level of the mass of the race is responsible for much discrimination against it, but they also know, and the nation knows, that relentless color-prejudice is more often a cause than a result of the Negro's degradation; they seek the abatement of this relic of barbarism, and not its systematic encouragement and pampering by all agencies of social power from the Associated Press to the Church of Christ. They advocate, with Mr. Washington, a broad system of Negro common schools supplemented by thorough industrial training; but they are surprised that a man of Mr. Washington's insight cannot see that no such educational system ever has rested or can rest on any other basis than that of the well-equipped college and university, and they insist that there is a demand for a few such institutions throughout the South to train the best of the Negro youth as teachers, professional men, and leaders.

This group of men honor Mr. Washington for his attitude of conciliation toward the white South; they accept the "Atlanta Compromise" in its broadest interpretation; they recognize, with him, many signs of promise, many men of high purpose and fair judgment, in this section; they know that no easy task has been laid upon a region already tottering under heavy burdens. But, nevertheless, they insist that the way to truth and right lies in straightforward honesty, not in indiscriminate flattery; in praising those of the South who do well and criticising uncompromisingly those who do ill; in taking advantage of the opportunities at hand and urging their fellows to do the same, but at the same time in remembering that only a firm adherence to their higher ideals and aspirations will ever keep those ideals within the realm of possibility. They do not expect that the free right to vote, to enjoy civic rights, and to be educated, will come in a moment; they do not expect to see the bias and prejudices of years disappear at the blast of a trumpet; but they are absolutely certain that the way for a people to gain their reasonable rights is not by voluntarily throwing them away and insisting that they do not want them; that the way for a people to gain respect is not by continually belittling and ridiculing themselves; that, on the contrary, Negroes must insist continually, in season and out of season, that voting is necessary to modern manhood, that color discrimination is barbarism, and that black boys need education as well as white boys.

In failing thus to state plainly and unequivocally the legitimate demands of their people, even at the cost of opposing an honored leader, the thinking classes of American Negroes would shirk a heavy responsibility,—a responsibility to themselves, a responsibility to the struggling masses, a responsibility to the darker races of men whose future depends so largely on this American experiment, but especially a responsibility to this nation,—this common Fatherland. It is wrong to encourage a man or a people in evil-doing; it is wrong to aid and abet a national crime simply because it is unpopular not to do so. The growing spirit of kindliness and reconciliation between the North and South after the frightful difference of a generation ago ought to be a source of deep congratulation to all, and especially to those whose mistreatment caused the war; but if that reconciliation is to be marked by the industrial slavery and civic death of those same black men, with permanent legislation into a position of inferiority, then those black men, if they are really men, are called upon by every consideration of patriotism and loyalty to oppose such a course by all civilized methods, even though such opposition involves disagreement with Mr. Booker T. Washington. We have no right to sit silently by while the inevitable seeds are sown for a harvest of disaster to our children, black and white.

First, it is the duty of black men to judge the South discriminatingly. The present generation of Southerners are not responsible for the past, and they should not be blindly hated or blamed for it. Furthermore, to no class is the indiscriminate endorsement of the recent course of the South toward Negroes more nauseating than to the best thought of the South. The South is not "solid"; it is a land in the ferment of social change, wherein forces of all kinds are fighting for supremacy; and to praise the ill the South is today perpetrating is just as wrong as to condemn the good. Discriminating and broad-minded criticism is what the South needs,—needs it for the sake of her own white sons and daughters, and for the insurance of robust, healthy mental and moral development.

Today even the attitude of the Southern whites toward the blacks is not, as so many assume, in all cases the same; the ignorant Southerner hates the Negro, the workingmen fear his competition, the money-makers wish to use him as a laborer, some of the educated see a menace in his upward development, while others—usually the sons of the masters—wish to help him to rise. National opinion has enabled this last class to maintain the Negro common schools, and to protect the Negro partially in property, life, and limb. Through the pressure of the money-makers, the Negro is in danger of being reduced to semi-slavery, especially in the country districts; the workingmen, and those of the educated who fear the Negro, have united to disfranchise him, and some have urged his deportation; while the passions of the ignorant are easily aroused to lynch and abuse any black man. To praise this intricate whirl of thought and prejudice is nonsense; to inveigh indiscriminately against "the South" is unjust; but to use the same breath in praising Governor Aycock*, exposing Senator Morgan†, arguing with Mr. Thomas Nelson Page‡, and denouncing Senator Ben Tillman⨎, is not only sane, but the imperative duty of thinking black men.

It would be unjust to Mr. Washington not to acknowledge that in several instances he has opposed movements in the South which were unjust to the Negro; he sent memorials to the Louisiana and Alabama constitutional conventions, he has spoken against lynching, and in other ways has openly or silently set his influence against sinister schemes and unfortunate happenings. Notwithstanding this, it is equally true to assert that on the whole the distinct impression left by Mr. Washington's propaganda is, first, that the South is justified in its present attitude toward the Negro because of the Negro's degradation; secondly, that the prime cause of the Negro's failure to rise more quickly is his wrong education in the past; and, thirdly, that his future rise depends primarily on his own efforts. Each of these propositions is a dangerous half-truth. The supplementary truths must never be lost sight of: first, slavery and race-prejudice are potent if not sufficient causes of the Negro's position; second, industrial and common-school training were necessarily slow in planting because they had to await the black teachers trained by higher institutions,—it being extremely doubtful if any essentially differ-

---

*Charles Brantley Aycock (1859–1912); supporter of public education.
†Edwin Denison Morgan (1811–83); businessman & politician.
‡(1893–1922) diplomat and author.
⨎(1847–1918); known for his extremist views on race.

ent development was possible, and certainly a Tuskegee was unthinkable before 1880; and, third, while it is a great truth to say that the Negro must strive and strive mightily to help himself, it is equally true that unless his striving be not simply seconded, but rather aroused and encouraged, by the initiative of the richer and wiser environing group, he cannot hope for great success.

In his failure to realize and impress this last point, Mr. Washington is especially to be criticised. His doctrine has tended to make the whites, North and South, shift the burden of the Negro problem to the Negro's shoulders and stand aside as critical and rather pessimistic spectators; when in fact the burden belongs to the nation, and the hands of none of us are clean if we bend not our energies to righting these great wrongs.

The South ought to be led, by candid and honest criticism, to assert her better self and do her full duty to the race she has cruelly wronged and is still wronging. The North—her co-partner in guilt—cannot salve her conscience by plastering it with gold. We cannot settle this problem by diplomacy and suaveness, by "policy" alone. If worse come to worst, can the moral fibre of this country survive the slow throttling and murder of nine millions of men?

The black men of America have a duty to perform, a duty stern and delicate,—a forward movement to oppose a part of the work of their greatest leader. So far as Mr. Washington preaches Thrift, Patience, and Industrial Training for the masses, we must hold up his hands and strive with him, rejoicing in his honors and glorying in the strength of this Joshua called of God and of man to lead the headless host. But so far as Mr. Washington apologizes for injustice, North or South, does not rightly value the privilege and duty of voting, belittles the emasculating effects of caste distinctions, and opposes the higher training and ambition of our brighter minds,—so far as he, the South, or the Nation, does this,—we must unceasingly and firmly oppose them. By every civilized and peaceful method we must strive for the rights which the world accords to men, clinging unwaveringly to those great words which the sons of the Fathers would fain forget: "We hold these truths to be self-evident: That all men are created equal; that they are endowed by their Creator with certain unalienable rights; that among these are life, liberty, and the pursuit of happiness."

IV
Of the Meaning of Progress

Willst Du Deine Macht verkünden,
Wähle sie die frei von Sünden,
Steh'n in Deinem ew'gen Haus!
Deine Geister sende aus!
Die Unsterblichen, die Reinen,
Die nicht fühlen, die nicht weinen!

Nicht die zarte Jungfrau wähle,
Nicht der Hirtin weiche Seele!*
 Friedrich von Schiller. (1759–1805) from *Die Jungfrau von Orleans*

Once upon a time I taught school in the hills of Tennessee, where the broad dark vale of the Mississippi begins to roll and crumple to greet the Alleghanies. I was a Fisk student then, and all Fisk men thought that Tennessee—beyond the Veil—was theirs alone, and in vacation time they sallied forth in lusty bands to meet the county school-commissioners. Young and happy, I too went, and I shall not soon forget that summer, seventeen years ago.

First, there was a Teachers' Institute at the county-seat; and there distinguished guests of the superintendent taught the teachers fractions and spelling and other mysteries,—white teachers in the morning, Negroes at night. A picnic now and then, and a supper, and the rough world was softened by laughter and song. I remember how—But I wander.

There came a day when all the teachers left the Institute and began the hunt for schools. I learn from hearsay (for my mother was mortally afraid of firearms) that the hunting of ducks and bears and men is wonderfully interesting, but I am sure that the man who has never hunted a country school has something to learn of the pleasures of the chase. I see now the white, hot roads lazily rise and fall and wind before me under the burning July sun; I feel the deep weariness of heart and limb as ten, eight, six miles stretch relentlessly ahead; I feel my heart sink heavily as I hear again and again, "Got a teacher? Yes." So I walked on and on—horses were too expensive—until I had wandered beyond railways, beyond stage lines, to a land of "varmints" and rattlesnakes, where the coming of a stranger was an event, and men lived and died in the shadow of one blue hill.

Sprinkled over hill and dale lay cabins and farmhouses, shut out from the world by the forests and the rolling hills toward the east. There I found at last a little school. Josie told me of it; she was a thin, homely girl of twenty, with a dark-brown face and thick, hard hair. I had crossed the stream at Watertown, and rested under the great willows; then I had gone to the little cabin in the lot where Josie was resting on her way to town. The gaunt farmer made me

*If you would proclaim your power choose the sinless within your Eternal house! The ones who are immortal and pure, who neither feel nor weep! Do not choose the tender virgin, nor the gentle soul's shepherdess.

welcome, and Josie, hearing my errand, told me anxiously that they wanted a school over the hill; that but once since the war had a teacher been there; that she herself longed to learn,—and thus she ran on, talking fast and loud, with much earnestness and energy.

Next morning I crossed the tall round hill, lingered to look at the blue and yellow mountains stretching toward the Carolinas, then plunged into the wood, and came out at Josie's home. It was a dull frame cottage with four rooms, perched just below the brow of the hill, amid peach-trees. The father was a quiet, simple soul, calmly ignorant, with no touch of vulgarity. The mother was different,—strong, bustling, and energetic, with a quick, restless tongue, and an ambition to live "like folks." There was a crowd of children. Two boys had gone away. There remained two growing girls; a shy midget of eight; John, tall, awkward, and eighteen; Jim, younger, quicker, and better looking; and two babies of indefinite age. Then there was Josie herself. She seemed to be the centre of the family: always busy at service, or at home, or berry-picking; a little nervous and inclined to scold, like her mother, yet faithful, too, like her father. She had about her a certain fineness, the shadow of an unconscious moral heroism that would willingly give all of life to make life broader, deeper, and fuller for her and hers. I saw much of this family afterwards, and grew to love them for their honest efforts to be decent and comfortable, and for their knowledge of their own ignorance. There was with them no affectation. The mother would scold the father for being so "easy"; Josie would roundly berate the boys for carelessness; and all knew that it was a hard thing to dig a living out of a rocky side-hill.

I secured the school. I remember the day I rode horseback out to the commissioner's house with a pleasant young white fellow who wanted the white school. The road ran down the bed of a stream; the sun laughed and the water jingled, and we rode on. "Come in," said the commissioner,— "come in. Have a seat. Yes, that certificate will do. Stay to dinner. What do you want a month?" "Oh," thought I, "this is lucky"; but even then fell the awful shadow of the Veil, for they ate first, then I—alone.

The schoolhouse was a log hut, where Colonel Wheeler used to shelter his corn. It sat in a lot behind a rail fence and thorn bushes, near the sweetest of springs. There was an entrance where a door once was, and within, a massive rickety fireplace; great chinks between the logs served as windows. Furniture was scarce. A pale blackboard crouched in the corner. My desk was made of three boards, reinforced at critical points, and my chair, borrowed from the landlady, had to be returned every night. Seats for the children—these puzzled me much. I was haunted by a New England vision of neat little desks and chairs, but, alas! the reality was rough plank benches without backs, and at times without legs. They had the one virtue of making naps dangerous,— possibly fatal, for the floor was not to be trusted.

It was a hot morning late in July when the school opened. I trembled when I heard the patter of little feet down the dusty road, and saw the growing row of dark solemn faces and bright eager eyes facing me. First came Josie and her brothers and sisters. The longing to know, to be a student in the great school at Nashville, hovered like a star above this child-woman amid her work and worry, and she studied doggedly. There were the Dowells from their farm over toward Alexandria,—Fanny, with her smooth black face and wondering eyes; Martha, brown and dull; the pretty girl-wife of a brother, and the younger brood.

There were the Burkes,—two brown and yellow lads, and a tiny haughty-eyed girl. Fat Reuben's little chubby girl came, with golden face and old-gold hair, faithful and solemn. 'Thenie was on hand early,—a jolly, ugly, good-hearted girl, who slyly dipped snuff and looked after her little bow-legged brother. When her mother could spare her, 'Tildy came,—a midnight beauty, with starry eyes and tapering limbs; and her brother, correspondingly homely. And then the big boys,—the hulking Lawrences; the lazy Neills, unfathered sons of mother and daughter; Hickman, with a stoop in his shoulders; and the rest.

There they sat, nearly thirty of them, on the rough benches, their faces shading from a pale cream to a deep brown, the little feet bare and swinging, the eyes full of expectation, with here and there a twinkle of mischief, and the hands grasping Webster's blue-black spelling-book. I loved my school, and the fine faith the children had in the wisdom of their teacher was truly marvellous. We read and spelled together, wrote a little, picked flowers, sang, and listened to stories of the world beyond the hill. At times the school would dwindle away, and I would start out. I would visit Mun Eddings, who lived in two very dirty rooms, and ask why little Lugene, whose flaming face seemed ever ablaze with the dark-red hair uncombed, was absent all last week, or why I missed so often the inimitable rags of Mack and Ed. Then the father, who worked Colonel Wheeler's farm on shares, would tell me how the crops needed the boys; and the thin, slovenly mother, whose face was pretty when washed, assured me that Lugene must mind the baby. "But we'll start them again next week." When the Lawrences stopped, I knew that the doubts of the old folks about book-learning had conquered again, and so, toiling up the hill, and getting as far into the cabin as possible, I put Cicero "pro Archia Poeta" into the simplest English with local applications, and usually convinced them—for a week or so.

On Friday nights I often went home with some of the children,—some-times to Doc Burke's farm. He was a great, loud, thin Black, ever working, and trying to buy the seventy-five acres of hill and dale where he lived; but people said that he would surely fail, and the "white folks would get it all." His wife was a magnificent Amazon, with saffron face and shining hair, uncorseted and barefooted, and the children were strong and beautiful. They lived in a one-and-a-half-room cabin in the hollow of the farm, near the spring. The front room was full of great fat white beds, scrupulously neat; and there were bad chromos on the walls, and a tired centre-table. In the tiny back kitchen I was often invited to "take out and help" myself to fried chicken and wheat biscuit, "meat" and corn pone, string-beans and berries. At first I used to be a little alarmed at the approach of bedtime in the one lone bedroom, but embarrassment was very deftly avoided. First, all the children nodded and slept, and were stowed away in one great pile of goose feathers; next, the mother and the father discreetly slipped away to the kitchen while I went to bed; then, blowing out the dim light, they retired in the dark. In the morning all were up and away before I thought of awaking. Across the road, where fat Reuben lived, they all went outdoors while the teacher retired, because they did not boast the luxury of a kitchen.

I liked to stay with the Dowells, for they had four rooms and plenty of good country fare. Uncle Bird had a small, rough farm, all woods and hills, miles from the big road; but he was full of tales,—he preached now and then,—and with his children, berries, horses, and wheat he was happy and prosperous. Often, to keep the peace, I must go where life was less lovely; for instance, 'Tildy's mother was incorrigibly dirty, Reuben's larder was limited seriously, and herds of untamed insects wandered over the Eddingses' beds. Best of all I loved to go to Josie's, and sit on the porch, eating peaches, while the mother bustled and talked: how Josie had bought the sewing-machine; how Josie worked at service in winter, but that four dollars a month was "mighty little" wages; how Josie longed to go away to school, but that it "looked like" they never could get far enough ahead to let her; how the crops failed and the well was yet unfinished; and, finally, how "mean" some of the white folks were.

For two summers I lived in this little world; it was dull and humdrum. The girls looked at the hill in wistful longing, and the boys fretted and haunted Alexandria. Alexandria was "town,"—a straggling, lazy village of houses, churches, and shops, and an aristocracy of Toms, Dicks, and Captains. Cuddled on the hill to the north was the village of the colored folks, who lived in three- or four-room unpainted cottages, some neat and homelike, and some dirty. The dwellings were scattered rather aimlessly, but they centred about the twin temples of the hamlet, the Methodist, and the Hard-Shell Baptist churches. These, in turn, leaned gingerly on a sad-colored schoolhouse. Hither my little world wended its crooked way on Sunday to meet other worlds, and gossip, and wonder, and make the weekly sacrifice with frenzied priest at the altar of the "old-time religion." Then the soft melody and mighty cadences of Negro song fluttered and thundered.

I have called my tiny community a world, and so its isolation made it; and yet there was among us but a half-awakened common consciousness, sprung from common joy and grief, at burial, birth, or wedding; from a common hardship in poverty, poor land, and low wages; and, above all, from the sight of the Veil that hung between us and Opportunity. All this caused us to think some thoughts together; but these, when ripe for speech, were spoken in various languages. Those whose eyes twenty-five and more years before had seen "the glory of the coming of the Lord," saw in every present hindrance or help a dark fatalism bound to bring all things right in His own good time. The mass of those to whom slavery was a dim recollection of childhood found the world a puzzling thing: it asked little of them, and they answered with little, and yet it ridiculed their offering. Such a paradox they could not understand, and therefore sank into listless indifference, or shiftlessness, or reckless bravado. There were, however, some—such as Josie, Jim, and Ben—to whom War, Hell, and Slavery were but childhood tales, whose young appetites had been whetted to an edge by school and story and half-awakened thought. Ill could they be content, born without and beyond the World. And their weak wings beat against their barriers,—barriers of caste, of youth, of life; at last, in dangerous moments, against everything that opposed even a whim.

The ten years that follow youth, the years when first the realization comes that life is leading somewhere,—these were the years that passed after I left my little school. When they were past, I came by chance once more to the walls of Fisk University, to the halls of the chapel of melody. As I lingered there in the joy and pain of meeting old school-friends, there swept over me a sudden longing to pass again beyond the blue hill, and to see the homes and the school of other days, and to learn how life had gone with my school-children; and I went.

Josie was dead, and the gray-haired mother said simply, "We've had a heap of trouble since you've been away." I had feared for Jim. With a cultured parentage and a social caste to uphold him, he might have made a venture-some merchant or a West Point cadet. But here he was, angry with life and reckless; and when Farmer Durham charged him with stealing wheat, the old man had to ride fast to escape the stones which the furious fool hurled after him. They told Jim to run away; but he would not run, and the constable came that afternoon. It grieved Josie, and great awkward John walked nine miles every day to see his little brother through the bars of Lebanon jail. At last the two came back together in the dark night. The mother cooked supper, and Josie emptied her purse, and the boys stole away. Josie grew thin and silent, yet worked the more. The hill became steep for the quiet old father, and with the boys away there was little to do in the valley. Josie helped them to sell the old farm, and they moved nearer town. Brother Dennis, the carpenter, built a new house with six rooms; Josie toiled a year in Nashville, and brought back ninety dollars to furnish the house and change it to a home.

When the spring came, and the birds twittered, and the stream ran proud and full, little sister Lizzie, bold and thoughtless, flushed with the passion of youth, bestowed herself on the tempter, and brought home a nameless child. Josie shivered and worked on, with the vision of schooldays all fled, with a face wan and tired,—worked until, on a summer's day, some one married another; then Josie crept to her mother like a hurt child, and slept—and sleeps.

I paused to scent the breeze as I entered the valley. The Lawrences have gone,—father and son forever,—and the other son lazily digs in the earth to live. A new young widow rents out their cabin to fat Reuben. Reuben is a Baptist preacher now, but I fear as lazy as ever, though his cabin has three rooms; and little Ella has grown into a bouncing woman, and is ploughing corn on the hot hillside. There are babies a-plenty, and one half-witted girl. Across the valley is a house I did not know before, and there I found, rocking one baby and expecting another, one of my schoolgirls, a daughter of Uncle Bird Dowell. She looked somewhat worried with her new duties, but soon bristled into pride over her neat cabin and the tale of her thrifty husband, and the horse and cow, and the farm they were planning to buy.

My log schoolhouse was gone. In its place stood Progress; and Progress, I understand, is necessarily ugly. The crazy foundation stones still marked the former site of my poor little cabin, and not far away, on six weary boulders, perched a jaunty board house, perhaps twenty by thirty feet, with three windows and a door that locked. Some of the window-glass was broken, and part of an old iron stove lay mournfully under the house. I peeped through the window half reverently, and found things that were more familiar. The blackboard had grown by about two feet, and the seats were still without backs. The county owns the lot now, I hear, and every year there is a session of school. As I sat by the spring and looked on the Old and the New I felt glad, very glad, and yet—

After two long drinks I started on. There was the great double log-house on the corner. I remembered the broken, blighted family that used to live there. The strong, hard face of the mother, with its wilderness of hair, rose before me. She had driven her husband away, and while I taught school a strange man lived there, big and jovial, and people talked. I felt sure that Ben and 'Tildy would come to naught from such a home. But this is an odd world; for Ben is a busy farmer in Smith County, "doing well, too," they say, and he had cared for little 'Tildy until last spring, when a lover married her. A hard life the lad had led, toiling for meat, and laughed at because he was homely and crooked. There was Sam Carlon, an impudent old skinflint, who had definite notions about "niggers," and hired Ben a summer and would not pay him. Then the hungry boy gathered his sacks together, and in broad daylight went into Carlon's corn; and when the hard-fisted farmer set upon him, the angry boy flew at him like a beast. Doc Burke saved a murder and a lynching that day.

The story reminded me again of the Burkes, and an impatience seized me to know who won in the battle, Doc or the seventy-five acres. For it is a hard thing to make a farm out of nothing, even in fifteen years. So I hurried on, thinking of the Burkes. They used to have a certain magnificent barbarism about them that I liked. They were never vulgar, never immoral, but rather rough and primitive, with an unconventionality that spent itself in loud guffaws, slaps on the back, and naps in the corner. I hurried by the cottage of the misborn Neill boys. It was empty, and they were grown into fat, lazy farm-hands. I saw the home of the Hickmans, but Albert, with his stooping shoulders, had passed from the world. Then I came to the Burkes' gate and peered through; the inclosure looked rough and untrimmed, and yet there were the same fences around the old farm save to the left, where lay twenty-five other acres. And lo! the cabin in the hollow had climbed the hill and swollen to a half-finished six-room cottage.

The Burkes held a hundred acres, but they were still in debt. Indeed, the gaunt father who toiled night and day would scarcely be happy out of debt, being so used to it. Some day he must stop, for his massive frame is showing decline. The mother wore shoes, but the lion-like physique of other days was broken. The children had grown up. Rob, the image of his father, was loud and rough with laughter. Birdie, my school baby of six, had grown to a picture of maiden beauty, tall and tawny. "Edgar is gone," said the mother, with head half bowed,—"gone to work in Nashville; he and his father couldn't agree."

Little Doc, the boy born since the time of my school, took me horseback down the creek next morning toward Farmer Dowell's. The road and the stream were battling for mastery, and the stream had the better of it. We splashed and waded, and the merry boy, perched behind me, chattered and laughed. He showed me where Simon Thompson had bought a bit of ground and a home; but his daughter Lana, a plump, brown, slow girl, was not there. She had married a man and a farm twenty miles away. We wound on down the stream till we came to a gate that I did not recognize, but the boy insisted that it was "Uncle Bird's." The farm was fat with the growing crop. In that little valley was a strange stillness as I rode up; for death and marriage had stolen youth and left age and childhood there. We sat and talked that night after the chores were done. Uncle Bird was grayer, and his eyes did not see so well, but he was still jovial. We talked of the acres bought,—one hundred and twenty-five,—of the new guest-chamber added, of Martha's marrying. Then we talked of death: Fanny and Fred were gone; a shadow hung over the other daughter, and when it lifted she was to go to Nashville to school. At last we spoke of the neighbors, and as night fell, Uncle Bird told me how, on a night like that, 'Thenie came wandering back to her home over yonder, to escape the blows of her husband. And next morning she died in the home that her little bow-legged brother, working and saving, had bought for their widowed mother.

My journey was done, and behind me lay hill and dale, and Life and Death. How shall man measure Progress there where the dark-faced Josie lies? How many heartfuls of sorrow shall balance a bushel of wheat? How hard a thing is life to the lowly, and yet how human and real! And all this life and love and strife and failure,—is it the twilight of nightfall or the flush of some faint-dawning day?

Thus sadly musing, I rode to Nashville in the Jim Crow car.

V

Of the Wings of Atalanta

> O black boy of Atlanta!
>   But half was spoken;
> The slave's chains and the master's
>   Alike are broken;
> The one curse of the races
>   Held both in tether;
> They are rising—all are rising—
>   The black and white together.
>
> John Greenleaf Whittier. (1807–92)

South of the North, yet north of the South, lies the City of a Hundred Hills, peering out from the shadows of the past into the promise of the future. I have seen her in the morning, when the first flush of day had half-roused her; she lay gray and still on the crimson soil of Georgia; then the blue smoke began to curl from her chimneys, the tinkle of bell and scream of whistle broke the silence, the rattle and roar of busy life slowly gathered and swelled, until the seething whirl of the city seemed a strange thing in a sleepy land.

Once, they say, even Atlanta slept dull and drowsy at the foot-hills of the Alleghanies, until the iron baptism of war awakened her with its sullen waters, aroused and maddened her, and left her listening to the sea. And the sea cried to the hills and the hills answered the sea, till the city rose like a widow and cast away her weeds, and toiled for her daily bread; toiled steadily, toiled cunningly,—perhaps with some bitterness, with a touch of *réclame*,— and yet with real earnestness, and real sweat.

It is a hard thing to live haunted by the ghost of an untrue dream; to see the wide vision of empire fade into real ashes and dirt; to feel the pang of the conquered, and yet know that with all the Bad that fell on one black day, something was vanquished that deserved to live, something killed that in justice had not dared to die; to know that with the Right that triumphed, triumphed something of Wrong, something sordid and mean, something less than the broadest and best. All this is bitter hard; and many a man and city and people have found in it excuse for sulking, and brooding, and listless waiting.

Such are not men of the sturdier make; they of Atlanta turned resolutely toward the future; and that future held aloft vistas of purple and gold:— Atlanta, Queen of the cotton kingdom; Atlanta, Gateway to the Land of the Sun; Atlanta, the new Lachesis, spinner of web and woof for the world. So the city crowned her hundred hills with factories, and stored her shops with cunning handiwork, and stretched long iron ways to greet the busy Mercury in his coming. And the Nation talked of her striving.

Perhaps Atlanta was not christened for the winged maiden of dull Bœotia; you know the tale,—how swarthy Atalanta, tall and wild, would marry only him who out-raced her; and how the wily Hippomenes laid three apples of gold in the way. She fled like a shadow, paused, startled over the first apple, but even as he stretched his hand, fled again; hovered over the second, then, slipping from his hot grasp, flew over river, vale, and hill; but as she lingered over the third, his arms fell round her, and looking on each other, the blazing passion of their love profaned the sanctuary of Love, and they were cursed. If Atlanta be not named for Atalanta, she ought to have been.

Atalanta is not the first or the last maiden whom greed of gold has led to defile the temple of Love; and not maids alone, but men in the race of life, sink from the high and generous ideals of youth to the gambler's code of the Bourse; and in all our Nation's striving is not the Gospel of Work befouled by the Gospel of Pay? So common is this that one-half think it normal; so unquestioned, that we almost fear to question if the end of racing is not gold, if the aim of man is not rightly to be rich. And if this is the fault of America, how dire a danger lies before a new land and a new city, lest Atlanta, stooping for mere gold, shall find that gold accursed!

It was no maiden's idle whim that started this hard racing; a fearful wilderness lay about the feet of that city after the War,—feudalism, poverty, the rise of the Third Estate, serfdom, the re-birth of Law and Order, and above and between all, the Veil of Race. How heavy a journey for weary feet! what wings must Atalanta have to flit over all this hollow and hill, through sour wood and sullen water, and by the red waste of sun-baked clay! How fleet must Atalanta be if she will not be tempted by gold to profane the Sanctuary!

The Sanctuary of our fathers has, to be sure, few Gods,—some sneer, "all too few." There is the thrifty Mercury of New England, Pluto of the North, and Ceres of the West; and there, too, is the half-forgotten Apollo of the South, under whose ægis the maiden ran,—and as she ran she forgot him, even as there in Bœotia Venus was forgot. She forgot the old ideal of the Southern gentleman,—that new-world heir of the grace and courtliness of patrician, knight, and noble; forgot his honor with his foibles, his kindliness with his carelessness, and stooped to apples of gold,—to men busier and sharper, thriftier and more unscrupulous. Golden apples are beautiful—I remember the lawless days of boyhood, when orchards in crimson and gold tempted me over fence and field—and, too, the merchant who has dethroned the planter is no despicable *parvenu*. Work and wealth are the mighty levers to lift this old new land; thrift and toil and saving are the highways to new hopes and new possibilities; and yet the warning is needed lest the wily Hippomenes tempt Atalanta to thinking that golden apples are the goal of racing, and not mere incidents by the way.

Atlanta must not lead the South to dream of material prosperity as the touchstone of all success; already the fatal might of this idea is beginning to spread; it is replacing the finer type of Southerner with vulgar money-getters; it is burying the sweeter beauties of Southern life beneath pretence and ostentation. For every social ill the panacea of Wealth has been urged,—wealth to overthrow the remains of the slave feudalism; wealth to raise the "cracker" Third Estate; wealth to employ the black serfs, and the prospect of wealth to keep them working; wealth as the end and aim of politics, and as the legal tender for law and order; and, finally, instead of Truth, Beauty, and Goodness, wealth as the ideal of the Public School.

Not only is this true in the world which Atlanta typifies, but it is threatening to be true of a world beneath and beyond that world,—the Black World beyond the Veil. Today it makes little difference to Atlanta, to the South, what the Negro thinks or dreams or wills. In the soul-life of the land he is to-day, and naturally will long remain, unthought of, half forgotten; and yet when he does come to think and will and do for himself,—and let no man dream that day will never come,—then the part he plays will not be one of sudden learning, but words and thoughts he has been taught to lisp in his race-childhood. To-day the ferment of his striving toward self-realization is to the strife of the white world like a wheel within a wheel: beyond the Veil are smaller but like problems of ideals, of leaders and the led, of serfdom, of poverty, of order and subordination, and, through all, the Veil of Race. Few know of these problems, few who know notice them; and yet there they are, awaiting student, artist, and seer,—a field for somebody sometime to discover. Hither has the temptation of Hippomenes penetrated; already in this smaller world, which now indirectly and anon directly must influence the larger for good or ill, the habit is forming of interpreting the world in dollars. The old leaders of Negro opinion, in the little groups where there is a Negro social consciousness, are being replaced by new; neither the black preacher nor the black teacher leads as he did two decades ago. Into their places are pushing the farmers and gardeners, the well-paid porters and

Greek marble statue of Atalanta in flight. "If Atlanta be not named for Atalanta, she ought to have been."

artisans, the business-men,—all those with property and money. And with all this change, so curiously parallel to that of the Other-world, goes too the same inevitable change in ideals. The South laments to-day the slow, steady disappearance of a certain type of Negro,—the faithful, courteous slave of other days, with his incorruptible honesty and dignified humility. He is passing away just as surely as the old type of Southern gentleman is passing, and from not dissimilar causes,—the sudden transformation of a fair far-off ideal of Freedom into the hard reality of bread-winning and the consequent deification of Bread.

In the Black World, the Preacher and Teacher embodied once the ideals of this people—the strife for another and a juster world, the vague dream of righteousness, the mystery of knowing; but to-day the danger is that these ideals, with their simple beauty and weird inspiration, will suddenly sink to a question of cash and a lust for gold. Here stands this black young Atalanta, girding herself for the race that must run; and if her eyes be still toward the hills and sky as in the days of old, then we may look for noble running; but what if some ruthless or wily or even thoughtless Hippomenes lay golden apples before her? What if the Negro people be wooed from a strife for righteousness, from a love of knowing, to regard dollars as the be-all and end-all of life? What if to the Mammonism of America be added the rising Mammonism of the re-born South, and the Mammonism of this South be reinforced by the budding Mammonism of its half-wakened black millions? Whither, then, is the new-world quest of Goodness and Beauty and Truth gone glimmering? Must this, and that fair flower of Freedom which, despite the jeers of latter-day striplings, sprung from our fathers' blood, must that too degenerate into a dusty quest of gold,—into lawless lust with Hippomenes?

The hundred hills of Atlanta are not all crowned with factories. On one, toward the west, the setting sun throws three buildings in bold relief against the sky. The beauty of the group lies in its simple unity:—a broad lawn of green rising from the red street and mingled roses and peaches; north and south, two plain and stately halls; and in the midst, half hidden in ivy, a larger building, boldly graceful, sparingly decorated, and with one low spire. It is a restful group,—one never looks for more; it is all here, all intelligible. There I live, and there I hear from day to day the low hum of restful life. In winter's twilight, when the red sun glows, I can see the dark figures pass between the halls to the music of the night-bell. In the morning, when the sun is golden, the clang of the day-bell brings the hurry and laughter of three hundred young hearts from hall and street, and from the busy city below,— children all dark and heavy-haired,—to join their clear young voices in the music of the morning sacrifice. In a half-dozen class-rooms they gather then,—here to follow the love-song of Dido, here to listen to the tale of Troy divine; there to wander among the stars, there to wander among men and nations,—and elsewhere other well-worn ways of knowing this queer world. Nothing new, no time-saving devices,—simply old time-glorified methods of delving for Truth, and searching out the hidden beauties of life, and learning the good of living. The riddle of existence is the college curriculum that was laid before the Pharaohs, that was taught in the groves by Plato, that formed the *trivium* and *quadrivium,* and is to-day laid before the freedmen's sons by Atlanta University. And this course of study will not change; its methods will grow more deft and effectual, its content richer by toil of scholar and sight of seer; but the true college will ever have one goal,—not to earn meat, but to know the end and aim of that life which meat nourishes.

The vision of life that rises before these dark eyes has in it nothing mean or selfish. Not at Oxford or at Leipsic, not at Yale or Columbia, is there an air of higher resolve or more unfettered striving; the determination to realize for men, both black and white, the broadest possibilities of life, to seek the better and the best, to spread with their own hands the Gospel of Sacrifice,—all this is the burden of their talk and dream. Here, amid a wide desert of caste and proscription, amid the heart-hurting slights and jars and vagaries of a deep race-dislike, lies this green oasis, where hot anger cools, and the bitterness of disappointment is sweetened by the springs and breezes of Parnassus; and here men may lie and listen, and learn of a future fuller than the past, and hear the voice of Time:

"Entbehren sollst du, sollst entbehren."*

They made their mistakes, those who planted Fisk and Howard and Atlanta before the smoke of battle had lifted; they made their mistakes, but those mistakes were not the things at which we lately laughed somewhat uproariously. They were right when they sought to found a new educational system upon the University: where, forsooth, shall we ground knowledge save on the broadest and deepest knowledge? The roots of the tree, rather than the leaves, are the sources of its life; and from the dawn of history, from Academus to Cambridge, the culture of the University has been the broad foundation-stone on which is built the kindergarten's A B C.

But these builders did make a mistake in minimizing the gravity of the problem before them; in thinking it a matter of years and decades; in there-fore building quickly and laying their foundation carelessly, and lowering the standard of knowing, until they had scattered haphazard through the South some dozen poorly equipped high schools and miscalled them universities. They forgot, too, just as their successors are forgetting, the rule of inequal-ity:—that of the million black youth, some were fitted to know and some to dig; that some had the talent and capacity of university men, and some the talent and capacity of blacksmiths; and that true training meant neither that all should be college men nor all artisans, but that the one should be made a missionary of culture to an untaught people, and the other a free work-man among serfs. And to seek to make the blacksmith a scholar is almost as silly as the more modern scheme of making the scholar a blacksmith; almost, but not quite.

---

*"Deny yourself, you must deny yourself." Johann Wolfgang von Goethe from *Faust I Studierzimmer.*

The remains of Atlanta's Georgia Railroad roadhouse after the Civil War.

The function of the university is not simply to teach bread-winning, or to furnish teachers for the public schools or to be a centre of polite society; it is, above all, to be the organ of that fine adjustment between real life and the growing knowledge of life, an adjustment which forms the secret of civilization. Such an institution the South of to-day sorely needs. She has religion, earnest, bigoted:—religion that on both sides the Veil often omits the sixth, seventh, and eighth commandments, but substitutes a dozen supplementary ones. She has, as Atlanta shows, growing thrift and love of toil; but she lacks that broad knowledge of what the world knows and knew of human living and doing, which she may apply to the thousand problems of real life to-day confronting her. The need of the South is knowledge and culture,—not in dainty limited quantity, as before the war, but in broad busy abundance in the world of work; and until she has this, not all the Apples of Hesperides, be they golden and bejewelled, can save her from the curse of the Bœotian lovers.

The Wings of Atalanta are the coming universities of the South. They alone can bear the maiden past the temptation of golden fruit. They will not guide her flying feet away from the cotton and gold; for—ah, thoughtful Hippomenes!—do not the apples lie in the very Way of Life? But they will guide her over and beyond them, and leave her kneeling in the Sanctuary of Truth and Freedom and broad Humanity, virgin and undefiled. Sadly did the Old South err in human education, despising the education of the masses, and niggardly in the support of colleges. Her ancient university foundations dwindled and withered under the foul breath of slavery; and even since the war they have fought a failing fight for life in the tainted air of social unrest and commercial selfishness, stunted by the death of criticism, and starving for lack of broadly cultured men. And if this is the white South's need and danger, how much heavier the danger and need of the freedmen's sons! how pressing here the need of broad ideals and true culture, the conservation of soul from sordid aims and petty passions! Let us build the Southern university—William and Mary, Trinity, Georgia, Texas, Tulane, Vanderbilt, and the others—fit to live; let us build, too, the Negro universities:—Fisk, whose foundation was ever broad; Howard, at the heart of the Nation; Atlanta at Atlanta, whose ideal of scholarship has been held above the temptation of numbers. Why not here, and perhaps elsewhere, plant deeply and for all time centres of learning and living, colleges that yearly would send into the life of the South a few white men and a few black men of broad culture, catholic tolerance, and trained ability, joining their hands to other hands, and giving to this squabble of the Races a decent and dignified peace?

Patience, Humility, Manners, and Taste, common schools and kindergartens, industrial and technical schools, literature and tolerance,—all these spring from knowledge and culture, the children of the university. So must men and nations build, not otherwise, not upside down.

Teach workers to work,—a wise saying; wise when applied to German boys and American girls; wiser when said of Negro boys, for they have less knowledge of working and none to teach them. Teach thinkers to think,—a needed knowledge in a day of loose and careless logic; and they whose lot is gravest must have the carefulest training to think aright. If these things are so, how foolish to ask what is the best education for one or seven or sixty million souls! shall we teach them trades, or train them in liberal arts? Neither and both: teach the workers to work and the thinkers to think; make carpenters of carpenters, and philosophers of philosophers, and fops of fools. Nor can we pause here. We are training not isolated men but a living group of men,—nay, a group within a group. And the final product of our training must be neither a psychologist nor a brickmason, but a man. And to make men, we must have ideals, broad, pure, and inspiring ends of living,— not sordid money-getting, not apples of gold. The worker must work for the glory of his handiwork, not simply for pay; the thinker must think for truth, not for fame. And all this is gained only by human strife and longing; by ceaseless training and education; by founding Right on righteousness and Truth on the unhampered search for Truth; by founding the common school on the university, and the industrial school on the common school; and weaving thus a system, not a distortion, and bringing a birth, not an abortion.

When night falls on the City of a Hundred Hills, a wind gathers itself from the seas and comes murmuring westward. And at its bidding, the smoke of the drowsy factories sweeps down upon the mighty city and covers it like a pall, while yonder at the University the stars twinkle above Stone Hall. And they say that yon gray mist is the tunic of Atalanta pausing over her golden apples. Fly, my maiden, fly, for yonder comes Hippomenes!

VI
Of the Training of Black Men

Why, if the Soul can fling the Dust aside,
And naked on the Air of Heaven ride,
   Were't not a Shame—were't not a Shame for him
In this clay carcase crippled to abide?

Omar Khayyām (1048–1131) from
The Rubāiyāt of Omar Khayyām of Naishāpūr

From the shimmering swirl of waters where many, many thoughts ago the slave-ship first saw the square tower of Jamestown, have flowed down to our day three streams of thinking: one swollen from the larger world here and overseas, saying, the multiplying of human wants in culture-lands calls for the world-wide cooperation of men in satisfying them. Hence arises a new human unity, pulling the ends of earth nearer, and all men, black, yellow, and white. The larger humanity strives to feel in this contact of living Nations and sleeping hordes a thrill of new life in the world, crying, "If the contact of Life and Sleep be Death, shame on such Life." To be sure, behind this thought lurks the afterthought of force and dominion,—the making of brown men to delve when the temptation of beads and red calico cloys.

The second thought streaming from the death-ship and the curving river is the thought of the older South,—the sincere and passionate belief that somewhere between men and cattle, God created a *tertium quid,* and called it a Negro,—a clownish, simple creature, at times even lovable within its limitations, but straitly foreordained to walk within the Veil. To be sure, behind the thought lurks the afterthought,—some of them with favoring chance might become men, but in sheer self-defence we dare not let them, and we build about them walls so high, and hang between them and the light a veil so thick, that they shall not even think of breaking through.

And last of all there trickles down that third and darker thought,—the thought of the things themselves, the confused, half-conscious mutter of men who are black and whitened, crying "Liberty, Freedom, Opportunity— vouchsafe to us, O boastful World, the chance of living men!" To be sure, behind the thought lurks the afterthought,—suppose, after all, the World is right and we are less than men? Suppose this mad impulse within is all wrong, some mock mirage from the untrue?

So here we stand among thoughts of human unity, even through conquest and slavery; the inferiority of black men, even if forced by fraud; a shriek in the night for the freedom of men who themselves are not yet sure of their right to demand it. This is the tangle of thought and afterthought wherein we are called to solve the problem of training men for life.

Behind all its curiousness, so attractive alike to sage and *dilettante,* lie its dim dangers, throwing across us shadows at once grotesque and awful. Plain it is to us that what the world seeks through desert and wild we have within our threshold,—a stalwart laboring force, suited to the semi-tropics; if, deaf to the voice of the Zeitgeist, we refuse to use and develop these men, we risk poverty and loss. If, on the other hand, seized by the brutal afterthought, we debauch the race thus caught in our talons, selfishly sucking their blood and brains in the future as in the past, what shall save us from national decadence? Only that saner selfishness, which Education teaches, can find the rights of all in the whirl of work.

Again, we may decry the color-prejudice of the South, yet it remains a heavy fact. Such curious kinks of the human mind exist and must be reckoned with soberly. They cannot be laughed away, nor always successfully stormed at, nor easily abolished by act of legislature. And yet they must not be encouraged by being let alone. They must be recognized as facts, but unpleasant facts; things that stand in the way of civilization and religion and common decency. They can be met in but one way,—by the breadth and broadening of human reason, by catholicity of taste and culture. And so, too, the native ambition and aspiration of men, even though they be black, backward, and ungraceful, must not lightly be dealt with. To stimulate wildly weak and untrained minds is to play with mighty fires; to flout their striving idly is to welcome a harvest of brutish crime and shameless lethargy in our very laps. The guiding of thought and the deft coordination of deed is at once the path of honor and humanity.

And so, in this great question of reconciling three vast and partially contradictory streams of thought, the one panacea of Education leaps to the lips of all:—such human training as will best use the labor of all men without enslaving or brutalizing; such training as will give us poise to encourage the prejudices that bulwark society, and to stamp out those that in sheer barbarity deafen us to the wail of prisoned souls within the Veil, and the mounting fury of shackled men.

But when we have vaguely said that Education will set this tangle straight, what have we uttered but a truism? Training for life teaches living; but what training for the profitable living together of black men and white? A hundred and fifty years ago our task would have seemed easier. Then Dr. Johnson blandly assured us that education was needful solely for the embellishments of life, and was useless for ordinary vermin. To-day we have climbed to heights where we would open at least the outer courts of knowledge to all, display its treasures to many, and select the few to whom its mystery of Truth is revealed, not wholly by birth or the accidents of the stock market, but at least in part according to deftness and aim, talent and character. This programme, however, we are sorely puzzled in carrying out through that part of the land where the blight of slavery fell hardest, and where we are dealing with two backward peoples. To make here in human education that ever necessary combination of the permanent and the contingent—of the ideal and the practical in workable equilibrium—has been there, as it ever must be in every age and place, a matter of infinite experiment and frequent mistakes.

In rough approximation we may point out four varying decades of work in Southern education since the Civil War. From the close of the war until 1876, was the period of uncertain groping and temporary relief. There were army schools, mission schools, and schools of the Freedmen's Bureau in chaotic disarrangement seeking system and cooperation. Then followed ten years of constructive definite effort toward the building of complete school systems in the South. Normal schools and colleges were founded for the freedmen, and teachers trained there to man the public schools. There was the inevitable tendency of war to underestimate the prejudices of the master and the ignorance of the slave, and all seemed clear sailing out of the wreckage of the storm. Meantime, starting in this decade yet especially developing from 1885 to 1895, began the industrial revolution of the South. The land saw glimpses of a new destiny and the stirring of new ideals. The educational system striving to complete itself saw new obstacles and a field of work ever broader and deeper. The Negro colleges, hurriedly founded, were inadequately equipped, illogically distributed, and of varying efficiency and grade; the normal and high schools were doing little more than common-school work, and the common schools were training but a third of the children who ought to be in them, and training these too often poorly. At the same time the white South, by reason of its sudden conversion from the slavery ideal, by so much the more became set and strengthened in its racial prejudice, and crystallized it into harsh law and harsher custom; while the marvellous pushing forward of the poor white daily threatened to take even bread and butter from the mouths of the heavily handicapped sons of the freedmen. In the midst, then, of the larger problem of Negro education sprang up the more practical question of work, the inevitable economic quandary that faces a people in the transition from slavery to freedom, and especially those who make that change amid hate and prejudice, lawlessness and ruthless competition.

The industrial school springing to notice in this decade, but coming to full recognition in the decade beginning with 1895, was the proffered answer to this combined educational and economic crisis, and an answer of singular wisdom and timeliness. From the very first in nearly all the schools some attention had been given to training in handiwork, but now was this training first raised to a dignity that brought it in direct touch with the South's magnificent industrial development, and given an emphasis which reminded black folk that before the Temple of Knowledge swing the Gates of Toil.

Yet after all they are but gates, and when turning our eyes from the temporary and the contingent in the Negro problem to the broader question of the permanent uplifting and civilization of black men in America, we have a right to inquire, as this enthusiasm for material advancement mounts to its height, if after all the industrial school is the final and sufficient answer in the training of the Negro race; and to ask gently, but in all sincerity, the ever-recurring query of the ages, Is not life more than meat, and the body more than raiment? And men ask this to-day all the more eagerly because of sinister signs in recent educational movements. The tendency is here, born of slavery and quickened to renewed life by the crazy imperialism of the day, to regard human beings as among the material resources of a land to be trained with an eye single to future dividends. Race-prejudices, which keep brown and black men in their "places," we are coming to regard as useful allies with such a theory, no matter how much they may dull the ambition and sicken the hearts of struggling human beings. And above all, we daily hear that an education that encourages aspiration, that sets the loftiest of ideals and seeks as an end culture and character rather than bread-winning, is the privilege of white men and the danger and delusion of black.

Especially has criticism been directed against the former educational efforts to aid the Negro. In the four periods I have mentioned, we find first, boundless, planless enthusiasm and sacrifice; then the preparation of teachers for a vast public-school system; then the launching and expansion of that school system amid increasing difficulties; and finally the training of workmen for the new and growing industries. This development has been sharply ridiculed as a logical anomaly and flat reversal of nature. Soothly we have been told that first industrial and manual training should have taught the Negro to work, then simple schools should have taught him to read and write, and finally, after years, high and normal schools could have completed the system, as intelligence and wealth demanded.

That a system logically so complete was historically impossible, it needs but a little thought to prove. Progress in human affairs is more often a pull than a push, a surging forward of the exceptional man, and the lifting of his duller brethren slowly and painfully to his vantage-ground. Thus it was no accident that gave birth to universities centuries before the common schools, that made fair Harvard the first flower of our wilderness. So in the South: the mass of the freedmen at the end of the war lacked the intelligence so necessary to modern workingmen. They must first have the common school to teach them to read, write, and cipher; and they must have higher schools to teach teachers for the common schools. The white teachers who flocked South went to establish such a common-school system. Few held the idea of founding colleges; most of them at first would have laughed at the idea. But they faced, as all men since them have faced, that central paradox of the South,—the social separation of the races. At that time it was the sudden volcanic rupture of nearly all relations between black and white, in work and government and family life. Since then a new adjustment of relations in economic and political affairs has grown up,—an adjustment subtle and difficult to grasp, yet singularly ingenious, which leaves still that frightful chasm at the color-line across which men pass at their peril. Thus, then and now, there stand in the South two separate worlds; and separate not simply in the higher realms of social intercourse, but also in church and school, on railway and street-car, in hotels and theatres, in streets and city sections, in books and newspapers, in asylums and jails, in hospitals and graveyards. There is still enough of contact for large economic and group cooperation, but the separation is so thorough and deep that it absolutely precludes for the present between the races anything like that sympathetic and effective group-training and leadership of the one by the other, such as the American Negro and all backward peoples must have for effectual progress.

This the missionaries of '68 soon saw; and if effective industrial and trade schools were impracticable before the establishment of a common-school system, just as certainly no adequate common schools could be founded until there were teachers to teach them. Southern whites would not teach them; Northern whites in sufficient numbers could not be had. If the Negro was to learn, he must teach himself, and the most effective help that could be given him was the establishment of schools to train Negro teachers. This conclusion was slowly but surely reached by every student of the situation until simultaneously, in widely separated regions, without consultation or systematic plan, there arose a series of institutions designed to furnish teachers for the untaught. Above the sneers of critics at the obvious defects of this procedure must ever stand its one crushing rejoinder: in a single generation they put thirty thousand black teachers in the South; they wiped out the illiteracy of the majority of the black people of the land, and they made Tuskegee possible.

Such higher training-schools tended naturally to deepen broader development: at first they were common and grammar schools, then some became high schools. And finally, by 1900, some thirty-four had one year or more of studies of college grade. This development was reached with different degrees of speed in different institutions: Hampton is still a high school, while Fisk University started her college in 1871, and Spelman Seminary about 1896. In all cases the aim was identical,—to maintain the standards of the lower training by giving teachers and leaders the best practicable training; and above all, to furnish the black world with adequate standards of human culture and lofty ideals of life. It was not enough that the teachers of teachers should be trained in technical normal methods; they must also, so far as possible, be broad-minded, cultured men and women, to scatter civilization among a people whose ignorance was not simply of letters, but of life itself.

It can thus be seen that the work of education in the South began with higher institutions of training, which threw off as their foliage common schools, and later industrial schools, and at the same time strove to shoot their roots ever deeper toward college and university training. That this was an inevitable and necessary development, sooner or later, goes without saying; but there has been, and still is, a question in many minds if the natural growth was not forced, and if the higher training was not either overdone or done with cheap and unsound methods. Among white Southerners this feeling is widespread and positive. A prominent Southern journal voiced this in a recent editorial.

"The experiment that has been made to give the colored students classical training has not been satisfactory. Even though many were able to pursue the course, most of them did so in a parrot-like way, learning what was taught, but not seeming to appropriate the truth and import of their instruction, and graduating without sensible aim or valuable occupation for their future. The whole scheme has proved a waste of time, efforts, and the money of the state."

While most fair-minded men would recognize this as extreme and overdrawn, still without doubt many are asking, Are there a sufficient number of Negroes ready for college training to warrant the undertaking? Are not too many students prematurely forced into this work? Does it not have the effect of dissatisfying the young Negro with his environment? And do these graduates succeed in real life? Such natural questions cannot be evaded, nor on the other hand must a Nation naturally skeptical as to Negro ability assume an unfavorable answer without careful inquiry and patient openness to conviction. We must not forget that most Americans answer all queries regarding the Negro *a priori,* and that the least that human courtesy can do is to listen to evidence.

The advocates of the higher education of the Negro would be the last to deny the incompleteness and glaring defects of the present system: too many institutions have attempted to do college work, the work in some cases has not been thoroughly done, and quantity rather than quality has sometimes been sought. But all this can be said of higher education throughout the land; it is the almost inevitable incident of educational growth, and leaves the deeper question of the legitimate demand for the higher training of Negroes untouched. And this latter question can be settled in but one way,—by a first-hand study of the facts. If we leave out of view all institutions which have not actually graduated students from a course higher than that of a New England high school, even though they be called colleges; if then we take the thirty-four remaining institutions, we may clear up many misapprehensions by asking searchingly, What kind of institutions are they? what do they teach? and what sort of men do they graduate?

And first we may say that this type of college, including Atlanta, Fisk, and Howard, Wilberforce and Claflin, Shaw, and the rest, is peculiar, almost unique. Through the shining trees that whisper before me as I write, I catch glimpses of a boulder of New England granite, covering a grave, which graduates of Atlanta University have placed there,—

"GRATEFUL MEMORY OF THEIR FORMER TEACHER
AND FRIEND AND OF THE UNSELFISH LIFE HE LIVED,
AND THE NOBLE WORK HE WROUGHT; THAT THEY,
THEIR CHILDREN, AND THEIR CHILDREN'S CHILDREN
MIGHT BE BLESSED."

This was the gift of New England to the freed Negro: not alms, but a friend; not cash, but character. It was not and is not money these seething millions want, but love and sympathy, the pulse of hearts beating with red blood;—a gift which to-day only their own kindred and race can bring to the masses, but which once saintly souls brought to their favored children in the crusade of the sixties, that finest thing in American history, and one of the few things untainted by sordid greed and cheap vainglory. The teachers in these institutions came not to keep the Negroes in their place, but to raise them out of the defilement of the places where slavery had wallowed them. The colleges they founded were social settlements; homes where the best of the sons of the freedmen came in close and sympathetic touch with the best traditions of New England. They lived and ate together, studied and worked, hoped and harkened in the dawning light. In actual formal content their curriculum was doubtless old-fashioned, but in educational power it was supreme, for it was the contact of living souls.

From such schools about two thousand Negroes have gone forth with the bachelor's degree. The number in itself is enough to put at rest the argument that too large a proportion of Negroes are receiving higher training. If the ratio to population of all Negro students throughout the land, in both college and secondary training, be counted, Commissioner Harris assures us "it must be increased to five times its present average" to equal the average of the land.

Fifty years ago the ability of Negro students in any appreciable numbers to master a modern college course would have been difficult to prove. To-day it is proved by the fact that four hundred Negroes, many of whom have been reported as brilliant students, have received the bachelor's degree from Harvard, Yale, Oberlin, and seventy other leading colleges. Here we have, then, nearly twenty-five hundred Negro graduates, of whom the crucial query must be made, How far did their training fit them for life? It is of course extremely difficult to collect satisfactory data on such a point,—difficult to reach the men, to get trustworthy testimony, and to gauge that testimony by any generally acceptable criterion of success. In 1900, the Conference at Atlanta University undertook to study these graduates, and published the results. First they sought to know what these graduates were doing, and succeeded in getting answers from nearly two-thirds of the living. The direct testimony was in almost all cases corroborated by the reports of the colleges where they graduated, so that in the main the reports were worthy of credence. Fifty-three per cent of these graduates were teachers,—presidents of institutions, heads of normal schools, principals of city school-systems, and the like. Seventeen per cent were clergymen; another seventeen per cent were in the professions, chiefly as physicians. Over six per cent were merchants, farmers, and artisans, and four per cent were in the government civil-service. Granting even that a considerable proportion of the third unheard from are unsuccessful, this is a record of usefulness. Personally I know many hundreds of these graduates, and have corresponded with more than a thousand; through others I have followed carefully the life-work of scores; I have taught some of them and some of the pupils whom they have taught, lived in homes which they have builded, and looked at life through their eyes. Comparing them as a class with my fellow students in New England and in Europe, I cannot hesitate in saying that nowhere have I met men and women with a broader spirit of helpfulness, with deeper devotion to their life-work, or with more consecrated determination to succeed in the face of bitter difficulties than among Negro college-bred men. They have, to be sure, their proportion of ne'er-do-wells, their pedants and lettered fools, but they have a surprisingly small proportion of them; they have not that culture of manner which we instinctively associate with university men, forgetting that in reality it is the heritage from cultured homes, and that no people a generation removed from slavery can escape a certain unpleasant rawness and *gaucherie,* despite the best of training.

With all their larger vision and deeper sensibility, these men have usually been conservative, careful leaders. They have seldom been agitators, have withstood the temptation to head the mob, and have worked steadily and faithfully in a thousand communities in the South. As teachers, they have given the South a commendable system of city schools and large numbers of private normal-schools and academies. Colored college-bred men have worked side by side with white college graduates at Hampton; almost from the beginning the backbone of Tuskegee's teaching force has been formed of graduates from Fisk and Atlanta. And to-day the institute is filled with college graduates, from the energetic wife of the principal down to the teacher of agriculture, including nearly half of the executive council and a majority of the heads of departments. In the professions, college men are slowly but surely leavening the Negro church, are healing and preventing the devastations of disease, and beginning to furnish legal protection for the liberty and property of the toiling masses. All this is needful work. Who would do it if Negroes did not? How could Negroes do it if they were not trained carefully for it? If white people need colleges to furnish teachers, ministers, lawyers, and doctors, do black people need nothing of the sort?

If it is true that there are an appreciable number of Negro youth in the land capable by character and talent to receive that higher training, the end of which is culture, and if the two and a half thousand who have had something of this training in the past have in the main proved themselves useful to their race and generation, the question then comes, What place in the future development of the South ought the Negro college and college-bred man to occupy? That the present social separation and acute race-sensitiveness must eventually yield to the influences of culture, as the South grows civilized, is clear. But such transformation calls for singular wisdom and patience. If, while the healing of this vast sore is progressing, the races are to live for many years side by side, united in economic effort, obeying a common government, sensitive to mutual thought and feeling, yet subtly and silently separate in many matters of deeper human intimacy,—if this unusual and dangerous development is to progress amid peace and order, mutual respect and growing intelligence, it will call for social surgery at once the delicatest and nicest in modern history. It will demand broad-minded, upright men, both white and black, and in its final accomplishment American civilization will triumph. So far as white men are concerned, this fact is to-day being recognized in the South, and a happy renaissance of university education seems imminent. But the very voices that cry hail to this good work are, strange to relate, largely silent or antagonistic to the higher education of the Negro.

Strange to relate! for this is certain, no secure civilization can be built in the South with the Negro as an ignorant, turbulent proletariat. Suppose we seek to remedy this by making them laborers and nothing more: they are not fools, they have tasted of the Tree of Life, and they will not cease to think, will not cease attempting to read the riddle of the world. By taking away their best equipped teachers and leaders, by slamming the door of opportunity in the faces of their bolder and brighter minds, will you make them satisfied with their lot? or will you not rather transfer their leading from the hands of men taught to think to the hands of untrained demagogues? We ought not to forget that despite the pressure of poverty, and despite the active discouragement and even ridicule of friends, the demand for higher training steadily increases among Negro youth: there were, in the years from 1875 to 1880, 22 Negro graduates from Northern colleges; from 1885 to 1890 there were 43, and from 1895 to 1900, nearly 100 graduates. From Southern Negro colleges there were, in the same three periods, 143, 413, and over 500 graduates. Here, then, is the plain thirst for training; by refusing to give this Talented Tenth the key to knowledge, can any sane man imagine that they will lightly lay aside their yearning and contentedly become hewers of wood and drawers of water?

No. The dangerously clear logic of the Negro's position will more and more loudly assert itself in that day when increasing wealth and more intricate social organization preclude the South from being, as it so largely is, simply an armed camp for intimidating black folk. Such waste of energy cannot be spared if the South is to catch up with civilization. And as the black third of the land grows in thrift and skill, unless skillfully guided in its larger philosophy, it must more and more brood over the red past and the creeping, crooked present, until it grasps a gospel of revolt and revenge and throws its new-found energies athwart the current of advance. Even to-day the masses of the Negroes see all too clearly the anomalies of their position and the moral crookedness of yours. You may marshal strong indictments against them, but their counter-cries, lacking though they be in formal logic, have burning truths within them which you may not wholly ignore, O Southern Gentlemen! If you deplore their presence here, they ask, Who brought us? When you cry, Deliver us from the vision of intermarriage, they answer that legal marriage is infinitely better than systematic concubinage and prostitution. And if in just fury you accuse their vagabonds of violating women, they also in fury quite as just may reply: The rape which your gentlemen have done against helpless black women in defiance of your own laws is written on the foreheads of two millions of mulattoes, and written in ineffaceable blood. And finally, when you fasten crime upon this race as its peculiar trait, they answer that slavery was the arch-crime, and lynching and lawlessness its twin abortions; that color and race are not crimes, and yet it is they which in this land receive most unceasing condemnation, North, East, South, and West.

I will not say such arguments are wholly justified,—I will not insist that there is no other side to the shield; but I do say that of the nine millions of Negroes in this nation, there is scarcely one out of the cradle to whom these arguments do not daily present themselves in the guise of terrible truth. I insist that the question of the future is how best to keep these millions from brooding over the wrongs of the past and the difficulties of the present, so that all their energies may be bent toward a cheerful striving and cooperation with their white neighbors toward a larger, juster, and fuller future. That one wise method of doing this lies in the closer knitting of the Negro to the great industrial possibilities of the South is a great truth. And this the common schools and the manual training and trade schools are working to accomplish. But these alone are not enough. The foundations of knowledge in this race, as in others, must be sunk deep in the college and university if we would build a solid, permanent structure. Internal problems of social advance must inevitably come,—problems of work and wages, of families and homes, of morals and the true valuing of the things of life; and all these and other inevitable problems of civilization the Negro must meet and solve largely for himself, by reason of his isolation; and can there be any possible solution other than by study and thought and an appeal to the rich experience of the past? Is there not, with such a group and in such a crisis, infinitely more danger to be apprehended from half-trained minds and shallow thinking than from over-education and over-refinement? Surely we have wit enough to found a Negro college so manned and equipped as to steer successfully between the *dilettante* and the fool. We shall hardly induce black men to believe that if their stomachs be full, it matters little about their brains. They already dimly perceive that the paths of peace winding between honest toil and dignified manhood call for the guidance of skilled thinkers, the loving, reverent comradeship between the black lowly and the black men emancipated by training and culture.

The function of the Negro college, then, is clear: it must maintain the standards of popular education, it must seek the social regeneration of the Negro, and it must help in the solution of problems of race contact and cooperation. And finally, beyond all this, it must develop men. Above our modern socialism, and out of the worship of the mass, must persist and evolve that higher individualism which the centres of culture protect; there must come a loftier respect for the sovereign human soul that seeks to know itself and the world about it; that seeks a freedom for expansion and self-development; that will love and hate and labor in its own way, untrammeled alike by old and new. Such souls aforetime have inspired and guided worlds, and if we be not wholly bewitched by our Rhinegold, they shall again. Herein the longing of black men must have respect: the rich and bitter depth of their experience, the unknown treasures of their inner life, the strange rendings of nature they have seen, may give the world new points of view and make their loving, living, and doing precious to all human hearts. And to themselves in these the days that try their souls, the chance to soar in the dim blue air above the smoke is to their finer spirits boon and guerdon for what they lose on earth by being black.

I sit with Shakespeare and he winces not. Across the color line I move arm in arm with Balzac and Dumas, where smiling men and welcoming women glide in gilded halls. From out the caves of evening that swing between the strong-limbed earth and the tracery of the stars, I summon Aristotle and Aurelius and what soul I will, and they come all graciously with no scorn nor condescension. So, wed with Truth, I dwell above the Veil. Is this the life you grudge us, O knightly America? Is this the life you long to change into the dull red hideousness of Georgia? Are you so afraid lest peering from this high Pisgah, between Philistine and Amalekite, we sight the Promised Land?

VII

Of the Black Belt

I am black but comely, O ye daughters of Jerusalem,
As the tents of Kedar, as the curtains of Solomon.
Look not upon me, because I am black,
Because the sun hath looked upon me:
My mother's children were angry with me;
They made me the keeper of the vineyards;
But mine own vineyard have I not kept.

The Song of Solomon.

Out of the North the train thundered, and we woke to see the crimson soil of Georgia stretching away bare and monotonous right and left. Here and there lay straggling, unlovely villages, and lean men loafed leisurely at the depots; then again came the stretch of pines and clay. Yet we did not nod, nor weary of the scene; for this is historic ground. Right across our track, three hundred and sixty years ago, wandered the cavalcade of Hernando de Soto, looking for gold and the Great Sea; and he and his foot-sore captives disappeared yonder in the grim forests to the west. Here sits Atlanta, the city of a hundred hills, with something Western, something Southern, and something quite its own, in its busy life. Just this side of Atlanta is the land of the Cherokees and to the southwest, not far from where Sam Hose was crucified, you may stand on a spot which is to-day the centre of the Negro problem,—the centre of those nine million men who are America's dark heritage from slavery and the slave-trade.

Not only is Georgia thus the geographical focus of our Negro population, but in many other respects, both now and yesterday, the Negro problems have seemed to be centered in this state. No other State in the Union can count a million Negroes among its citizens,—a population as large as the slave population of the whole Union in 1800; no other State fought so long and strenuously to gather this host of Africans. Oglethorpe thought slavery against law and gospel; but the circumstances which gave Georgia its first inhabitants were not calculated to furnish citizens over-nice in their ideas about rum and slaves. Despite the prohibitions of the trustees, these Georgians, like some of their descendants, proceeded to take the law into their own hands; and so pliant were the judges, and so flagrant the smuggling, and so earnest were the prayers of Whitefield, that by the middle of the eighteenth century all restrictions were swept away, and the slave-trade went merrily on for fifty years and more.

Down in Darien, where the Delegal riots took place some summers ago, there used to come a strong protest against slavery from the Scotch Highlanders; and the Moravians of Ebenezer did not like the system. But not till the Haytian Terror of Toussaint was the trade in men even checked; while the national statute of 1808 did not suffice to stop it. How the Africans poured in!—fifty thousand between 1790 and 1810, and then, from Virginia and from smugglers, two thousand a year for many years more. So the thirty thousand Negroes of Georgia in 1790 doubled in a decade,—were over a hundred thousand in 1810, had reached two hundred thousand in 1820, and half a million at the time of the war. Thus like a snake the black population writhed upward.

But we must hasten on our journey. This that we pass as we near Atlanta is the ancient land of the Cherokees,—that brave Indian nation which strove so long for its fatherland, until Fate and the United States Government drove them beyond the Mississippi. If you wish to ride with me you must come into the "Jim Crow Car." There will be no objection,—already four other white men, and a little white girl with her nurse, are in there. Usually the races are mixed in there; but the white coach is all white. Of course this car is not so good as the other, but it is fairly clean and comfortable. The discomfort lies chiefly in the hearts of those four black men yonder—and in mine.

We rumble south in quite a business-like way. The bare red clay and pines of Northern Georgia begin to disappear, and in their place appears a rich rolling land, luxuriant, and here and there well tilled. This is the land of the Creek Indians; and a hard time the Georgians had to seize it. The towns grow more frequent and more interesting, and brand-new cotton mills rise on every side. Below Macon the world grows darker; for now we approach the Black Belt,—that strange land of shadows, at which even slaves paled in the past, and whence come now only faint and half-intelligible murmurs to the world beyond. The "Jim Crow Car" grows larger and a shade better; three rough field-hands and two or three white loafers accompany us, and the newsboy still spreads his wares at one end. The sun is setting, but we can see the great cotton country as we enter it,—the soil now dark and fertile, now thin and gray, with fruit-trees and dilapidated buildings,—all the way to Albany.

At Albany, in the heart of the Black Belt, we stop. Two hundred miles south of Atlanta, two hundred miles west of the Atlantic, and one hundred miles north of the Great Gulf lies Dougherty County, with ten thousand Negroes and two thousand whites. The Flint River winds down from Andersonville, and, turning suddenly at Albany, the county-seat, hurries on to join the Chattahoochee and the sea. Andrew Jackson knew the Flint well, and marched across it once to avenge the Indian Massacre at Fort Mims. That was in 1814, not long before the battle of New Orleans; and by the Creek treaty that followed this campaign, all Dougherty County, and much other rich land, was ceded to Georgia. Still, settlers fought shy of this land, for the Indians were all about, and they were unpleasant neighbors in those days. The panic of 1837, which Jackson bequeathed to Van Buren, turned the planters from the impoverished lands of Virginia, the Carolinas, and east Georgia, toward the West. The Indians were removed to Indian Territory, and settlers poured into these coveted lands to retrieve their broken fortunes. For a radius of a hundred miles about Albany, stretched a great fertile land, luxuriant with forests of pine, oak, ash, hickory, and poplar; hot with the sun and damp with the rich black swamp-land; and here the corner-stone of the Cotton Kingdom was laid.

Albany is to-day a wide-streeted, placid, Southern town, with a broad sweep of stores and saloons, and flanking rows of homes,—whites usually to the north, and blacks to the south. Six days in the week the town looks decidedly too small for itself, and takes frequent and prolonged naps. But upon Saturday suddenly the whole county disgorges itself upon the place, and a perfect flood of black peasantry pours through the streets, fills the stores, blocks the sidewalks, chokes the thoroughfares, and takes full possession of the town. They are black, sturdy, uncouth country folk, good-natured and simple, talkative to a degree, and yet far more silent and brooding than the crowds of the Rhine-pfalz, or Naples, or Cracow. They drink considerable quantities of whiskey, but do not get very drunk; they talk and laugh loudly at times, but seldom quarrel or fight. They walk up and down the streets, meet and gossip with friends, stare at the shop windows, buy coffee, cheap candy, and clothes, and at dusk drive home—happy? well no, not exactly happy, but much happier than as though they had not come.

Thus Albany is a real capital,—a typical Southern county town, the centre of the life of ten thousand souls; their point of contact with the outer world, their centre of news and gossip, their market for buying and selling, borrowing and lending, their fountain of justice and law. Once upon a time we knew country life so well and city life so little, that we illustrated city life as that of a closely crowded country district. Now the world has well-nigh forgotten what the country is, and we must imagine a little city of black people scattered far and wide over three hundred lonesome square miles of land, without train or trolley, in the midst of cotton and corn, and wide patches of sand and gloomy soil.

It gets pretty hot in Southern Georgia in July,—a sort of dull, determined heat that seems quite independent of the sun; so it took us some days to muster courage enough to leave the porch and venture out on the long country roads, that we might see this unknown world. Finally we started. It was about ten in the morning, bright with a faint breeze, and we jogged leisurely southward in the valley of the Flint. We passed the scattered box-like cabins of the brickyard hands, and the long tenement-row facetiously called "The Ark," and were soon in the open country, and on the confines of the great plantations of other days. There is the "Joe Fields place"; a rough old fellow was he, and had killed many a "nigger" in his day. Twelve miles his plantation used to run,—a regular barony. It is nearly all gone now; only straggling bits belong to the family, and the rest has passed to Jews and Negroes. Even the bits which are left are heavily mortgaged, and, like the rest of the land, tilled by tenants. Here is one of them now,—a tall brown man, a hard worker and a hard drinker, illiterate, but versed in farmlore, as his nodding crops declare. This distressingly new board house is his, and he has just moved out of yonder moss-grown cabin with its one square room.

From the curtains in Benton's house, down the road, a dark comely face is staring at the strangers; for passing carriages are not every-day occurrences here. Benton is an intelligent yellow man with a good-sized family, and manages a plantation blasted by the war and now the broken staff of the widow.

He might be well-to-do, they say; but he carouses too much in Albany. And the half-desolate spirit of neglect born of the very soil seems to have settled on these acres. In times past there were cotton-gins and machinery here; but they have rotted away.

The whole land seems forlorn and forsaken. Here are the remnants of the vast plantations of the Sheldons, the Pellots, and the Rensons; but the souls of them are passed. The houses lie in half ruin, or have wholly disappeared; the fences have flown, and the families are wandering in the world. Strange vicissitudes have met these whilom masters. Yonder stretch the wide acres of Bildad Reasor; he died in war-time, but the upstart overseer hastened to wed the widow. Then he went, and his neighbors too, and now only the

Slaves on a South Carolina plantation in 1862 prepare cotton for processing in a cotton gin.

black tenant remains; but the shadow-hand of the master's grand-nephew or cousin or creditor stretches out of the gray distance to collect the rack-rent remorselessly, and so the land is uncared-for and poor. Only black tenants can stand such a system, and they only because they must. Ten miles we have ridden to-day and have seen no white face.

A resistless feeling of depression falls slowly upon us, despite the gaudy sunshine and the green cottonfields. This, then, is the Cotton Kingdom,— the shadow of a marvellous dream. And where is the King? Perhaps this is he,—the sweating ploughman, tilling his eighty acres with two lean mules, and fighting a hard battle with debt. So we sit musing, until, as we turn a corner on the sandy road, there comes a fairer scene suddenly in view,—a neat cottage snugly ensconced by the road, and near it a little store. A tall bronzed man rises from the porch as we hail him, and comes out to our carriage. He is six feet in height, with a sober face that smiles gravely. He walks too straight to be a tenant,—yes, he owns two hundred and forty acres. "The land is run down since the boom-days of eighteen hundred and fifty," he explains, and cotton is low. Three black tenants live on his place, and in his little store he keeps a small stock of tobacco, snuff, soap, and soda, for the neighborhood. Here is his gin-house with new machinery just installed. Three hundred bales of cotton went through it last year. Two children he has sent away to school. Yes, he says sadly, he is getting on, but cotton is down to four cents; I know how Debt sits staring at him.

Wherever the King may be, the parks and palaces of the Cotton Kingdom have not wholly disappeared. We plunge even now into great groves of oak and towering pine, with an undergrowth of myrtle and shrubbery. This was the "home-house" of the Thompsons,—slave-barons who drove their coach and four in the merry past. All is silence now, and ashes, and tangled weeds. The owner put his whole fortune into the rising cotton industry of the fifties, and with the falling prices of the eighties he packed up and stole away. Yonder is another grove, with unkempt lawn, great magnolias, and grass-grown paths. The Big House stands in half-ruin, its great front door staring blankly at the street, and the back part grotesquely restored for its black tenant. A shabby, well-built Negro he is, unlucky and irresolute. He digs hard to pay rent to the white girl who owns the remnant of the place. She married a policeman, and lives in Savannah.

Now and again we come to churches. Here is one now,—Shepherds, they call it,—a great whitewashed barn of a thing, perched on stilts of stone, and looking for all the world as though it were just resting here a moment and might be expected to waddle off down the road at almost any time. And yet it is the centre of a hundred cabin homes; and sometimes, of a Sunday, five hundred persons from far and near gather here and talk and eat and sing. There is a schoolhouse near,—a very airy, empty shed; but even this is an improvement, for usually the school is held in the church. The churches vary from log-huts to those like Shepherd's, and the schools from nothing to this little house that sits demurely on the county line. It is a tiny plank-house, perhaps ten by twenty, and has within a double row of rough unplaned benches, resting mostly on legs, sometimes on boxes. Opposite the door is a square home-made desk. In one corner are the ruins of a stove, and in the other a dim blackboard. It is the cheerfulest schoolhouse I have seen in Dougherty, save in town. Back of the schoolhouse is a lodgehouse two stories high and not quite finished. Societies meet there,—societies "to care for the sick and bury the dead"; and these societies grow and flourish.

We had come to the boundaries of Dougherty, and were about to turn west along the county-line, when all these sights were pointed out to us by a kindly old man, black, white-haired, and seventy. Forty-five years he had lived here, and now supports himself and his old wife by the help of the steer tethered yonder and the charity of his black neighbors. He shows us the farm of the Hills just across the county line in Baker,—a widow and two strapping sons, who raised ten bales (one need not add "cotton" down here) last year. There are fences and pigs and cows, and the soft-voiced, velvet-skinned young Memnon, who sauntered half-bashfully over to greet the strangers, is proud of his home. We turn now to the west along the county line. Great dismantled trunks of pines tower above the green cottonfields, cracking their naked gnarled fingers toward the border of living forest beyond. There is little beauty in this region, only a sort of crude abandon that suggests power,—a naked grandeur, as it were. The houses are bare and straight; there are no hammocks or easy-chairs, and few flowers. So when, as here at Rawdon's, one sees a vine clinging to a little porch, and home-like windows peeping over the fences, one takes a long breath. I think I never before quite realized the place of the Fence in civilization. This is the Land of the Unfenced, where crouch on either hand scores of ugly one-room cabins, cheerless and dirty. Here lies the Negro problem in its naked dirt and penury. And here are no fences. But now and then the criss-cross rails or straight palings break into view, and then we know a touch of culture is near. Of course Harrison Gohagen,—a quiet yellow man, young, smooth-faced, and diligent,—of course he is lord of some hundred acres, and we expect to see a vision of well-kept rooms and fat beds and laughing children. For has he not fine fences? And those over yonder, why should they build fences on the rack-rented land? It will only increase their rent.

On we wind, through sand and pines and glimpses of old plantations, till there creeps into sight a cluster of buildings,—wood and brick, mills and houses, and scattered cabins. It seemed quite a village. As it came nearer and nearer, however, the aspect changed: the buildings were rotten, the bricks were falling out, the mills were silent, and the store was closed. Only in the cabins appeared now and then a bit of lazy life. I could imagine the place under some weird spell, and was half-minded to search out the princess. An old ragged black man, honest, simple, and improvident, told us the tale. The Wizard of the North—the Capitalist—had rushed down in the seventies to woo this coy dark soil. He bought a square mile or more, and for a time the field-hands sang, the gins groaned, and the mills buzzed. Then came a change. The agent's son embezzled the funds and ran off with them. Then the agent himself disappeared. Finally the new agent stole even the books, and the company in wrath closed its business and its houses, refused to sell, and let houses and furniture and machinery rust and rot. So the Waters-

Loring plantation was stilled by the spell of dishonesty, and stands like some gaunt rebuke to a scarred land.

Somehow that plantation ended our day's journey; for I could not shake off the influence of that silent scene. Back toward town we glided, past the straight and thread-like pines, past a dark tree-dotted pond where the air was heavy with a dead sweet perfume. White slender-legged curlews flitted by us, and the garnet blooms of the cotton looked gay against the green and purple stalks. A peasant girl was hoeing in the field, white-turbaned and black-limbed. All this we saw, but the spell still lay upon us.

How curious a land is this,—how full of untold story, of tragedy and laughter, and the rich legacy of human life; shadowed with a tragic past, and big with future promise! This is the Black Belt of Georgia. Dougherty County is the west end of the Black Belt, and men once called it the Egypt of the Confederacy. It is full of historic interest. First there is the Swamp, to the west, where the Chickasawhatchee flows sullenly southward. The shadow of an old plantation lies at its edge, forlorn and dark. Then comes the pool; pendent gray moss and brackish waters appear, and forest filled with wildfowl. In one place the wood is on fire, smouldering in dull red anger; but nobody minds. Then the swamp grows beautiful; a raised road, built by chained Negro convicts, dips down into it, and forms a way walled and almost covered in living green. Spreading trees spring from a prodigal luxuriance of undergrowth; great dark green shadows fade into the black background, until all is one mass of tangled semi-tropical foliage, marvellous in its weird savage splendor. Once we crossed a black silent stream, where the sad trees and writhing creepers, all glinting fiery yellow and green, seemed like some vast cathedral,—some green Milan builded of wildwood. And as I crossed, I seemed to see again that fierce tragedy of seventy years ago. Osceola, the Indian-Negro chieftain, had risen in the swamps of Florida, vowing vengeance. His war-cry reached the red Creeks of Dougherty, and their war-cry rang from the Chattahoochee to the sea. Men and women and children fled and fell before them as they swept into Dougherty. In yonder shadows a dark and hideously painted warrior glided stealthily on,—another and another, until three hundred had crept into the treacherous swamp. Then the false slime closing about them called the white men from the east. Waist-deep, they fought beneath the tall trees, until the war-cry was hushed and the Indians glided back into the west. Small wonder the wood is red.

Then came the black slaves. Day after day the clank of chained feet marching from Virginia and Carolina to Georgia was heard in these rich swamp lands. Day after day the songs of the callous, the wail of the motherless, and the muttered curses of the wretched echoed from the Flint to the Chickasawhatchee, until by 1860 there had risen in West Dougherty perhaps the richest slave kingdom the modern world ever knew. A hundred and fifty barons commanded the labor of nearly six thousand Negroes, held sway over farms with ninety thousand acres tilled land, valued even in times of cheap soil at three millions of dollars. Twenty thousand bales of ginned cotton went yearly to England, New and Old; and men that came there bankrupt made money and grew rich. In a single decade the cotton output increased fourfold and the value of lands was tripled. It was the heyday of the *nouveau riche,* and a life of careless extravagance among the masters. Four and six bobtailed thoroughbreds rolled their coaches to town; open hospitality and gay entertainment were the rule. Parks and groves were laid out, rich with flower and vine, and in the midst stood the low wide-halled "big house," with its porch and columns and great fireplaces.

And yet with all this there was something sordid, something forced,—a certain feverish unrest and recklessness; for was not all this show and tinsel built upon a groan? "This land was a little Hell," said a ragged, brown, and grave-faced man to me. We were seated near a roadside blacksmith shop, and behind was the bare ruin of some master's home. "I've seen niggers drop dead in the furrow, but they were kicked aside, and the plough never stopped. Down in the guard-house, there's where the blood ran."

With such foundations a kingdom must in time sway and fall. The masters moved to Macon and Augusta, and left only the irresponsible overseers on the land. And the result is such ruin as this, the Lloyd "home-place":— great waving oaks, a spread of lawn, myrtles and chestnuts, all ragged and wild; a solitary gate-post standing where once was a castle entrance; an old rusty anvil lying amid rotting bellows and wood in the ruins of a blacksmith shop; a wide rambling old mansion, brown and dingy, filled now with the grandchildren of the slaves who once waited on its tables; while the family of the master has dwindled to two lone women, who live in Macon and feed hungrily off the remnants of an earldom. So we ride on, past phantom gates and falling homes,—past the once flourishing farms of the Smiths, the Gandys, and the Lagores,—and find all dilapidated and half ruined, even there where a solitary white woman, a relic of other days, sits alone in state among miles of Negroes and rides to town in her ancient coach each day.

This was indeed the Egypt of the Confederacy,—the rich granary whence potatoes and corn and cotton poured out to the famished and ragged Confederate troops as they battled for a cause lost long before 1861. Sheltered and secure, it became the place of refuge for families, wealth, and slaves. Yet even then the hard ruthless rape of the land began to tell. The red-clay sub-soil already had begun to peer above the loam. The harder the slaves were driven the more careless and fatal was their farming. Then came the revolution of war and Emancipation, the bewilderment of Reconstruction,— and now, what is the Egypt of the Confederacy, and what meaning has it for the nation's weal or woe?

It is a land of rapid contrasts and of curiously mingled hope and pain. Here sits a pretty blue-eyed quadroon hiding her bare feet; she was married only last week, and yonder in the field is her dark young husband, hoeing to support her, at thirty cents a day without board. Across the way is Gatesby, brown and tall, lord of two thousand acres shrewdly won and held. There is a store conducted by his black son, a blacksmith shop, and a ginnery. Five miles below here is a town owned and controlled by one white New Englander. He owns almost a Rhode Island county, with thousands of acres and hundreds of black laborers. Their cabins look better than most, and the farm, with machinery and fertilizers, is much more business-like than any in the county, although the manager drives hard bargains in wages. When now we turn and look five miles above, there on the edge of town are five houses of prostitutes,—two of blacks and three of whites; and in one of the houses of the whites a worthless black boy was harbored too openly two years ago; so he was hanged for rape. And here, too, is the high whitewashed fence of the "stockade," as the county prison is called; the white folks say it is ever full of black criminals,—the black folks say that only colored boys are sent to jail, and they not because they are guilty, but because the State needs criminals to eke out its income by their forced labor.

Immigrants are heirs of the slave baron in Dougherty; and as we ride westward, by wide stretching cornfields and stubby orchards of peach and pear, we see on all sides within the circle of dark forest a Land of Canaan. Here and there are tales of projects for money-getting, born in the swift days of Reconstruction,—"improvement" companies, wine companies, mills and factories; most failed, and foreigners fell heir. It is a beautiful land, this Dougherty, west of the Flint. The forests are wonderful, the solemn pines have disappeared, and this is the "Oakey Woods," with its wealth of hickories, beeches, oaks and palmettos. But a pall of debt hangs over the beautiful land; the merchants are in debt to the wholesalers, the planters are in debt to the merchants, the tenants owe the planters, and laborers bow and bend beneath the burden of it all. Here and there a man has raised his head above these murky waters. We passed one fenced stock-farm with grass and grazing cattle, that looked very home-like after endless corn and cotton. Here and there are black free-holders; there is the gaunt dull-black Jackson, with his hundred acres. "I says, 'Look up! If you don't look up you can't get up,'" remarks Jackson, philosophically. And he's gotten up. Dark Carter's neat barns would do credit to New England. His master helped him to get a start, but when the black man died last fall the master's sons immediately laid claim to the estate. "And them white folks will get it, too," said my yellow gossip.

I turn from these well-tended acres with a comfortable feeling that the Negro is rising. Even then, however, the fields, as we proceed, begin to redden and the trees disappear. Rows of old cabins appear filled with renters and laborers,—cheerless, bare, and dirty, for the most part, although here and there the very age and decay makes the scene picturesque. A young black fellow greets us. He is twenty-two, and just married. Until last year he had good luck renting; then cotton fell, and the sheriff seized and sold all he had. So he moved here, where the rent is higher, the land poorer, and the owner inflexible; he rents a forty-dollar mule for twenty dollars a year. Poor lad!— a slave at twenty-two. This plantation, owned now by a foreigner, was a part of the famous Bolton estate. After the war it was for many years worked by gangs of Negro convicts,—and black convicts then were even more plentiful than now; it was a way of making Negroes work, and the question of guilt was a minor one. Hard tales of cruelty and mistreatment of the chained freemen are told, but the county authorities were deaf until the free-labor market was nearly ruined by wholesale migration. Then they took the convicts from the plantations, but not until one of the fairest regions of the "Oakey Woods" had been ruined and ravished into a red waste, out of which only a Yankee or an immigrant could squeeze more blood from debt-cursed tenants.

No wonder that Luke Black, slow, dull, and discouraged, shuffles to our carriage and talks hopelessly. Why should he strive? Every year finds him deeper in debt. How strange that Georgia, the world-heralded refuge of poor debtors, should bind her own to sloth and misfortune as ruthlessly as ever England did! The poor land groans with its birth-pains, and brings forth scarcely a hundred pounds of cotton to the acre, where fifty years ago it yielded eight times as much. Of his meagre yield the tenant pays from a quarter to a third in rent, and most of the rest in interest on food and supplies bought on credit. Twenty years yonder sunken-cheeked, old black man has labored under that system, and now, turned day-laborer, is supporting his wife and boarding himself on his wages of a dollar and a half a week, received only part of the year.

The Bolton convict farm formerly included the neighboring plantation. Here it was that the convicts were lodged in the great log prison still standing. A dismal place it still remains, with rows of ugly huts filled with surly ignorant tenants. "What rent do you pay here?" I inquired. "I don't know,—what is it, Sam?" "All we make," answered Sam. It is a depressing place,—bare, unshaded, with no charm of past association, only a memory of forced human toil,—now, then, and before the war. They are not happy, these black men whom we meet throughout this region. There is little of the joyous abandon and playfulness which we are wont to associate with the plantation Negro. At best, the natural good-nature is edged with complaint or has changed into sullenness and gloom. And now and then it blazes forth in veiled but hot anger. I remember one big red-eyed black whom we met by the roadside. Forty-five years he had labored on this farm, beginning with nothing, and still having nothing. To be sure, he had given four children a common-school training, and perhaps if the new fence-law had not allowed unfenced crops in West Dougherty he might have raised a little stock and kept ahead. As it is, he is hopelessly in debt, disappointed, and embittered. He stopped us to inquire after the black boy in Albany, whom it was said a policeman had shot and killed for loud talking on the sidewalk. And then he said slowly: "Let a white man touch me, and he dies; I don't boast this,— I don't say it around loud, or before the children,—but I mean it. I've seen them whip my father and my old mother in them cotton-rows till the blood ran; by—" and we passed on.

Now Sears, whom we met next lolling under the chubby oak-trees, was of quite different fibre. Happy?—Well, yes; he laughed and flipped pebbles, and thought the world was as it was. He had worked here twelve years and has nothing but a mortgaged mule. Children? Yes, seven; but they hadn't been to school this year,—couldn't afford books and clothes, and couldn't spare their work. There go part of them to the fields now,—three big boys astride mules, and a strapping girl with bare brown legs. Careless ignorance and laziness here, fierce hate and vindictiveness there;—these are the extremes of the Negro problem which we met that day, and we scarce knew which we preferred.

Here and there we meet distinct characters quite out of the ordinary. One came out of a piece of newly cleared ground, making a wide detour to avoid the snakes. He was an old, hollow-cheeked man, with a drawn and character-ful brown face. He had a sort of self-contained quaintness and rough humor impossible to describe; a certain cynical earnestness that puzzled one. "The niggers were jealous of me over on the other place," he said, "and so me and the old woman begged this piece of woods, and I cleared it up myself. Made nothing for two years, but I reckon I've got a crop now." The cotton looked tall and rich, and we praised it. He curtsied low, and then bowed almost to the ground, with an imperturbable gravity that seemed almost suspicious. Then he continued, "My mule died last week,"—a calamity in this land equal to a devastating fire in town,—"but a white man loaned me another." Then he added, eyeing us, "Oh, I gets along with white folks." We turned the conversation. "Bears? deer?" he answered, "well, I should say there were," and he let fly a string of brave oaths, as he told hunting-tales of the swamp. We left him standing still in the middle of the road looking after us, and yet apparently not noticing us.

The Whistle place, which includes his bit of land, was bought soon after the war by an English syndicate, the "Dixie Cotton and Corn Company." A marvellous deal of style their factor put on, with his servants and coach-and-six; so much so that the concern soon landed in inextricable bankruptcy. Nobody lives in the old house now, but a man comes each winter out of the North and collects his high rents. I know not which are the more touching,— such old empty houses, or the homes of the masters' sons. Sad and bitter tales lie hidden back of those white doors,—tales of poverty, of struggle, of disappointment. A revolution such as that of '63 is a terrible thing; they that rose rich in the morning often slept in paupers' beds. Beggars and vulgar speculators rose to rule over them, and their children went astray. See yonder sad-colored house, with its cabins and fences and glad crops! It is not glad within; last month the prodigal son of the struggling father wrote home from the city for money. Money! Where was it to come from? And so the son rose in the night and killed his baby, and killed his wife, and shot himself dead. And the world passed on.

I remember wheeling around a bend in the road beside a graceful bit of forest and a singing brook. A long low house faced us, with porch and flying pillars, great oaken door, and a broad lawn shining in the evening sun. But the window-panes were gone, the pillars were worm-eaten, and the moss-grown roof was falling in. Half curiously I peered through the unhinged door, and saw where, on the wall across the hall, was written in once gay letters a faded "Welcome."

Quite a contrast to the southwestern part of Dougherty County is the northwest. Soberly timbered in oak and pine, it has none of that half-tropical luxuriance of the southwest. Then, too, there are fewer signs of a romantic past, and more of systematic modern land-grabbing and money-getting. White people are more in evidence here, and farmer and hired labor replace to some extent the absentee landlord and rack-rented tenant. The crops have neither the luxuriance of the richer land nor the signs of neglect so often seen, and there were fences and meadows here and there. Most of this land was poor, and beneath the notice of the slave-baron, before the war. Since then his poor relations and foreign immigrants have seized it. The returns of the farmer are too small to allow much for wages, and yet he will not sell off small farms. There is the Negro Sanford; he has worked fourteen years as overseer on the Ladson place, and "paid out enough for fertilizers to have bought a farm," but the owner will not sell off a few acres.

Two children—a boy and a girl—are hoeing sturdily in the fields on the farm where Corliss works. He is smooth-faced and brown, and is fencing up his pigs. He used to run a successful cotton-gin, but the Cotton Seed Oil Trust has forced the price of ginning so low that he says it hardly pays him. He points out a stately old house over the way as the home of "Pa Willis." We eagerly ride over, for "Pa Willis" was the tall and powerful black Moses who led the Negroes for a generation, and led them well. He was a Baptist preacher, and when he died, two thousand black people followed him to the grave; and now they preach his funeral sermon each year. His widow lives here,—a weazened, sharp-featured little woman, who curtsied quaintly as we greeted her. Further on lives Jack Delson, the most prosperous Negro farmer in the county. It is a joy to meet him,—a great broad-shouldered, handsome black man, intelligent and jovial. Six hundred and fifty acres he owns, and has eleven black tenants. A neat and tidy home nestled in a flower-garden, and a little store stands beside it.

We pass the Munson place, where a plucky white widow is renting and struggling; and the eleven hundred acres of the Sennet plantation, with its Negro overseer. Then the character of the farms begins to change. Nearly all the lands belong to Russian Jews; the overseers are white, and the cabins are bare board-houses scattered here and there. The rents are high, and day-laborers and "contract" hands abound. It is a keen, hard struggle for living here, and few have time to talk. Tired with the long ride, we gladly drive into Gillonsville. It is a silent cluster of farmhouses standing on the crossroads, with one of its stores closed and the other kept by a Negro preacher. They tell great tales of busy times at Gillonsville before all the railroads came to Albany; now it is chiefly a memory. Riding down the street, we stop at the preacher's and seat ourselves before the door. It was one of those scenes one cannot soon forget:—a wide, low, little house, whose motherly roof reached over and sheltered a snug little porch. There we sat, after the long hot drive, drinking cool water,—the talkative little storekeeper who is my daily companion; the silent old black woman patching pantaloons and saying never a word; the ragged picture of helpless misfortune who called in just to see the preacher; and finally the neat matronly preacher's wife, plump, yellow, and intelligent. "Own land?" said the wife; "well, only this house." Then she added quietly, "We did buy seven hundred acres across up yonder, and paid for it; but they cheated us out of it. Sells was the owner." "Sells!" echoed the ragged misfortune, who was leaning against the balustrade and listening, "he's a regular cheat. I worked for him thirty-seven days this spring, and he paid me in cardboard checks which were to be cashed at the end of the month. But he never cashed them,—kept putting me off. Then the sheriff came and took my mule and corn and furniture—" "Furniture? But furniture is exempt from seizure by law." "Well, he took it just the same," said the hard-faced man.

VIII
Of the Quest of the Golden Fleece

But the Brute said in his breast, "Till the mills I grind have ceased,
The riches shall be dust of dust, dry ashes be the feast!

    "On the strong and cunning few
    Cynic favors I will strew;
I will stuff their maw with overplus until their spirit dies;
    From the patient and the low
    I will take the joys they know;
    They shall hunger after vanities and still an-hungered go.
Madness shall be on the people, ghastly jealousies arise;
Brother's blood shall cry on brother up the dead and empty skies."
William Vaughn Moody. (1869–1910)

Have you ever seen a cotton-field white with harvest,—its golden fleece hovering above the black earth like a silvery cloud edged with dark green, its bold white signals waving like the foam of billows from Carolina to Texas across that Black and human Sea? I have sometimes half suspected that here the winged ram Chrysomallus left that Fleece after which Jason and his Argonauts went vaguely wandering into the shadowy East three thousand years ago; and certainly one might frame a pretty and not far-fetched analogy of witchery and dragons' teeth, and blood and armed men, between the ancient and the modern quest of the Golden Fleece in the Black Sea.

And now the golden fleece is found; not only found, but, in its birthplace, woven. For the hum of the cotton-mills is the newest and most significant thing in the New South to-day. All through the Carolinas and Georgia, away down to Mexico, rise these gaunt red buildings, bare and homely, and yet so busy and noisy withal that they scarce seem to belong to the slow and sleepy land. Perhaps they sprang from dragons' teeth. So the Cotton Kingdom still lives; the world still bows beneath her sceptre. Even the markets that once defied the *parvenu* have crept one by one across the seas, and then slowly and reluctantly, but surely, have started toward the Black Belt.

To be sure, there are those who wag their heads knowingly and tell us that the capital of the Cotton Kingdom has moved from the Black to the White Belt,—that the Negro of to-day raises not more than half of the cotton crop. Such men forget that the cotton crop has doubled, and more than doubled, since the era of slavery, and that, even granting their contention, the Negro is still supreme in a Cotton Kingdom larger than that on which the Confederacy builded its hopes. So the Negro forms to-day one of the chief figures in a great world-industry; and this, for its own sake, and in the light of historic interest, makes the field-hands of the cotton country worth studying.

We seldom study the condition of the Negro to-day honestly and carefully. It is so much easier to assume that we know it all. Or perhaps, having already reached conclusions in our own minds, we are loth to have them disturbed by facts. And yet how little we really know of these millions,—of their daily lives and longings, of their homely joys and sorrows, of their real shortcomings and the meaning of their crimes! All this we can only learn by intimate contact with the masses, and not by wholesale arguments covering millions separate in time and space, and differing widely in training and culture. To-day, then, my reader, let us turn our faces to the Black Belt of Georgia and seek simply to know the condition of the black farm-laborers of one county there.

Here in 1890 lived ten thousand Negroes and two thousand whites. The country is rich, yet the people are poor. The keynote of the Black Belt is debt; not commercial credit, but debt in the sense of continued inability on the part of the mass of the population to make income cover expense. This is the direct heritage of the South from the wasteful economies of the slave *régime;* but it was emphasized and brought to a crisis by the Emancipation of the slaves. In 1860, Dougherty County had six thousand slaves, worth at least two and a half millions of dollars; its farms were estimated at three millions,—making five and a half millions of property, the value of which depended largely on the slave system, and on the speculative demand for land once marvellously rich but already partially devitalized by careless and exhaustive culture. The war then meant a financial crash; in place of the five and a half millions of 1860, there remained in 1870 only farms valued at less than two millions. With this came increased competition in cotton culture from the rich lands of Texas; a steady fall in the normal price of cotton followed, from about fourteen cents a pound in 1860 until it reached four cents in 1898. Such a financial revolution was it that involved the owners of the cotton-belt in debt. And if things went ill with the master, how fared it with the man?

The plantations of Dougherty County in slavery days were not as imposing and aristocratic as those of Virginia. The Big House was smaller and usually one-storied, and sat very near the slave cabins. Sometimes these cabins stretched off on either side like wings; sometimes only on one side, forming a double row, or edging the road that turned into the plantation from the main thoroughfare. The form and disposition of the laborers' cabins throughout the Black Belt is to-day the same as in slavery days. Some live in the self-same cabins, others in cabins rebuilt on the sites of the old. All are sprinkled in little groups over the face of the land, centering about some dilapidated

Big House where the head-tenant or agent lives. The general character and arrangement of these dwellings remains on the whole unaltered. There were in the county, outside the corporate town of Albany, about fifteen hundred Negro families in 1898. Out of all these, only a single family occupied a house with seven rooms; only fourteen have five rooms or more. The mass live in one- and two-room homes.

The size and arrangements of a people's homes are no unfair index of their condition. If, then, we inquire more carefully into these Negro homes, we find much that is unsatisfactory. All over the face of the land is the one-room cabin,—now standing in the shadow of the Big House, now staring at the dusty road, now rising dark and sombre amid the green of the cotton-fields. It is nearly always old and bare, built of rough boards, and neither plastered nor ceiled. Light and ventilation are supplied by the single door and by the square hole in the wall with its wooden shutter. There is no glass, porch, or ornamentation without. Within is a fireplace, black and smoky, and usually unsteady with age. A bed or two, a table, a wooden chest, and a few chairs compose the furniture; while a stray show-bill or a newspaper makes up the

Crowded, impoverished living conditions were common for black families living in rural areas at the turn of the century.

decorations for the walls. Now and then one may find such a cabin kept scrupulously neat, with merry steaming fireplaces and hospitable door; but the majority are dirty and dilapidated, smelling of eating and sleeping, poorly ventilated, and anything but homes.

Above all, the cabins are crowded. We have come to associate crowding with homes in cities almost exclusively. This is primarily because we have so little accurate knowledge of country life. Here in Dougherty County one may find families of eight and ten occupying one or two rooms, and for every ten rooms of house accommodation for the Negroes there are twenty-five persons. The worst tenement abominations of New York do not have above twenty-two persons for every ten rooms. Of course, one small, close room in a city, without a yard, is in many respects worse than the larger single country room. In other respects it is better; it has glass windows, a decent chimney, and a trustworthy floor. The single great advantage of the Negro peasant is that he may spend most of his life outside his hovel, in the open fields.

There are four chief causes of these wretched homes: First, long custom born of slavery has assigned such homes to Negroes; white laborers would be offered better accommodations, and might, for that and similar reasons, give better work. Secondly, the Negroes, used to such accommodations, do not as a rule demand better; they do not know what better houses mean. Thirdly, the landlords as a class have not yet come to realize that it is a good business investment to raise the standard of living among labor by slow and judicious methods; that a Negro laborer who demands three rooms and fifty cents a day would give more efficient work and leave a larger profit than a discouraged toiler herding his family in one room and working for thirty cents. Lastly, among such conditions of life there are few incentives to make the laborer become a better farmer. If he is ambitious, he moves to town or tries other labor; as a tenant-farmer his outlook is almost hopeless, and following it as a makeshift, he takes the house that is given him without protest.

In such homes, then, these Negro peasants live. The families are both small and large; there are many single tenants,—widows and bachelors, and remnants of broken groups. The system of labor and the size of the houses both tend to the breaking up of family groups: the grown children go away as contract hands or migrate to town, the sister goes into service; and so one finds many families with hosts of babies, and many newly married couples, but comparatively few families with half-grown and grown sons and daughters. The average size of Negro families has undoubtedly decreased since the war, primarily from economic stress. In Russia over a third of the bridegrooms and over half the brides are under twenty; the same was true of the ante-bellum Negroes. To-day, however, very few of the boys and less than a fifth of the Negro girls under twenty are married. The young men marry between the ages of twenty-five and thirty-five; the young women between twenty and thirty. Such postponement is due to the difficulty of earning sufficient to rear and support a family; and it undoubtedly leads, in the country districts, to sexual immorality. The form of this immorality, however, is very seldom that of prostitution, and less frequently that of illegitimacy than one would imagine. Rather, it takes the form of separation and desertion after a family group has been formed. The number of separated persons is thirty-five to the thousand,—a very large number. It would of course be unfair to compare this number with divorce statistics, for many of these separated women are in reality widowed, were the truth known, and in other cases the separation is not permanent. Nevertheless, here lies the seat of greatest moral danger. There is little or no prostitution among these Negroes, and over three-fourths of the families, as found by house-to-house investigation, deserve to be classed as decent people with considerable regard for female chastity. To be sure, the ideas of the mass would not suit New England, and there are many loose habits and notions. Yet the rate of illegitmacy is undoubtedly lower than in Austria or Italy, and the women as a class are modest. The plague-spot in sexual relations is easy marriage and easy separation. This is no sudden development, nor the fruit of Emancipation. It is the plain heritage from slavery. In those days Sam, with his master's consent, "took up" with Mary. No ceremony was necessary, and in the busy life of the great plantations of the Black Belt it was usually dispensed with. If now the master needed Sam's work in another plantation or in another part of the same plantation, or if he took a notion to sell the slave, Sam's married life with Mary was usually unceremoniously broken, and then it was clearly to the master's interest to have both of them take new mates. This widespread custom of two centuries has not been eradicated in thirty years. To-day Sam's grandson "takes up" with a woman without license or ceremony; they live together decently and honestly, and are, to all intents and purposes, man and wife. Sometimes these unions are never broken until death; but in too many cases family quarrels, a roving spirit, a rival suitor, or perhaps more frequently the hopeless battle to support a family, lead to separation, and a broken household is the result. The Negro church has done much to stop this practice, and now most marriage ceremonies are performed by the pastors. Nevertheless, the evil is still deep seated, and only a general raising of the standard of living will finally cure it.

Looking now at the county black population as a whole, it is fair to characterize it as poor and ignorant. Perhaps ten per cent compose the well-to-do and the best of the laborers, while at least nine per cent are thoroughly lewd and vicious. The rest, over eighty per cent, are poor and ignorant, fairly honest and well meaning, plodding, and to a degree shiftless, with some but not great sexual looseness. Such class lines are by no means fixed; they vary, one might almost say, with the price of cotton. The degree of ignorance cannot easily be expressed. We may say, for instance, that nearly two-thirds of them cannot read or write. This but partially expresses the fact. They are ignorant of the world about them, of modern economic organization, of the function of government, of individual worth and possibilities,—of nearly all those things which slavery in self-defence had to keep them from learning. Much that the white boy imbibes from his earliest social atmosphere forms the puzzling problems of the black boy's mature years. America is not another word for Opportunity to *all* her sons.

It is easy for us to lose ourselves in details in endeavoring to grasp and comprehend the real condition of a mass of human beings. We often forget that each unit in the mass is a throbbing human soul. Ignorant it may be, and poverty stricken, black and curious in limb and ways and thought; and yet it loves and hates, it toils and tires, it laughs and weeps its bitter tears, and looks in vague and awful longing at the grim horizon of its life,—all this, even as you and I. These black thousands are not in reality lazy; they are improvident and careless; they insist on breaking the monotony of toil with a glimpse at the great town-world on Saturday; they have their loafers and their rascals; but the great mass of them work continuously and faithfully for a return, and under circumstances that would call forth equal voluntary effort from few if any other modern laboring class. Over eighty-eight per cent of them—men, women, and children—are farmers. Indeed, this is almost the only industry. Most of the children get their schooling after the "crops are laid by," and very few there are that stay in school after the spring work has begun. Child-labor is to be found here in some of its worst phases, as fostering ignorance and stunting physical development. With the grown men of the county there is little variety in work: thirteen hundred are farmers, and two hundred are laborers, teamsters, etc., including twenty-four artisans, ten merchants, twenty-one preachers, and four teachers. This narrowness of life reaches its maximum among the women: thirteen hundred and fifty of these are farm laborers, one hundred are servants and washerwomen, leaving sixty-five housewives, eight teachers, and six seamstresses.

Among this people there is no leisure class. We often forget that in the United States over half the youth and adults are not in the world earning incomes, but are making homes, learning of the world, or resting after the heat of the strife. But here ninety-six per cent are toiling; no one with leisure to turn the bare and cheerless cabin into a home, no old folks to sit beside the fire and hand down traditions of the past; little of careless happy childhood and dreaming youth. The dull monotony of daily toil is broken only by the gayety of the thoughtless and the Saturday trip to town. The toil, like all farm toil, is monotonous, and here there are little machinery and few tools to relieve its burdensome drudgery. But with all this, it is work in the pure open air, and this is something in a day when fresh air is scarce.

The land on the whole is still fertile, despite long abuse. For nine or ten months in succession the crops will come if asked: garden vegetables in April, grain in May, melons in June and July, hay in August, sweet potatoes in September, and cotton from then to Christmas. And yet on two-thirds of the land there is but one crop, and that leaves the toilers in debt. Why is this?

Away down the Baysan road, where the broad flat fields are flanked by great oak forests, is a plantation; many thousands of acres it used to run, here and there, and beyond the great wood. Thirteen hundred human beings here obeyed the call of one,—were his in body, and largely in soul. One of them lives there yet,—a short, stocky man, his dull-brown face seamed and drawn, and his tightly curled hair gray-white. The crop? Just tolerable, he said; just tolerable. Getting on? No—he wasn't getting on at all. Smith of Albany "furnishes" him, and his rent is eight hundred pounds of cotton. Can't make anything at that. Why didn't he buy land! Humph! Takes money to buy land. And he turns away. Free! The most piteous thing amid all the black ruin of war-time, amid the broken fortunes of the masters, the blighted hopes of mothers and maidens, and the fall of an empire,—the most piteous thing amid all this was the black freedman who threw down his hoe because the world called him free. What did such a mockery of freedom mean? Not a cent of money, not an inch of land, not a mouthful of victuals,—not even ownership of the rags on his back. Free! On Saturday, once or twice a month, the old master, before the war, used to dole out bacon and meal to his Negroes. And after the first flush of freedom wore off, and his true helplessness dawned on the freedman, he came back and picked up his hoe, and old master still doled out his bacon and meal. The legal form of service was theoretically far different; in practice, task-work or "cropping" was substituted for daily toil in gangs; and the slave gradually became a metayer, or tenant on shares, in name, but a laborer with indeterminate wages in fact.

Still the price of cotton fell, and gradually the landlords deserted their plantations, and the reign of the merchant began. The merchant of the Black Belt is a curious institution,—part banker, part landlord, part contractor, and part despot. His store, which used most frequently to stand at the crossroads and become the centre of a weekly village, has now moved to town; and thither the Negro tenant follows him. The merchant keeps everything, — clothes and shoes, coffee and sugar, pork and meal, canned and dried goods, wagons and ploughs, seed and fertilizer,—and what he has not in stock he can give you an order for at the store across the way. Here, then, comes the tenant, Sam Scott, after he has contracted with some absent landlord's agent for hiring forty acres of land; he fingers his hat nervously until the merchant finishes his morning chat with Colonel Saunders, and calls out, "Well, Sam, what do you want?" Sam wants him to "furnish" him,—*i.e.,* to advance him food and clothing for the year, and perhaps seed and tools, until his crop is raised and sold. If Sam seems a favorable subject, he and the merchant go to a lawyer, and Sam executes a chattel mortgage on his mule and wagon in return for seed and a week's rations. As soon as the green cotton-leaves appear above the ground, another mortgage is given on the "crop." Every Saturday, or at longer intervals, Sam calls upon the merchant for his "rations"; a family of five usually gets about thirty pounds of fat side-pork and a couple of bushels of cornmeal a month. Besides this, clothing and shoes must be furnished; if Sam or his family is sick, there are orders on the druggist and doctor; if the mule wants shoeing, an order on the blacksmith, etc. If Sam is a hard worker and crops promise well, he is often encouraged to buy more,— sugar, extra clothes, perhaps a buggy. But he is seldom encouraged to save. When cotton rose to ten cents last fall, the shrewd merchants of Dougherty County sold a thousand buggies in one season, mostly to black men.

The security offered for such transactions—a crop and chattel mortgage— may at first seem slight. And, indeed, the merchants tell many a true tale of shiftlessness and cheating; of cotton picked at night, mules disappearing, and tenants absconding. But on the whole the merchant of the Black Belt is the most prosperous man in the section. So skillfully and so closely has he drawn the bonds of the law about the tenant, that the black man has often simply to choose between pauperism and crime; he "waives" all homestead exemptions in his contract; he cannot touch his own mortgaged crop, which the laws put almost in the full control of the land-owner and of the merchant. When the crop is growing the merchant watches it like a hawk; as soon as it is ready for market he takes possession of it, sells it, pays the landowner his rent, subtracts his bill for supplies, and if, as sometimes happens, there is anything left, he hands it over to the black serf for his Christmas celebration.

The direct result of this system is an all-cotton scheme of agriculture and the continued bankruptcy of the tenant. The currency of the Black Belt is cotton. It is a crop always salable for ready money, not usually subject to great yearly fluctuations in price, and one which the Negroes know how to raise. The landlord therefore demands his rent in cotton, and the merchant will accept mortgages on no other crop. There is no use asking the black tenant, then, to diversify his crops,—he cannot under this system. Moreover, the system is bound to bankrupt the tenant. I remember once meeting a little one-mule wagon on the River road. A young black fellow sat in it driving listlessly, his elbows on his knees. His dark-faced wife sat beside him, stolid, silent.

"Hello!" cried my driver,—he has a most imprudent way of addressing these people, though they seem used to it,—"what have you got there?"

"Meat and meal," answered the man, stopping. The meat lay uncovered in the bottom of the wagon,—a great thin side of fat pork covered with salt; the meal was in a white bushel bag.

"What did you pay for that meat?"

"Ten cents a pound." It could have been bought for six or seven cents cash.

"And the meal?"

"Two dollars." One dollar and ten cents is the cash price in town. Here was a man paying five dollars for goods which he could have bought for three dollars cash, and raised for one dollar or one dollar and a half.

Yet it was not wholly his fault. The Negro farmer started behind,—started in debt. This was not his choosing, but the crime of this happy-go-lucky nation which goes blundering along with its Reconstruction tragedies, its Spanish war interludes and Philippine matinees, just as though God really were dead. Once in debt, it is no easy matter for a whole race to emerge.

In the year of low-priced cotton, 1898, out of three hundred tenant families one hundred and seventy-five ended their year's work in debt to the extent of fourteen thousand dollars; fifty cleared nothing, and the remaining seventy-five made a total profit of sixteen hundred dollars. The net indebtedness of the black tenant families of the whole county must have been at least sixty thousand dollars. In a more prosperous year the situation is far better; but on the average the majority of tenants end the year even, or in debt, which means that they work for board and clothes. Such an economic organization is radically wrong. Whose is the blame?

The underlying causes of this situation are complicated but discernible. And one of the chief, outside the carelessness of the nation in letting the slave start with nothing, is the widespread opinion among the merchants and employers of the Black Belt that only by the slavery of debt can the Negro be kept at work. Without doubt, some pressure was necessary at the beginning of the free-labor system to keep the listless and lazy at work; and even to-day the mass of the Negro laborers need stricter guardianship than most Northern laborers. Behind this honest and widespread opinion dishonesty and cheating of the ignorant laborers have a good chance to take refuge. And to all this must be added the obvious fact that a slave ancestry and a system of unrequited toil has not improved the efficiency or temper of the mass of black laborers. Nor is this peculiar to Sambo; it has in history been just as true of John and Hans, of Jacques and Pat, of all ground-down peasantries. Such is the situation of the mass of the Negroes in the Black Belt to-day; and they are thinking about it. Crime, and a cheap and dangerous socialism, are the inevitable results of this pondering. I see now that ragged black man sitting on a log, aimlessly whittling a stick. He muttered to me with the murmur of many ages, when he said: "White man sit down whole year; Nigger work day and night and make crop; Nigger hardly gits bread and meat; white man sittin' down gits all. *It's wrong.*" And what do the better classes of Negroes do to improve their situation? One of two things: if any way possible, they buy land; if not, they migrate to town. Just as centuries ago it was no easy thing for the serf to escape into the freedom of town-life, even so to-day there are hindrances laid in the way of county laborers. In considerable parts of all the Gulf States, and especially in Mississippi, Louisiana, and Arkansas, the Negroes on the plantations in the back-country districts are still held at forced labor practically without wages. Especially is this true in districts where the farmers are composed of the more ignorant class of poor whites, and the Negroes are beyond the reach of schools and intercourse with their advancing fellows. If such a peon should run away, the sheriff, elected by white suffrage, can usually be depended on to catch the fugitive, return him, and ask no questions. If he escapes to another county, a charge of petty thieving, easily true, can be depended upon to secure his return. Even if some unduly officious person insists upon a trial, neighborly comity will probably make his conviction sure, and then the labor due the county can easily be bought by the master. Such a system is impossible in the more civilized parts of the South, or near the large towns and cities; but in those vast stretches of land beyond the telegraph and the newspaper the spirit of the Thirteenth Amendment is sadly broken. This represents the lowest economic depths of the black American peasant; and in a study of the rise and condition of the Negro freeholder we must trace his economic progress from the modern serfdom.

Even in the better-ordered country districts of the South the free movement of agricultural laborers is hindered by the migration-agent laws. The "Associated Press" recently informed the world of the arrest of a young white man in Southern Georgia who represented the "Atlantic Naval Supplies Company," and who "was caught in the act of enticing hands from the turpentine farm of Mr. John Greer." The crime for which this young man was arrested is taxed five hundred dollars for each county in which the employment agent proposes to gather laborers for work outside the State. Thus the Negroes' ignorance of the labor-market outside his own vicinity is increased rather than diminished by the laws of nearly every Southern State.

Similar to such measures is the unwritten law of the back districts and small towns of the South, that the character of all Negroes unknown to the mass of the community must be vouched for by some white man. This is really a revival of the old Roman idea of the patron under whose protection the new-made freedman was put. In many instances this system has been of great good to the Negro, and very often under the protection and guidance of the former master's family, or other white friends, the freedman progressed in wealth and morality. But the same system has in other cases resulted in the refusal of whole communities to recognize the right of a Negro to change his habitation and to be master of his own fortunes. A black stranger in Baker County, Georgia, for instance, is liable to be stopped anywhere on the public highway and made to state his business to the satisfaction of any white interrogator. If he fails to give a suitable answer, or seems too independent or "sassy," he may be arrested or summarily driven away.

Thus it is that in the country districts of the South, by written or unwritten law, peonage, hindrances to the migration of labor, and a system of white patronage exists over large areas. Besides this, the chance for lawless oppression and illegal exactions is vastly greater in the country than in the city, and nearly all the more serious race disturbances of the last decade have arisen from disputes in the count between master and man,—as, for instance, the Sam Hose affair. As a result of such a situation, there arose, first, the Black Belt; and, second, the Migration to Town. The Black Belt was not, as many assumed, a movement toward fields of labor under more genial climatic conditions; it was primarily a huddling for self-protection,—a massing of the black population for mutual defence in order to secure the peace and tranquility necessary to economic advance. This movement took place between Emancipation and 1880, and only partially accomplished the desired results. The rush to town since 1880 is the counter-movement of men disappointed in the economic opportunities of the Black Belt.

In Dougherty County, Georgia, one can see easily the results of this experiment in huddling for protection. Only ten per cent of the adult population was born in the county, and yet the blacks outnumber the whites four or five to one. There is undoubtedly a security to the blacks in their very numbers,—a personal freedom from arbitrary treatment, which makes hundreds of laborers cling to Dougherty in spite of low wages and economic distress. But a change is coming, and slowly but surely even here the agricultural laborers are drifting to town and leaving the broad acres behind. Why is this? Why do not the Negroes become land-owners, and build up the black landed peasantry, which has for a generation and more been the dream of philanthropist and statesman?

To the car-window sociologist, to the man who seeks to understand and know the South by devoting the few leisure hours of a holiday trip to unravelling the snarl of centuries,—to such men very often the whole trouble with the black field-hand may be summed up by Aunt Ophelia's word, "Shiftless!" They have noted repeatedly scenes like one I saw last summer. We were riding along the highroad to town at the close of a long hot day. A couple of young black fellows passed us in a muleteam, with several bushels of loose corn in the ear. One was driving, listlessly bent forward, his elbows on his knees,—a happy-go-lucky, careless picture of irresponsibility. The other was fast asleep in the bottom of the wagon. As we passed we noticed an ear of corn fall from the wagon. They never saw it,—not they. A rod farther on we noted another ear on the ground; and between that creeping mule and town we counted twenty-six ears of corn. Shiftless? Yes, the personification of shiftlessness. And yet follow those boys: they are not lazy; to-morrow morning they'll be up with the sun; they work hard when they do work, and they work willingly. They have no sordid, selfish, money-getting ways, but rather a fine disdain for mere cash. They'll loaf before your face and work behind your back with good-natured honesty. They'll steal a watermelon, and hand you back your lost purse intact. Their great defect as laborers lies in their lack of incentive beyond the mere pleasure of physical exertion. They are careless because they have not found that it pays to be careful; they are improvident because the improvident ones of their acquaintance get on about as well as the provident. Above all, they cannot see why they should take unusual pains to make the white man's land better, or to fatten his mule, or save his corn. On the other hand, the white land-owner argues that any attempt to improve these laborers by increased responsibility, or higher wages, or better homes, or land of their own, would be sure to result in failure. He shows his Northern visitor the scarred and wretched land; the ruined mansions, the worn-out soil and mortgaged acres, and says, This is Negro freedom!

Now it happens that both master and man have just enough argument on their respective sides to make it difficult for them to understand each other. The Negro dimly personifies in the white man all his ills and misfortunes; if he is poor, it is because the white man seizes the fruit of his toil; if he is ignorant, it is because the white man gives him neither time nor facilities to learn; and, indeed, if any misfortune happens to him, it is because of some hidden machinations of "white folks." On the other hand, the masters and the masters' sons have never been able to see why the Negro, instead of settling down to be day-laborers for bread and clothes, are infected with a silly desire to rise in the world, and why they are sulky, dissatisfied, and careless, where their fathers were happy and dumb and faithful. "Why, you niggers have an easier time than I do," said a puzzled Albany merchant to his black customer. "Yes," he replied, "and so does yo' hogs."

Taking, then, the dissatisfied and shiftless field-hand as a starting-point, let us inquire how the black thousands of Dougherty have struggled from him up toward their ideal, and what that ideal is. All social struggle is evidenced by the rise, first of economic, then of social classes, among a homogeneous

population. To-day the following economic classes are plainly differentiated among these Negroes.

A "submerged tenth" of croppers, with a few paupers; forty per cent who are metayers and thirty-nine per cent of semi-metayers and wage laborers. There are left five per cent of money-renters and six per cent of free-holders,—the "Upper Ten" of the land. The croppers are entirely without capital, even in the limited sense of food or money to keep them from seed-time to harvest. All they furnish is their labor; the land-owner furnishes land, stock, tools, seed, and house; and at the end of the year the laborer gets from a third to half of the crop. Out of his share, however, comes pay and interest for food and clothing advanced him during the year. Thus we have a laborer without capital and without wages, and an employer whose capital is largely his employees' wages. It is an unsatisfactory arrangement, both for hirer and hired, and is usually in vogue on poor land with hard-pressed owners.

Above the croppers come the great mass of the black population who work

Cotton being harvested in a Georgia field in 1913.

the land on their own responsibility, paying rent in cotton and supported by the crop-mortgage system. After the war this system was attractive to the freedmen on account of its larger freedom and its possibility for making a surplus. But with the carrying out of the crop-lien system, the deterioration of the land, and the slavery of debt, the position of the metayers has sunk to a dead level of practically unrewarded toil. Formerly all tenants had some capital, and often considerable; but absentee landlordism, rising rack-rent, and falling cotton have stripped them well-nigh of all, and probably not over half of them to-day own their mules. The change from cropper to tenant was accomplished by fixing the rent. If, now, the rent fixed was reasonable, this was an incentive to the tenant to strive. On the other hand, if the rent was too high, or if the land deteriorated, the result was to discourage and check the efforts of the black peasantry. There is no doubt that the latter case is true; that in Dougherty County every economic advantage of the price of cotton in market and of the strivings of the tenant has been taken advantage of by the landlords and merchants, and swallowed up in rent and interest. If cotton rose in price, the rent rose even higher; if cotton fell, the rent remained or followed reluctantly. If the tenant worked hard and raised a large crop, his rent was raised the next year; if that year the crop failed, his corn was confiscated and his mule sold for debt. There were, of course, exceptions to this,—cases of personal kindness and forbearance; but in the vast majority of cases the rule was to extract the uttermost farthing from the mass of the black farm laborers.

The average metayer pays from twenty to thirty per cent of his crop in rent. The result of such rack-rent can only be evil,—abuse and neglect of the soil, deterioration in the character of the laborers, and a widespread sense of injustice. "Wherever the country is poor," cried Arthur Young, "it is in the hands of metayers," and "their condition is more wretched than that of day-laborers." He was talking of Italy a century ago; but he might have been talking of Dougherty County to-day. And especially is that true to-day which he declares was true in France before the Revolution: "The metayers are considered as little better than menial servants, removable at pleasure, and obliged to conform in all things to the will of the landlords." On this low plane half the black population of Dougherty County—perhaps more than half the black millions of this land—are to-day struggling.

A degree above these we may place those laborers who receive money wages for their work. Some receive a house with perhaps a garden spot; then supplies of food and clothing are advanced, and certain fixed wages are given at the end of the year, varying from thirty to sixty dollars, out of which the supplies must be paid for, with interest. About eighteen per cent of the population belong to this class of semi-metayers, while twenty-two per cent are laborers paid by the month or year, and are either "furnished" by their own savings or perhaps more usually by some merchant who takes his chances of payment. Such laborers receive from thirty-five to fifty cents a day during the working season. They are usually young unmarried persons, some being women; and when they marry they sink to the class of metayers, or, more seldom, become renters.

The renters for fixed money rentals are the first of the emerging classes, and form five per cent of the families. The sole advantage of this small class is their freedom to choose their crops, and the increased responsibility which comes through having money transactions. While some of the renters differ little in condition from the metayers, yet on the whole they are more intelligent and responsible persons, and are the ones who eventually become land-owners. Their better character and greater shrewdness enable them to gain, perhaps to demand, better terms in rents; rented farms, varying from forty to a hundred acres, bear an average rental of about fifty-four dollars a year. The men who conduct such farms do not long remain renters; either they sink to metayers, or with a successful series of harvests rise to be land-owners.

In 1870 the tax-books of Dougherty report no Negroes as landholders. If there were any such at that time,—and there may have been a few,—their land was probably held in the name of some white patron,—a method not uncommon during slavery. In 1875 ownership of land had begun with seven hundred and fifty acres; ten years later this had increased to over sixty-five hundred acres, to nine thousand acres in 1890 and ten thousand in 1900. The total assessed property has in this same period risen from eighty thousand dollars in 1875 to two hundred and forty thousand dollars in 1900.

Two circumstances complicate this development and make it in some respects difficult to be sure of the real tendencies; they are the panic of 1893, and the low price of cotton in 1898. Besides this, the system of assessing property in the country districts of Georgia is somewhat antiquated and of uncertain statistical value; there are no assessors, and each man makes a sworn return to a tax-receiver. Thus public opinion plays a large part, and the returns vary strangely from year to year. Certainly these figures show the small amount of accumulated capital among the Negroes, and the consequent large dependence of their property on temporary prosperity. They have little to tide over a few years of economic depression, and are at the mercy of the cotton-market far more than the whites. And thus the land-owners, despite their marvellous efforts, are really a transient class, continually being depleted by those who fall back into the class of renters or metayers, and augmented by newcomers from the masses. Of one hundred land-owners in 1898, half had bought their land since 1893, a fourth between 1890 and 1893, a fifth between 1884 and 1890, and the rest between 1870 and 1884. In all, one hundred and eighty-five Negroes have owned land in this county since 1875.

If all the black land-owners who had ever held land here had kept it or left it in the hands of black men, the Negroes would have owned nearer thirty thousand acres than the fifteen thousand they now hold. And yet these fifteen thousand acres are a creditable showing,—a proof of no little weight of the worth and ability of the Negro people. If they had been given an economic start at Emancipation, if they had been in an enlightened and rich community which really desired their best good, then we might perhaps call such a result small or even insignificant. But for a few thousand poor ignorant field-hands, in the face of poverty, a falling market, and social stress, to save and capitalize two hundred thousand dollars in a generation has meant a tremendous effort. The rise of a nation, the pressing forward of a social class, means a bitter struggle, a hard and soul-sickening battle with the world such as few of the more favored classes know or appreciate.

Out of the hard economic conditions of this portion of the Black Belt, only six per cent of the population have succeeded in emerging into peasant proprietorship; and these are not all firmly fixed, but grow and shrink in number with the wavering of the cotton-market. Fully ninety-four per cent have struggled for land and failed, and half of them sit in hopeless serfdom. For these there is one other avenue of escape toward which they have turned in increasing numbers, namely, migration to town. A glance at the distribution of land among the black owners curiously reveals this fact. In 1898 the holdings were as follows: Under forty acres, forty-nine families; forty to two hundred and fifty acres, seventeen families; two hundred and fifty to one thousand acres, thirteen families; one thousand or more acres, two families. Now in 1890 there were forty-four holdings, but only nine of these were under forty acres. The great increase of holdings, then, has come in the buying of small homesteads near town, where their owners really share in the town life; this is a part of the rush to town. And for every land-owner who has thus hurried away from the narrow and hard conditions of country life, how many field-hands, how many tenants, how many ruined renters, have joined that long procession? Is it not strange compensation? The sin of the country districts is visited on the town, and the social sores of city life to-day may, here in Dougherty County, and perhaps in many places near and far, look for their final healing without the city walls.

IX
Of the Sons of Master and Man

Life treads on life, and heart on heart;
We press too close in church and mart
To keep a dream or grave apart.
    Elizabeth Barrett Browning. (1806–61) from *A Vision of Poets*

The world-old phenomenon of the contact of diverse races of men is to have new exemplification during the new century. Indeed, the characteristic of our age is the contact of European civilization with the world's undeveloped peoples. Whatever we may say of the results of such contact in the past, it certainly forms a chapter in human action not pleasant to look back upon.

War, murder, slavery, extermination, and debauchery,—this has again and again been the result of carrying civilization and the blessed gospel to the isles of the sea and the heathen without the law. Nor does it altogether satisfy the conscience of the modern world to be told complacently that all this has been right and proper, the fated triumph of strength over weakness, of righteousness over evil, of superiors over inferiors. It would certainly be soothing if one could readily believe all this; and yet there are too many ugly facts for everything to be thus easily explained away. We feel and know that there are many delicate differences in race psychology, numberless changes that our crude social measurements are not yet able to follow minutely, which explain much of history and social development. At the same time, too, we know that these considerations have never adequately explained or excused the triumph of brute force and cunning over weakness and innocence.

It is, then, the strife of all honorable men of the twentieth century to see that in the future competition of races the survival of the fittest shall mean the triumph of the good, the beautiful, and the true; that we may be able to preserve for future civilization all that is really fine and noble and strong, and not continue to put a premium on greed and impudence and cruelty. To bring this hope to fruition, we are compelled daily to turn more and more to a conscientious study of the phenomena of race-contact,—to a study frank and fair, and not falsified and colored by our wishes or our fears. And we have in the South as fine a field for such a study as the world affords,— a field, to be sure, which the average American scientist deems somewhat beneath his dignity, and which the average man who is not a scientist knows all about, but nevertheless a line of study which by reason of the enormous race complications with which God seems about to punish this nation must increasingly claim our sober attention, study, and thought, we must ask, what are the actual relations of whites and blacks in the South? and we must be answered, not by apology or fault-finding, but by a plain, unvarnished tale.

In the civilized life of to-day the contact of men and their relations to each other fall in a few main lines of action and communication: there is, first, the physical proximity of home and dwelling-places, the way in which neighborhoods group themselves, and the contiguity of neighborhoods. Secondly, and in our age chiefest, there are the economic relations,—the methods by which individuals cooperate for earning a living, for the mutual satisfaction of wants, for the production of wealth. Next, there are the political relations, the cooperation in social control, in group government, in laying and paying the burden of taxation. In the fourth place there are the less tangible but highly important forms of intellectual contact and commerce, the interchange of ideas through conversation and conference, through periodicals and libraries; and, above all, the gradual formation for each community of that curious *tertium quid* which we call public opinion. Closely allied with this come the various forms of social contact in everyday life, in travel, in theatres, in house gatherings, in marrying and giving in marriage. Finally, there are the varying forms of religious enterprise, of moral teaching and benevolent endeavor. These are the principal ways in which men living in the same communities are brought into contact with each other. It is my present task, therefore, to indicate, from my point of view, how the black race in the South meet and mingle with the whites in these matters of everyday life.

First, as to physical dwelling. It is usually possible to draw in nearly every Southern community a physical color-line on the map, on the one side of which whites dwell and on the other Negroes. The winding and intricacy of the geographical color-line varies, of course, in different communities. I know some towns where a straight line drawn through the middle of the main street separates nine-tenths of the whites from nine-tenths of the blacks. In other towns the older settlement of whites has been encircled by a broad band of blacks; in still other cases little settlements or nuclei of blacks have sprung up amid surrounding whites. Usually in cities each street has its distinctive color, and only now and then do the colors meet in close proximity. Even in the country something of this segregation is manifest in the smaller areas, and of course in the larger phenomena of the Black Belt.

All this segregation by color is largely independent of that natural clustering by social grades common to all communities. A Negro slum may be in dangerous proximity to a white residence quarter, while it is quite common to find a white slum planted in the heart of a respectable Negro district. One thing, however, seldom occurs: the best of the whites and the best of the Negroes almost never live in anything like close proximity. It thus happens that in nearly every Southern town and city, both whites and blacks see commonly the worst of each other. This is a vast change from the situation in the past, when, through the close contact of master and house-servant in the patriarchal big house, one found the best of both races in close contact and sympathy, while at the same time the squalor and dull round of toil among the field-hands was removed from the sight and hearing of the family. One can easily see how a person who saw slavery thus from his father's parlors, and sees freedom on the streets of a great city, fails to grasp or comprehend the whole of the new picture. On the other hand, the settled belief of the mass of the Negroes that the Southern white people do not have the black man's best interests at heart has been intensified in later years by this continual daily contact of the better class of blacks with the worst representatives of the white race.

Coming now to the economic relations of the races, we are on ground made familiar by study, much discussion, and no little philanthropic effort. And yet with all this there are many essential elements in the cooperation of Negroes and whites for work and wealth that are too readily overlooked or not thoroughly understood. The average American can easily conceive of a rich land awaiting development and filled with black laborers. To him the Southern problem is simply that of making efficient workingmen out of this material, by giving them the requisite technical skill and the help of invested capital. The problem, however, is by no means as simple as this, from the obvious fact that these workingmen have been trained for centuries as slaves. They exhibit, therefore, all the advantages and defects of such training; they are willing and good-natured, but not self-reliant, provident, or careful. If now the economic development of the South is to be pushed to the verge of exploitation, as seems probable, then we have a mass of workingmen thrown into relentless competition with the workingmen of the world, but handicapped by a training the very opposite to that of the modern self-reliant democratic laborer. What the black laborer needs is careful personal guidance, group leadership of men with hearts in their bosoms, to train them to foresight, carefulness, and honesty. Nor does it require any fine-spun theories of racial differences to prove the necessity of such group training after the brains of the race have been knocked out by two hundred and fifty years of assiduous education in submission, carelessness, and stealing. After Emancipation, it was the plain duty of some one to assume this group leadership and training of the Negro laborer. I will not stop here to inquire whose duty it was—whether that of the white ex-master who had profited by unpaid toil, or the Northern philanthropist whose persistence brought on the crisis, or the National Government whose edict freed the bondmen; I will not stop to ask whose duty it was, but I insist it was the duty of some one to see that these workingmen were not left alone and unguided, without capital, without land, without skill, without economic organization, without even the bald protection of law, order, and decency,—left in a great land, not to settle down to slow and careful internal development, but destined to be thrown almost immediately into relentless and sharp competition with the best of modern workingmen under an economic system where every participant is fighting for himself, and too often utterly regardless of the rights or welfare of his neighbor.

For we must never forget that the economic system of the South to-day which has succeeded the old regime is not the same system as that of the old industrial North, of England, or of France, with their trade-unions, their restrictive laws, their written and unwritten commercial customs, and their long experience. It is, rather, a copy of that England of the early nineteenth century, before the factory acts,—the England that wrung pity from thinkers and fired the wrath of Carlyle. The rod of empire that passed from the hands of Southern gentlemen in 1865, partly by force, partly by their own petulance, has never returned to them. Rather it has passed to those men who have come to take charge of the industrial exploitation of the New South,—the sons of poor whites fired with a new thirst for wealth and power, thrifty and avaricious Yankees, and unscrupulous immigrants. Into the hands of these men the Southern laborers, white and black, have fallen; and this to their sorrow. For the laborers as such, there is in these new captains of industry neither love nor hate, neither sympathy nor romance; it is a cold question of dollars and dividends. Under such a system all labor is bound to suffer. Even the white laborers are not yet intelligent, thrifty, and well trained enough to maintain themselves against the powerful inroads of organized capital. The results among them, even, are long hours of toil, low wages, child labor, and lack of protection against usury and cheating. But among the black laborers all this is aggravated, first, by a race prejudice which varies from a doubt and distrust among the best element of whites to a frenzied hatred among the worst; and, secondly, it is aggravated, as I have said before, by the wretched economic heritage of the freemen from slavery. With this training it is difficult for the freedman to learn to grasp the opportunities already opened to him, and the new opportunities are seldom given him, but go by favor to the whites.

Left by the best elements of the South with little protection or oversight, he has been made in law and custom the victim of the worst and most unscrupulous men in each community. The crop-lien system which is depopulating the fields of the South is not simply the result of shiftlessness on the part of Negroes, but is also the result of cunningly devised laws as to mortgages, liens, and misdemeanors, which can be made by conscienceless men to entrap and snare the unwary until escape is impossible, further toil a farce, and protest a crime. I have seen, in the Black Belt of Georgia, an ignorant, honest Negro buy and pay for a farm in installments three separate times, and then in the face of law and decency the enterprising American who sold it to him pocketed the money and deed and left the black man landless, to labor on his own land at thirty cents a day. I have seen a black farmer fall in debt to a white storekeeper, and that storekeeper go to his farm and strip it of every single marketable article,—mules, ploughs, stored crops, tools, furniture, bedding, clocks, looking-glass,—and all this without a sheriff or officer, in the face of the law for homestead exemptions, and without rendering to a single responsible person any account or reckoning. And such proceedings can happen, and will happen, in any community where a class of ignorant toilers are placed by custom and race-prejudice beyond the pale of sympathy and race-brotherhood. So long as the best elements of a community do not feel in duty bound to protect and train and care for the weaker members of their group, they leave them to be preyed upon by these swindlers and rascals.

This unfortunate economic situation does not mean the hindrance of all advance in the black South, or the absence of a class of black landlords and mechanics who, in spite of disadvantages, are accumulating property and making good citizens. But it does mean that this class is not nearly so large as a fairer economic system might easily make it, that those who survive in the competition are handicapped so as to accomplish much less than they deserve to, and that, above all, the *personnel* of the successful class is left to chance and accident, and not to any intelligent culling or reasonable methods of selection. As a remedy for this, there is but one possible procedure. We must accept some of the race prejudice in the South as a fact,—deplorable in its intensity, unfortunate in results, and dangerous for the future, but nevertheless a hard fact which only time can efface. We cannot hope, then, in this generation, or for several generations, that the mass of the whites can be brought to assume that close sympathetic and self-sacrificing leadership of the blacks which their present situation so eloquently demands. Such leadership, such social teaching and example, must come from the blacks themselves. For some time men doubted as to whether the Negro could develop such leaders; but to-day no one seriously disputes the capability of individual Negroes to assimilate the culture and common sense of modern civilization, and to pass it on, to some extent at least, to their fellows. If this is true, then here is the path out of the economic situation, and here is the imperative demand for trained Negro leaders of character and intelligence,—men of skill, men of light and leading, college-bred men, black captains of industry, and missionaries of culture; men who thoroughly comprehend and know modern civilization, and can take hold of Negro communities and raise and train them by force of precept and example, deep sympathy, and the inspiration of common blood and ideals. But if such men are to be effective they must have some power,—they must be backed by the best public opinion of these communities, and able to wield for their objects and aims such weapons as the experience of the world has taught are indispensable to human progress.

Of such weapons the greatest, perhaps, in the modern world is the power of the ballot; and this brings me to a consideration of the third form of contact between whites and blacks in the South,—political activity.

In the attitude of the American mind toward Negro suffrage can be traced with unusual accuracy the prevalent conceptions of government. In the fifties we were near enough the echoes of the French Revolution to believe pretty thoroughly in universal suffrage. We argued, as we thought then rather logically, that no social class was so good, so true, and so disinterested as to be trusted wholly with the political destiny of its neighbors; that in every state the best arbiters of their own welfare are the persons directly affected; consequently that it is only by arming every hand with a ballot,—with the right to have a voice in the policy of the state,—that the greatest good to the greatest number could be attained. To be sure, there were objections to these arguments, but we thought we had answered them tersely and convincingly; if some one complained of the ignorance of voters, we answered, "Educate them." If another complained of their venality, we replied, "Disfranchise them or put them in jail." And, finally, to the men who feared demagogues and the natural perversity of some human beings we insisted that time and bitter experience would teach the most hardheaded. It was at this time that the question of Negro suffrage in the South was raised. Here was a defence-less people suddenly made free. How were they to be protected from those who did not believe in their freedom and were determined to thwart it? Not by force, said the North; not by government guardianship, said the South; then by the ballot, the sole and legitimate defence of a free people, said the Common Sense of the Nation. No one thought, at the time, that the ex-slaves could use the ballot intelligently or very effectively; but they did think that the possession of so great power by a great class in the nation would compel their fellows to educate this class to its intelligent use.

Meantime, new thoughts came to the nation: the inevitable period of moral retrogression and political trickery that ever follows in the wake of war overtook us. So flagrant became the political scandals that reputable men began to leave politics alone, and politics consequently became disreputable. Men began to pride themselves on having nothing to do with their own government, and to agree tacitly with those who regarded public office as a private perquisite. In this state of mind it became easy to wink at the suppression of the Negro vote in the South, and to advise self-respecting Negroes to leave politics entirely alone. The decent and reputable citizens of the North who neglected their own civic duties grew hilarious over the exaggerated importance with which the Negro regarded the franchise. Thus it easily happened that more and more the better class of Negroes followed the advice from abroad and the pressure from home, and took no further interest in politics, leaving to the careless and the venal of their race the exercise of their rights as voters. The black vote that still remained was not trained and educated, but further debauched by open and unblushing bribery, or force and fraud; until the Negro voter was thoroughly inoculated with the idea that politics was a method of private gain by disreputable means.

And finally, now, to-day, when we are awakening to the fact that the perpetuity of republican institutions on this continent depends on the purification of the ballot, the civic training of voters, and the raising of voting to the plane of a solemn duty which a patriotic citizen neglects to his peril and to the peril of his children's children,—in this day, when we are striving for a renaissance of civic virtue, what are we going to say to the black voter of the South? Are we going to tell him still that politics is a disreputable and useless form of human activity? Are we going to induce the best class of Negroes to take less and less interest in government, and to give up their right to take such an interest, without a protest? I am not saying a word against all legitimate efforts to purge the ballot of ignorance, pauperism, and crime. But few have pretended that the present movement for disfranchisement in the South is for such a purpose; it has been plainly and frankly declared in nearly every case that the object of the disfranchising laws is the elimination of the black man from politics.

Now, is this a minor matter which has no influence on the main question of the industrial and intellectual development of the Negro? Can we establish a mass of black laborers and artisans and landholders in the South who, by law and public opinion, have absolutely no voice in shaping the laws under which they live and work? Can the modern organization of industry, assuming as it does free democratic government and the power and ability of the laboring classes to compel respect for their welfare,—can this system be carried out in the South when half its laboring force is voiceless in the public councils and powerless in its own defence? To-day the black man of the South has almost nothing to say as to how much he shall be taxed, or how those taxes shall be expended; as to who shall execute the laws, and how they shall do it; as to who shall make the laws, and how they shall be made. It is pitiable that frantic efforts must be made at critical times to get law-makers in some States even to listen to the respectful presentation of the black man's side of a current controversy. Daily the Negro is coming more and more to look upon law and justice, not as protecting safeguards, but as sources of humiliation and oppression. The laws are made by men who have little interest in him; they are executed by men who have absolutely no motive for treating the black people with courtesy or consideration; and, finally, the accused law-breaker is tried, not by his peers, but too often by men who would rather punish ten innocent Negroes than let one guilty one escape.

I should be the last one to deny the patent weaknesses and shortcomings of the Negro people; I should be the last to withhold sympathy from the white South in its efforts to solve its intricate social problems. I freely acknowledged that it is possible, and sometimes best, that a partially undeveloped people should be ruled by the best of their stronger and better neighbors for their own good, until such time as they can start and fight the world's battles alone. I have already pointed out how sorely in need of such economic and spiritual guidance the emancipated Negro was, and I am quite willing to admit that if the representatives of the best white Southern public opinion were the ruling and guiding powers in the South to-day the conditions indicated would be fairly well fulfilled. But the point I have insisted upon and now emphasize again, is that the best opinion of the South to-day is not the ruling opinion. That to leave the Negro helpless and without a ballot to-day is to leave him not to the guidance of the best, but rather to the exploitation and debauchment of the worst; that this is no truer of the South than of the North,—of the North than of Europe: in any land, in any country under modern free competition, to lay any class of weak and despised people, be they white, black, or blue, at the political mercy of their stronger, richer, and more resourceful fellows, is a temptation which human nature seldom has withstood and seldom will withstand.

Moreover, the political status of the Negro in the South is closely connected with the question of Negro crime. There can be no doubt that crime among Negroes has sensibly increased in the last thirty years, and that there has appeared in the slums of great cities a distinct criminal class among the blacks. In explaining this unfortunate development, we must note two things: (1) that the inevitable result of Emancipation was to increase crime and criminals, and (2) that the police system of the South was primarily designed to control slaves. As to the first point, we must not forget that under a strict slave system there can scarcely be such a thing as crime. But when these variously constituted human particles are suddenly thrown broadcast on the sea of life, some swim, some sink, and some hang suspended, to be forced up or down by the chance currents of a busy hurrying world. So great an economic and social revolution as swept the South in '63 meant a weeding out among the Negroes of the incompetents and vicious, the beginning of a differentiation of social grades. Now a rising group of people are not lifted bodily from the ground like an inert solid mass, but rather stretch upward like a living plant with its roots still clinging in the mould. The appearance, therefore, of the Negro criminal was a phenomenon to be awaited; and while it causes anxiety, it should not occasion surprise.

Here again the hope for the future depended peculiarly on careful and delicate dealing with these criminals. Their offences at first were those of laziness, carelessness, and impulse, rather than of malignity or ungoverned viciousness. Such misdemeanors needed discriminating treatment, firm but reformatory, with no hint of injustice, and full proof of guilt. For such dealing with criminals, white or black, the South had no machinery, no adequate jails or reformatories; its police system was arranged to deal with blacks alone, and tacitly assumed that every white man was *ipso facto* a member of that police. Thus grew up a double system of justice, which erred on the white side by undue leniency and the practical immunity of red-handed criminals, and erred on the black side by undue severity, injustice, and lack of discrimination. For, as I have said, the police system of the South was originally designed to keep track of all Negroes, not simply of criminals; and when the Negroes were freed and the whole South was convinced of the impossibility of free Negro labor, the first and almost universal device was to use the courts as a means of reenslaving the blacks. It was not then a question of crime, but rather one of color, that settled a man's conviction on almost any charge. Thus Negroes came to look upon courts as instruments of injustice and oppression, and upon those convicted in them as martyrs and victims.

When, now, the real Negro criminal appeared, and instead of petty stealing and vagrancy we began to have highway robbery, burglary, murder, and rape, there was a curious effect on both sides the color-line: the Negroes refused to believe the evidence of white witnesses or the fairness of white juries, so that the greatest deterrent to crime, the public opinion of one's own social caste, was lost, and the criminal was looked upon as crucified rather than hanged. On the other hand, the whites, used to being careless as to the guilt or innocence of accused Negroes, were swept in moments of passion beyond law, reason, and decency. Such a situation is bound to increase crime, and has increased it. To natural viciousness and vagrancy are being daily added motives of revolt and revenge which stir up all the latent savagery of both races and make peaceful attention to economic development often impossible.

But the chief problem in any community cursed with crime is not the punishment of the criminals, but the preventing of the young from being trained to crime. And here again the peculiar conditions of the South have prevented proper precautions. I have seen twelve-year-old boys working in chains on the public streets of Atlanta, directly in front of the schools, in company with old and hardened criminals; and this indiscriminate mingling of men and women and children makes the chain-gangs perfect schools of crime and debauchery. The struggle for reformatories, which has gone on in Virginia, Georgia, and other States, is the one encouraging sign of the awakening of some communities to the suicidal results of this policy.

It is the public schools, however, which can be made, outside the homes, the greatest means of training decent self-respecting citizens. We have been so hotly engaged recently in discussing trade-schools and the higher education that the pitiable plight of the public-school system in the South has almost dropped from view. Of every five dollars spent for public education in the State of Georgia, the white schools get four dollars and the Negro one dollar; and even then the white public-school system, save in the cities, is bad and cries for reform. If this is true of the whites, what of the blacks? I am becoming more and more convinced, as I look upon the system of common-school training in the South, that the national government must soon step in and aid popular education in some way. To-day it has been only by the most strenuous efforts on the part of the thinking men of the South that the Negro's share of the school fund has not been cut down to a pittance in some half-dozen States; and that movement not only is not dead, but in many communities is gaining strength. What in the name of reason does this nation expect of a people, poorly trained and hard pressed in severe economic competition, without political rights, and with ludicrously inadequate common-school facilities? What can it expect but crime and listlessness, offset here and there by the dogged struggles of the fortunate and more determined who are themselves buoyed by the hope that in due time the country will come to its senses?

I have thus far sought to make clear the physical, economic, and political relations of the Negroes and whites in the South, as I have conceived them, including, for the reasons set forth, crime and education. But after all that has been said on these more tangible matters of human contact, there still remains a part essential to a proper description of the South which it is difficult to describe or fix in terms easily understood by strangers. It is, in fine, the atmosphere of the land, the thought and feeling, the thousand and one little actions which go to make up life. In any community or nation it is these little things which are most elusive to the grasp and yet most essential to any clear conception of the group life taken as a whole. What is thus true of all communities is peculiarly true of the South, where, outside of written history and outside of printed law, there has been going on for a generation as deep a storm and stress of human souls, as intense a ferment of feeling, as intricate a writhing of spirit, as ever a people experienced. Within and without the sombre veil of color vast social forces have been at work,— efforts for human betterment, movements toward disintegration and despair, tragedies and comedies in social and economic life, and a swaying and lifting and sinking of human hearts which have made this land a land of mingled sorrow and joy, of change and excitement and unrest.

The centre of this spiritual turmoil has ever been the millions of black freedmen and their sons, whose destiny is so fatefully bound up with that of the nation. And yet the casual observer visiting the South sees at first little of this. He notes the growing frequency of dark faces as he rides along,—but otherwise the days slip lazily on, the sun shines, and this little world seems as happy and contented as other worlds he has visited. Indeed, on the question of questions—the Negro problem—he hears so little that there almost seems to be a conspiracy of silence; the morning papers seldom mention it, and then usually in a far-fetched academic way, and indeed almost every one seems to forget and ignore the darker half of the land, until the astonished visitor is inclined to ask if after all there *is* any problem here. But if he lingers long enough there comes the awakening: perhaps in a sudden whirl of passion which leaves him gasping at its bitter intensity; more likely in a gradually dawning sense of things he had not at first noticed. Slowly but surely his eyes begin to catch the shadows of the color-line: here he meets crowds of Negroes and whites; then he is suddenly aware that he cannot discover a single dark face; or again at the close of a day's wandering he may find himself in some strange assembly, where all faces are tinged brown or black, and where he has the vague, uncomfortable feeling of the stranger. He realizes at last that silently, resistlessly, the world about flows by him in two great streams: they ripple on in the same sunshine, they approach and mingle their waters in seeming carelessness,—then they divide and flow wide apart. It is done quietly; no mistakes are made, or if one occurs, the swift arm of the law and of public opinion swings down for a moment, as when the other day a black man and a white woman were arrested for talking together on Whitehall Street in Atlanta.

Now if one notices carefully one will see that between these two worlds, despite much physical contact and daily intermingling, there is almost no community of intellectual life or point of transference where the thoughts and feelings of one race can come into direct contact and sympathy with the thoughts and feelings of the other. Before and directly after the war, when all the best of the Negroes were domestic servants in the best of the white families, there were bonds of intimacy, affection, and sometimes blood relationship, between the races. They lived in the same home, shared in the family life, often attended the same church, and talked and conversed with each other. But the increasing civilization of the Negro since then has naturally meant the development of higher classes: there are increasing numbers of ministers, teachers, physicians, merchants, mechanics, and independent farmers, who by nature and training are the aristocracy and leaders of the blacks. Between them, however, and the best element of the whites, there is little or no intellectual commerce. They go to separate churches, they live in separate sections, they are strictly separated in all public gatherings, they travel separately, and they are beginning to read different papers and books. To most libraries, lectures, concerts, and museums, Negroes are either not admitted at all, or on terms peculiarly galling to the pride of the very classes who might otherwise be attracted. The daily paper chronicles the doings of the black world from afar with no great regard for accuracy; and so on, throughout the category of means for intellectual communication,—schools, conferences, efforts for social betterment, and the like,—it is usually true that the very representatives of the two races, who for mutual benefit and the welfare of the land ought to be in complete understanding and sympathy, are so far strangers that one side thinks all whites are narrow and prejudiced, and the other thinks educated Negroes dangerous and insolent. Moreover, in a land where the tyranny of public opinion and the intolerance of criticism is for obvious historical reasons so strong as in the South, such a situation is extremely difficult to correct. The white man, as well as the Negro, is bound and barred by the color-line, and many a scheme of friendliness and philanthropy, of broad-minded sympathy and generous fellowship between the two has dropped still-born because some busy-body has forced the color-question to the front and brought the tremendous force of unwritten law against the innovators.

It is hardly necessary for me to add very much in regard to the social contact between the races. Nothing has come to replace that finer sympathy and love between some masters and house servants which the radical and more uncompromising drawing of the color-line in recent years has caused almost completely to disappear. In a world where it means so much to take a man by the hand and sit beside him, to look frankly into his eyes and feel his heart beating with red blood; in a world where a social cigar or a cup of tea together means more than legislative halls and magazine articles and speeches,—one can imagine the consequences of the almost utter absence of such social amenities between estranged races, whose separation extends even to parks and streetcars.

Here there can be none of that social going down to the people,—the opening of heart and hand of the best to the worst, in generous acknowledgment of a common humanity and a common destiny. On the other hand, in matters of simple almsgiving, where there can be no question of social contact, and in the succor of the aged and sick, the South, as if stirred by a feeling of its unfortunate limitations, is generous to a fault. The black beggar is never turned away without a good deal more than a crust, and a call for help for the unfortunate meets quick response. I remember, one cold winter, in Atlanta, when I refrained from contributing to a public relief fund lest Negroes should be discriminated against, I afterward inquired of a friend: "Were any black people receiving aid?" "Why," said he, "they were *all* black."

And yet this does not touch the kernel of the problem. Human advancement is not a mere question of almsgiving, but rather of sympathy and cooperation among classes who would scorn charity. And here is a land where, in the higher walks of life, in all the higher striving for the good and noble and true, the color-line comes to separate natural friends and co-workers; while at the bottom of the social group, in the saloon, the gambling-hell, and the brothel, that same line wavers and disappears.

I have sought to paint an average picture of real relations between the sons of master and man in the South. I have not glossed over matters for policy's sake, for I fear we have already gone too far in that sort of thing. On the other hand, I have sincerely sought to let no unfair exaggerations creep in. I do not doubt that in some Southern communities conditions are better than those I have indicated; while I am no less certain that in other communities they are far worse.

Nor does the paradox and danger of this situation fail to interest and perplex the best conscience of the South. Deeply religious and intensely democratic as are the mass of the whites, they feel acutely the false position in which the Negro problems place them. Such an essentially honest-hearted and generous people cannot cite the caste-levelling precepts of Christianity, or believe in equality of opportunity for all men, without coming to feel more and more with each generation that the present drawing of the color-line is a flat contradiction to their beliefs and professions. But just as often as they come to this point, the present social condition of the Negro stands as a menace and a portent before even the most open-minded: if there were nothing to charge against the Negro but his blackness or other physical peculiarities, they argue, the problem would be comparatively simple; but what can we say to his ignorance, shiftlessness, poverty, and crime? can a self-respecting group hold anything but the least possible fellowship with such persons and survive? and shall we let a mawkish sentiment sweep away the culture of our fathers or the hope of our children? The argument so put is of great strength, but it is not a whit stronger than the argument of thinking Negroes: granted, they reply, that the condition of our masses is bad; there is certainly on the one hand adequate historical cause for this, and unmistakable evidence that no small number have, in spite of tremendous disadvantages, risen to the level of American civilization. And when, by proscription and prejudice, these same Negroes are classed with and treated like the lowest of their people, simply *because* they are Negroes, such a policy not only discourages thrift and intelligence among black men, but puts a direct premium on the very things you complain of,—inefficiency and crime. Draw lines of crime, of incompetency, of vice, as tightly and uncompromisingly as you will, for these things must be proscribed; but a color-line not only does not accomplish this purpose, but thwarts it.

In the face of two such arguments, the future of the South depends on the ability of the representatives of these opposing views to see and appreciate and sympathize with each other's position,—for the Negro to realize more deeply than he does at present the need of uplifting the masses of his people, for the white people to realize more vividly than they have yet done the deadening and disastrous effect of a color-prejudice that classes Phillis Wheatley and Sam Hose in the same despised class.

It is not enough for the Negroes to declare that color-prejudice is the sole cause of their social condition, nor for the white South to reply that their social condition is the main cause of prejudice. They both act as reciprocal cause and effect, and a change in neither alone will bring the desired effect. Both must change, or neither can improve to any great extent. The Negro cannot stand the present reactionary tendencies and unreasoning drawing of the color-line indefinitely without discouragement and retrogression. And the condition of the Negro is ever the excuse for further discrimination. Only by a union of intelligence and sympathy across the color-line in this critical period of the Republic shall justice and right triumph,

> "That mind and soul according well,
> May make one music as before,
> But vaster."

X
Of the Faith of the Fathers

Dim face of Beauty haunting all the world,
    Fair face of Beauty all too fair to see,
Where the lost stars adown the heavens are hurled,—
      There, there alone for thee
      May white peace be,

Beauty, sad face of Beauty, Mystery, Wonder,
    What are these dreams to foolish babbling men
Who cry with little noises 'neath the thunder
      Of Ages ground to sand,
      To a little sand,
        Fiona Macleod. (1855–1905) from *Pseudonym of William Sharp*

It was out in the country, far from home, far from my foster home, on a dark Sunday night. The road wandered from our rambling log-house up the stony bed of a creek, past wheat and corn, until we could hear dimly across the fields a rhythmic cadence of song,—soft, thrilling, powerful, that swelled and died sorrowfully in our ears. I was a country schoolteacher then, fresh from the East, and had never seen a Southern Negro revival. To be sure, we in Berkshire were not perhaps as stiff and formal as they in Suffolk of olden time; yet we were very quiet and subdued, and I know not what would have happened those clear Sabbath mornings had some one punctuated the sermon with a wild scream, or interrupted the long prayer with a loud Amen! And so most striking to me, as I approached the village and the little plain church perched aloft, was the air of intense excitement that possessed that mass of black folk. A sort of suppressed terror hung in the air and seemed to seize us,—a pythian madness, a demoniac possession, that lent terrible reality to song and word. The black and massive form of the preacher swayed and quivered as the words crowded to his lips and flew at us in singular eloquence. The people moaned and fluttered, and then the gaunt-cheeked brown woman beside me suddenly leaped straight into the air and shrieked like a lost soul, while round about came wail and groan and outcry, and a scene of human passion such as I had never conceived before.

Those who have not thus witnessed the frenzy of a Negro revival in the untouched backwoods of the South can but dimly realize the religious feeling of the slave; as described, such scenes appear grotesque and funny, but as seen they are awful. Three things characterized this religion of the slave,— the Preacher, the Music, and the Frenzy. The Preacher is the most unique personality developed by the Negro on American soil. A leader, a politician, an orator, a "boss," an intriguer, an idealist,—all these he is, and ever, too, the centre of a group of men, now twenty, now a thousand in number. The combination of a certain adroitness with deep-seated earnestness, of tact with consummate ability, gave him his preeminence, and helps him maintain it. The type, of course, varies according to time and place, from the West Indies in the sixteenth century to New England in the nineteenth, and from the Mississippi bottoms to cities like New Orleans or New York.

The Music of Negro religion is that plaintive rhythmic melody, with its touching minor cadences, which, despite caricature and defilement, still remains the most original and beautiful expression of human life and long- ing yet born on American soil. Sprung from the African forests, where its counterpart can still be heard, it was adapted, changed, and intensified by the tragic soul-life of the slave, until, under the stress of law and whip, it became the one true expression of a people's sorrow, despair, and hope.

Finally the Frenzy of "Shouting," when the Spirit of the Lord passed by, and, seizing the devotee, made him mad with supernatural joy, was the last essential of Negro religion and the one more devoutly believed in than all the rest. It varied in expression from the silent rapt countenance or the low murmur and moan to the mad abandon of physical fervor,—the stamping, shrieking, and shouting, the rushing to and fro and wild waving of arms, the weeping and laughing, the vision and the trance. All this is nothing new in the world, but old as religion, as Delphi and Endor. And so firm a hold did it have on the Negro, that many generations firmly believed that without this visible manifestation of the God there could be no true communion with the Invisible.

These were the characteristics of Negro religious life as developed up to the time of Emancipation. Since under the peculiar circumstances of the black man's environment they were the one expression of his higher life, they are of deep interest to the student of his development, both socially and psychologically. Numerous are the attractive lines of inquiry that here group themselves. What did slavery mean to the African savage? What was his attitude toward the World and Life? What seemed to him good and evil,—God and Devil? Whither went his longings and strivings, and wherefore were his heart-burnings and disappointments? Answers to such questions can come only from a study of Negro religion as a development, through its gradual changes from the heathenism of the Gold Coast to the institutional Negro church of Chicago.

Moreover, the religious growth of millions of men, even though they be slaves, cannot be without potent influence upon their contemporaries. The Methodists and Baptists of America owe much of their condition to the silent but potent influence of their millions of Negro converts. Especially is this noticeable in the South, where theology and religious philosophy are on this account a long way behind the North, and where the religion of the poor whites is a plain copy of Negro thought and methods. The mass of "gospel" hymns which has swept through American churches and well-nigh ruined our sense of song consists largely of debased imitations of Negro melodies made by ears that caught the jingle but not the music, the body but not the soul, of the Jubilee songs. It is thus clear that the study of Negro religion is not only a vital part of the history of the Negro in America, but no uninteresting part of American history.

The Negro church of to-day is the social centre of Negro life in the United States, and the most characteristic expression of African character. Take a typical church in a small Virginia town: it is the "First Baptist"—a roomy brick edifice seating five hundred or more persons, tastefully finished in Georgia pine, with a carpet, a small organ, and stained-glass windows. Underneath is a large assembly room with benches. This building is the central club-house of a community of a thousand or more Negroes. Various organizations meet here,—the church proper, the Sunday-school, two or three insurance societies, women's societies, secret societies, and mass meetings of various kinds. Entertainments, suppers, and lectures are held beside the five or six regular weekly religious services. Considerable sums of money are collected and expended here, employment is found for the idle, strangers are introduced, news is disseminated and charity distributed. At the same time this social, intellectual, and economic centre is a religious centre of great power. Depravity, Sin, Redemption, Heaven, Hell, and Damnation are preached twice a Sunday after the crops are laid by; and few indeed of the community have the hardihood to withstand conversion. Back of this more formal religion, the Church often stands as a real conserver of morals, a strengthener of family life, and the final authority on what is Good and Right.

Thus one can see in the Negro church to-day, reproduced in microcosm, all the great world from which the Negro is cut off by color-prejudice and social condition. In the great city churches the same tendency is noticeable and in many respects emphasized. A great church like the Bethel of Philadelphia has over eleven hundred members, an edifice seating fifteen hundred persons and valued at one hundred thousand dollars, an annual budget of five thousand dollars, and a government consisting of a pastor with several assisting local preachers, an executive and legislative board, financial boards and tax collectors; general church meetings for making laws; sub-divided groups led by class leaders, a company of militia, and twenty-four auxiliary societies. The activity of a church like this is immense and far-reaching, and the bishops who preside over these organizations throughout the land are among the most powerful Negro rulers in the world.

Such churches are really governments of men, and consequently a little investigation reveals the curious fact that, in the South, at least, practically every American Negro is a church member. Some, to be sure, are not regularly enrolled, and a few do not habitually attend services; but, practically, a proscribed people must have a social centre, and that centre for this people is the Negro church. The census of 1890 showed nearly twenty-four thousand Negro churches in the country, with a total enrolled membership of over two and a half millions, or ten actual church members to every twenty-eight persons, and in some Southern States one in every two persons. Besides these there is the large number who, while not enrolled as members, attend and take part in many of the activities of the church. There is an organized Negro church for every sixty black families in the nation, and in some States for every forty families, owning, on an average, a thousand dollars' worth of property each, or nearly twenty-six million dollars in all.

Such, then, is the large development of the Negro church since Emancipation. The question now is, What have been the successive steps of this social history and what are the present tendencies? First, we must realize that no such institution as the Negro church could rear itself without definite historical foundations. These foundations we can find if we remember that the social history of the Negro did not start in America. He was brought from a definite social environment,—the polygamous clan life under the headship of the chief and the potent influence of the priest. His religion was nature-worship, with profound belief in invisible surrounding influences, good and bad, and his worship was through incantation and sacrifice. The first rude change in this life was the slave ship and the West Indian sugar-fields. The plantation organization replaced the clan and tribe, and the white master replaced the chief with far greater and more despotic powers. Forced and long-continued toil became the rule of life, the old ties of blood relationship and kinship disappeared, and instead of the family appeared a new polygamy and polyandry, which, in some cases, almost reached promiscuity. It was a terrific social revolution, and yet some traces were retained of the former group life, and the chief remaining institution was the Priest or Medicine-man. He early appeared on the plantation and found his function as the healer of the sick, the interpreter of the Unknown, the comforter of the sorrowing, the supernatural avenger of wrong, and the one who rudely but picturesquely expressed the longing, disappointment, and resentment of a stolen and oppressed people. Thus, as bard, physician, judge, and priest, within the narrow limits allowed by the slave system, rose the Negro preacher, and under him the first church was not at first by any means Christian nor definitely organized; rather it was an adaptation and mingling of heathen rites among the members of each plantation, and roughly designated as Voodooism. Association with the masters, missionary effort and motives of expediency gave these rites an early veneer of Christianity, and after the lapse of many generations the Negro church became Christian.

Two characteristic things must be noticed in regard to the church. First, it became almost entirely Baptist and Methodist in faith; secondly, as a social institution it antedated by many decades the monogamic Negro home. From the very circumstances of its beginning, the church was confined to the plantation, and consisted primarily of a series of disconnected units; although, later on, some freedom of movement was allowed, still this geographical limitation was always important and was one cause of the spread of the decentralized and democratic Baptist faith among the slaves. At the same time, the visible rite of baptism appealed strongly to their mystic temperament. To-day the Baptist Church is still largest in membership among Negroes, and has a million and a half communants. Next in popularity came the churches organized in connection with the white neighboring churches, chiefly Baptist and Methodist, with a few Episcopalian and others. The Methodists still form the second greatest denomination, with nearly a million members. The faith of these two leading denominations was more suited to the slave church from the prominence they gave to religious feeling and fervor. The Negro membership in other denominations has always been small and relatively unimportant, although the Episcopalians and Presbyterians are gaining among the more intelligent classes to-day, and the Catholic Church is making headway in certain sections. After Emancipation, and still earlier in the North, the Negro churches largely served such affiliations as they had had with the white churches, either by choice or by compulsion. The Baptist churches became independent, but the Methodists were compelled early to unite for purposes of episcopal government. This gave rise to the great African Methodist Church, the greatest Negro organization in the world, to the Zion Church and the Colored Methodist, and to the black conferences and churches in this and other denominations.

The second fact noted, namely, that the Negro church antedates the Negro home, leads to an explanation of much that is paradoxical in this communistic institution and in the morals of its members. But especially it leads us to regard this institution as peculiarly the expression of the inner ethical life of a people in a sense seldom true elsewhere. Let us turn, then, from the outer physical development of the church to the more important inner ethical life of the people who compose it. The Negro has already been pointed out many times as a religious animal,—a being of that deep emotional nature which turns instinctively toward the supernatural. Endowed with a rich tropical imagination and a keen, delicate appreciation of Nature, the transplanted African lived in a world animate with gods and devils, elves and witches; full of strange influences,—of Good to be implored, of Evil to be propitiated. Slavery, then, was to him the dark triumph of Evil over him. All the hateful powers of the Under-world were striving against him, and a spirit of revolt and revenge filled his heart. He called up all the resources of heathenism to aid,—exorcism and witch-craft, the mysterious Obi worship with its barbarious rites, spells, and blood-sacrifice even, now and then, of human victims. Weird midnight orgies and mystic conjurations were invoked, the witch-woman and the voodoo-priest became the centre of Negro group life, and that vein of vague superstition which characterizes the unlettered Negro even to-day was deepened and strengthened.

In spite, however, of such success as that of the fierce Maroons, the Danish blacks, and others, the spirit of revolt gradually died away under the untiring energy and superior strength of the slave masters. By the middle of the eighteenth century the black slave had sunk, with hushed murmurs, to his place at the bottom of a new economic system, and was unconsciously ripe for a new philosophy of life. Nothing suited his condition then better than the doctrines of passive submission embodied in the newly learned Christianity. Slave masters early realized this, and cheerfully aided religious propaganda within certain bounds. The long system of repression and degradation of the Negro tended to emphasize the elements of his character which made him a valuable chattel: courtesy became humility, moral strength degenerated into submission, and the exquisite native appreciation of the beautiful became an infinite capacity for dumb suffering. The Negro, losing the joy of this world, eagerly seized upon the offered conceptions of the next; the avenging Spirit of the Lord enjoining patience in this world, under sorrow and tribulation until the Great Day when He should lead His dark children home,—this became his comforting dream. His preacher repeated the prophecy, and his bards sang,—

"Children, we all shall be free
    When the Lord shall appear!

This deep religious fatalism, painted so beautifully in "Uncle Tom," came soon to breed, as all fatalistic faiths will, the sensualist side by side with the martyr. Under the lax moral life of the plantation, where marriage was a farce, laziness a virtue, and property a theft, a religion of resignation and submission degenerated easily, in less strenuous minds, into a philosophy of indulgence and crime. Many of the worst characteristics of the Negro masses of to-day had their seed in this period of the slave's ethical growth. Here it was that the Home was ruined under the very shadow of the Church, white and black; here habits of shiftlessness took root, and sullen hopelessness replaced hopeful strife.

With the beginning of the abolition movement and the gradual growth of a class of free Negroes came a change. We often neglect the influence of the freedman before the war, because of the paucity of his numbers and the small weight he had in the history of the nation. But we must not forget that his chief influence was internal,—was exerted on the black world; and that there he was the ethical and social leader. Huddled as he was in a few centres like Philadelphia, New York, and New Orleans, the masses of the freedmen sank into poverty and listlessness; but not all of them. The free Negro leader early arose and his chief characteristic was intense earnestness and deep feeling on the slavery question. Freedom became to him a real thing and not a dream. His religion became darker and more intense, and into his ethics crept a note of revenge, into his songs a day of reckoning close at hand. The

"Coming of the Lord" swept this side of Death, and came to be a thing to be hoped for in this day. Through fugitive slaves and irrepressible discussion this desire for freedom seized the black millions still in bondage, and became their one ideal of life. The black bards caught new notes, and sometimes even dared to sing,—

"O Freedom, O Freedom, O Freedom over me!
  Before I'll be a slave
  I'll be buried in my grave,
  And go home to my Lord
  And be free."

For fifty years Negro religion thus transformed itself and identified itself with the dream of Abolition, until that which was a radical fad in the white North and an anarchistic plot in the white South had become a religion to the black world. Thus, when Emancipation finally came, it seemed to the freedman a literal Coming of the Lord. His fervid imagination was stirred as never before, by the tramp of armies, the blood and dust of battle, and the wail and whirl of social upheaval. He stood dumb and motionless before the whirlwind: what had he to do with it? Was it not the Lord's doing, and marvellous in his eyes? Joyed and bewildered with what came, he stood awaiting new wonders till the inevitable Age of Reaction swept over the nation and brought the crisis of to-day.

It is difficult to explain clearly the present critical stage of Negro religion. First, we must remember that living as the blacks do in close contact with a great modern nation, and sharing, although imperfectly, the soul-life of that nation, they must necessarily be affected more or less directly by all the religious and ethical forces that are to-day moving the United States. These questions and movements are, however, overshadowed and dwarfed by the (to them) all-important question of their civil, political, and economic status. They must perpetually discuss the "Negro Problem,"—must live, move, and have their being in it, and interpret all else in its light or darkness. With this come, too, peculiar problems of their inner life,—of the status of women, the maintenance of Home, the training of children, the accumulation of wealth, and the prevention of crime. All this must mean a time of intense ethical ferment, of religious heart-searching and intellectual unrest. From the double life every American Negro must live, as a Negro and as an American, as swept on by the current of the nineteenth while yet struggling in the eddies of the fifteenth century,—from this must arise a painful self-consciousness, an almost morbid sense of personality and a moral hesitancy which is fatal to self-confidence. The worlds within and without the Veil of Color are changing, and changing rapidly, but not at the same rate, not in the same way; and this must produce a peculiar wrenching of the soul, a peculiar sense of doubt and bewilderment. Such a double life, with double thoughts, double duties, and double social classes, must give rise to double words and double ideals, and tempt the mind to pretence or revolt, to hypocrisy or radicalism.

In some such doubtful words and phrases can one perhaps most clearly picture the peculiar ethical paradox that faces the Negro of to-day and is tingeing and changing his religious life. Feeling that his rights and his dearest ideals are being trampled upon, that the public conscience is ever more deaf to his righteous appeal, and that all the reactionary forces of prejudice, greed, and revenge are daily gaining new strength and fresh allies, the Negro faces no enviable dilemma. Conscious of his impotence, and pessimistic, he often becomes bitter and vindictive; and his religion, instead of a worship, is a complaint and a curse, a wail rather than a hope, a sneer rather than a faith. On the other hand, another type of mind, shrewder and keener and more tortuous too, sees in the very strength of the anti-Negro movement it patent weaknesses, and with Jesuitic casuistry is deterred by no ethical considerations in the endeavor to turn this weakness to the black man's strength. Thus we have two great and hardly reconcilable streams of thought and ethical strivings; the danger of the one lies in anarchy, that of the other in hypocrisy. The one type of Negro stands almost ready to curse God and die, and the other is too often found a traitor to right and a coward before force; the one is wedded to ideals remote, whimsical, perhaps impossible of realization; the other forgets that life is more than meat and the body more than raiment. But, after all, is not this simply the writhing of the age translated into black,—the triumph of the Lie which today, with its false culture, faces the hideousness of the anarchist assassin?

To-day the two groups of Negroes, the one in the North, the other in the South, represent these divergent ethical tendencies, the first tending toward radicalism, the other toward hypocritical compromise. It is no idle regret with which the white South mourns the loss of the old-time Negro,—the frank, honest, simple old servant who stood for the earlier religious age of submission and humility. With all his laziness and lack of many elements of true manhood, he was at least open-hearted, faithful, and sincere. To-day he is gone, but who is to blame for his going? Is it not those very persons who mourn for him? Is it not the tendency, born of Reconstruction and Reaction, to found a society on lawlessness and deception, to tamper with the moral fibre of a naturally honest and straightforward people until the whites threaten to become ungovernable tyrants and the blacks criminals and hypocrites? Deception is the natural defence of the weak against the strong, and the South used it for many years against its conquerors; to-day it must be prepared to see its black proletariat turn that same two-edged weapon against itself. And how natural this is! The death of Denmark Vesey and Nat Turner proved long since to the Negro the present hopelessness of physical defence. Political defence is becoming less and less available, and economic defence is still only partially effective. But there is a patent defence at hand,—the defence of deception and flattery, of cajoling and lying. It is the same defence which peasants of the Middle Age used and which left its stamp on their character for centuries. To-day the young Negro of the South who would succeed cannot be frank and outspoken, honest and self-assertive, but rather he is daily tempted to be silent and wary, politic and sly; he must flatter and be pleasant, endure petty insults with a smile, shut his eyes to wrong; in too many cases he sees positive personal advantage in deception and lying. His real thoughts, his real aspirations, must be guarded in whispers; he must not criticise, he must not complain. Patience, humility, and adroitness must, in these growing black youth, replace impulse, manliness, and courage. With this sacrifice there is an economic opening, and perhaps peace and some prosperity. Without this there is riot, migration, or crime. Nor is this situation peculiar to the Southern United States, is it not rather the only method by which undeveloped races have gained the right to share modern culture? The price of culture is a Lie.

On the other hand, in the North the tendency is to emphasize the radicalism of the Negro. Driven from his birthright in the South by a situation at which every fibre of his more outspoken and assertive nature revolts, he finds himself in a land where he can scarcely earn a decent living amid the harsh competition and the color discrimination. At the same time, through schools and periodicals, discussions and lectures, he is intellectually quickened and awakened. The soul, long pent up and dwarfed, suddenly expands in new-found freedom. What wonder that every tendency is to excess,—radical complaint, radical remedies, bitter denunciation or angry silence. Some sink, some rise. The criminal and the sensualist leave the church for the gambling-hell and the brothel, and fill the slums of Chicago and Baltimore; the better classes segregate themselves from the group-life of both white and black, and form an aristocracy, cultured but pessimistic, whose bitter criticism stings while it points out no way of escape. They despise the submission and subserviency of the Southern Negroes, but offer no other means by which a poor and oppressed minority can exist side by side with its masters. Feeling deeply and keenly the tendencies and opportunities of the age in which they live, their souls are bitter at the fate which drops the Veil between; and the very fact that this bitterness is natural and justifiable only serves to intensify it and make it more maddening.

Between the two extreme types of ethical attitude which I have thus sought to make clear wavers the mass of the millions of Negroes, North and South; and their religious life and activity partake of this social conflict within their ranks. Their churches are differentiating,—now into groups of cold, fashionable devotees, in no way distinguishable from similar white groups save in color of skin; now into large social and business institutions catering to the desire for information and amusement of their members, warily avoiding unpleasant questions both within and without the black world, and preaching in effect if not in word: *Dum vivimus, vivamus.*

But back of this still broods silently the deep religious feeling of the real Negro heart, the stirring, unguided might of powerful human souls who have lost the guiding star of the past and seek in the great night a new religious ideal. Some day the Awakening will come, when the pent-up vigor of ten million souls shall sweep irresistibly toward the Goal, out of the Valley of the Shadow of Death, where all that makes life worth living—Liberty, Justice, and Right—is marked "For White People Only."

XI

Of the Passing of the First-Born

O sister, sister, thy first-begotten,
The hands that cling and the feet that follow,

The voice of the child's blood crying yet,
Who hath remembered me? who hath forgotten?
Thou hast forgotten, O summer swallow,
But the world shall end when I forget.
Algernon Charles Swinburne. (1837–1909) from *Itylus*

"Unto you a child is born," sang the bit of yellow paper that fluttered into my room one brown October morning. Then the fear of fatherhood mingled wildly with the joy of creation; I wondered how it looked and how it felt—what were its eyes, and how its hair curled and crumpled itself. And I thought in awe of her,—she who had slept with Death to tear a man-child from underneath her heart, while I was unconsciously wandering. I fled to my wife and child, repeating the while to myself half wonderingly, "Wife and child? Wife and child?"—fled fast and faster than boat and steam-car, and yet must ever impatiently await them; away from the hard-voiced city, away from the flickering sea into my own Berkshire Hills that sit all sadly guarding the gates of Massachusetts.

Up the stairs I ran to the wan mother and whimpering babe, to the sanctuary on whose altar a life at my bidding had offered itself to win a life, and won. What is this tiny formless thing, this newborn wail from an unknown world,—all head and voice? I handle it curiously, and watch perplexed its winking, breathing, and sneezing. I did not love it then; it seemed a ludicrous thing to love; but her I loved, my girl-mother, she whom now I saw unfolding like the glory of the morning—the transfigured woman. Through her I came to love the wee thing, as it grew strong; as its little soul unfolded itself in twitter and cry and half-formed word, and as its eyes caught the gleam and flash of life. How beautiful he was, with his olive-tinted flesh and dark gold ringlets, his eyes of mingled blue and brown, his perfect little limbs, and the soft voluptuous roll which the blood of Africa had moulded into his features! I held him in my arms, after we had sped far away from our Southern home,—held him, and glanced at the hot red soil of Georgia and the breathless city of a hundred hills, and felt a vague unrest. Why was his hair tinted with gold? An evil omen was golden hair in my life. Why had not the brown of his eyes crushed out and killed the blue?—for brown were his father's eyes, and his father's father's. And thus in the Land of the Color-line I saw, as it fell across my baby, the shadow of the Veil.

Within the Veil was he born, said I; and there within shall he live,—a Negro and a Negro's son. Holding in that little head—ah, bitterly!—the unbowed pride of a hunted race, clinging with that tiny dimpled hand—ah, wearily!—

to a hope not hopeless but unhopeful, and seeing with those bright wondering eyes that peer into my soul a land whose freedom is to us a mockery and whose liberty a lie. I saw the shadow of the Veil as it passed over my baby, I saw the cold city towering above the blood-red land. I held my face beside his little cheek, showed him the star-children and the twinkling lights as they began to flash, and stilled with an even-song the unvoiced terror of my life.

So sturdy and masterful he grew, so filled with bubbling life, so tremulous with the unspoken wisdom of a life but eighteen months distant from the All-life,—we were not far from worshipping this revelation of the divine, my wife and I. Her own life builded and moulded itself upon the child; he tinged her every dream and idealized her every effort. No hands but hers must touch and garnish those little limbs; no dress or frill must touch them that had not wearied her fingers; no voice but hers could coax him off to Dreamland, and she and he together spoke some soft and unknown tongue and in it held communion. I too mused above his little white bed; saw the strength of my own arm stretched onward through the ages through the newer strength of his; saw the dream of my black fathers stagger a step onward in the wild phantasm of the world; heard in his baby voice the voice of the Prophet that was to rise within the Veil.

And so we dreamed and loved and planned by fall and winter, and the full flush of the long Southern spring, till the hot winds rolled from the fetid Gulf, till the roses shivered and the still stern sun quivered its awful light over the hills of Atlanta. And then one night the little feet pattered wearily to the wee white bed, and the tiny hands trembled; and a warm flushed face tossed on the pillow, and we knew baby was sick. Ten days he lay there,—a swift week and three endless days, wasting, wasting away. Cheerily the mother nursed him the first days, and laughed into the little eyes that smiled again. Tenderly then she hovered round him, till the smile fled away and Fear crouched beside the little bed.

Then the day ended not, and night was a dreamless terror, and joy and sleep slipped away. I hear now that Voice at midnight calling me from dull and dreamless trance,—crying, "The Shadow of Death! The Shadow of Death!" Out into the starlight I crept, to rouse the gray physician,—the Shadow of Death, the Shadow of Death. The hours trembled on; the night listened; the ghastly dawn glided like a tired thing across the lamplight. Then we two alone looked upon the child as he turned toward us with great eyes, and stretched his stringlike hands,—the Shadow of Death! And we spoke no word, and turned away.

He died at eventide, when the sun lay like a brooding sorrow above the western hills, veiling its face; when the winds spoke not, and the trees, the great green trees he loved, stood motionless. I saw his breath beat quicker and quicker, pause, and then his little soul leapt like a star that travels in the night and left a world of darkness in its train. The day changed not; the same tall trees peeped in at the windows, the same green grass glinted in the setting sun. Only in the chamber of death writhed the world's most piteous thing—a childless mother.

I shirk not. I long for work. I pant for a life full of striving. I am no coward, to shrink before the rugged rush of the storm, nor even quail before the awful shadow of the Veil. But hearken, O Death! Is not this my life hard enough,—is not that dull land that stretches its sneering web about me cold enough,—is not all the world beyond these four little walls pitiless enough, but that thou must needs enter here,—thou, O Death? About my head the thundering storm beat like a heartless voice, and the crazy forest pulsed with the curses of the weak; but what cared I, within my home beside my wife and baby boy? Wast thou so jealous of one little coign of happiness that thou must needs enter there,—thou, O Death?

A perfect life was his, all joy and love, with tears to make it brighter,—sweet as a summer's day beside the Housatonic. The world loved him; the women kissed his curls, the men looked gravely into his wonderful eyes, and the children hovered and fluttered about him. I can see him now, changing like the sky from sparkling laughter to darkening frowns, and then to wondering thoughtfulness as he watched the world. He knew no color-line, poor dear—and the Veil, though it shadowed him, had not yet darkened half his sun. He loved the white matron, he loved his black nurse; and in his little world walked souls alone, uncolored and unclothed. I—yea, all men—are larger and purer by the infinite breadth of that one little life. She who in simple clearness of vision sees beyond the stars said when he had flown, "He will be happy There; he ever loved beautiful things." And I, far more ignorant, and blind by the web of mine own weaving, sit alone winding words and muttering, "If still he be, and he be There, and there be a There, let him be happy, O Fate!"

Blithe was the morning of his burial, with bird and song and sweet-smelling flowers. The trees whispered to the grass, but the children sat with hushed faces. And yet it seemed a ghostly unreal day,—the wraith of Life. We seemed to rumble down an unknown street behind a little white bundle of posies, with the shadow of a song in our ears. The busy city dinned about us; they did not say much, those pale-faced hurrying men and women; they did not say much,—they only glanced and said, "Niggers!"

We could not lay him in the ground there in Georgia, for the earth there is strangely red; so we bore him away to the northward, with his flowers and his little folded hands. In vain, in vain!—for where, O God! beneath thy broad blue sky shall my dark baby rest in peace,—where Reverence dwells, and Goodness, and a Freedom that is free?

All that day and all that night there sat an awful gladness in my heart,—nay, blame me not if I see the world thus darkly through the Veil,—and my soul whispers ever to me saying, "Not dead, not dead, but escaped; not bond, but free." No bitter meanness now shall sicken his baby heart till it die a living death, no taunt shall madden his happy boyhood. Fool that I was to think or wish that this little soul should grow choked and deformed within the Veil! I might have known that yonder deep unworldly look that ever and anon floated past his eyes was peering far beyond this narrow Now. In the poise of his little curl-crowned head did there not sit all that wild pride of being which his father had hardly crushed in his own heart? For what, forsooth, shall a Negro want with pride amid the studied humiliations of fifty million fellows? Well sped, my boy, before the world had dubbed your ambition insolence, had held your ideals unattainable, and taught you to cringe and bow. Better far this nameless void that stops my life than a sea of sorrow for you.

Idle words; he might have borne his burden more bravely than we,—aye, and found it lighter too, some day; for surely, surely this is not the end. Surely there shall yet dawn some mighty morning to lift the Veil and set the prisoned free. Not for me,—I shall die in my bonds,—but for fresh young souls who have not known the night and waken to the morning; a morning when men ask of the workman, not "Is he white?" but "Can he work?" When men ask artists, not "Are they black?" but "Do you know?" Some morning this may be, long, long years to come. But now there wails, on that dark shore within the Veil, the same deep voice, *Thou shalt forego!* And all have I foregone at that command, and with small complaint,—all save that fair young form that lies so coldly wed with death in the nest I had builded.

If one must have gone, why not I? Why may I not rest me from this restlessness and sleep from this wide waking? Was not the world's alembic, Time, in his young hands, and is not my time waning? Are there so many workers in the vineyard that the fair promise of this little body could lightly be tossed away? The wretched of my race that line the alleys of the nation sit fatherless and unmothered; but Love sat beside his cradle, and in his ear Wisdom waited to speak. Perhaps now he knows the All-love, and needs not to be wise. Sleep, then, child,—sleep till I sleep and waken to a baby voice and the ceaseless patter of little feet—above the Veil.

XII
Of Alexander Crummell

Then from the Dawn it seemed there came, but faint
As from beyond the limit of the world,
Like the last echo born of a great cry,
Sounds, as if some fair city were one voice
Around a king returning from his wars.
Lord Alfred Tennyson. (1809–92) from In Memorium

This is the story of a human heart,—the tale of a black boy who many long years ago began to struggle with life that he might know the world and know himself. Three temptations he met on those dark dunes that lay gray and dismal before the wonder-eyes of the child: the temptation of Hate, that stood out against the red dawn; the temptation of Despair, that darkened noonday; and the temptation of Doubt, that ever steals along with twilight.

Above all, you must hear of the vales he crossed,—the Valley of Humiliation and the Valley of the Shadow of Death.

I saw Alexander Crummell first at a Wilberforce commencement season, amid its bustle and crush. Tall, frail, and black he stood, with simple dignity and an unmistakable air of good breeding. I talked with him apart, where the storming of the lusty young orators could not harm us. I spoke to him politely, then curiously, then eagerly, as I began to feel the fineness of his character,—his calm courtesy, the sweetness of his strength, and his fair blending of the hope and truth of life. Instinctively I bowed before this man, as one bows before the prophets of the world. Some seer he seemed, that came not from the crimson Past or the gray To-come, but from the pulsing Now,—that mocking world which seemed to me at once so light and dark, so splendid and sordid. Fourscore years had he wandered in this same world of mine, within the Veil.

He was born with the Missouri Compromise and lay a-dying amid the echoes of Manila and El Caney: stirring times for living, times dark to look back upon, darker to look forward to. The black-faced lad that paused over his mud and marbles seventy years ago saw puzzling vistas as he looked down the world. The slave-ship still groaned across the Atlantic, faint cries burdened the Southern breeze, and the great black father whispered mad tales of cruelty into those young ears. From the low doorway the mother silently watched her boy at play, and at nightfall sought him eagerly lest the shadows bear him away to the land of slaves.

So his young mind worked and winced and shaped curiously a vision of Life; and in the midst of that vision ever stood one dark figure alone,—ever with the hard, thick countenance of that bitter father, and a form that fell in vast and shapeless folds. Thus the temptation of Hate grew and shadowed the growing child,—gliding stealthily into his laughter, fading into his play, and seizing his dreams by day and night with rough, rude turbulence. So the black boy asked of sky and sun and flower the never-answered Why? and loved, as he grew, neither the world nor the world's rough ways.

Strange temptation for a child, you may think; and yet in this wide land to-day a thousand thousand dark children brood before this same temptation, and feel its cold and shuddering arms. For them, perhaps, some one will some day lift the Veil,—will come tenderly and cheerily into those sad little lives and brush the brooding hate away, just as Beriah Green strode in upon the life of Alexander Crummell. And before the bluff, kind-hearted man the shadow seemed less dark. Beriah Green had a school in Oneida County, New York, with a score of mischievous boys. "I'm going to bring a black boy here to educate," said Beriah Green, as only a crank and an abolitionist would have dared to say. "Oho!" laughed the boys. "Ye-es," said his wife; and Alexander came. Once before, the black boy had sought a school, had travelled, cold and hungry, four hundred miles up into free New Hampshire, to Canaan. But the godly farmers hitched ninety yoke of oxen to the abolition schoolhouse and dragged it into the middle of the swamp. The black boy trudged away.

The nineteenth was the first century of human sympathy,—the age when half wonderingly we began to descry in others that transfigured spark of divinity which we call Myself; when clodhoppers and peasants, and tramps and thieves, and millionaires and—sometimes—Negroes, became throbbing souls whose warm pulsing life touched us so nearly that we half gasped with surprise, crying, "Thou too! Hast Thou seen Sorrow and the dull waters of Hopelessness? Hast Thou known Life?" And then all helplessly we peered into those Other-worlds, and wailed, "O World of Worlds, how shall man make you one?"

So in that little Oneida school there came to those school-boys a revelation of thought and longing beneath one black skin, of which they had not dreamed before. And to the lonely boy came a new dawn of sympathy and inspiration. The shadowy, formless thing—the temptation of Hate, that hovered between him and the world—grew fainter and less sinister. It did not wholly fade away, but diffused itself and lingered thick at the edges. Through it the child now first saw the blue and gold of life,—the sun-swept road that ran 'twixt heaven and earth until in one far-off wan wavering line they met and kissed. A vision of life came to the growing boy,—mystic, wonderful. He raised his head, stretched himself, breathed deep of the fresh new air. Yonder, behind the forests, he heard strange sounds; then glinting through the trees he saw, far, far away, the bronzed hosts of a nation calling,—calling faintly, calling loudly. He heard the hateful clank of their chains; he felt them cringe and grovel, and there rose within him a protest and a prophecy. And he girded himself to walk down the world.

A voice and vision called him to be a priest,—a seer to lead the uncalled out of the house of bondage. He saw the headless host turn toward him like the whirling of mad waters,—he stretched forth his hands eagerly, and then, even as he stretched them, suddenly there swept across the vision the temptation of Despair.

They were not wicked men,—the problem of life is not the problem of the wicked,—they were calm, good men, Bishops of the Apostolic Church of God, and strove toward righteousness. They said slowly, "It is all very natural—it is even commendable; but the General Theological Seminary of the Episcopal Church cannot admit a Negro." And when that thin, half-grotesque figure still haunted their doors, they put their hands kindly, half sorrowfully, on his shoulders, and said, "Now,—of course, we—we know how *you* feel about it; but you see it is impossible,—that is—well—it is premature. Sometime, we trust—sincerely trust—all such distinctions will fade away; but now the world is as it is."

This was the temptation of Despair; and the young man fought it doggedly. Like some grave shadow he flitted by those halls, pleading, arguing, half angrily demanding admittance, until there came the final *No:* until men hustled the disturber away, marked him as foolish, unreasonable, and injudicious, a vain rebel against God's law. And then from that Vision Splendid all the glory faded slowly away, and left an earth gray and stern rolling on beneath a dark despair. Even the kind hands that stretched themselves toward him from out the depths of that dull morning seemed but parts of the purple shadows. He saw them coldly, and asked, "Why should I strive by special grace when the way of the world is closed to me?" All gently yet, the hands urged him on,—the hands of young John Jay, that daring father's daring son; the hands of the good folk of Boston, that free city. And yet, with a way to the priesthood of the Church open at last before him, the cloud lingered there; and even when in old St. Paul's the venerable Bishop raised his white arms above the Negro deacon—even then the burden had not lifted from that heart, for there had passed a glory from the earth.

And yet the fire through which Alexander Crummell went did not burn in vain. Slowly and more soberly he took up again his plan of life. More critically he studied the situation. Deep down below the slavery and servitude of the Negro people he saw their fatal weaknesses, which long years of mistreatment had emphasized. The dearth of strong moral character, of unbending righteousness, he felt, was their great shortcoming, and here he would begin. He would gather the best of his people into some little Episcopal chapel and there lead, teach, and inspire them, till the leaven spread, till the children grew, till the world hearkened, till—till—and then across his dream gleamed some faint after-glow of that first fair vision of youth—only an after-glow, for there had passed a glory from the earth.

One day—it was in 1842, and the springtide was struggling merrily with the May winds of New England—he stood at last in his own chapel in Providence, a priest of the Church. The days sped by, and the dark young clergyman labored; he wrote his sermons carefully; he intoned his prayers with a soft, earnest voice; he haunted the streets and accosted the wayfarers; he visited the sick, and knelt beside the dying. He worked and toiled, week by week, day by day, month by month. And yet month by month the congregation dwindled, week by week the hollow walls echoed more sharply, day by day the calls came fewer and fewer, and day by day the third temptation sat clearer and still more clearly within the Veil; a temptation, as it were, bland and smiling, with just a shade of mockery in its smooth tones. First it came casually, in the cadence of a voice: "Oh, colored folks? Yes." Or perhaps more definitely: "What do you *expect?*" In voice and gesture lay the doubt— the temptation of Doubt. How he hated it, and stormed at it furiously! "Of course they are capable," he cried; "of course they can learn and strive and achieve—" and "Of course," added the temptation softly, "they do nothing of the sort." Of all the three temptations, this one struck the deepest. Hate? He had outgrown so childish a thing. Despair? He had steeled his right arm against it, and fought it with the vigor of determination. But to doubt the worth of his life-work,—to doubt the destiny and capability of the race his soul loved because it was his; to find listless squalor instead of eager endeavor; to hear his own lips whispering, "They do not care; they cannot know; they are dumb driven cattle,—why cast your pearls before swine?"—this, this seemed more than man could bear; and he closed the door, and sank upon the steps of the chancel, and cast his robe upon the floor and writhed.

The evening sunbeams had set the dust to dancing in the gloomy chapel when he arose. He folded his vestments, put away the hymn-books, and closed the great Bible. He stepped out into the twilight, looked back upon the narrow little pulpit with a weary smile, and locked the door. Then he walked briskly to the Bishop, and told the Bishop what the Bishop already knew. "I have failed," he said simply. And gaining courage by the confession, he added: "What I need is a larger constituency. There are comparatively few

Negroes here, and perhaps they are not of the best. I must go where the field is wider, and try again." So the Bishop sent him to Philadelphia, with a letter to Bishop Onderdonk.

Bishop Onderdonk lived at the head of six white steps,—corpulent, red-faced, and the author of several thrilling tracts on Apostolic Succession. It was after dinner, and the Bishop had settled himself for a pleasant season of contemplation, when the bell must needs ring, and there must burst in upon the Bishop a letter and a thin, ungainly Negro. Bishop Onderdonk read the letter hastily and frowned. Fortunately, his mind was already clear on this point; and he cleared his brow and looked at Crummell. Then he said, slowly and impressively: "I will receive you into this diocese on one condition: no Negro priest can sit in my church convention, and no Negro church must ask for representation there."

I sometimes fancy I can see that tableau: the frail black figure, nervously twitching his hat before the massive abdomen of Bishop Onderdonk; his threadbare coat thrown against the dark woodwork of the bookcases, where Fox's "Lives of the Martyrs" nestled happily beside "The Whole Duty of Man." I seem to see the wide eyes of the Negro wander past the Bishop's broadcloth to where the swinging glass doors of the cabinet glow in the sunlight. A little blue fly is trying to cross the yawning keyhole. He marches briskly up to it, peers into the chasm in a surprised sort of way, and rubs his feelers reflectively; then he essays its depths, and, finding it bottomless, draws back again. The dark-faced priest finds himself wondering if the fly too has faced its Valley of Humiliation, and if it will plunge into it,—when lo! it spreads its tiny wings and buzzes merrily across, leaving the watcher wingless and alone.

Then the full weight of his burden fell upon him. The rich walls wheeled away, and before him lay the cold rough moor winding on through life, cut in twain by one thick granite ridge,—here, the Valley of Humiliation; yonder, the Valley of the Shadow of Death. And I know not which be darker,—no, not I. But this I know: in yonder Vale of the Humble stand to-day a million swarthy men, who willingly would

"... bear the whips and scorns of time,
The oppressor's wrong, the proud man's contumely,
The pangs of despised love, the law's delay,
The insolence of office, and the spurns
That patient merit of the unworthy takes,"—

all this and more would they bear did they but know that this were sacrifice and not a meaner thing. So surged the thought within that lone black breast. The Bishop cleared his throat suggestively; then, recollecting that there was really nothing to say, considerately said nothing, only sat tapping his foot impatiently. But Alexander Crummell said, slowly and heavily: "I will never enter your diocese on such terms." And saying this, he turned and passed into the Valley of the Shadow of Death. You might have noted only the phys-ical dying, the shattered frame and hacking cough; but in that soul lay deeper death than that. He found a chapel in New York,—the church of his father;

he labored for it in poverty and starvation, scorned by his fellow priests. Half in despair, he wandered across the sea, a beggar with outstretched hands. Englishmen clasped them,—Wilberforce and Stanley, Thirwell and Ingles, and even Froude and Macaulay; Sir Benjamin Brodie bade him rest awhile at Queen's College in Cambridge, and there he lingered, struggling for health of body and mind, until he took his degree in '53. Restless still, and unsatisfied, he turned toward Africa, and for long years, amid the spawn of the slave-smugglers, sought a new heaven and a new earth.

So the man groped for light; all this was not Life,—it was the world-wandering of a soul in search of itself, the striving of one who vainly sought his place in the world, ever haunted by the shadow of a death that is more than death,—the passing of a soul that has missed its duty. Twenty years he wandered,—twenty years and more; and yet the hard rasping question kept gnawing within him. "What, in God's name, am I on earth for?" In the nar-row New York parish his soul seemed cramped and smothered. In the fine old air of the English University he heard the millions wailing over the sea. In the wild fever-cursed swamps of West Africa he stood helpless and alone.

You will not wonder at his weird pilgrimage,—you who in the swift whirl of living, amid its cold paradox and marvellous vision, have fronted life and asked its riddle face to face. And if you find that riddle hard to read, remember that yonder black boy finds it just a little harder; if it is difficult for you to find and face your duty, it is a shade more difficult for him; if your heart sickens in the blood and dust of battle, remember that to him the dust is thicker and the battle fiercer. No wonder the wanderers fall! No wonder we point to thief and murderer, and haunting prostitute, and the never-ending throng of unhearsed dead! The Valley of the Shadow of Death gives few of its pilgrims back to the world.

But Alexander Crummell it gave back. Out of the temptation of Hate, and burned by the fire of Despair, triumphant over Doubt, and steeled by Sacrifice against Humiliation, he turned at last home across the waters, humble and strong, gentle and determined. He bent to all the gibes and prejudices, to all hatred and discrimination, with that rare courtesy which is the armor of pure souls. He fought among his own, the low, the grasping, and the wicked, with that unbending righteousness which is the sword of the just. He never faltered, he seldom complained; he simply worked, inspiring the young, rebuking the old, helping the weak, guiding the strong.

So he grew, and brought within his wide influence all that was best of those who walk within the Veil. They who live without knew not nor dreamed of that full power within, that mighty inspiration which the dull gauze of caste decreed that most men should not know. And now that he is gone, I sweep the Veil away and cry, Lo! the soul to whose dear memory I bring this little tribute. I can see his face still, dark and heavy-lined beneath his snowy hair; lighting and shading, now with inspiration for the future, now in innocent pain at some human wickedness, now with sorrow at some hard memory from the past. The more I met Alexander Crummell, the more I felt how much that world was losing which knew so little of him. In another age he might have sat among the elders of the land in purple-bordered toga; in another country mothers might have sung him to the cradles.

He did his work,—he did it nobly and well; and yet I sorrow that here he worked alone, with so little human sympathy. His name to-day, in this broad land, means little, and comes to fifty million ears laden with no incense of memory or emulation. And herein lies the tragedy of the age: not that men are poor,—all men know something of poverty; not that men are wicked,—who is good? not that men are ignorant,—what is Truth? Nay, but that men know so little of men.

He sat one morning gazing toward the sea. He smiled and said, "The gate is rusty on the hinges." That night at star-rise a wind came moaning out of the west to blow the gate ajar, and then the soul I loved fled like a flame across the Seas, and in its seat sat Death.

I wonder where he is to-day? I wonder if in that dim world beyond, as he came gliding in, there rose on some wan throne a King,—a dark and pierced Jew, who knows the writhings of the earthly damned, saying, as he laid those heart-wrung talents down, "Well done!" while round about the morning stars sat singing.

XIII
Of the Coming of John

> What bring they 'neath the midnight,
>   Beside the River-sea?
> They bring the human heart wherein
>   No nightly calm can be;
> That droppeth never with the wind,
>   Nor drieth with the dew;
> O calm it, God; thy calm is broad
>   To cover spirits too,
> The river floweth on.
>
>   Elizabeth Barrett Browning. (1806–61)

Carlisle Street runs westward from the centre of Johnstown, across a great black bridge, down a hill and up again, by little shops and meat-markets, past single-storied homes, until suddenly it stops against a wide green lawn. It is a broad, restful place, with two large buildings outlined against the west.

When at evening the winds come swelling from the east, and the great pall of the city's smoke hangs wearily above the valley, then the red west glows like a dreamland down Carlisle Street, and, at the tolling of the supper-bell, throws the passing forms of students in dark silhouette against the sky. Tall and black, they move slowly by, and seem in the sinister light to flit before the city like dim warning ghosts. Perhaps they are; for this is Wells Institute, and these black students have few dealings with the white city below.

And if you will notice, night after night, there is one dark form that ever hurries last and late toward the twinkling lights of Swain Hall,—for Jones is never on time. A long, straggling fellow he is, brown and hard-haired, who seems to be growing straight out of his clothes, and walks with a half-apologetic roll. He used perpetually to set the quiet dining-room into waves of merriment, as he stole to his place after the bell had tapped for prayers; he seemed so perfectly awkward. And yet one glance at his face made one forgive him much,—that broad, good-natured smile in which lay no bit of art or artifice, but seemed just bubbling good-nature and genuine satisfaction with the world.

He came to us from Altamaha, away down there beneath the gnarled oaks of Southeastern Georgia, where the sea croons to the sands and the sands listen till they sink half drowned beneath the waters, rising only here and there in long, low islands. The white folk of Altamaha voted John a good boy,—fine plough-hand, good in the rice-fields, handy everywhere, and always good-natured and respectful. But they shook their heads when his mother wanted to send him off to school. "It'll spoil him,—ruin him," they said; and they talked as though they knew. But full half the black folk followed him proudly to the station, and carried his queer little trunk and many bundles. And there they shook and shook hands, and the girls kissed him shyly and the boys clapped him on the back. So the train came, and he pinched his little sister lovingly, and put his great arms about his mother's neck, and then was away with a puff and a roar into the great yellow world that flamed and flared about the doubtful pilgrim. Up the coast they hurried, past the squares and palmettos of Savannah, through the cotton-fields and through the weary night, to Millville, and came with the morning to the noise and bustle of Johnstown.

And they that stood behind, that morning in Altamaha, and watched the train as it noisily bore playmate and brother and son away to the world, had thereafter one ever-recurring word,—"When John comes." Then what parties were to be, and what speakings in the churches; what new furniture in the front room,—perhaps even a new front room; and there would be a new schoolhouse, with John as teacher; and then perhaps a big wedding; all this and more—when John comes. But the white people shook their heads.

At first he was coming at Christmas-time,—but the vacation proved too short; and then, the next summer,—but times were hard and schooling costly, and so, instead, he worked in Johnstown. And so it drifted to the next summer, and the next,—till playmates scattered, and mother grew gray, and sister went up to the Judge's kitchen to work. And still the legend lingered,—"When John comes."

Up at the Judge's they rather liked this refrain; for they too had a John—a fair-haired, smooth-faced boy, who had played many a long summer's day to its close with his darker namesake. "Yes, sir! John is at Princeton, sir," said the broad-shouldered gray-haired Judge every morning as he marched down to the post-office. "Showing the Yankees what a Southern gentleman can do," he added; and strode home again with his letters and papers. Up at the great pillared house they lingered long over the Princeton letter,—the judge and his frail wife, his sister and growing daughters. "It'll make a man of him," said the Judge, "college is the place." And then he asked the shy little waitress, "Well, Jennie, how's your John?" and added reflectively, "Too bad, too bad your mother sent him off,—it will spoil him." And the waitress wondered.

Thus in the far-away Southern village the world lay waiting, half consciously, the coming of two young men, and dreamed in an inarticulate way of new things that would be done and new thoughts that all would think. And yet it was singular that few thought of two Johns,—for the black folk thought of one John, and he was black; and the white folk thought of another John, and he was white. And neither world thought the other world's thought, save with a vague unrest.

Up in Johnstown, at the Institute, we were long puzzled at the case of John Jones. For a long time the clay seemed unfit for any sort of moulding. He was loud and boisterous, always laughing and singing, and never able to work consecutively at anything. He did not know how to study; he had no idea of thoroughness; and with his tardiness, carelessness, and appalling good-humor, we were sore perplexed. One night we sat in faculty-meeting, worried and serious; for Jones was in trouble again. This last escapade was too much, and so we solemnly voted "that Jones, on account of repeated disorder and inattention to work, be suspended for the rest of the term."

It seemed to us that the first time life ever struck Jones as a really serious thing was when the Dean told him he must leave school. He stared at the gray-haired man blankly, with great eyes, "Why,—why," he faltered, "but—I haven't graduated!" Then the Dean slowly and clearly explained, reminding him of the tardiness and the carelessness, of the poor lessons and neglected work, of the noise and disorder, until the fellow hung his head in confusion. Then he said quickly, "But you won't tell mammy and sister,—you won't write mammy, now will you? For if you won't I'll go out into the city and work, and come back next term and show you something." So the Dean promised faithfully, and John shouldered his little trunk, giving neither word nor look to the giggling boys, and walked down Carlisle Street to the great city, with sober eyes and a set and serious face.

Perhaps we imagined it, but someway it seemed to us that the serious look that crept over his boyish face that afternoon never left it again. When he came back to us he went to work with all his rugged strength. It was a hard struggle, for things did not come easily to him,—few crowding memories of early life and teaching came to help him on his new way; but all the world toward which he strove was of his own building, and he builded slow and hard. As the light dawned lingeringly on his new creations, he sat rapt and silent before the vision, or wandered alone over the green campus peering through and beyond the world of men into a world of thought. And the thoughts at times puzzled him sorely; he could not see just why the circle was not square, and carried it out fifty-six decimal places one midnight,—would have gone further, indeed, had not the matron rapped for lights out. He caught terrible colds lying on his back in the meadows of nights, trying to think out of the solar system; he had grave doubts as to the ethics of the Fall of Rome, and strongly suspected the Germans of being thieves and rascals, despite his textbooks; he pondered long over every new Greek word, and wondered why this meant that and why it couldn't mean something else, and how it must have felt to think all things in Greek. So he thought and puzzled along for himself,—pausing perplexed where others skipped merrily, and walking steadily through the difficulties where the rest stopped and surrendered.

Thus he grew in body and soul, and with him his clothes seemed to grow and arrange themselves; coat sleeves got longer, cuffs appeared, and collars got less soiled. Now and then his boots shone, and a new dignity crept into his walk. And we who saw daily a new thoughtfulness growing in his eyes began to expect something of this plodding boy. Thus he passed out of the preparatory school into college, and we who watched him felt four more years of change, which almost transformed the tall, grave man who bowed to us commencement morning. He had left his queer thought-world and come back to a world of motion and of men. He looked now for the first time sharply about him, and wondered he had seen so little before. He grew slowly to feel almost for the first time the Veil that lay between him and the white world; he first noticed now the oppression that had not seemed oppression before, differences that erstwhile seemed natural, restraints and slights that in his boyhood days had gone unnoticed or been greeted with a laugh. He felt angry now when men did not call him "Mister," he clenched his hands at the "Jim Crow" cars, and chafed at the color-line that hemmed in him and his. A tinge of sarcasm crept into his speech, and a vague bitterness into his life; and he sat long hours wondering and planning a way around these crooked things. Daily he found himself shrinking from the choked and narrow life of his native town. And yet he always planned to go back to Altamaha,— always planned to work there. Still, more and more as the day approached he hesitated with a nameless dread; and even the day after graduation he seized with eagerness the offer of the Dean to send him North with the quartette during the summer vacation, to sing for the Institute. A breath of air before the plunge, he said to himself in half apology.

It was a bright September afternoon, and the streets of New York were brilliant with moving men. They reminded John of the sea, as he sat in the square and watched them, so changelessly changing, so bright and dark, so grave and gay. He scanned their rich and faultless clothes, the way they carried their hands, the shape of their hats; he peered into the hurrying carriages. Then, leaning back with a sigh, he said, "This is the World." The notion suddenly seized him to see where the world was going; since many of the richer and brighter seemed hurrying all one way. So when a tall, light-haired young man and a little talkative lady came by, he rose half hesitatingly and followed them. Up the street they went, past stores and gay shops, across a broad square, until with a hundred others they entered the high portal of a great building.

He was pushed toward the ticket-office with the others, and felt in his pocket for the new five-dollar bill he had hoarded. There seemed really no time for hesitation, so he drew it bravely out, passed it to the busy clerk, and received simply a ticket but no change. When at last he realized that he had paid five dollars to enter he knew not what, he stood stockstill amazed. "Be careful," said a low voice behind him; "you must not lynch the colored gentleman simply because he's in your way," and a girl looked up roguishly into the eyes of her fair-haired escort. A shade of annoyance passed over the escort's face. "You *will* not understand us at the South," he said half impatiently, as if continuing an argument. "With all your professions, one never sees in the North so cordial and intimate relations between white and black as are everyday occurrences with us. Why, I remember my closest playfellow in boyhood was a little Negro named after me, and surely no two,—*well!*" The man stopped short and flushed to the roots of his hair, for there directly beside his reserved orchestra chairs sat the Negro he had stumbled over in the hallway. He hesitated and grew pale with anger, called the usher and gave him his card, with a few peremptory words, and slowly sat down. The lady deftly changed the subject.

All this John did not see, for he sat in a half-daze minding the scene about him; the delicate beauty of the hall, the faint perfume, the moving myriad of men, the rich clothing and low hum of talking seemed all a part of a world so different from his, so strangely more beautiful than anything he had known, that he sat in dreamland, and started when, after a hush, rose high and clear the music of Lohengrin's swan. The infinite beauty of the wail lingered and swept through every muscle of his frame, and put it all a-tune. He closed his eyes and grasped the elbows of the chair, touching unwittingly the lady's arm. And the lady drew away. A deep longing swelled in all his heart to rise with that clear music out of the dirt and dust of that low life that held him prisoned and befouled. If he could only live up in the free air where birds sang and setting suns had no touch of blood! Who had called him to be the slave and butt of all? And if he had called, what right had he to call when a world like this lay open before men?

Then the movement changed, and fuller, mightier harmony swelled away. He looked thoughtfully across the hall, and wondered why the beautiful gray-haired woman looked so listless, and what the little man could be whispering about. He would not like to be listless and idle, he thought, for he felt with the music the movement of power within him. If he but had some master-work, some life-service, hard,—aye, bitter hard, but without the cringing and sickening servility, without the cruel hurt that hardened his heart and soul. When at last a soft sorrow crept across the violins, there came to him the vision of a far-off home, the great eyes of his sister, and the dark drawn face of his mother. And his heart sank below the waters, even as the sea-sand sinks by the shores of Altamaha, only to be lifted aloft again with that last ethereal wail of the swan that quivered and faded away into the sky.

It left John sitting so silent and rapt that he did not for some time notice the usher tapping him lightly on the shoulder and saying politely, "Will you step this way, please, sir?" A little surprised, he arose quickly at the last tap, and, turning to leave his seat, looked full into the face of the fair-haired young man. For the first time the young man recognized his dark boyhood playmate, and John knew that it was the Judge's son. The White John started, lifted his hand, and then froze into his chair; the black John smiled lightly, then grimly, and followed the usher down the aisle. The manager was sorry, very, very sorry,—but he explained that some mistake had been made in selling the gentleman a seat already disposed of; he would refund the money, of course,—and indeed felt the matter keenly, and so forth, and—before he had finished John was gone, walking hurriedly across the square and down the broad streets, and as he passed the park he buttoned his coat and said, "John Jones, you're a natural-born fool." Then he went to his lodgings and wrote a letter, and tore it up; he wrote another, and threw it in the fire. Then he seized a scrap of paper and wrote: "Dear Mother and Sister—I am coming—John."

"Perhaps," said John, as he settled himself on the train, "perhaps I am to blame myself in struggling against my manifest destiny simply because it looks hard and unpleasant. Here is my duty to Altamaha plain before me; perhaps they'll let me help settle the Negro problems there,—perhaps they won't. 'I will go in to the King, which is not according to the law; and if I perish, I perish.' " And then he mused and dreamed, and planned a life-work; and the train flew south.

Down in Altamaha, after seven long years, all the world knew John was coming. The homes were scrubbed and scoured,—above all, one; the gardens and yards had an unwonted trimness, and Jennie bought a new gingham. With some finesse and negotiation, all the dark Methodists and Presbyterians were induced to join in a monster welcome at the Baptist Church; and as the day drew near, warm discussions arose on every corner as to the exact extent and nature of John's accomplishments. It was noontide on a gray and cloudy day when he came. The black town flocked to the depot, with a little of the white at the edges,—a happy throng, with "Goodmawnings" and "Howdys" and laughing and joking and jostling. Mother sat yonder in the window watching; but sister Jennie stood on the platform, nervously fingering her dress, tall and lithe, with soft brown skin and loving eyes peering from out a tangled wilderness of hair. John rose gloomily as the train stopped, for he was thinking of the "Jim Crow" car; he stepped to the platform, and paused: a little dingy station, a black crowd gaudy and dirty, a half-mile of dilapidated shanties along a straggling ditch of mud. An overwhelming sense of the sordidness and narrowness of it all seized him; he looked in vain for his mother, kissed coldly the tall, strange girl who called him brother, spoke a short, dry word here and there; then, lingering neither for hand-shaking nor gossip, started silently up the street, raising his hat merely to the last eager old aunty, to her open-mouthed astonishment. The people were distinctly bewildered. This silent, cold man,—was this John? Where was his smile and hearty hand-grasp? " 'Peared kind o' down in the mouf," said the Methodist preacher thoughtfully. "Seemed monstus stuck up," complained a Baptist sister. But the white postmaster from the edge of the crowd expressed the opinion of his folks plainly. "That damn Nigger," said he, as he shouldered the mail and arranged his tobacco, "has gone North and got plum full o' fool notions; but they won't work in Altamaha." And the crowd melted away.

The meeting of welcome at the Baptist Church was a failure. Rain spoiled the barbecue, and thunder turned the milk in the ice-cream. When the speaking came at night, the house was crowded to overflowing. The three preachers had especially prepared themselves, but somehow John's manner seemed to throw a blanket over everything,—he seemed so cold and preoccupied, and had so strange an air of restraint that the Methodist brother could not warm up to his theme and elicited not a single "Amen"; the Presbyterian prayer was but feebly responded to, and even the Baptist preacher, though he wakened faint enthusiasm, got so mixed up in his favorite sentence that he had to close it by stopping fully fifteen minutes sooner than he meant. The people moved uneasily in their seats as John rose to reply. He spoke slowly and methodically. The age, he said, demanded new ideas; we were far different from those men of the seventeenth and eighteenth centuries,—with broader ideas of human brotherhood and destiny. Then he spoke of the rise of charity and popular education, and particularly of the spread of wealth and work. The question was, then, he added reflectively, looking at the low discolored ceiling, what part the Negroes of this land would take in the striving of the new century. He sketched in vague outline the new Industrial School that might rise among these pines, he spoke in detail of the charitable and philanthropic work that might be organized, of money that might be saved for banks and business. Finally he urged unity, and deprecated especially religious and denominational bickering. "To-day," he said, with a smile, "the world cares little whether a man be Baptist or Methodist, or indeed a churchman at all, so long as he is good and true. What difference does it make whether a man he baptized in river or washbowl, or not at all? Let's leave all that littleness, and look higher." Then, thinking of nothing else, he slowly sat down. A painful hush seized that crowded mass. Little had they understood of what he said, for he spoke an unknown tongue, save the last word about baptism; that they knew, and they sat very still while the clock ticked. Then at last a low suppressed snarl came from the Amen corner, and an old bent man arose, walked over the seats, and climbed straight up into the pulpit. He was wrinkled and black, with scant gray and tufted hair; his voice and hands shook as with palsy; but on his face lay the intense rapt look of the religious fanatic. He seized the Bible with his rough, huge hands; twice he raised it inarticulate, and then fairly burst into words, with rude and awful eloquence. He quivered, swayed, and bent; then rose aloft in perfect majesty, till the people moaned and wept, wailed and shouted, and a wild shrieking arose from the corners where all the pent-up feeling of the hour gathered itself and rushed into the air. John never knew clearly what the old man said; he only felt himself held up to scorn and scathing denunciation for trampling on the true Religion, and he realized with amazement that all unknowingly he had put rough, rude hands on something this little world held sacred. He arose silently, and passed out into the night. Down toward the sea he went, in the fitful starlight, half conscious of the girl who followed timidly after him. When at last he stood upon the bluff, he turned to his little sister and looked upon her sorrowfully, remembering with sudden pain how little thought he had given her. He put his arm about her and let her passion of tears spend itself on his shoulder.

Long they stood together, peering over the gray unresting water.

"John," she said, "does it make every one—unhappy when they study and learn lots of things?"

He paused and smiled. "I am afraid it does," he said.

"And, John, are you glad you studied?"

"Yes," came the answer, slowly but positively.

She watched the flickering lights upon the sea, and said thoughtfully, "I wish I was unhappy,—and—and," putting both arms about his neck, "I think I am, a little, John."

It was several days later that John walked up to the Judge's house to ask for the privilege of teaching the Negro school. The Judge himself met him at the front door, stared a little hard at him, and said brusquely, "Go 'round to the kitchen door, John, and wait." Sitting on the kitchen steps, John stared at the corn, thoroughly perplexed. What on earth had come over him? Every step he made offended some one. He had come to save his people, and before he left the depot he had hurt them. He sought to teach them at the church, and had outraged their deepest feelings. He had schooled himself to be respectful to the Judge, and then blundered into his front door. And all the time he had meant right,—and yet, and yet, somehow he found it so hard and strange to fit his old surroundings again, to find his place in the world about him. He could not remember that he used to have any difficulty in the past, when life was glad and gay. The world seemed smooth and easy then. Perhaps,—but his sister came to the kitchen door just then and said the Judge awaited him.

The Judge sat in the dining-room amid his morning's mail, and he did not ask John to sit down. He plunged squarely into the business. "You've come for the school, I suppose. Well, John, I want to speak to you plainly. You know I'm a friend to your people. I've helped you and your family, and would have done more if you hadn't got the notion of going off. Now I like the colored people, and sympathize with all their reasonable aspirations; but you and I both know, John, that in this country the Negro must remain subordinate, and can never expect to be the equal of white men. In their place, your people can be honest and respectful; and God knows, I'll do what I can to help them. But when they want to reverse nature, and rule white men, and marry white women, and sit in my parlor, then, by God! we'll hold them under if we have to lynch every Nigger in the land. Now, John, the question is, are you, with your education and Northern notions, going to accept the situation and teach the darkies to be faithful servants and laborers as your fathers were,—I knew your father, John, he belonged to my brother, and he was a good Nigger. Well—well, are you going to be like him, or are you going to try to put fool ideas of rising and equality into these folks' heads, and make them discontented and unhappy?"

"I am going to accept the situation, Judge Henderson," answered John, with a brevity that did not escape the keen old man. He hesitated a moment, and then said shortly, "Very well,—we'll try you awhile. Good-morning."

It was a full month after the opening of the Negro school that the other John came home, tall, gay, and headstrong. The mother wept, the sisters sang. The whole white town was glad. A proud man was the Judge, and it was a goodly sight to see the two swinging down Main Street together. And yet all did not go smoothly between them, for the younger man could not and did not veil his contempt for the little town, and plainly had his heart set on New York. Now the one cherished ambition of the Judge was to see his son mayor of Altamaha, representative to the legislature, and—who could say?—

governor of Georgia. So the argument often waxed hot between them. "Good heavens, father," the younger man would say after dinner, as he lighted a cigar and stood by the fireplace, "you surely don't expect a young fellow like me to settle down permanently in this—this God-forgotten town with nothing but mud and Negroes?" "*I* did," the Judge would answer laconically; and on this particular day it seemed from the gathering scowl that he was about to add something more emphatic, but neighbors had already begun to drop in to admire his son, and the conversation drifted.

"Heah that John is livenin' things up at the darky school," volunteered the postmaster, after a pause.

"What now?" asked the Judge, sharply.

"Oh, nothin' in particulah,—just his almighty air and uppish ways. B'lieve I did heah somethin' about his givin' talks on the French Revolution, equality, and such like. He's what I call a dangerous Nigger."

"Have you heard him say anything out of the way?"

"Why, no,—but Sally, our girl, told my wife a lot of rot. Then, too, I don't need to heah: a Nigger what won't say 'sir' to a white man, or—"

"Who is this John?" interrupted the son.

"Why, it's little black John, Peggy's son,—your old playfellow."

The young man's face flushed angrily, and then he laughed.

"Oh," said he, "it's the darky that tried to force himself into a seat beside the lady I was escorting—"

But Judge Henderson waited to hear no more. He had been nettled all day, and now at this he rose with a half-smothered oath, took his hat and cane, and walked straight to the schoolhouse.

For John, it had been a long, hard pull to get things started in the rickety old shanty that sheltered his school. The Negroes were rent into factions for and against him, the parents were careless, the children irregular and dirty, and books, pencils, and slates largely missing. Nevertheless, he struggled hopefully on, and seemed to see at last some glimmering of dawn. The attendance was larger and the children were a shade cleaner this week. Even the booby class in reading showed a little comforting progress. So John settled himself with renewed patience this afternoon.

"Now, Mandy," he said cheerfully, "that's better; but you mustn't chop your words up so: 'If—the—man—goes.' Why, your little brother even wouldn't tell a story that way, now would he?"

"Naw, suh, he cain't talk."

"All right; now let's try again: 'If the man—' "

"John!"

The whole school started in surprise, and the teacher half arose, as the red, angry face of the Judge appeared in the open doorway.

"John, this school is closed. You children can go home and get to work. The white people of Altamaha are not spending their money on black folks to have their heads crammed with impudence and lies. Clear out! I'll lock the door myself."

Up at the great pillared house the tall young son wandered aimlessly about after his father's abrupt departure. In the house there was little to interest him; the books were old and stale, the local newspaper flat, and the women had retired with headaches and sewing. He tried a nap, but it was too warm. So he sauntered out into the fields, complaining disconsolately, "Good Lord! how long will this imprisonment last!" He was not a bad fellow,—just a little spoiled and self-indulgent, and as headstrong as his proud father. He seemed a young man pleasant to look upon, as he sat on the great black stump at the edge of the pines idly swinging his legs and smoking. "Why, there isn't even a girl worth getting up a respectable flirtation with," he growled. Just then his eye caught a tall, willowy figure hurrying toward him on the narrow path. He looked with interest at first, and then burst into a laugh as he said, "Well, I declare, if it isn't Jennie, the little brown kitchen-maid! Why, I never noticed before what a trim little body she is. Hello, Jennie! Why, you haven't kissed me since I came home," he said gaily. The young girl stared at him in surprise and confusion,—faltered something inarticulate, and attempted to pass. But a wilful mood had seized the young idler, and he caught at her arm. Frightened, she slipped by; and half mischievously he turned and ran after her through the tall pines.

Yonder, toward the sea, at the end of the path, came John slowly, with his head down. He had turned wearily homeward from the schoolhouse; then, thinking to shield his mother from the blow, started to meet his sister as she came from work and break the news of his dismissal to her. "I'll go away," he said slowly; "I'll go away and find work, and send for them. I cannot live here longer." And then the fierce, buried anger surged up into his throat. He waved his arms and hurried wildly up the path.

The great brown sea lay silent. The air scarce breathed. The dying day bathed the twisted oaks and mighty pines in black and gold. There came from the wind no warning, not a whisper from the cloudless sky. There was only a black man hurrying on with an ache in his heart, seeing neither sun nor sea, but starting as from a dream at the frightened cry that woke the pines, to see his dark sister struggling in the arms of a tall and fair-haired man.

He said not a word, but, seizing a fallen limb, struck him with all the pent-up hatred of his great black arm, and the body lay white and still beneath the pines, all bathed in sunshine and in blood. John looked at it dreamily, then walked back to the house briskly, and said in a soft voice, "Mammy, I'm going away—I'm going to be free."

She gazed at him dimly and faltered, "No'th, honey, is yo' gwine No'th agin?"

He looked out where the North Star glistened pale above the waters, and said, "Yes, mammy, I'm going—North."

Then, without another word, he went out into the narrow lane, up by the straight pines, to the same winding path, and seated himself on the great black stump, looking at the blood where the body had lain. Yonder in the gray past he had played with that dead boy, romping together under the solemn trees. The night deepened; he thought of the boys at Johnstown. He wondered how Brown had turned out, and Carey? and Jones,—Jones? Why, *he* was Jones, and he wondered what they would all say when they knew, when they knew, in that great long dining-room with its hundreds of merry eyes. Then as the sheen of the starlight stole over him, he thought of the gilded ceiling of that vast concert hall, heard stealing toward him the faint sweet music of the swan. Hark! was it music, or the hurry and shouting of men? Yes, surely! Clear and high the faint sweet melody rose and fluttered like a living thing, so that the very earth trembled as with the tramp of horses and murmur of angry men.

He leaned back and smiled toward the sea, whence rose the strange melody, away from the dark shadows where lay the noise of horses galloping, galloping on. With an effort he roused himself, bent forward, and looked steadily down the pathway, softly humming the "Song of the Bride,"—

"Freudig geführt, ziehet dahin."*

Amid the trees in the dim morning twilight he watched their shadows dancing and heard their horses thundering toward him, until at last they came sweeping like a storm, and he saw in front that haggard white-haired man, whose eyes flashed red with fury. Oh, how he pitied him,—pitied him,—and wondered if he had the coiling twisted rope. Then, as the storm burst round him, he rose slowly to his feet and turned his closed eyes toward the Sea.

And the world whistled in his ears.

XIV
Of the Sorrow Songs

    I walk through the churchyard
      To lay this body down;
    I know moon-rise, I know star-rise;
    I walk in the moonlight, I walk in the starlight;
    I'll lie in the grave and stretch out my arms,
    I'll go to judgment in the evening of the day,
    And my soul and thy soul shall meet that day,
      When I lay this body down.
                    Negro Song.

They that walked in darkness sang songs in the olden days—Sorrow Songs—for they were weary at heart. And so before each thought that I have written

    *"Joyfully led, be drawn to that place where the blessings of love watch over you!" from "The Wedding March," Richard Wagner, *Lohengrin III,* i. Du Bois altered the quote to read "joyfully led" instead of the original "faithfully led."

in this book I have set a phrase, a haunting echo of these weird old songs in which the soul of the black slave spoke to men. Ever since I was a child these songs have stirred me strangely. They came out of the South unknown to me, one by one, and yet at once I knew them as of me and of mine. Then in after years when I came to Nashville I saw the great temple builded of these songs towering over the pale city. To me Jubilee Hall seemed ever made of the songs themselves, and its bricks were red with the blood and dust of toil. Out of them rose for me morning, noon, and night, bursts of wonderful melody, full of the voices of my brothers and sisters, full of the voices of the past.

Little of beauty has America given the world save the rude grandeur God himself stamped on her bosom; the human spirit in this new world has expressed itself in vigor and ingenuity rather than in beauty. And so by fateful chance the Negro folk-song—the rhythmic cry of the slave—stands to-day not simply as the sole American music, but as the most beautiful expression of human experience born this side the seas. It has been neglected, it has been, and is, half despised, and above all it has been persistently mistaken and misunderstood; but notwithstanding, it still remains as the singular spiritual heritage of the nation and the greatest gift of the Negro people.

Away back in the thirties the melody of these slave songs stirred the nation, but the songs were soon half forgotten. Some, like "Near the lake where drooped the willow," passed into current airs and their source was forgotten; others were caricatured on the "minstrel" stage and their memory died away. Then in war-time came the singular Port Royal experiment after the capture of Hilton Head, and perhaps for the first time the North met the Southern slave face to face and heart to heart with no third witness. The Sea Islands of the Carolinas, where they met, were filled with a black folk of primitive type, touched and moulded less by the world about them than any others outside the Black Belt. Their appearance was uncouth, their language funny, but their hearts were human and their singing stirred men with a mighty power. Thomas Wentworth Higginson hastened to tell of these songs, and Miss McKim and others urged upon the world their rare beauty. But the world listened only half credulously until the Fisk Jubilee Singers sang the slave songs so deeply into the world's heart that it can never wholly forget them again.

There was once a blacksmith's son born at Cadiz, New York, who in the changes of time taught school in Ohio and helped defend Cincinnati from Kirby Smith. Then he fought at Chancellorsville and Gettysburg and finally served in the Freedmen's Bureau at Nashville. Here he formed a Sunday-school class of black children in 1866, and sang with them and taught them to sing. And then they taught him to sing, and when once the glory of the Jubilee songs passed into the soul of George L. White, he knew his life-work was to let those Negroes sing to the world as they had sung to him. So in 1871 the pilgrimage of the Fisk Jubilee Singers began. North to Cincinnati they rode,—four half-clothed black boys and five girl-women,—led by a man with a cause and a purpose. They stopped at Wilberforce, the oldest of Negro schools, where a black bishop blessed them. Then they went, fighting cold and starvation, shut out of hotels, and cheerfully sneered at, ever northward; and ever the magic of their song kept thrilling hearts, until a burst of applause in the Congregational Council at Oberlin revealed them to the world. They came to New York and Henry Ward Beecher dared to welcome them, even though the metropolitan dailies sneered at his "Nigger Minstrels." So their songs conquered till they sang across the land and across the sea, before Queen and Kaiser, in Scotland and Ireland, Holland and Switzerland. Seven years they sang, and brought back a hundred and fifty thousand dollars to found Fisk University.

Since their day they have been imitated—sometimes well, by the singers of Hampton and Atlanta, sometimes ill, by straggling quartettes. Caricature has sought again to spoil the quaint beauty of the music, and has filled the air with many debased melodies which vulgar ears scarce know from the real. But the true Negro folk-song still lives in the hearts of those who have heard them truly sung and in the hearts of the Negro people.

What are these songs, and what do they mean? I know little of music and can say nothing in technical phrase, but I know something of men, and knowing them, I know that these songs are the articulate message of the slave to the world. They tell us in these eager days that life was joyous to the black slave, careless and happy. I can easily believe this of some, of many. But not all the past South, though it rose from the dead, can gainsay the heart-touching witness of these songs. They are the music of an unhappy people, of the children of disappointment; they tell of death and suffering and unvoiced longing toward a truer world, of misty wanderings and hidden ways.

The songs are indeed the siftings of centuries; the music is far more ancient than the words, and in it we can trace here and there signs of development. My grandfather's grandmother was seized by an evil Dutch trader two centuries ago; and coming to the valleys of the Hudson and Housatonic, black, little, and lithe, she shivered and shrank in the harsh north winds, looked longingly at the hills, and often crooned a heathen melody to the child between her knees, thus:

The Fisk Jubilee Singers in 1871.

The child sang it to his children and they to their children's children, and so two hundred years it has travelled down to us and we sing it to our children, knowing as little as our fathers what its words may mean, but knowing well the meaning of its music.

This was primitive African music; it may be seen in larger form in the strange chant which heralds "The Coming of John":

> "You may bury me in the East,
>   You may bury me in the West,
>   But I'll hear the trumpet sound in that morning,"

—the voice of exile.

Ten master songs, more or less, one may pluck from the forest of melody—songs of undoubted Negro origin and wide popular currency, and songs peculiarly characteristic of the slave. One of these I have just mentioned. Another whose strains begin this book is "Nobody knows the trouble I've seen." When, struck with a sudden poverty, the United States refused to fulfill its promises of land to the freedmen, a brigadier-general went down to the Sea Islands to carry the news. An old woman on the outskirts of the throng began singing this song; all the mass joined with her, swaying. And the soldier wept.

The third song is the cradle-song of death which all men know,—"Swing low, sweet chariot,"—whose bars begin the life story of "Alexander Crummell." Then there is the song of many waters, "Roll, Jordan, roll," a mighty chorus with minor cadences. There were many songs of the fugitive like that which opens "The Wings of Atalanta," and the more familiar "Been a-listening." The seventh is the song of the End and the Beginning—"My Lord, what a mourning! when the stars begin to fall"; a strain of this is placed before "The Dawn of Freedom." The song of groping—"My way's cloudy"—begins "The Meaning of Progress"; the ninth is the song of this chapter—"Wrestlin' Jacob, the day is a-breaking,"—a pæan of hopeful strife. The last master song is the song of songs—"Steal away,"—sprung from "The Faith of the Fathers."

There are many others of the Negro folk-songs as striking and characteristic as these, as, for instance, the three strains in the third, eighth, and ninth chapters; and others I am sure could easily make a selection on more scientific principles. There are, too, songs that seem to be a step removed from the more primitive types: there is the maze-like medley, "Bright sparkles," one phrase of which heads "The Black Belt"; the Easter carol, "Dust, dust and ashes"; the dirge, "My mother's took her flight and gone home"; and that burst of melody hovering over "The Passing of the First-Born"—"I hope my mother will be there in that beautiful world on high."

These represent a third step in the development of the slave song, of which "You may bury me in the East" is the first, and songs like "March on" (chapter six) and "Steal away" are the second. The first is African music, the second Afro-American, while the third is a blending of Negro music with the music heard in the foster land. The result is still distinctively Negro and the method of blending original, but the elements are both Negro and Caucasian. One might go further and find a fourth step in this development, where the songs of white America have been distinctively influenced by the slave songs or have incorporated whole phrases of Negro melody, as "Swanee River" and "Old Black Joe." Side by side, too, with the growth has gone the debasements and imitations—the Negro "minstrel" songs, many of the "gospel" hymns, and some of the contemporary "coon" songs,—a mass of music in which the novice may easily lose himself and never find the real Negro melodies.

In these songs, I have said, the slave spoke to the world. Such a message is naturally veiled and half articulate. Words and music have lost each other and new and cant phrases of a dimly understood theology have displaced the older sentiment. Once in a while we catch a strange word of an unknown tongue, as the "Mighty Myo," which figures as a river of death; more often slight words or mere doggerel are joined to music of singular sweetness. Purely secular songs are few in number, partly because many of them were turned into hymns by a change of words, partly because the frolics were seldom heard by the stranger, and the music less often caught. Of nearly all the songs, however, the music is distinctly sorrowful. The ten master songs I have mentioned tell in word and music of trouble and exile, of strife and hiding; they grope toward some unseen power and sigh for rest in the End.

The words that are left to us are not without interest, and, cleared of evident dross, they conceal much of real poetry and meaning beneath conventional theology and unmeaning rhapsody. Like all primitive folk, the slave stood near to Nature's heart. Life was a "rough and rolling sea" like the brown Atlantic of the Sea Islands; the "Wilderness" was the home of God, and the "lonesome valley" led to the way of life. "Winter'll soon be over," was the picture of life and death to a tropical imagination. The sudden wild thunder-storms of the South awed and impressed the Negroes,—at times the rumbling seemed to them "mournful," at times imperious:

"My Lord calls me,
   He calls me by the thunder,
   The trumpet sounds it in my soul."

The monotonous toil and exposure is painted in many words. One sees the ploughmen in the hot, moist furrow, singing:

"Dere's no rain to wet you,
   Dere's no sun to burn you,
   Oh, push along, believer,
   I want to go home."

The bowed and bent old man cries, with thrice-repeated wail:

"O Lord, keep me from sinking down,"

and he rebukes the devil of doubt who can whisper:

"Jesus is dead and God's gone away."

Yet the soul-hunger is there, the restlessness of the savage, the wail of the wanderer, and the plaint is put in one little phrase:

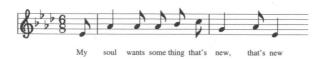

My soul wants some thing that's new, that's new

Over the inner thoughts of the slaves and their relations one with another the shadow of fear ever hung, so that we get but glimpses here and there, and also with them, eloquent omissions and silences. Mother and child are sung, but seldom father; fugitive and weary wanderer call for pity and affection, but there is little of wooing and wedding; the rocks and the mountains are well known, but home is unknown. Strange blending of love and helplessness sings through the refrain:

> "Yonder's my ole mudder,
> Been waggin' at de hill so long;
> 'Bout time she cross over,
> Git home bime-by."

Elsewhere comes the cry of the "motherless" and the "Farewell, farewell, my only child."

Love-songs are scarce and fall into two categories—the frivolous and light, and the sad. Of deep successful love there is ominous silence, and in one of the oldest of these songs there is a depth of history and meaning:

Poor Ro - sy, poor gal; Poor Ro - sy,
poor gal; Ro - sy break my poor heart.
Heav'n shall - a - be my home.

A black woman said of the song, "It can't be sung without a full heart and a troubled sperrit." The same voice sings here that sings in the German folk-song:

> "Jetz Geh i' an's brunele, trink' aber net."

Of death the Negro showed little fear, but talked of it familiarly and even fondly as simply a crossing of the waters, perhaps—who knows?—back to his ancient forests again. Later days transfigured his fatalism, and amid the dust and dirt the toiler sang:

"Dust, dust and ashes, fly over my grave,
But the Lord shall bear my spirit home."

The things evidently borrowed from the surrounding world undergo characteristic change when they enter the mouth of the slave. Especially is this true of Bible phrases. "Weep, O captive daughter of Zion," is quaintly turned into "Zion, weep-a-low," and the wheels of Ezekiel are turned every way in the mystic dreaming of the slave, till he says:

"There's a little wheel a turnin' in-a-my heart."

As in olden time, the words of these hymns were improvised by some leading minstrel of the religious band. The circumstances of the gathering, however, the rhythm of the songs, and the limitations of allowable thought, confined the poetry for the most part to single or double lines, and they seldom were expanded to quatrains or longer tales, although there are some few examples of sustained efforts, chiefly paraphrases of the Bible. Three short series of verses have always attracted me,—the one that heads this chapter, of one line of which Thomas Wentworth Higginson has fittingly said, "Never, it seems to me, since man first lived and suffered was his infinite longing for peace uttered more plaintively." The second and third are descriptions of the Last Judgment,—the one a late improvisation, with some traces of outside influence:

"Oh, the stars in the elements are falling,
And the moon drips away into blood,
And the ransomed of the Lord are returning unto God,
Blessed be the name of the Lord."

And the other earlier and homelier picture from the low coast lands:

"Michael, haul the boat ashore,
Then you'll hear the horn they blow,
Then you'll hear the trumpet sound,
Trumpet sound the world around,
Trumpet sound for rich and poor,
Trumpet sound the Jubilee,
Trumpet sound for you and me."

Through all the sorrow of the Sorrow Songs there breathes a hope—a faith in the ultimate justice of things. The minor cadences of despair change often to triumph and calm confidence. Sometimes it is faith in life, sometimes a faith in death, sometimes assurance of boundless justice in some fair world beyond. But whichever it is, the meaning is always clear: that sometime, somewhere, men will judge men by their souls and not by their skins. Is such a hope justified? Do the Sorrow Songs sing true?

The silently growing assumption of this age is that the probation of races is past, and that the backward races of to-day are of proven inefficiency and not worth the saving. Such an assumption is the arrogance of peoples irreverent toward Time and ignorant of the deeds of men. A thousand years ago such an assumption, easily possible, would have made it difficult for the Teuton to prove his right to life. Two thousand years ago such dogmatism, readily welcome, would have scouted the idea of blond races ever leading civilization. So wofully unorganized is sociological knowledge that the meaning of progress, the meaning of "swift" and "slow" in human doing, and the limits of human perfectability, are veiled, unanswered sphinxes on the shores of science. Why should Æschylus have sung two thousand years before Shakespeare was born? Why has civilization flourished in Europe, and flickered, flamed, and died in Africa? So long as the world stands meekly dumb before such questions, shall this nation proclaim its ignorance and unhallowed prejudices by denying freedom of opportunity to those who brought the Sorrow Songs to the Seats of the Mighty?

Your country? How came it yours? Before the Pilgrims landed we were here. Here we have brought our three gifts and mingled them with yours: a gift of story and song—soft, stirring melody in an ill-harmonized and unmelodious land; the gift of sweat and brawn to beat back the wilderness, conquer the soil, and lay the foundations of this vast economic empire two hundred years earlier than your weak hands could have done it; the third, a gift of the Spirit. Around us the history of the land has centred for thrice a hundred years; out of the nation's heart we have called all that was best to throttle and subdue all that was worst; fire and blood, prayer and sacrifice, have billowed over this people, and they have found peace only in the altars of the God of Right. Nor has our gift of the Spirit been merely passive. Actively we have woven ourselves with the very warp and woof of this nation,—we fought their battles, shared their sorrow, mingled our blood with theirs, and generation after generation have pleaded with a headstrong, careless people to despise not Justice, Mercy, and Truth, lest the nation be smitten with a curse. Our song, our toil, our cheer, and warning have been given to this nation in blood-brotherhood. Are not these gifts worth the giving? Is not this work and striving? Would America have been America without her Negro people?

Even so is the hope that sang in the songs of my fathers well sung. If somewhere in this whirl and chaos of things there dwells Eternal Good, pitiful yet masterful, then anon in His good time America shall rend the Veil and the prisoned shall go free. Free, free as the sunshine trickling down the morning into these high windows of mine, free as yonder fresh young voices welling up to me from the caverns of brick and mortar below—swelling with song, instinct with life, tremulous treble and darkening bass. My children, my little children, are singing to the sunshine, and thus they sing:

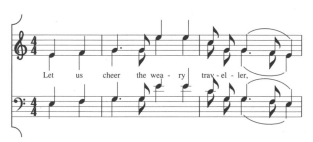

Let us cheer the wea - ry trav - el - ler,

Cheer the wea - ry trav-el - ler, Let us

cheer the wea - ry trav-el - ler A -

- long the heav - en - ly way,

And the traveller girds himself, and sets his face toward the Morning, and goes his way.

The Afterthought

Hear my cry, O God the Reader; vouchsafe that this my book fall not still-born into the world wilderness. Let there spring, Gentle One, from out its leaves vigor of thought and thoughtful deed to reap the harvest wonderful. Let the ears of a guilty people tingle with truth, and seventy millions sigh for the righteousness which exalteth nations, in this drear day when human brother-hood is mockery and a snare. Thus in Thy good time may infinite reason turn the tangle straight, and these crooked marks on a fragile leaf be not indeed

THE END

Editor's Notes

Within the last year, an issue of *Harper's Magazine* devoted itself to a group of young American intellectuals who seem lately to have "arrived" in importance—"opinion makers," we may call them, with influential views on social questions which have been expressed in writings and public appearances of various kinds. The views are far from always the same, but they reflect shared preoccupations, and these are a consequence of the fact that, as the editors observed, all the intellectuals are black—that is, they are African-Americans, as we now say. The editors could not recall an earlier time when so many important social ideas could be located in this sector of the population.

Certainly a hundred, even fifty years ago, there would have been far fewer such names to list, and perhaps only one would have been regarded as highly influential—that of W. E. B. Du Bois (the name is pronounced to rhyme with "rejoice"). An academically distinguished pioneer in black studies who wrote tirelessly and powerfully in his field, where his own views were disturbingly radical to some, Du Bois was the preeminent American Negro thinker (as the term was) of his day. His works and reputation were of incalculable importance to the development of black writers who came after him, for whom he was "the public 'voice,' " as Henry Louis Gates, Jr. has said, "of the American Negro intellectual."

Born in 1868 at Great Barrington, Massachusetts, of French, Dutch, and African ancestry, Du Bois studied despite meager means at Fisk University, after that at Harvard, and then at the Friedrich Wilhelm University of Berlin. Among his teachers were George Santayana, William James, and Max Weber, the great sociologist who became a friend. In 1897 Du Bois was made a professor of history and economics at Atlanta University where he undertook unprecedented research into the condition of the black person in America. He also wrote trenchant articles on the same subject for popular magazines. By the turn of the century, or not long after, he was the most widely published black author in the United States.

From 1910 to 1934, still teaching, he edited *The Crisis,* the official publication of the NAACP, an organization he had helped to create. This became a major outlet for black opinion throughout the world, and the chief voice of opposition to Booker T. Washington, the founder of Tuskegee Institute, who advocated economic advancement for the Negro without making troublesome social or political claims—a policy Du Bois thought pernicious because of its failure to address the lack of self-respect and sense of powerlessness which he regarded as the Negro's chief problem.

Over a long life, Du Bois published many writings (his bibliography runs to nearly 2,000 titles), including poems and novels as well as scholarly works. Among the latter were *Black Reconstruction* (1935, still a standard work on its subject), and numerous essays, a form in which he particularly excelled. Nothing else he wrote had the sustained impact of *The Souls of Black Folk* (1903), however, a book that, if it were published now would probably be called (or have some such subtitle as) "The Sense of Self in African-Americans," that being in great part what it is about. Gates believes that no other text, save possibly the King James version of the Bible, has done more to shape the Afro-American literary tradition. Langston Hughes seems to agree when he says that his "earliest memories of written words are those of Du Bois and the Bible." James Weldon Johnson, himself a distinguished black writer and for many years executive secretary of the NAACP, said that *The Souls* had "a greater effect upon and within the Negro race in America than any other single book published in this country since *Uncle Tom's Cabin.*"

It is the "silent second text," Gates says, in Johnson's own *Autobiography of an Ex-Colored Man* (1912), Jean Toomer's *Cane* (1923), Zora Neale Hurston's *Their Eyes Were Watching God* (1937), Richard Wright's *Black Boy,* (1945), and Ralph Ellison's *Invisible Man* (1952). "In this way," Gates says, "*The Souls* has functioned as an urtext of the African-American experience."

Du Bois's politics were radical—that is, his sympathies were first socialist and then, toward the end of his life, communist (because he thought the Soviet Union less racist and colonialist in its policies than the United States). His expressions of opinion, always frank, had predictable consequences. As early as 1918 he was threatened by the Department of Justice for attacking racism in the military; in 1934 he was censored by the NAACP, from which he resigned; he lost his professorship at Atlanta in 1944; in 1951 he was indicted by the United States Government as a foreign agent (but was acquitted), and in 1952 he was refused a passport to travel abroad, permission he did not receive until 1958 after constant harassment by Government officials.

These trials did not prevent Du Bois from political protests on occasions that moved him, nor from running for the United States Senate from New York in 1950. Nevertheless, he decided at last to join the communist party, and did in 1961, after a world tour in which he was widely celebrated. At that point, having relinquished his American citizenship, he became a citizen of Ghana. Whatever his standing in the United States, he had long since become a world figure, and was recognized as such at his 90th birthday celebration in New York, when Prime Minister Jawaharlal Nehru of India, leader of a nation of seven hundred and fifty million dark-skinned human beings, greeted him, in words no one present ever forgot, as "the greatest living colored man." He died at Accra, Ghana, where he is buried, in 1963.

PICTURE CREDITS

GB

Angel   Animal   Aristocr

Beauty   Being   Cause   Chance

        Courage   Custom and Con

   Desire   Dialectic   Duty

Eternity   Evolution   Experience

     Good and Evil   Government

Honor   Hypothesis   Idea

Judgment   Justice   Knowledge

                    The

Life and Death   Logic   Love   Man

                    Great

   Medicine   Memory and Imaginatic

   Nature   Necessity and Contingency

        Opinion   Opposition   Philoso

Poetry   Principle   Progress   P

   Quality   Quantity   Reasoning

     Rhetoric   Same and Other   S

Sin   Slavery   Soul   Space   Sta

        Truth   Tyranny and Despo

Virtue and Vice   War and Peace